CORPORATE ENVIRONMENTAL ACCOUNTABILITY IN INTERNATIONAL LAW

Corporate Environmental Accountability in International Law

Second Edition

ELISA MORGERA

Great Clarendon Street, Oxford, OX2 6DP,
United Kingdom

Oxford University Press is a department of the University of Oxford.
It furthers the University's objective of excellence in research, scholarship,
and education by publishing worldwide. Oxford is a registered trade mark of
Oxford University Press in the UK and in certain other countries

© Elisa Morgera 2020

The moral rights of the author have been asserted

First Edition published in 2009
Second Edition published in 2020

Impression: 2

Some rights reserved. No part of this publication may be reproduced, stored in
a retrieval system, or transmitted, in any form or by any means, for commercial purposes,
without the prior permission in writing of Oxford University Press, or as expressly
permitted by law, by licence or under terms agreed with the appropriate
reprographics rights organization.

This is an open access publication, available online and distributed under the terms of a
Creative Commons Attribution – Non Commercial – No Derivatives 4.0
International licence (CC BY-NC-ND 4.0), a copy of which is available at
http://creativecommons.org/licenses/by-nc-nd/4.0/.

Enquiries concerning reproduction outside the scope of this licence
should be sent to the Rights Department, Oxford University Press, at the address above

Published in the United States of America by Oxford University Press
198 Madison Avenue, New York, NY 10016, United States of America

British Library Cataloguing in Publication Data
Data available

Library of Congress Control Number: 2020932773

ISBN 978–0–19–873804–6

Printed and bound by
CPI Group (UK) Ltd, Croydon, CR0 4YY

Links to third party websites are provided by Oxford in good faith and
for information only. Oxford disclaims any responsibility for the materials
contained in any third party website referenced in this work.

To my family

Preface to the Second Edition (2019)

An international debate started in the 1970s and continues to haunt the international community in coming to grips first with de-colonization and now with globalization. This ongoing debate is vividly represented by the decision taken on 26 June 2014 by the Human Rights Council to establish a process to elaborate an international, legally binding instrument on transnational corporations and other business enterprises.[1] Significantly, the resolution was adopted by a majority vote with twenty countries in favour, fourteen against (including the US and Member States of the European Union), and thirteen abstentions.[2] The proponents of the resolution pointed to an imbalance in the current international legal system: binding international law affords significant protection to foreign companies, whereas the victims of harmful corporate activities can only rely on international voluntary instruments, with national law often being inadequate to sufficiently protect them. Those that voted against the resolution argued that international guidelines and national law, rather than an international treaty, are the most suitable approaches to address harmful corporate conduct.[3]

This book aims to assess the degree to which corporate environmental accountability is addressed in public international law.[4] It explores the evolving role of international law in directing and controlling the conduct of business enterprises, in particular multinational corporations. It focuses on the identification of international standards of corporate environmental accountability and their implementation by international organizations. This assessment aims to contribute to the ongoing international debate[5] on the need for international oversight of private

---

[1] Res. 26/9 of 26 June 2014 on the elaboration of an International Legally Binding Instrument on Transnational Corporations and Other Business Enterprises.

[2] 'Council extends mandates on extreme poverty, international solidarity, independence of judges, and trafficking in persons' (26 June 2014), at http://www.ohchr.org/en/NewsEvents/Pages/DisplayNews.aspx?NewsID=14785&LangID=E#sthash.oEXXs44o.dBWOFzwf.dpuf.

[3] Ibid.

[4] The difficulty in ascertaining precisely what 'binds together' the disparate developments on global corporate accountability is affirmed by P. Muchlinski, 'Human Rights, Social Responsibility and the Regulation of International Business: The Development of International Standards by Intergovernmental Organizations' (2003) 3 *Non-State Actors and International Law* 23, 130.

[5] Eg P. Hansen and V. Aranda, 'An Emerging International Framework for Transnational Corporations' (1990) 14 *Fordham International Law Journal* 881; J. Bendell and D. Murphy, 'Towards Civil Regulation: NGOs and the Politics of Corporate Environmentalism' in P. Utting (ed.), *The Greening of Business in Developing Countries* (London: Zed Books in association with UNRISD, 2002) 244, 264; The International Council on Human Rights Policy, *Beyond Voluntarism: Human Rights and the Developing International Legal Obligations for Companies* (Versoix: International Council on Human Rights Policy, 2002) 8; M. Mason, *The New Accountability: Environmental Responsibility Across Borders* (London: Earthscan, 2005) 15.

companies, particularly multinationals, in order to avoid the most serious environmental harm caused by them. It also serves to appreciate the progress already made at the international level, through the growing practice of international organizations, to increasingly engage the private sector in attaining global goals for the protection of the environment and to conceptually and operationally clarifying the international community's expectations about acceptable corporate conduct.

The first edition of this book concluded that international standard-setting initiatives on corporate environmental accountability were increasingly characterized by a significant degree of normative convergence.[6] Since the early 2010s, this trend has accelerated and became more explicit. The current edition explores the intensification of the convergence of international standard-setting efforts on corporate environmental accountability, in light of the prominent role now played by international developments in business and human rights, and advances in the understanding of the inter-relationship between human rights and the environment. The second edition also explores the emergence of substantive international standards of corporate environmental responsibility, as a result of the development of international sectoral guidelines. As standards become more detailed, the remaining divergences reflect differing views among States and other actors about the degree to which evolving international law has sufficiently settled on a certain substantive point. Furthermore, the second edition explores the extent to which the outcomes of international monitoring activities, which are carried out by a plethora of actors, also show increasing signs of cross-fertilization.

Similar to the first edition, the current edition builds both on doctrinal research and on empirical observation of international standard-setting activities. In the early 2000s, I had the opportunity to assist with legal research feeding into a non-governmental organization (NGO) position paper for the World Summit on Sustainable Development, calling for the launch of international negotiations for a binding convention on corporate accountability and liability.[7] Since 2004 I have attended international environmental negotiations on behalf of the International Institute for Sustainable Development/Reporting Services[8] that have allowed me to monitor the development of relevant international guidelines under the Convention on Biological Diversity (CBD). Furthermore, since the publication of the first edition, I have served as an international consultant for the European Commission, the Organization for Economic Cooperation and Development (OECD), and the Food and Agriculture Organization of the United Nations (FAO) on questions related to the evolution of international law and corporate

---

[6] E. Morgera, 'From Corporate Social Responsibility to Accountability Mechanisms' in P.-M. Dupuy and J. Viñuales (eds), *Harnessing Foreign Investment to Promote Environmental Protection: Incentives and Safeguards* (Cambridge: Cambridge University Press, 2013) 321.

[7] As an intern at the London-based Foundation for International Environmental Law and Development.

[8] http://www.iisd.ca.

environmental accountability. In particular, I have been involved in the preparatory studies for the adoption of two sets of international guidance: the 2014 Principles on Responsible Investment in Agriculture and Food Systems of the Committee on Food Security,[9] and the 2016 FAO-OECD Guidance on Responsible Agricultural Supply Chains.[10] In parallel, thanks to a five-year research programme funded by the European Research Council,[11] I have been able to deepen my understanding of the interactions of international biodiversity and human rights law on corporate accountability in a dialogue with UN negotiators in different international fora (through side-events) and with community activists and advisors in Argentina, Greece, Malaysia, Namibia, and South Africa.

Assessing the growing, multi-faceted—yet largely convergent—international practice, this book examines the progress, limitations, and tensions in the progressive development of international law in light of social change.[12] The gradual emergence of international standards on corporate environmental accountability and responsibility may be understood as part of the constant evolution of international law in general, and of international environmental law in particular, in response to societal concerns that are increasingly expected to be formally addressed by law.[13]

Between widespread expectations that public international law needs to provide oversight of corporate conduct and the perception of the limitations of existing law to address harmful corporate activities, the fine line between positive law and law *in fieri* may not be clearly defined.[14] This book, therefore, explores the borderline between current and developing international law, from where international standards emerge as the current response to the calls for 'a new legal order that brings multinational actors within ... the principle of accountability'.[15]

E.M. April 2020

---

[9] The Committee on World Food Security (CFS) endorsed the Principles for Responsible Investment in Agriculture and Food Systems on 15 October 2014, at http://www.fao.org/3/a-au866e.pdf.

[10] FAO-OECD, Guidance on Responsible Agricultural Supply Chains (2016) https://www.oecd-ilibrary.org/agriculture-and-food/oecd-fao-guidance-for-responsible-agricultural-supply-chains_9789264251052-en.

[11] 'BENELEX: Benefit-sharing for an equitable transition to the green economy—the role of law', which is funded by the European Research Council Starting Grant (November 2013–October 2018)—Grant Number: 335592: https://www.strath.ac.uk/research/strathclydecentreenvironmentallawgovernance/benelex/

[12] N. Bobbio, *Dalla struttura alla funzione: nuovi studi di teoria del diritto* (Milano: Edizioni di Comunità, 1977) 53 and G. Abi-Saab, 'Cours general de droit international public' (1987) 207 *Recueil des cours* 9, 33.

[13] Paraphrasing Abi-Saab, ibid. 204–05.

[14] Ibid.

[15] C. Weeramantry, 'Human Rights and the Global Marketplace' (1999) 25 *Brooklyn Journal of International Law* 27.

Acknowledgements

I wish to express my gratitude to the supervisors of my PhD research at the European University Institute, upon which this book is largely based. My gratitude thus goes to Professor Pierre-Marie Dupuy, for sharing his views about legal standards, the social function of international lawyers, and the importance of linking legal theory to empirical research in international law. Many sincere thanks are also owed to Professor Francesco Francioni for his support before and after the PhD, his rigour in assessing legal research, and his unfaltering encouragement. It has been a privilege to receive the comments and suggestions of Professors Alan Boyle and Tullio Scovazzi, who served as external jury members of on the PhD thesis upon which this book is based. I am further very grateful to Professors Fabrizio Cafaggi and Marie-Ange Moreau for having engaged me in multidisciplinary debates on corporate accountability during my PhD studies. I have also benefitted from the comments of the reviewers of the first edition, particularly Professor Gunther Handl[1] and Sergio Peña Neira.[2]

I am very thankful to the Italian granting authorities for giving me the opportunity to undertake a PhD programme at the European University Institute (EUI), an environment that prevented my academic research from becoming a solitary endeavour and spoiled me with its beauty and history. It had been a pleasure to be part of the EUI Environmental Law Working Group, and I wish to thank Patricia Quillacq, Emanuela Orlando, and the other members.

I am also grateful to the friends and colleagues of the International Institute for Sustainable Development (IISD), with whom I attended and analysed inter-governmental negotiations—particularly those in the framework of the Convention on Biological Diversity (CBD)—which have significantly contributed to the reflections in this book.

I wish to thank for the stimulating exchanges of ideas on UN initiatives Peter Utting (UN Research Institute on Social Development), Simon Walker (UN High Commissioner's Office for Human Rights), and Khalil Hamdani and Ludger Odenthal (UN Conference on Trade and Development), whom I met during a mission to the UN Office in Geneva, Switzerland, in July 2004, which was funded by the EUI.

I also wish to express my gratitude to the Foundation for International Environmental Law and Development, where I first undertook research on

---

[1] (2010) 19 *RECIEL* 128.
[2] (2015) 24 *RECIEL* 241.

corporate environmental accountability under the guidance of Alice Palmer. I am indebted to Professor Philippe Sands at University College London (UCL), with whom I first explored the links between international environmental law, and the work of international organizations.

A million thanks are also due to the friends I made while at the EUI—Graciela, Louisa, Tom, and Clemens; at UCL—Rika and Harry; and to my old friends Francesca and Lorraine, who have always been there for me and for whom distance makes no difference. Finally, my lasting gratitude to my family, to whom this book is dedicated: i miei genitori, Francesca, Andrea, Margherita e Tommaso.

Contents

Table of Cases	xvii
Table of Treaties	xxi
List of Acronyms	xxiii

1 Introduction	1
1 The case for an international approach to corporate environmental accountability	2
2 The case for corporate engagement in environmental protection	6
3 History and definitions	8
3.1 From Stockholm to Johannesburg	8
3.2 Rio+20 and the green economy	13
4 Corporate responsibility and/or corporate accountability?	15
4.1 The concept of corporate responsibility	16
4.2 The concept of corporate accountability	18
5 Aim and structure of the book	22
2 The Shortcomings of Traditional Legal Solutions	24
1 The shortcomings of national control	24
1.1 Host State control	25
1.2 Home State control	28
1.2.1 Application of international law by national courts	33
2 The limits of international law	38
2.1 International law on State responsibility	39
2.2 International regimes on civil liability for environmental damage: *en impasse*?	44
2.3 International environmental crimes?	46
2.4 Balancing the international protection of foreign investment	49
2.5 Synergies with international human rights law	53
2.5.1 Legal arguments	56
2.6 The status of multinational companies in international law	60
3 Concluding remarks	67
3 The Emergence of International Standards	69
1 International standards and the sources of international law	70
1.1 The distinctive nature of legal standards	73
1.2 International standards as soft law	78
1.3 The functions of international standards	81
2 Attempts at international regulation: the UN draft Code of Conduct on Transnational Corporations	83
2.1 Environmental content	86
2.2 Legacy	88

3　Subsequent practice of the UN in the 1990s: the partnership approach　91
　　　　3.1　The UN Global Compact　93
　　　　　　3.1.1　Legal significance　95
　　　　　　3.1.2　Environmental content　98
　　4　The human rights-based approach　99
　　　　4.1　The Norms on the Responsibilities of Transnational Corporations and Other Business Enterprises with regard to Human Rights　101
　　　　　　4.1.1　Legal significance　102
　　　　　　4.1.2　Environmental content　105
　　　　　　4.1.3　Legacy　106
　　　　4.2　The UN Framework and Guiding Principles on Business and Human Rights　108
　　　　　　4.2.1　Conceptual and normative contributions　110
　　　　　　4.2.2　Legacy: the Working Group on Business and Human Rights　114
　　　　　　4.2.3　Environmental relevance?　117
　　5　The OECD Guidelines for Multinational Enterprises　120
　　　　5.1　Conceptual approach and legal significance　121
　　　　5.2　Environmental content　124
　　　　5.3　Legacy　127
　　6　The Performance Standards of the International Finance Corporation　129
　　　　6.1　The IFC　129
　　　　6.2　The IFC environmental standards　132
　　　　6.3　Operational distinctiveness and broader trend-setting value　134
　　7　Preliminary conclusions and their relevance for a new treaty on business and human rights　136

4　Assessing the Convergence of International Standards on Corporate Environmental Accountability　140
　　1　The Convention on Biodiversity and the private sector　141
　　　　1.1　The extent to which the CBD has addressed corporate environmental accountability and responsibility　144
　　2　International standards on corporate environmental accountability　147
　　　　2.1　Environmental integration　147
　　　　　　2.1.1　(Self-)assessment of environmental impacts　148
　　　　　　　　2.1.1.1　Cumulative impacts　151
　　　　　　　　2.1.1.2　Outcomes　153
　　　　　　　　2.1.1.3　Links with consultation　154
　　　　　　2.1.2　Environmental management system　155
　　　　　　　　2.1.2.1　Substantive dimensions　156
　　　　2.2　Prevention　158
　　　　　　2.2.1　Substantive dimensions　161
　　　　2.3　Precaution　165
　　　　2.4　Disclosure of environmental information　168
　　　　　　2.4.1　Recipients of information　170
　　　　　　2.4.2　Types of information　171
　　　　　　2.4.3　Degree of disclosure　173

		2.5 Consultation with potentially affected communities	174
		2.6 Grievance	177
	3	Preliminary conclusions	179
5	Assessing the Convergence of International Standards on Corporate Environmental Responsibility		181
	1	Indigenous peoples and local communities	181
		1.1 Environmental and socio-cultural impact (self-)assessment	188
		1.2 Free prior informed consent	192
		1.2.1 Meaning of consent	195
		1.2.2 Appropriate representation	196
		1.2.3 Iterative and culturally appropriate modalities	197
		1.2.4 Documentation and community protocols	199
		1.3 Fair and equitable benefit-sharing	202
		1.3.1 Kinds of benefits	203
		1.3.2 Cautions	206
		1.3.3 Business-community agreements	208
	2	Protected areas	211
		2.1 Natural and cultural heritage	211
		2.2 Natural areas	214
	3	Sustainable use of natural resources	216
		3.1 Threatened or endangered species	217
		3.2 Sustainable production	218
		3.3 Ecosystem services	220
		3.4 Invasive alien species	221
		3.5 Habitats	221
		3.6 Sustainable agri-business	223
	4	Preliminary conclusions	224
6	International Oversight		227
	1	Tools for compliance?	228
	2	The implementation procedure of the OECD Guidelines	231
		2.1 Evolution of the procedure	233
		2.2 Variation in outcomes	235
		2.3 Promoting normative coherence	240
		2.4 Inter-institutional cooperation	242
		2.5 Continued challenges	244
	3	Compliance under the IFC	247
		3.1 Contract-related procedures	248
		3.1.1 Internal assessment	251
		3.1.1.1 Implementation of biodiversity standards	255
		3.2 Ombudsman function of the CAO	257
		3.2.1 Variation in outcomes	261
		3.2.2 Mediation and fair and equitable benefit-sharing	267

xvi CONTENTS

    4 Human rights monitoring bodies and special procedures   271
        4.1 Country visits by UN Special Rapporteurs   273
            4.1.1 UN Special Rapporteur on Indigenous Peoples' Rights   275
            4.1.2 UN Special Rapporteur on Toxics   279
    5 Complaints before the UN Global Compact   282
    6 Concluding remarks   285

Conclusions: Contributions and Areas for Further Research   287

Bibliography   291
Index   317

Table of Cases

(A) NATIONAL

Canada

Recherches Internationales Quebec (RIQ) v. Cambior Inc., Canada Superior
  Court, Quebec, no. 500-06-000034-971)] 1998 Q.J. N.2554 (Q.L.) 28............. 27

Italy

Cassazione, Sez. Unite, 25 January 1989, n.440, reprinted in 1989 *Rivista
  Giuridica dell'Ambiente* 97 27

USA

Aguinda v. Texaco, No. 93 Civ 7527 (VLB), 1994 U.S. Dist.
  (S.D.N.Y. Apr. 11, 1994) 22–23) 29, 34
Aguinda v. Texaco, Inc., 1994 WL 142006 (S.D.N.Y. 1994) 34, 71–72
Aguinda v. Texaco, Inc., 945 F. Supat 625, 627 (S.D.N.Y. 1996) 31–32
Aguinda v. Texaco, 303 F.3d 470, (SDNY 11 March2002) 31–32
AmlonMetals, Inc. v. FMC Corp., 775 F. Sup 668, 669 (S.D.N.Y. 1991) 34, 61–62
Amoco Cadiz, District Court of Chicago, 18 April 1984 in Lloyd's Review
  Report 1984... 32
Bano v. Union Carbide Corat, No. 99 Civ. 11329 (JFK) (S.D.N.Y., March 18, 2003) 33
Bano v. Union Carbide Corat, No. 03-7416 (S.D.N.Y., March 17, 2004) 33
Beanal v. Freeport-McMoRan, Inc., 969 F. Supat 362 (E.D. La. 1997) (No. 96-1474)...... 35
Doe v. Unocal, 963 F. Supat 880 (C.D. Cal. 1997)..................................... 36
Flores v. Southern Peru Copper Corp., 2002 U.S. Dist. (S.D.N.Y. 2002) 35, 36
In re Union Carbide Corp Gas Plant Disaster, 634 F. Supat 842, 844
  (S.D.N.Y. 1986), aff'd, 809 F.2d 195 (2d Cir. 1987) 29
Esther Kiobel v Royal Dutch Petroleum Co, 133 S. Ct. 1659 (2013) 36–37
Sarei v. Rio Tinto PLC., 221 F. Supat 2d 1116 (C.D. Cal. 2001) 32–33
Sosa v. Alvarez-Machain, 542 U.S. 692 (2004) 36–37

(B) INTERNATIONAL

Court of Justice of the European Union

Case C-128/01, *Owusu v Jackson* [2005] ECR I-553 37–38

European Court of Human Rights

Costello-Roberts v. UK, App. No. 13134/87 (1993)................................ 57
Lopez Ostra v. Spain, App. No. 16798/90 (1994) 56
Onereyldiz v. Turkey, App.No. 36022/97 (2003) 56
International Federation for Human Rights v Greece, App. No. 72/2011 (2013).......... 56

xviii   TABLE OF CASES

International Court of Justice (ICJ)

Gabčíkovo-Nagymaros Project (Hungary-Slovakia), Judgment (25 September 1997) 34
Pulp Mills on the River Uruguay (Argentina v. Uruguay), Order (13 July 2006) 261–62
Pulp Mills on the River Uruguay (Argentina v Uruguay), Judgment
  (20 April 2010) 134, 148–49
Reparations for Injuries Suffered in the Service of the United Nations, ICJ,
  Advisory Opinion (11 April 1949) 61–62
Construction of a Road Case (Nicaragua v Costa Rica) (merit) Judgment
  (16 December 2015) 149

Permanent Court of Arbitration

Iron Rhine Railway Arbitration (Belgium and the Netherlands), Award of the Arbitral
  Tribunal (24 May 2005) 29
Chevron and Texaco v Ecuador, Second Partial Award on Track II
  (30 August 2018) 52–53

Inter-American Commission of Human Rights

'Report on the Situation of Human Rights in Ecuador' Inter-American Commission
  of Human Rights, (24 April 1997) OEA/ser. L/V/II.96, doc10 rev1 54–55

Inter-American Court of Human Rights

Mayagna (Sumo) Indigenous Community of Awas Tingni v Nicaragua, judgment
  (31 August 2001) 55
Pueblo Indígena Kichwa de Sarayaku vs. Ecuador, provisional measures order
  (6 July 2004) 56, 189–90, 206
Case of the Saramaka People v. Suriname, Judgment (Preliminary Objections,
  Merits, Reparations and Costs), 28 November 2007 .... 186, 189, 199
Saramaka People v. Suriname, judgment (interpretation of the judgment on
  preliminary objections, merits, reparations and costs) (12 August 2008) 185–86
Kaliña and Lokono Peoples v Suriname, judgment (merits, reparations and
  costs: 25 November 2015) 56, 188–90, 198, 208, 213
Medio Ambiente y Derechos Humanos, Oc-23/17, opinión consultiva
  (15 November 2017) 56, 165

International Centre for Settling Investment Disputes (ICSID)

Compañía del Desarrollo de Santa Elena S.A. v. Republic of Costa Rica,
  Case ARB/96/1, Final Award (17 February 2000) 52–53
ICSID, *Metalclad Corporation v United Mexican States*, Case ARB (AF)/97/1,
  Award (30 August 2000) 52–53
S. D. Myers Inc. v Government of Canada, NAFTA Arbitration under UNCITRAL
  Arbitration Rules, Partial Award (17 November 2000) 50–52
Mondev International Ltd. v. USA, Case ARB/(AF)/99/2, Award
  (11 October 2002) 59–60

Human Rights Committee

Lubicon Lake Band v. Canada, Human Rights Committee, Communication
  No. 167/1984 (26 March 1990) UN Doc A/45/40 56

African Commission on Human and Peoples' Rights

'The Social and Economic Rights Action Centre and the Centre for Economic and Social Rights/Nigeria' (2001) Communication 155/96, Case No. ACHPR/COMM/A044/1 55

Centre for Minority Rights Development (Kenya) and Minority Rights Group International on Behalf of Endorois Welfare Council v Kenya (2009) Communication 276/03 .... 54–55, 193–94, 210–13

UNCITRAL Ad Hoc Tribunal

Chematura Corp v Government of Canada, Award (2 August 2010) 52–53

Table of Treaties

(European) Convention for the Protection of Human Rights and Fundamental Freedoms
(Rome, 4 November 1950, in force 3 September 1953) 63
Protocol to the (European) Convention for the Protection of Human Rights and
Fundamental Freedoms (Paris, 20 March 1952, in force 18 May 1954) 63
Articles of Agreement of the International Finance Corporation (20 July 1956,
as amended by resolutions effective 21 September 1961 and 1 September
1965) 129–30
Convention on the Organisation for Economic Co-operation and Development
(Paris, 14 December 1960, in force 30 September 1961) 120
Convention on Civil Liability for Nuclear Damage (Vienna, 29 May 1963, into
force 12 November 1977) 8–9, 36–37
Convention on the Settlement of Investment Disputes between States and
Nationals of Other States (ICSID Convention) (Washington, 18 March
1965, in force 14 October 1966) 50
International Convention on the Elimination of All Forms of Racial Discrimination
(New York, 7 March 1966, in force 4 January 1969) 192
Convention on the Law of the Treaties (Vienna, 23 May 1969, in force
27 January 1980) 142–43, 181–82
International Convention on Civil Liability for Oil Pollution Damage (Brussels,
29 November 1969, in force 19 June 1975) 8, 45, 140
Ramsar Convention on Wetlands of International Importance (Ramsar Convention)
(Ramsar, 2 February 1971, in force 21 December 1975) 211
International Convention on the Establishment of an International Fund for
Compensation for Oil Pollution Damage (Brussels, 18 December 1971, in
force 16 October 1978) 45–46
Convention for the Protection of the World Cultural and Natural Heritage
(World Heritage Convention) (Paris, 16 November 1972, in force
17 December 1975) 132–33, 211–12
Convention on the Prevention of Marine Pollution by Dumping of Wastes and Other
Matter (London Convention on Ocean Dumping) (London, 29 December 1972,
in force 30 August 1975) 162
Convention on International Trade in Endangered Species of Wild Fauna and Flora
(CITES) (Washington, 3 March 1973, in force 1 July 1975) 217–18
Convention on the Conservation of Migratory Species of Wild Animals (CMS) (Bonn, 23
June 1979, in force 1 November 1983) 217
Convention on Long-range Transboundary Air Pollution (Geneva, 13 November
1979, in force 16 March 1983) 132–33, 162–63
Montreal Protocol on Substances that Deplete the Ozone Layer (Montreal,
16 September 1987, in force 1 January 1989) 132–33
Convention on the Control of Transboundary Movements of Hazardous Wastes
and Their Disposal (Basel Convention) (Basel, 22 March 1989, in force
24 May 1992) 52, 132–33, 162
International Labour Organization's (ILO) Convention no. 169 Concerning Indigenous
and Tribal Peoples in Independent Countries (Geneva, 27 June 1989, in force 5
September 1991) 192

Protocol to the Antarctic Treaty on Environmental Protection (Madrid, 4 October 1991, in force 14 January 1998) as amended by the 28th Antarctic Treaty Consultative Meeting on 14 June 2005, to include Annex VI on Liability Arising from Environmental Emergencies 45–46
United Nations Convention on the Law of the Sea (UNCLOS) (Montego Bay, 10 December 1992, in force 16 November 1994) 61–62, 217
UNECE Convention on the Transboundary Effects of Industrial Accidents (Helsinki, 17 March 1992, in force 19 April 2000) 45
United Nations Framework Convention on Climate Change (New York, 9 May 1992, in force 21 March 1994) 132–33
Convention on Biological Diversity (CBD) (Rio de Janeiro, 5 June 1992, in force 29 December 1993) 105, 119, 132–33, 137, 140, 141–42, 166, 181, 192, 240–41, 261, 287–88
Convention on Civil Liability for Damage resulting from Activities Dangerous to the Environment (Lugano, 21 June 1993, not in force) 45–46, 140
Convention on Liability and Compensation for Damage in Connection with the Carriage of Hazardous and Noxious Substances by Sea (London, 3 May 1996, not in force) 45–46
Convention on Access to Information, Public Participation in Decision-Making and Access to Justice in Environmental Matters (Aarhus Convention) (Aarhus, 25 June 1998, in force 30 October 2001) 125–26, 172
Statute of the International Criminal Court (Rome, 17 July 1998, in force 1 July 2002) 47–49
Protocol on Liability and Compensation for Damage Resulting from the Transboundary Movement of Hazardous Wastes and their Disposal (Basel, 10 December 1999, not in force) 45–46
International Convention for the Suppression of Financing of Terrorism (New York, 9 December 1999, in force 10 April 2002) 49
Convention against Transnational Organized Crime (15 November 2000, in force 29 September 2003) 48–49
Optional Protocol to the Convention on the Rights of the Child on the Sale of Children and Child Pornography (New York, 25 May 2000, in force 18 January 2002)... 53
International Treaty on Plant Genetic Resources for Food and Agriculture (Rome, 3 November 2001, in force 29 June 2004) 186–88, 204–5
International Convention on Civil Liability for Bunker Oil Pollution Damage, (London, 23 May 2001, in force 21 November 2008)........................... 45
Stockholm Convention on Persistent Organic Pollutants (Stockholm, 22 May 2002, in force 17 May 2004) 132–33
United Nations Convention against Corruption (New York, 31 October 2003, in force 14 December 2005) 48–49, 96
Protocol on Civil Liability and Compensation for Damage Caused by the Transboundary Effects of Industrial Accidents on Transboundary Waters to the 1992 Convention on the Protection and Use of Transboundary Watercourses and International Lakes and to the 1992 Convention on the Transboundary Effects of Industrial Accidents (Kiev, 21 May 2003, not in force) 45
Nagoya Protocol on Access to Genetic Resources and the Fair and Equitable Sharing of Benefits Arising from Their Utilization to the Convention on Biological Diversity (Nagoya, 29 October 2010, in force 12 October 2014) 183, 185, 192, 204
Nagoya–Kuala Lumpur Supplementary Protocol on Liability and Redress to the Cartagena Protocol on Biosafety (Nagoya, 15 October 2010; in force 5 March 2018) 45–46
Protocol on Amendments to the Protocol on the Statute of the African Court of Justice and Human Rights (Malabo, 27 June 2014, not in force)........................ 47

List of Acronyms

ADR	Alternative dispute resolution
ATCA	Alien Tort Claim Act
BITs	Bilateral investment treaties
CAO	Compliance Advisor/Ombudsman of the IFC
CBD	Convention on Biological Diversity
CIME	OECD Committee on International Investment and Multilateral Enterprises
CITES	Convention on International Trade in Endangered Species
CMS	Convention on Migratory Species
CoE	Council of Europe
COP	Conference of the Parties
CSD	Commission on Sustainable Development
CSR	Corporate Social Responsibility
EBRD	European Bank for Reconstruction and Development
ECHR	European Court of Human Rights
EIA	Environmental impact assessment
EMS	Environmental management systems
FDI	Foreign direct investment
FOE	Friends of the Earth
GATS	General Agreement on Trade and Services
GDP	Gross domestic product
G-77	Group of Developing Countries
HRC	Human Rights Council
ICJ	International Court of Justice
ICSID	International Centre for Settlement of Investment Disputes
IDB	Inter-American Development Bank
IFC	International Finance Corporation
ILC	International Law Commission
ILO	International Labour Organization
IPBES	Intergovernmental Science-Policy Platform on Biodiversity and Ecosystem Services
IPCC	Intergovernmental Panel on Climate Change
IPR	Intellectual property rights
ISO	International Standards Organization
IUCN	International Union for Conservation of Nature
MAI	Multilateral Agreement on Investment
MDGs	Millennium Development Goals
MEAs	Multilateral environmental agreements
MNCs	Multinational corporations/companies

MNEs	Multinational enterprises
NAFTA	North American Free Trade Agreement
NCPs	National contact points
NGOs	Non-Governmental Organizations
NIEO	New International Economic Order
ODA	Official Development Assistance
OECD	Organization for Economic Cooperation and Development
OHCHR	Office of the High Commissioner for Human Rights
PRTRs	Pollution release and transfer registers
TEEB	The Economics of Ecosystems and Biodiversity
UDHR	Universal Declaration of Human Rights
UN	United Nations
UNCLOS	United Nations Convention on the Law of the Sea
UNCHR	United Nations Human Rights Council
UNCTAD	United Nations Conference on Trade and Development
UNCTC	United Nations Commission on Transnational Corporations
UNDESA	United Nations Department of Economic and Social Affairs
UNECE	United Nations Economic Commission for Europe
UNECOSOC	United Nations Economic and Social Council
UNESCO	United Nations Educational, Scientific and Cultural Organization
UNESCRC	UN Economic, Social and Cultural Rights Committee
UNGC	United Nations Global Compact
UNGA	United Nations General Assembly
UNRISD	United Nations Research Institute for Social Development
WHO	World Health Organization
WSSD	World Summit on Sustainable Development
WTO	World Trade Organization
WWF	World Wide Fund for Nature

1
Introduction

The international community has debated the need for international regulation and oversight of multinational companies for about fifty years.[1] While States have hitherto resisted developing an international legally binding instrument on the matter,[2] voluntary multi-stakeholder initiatives[3] and international soft-law instruments with inter-governmental backing have proliferated to support and encourage an environmentally sound conduct of multinational and other companies.

This chapter illustrates the need for an international approach to address the question of acceptable corporate environmental conduct. It explains such need both on the basis of egregious cases of environmental damage and day-to-day negative impacts of corporations that appear to defy States' regulations and controls. It also points to the desirability of private companies' proactive contribution to the attainment of internationally agreed goals. The chapter then provides a historical and conceptual introduction to evolving approaches in addressing corporate environmental conduct in the framework of public international law,[4] with a view to introducing two key concepts in this study—corporate responsibility and corporate accountability. The chapter explains how these two concepts have emerged, and how they have reached different stages of development and acceptance in international environmental law. The chapter further relates these concepts to what has become the mainstream term of reference—'business *responsibility* to respect human rights' under the influential UN Framework on Business and Human Rights.[5] These factual, historical, and conceptual premises will serve to explain the aims and approach of this book.

---

[1] Eg ECOSOC Res. 1721 (LIII) 28 July 1972; see discussion in Ch. 3.

[2] Although in 2014, a process to develop an international legally binding instrument on transnational corporations and other business enterprises got underway (Human Rights Council, Res. 26/9, 26 June 2014), the outcome of the negotiations is uncertain at the time of writing.

[3] This is notably the case of international public-private partnerships, which were endorsed as an official outcome of the World Summit on Sustainable Development in 2002. See C. Streck, 'The World Summit on Sustainable Development: Partnerships as the New Tool in Environmental Governance' (2003) 13 *Yearbook of International Environmental Law* 21.

[4] An early version of this chapter was published as 'From Stockholm to Johannesburg: From Corporate Responsibility to Corporate Accountability for the Global Protection of the Environment?' (2004) 13 *Review of European Community and International Environmental Law* 214.

[5] Report of the Special Representative of the Secretary-General on the Issue of Human Rights and Transnational Corporations and Other Business Enterprises, John Ruggie. 'Protect, Respect and Remedy: A Framework for Business and Human Rights' (2008) UN Doc. A/HRC/8/35, paras 25 and 58 (the Human Rights Council recognized the need to operationalize the framework through Resolution 8/7 of 2008, para. 2)—Hereinafter, UN Framework on Business and Human Rights. This is discussed in more detail in Ch. 3.

1. The case for an international approach to corporate environmental accountability

Multinational corporations have established themselves as major actors in the world economy since the 1940s, through their ability to combine factors of production around the world and achieve economic efficiency on a global scale.[6] More than 80,000 corporations, 800,000 subsidiaries, and millions of suppliers dominate the world's economic growth.[7] New investment policy measures tend to focus on investment liberalization and promotion, while controls over corporations become more and more challenging due to the increasing complexity of internal ownership structures and the resulting blurring of investor nationality.[8] As a result, the global reach of multinational corporations has significantly and rapidly increased their capacity to act at a pace and scale that neither governments nor international organizations can match.[9] Multinationals have long been seen as:

> [a] triumph of economic power and legal ingenuity operating on a scale, which transcends and at time dwarfs the authority of individual States and for which the existing legal order makes no appropriate provision. It is inevitable that … so much economic power and so much legal ingenuity should sometimes be tempted to take advantage of the complexity of political and legal systems to create a world of their own which must accommodate itself in the conduct of its operations to many legal systems but is not in any real sense subject to any of them.[10]

McBarnet explains the phenomenon from a socio-legal perspective. Multinationals take advantage of the limited development of global institutions regulating business to experiment in 'regulatory arbitrage', choosing to base their operations in countries with limited regulation and enforcement, and in 'creative compliance'[11] by 'fall[ing] outside the ambit of disadvantageous law and beyond the reach of

---

[6] K. P. Sauvant and V. Aranda, 'The International Legal Framework for Transnational Corporations' in A. A. Fatouros (ed.), *Transnational Corporations: The International Legal Framework* (London: Routledge, 1994) 83, 88; and A. Perry-Kessaris, 'Corporate Liability for Environmental Harm' in M. Fitzmaurice, D. Ong, and P. Merkouris (ed.), *Research Handbook on International Environmental Law* (Cheltenham: Edward Elgar, 2010) 361.

[7] Human Rights Council, 'Report of the Special Representative of the Secretary-General on the issue of Human Rights and Transnational Corporations and Other Business Enterprises' (21 March 2011) UN Doc. A/HRC/17/31, para. 15.

[8] UNCTAD, Key Messages in World Investment Report 2016—Investor Nationality: Policy Challenges (UNCTAD/WIR/2016).

[9] UN Commission on Human Rights, 'Interim Report of the Special Representative of the Secretary-General on the issue of Human Rights and Transnational Corporations and Other Business Enterprises' (22 February 2006) UN Doc. E/CN.4/2006/97, paras 12 and 16.

[10] C. W. Jenks, 'Multinational Entities in the Law of Nations' in W. Friedmann, L. Henkin, and O. Lissitzyn (eds), *Essays in Honor of Philip C. Jessup* (New York: Columbia University Press, 1972) 70, 73.

[11] D. McBarnet, 'Corporate Social Responsibility Beyond Law, Through Law and For Law' in D. McBarnet, A. Voiculescu, and T. Campbell (eds), *The New Corporate Accountability: Corporate Social Responsibility and the Law* (Cambridge: Cambridge University Press, 2007) 1.

legal control'.¹² In addition, multinational companies are notoriously able to influence the development and implementation of both national and international law through lobbying, negotiations, compromise, and weakening of controls.¹³ In response, the law has increasingly been used in 'subtle, indirect and creative ways', also in the absence of government action,¹⁴ to shift corporate focus from profit maximization to responsibility towards a broader range of stakeholders.¹⁵ This is ultimately seen as having the potential to lead business to review its attitude to law, shifting from minimum compliance with the letter of the law to compliance with the spirit of the law.¹⁶

Due to multinational corporations' economic power, often shadowing States' gross domestic product (GDP), and worldwide scale of activities, their impacts have been considered highly significant for the global protection of the environment. They adversely affect globally relevant resources through the release of greenhouse gases, the unsustainable use of biodiversity, and the production of toxic and hazardous substances and waste.¹⁷ At the same time, the increasing acceleration of international financial flows linked with foreign investments has outpaced States' capacity or delayed their efforts to regulate or control multinationals for the protection of the environment.¹⁸ Privatization of services related to the management of natural resources (such as water utilities) raises particular concerns, for instance governments may not be able to regulate multinationals appropriately so as to ensure fair prices for basic services and the proper consideration of environmental impacts.¹⁹ In all, 'the internationalisation of production of goods and services by multinationals increases the likelihood of any related environmental damage to a greater number of countries and to a larger part of the world's environment'.²⁰ Concerns over the negative impacts of multinationals on the global environment are usually justified with reference to their institutional functioning, guided by preoccupations for short-term performance, competition, and a piecemeal or minimalistic approach to environmental management.²¹

---

[12] Ibid. 48.
[13] Ibid.
[14] Ibid. 5.
[15] Ibid. 1.
[16] Ibid. 61.
[17] For an early overview of perceived unsustainable practices of multinational corporations, D. Santillo and P. Johnston, 'Ethical Standards and Principles of Sustainability' in M. K. Addo (ed.), *Human Rights Standards and the Responsibility of Transnational Corporations* (The Hague: Kluwer Law International, 1999) 351. UN Commission on Transnational Corporations (UNCTC), *Climate Change and Transnational Corporations: Analysis and Trends* (Geneva: UN, 1993); cited in UNCTAD, *Environmental Management in Transnational Corporations. Report on the Benchmark Corporate Environmental Survey* (New York: UN, 1993) 101.
[18] World Resources Institute, *World Resources 2002–2004: Decisions for the Earth: Balance, Voice, and Power* (Washington DC: World Resources Institute, 2003) 164.
[19] Ibid. 94.
[20] UNCTAD, *Environment* (Geneva: UNCTAD, 2001) 7.
[21] R. Welford, *Environmental Strategy and Sustainable Development: The Corporate Challenge for the 21st Century* (London: Routledge, 1995) 39.

Major accidents due to substandard operations of multinationals have illustrated these points. Between 1983 and 2002, there were 150 significant environmental accidents in the mining sector alone: in many cases companies, response bodies, and communities were not fully prepared or sufficiently informed to deal with the incidents, so companies exacerbated environmental contamination problems and public health risks.[22] To name but a few specific examples, widespread water pollution, deforestation, over-exploitation of natural resources, and soil erosion was caused by Texaco's oil extracting practices in Ecuador in the 1990s. Texaco's operations resulted in 464 million barrels of wastewater contaminated with hydrocarbon and other carcinogenic metals being discharged into the river systems. This affected not only the Ecuadorian indigenous peoples' ancestral lands and a national park, but also some of Peru's river systems.[23] As a result, 30,000 representatives of indigenous peoples and farmers from Ecuador and 25,000 downstream residents in Peru filed a class action lawsuit in the US against the multinational oil company Texaco, seeking personal and environmental damages. A transnational litigation saga has ensued for over twenty years, which has not yet provided an appropriate response.[24]

Another egregious environmental disaster resulted from the massive pollution of the Ok Tedi River in Papua New Guinea, due to the direct release in the 1990s of about 40 million tons of waste rock and 30 million tons of mine tailings per year by the subsidiary of an Australian mining company.[25] This irreparably damaged the river ecosystem and the adjacent rain forest, destroying the traditional livelihoods of indigenous peoples living along the watercourse.[26] More than twenty years later, the mine waste has continued to be disposed into the river, and while communities received some compensation, this did not include mitigation of environmental impacts.[27]

---

[22] World Bank, 'Striking a Better Balance: The World Bank Group and the Extractive Industry' in World Bank, *The Final Report of the Extractive Industries Review* (Washington DC: World Bank, 2003) 26; and World Resources Institute, *Mining and Critical Ecosystems: Mapping the Risks* (Washington DC: World Bank, 2003).

[23] Inter-American Commission on Human Rights, *Report on the Situation of Human Rights in Ecuador*, OEA/ser. L/V/II.96, doc.10 rev. 1, 24 April 1997. See J. Kimerling, 'Disregarding Environmental Law: Petroleum Development in Protected Natural Areas and Indigenous Homelands in the Ecuadorian Amazon' (1991) 14 *Hastings International and Comparative Law Review* 849; and S. Holwick, 'Transnational Corporate Behaviour and its Disparate and Unjust Effects on the Indigenous Cultures and the Environment of Developing Nations: Jota v. Texaco, a Case Study' (2000) 11 *Colorado Journal of International Environmental Law and Policy* 183.

[24] For updates, see https://business-humanrights.org/en/texacochevron-lawsuits-re-ecuador. See T. Lambooy, A. Argyrou, and M. Varner, 'An Analysis and Practical Application of the Guiding Principles on Providing Remedies with Special Reference to Case Studies Related to Oil Companies' in S. Deva and D. Bilchitz (eds), *Human Rights Obligations of Business: Beyond Corporate Responsibility to Respect?* (Cambridge: Cambridge University Press, 2013) 329, 335–70.

[25] Amnesty International, *Injustice Incorporated: Corporate Abuses and the Human Right to Remedy* (London: Amnesty International, 2014) 81–96.

[26] Ibid.

[27] Ibid.

Another paradigmatic case was caused by the leak of lethal gas from a chemical storage facility of an American multinational company's subsidiary in Bhopal, India in 1984. The leak resulted in the deaths of between 7,000 and 10,000 people within three days; the chronic, debilitating illness of at least 12,000 people; and pollution of groundwater and soil with toxins in concentrations exceeding six to 600 times the limits recommended.[28] Much of the environmental damage had not been redressed twenty years after the accident.[29] The lack of comprehensive clean-up is allegedly still causing damage to the environment and people's health, and transnational litigation spanning over twenty-five years is still ongoing.[30]

While corporate activity has led to significant environmental damage, deterioration of environmental conditions in turn negatively affects business opportunities. The 2005 Millennium Ecosystem Assessment—a global scientific process commissioned by the UN Secretary-General to assess the consequences of ecosystem change on human well-being—indicated that the decline or increased cost of natural resources that have been freely available will affect the framework conditions with which businesses operate. Environmental degradation may lead to increased regulatory constraints, risk to reputation and brand image that could affect business most directly tied to threatened ecosystems and services, substantially higher costs of inputs, increased vulnerability of assets to floods and disasters, as well as conflict and corruption.[31] Corporate access to capital and insurance can also be impacted by environmental conduct. Biodiversity loss is increasingly recognized as a material risk for business by investors, financial institutions, and insurance companies. For industries that depend for their operations on biodiversity, its components, or on the ecosystem services supported by biodiversity, the decline in the availability of these resources and services is a production risk that could lead to insecure supply chains, decreased productivity, unreliable service, and poor product quality. Insurance companies are taking new approaches to setting rates that reflect growing risks from degradation of ecosystem services and reflecting the environmental uncertainties and potential for proximate cause in pricing and coverage exclusions.[32] Consequently, companies that minimize their negative impacts on the environment are helping to guarantee the sustainability of their own businesses. A company's biodiversity positive record, for instance, may influence

---

[28] Amnesty International, *Clouds of Injustice: Bhopal Twenty Years On* (London: Amnesty International, 2004).
[29] Greenpeace, *The Bhopal Legacy: Toxic Contaminants at the Former Union Carbide Factory Site, Bhopal, India* (1999) <https://www.cseindia.org/the-bhopal-legacy-greenpeace-international-1999-7847>. See also comments in S. Deva, *Regulating Corporate Human Rights Violations: Humanizing Business* (Abingdon: Routledge, 2012) ch. 2.
[30] Amnesty International (n. 25) 33–64.
[31] Millennium Ecosystem Assessment, *Ecosystems and Human Well-Being: Opportunities and Challenges for Business and Industry* (Washington DC: World Resources Institute, 2005) 9.
[32] Ibid. 17–18.

6 INTRODUCTION

its ability to access land, sea, and other natural resources essential for its operations, as well as its ability to obtain both the legal and social right to operate in an area.³³

2. The case for corporate engagement in environmental protection

Conversely, 'multinational corporations can play a critical role in a sustainable managed world'.³⁴ Multinationals financial, managerial, and research and development (R&D) resources may significantly contribute to the development and transfer of clean technologies and environmentally sound management practices.³⁵ Arguably sustainable development provides an opportunity for corporations to do 'what they do best, innovation, creativity, adaptation to new conditions and shaping new markets and new production possibilities'.³⁶

To get 'business on board' of the global environmental agenda, emphasis has been increasingly placed on the opportunities that global environmental protection can create for business, including renewable energy, agroforestry, eco-tourism, and ecological restoration.³⁷ The Millennium Ecosystem Assessment underlined the growing demand for more efficient or different ways to use ecosystem services³⁸ for mitigating impacts or to track or trade services.³⁹ It also indicated that new markets and product opportunities may be identified in an effort to address

---

³³ Secretariat of the Convention on Biological Diversity (CBD Secretariat), *Private Sector Engagement in the Implementation of the Convention*, (2005) UN Doc. UNEP/CBD/WG-RI/1/8, paras 12–15.

³⁴ H. Gleckman, 'Transnational Corporations' Strategic Responses to "Sustainable Development"' in H. O. Bergenses, G. Parmann, and Ø. B. Thommessen (eds), *Green Globe Yearbook of International Cooperation on Environment and Development* (Oxford: Oxford University Press, 1995) 93.

³⁵ UNCTAD (n. 20) 7. Welford (n. 21) 89; and J. H. Faulkner, 'The Role of Business in International Environmental Governance' in M. Rolén, H. Sjöberg, and U. Svedin (eds), *International Governance on Environmental Issues* (Dordrecht: Kluwer Academic Publishers, 1997) 150. E. Morgera and K. Kulovesi, 'Public-private Partnerships for Wider and Equitable Access to Climate Technologies' in A. Brown (ed.), *Environmental Technologies, Intellectual Property and Climate Change: Accessing, Obtaining and Protecting* (Cheltenham: Edward Elgar, 2013) 128.

³⁶ N. Choucri, 'Corporate Strategies toward Sustainability' in W. Lang (ed.), *Sustainable Development and International Law* (London: Graham & Trotman/Martinus Nijhoff, 1995) 189.

³⁷ CBD Secretariat (n. 33) paras 12–15.

³⁸ Ecosystem services are the benefits people obtain from ecosystems, such as: food, water, timber, and fibre; regulating services that affect climate, floods, diseases, wastes, and water quality; cultural services that provide recreational, aesthetic, and spiritual benefits; and supporting services such as soil formation, photosynthesis, and nutrient cycling: see generally Millennium Ecosystem Assessment (n. 31). Note that in 2017, the Intergovernmental Platform on Biodiversity and Ecosystem Services (IPBES) proposed replacing the term ecosystem services with 'nature's contributions to people' to refer to 'all the positive contributions or benefits, and occasionally negative contributions, losses or detriments, that people obtain from nature' and 'explicitly embracing concepts associated with other worldviews on human-nature relations and knowledge systems': IPBES-5/1: Implementation of the first work programme of the Platform (2017) III, paras 8–9, and discussion in U. Pascual, P. Balvanera, S. Díaz, G. Pataki, E. Roth, M. Stenseke, R. T. Watson, E. B. Dessane, M. Islar, E. Kelemen, and V. Maris, 'Valuing Nature's Contributions to People: The IPBES Approach' (2017) 26–27 *Current Opinion in Environmental Sustainability* 7, 15 and 8–9.

³⁹ Millennium Ecosystem Assessment (n. 32) 2.

scarcities in ecosystem services, with additional benefits in terms of enhanced corporate image and reputation, political capital, and brand value from genuine proactive management of environmental issues. There may be cost and operational advantages derived from early recognition and action with regard to ecosystem service scarcity,[40] in particular to address developing countries' needs and enhance or build local capacities sustainably.[41] The Millennium Ecosystem Assessment concluded that it is in business self-interest to promote and invest in technologies that can augment the availability of ecosystem services or reduce pressures on ecosystems, even if technology will not be able to provide a substitute for all ecosystem services.[42]

More recently, the Economics of Ecosystems and Biodiversity (TEEB)—a global study focusing on 'the global economic benefit of biological diversity, the costs of the loss of biodiversity and the failure to take protective measures versus the costs of effective conservation'—identified emerging business models that deliver biodiversity benefits and ecosystem services on a commercial basis, and reviewed the enabling frameworks needed to stimulate private investment and entrepreneurship to realize such opportunities, as well as obstacles.[43] It concluded that 'businesses that fail to assess their impacts and dependence on biodiversity and ecosystem services carry undefined risks and may neglect profitable opportunities'.[44]

In light of these predictions, certain voluntary changes in corporate behaviour have been observed, to limit negative impacts on the environment and take advantage of environment-related business, investment, and employment opportunities. Such modifications, however, are often seen as piecemeal and contradictory, leaving considerable gaps between corporate rhetoric and practice[45] and that 'the dominant strategy of economic growth continues to be business as usual'.[46] Even in the hypothesis of a strategic model of corporate social responsibility, whereby the expectation is that investment in stakeholders' well-being will lead to economic returns for shareholders in the long term, there are some 'built-in limits' due to reliance on cost-benefit analysis.[47]

---

[40] Ibid. 9.
[41] Ibid. 22.
[42] Ibid. 28.
[43] TEEB, *The Economics of Ecosystems and Biodiversity in Business and Enterprise* (London: Earthscan, 2012).
[44] TEEB—The Economics of Ecosystems and Biodiversity Report for Business: Executive Summary (TEEB, 2010) at http://img.teebweb.org/wp-content/uploads/Study%20and%20Reports/Reports/Business%20and%20Enterprise/Executive%20Summary/Business%20Executive%20Summary_English.pdf.
[45] P. Utting, 'Towards Corporate Environmental Responsibility' in P. Utting (ed.), *The Greening of Business in Developing Countries* (London: Zed Books in association with UNRISD, 2002) 1, 6.
[46] P. Utting, 'Corporate Environmentalism in the South: Assessing the Limits and Prospects' in Utting (n. 45) 268, 269.
[47] D. Millon, 'Corporate Social Responsibility and Environmental Sustainability' in B. Sjåfjell and B. Richardson (eds), *Company Law and Sustainability: Legal Barriers and Opportunities* (Cambridge: Cambridge University Press, 2015) 35, 37–38.

3. History and definitions

Against this background, the search for standards for corporate sustainable behaviour has received increasing attention at the international level. One way to assess this trend is by focusing on major UN summits on the environment: a textual analysis of their outcome documents (in different translations) highlights controversies and consensus-based choices among different conceptual approaches and their possible legal implications. These historical and conceptual insights will provide a basis to analyse more specific international legal materials on corporate environmental accountability in the following chapters.

3.1 From Stockholm to Johannesburg

As early as during the 1972 UN Conference on the Human Environment, the role of business in the global protection of the environment and the necessity of integrating environmental concerns into corporate decision-making were discussed.[48] As a result, the preamble of the Stockholm Declaration[49] made a broad reference to the environmental responsibility of business in the following terms:

> To achieve this environmental goal will demand the acceptance of *responsibility* by citizens and communities, and by *enterprises* and institutions at every level, *all sharing equitably in common efforts*. [Emphasis added.]

The role of private companies, particularly multinationals, and environmental protection was more extensively discussed at the UN Conference on Environment and Development in Rio de Janeiro in 1992.[50] Indeed the 'Earth Summit' was the first international conference where industrial leaders participated along with diplomats and scientists in discussing the role of business in aiming at sustainable development.[51] Nonetheless, the Rio Declaration[52] did not specify what the contribution

---

[48] 'Business and the UNCED Process' in UNCTC, 'Activities of Transnational Corporations and Management Division and its Joint Units: Follow-up to the UN Conference on Environment and Development as related to Transnational Corporations' (1993) UN Doc. E/C.10/1993/7, which indicated that more than 900 firms were involved in the preparatory process of the Conference on the Human Environment. Gleckman (n. 34) 95.

[49] 'Declaration of the United Nations Conference on the Human Environment' (16 June 1972) UN Doc. A/CONF.48/14/Rev.1, para. 7 (Stockholm Declaration).

[50] This was in accordance with the 1989 UN General Assembly resolution convening the Conference, which explicitly focused attention upon transnational corporations' 'activities in sectors that have an impact on the environment', and their correlated 'specific responsibility': UNGA Res. 44/228 (22 December 1989) para. 10.

[51] G. Thurdin, 'Political Dimensions of International Environmental Governance Issues' in Rolén, Sjöberg, and Svedin (eds), *International Governance on Environmental Issues* (Dordrecht: Kluwer Academic Publishers, 1997).

[52] 'Rio Declaration on Environment and Development' (13 June 1992) UN Doc. A/CONF.151/6/Rev.1 (Rio Declaration).

of multinationals to sustainable development should be, which has been considered a lost opportunity.[53] On the other hand, the emphasis placed in the Rio Declaration (Principle 16) upon the necessity of internalizing environmental costs through economic instruments has some direct relevance for corporations.[54] The polluter-pays principle[55] was in fact the underlying concept for the international provisions on civil liability of enterprises for nuclear damage[56] and oil pollution.[57]

Agenda 21, instead, dedicated a whole chapter (Chapter 30) to 'Strengthening the Role of Business and Industry', explicitly and implicitly[58] making reference to the role of transnational corporations. This has been considered as one of the most important contributions of the blueprint: it provided an unprecedented framework for corporate environmental responsibility[59] and acknowledged the importance of governments in encouraging improved corporate environmental management.[60] Agenda 21, therefore, is based upon the idea that sustainable development cannot be achieved without the cooperation of business.[61] In particular, Chapter 30 starts by requiring the 'full participation' of business 'in the implementation and evaluation of activities related to Agenda 21'.[62] Furthermore, the introduction to Chapter 30 exhorts business enterprises to recognize environmental management as among the highest corporate priorities and as a key determinant to sustainable development.[63] Some authors have recognized in this recommendation a reflection of the need for private companies to integrate sustainability concerns[64] and even the interests of future generations in their business operations.[65]

Agenda 21 Chapter 30 then put forward two programme areas for private companies. The first, 'Promoting Cleaner Production',[66] focused on efficient resource

---

[53] Gleckman (n. 34) 93–95.
[54] J. H. Faulkner, 'The Role of Business in International Environmental Governance' in Rolén, Sjöberg, and Svedin (n. 51) 150, 153.
[55] P. Schwartz, 'Principle 16: The Polluter-Pays Principle' in J. Viñuales (ed.), *The Rio Declaration on Environment and Development: A Commentary* (Oxford: Oxford University Press, 2015) 429.
[56] Vienna Convention on Civil Liability for Nuclear Damage (Vienna, 21 May 1963) Arts I(1)(k) and II(1).
[57] Brussels International Convention on Civil Liability for Oil Pollution Damage (Brussels, 29 November 1969) Arts II and III(1)).
[58] ECOSOC, 'Follow-up to the United Nations Conference on Environment and Development as related to Transnational Corporations: Report of the Secretary-General' (1993) UN Doc. E/C.10/1993/7, nn. 44, 35, indicates that multinational enterprises were referred to with the following terms 'foreign direct investment, multinationals, commerce and industry including multinational companies', etc.
[59] UNCTAD (n. 20) 42 and 51.
[60] UNCTAD (n. 17) 167.
[61] W. L. Thomas, 'Wither from Here? American Enterprise and the Journey towards Environmentally Sustainable Globalization following WSSD' (2003) 12 *Review of European Community and International Environmental Law* 39, 41; and M. Iovane, 'Soggetti privati, società civile e tutela internazionale dell'ambiente' in A. Del Vecchio and A. Dal Ri Jr (eds), *Il diritto internazionale dell'ambiente dopo il vertice di Johannesburg* (Napoli: Editoriale Scientifica, 2005) 133, 140–42.
[62] 'Agenda 21' (13 June 1992) UN Doc. A/CONF.151/6/Rev.1, para. 30.1.
[63] Ibid. para. 30.3.
[64] N. Choucri, 'Corporate Strategies toward Sustainability' in Lang (n 36), 189, 198.
[65] T. Juniper, 'The Corporate Transition to Sustainable Development' in Addo (n. 17) 77.
[66] Agenda 21, para. 30.5–16.

utilization (reuse and recycling of residues, and waste reduction); partnership; and reporting and codes of conduct on best environmental practices. More relevant for the purposes of this chapter is the second programme area, 'Promoting Responsible Entrepreneurship',[67] which requires the implementation of sustainable development policies by enterprises[68] and 'responsible and ethical management of products and processes from the point of view of health, safety and environmental aspects'.[69] It is noteworthy that while the Spanish text appears in line with the English version,[70] the French version lacks any reference to the concept of responsibility, but rather mentions 'rational and rigorous management of products and processes'.[71]

Overall, it has been observed that Agenda 21 made more substantial references to the responsibility of multinationals and other business enterprises in the area of sustainable development than any other area considered by the UN General Assembly in that period.[72] So much so, that expectations arising from the Rio process encompassed the inclusion, in accordance with the objectives of Agenda 21, of environmental norms in an international agreement on foreign investment that was, however, never concluded.[73] Nevertheless, what was expressed by Agenda 21 represented the explicit political intention of the vast majority of States[74] that the private sector should no longer avoid responding to the challenge of sustainable development.[75]

At the World Summit on Sustainable Development in Johannesburg in 2002, discussions on the role of the private sector were even more intense than in the previous international conferences. A broad coalition of non-governmental organizations (NGOs) presented a proposal for a legally binding treaty on corporate *accountability*, including provisions for corporate *liability*.[76] While not eliciting sufficient State support,[77] the proposal suggested that international minimum

---

[67] Ibid. para. 30.17–30.
[68] Ibid. para. 30.18(b).
[69] Ibid. para. 30.26.
[70] By referring to 'responsabilidad empresarial' and to 'gestión responsable y ética de los productos' (literally 'responsible entrepreneurship' and 'responsible and ethical management of products' respectively).
[71] The French translation only refers to an unqualified 'initiative des entrepreneurs' (literally 'entrepreneurship') in the title of the programme area, and then to 'gestione rationnelle et rigoureuse des produits et des procédés'.
[72] Gleckman (n. 34) 98.
[73] Juniper (n. 65) 80. This is the Multilateral Investment Agreement that was being negotiated under the aegis of the Organization for Economic Cooperation and Development (OECD), discussed in Ch. 3.
[74] D. Ong, 'The Impact of Environmental Law on Corporate Governance: International and Comparative Perspectives' (2001) 12 *European Journal of International Law* 685.
[75] Choucri (n. 64) 198.
[76] Friends of the Earth, *Towards Binding Corporate Accountability* (Position paper for the WSSD, January 2002). World Resources Institute, *World Resources 2002-2004: Decisions for the Earth: Balance, Voice, and Power* (Washington DC: World Resources Institute, 2003) 129.
[77] R. Annerberg, *General Overview of WSSD Outcomes on Globalisation, Trade, Corporate Accountability and the Hierarchy of Multilateral Environmental Agreements vs. Trade Rules* (Public Hearing organized by the European Parliament and Heinrich Böll Foundation, 6 March 2003) 3.

environmental standards were increasingly expected to be directly applicable to multinationals, based on existing international environmental treaties, with a view to imposing duties to take them into account in decision-making and report on their application.[78]

Notwithstanding the opposition of some national delegations,[79] both final texts of the Summit refer instead to corporate responsibility,[80] on the basis of the general recognition that the private sector has a 'duty to contribute to the evolution of equitable and sustainable communities and societies'.[81] This has been interpreted as an indication that the international community has 'recognized a responsibility to protect international public (environmental) values by influencing the private sector directly, not only through States'.[82]

The WSSD Political Declaration[83] includes two references to the role of business for sustainable development: a *'duty'* of the private sector 'to contribute to the evolution of equitable and sustainable communities and societies',[84] and a 'need for private sector corporations to enforce corporate *accountability*, which should take place within a transparent and stable regulatory environment'.[85] The latter was agreed after considerable controversy,[86] and was welcomed by civil society as a 'significant new basis on which to build stronger, binding standards for global companies'.[87] Interestingly, the term 'accountability' appears for the first time as a concept linking corporations and environmental and sustainable development concerns. Certain conceptual insights can be derived from comparing the different translations of the WSSD outcome documents, as the term 'accountability' does not have an exact equivalent in other official languages. Indeed, the words 'responsabilité' in French[88] and 'responsabilidad' in Spanish[89] encompass three

---

[78] K. Miles, *The Origins of International Investment Law* (Cambridge: Cambridge University Press, 2013) 238–370.

[79] See in particular the reservation expressed by the US delegation, specifying that the references to corporate accountability should only apply to existing agreements and not to new ones, in 'Report of the World Summit on Sustainable Development' (4 July 2002) UN Doc. A/CONF.199/20 (WSSD Report) 145, para. 20.

[80] Summary table in M. C. Cordonier Segger, 'Sustainability and Corporate Accountability Regimes: Implementing the Johannesburg Summit Agenda' (2003) 12 *Review of European Community and International Environmental Law* 295, 306.

[81] WSSD Report (n. 79) para. 27.

[82] A. Nollkaemper, 'Responsibility of Transnational Corporations in International Environmental Law: Three Perspectives' in G. Winter (ed.), *Multilevel Governance of Global Environmental Change: Perspectives from Science, Sociology and the Law* (Cambridge: Cambridge University Press, 2006) 179, 193.

[83] WSSD, Political Declaration (4 July 2002) UN Doc. A/CONF.199/20, 2002, Resolution 1 (WSSD Declaration).

[84] Ibid. para. 27

[85] Ibid. para. 29

[86] Cordonier Segger (n. 80) 305.

[87] T. Bigg, *The World Summit on Sustainable Development: Was it Worthwhile?* (Winnipeg: International Institute for the Environment and Development, 2003) 4.

[88] *Robert Collins French-English Dictionary* (Harper Collins Publishers, 1990) 5 and 619.

[89] *Collins Spanish Dictionary* (Harper Collins Publishers, 2002) 496 and 610.

different concepts expressed by the English language with: accountability, responsibility, and liability. Accountability is thus translated, inconsistently, in the French version as transparency,[90] and as responsibility in the Spanish version.[91] These discrepancies can also be found in the WSSD Plan of Implementation.[92] Paragraph 49 of the Plan of Implementation, whose significance has been emphasized by civil society[93] and scholars,[94] urges States to:

> [a]ctively promote corporate responsibility and accountability, based on the Rio principles including through the full development and effective implementation of intergovernmental agreements and measures, international initiatives and public-private partnerships and appropriate national regulations, and support continuous improvement in corporate practices in all countries.[95]

In this case, the French translation only refers to responsibility,[96] whereas in Spanish accountability has this time been translated as 'answerability'.[97] Finally, the Plan of Implementation states that '[T]he international community should ... promote corporate responsibility and accountability'.[98] In this case, the Spanish translation refers again to accountability as answerability,[99] whereas the French one to a 'reporting obligation'.[100]

Compared to the 1992 Rio Conference, the Johannesburg Summit more effectively drew attention to the international level of action, rather than solely focusing

---

[90] The French translation of para. 29 omits the first part of the sentence, namely the reference to 'corporate accountability', and highlights instead, in a rather weaker formulation, the need for a transparent and stable framework: 'nous accordons à penser que les entreprises du secteur privé doivent fonctionner dans un encadrement transparent et stable' (we agree to consider that private enterprises must function within a transparent and stable framework). Note that the French version of the Political Declaration does not diverge from the formulation of para. 27 in the English version.

[91] The Spanish translation in effect utilizes stronger language than the English version, stating the necessity for enterprises to assume 'plena responsabilidad de sus actos en un entorno regulatorio transparente y estable' (full responsibility for their acts within a transparent and stable regulatory framework).

[92] With accountability being translated as transparency in French ('Promouvoir la responsabilité écologique et sociale et la transparence dans le monde des affaires'—'promote the ecological and social responsibility and transparency of the business world'); and omitted in the Spanish version ('Promover la responsabilidad en los círculos empresariales'—'promote the responsibility of business circles').

[93] World Resources Institute (n. 76) 129.

[94] Cordonier Segger (n. 80) 305–07, where the author examines different options for an 'intergovernmental agreement'.

[95] It is worth noting how this paragraph was further endorsed by the General Assembly in 2005, in its resolution on the 'Role of the United Nations in Promoting Development in the context of Globalization and Interdependence', UNGA Res. 58/225 (23 December 2003) para. 11, albeit without reference to the Rio Principles.

[96] '[E]ncourager activement les entreprises à adopter une attitude responsable, sur la base des Principes de Rio' ('actively encourage companies to adopt a responsible attitude, on the basis of the Rio Principles').

[97] 'Rendición de cuentas', which is the equivalent to 'answering of one's actions'.

[98] Para. 140(f).

[99] 'la responsabilidad y la rendición de cuentas de las empresas'.

[100] 'la responsabilité et l'obligation redditionnelle des entreprises'.

on domestic measures for environmental liability.[101] In addition, the WSSD also expanded the scope of corporate responsibility delineated in Agenda 21, beyond purely environmental concerns, thus linking broader regimes for sustainable development to the concept of corporate accountability.[102]

Three conceptual observations can be made. First, all these instruments referred consistently to corporate 'responsibility' in the field of environment and sustainable development. Secondly, none of these instruments referred to 'liability' of multinational corporations in the field of environmental protection. This reflects preference in international law-making processes. States have preferred to strictly limit indications of liability of the private sector to a very narrow ambit of ultra-hazardous activities at the international level.[103] Thirdly, the concept of 'accountability', as discussed below,[104] was utilized for the first time during the negotiations in 2002, but its differing translations into Spanish and French reflect the difficulty in defining its legal implications.

3.2 Rio+20 and the green economy

The most recent UN environmental summit, the 'Rio+20' Conference on Sustainable Development[105] did not build upon the concepts of corporate responsibility and accountability. Attention was rather focused on the theme 'a green economy in the context of sustainable development and poverty eradication'.[106] This was seen as 'a lens for focusing on and seizing opportunities to advance economic and environmental goals simultaneously'.[107] But the concept of green economy proved controversial: delegates did not agree upon a consensus definition and merely 'encourage[d] each country to consider the implementation of green economy policies' as one of the different approaches available to achieve sustainable development.[108] This half-hearted outcome is due to challenges in framing the concept from the perspective not only of developed countries but also developing ones.[109] Nonetheless, related sections of the Rio+20 outcome document have

---

[101] Cordonier Segger (n. 80) 308.
[102] Ibid. 305 and 309.
[103] Ong (n. 74) 696–702. See Ch. 2.
[104] Section 4.2.
[105] This section draws on E. Morgera and A. Savaresi, 'A Conceptual and Legal Perspective on the Green Economy' (2012) 21 *Review of European, Comparative and International Environmental Law* 14–28.
[106] Implementation of Agenda 21, the Programme for the Further Implementation of Agenda 21, and the outcomes of the World Summit on Sustainable Development (UNGA Resolution A/RES/64/236, 24 December 2009) para. 20(a).
[107] Objective and Themes of the United Nations Conference on Sustainable Development, Report of the Secretary-General (UN Doc. A/CONF.216/PC/7, 22 December 2010) ('Objective and Themes') para. 24.
[108] The Future We Want (UN Doc. A/RES/66/288, 11 September 2012), Annex, paras 56 and 62.
[109] P. Kohona, 'The Future We Wanted—The Future We Will Get' (2012) 42 *Environmental Policy and Law* 137, 138.

contributed to provide the green economy with a broad environmental remit, as opposed to one limited to a low-carbon economy that was dominating the preparatory process leading to the Rio+20 Conference.[110] The outcome document emphasized also socio-cultural inclusiveness, taking into account human rights and the specific contributions of indigenous peoples and local communities to environmental management.[111] These are the two themes that reflect broader developments in other international initiatives on corporate environmental accountability.

Besides these general references to the interplay between economic development and environmental protection, however, the Rio+20 outcome did not take stock of more specific advances made by the international community on corporate responsibility and accountability since the WSSD. Norway and the EU attempted to include reference to international guidelines[112] such as the OECD Guidelines for Multinational Enterprises[113] and the UN Guiding Principles on Business and Human Rights,[114] without success. Similarly, a draft invitation to business to 'act in accordance with the UN Global Compact'[115] was replaced by a 'call on the private sector to engage in responsible business practices, such as those promoted by the United Nations Global Compact'.[116] Instead, the Rio+20 outcome document merely 'invite[s] business and industry as appropriate and in accordance with national legislation to contribute to sustainable development and to develop sustainability strategies that integrate, inter alia, green economy policies.'[117] It also focuses on the need for national regulatory and policy frameworks enabling business 'to

---

[110] See references to 'maintaining the healthy functioning of the Earth's ecosystems' in The Future We Want (n. 108) para. 56; to 'sustainable resource management, resource efficiency and waste reduction' at para. 60; and to 'sustainable production and consumption, and conservation and sustainable use of biodiversity and ecosystems' at para. 61. See also Report of the UN Secretary-General, Objective and themes of the United Nations Conference on Sustainable Development (UN Doc. A/CONF.216/PC/7), 22 December 2010, para. 118.

[111] See references to 'enhancing social inclusion, improving human welfare and creating opportunities for employment and decent work for all' at para. 56; to '[p]romote sustained and inclusive economic growth, foster innovation and provide opportunities, benefits and empowerment for all and respect of all human rights' at para. 58(d); to enhancing 'the welfare of indigenous peoples and their communities, other local and traditional communities and ethnic minorities, recognizing and supporting their identity, culture and interests, and avoid endangering their cultural heritage, practices and traditional knowledge, preserving and respecting non-market approaches that contribute to the eradication of poverty', at para. 58 (j); and to 'the welfare of women, children, youth, persons with disabilities, smallholder and subsistence farmers, fisherfolk and those working in small and medium-sized enterprises, and improve the livelihoods and empowerment of the poor and vulnerable groups in particular in developing countries' at para. 58(k).

[112] A. Schulz et al., 'Summary of the Third Round of UNCSD Informal Consultations: 29 May—2 June 2012' (2012) 27(40) *Earth Negotiation Bulletin* 6–7.

[113] OECD, *Guidelines for Multinational Enterprises* (OECD Publishing, 2011), which will be discussed in Ch. 3.

[114] 'Guiding Principles on Business and Human Rights to implement the UN Protect, Respect and Remedy Framework' (2011) UN Doc. A/HRC/17/31, adopted by the Human Rights Council in Res. 17/4 (6 July 2011), which will be discussed in Ch. 3—hereinafter, UN Guiding Principles.

[115] Draft of the Rio+20 Outcome Document (2 June 2012) para. 63 (bracketed language), on file with author. UN Global Compact, https://www.unglobalcompact.org/, discussed in Ch. 3.

[116] The Future We Want (n. 108) para. 46.

[117] Ibid. para. 69.

advance sustainable development initiatives, taking into account the importance of corporate social responsibility'.[118] Elsewhere, however, the Rio+20 outcome document employed more assertive language in specific relation to mining, by

> recogniz[ing] the importance of strong and effective legal and regulatory frameworks, policies and practices for the mining sector that ... include effective safeguards that reduce social and environmental impacts, as well as conserve biodiversity and ecosystems, including during post-mining closure, ... call[ing] on governments *and* business to promote the continuous improvement of accountability and transparency.[119]

It is arguably with regard to corporate sustainability reporting that the Rio+20 Summit made an original contribution to the international policy discourse on corporate environmental accountability.[120] Compared with WSSD, the Rio+20 outcome document 'encourage[s] industry, interested governments and relevant stakeholders with the support of the United Nations system, as appropriate, to develop models for best practice and facilitate action for the integration of sustainability reporting, taking into account experiences from already existing frameworks and paying particular attention to the needs of developing countries, including for capacity-building.'[121]

4. Corporate responsibility and/or corporate accountability?

As opposed to purely voluntary approaches (which are usually captured with the expression 'corporate social responsibility or CSR'),[122] it is argued here that the concepts of corporate responsibility and accountability refer to soft-law[123] approaches addressing the role of business, and multinationals in particular, in the global protection of the environment. Soft law fills the normative space between multinationals being oblivious to international law and their having obligations or being liable directly under international law. The above analysis

---

[118] Ibid. para. 46.
[119] Ibid. para. 228.
[120] Cordonier Segger (n. 80) 308.
[121] The Future We Want (n. 108) para. 47. This was followed up by the creation of a group of 'Friends of paragraph 47' led by Brazil, Denmark, France, and South Africa to support corporate sustainability reporting in their respective countries and the exchange of experiences with the rest of the world: UNEP press release, 'Brazil, Denmark, France and South Africa Join in Commitment to Sustainable Reporting, 20 June 2012, http://www.unepfi.org/fileadmin/events/2012/Rio20/Press_release_Rio_outcome_document.pdf.
[122] CSR is the label used to group efforts and initiatives that are purposely voluntary in their approach to sustainable corporate conduct. Even voluntary initiatives may have, however, legal implications or relevance. See McBarnet et al. (n. 11).
[123] The relevance of soft law for present purposes is discussed in Ch. 3.

of UN summit outcomes seems to point to an unspecified substantive expectation in as far as corporate responsibility is concerned, and a more defined procedural approach in as far as corporate accountability is concerned. The UN General Assembly implicitly recognized such duality in 2005, when framing the mandate of the UN Special Representative on Business and Human Rights in terms of 'identify[ing] and clarify[ing] standards of corporate responsibility *and* accountability'.[124] The following sections will propose an understanding of each expression and place them in the context of the 2008 UN Framework on Business and Human Rights and its second pillar on business responsibility to respect human rights.

4.1 The concept of corporate responsibility

The concept of corporate responsibility[125] is arguably based on the expectation that private companies should no longer base their actions on the needs of their shareholders alone, but be more broadly responsive to the needs of the society in which they operate on the basis of internationally recognized values.[126] This finds reflection in the work leading to the adoption of the UN Framework on Business and Human Rights. While the UN Framework emerged from the rejection of the idea that there are direct legal obligations arising of international law for companies,[127] the UN Special Representative on Business and Human Rights pointed to international standards that are in 'the process of being socially constructed'[128] in the face of the 'fluid' applicability of international legal principles to companies' acts.[129] He thus referred to corporate *responsibility* as 'the legal, social or moral *obligations* imposed on companies'.[130] In his subsequent report, the Special Representative referred to 'corporate responsibility to respect human rights' as the baseline expectation for all companies in all situations to do no harm, that is, 'to manage the risk of

---

[124] Commission on Human Rights Res. 2005/69 (20 April 2005).
[125] Standards of conduct, rather than the legal consequences arising out of a breach of international law (secondary rules), are understood with reference to primary rules, as pointed out by Nollkaemper (n. 82) 181.
[126] UNCTAD, *Social Responsibility* (Geneva: UN, 2001) 3.
[127] Report of the Special Representative of the Secretary-General on the issue of Human Rights and Transnational Corporations and Other Business Enterprises: Mapping International Standards of Responsibility and Accountability for Corporate Acts (2007) UN Doc A/HRC/4/35, paras 33–35, where it is stated '[the question as to whether] any legal responsibilities corporations may have for other human rights violations under international law is subject to far greater existential debate ... preliminary research has not identified the emergence of uniform and consistent State practice establishing corporate responsibilities under customary international law'.
[128] UNCHR, 'Interim Report of the Special Representative of the Secretary-General on the issue of Human Rights and Transnational Corporations and other Business Enterprises' UN Doc E/CN.4/2006/97 (2006) para. 55.
[129] Ibid. para. 64.
[130] Report of the Special Representative (n. 127) para. 6 (emphasis added).

human rights harm with a view to avoiding it'.[131] He substantiated his argument on the understanding that corporations are under growing scrutiny by international human rights mechanisms and have been the object of international standard-setting in light of 'social expectations by States and other actors'.[132] Such practice was considered by the Special Representative as 'blurring the lines between [what is] strictly voluntary, and mandatory' and recognizing the need to 'exercise shared responsibility'.[133]

While this has been criticized for lack of normative ambition,[134] it is a fair assessment of the current state of development of international law, as demonstrated by the continued opposition to the proposed treaty on business and human rights.[135] Nonetheless, this is a step forward conceptually from a traditional understanding that international law does not matter for corporations if not through the State. Critically, corporate responsibility expects companies to go beyond compliance with national laws, in order to respond to the international society's expectation that granting multinational companies their right to existence and the possibility of operating internationally through trade and investment liberalization should be balanced by proportionate responsibility.[136] The 2011 Guiding Principles on Business and Human Rights, which support the implementation of the UN Framework, have confirmed that there is a 'global standard of expected conduct for all business enterprises wherever they operate', that exists independently of States' abilities and willingness to fulfil their human rights obligations. Such global standard operates 'over and above compliance with national laws and regulations protecting human rights', basically requiring business entities to take adequate measures to prevent, mitigate, and remediate adverse human rights impacts.[137] In other words, companies can no longer be oblivious to international law.[138]

---

[131] J. Ruggie, 'Presentation of the work of the Special Representative of the UN Secretary-General on Business and Human Rights to the 7th Inter-Committee meeting of the Human Rights Treaty Bodies' (Geneva, 24 June 2008).
[132] Report of the Special Representative (n. 127) paras 6, 44–46.
[133] Ibid. paras 61–62.
[134] G. Handl, 'Book Review of *Corporate Accountability in International Environmental Law*' (2010) 19 *Review of European Community and International Environmental Law* 128.
[135] See the majority voting on Human Rights Council Res. 26/9 of 26 June 2014 on the elaboration of an International Legally Binding Instrument on Transnational Corporations and Other Business Enterprises.
[136] UNCTAD, *World Investment Report 1999*: *Foreign Direct Investment and the Challenge of Development* (Geneva: UN, 1999) 345–47.
[137] UN Special Representative on Human Rights and Business Enterprises, 'Guiding Principles on Business and Human Rights to implement the UN Protect, Respect and Remedy Framework', UN Doc. A/HRC/17/31 (2011) para. 11 (the Guiding Principles were adopted by the Human Rights Council by Resolution A/HRC/17/4 (2011); see also Office of the UN High Commissioner on Human Rights press release, 'New Guiding Principles on Business and human rights endorsed by the UN Human Rights Council', 16 June 2011).
[138] P. Muchlinski, 'Implementing the New UN Corporate Human Rights Framework: Implications for Corporate Law, Governance and Regulation' (2012) 22 *Business Ethics Quarterly* 145–77, argues that this may have legal consequences via company law and corporate governance.

As a substantive standard, business responsibility to respect human rights consists of the prevailing societal expectation that companies 'do no harm', which is an expectation of positive action rather than just 'passive avoidance'.[139] Former UN Special Representative on Business and Human Rights, John Ruggie, however, indicated that the scope of this substantive standard is to be defined on a case-by-case basis, depending on the actual and potential human rights impacts generated by business, in light of international recognized human rights.[140] Companies are expected to prioritize the prevention and mitigation of most severe impacts or those that a delayed response would make irremediable.[141] In other words, corporate responsibility presupposes an increasing demand on multinationals to consider implications of their actions regardless of whether specific legal obligations require them to do so at the national level.[142]

This resonates with the approach to corporate environmental responsibility, which aims at preventing environmental harm and promoting sustainable development, through environmentally sound policies, practices, and technologies.[143] But substantive environmental standards for multinationals have been slow to emerge internationally. It has mainly been since the 2010s that international standard-setting initiatives have focused more on substantive standards of corporate environmental responsibility, in connection with international developments on the linkages between human rights and the environment.[144]

4.2 The concept of corporate accountability

The concept of *accountability* has developed in the broader context of the debate on global environmental governance.[145] In the process of economic globalization

---

[139] Ibid. 148. Contra, on the negative content (rather than substantive nature) of the 'no harm' responsibility, and of the positive content (rather than procedural nature) of due diligence, see D. Cassell and A. Ramasastry, 'White Paper: Options for a Treaty on Business and Human Rights' (2016) 6 *Notre Dame Journal of International and Comparative Law* 1, 7.

[140] Report of the Special Representative of the Secretary-General on the issue of human rights and transnational corporations and other business enterprises, 'Business and Human Rights: Towards Operationalising the "Protect, Respect and Remedy" Framework' (2009) UN Doc. A/HRC/11/13, 15.

[141] UN Guiding Principles, para. 24.

[142] Ong (n. 74) 686. See contra Deva (n. 29), 22–23.

[143] UNCTAD (n. 20) 68.

[144] Chs 3–5.

[145] World Resources Institute (n. 76) and UNDP, *Human Development Report 1999* (New York: Oxford University Press, 1999) 100, where it was stated: 'Multinational corporations are already a dominant part of the global economy—yet many of their actions go unrecorded and unaccounted. They must however go far beyond reporting just to their shareholders. They need to be brought within the frame of global governance.' More generally on accountability as part of good governance, see E. Brown Weiss and A. Sornarajah, 'Good Governance' in R. Wolfrum (ed.), *Max Planck Encyclopedia of Public International Law* (Oxford: Oxford University Press, online edition, 2010) paras 16 and 28–29; and M. Bovens, 'Analysing and Assessing Accountability: A Conceptual Framework' (2007) 13 *European Law Journal* 447.

and its increasing demands on transboundary environmental management, multinationals as 'global citizens' are expected to be included in the design of a more coherent and effective global framework for environmentally relevant decision-making at all levels.[146] Against this background, 'accountability' refers in general to the way in which public and private actors are considered answerable for their decisions and operations, and are expected to explain them when they are asked by stakeholders.[147] They are required to be open in their decision-making processes to be examined and judged by other interested parties. This is reflected in the understanding of the concept of accountability emerging from the translations of the WSSD outcome documents: transparency, answerability, and reporting. It is also reflected in the definition of accountability proposed by UN Special Representative on Business and Human Rights as 'the *mechanisms* for holding corporations to [certain] obligations' based on participation, transparency and review.[148]

Consequently, corporate accountability implies, on the one hand, widening the scope of stakeholders within a company beyond shareholders, so as to include all interest groups affected by the company's activities, such as: governments, employees, boards of directors, investors, consumers, suppliers, local communities in and around areas where the company operates, civil society, and the public at large.[149] This aspect appears to be in line with the translation of accountability in Spanish as answerability.[150] It seems also in line with the plethora of voluntary codes of conduct enacted by several multinationals, that arguably reflect the acceptance by the corporate world that they must address public expectations of environmentally sound behaviour beyond their shareholders.[151] On the other hand, corporate accountability appears to be dependent on disclosure of information and, therefore, on the concept of transparency,[152] as suggested by the French translation of the WSSD Plan of Implementation. To connect business to stakeholders, public access to information and reporting[153] may serve as preconditions for enhanced public scrutiny, by enabling NGOs to play the role of 'watchdogs' for corporate accountability on at least three levels: demanding transparency of business operations; 'shaming' corporations into better environmental behaviour by widely informing about their conduct; and raising awareness about corporate behaviour at the local level.[154] These transparency approaches may encourage better

---
[146] N. Yamamoto, 'Comment on the Paper by Nazli Choucri' in Lang (n. 36), 203–06 (emphasis added).
[147] World Resources Institute (n. 31) 108.
[148] Report of the Special Representative (n. 127) paras 6 and 56.
[149] See generally Muchlinski (n. 138).
[150] M. Mason, *The New Accountability: Environmental Responsibility Across Borders* (London: Earthscan, 2005) 3.
[151] World Resources Institute (n. 76) 116.
[152] Ibid. 19. See also J. Harrison, 'Establishing a Meaningful Human Rights Due Diligence Process for Corporations: Learning from Experience of Human Rights Impact Assessment' (2013) 31 *Impact Assessment and Project Appraisal* 107–17.
[153] Mason (n. 150) 108.
[154] World Resources Institute (n. 76) 73.

environmental behaviour of corporations that depend on reputation and market power in the face of stakeholders.[155]

Overall, accountability, as opposed to responsibility, seems to make reference to the means rather than the result that should be achieved by environmentally sound corporate conduct in light of public expectations. Rather than referring to social control, accountability is more related to the idea of 'social direction' through incentives and prevention.[156] The concept of accountability takes into account that the protection of the environment cannot be the sole or main task of the private sector, given the importance of many other, also endogenous, factors. At the same time, it serves to define the reasonable efforts, including a transparent and participatory framework for decision-making, that are expected to be put in place, according to international standards, by private companies towards the protection of a certain interest or the attainment of a certain environmental result.

It can be argued that corporate accountability corresponds to the procedural dimension of the business responsibility to respect human rights—companies' 'due diligence".[157] In effect, due diligence has been broken down into its procedural elements in the 2011 UN Guiding Principles on Business and Human Rights as: (i) assessing actual and potential impacts with meaningful consultations with potentially affected groups and other stakeholders at regular intervals; (ii) integrating the assessment findings in internal decision-making, budget allocation, and oversight processes; (iii) tracking responses (including by drawing on feedback from affected stakeholders); and (iv) communicating how impacts are addressed to right-holders in a manner that is sufficient for stakeholders to evaluate the adequacy of the company's response.[158] These are all elements that have been identified in international environmental law.

An element that has not emerged quite as clearly in the context of international environmental law policy debates, however, is that, according to the UN Framework, enterprises 'should establish or participate in' grievance mechanisms. These should be legitimate, transparent, predictable, equitable, right-compatible, and directly accessible to individuals and communities that may directly be affected by their business operations. They seek both to support the identification of adverse impacts and systematic problems, and remedy adverse impacts.[159]

These international developments can be usefully related to the scholarly interpretation of accountability as a 'system of power control' – a means to furnish substantial reasons or a convincing explanation of one's actions, and a system of

---

[155] Ibid. 110; contra R. O. Keohane, 'The Concept of Accountability in World Politics and the Use of Force' (2003) 24 *Michigan Journal of International Law* 1121, where the author argued that the concept of accountability not only implies answering for one's own actions but also being exposed to sanctions.

[156] N. Bobbio, *Dalla struttura alla funzione: nuovi studi di teoria del diritto* (Milano: Edizioni di Comunità, 1977) 54.

[157] UN Framework on Business and Human Rights, paras 25 and 58.

[158] UN Guiding Principles, paras 17–21.

[159] Ibid. paras 29 and 31.

'quasi-juridical' answerability based on standards that are internationally defined and implemented.[160] Indeed, some authors assert that the international community is moving towards the implementation of a mechanism for enhanced democratic control over business, with a view to preventing corporate environmental damage.[161]

For present purposes, Boven's narrow concept of accountability appears particularly suitable: 'a relationship between an actor and a forum, in which the actor has an obligation to explain and justify his/her conduct, the forum can pose questions and pass judgement [on the adequacy of the information provided and or the legitimacy of a conduct], and the actor can face consequences.'[162] The latter includes 'implicit and informal' consequences such as having to render account publicly or being affected by negative publicity generated by the process.[163] Accordingly, accountability can be social, without hierarchical relations.[164] It can have a marked learning dimension, in that it is aimed at improving effectiveness, trust, and acceptance of power through openness and reflexivity that 'forces reflection on successes and failures, including for those [companies] that are not immediately involved in a particular accountability process'.[165]

Corporate accountability needs, therefore, to be differentiated from the concept of corporate governance, which in turn refers to an internal process within a business entity to respond to societal expectations concerning its environmentally sound conduct,[166] such as the 'organization of ownership, participation, disclosure and decision-making in corporations'.[167] Corporate governance refers to the phenomenon of self-regulation, to the policies and practices that business voluntarily adopts internally because of its perceptions of the relevance of international law to its operations and pressure from civil society.[168] Corporate accountability, conversely, is grounded in soft-law and quasi-judicial dimensions based on standard-setting and review mechanisms that function outside companies—without being, however, a formal part of the judicial institutions at the national or international

---

[160] N. Rosemann, *The UN Norms on Corporate Human Rights Responsibilities: An Innovating Instrument to Strengthen Business' Human Rights Performance*, Friedrich-Ebert-Stiftung Occasional Geneva Papers n. 20, 2005, 15.
[161] Ong (n. 74) 719.
[162] Bovens (n. 145) 451.
[163] Even if developed with actors exercising public powers in mind: ibid. 452.
[164] Ibid. 460.
[165] Ibid. 464.
[166] Definition in OECD, 'Principles of Corporate Governance' (2004) <http://www.oecd.org/dataoecd/32/18/31557724.pdf>, whose preamble reads: 'Corporate governance involves a set of relationships between a company's management, its board, its shareholders and other stakeholders. Corporate governance also provides the structure through which the objectives of the company are set, and the means of attaining those objectives and monitoring performance are determined.'
[167] P. Muchlinski, 'Corporate Social Responsibility' in P. Muhclinski, F. Ortino, and C. Schreuer (eds), *The Oxford Handbook of International Investment Law* (Oxford: Oxford University Press, 2008) 637, 645.
[168] Report of the Special Representative (n. 127) para. 63.

level. Nonetheless, corporate governance may experience a certain degree of cross-fertilization with corporate accountability, in adopting similar standards, and thus providing an indication of business' acceptance of international standards.[169] Corporate governance can provide tools for the implementation of international corporate environmental accountability and responsibility standards, by embedding them in the managerial decision-making structure of a company.[170]

5. Aim and structure of the book

As will be discussed in this book, corporate accountability has gathered quicker acceptance internationally than corporate responsibility. Several aspects of due diligence, as framed under the UN Framework on Business and Human Rights, have drawn on procedural environmental approaches[171] for private companies to be more transparent, participatory, and proactive in their efforts to respond to the expectations of the international community based on international law. More precise substantive standards of corporate environmental responsibility, in turn, have started to emerge internationally since the 2010s, including as a result of the advancements in the debate on human rights and the environment.

This book aims to assess the extent to which public international law has contributed to the identification of corporate accountability and responsibility standards against which multinationals have to explain their conduct, as well as the development of mechanisms to support transparency, prevention, monitoring, and learning. The analysis is premised and informed by the shortcomings of traditional legal solutions to ensure the environmentally sound conduct of multinational companies through national and international law (Chapter 2).

The central part of the book reveals the emergence of converging international standards for corporate environmental accountability and responsibility in various initiatives undertaken by different international organizations, at different points in time, and with varying degrees of inter-governmental involvement. Attention is first devoted to the elaboration of international standards of corporate environmental accountability and responsibility in the framework of the UN, the OECD, and the International Finance Corporation of the World Bank group (Chapter 3). The following chapters assesses the influence of the Convention on Biological Diversity on the level of normative detail and the degree of international

---

[169] Such weaknesses have been identified also by the UN Special Representative as follows: 'Companies do not necessarily recognize those [human] rights on which they may have the greatest impact, and when drawing from international instruments, the language they use is rarely identical and their interpretations are so elastic that the standards lose meaning.' Ibid. para. 74.

[170] Muchlinski (n. 167) 645.

[171] E. Morgera, 'From Corporate Social Responsibility to Accountability Mechanisms' in P.-M. Dupuy and J. Viñuales (eds), *Harnessing Foreign Investment to Promote Environmental Protection: Incentives and Safeguards* (Cambridge: Cambridge University Press, 2013) 321, 333.

acceptance of emerging international standards of corporate environmental accountability (Chapter 4) and corporate environmental responsibility (Chapter 5). The practical relevance of the international standards for corporate environmental accountability and responsibility is assessed in the final chapter of this book, which focuses on the tools for compliance that international organizations have at their disposal and the extent to which these tools provide consequences (Chapter 6). This provides an opportunity to assess convergence in the interpretation and application of international standards, as well as the advantages and disadvantages of these approaches vis-à-vis traditional legal solutions. The conclusions take stock of the overall state of development of international law on corporate environmental accountability and responsibility, and outlines areas for further research and more systematic dialogue with other areas of scholarship and practice.

2
The Shortcomings of Traditional Legal Solutions

The limitations inherent in relevant parts of national and international law are the reasons for the emergence of international standards of corporate environmental accountability and responsibility. This chapter will discuss how control over multinational enterprises at the national level—the legal control over a subsidiary of a multinational company by the host State, and the legal control over a multinational parent company by the home State—is ineffective. Despite the surge in efforts at the national level (by States and non-State actors) since the endorsement of the UN Guiding Principles on Business and Human Rights in 2011,[1] the proposal to develop a new international treaty in this area in 2014 indicates a continuing significant level of dissatisfaction with the current approaches at the national level.[2]

Even more significant limits affect the possibility of ensuring the environmentally sound conduct of business under the international law on State responsibility, civil and criminal liability in international environmental law, or international criminal law. Meanwhile, multinationals enjoy a significant degree of protection under international investment law, which adds to the reasons behind the recourse to international standards of corporate environmental accountability and responsibility. International human rights law, in turn, while also affording certain protection to private companies, has over the last decade emerged as the most dynamic area of international law to address unresolved questions about the conduct of multinational enterprises, including from an environmental perspective.

1 The shortcomings of national control

National control over private companies, in particular multinational companies, has proved ineffective, as a result of the fact that 'corporations are present nowhere; their activities through their agents may be present everywhere and the location of

---

[1] 'Guiding Principles on Business and Human Rights to implement the UN Protect, Respect and Remedy Framework' (2011) UN Doc. A/HRC/17/31, adopted by the Human Rights Council in Res. 17/4 (6 July 2011)—hereinafter, UN Guiding Principles, which will be discussed in detail in Ch. 3.

[2] Human Rights Council Res. 26/9 of 26 June 2014 on the elaboration of an International Legally Binding Instrument on Transnational Corporations and Other Business Enterprises.

these activities may change almost instantaneously'.³ The following sections will discuss the shortcomings of host and home State control, in turn.

1.1 Host State control

The most immediate legal system for ensuring the environmentally sound conduct of private enterprises is that of the State in which they operate. According to the principle of national sovereignty, foreign investors, such as multinationals, are also subject to the control of the host State—the State in which they operate.⁴ Control by the host State entails unilateral action for the protection of national interests in two stages: before the entry of a foreign investor into the host State and after its establishment there.

Before a multinational enters the host State, the latter enjoys great discretion in permitting or conditioning the company's entrance. This discretion is generally regulated by national foreign investment laws. They not only provide for guarantees against expropriation and for dispute settlement, and tax and non-tax incentives, but also detail a screening process of entry through administrative agencies and often require a feasibility study.⁵ Feasibility studies often include an environmental impact assessment.⁶ In concluding the screening process, conditions could be attached by the administrative agency to the entry of the foreign investor into the host State and to the manner in which it operates its business. Such conditions may include requirements on local collaborations, capitalization, export targets, local equity, and environmental protection.⁷ In this regard, it should be highlighted that an investment project or agreement can be cancelled, even after it has commenced, if it can be shown that an environmental condition has not been fulfilled, and, according to some authors, also if harm to the environment is irreversible or outweighs the benefits of the project.⁸

The second stage of host State control is after the establishment of the enterprise in the host State. Then, corporations have to abide by all national laws and regulations—including environmental ones, as the investor voluntarily subjects himself to the regime of the host State.⁹ In this phase, permits may need to be obtained and further administrative controls over foreign direct investment

---

[3] V. Lowe, 'Corporations as International Actors and International Law Makers' (2004) 13 *Italian Yearbook of International Law* 23, 32.
[4] M. Sornarajah, *The International Law on Foreign Investment* (Cambridge: Cambridge University Press, 2010) ch. 2.
[5] P. Muchlinski, *Multinational Enterprises and the Law* (Oxford: Oxford University Press, 2007) ch. 5.
[6] Sornarajah (n. 4) 109.
[7] Ibid. 109–11.
[8] Ibid.
[9] For a complete review of host State methods of controlling foreign investors, Muchlinski (n. 5) ch. 3; and C. D. Wallace, *The Multinational Enterprise and Legal Control* (The Hague: Martinus Nijhoff Publishers, 2002).

operations may take place. The pre- and post-establishment phases are strictly interlinked, as the first often leads to conditions to be applied in the second.

There exists no right of establishment for foreign investors in any country as a general rule of international law, and administrative screening of foreign direct investment is common prior to entry.[10] But the right of the State to control such entry often is limited by other international obligations to which the country has subjected itself. As will be discussed in more detail below, host States are usually parties to bilateral and multilateral investment treaties, under which they have accepted limitations to their discretion to allow the entry of foreign investors into their territory.

In addition, some significant factual constraints on States' exercise of their sovereignty in this realm should be considered. In light of the competition among host States to receiving foreign investment,[11] the bargaining power of the foreign investor is at its highest at the time of entry. The foreign investment contract, resulting from the acceptance of foreign direct investment by the host State, is therefore often drafted with as many contractual guarantees as possible for the protection of the investment after establishment in the host State, usually linking it to external legal systems or tribunals for protecting investors against risks.[12] As a result, the host State may be limited in its capacity to change (refine, or update) its environmental laws, because this may adversely affect the foreign investment and could entail the payment of compensation to foreign companies.[13]

Besides the international obligations embodied in bilateral and other investment treaties and contractual limitations agreed upon with specific investors, other significant shortcomings affect the capacity of host States to effectively control the environmental conduct of multinationals after their establishment in the host country. First, difficulties derive from the limited financial and human resources that the host State may have in effectively implementing and enforcing their national environmental laws.[14] Second, lack of information as to the technology and the risks of the activities of the multinationals within a State's territory may further hinder the control of the host State. Third, even when the host State is able to hold a multinational accountable for environmental damage, the very structure of the multinational may prevent the host State from obtaining full compensation and redress for victims. This is the case when a subsidiary with limited financial resources

---

[10] M. Sornarajah, *The Settlement of Foreign Investment Disputes* (The Hague: Kluwer Law International, 2000) 69.

[11] O. de Schutter, *Towards Corporate Accountability for Human and Environmental Rights Abuses*, discussion paper for the European Coalition for Corporate Justice (April 2007) 3.

[12] Sornarajah (n. 4) 102.

[13] Eg L. Cotula, 'Expropriation Clauses and Environmental Regulation: Diffusion of Law in the Era of Investment Treaties' (2015) 24 *Review of European, Comparative and International Environmental Law* 278.

[14] Eg M. Taylor, 'Putting *OK Tedi* in Perspective' in G. Banks and C. Ballard (eds), *The Ok Tedi Settlement: Issues, Outcomes and Implications* (Canberra: National Centre for Development Studies and Resource Management, 1997) 12.

causes environmental harm.[15] This is the effect of the 'corporate veil'—the separate legal personality between different entities of the same multinational group. It serves to protect one corporate entity from the liabilities of other corporate entities within the same multinational enterprise.[16]

Furthermore, conflicts of interests may arise for host State courts dealing with the environmental damage caused by the operations of a foreign company within their territory. Particularly in the case of developing countries, the revenues from the concessions to the multinational may well represent a considerable share of the State's gross domestic product (GDP)[17] and a far larger source of external finance than Official Development Assistance.[18,19] The host State may also have authorized the foreign company's operations causing environmental damage, so it may be considered at least partly responsible for the damage.[20] Or, host States may join the business venture, thus becoming even more directly involved in the operations of the multinational.[21]

---

[15] T. Scovazzi, 'Industrial Accidents and the Veil of Transnational Corporations' in F. Francioni and T. Scovazzi (eds), *International Responsibility for Environmental Harm* (London: Graham & Trotman, 1991) 395; O. De Schutter, 'Towards a New Treaty on Business and Human Rights' (2016) 1 *Business and Human Rights Journal* 41, 47–54.

[16] A. Palmer, *Community Redress and Multinational Enterprises* (London: Foundation for International Environmental Law and Development, 2003) 8–9.

[17] For instance, the case of pollution of Guyana's Essequibo River due to gold mining activities in 1995 by a Canadian multinational subsidiary. A class action was brought by 23,000 Guyanese victims before the Canadian Superior Court, which dismissed it on grounds of *forum non conveniens*. Since the mine was the source of 20 percent of Guyana's GDP, there were serious concerns as to whether a fair hearing could be held in the host country. *Recherches Internationales Quebec v. Cambior Inc.*, Canada Superior Court, Quebec, no. 500–06–000034–971)] 1998 QJ N2554 (QL). For a full account of the case, S. Seck, 'Environmental Harm in Developing Countries caused by Subsidiaries of Canadian Mining Corporations: The Interface of Public and Private International Law' (1999) 37 *The Canadian Yearbook of International Law* 139; and R. Unger, 'Brandishing the Precautionary Principle through the Alien Tort Claims Act' (2001) 9 *New York University School of Law Environmental Law Journal* 638, 638.

[18] P. Sands, *Principles of International Environmental Law*, 2nd edn (Cambridge: Cambridge University Press, 2003) 1056.

[19] This was explicitly stated, for instance, by the Superior Court of Bogotá when deciding that neither the State nor a multinational company were responsible for damage caused by oil drilling activities resulting in deforestation, pollution, ecosystem degradation, and damage to natural resources traditionally used by the U'wa indigenous tribe in an adjacent reservation, refusing to impair the host country's essential economic interest by suspending oil exploration. Initially, the Colombian Constitutional Court had revoked the oil company's environmental licence, holding that the relevant EIA did not take into consideration the impacts on the U'wa tribe of the oil operations, which threatened the people's ethnic, cultural, and economic identity. A. Gibson, 'The Real Price of Oil: Cultural Survival and the U'wa of Colombia' (2000) 34 *Colorado Journal of International Environmental Law and Policy* 139; J. A. Cohan, 'Environmental Rights of Indigenous Peoples under the Alien Tort Claims Act, the Public Trust Doctrine and Corporate Ethics, and Environmental Dispute Resolution' (2001–02) 20 *UCLA Journal of Environmental Law and Policy* 133, 142.

[20] In the *Montedison* case, for instance, public servants responsible for authorizing a private company to discharge industrial waste at sea, were held liable for environmental damage, as held by Cassazione, Sez. Unite, 25 January 1989, n. 440, reprinted in 1989 *Rivista Giuridica dell'Ambiente* 97. A. Postiglione, 'Danno ambientale e Corte di Cassazione' (1989) *Rivista giuridica dell'Ambiente* 97; A. Kiss, 'Un cas de pollution internationale: l'affaire des boues rouges' (1975) 102 *Journal du Droit International* 207; T. Scovazzi, 'Immersione di sostanze inquinanti in mare e risarcimento del danno' (1986) *Rivista giuridica dell' ambiente* 105.

[21] For instance, the case of the OK Tedi pollution in Papua New Guinea, discussed in Banks and Ballard (n. 14).

Moreover, there are several practical barriers to seeking redress in host countries when a multinational causes environmental damage.[22] For instance, plaintiffs may lack standing when the environmental damage is too general, or not specific to a certain individual/group. Or they may lack financial and legal resources to file the claim, if these are not provided by the State. Finally, in some countries the level of damages that can be awarded or the fines that can be imposed against companies are so low, that it is often cheaper for corporations to pay damages than to invest in management or structures to prevent environmental harm from occurring.[23]

The corporate veil, coupled with the transboundary character of multinationals' operations, makes it extremely difficult for the host State to effectively control corporate conduct. For all these reasons, the host State may not represent an available venue for the full protection of the interests of the victims of environmental degradation.[24] Yet host State control is often considered the most significant level of regulation of multinationals, because of the limited development of international initiatives on the matter.[25]

1.2 Home State control

Control over corporate environmental conduct even when companies operate abroad can be exercised by the State in which the multinational is incorporated or headquartered, through the extraterritorial application of national standards of the home State[26] or international standards[27] over the multinationals' operations abroad. Such control has already been put in place for promoting foreign direct investment through risk insurance, tax exemptions, and anti-trust and export control

---

[22] Committee on Economic, Social and Cultural Rights, General Comment No. 24 on State Obligations under the International Covenant on Economic, Social and Cultural Rights in the Context of Business Activities, section (2017) UN Doc. E/C.12/GC/24, paras 42–43.

[23] The International Council on Human Rights Policy, *Beyond Voluntarism: Human Rights and the Developing International Legal Obligations for Companies* (Versoix: International Council on Human Rights Policy, 2002) 79.

[24] The consideration has also been formulated in relation to the *Bhopal* case by H. Hosein, 'Unsettling: Bhopal and the Resolution of International Disputes Involving an Environmental Disaster' (1993) 16 *Boston College International and Comparative Law Review* 285, 299.

[25] Muchlinski (n. 5) 107.

[26] For a complete review of host State methods of controlling foreign investors, Sornarajah (n. 4) ch. 3; and Muchlinski (n. 5) ch. 5. See also J. Zerk, 'Corporate Liabilty for Gross Human Rights Abuses: Towards a Fairer and More Effective System of Domestic Law Remedies', report prepared for the Office of the High Commissioner for Human Rights (2012); Office of the High Commissioner for Human Rights, Report to the Human Rights Council: Improving accountability and access to remedy for victims of business-related human rights abuse (2016) UN Doc. A/HRC/32/19; and Improving Access to Remedy in the area of Business and Human Rights at the EU Level: Opinion of the European Union Agency for Fundamental Rights (10 April 2017).

[27] F. Francioni, *Imprese multinazionali, protezione diplomatica e responsabilità internazionale* (Milano: Giuffré Editore, 1979).

laws.[28] Accordingly, it has been argued that home State control could also include other areas of public interest, such as human rights and environmental liability.[29]

This may be justified on the assumption that developed States owe to the international community a duty of control over multinationals, because these States have better means of exercising such control. As multinationals' activities eventually benefit the home State's economic prosperity, they should not be secured through injury to other States or to the welfare of the international community as a whole.[30] This is particularly the case when the home State is not effectively ensuring compliance with international environmental law.[31] It can also be argued that the exercise of sovereignty resulting in negative impacts on the territory of another State requires 'by analogy' that considerations of environmental protection apply when the State exercises a right under international law within the territory of another State.[32]

Home State control of multinationals is, however, a limited way of ensuring the responsible conduct of multinationals. First and foremost, it poses a broad issue of respect for the national sovereignty of foreign countries. Extraterritorial jurisdiction is not prohibited by international law when there is enough connection with the home State to justify it, and as long as there are no protests from host States. While some States have manifested their willingness to have the home State controlling multinationals in their territory,[33] other countries, however, may view it with suspicion when home State standards conflict with the host State's regulation of foreign direct investment and protection of the environment.[34] In particular with regard to the extraterritorial protection of social, economic, and cultural rights, commentators have identified the risk of 'normative competency conflicts' between home and host States due the distributive justice questions inherent in this group of human rights. This arguably leads to the situation where 'what is considered a human rights violation in one (developed) country may be considered a legitimate exercise of state authority in another (developing) country'.[35]

In the case of home States willing to apply their domestic standards to their multinational operating abroad, this approach can also lead to the application of different environmental regulations to different multinationals operating in

---

[28] Ibid. 24 and 112–31; Sornarajah (n. 4) 144–71 Francioni (n. 27) 24.
[29] Sornarajah (n. 4) 149–53.
[30] Francioni (n. 27) 141; Sornarajah (n. 4) 164–68.
[31] *Iron Rhine Railway Arbitration* (Belgium and the Netherlands), Award of the Arbitral Tribunal (24 May 2005) para. 223.
[32] Ibid.
[33] India in the *Bhopal* case (*Re Union Carbide Corat Gas Plant Disaster*, 634 F. Supat 842, 844 (S.D.N.Y. 1986), aff'd, 809 F.2d 195 (2nd Cir. 1987) and Ecuador in the *Texaco* case (*Aguinda v. Texaco*, No. 93 Civ 7527 (VLB), 1994 U.S. Dist. (S.D.N.Y. Apr. 11, 1994) 22–23).
[34] Palmer (n. 16) 12; Muchlinski (n 5) 109.
[35] D. Augenstein and D. Kinley, 'Beyond the 100 Acre Wood: In Which International Human Rights Law Finds New Ways to Tame Global Corporate Power' (2015) 19 *International Journal of Human Rights* 828.

the same sector and same foreign country, depending on their country of origin, thereby conferring a competitive advantage to those multinationals whose home State has lower environmental standards.[36] Even where home States apply international standards endorsed also by the host State, this approach still gives rise to major logistical, financial, and technical questions in terms of monitoring compliance with home State norms in foreign countries.

Nevertheless, the difficulties in litigating environmental cases in host States have led victims to seek redress in home State courts,[37] based on the idea of a 'monolithic multinational', according to which victims of accidents are entitled to sue the multinational in the State where the decision-making centre of the corporation is located, because of the exclusive knowledge of the risks involved in the multinationals' activities and inherent obligation to provide warnings of potential hazards.[38] Home States have an international duty to provide access to remedies in their domestic courts for violations of international human rights and environmental law occurring in a host State when victims do not have access to effective judicial remedy in that State, as discussed below,[39] but there are objections to viewing this as settled in international law. The phenomenon of transnational litigation has thus emerged as an effort to bring to justice at the national level the decision-making centre of the multinational structure, in order to seek redress beyond the financial limitations of the corporate entities of the same group. This phenomenon, also labelled 'foreign direct liability',[40] has particularly concerned countries such as the US, the UK, the Netherlands, Canada, and Australia,[41] arguably allowing for 'a *de facto* globalization of law that is driven by necessity', in the absence of other effective remedies.[42]

---

[36] J. P. Eaton, 'The Nigerian Tragedy, Environmental Regulation of Transnational Corporations, and the Human Right to a Healthy Environment' (1997) 15 *Boston University International Law Journal* 261, 276; T. M. Kerr, 'What's Good for General Motors Is Not Always Good for Developing Nations: Standardizing Environmental Assessment of Foreign-Investment Projects in Developing Countries' (1995) 29 *The International Lawyer* 153, 153.

[37] A. Khokhryakova, 'Beanal v. Freeport-Mcmoran, Inc.: Liability of a Private Actor for an International Environmental Tort under the Alien Tort Claims Act' (1998) 9 *Colorado Journal of International Environmental Law* 463, 463.

[38] T. Gladwin, 'A Case Study of the Bhopal Tragedy' in C. Pearson (ed.), *Multinational Corporations, Environment, and the Third World* (Durham: Duke University Press, 1987) 223; Scovazzi (n. 15) 408 and 413; Hosein (n. 24) 295 and B. Desai, 'The Bhopal Gas Leak Disaster Litigation: An Overview' (1994) *Asian Yearbook of International Law* 163.

[39] Section 2.3. See De Schutter (n. 15) at 54–55, referring to UN High Commissioner for Human Rights 'Analytical Study on the Relationship between Human Rights and the Environment' (2011) UN A/HRC/19/34, para. 72.

[40] H. Ward, 'Securing Transnational Corporate Accountability through National Courts: Implications and Policy Options' (2001) 24 *Hastings International and Comparative Law Review* 451, 454.

[41] H. Ward, *Governing Multinationals: The Role of Foreign Direct Liability* (London: Royal Institute for International Affairs, 2001); F. Calder and M. Culverwell, *Following up the WSSD Commitments on Corporate Responsibility & Accountability* (London: Royal Institute of International Affairs, 2004) 50–51 <http://www.riia.org/pdf/research/sdp/WSSD.pdf>.

[42] H. Ward, 'Towards a New Convention on Corporate Accountability? Some Lessons from the Thor Chemicals and Cape PLC Cases' (2002) 13 *Yearbook of International Environmental Law* 105, 109.

There are several potential advantages to this level of action. Resort to foreign direct liability may help raise international attention on the alleged facts and putting international pressure for obtaining remedial action on the multinational.[43] Secondly, the preparation of a foreign direct liability claim usually leads to the building of global alliances with international non-governmental organizations (NGOs) and leading experts, exposing new audiences to questions about corporate accountability and the protection of the environment. Finally, prospects of home State litigation may serve as a deterrent for multinationals' environmentally irresponsible conduct,[44] particularly if punitive damages may be awarded.[45] Foreign direct liability may also play a role in reducing the incentive for multinationals to lobby against higher environmental standards in host countries, because of the availability of home country levels of compensation even for damages caused abroad.[46]

Many limitations, however, characterize the resort to foreign direct liability.[47] First and foremost, home State courts are in a conflict of interests as to deciding cases involving national companies abroad. This attitude is exemplified by the use of the doctrine of *forum non conveniens*, namely the discretion of a court to refuse to hear a case if the forum is inappropriate or inconvenient to the defendant. In the case of Texaco/Chevron oil pollution in Ecuador, for instance, after several unsuccessful attempts,[48] a US court[49] established in 2002 the jurisdiction of the Ecuador courts so that their judgment could be enforceable against Texaco's assets in the US.[50] This led an Ecuadorian court in 2011 to award damages of $8.6 billion and clean-up costs. This was, however, followed by a US court ruling that the Ecuadorian judgment should not be enforced as it was obtained by corrupt means.[51] Questions of jurisdiction have placed unfair obstacles in the way of foreign plaintiffs, thereby implicitly favouring multinationals.[52] Undeniably, this

---

[43] In the case of mine waste pollution of OK Tedi River in Papua New Guinea, for instance, the company reviewed and modified its environmental management policies voluntarily, due to the significant public attention attracted by a case brought before Australian courts: Palmer (n. 16) 11.

[44] S. Zia-Zarifi, 'Suing Multinational Corporations in the US for Violating International Law' (1999) 4 *UCLA Journal of International Law and Foreign Affairs* 81, 146.

[45] F. Rivera, 'A Response to the Corporate Campaign against the Alien Tort Claims Act' (2003) 14 *Indiana International and Comparative Law Review* 251, 258.

[46] Ward (n. 41) 137.

[47] G. Skinner, R. McCorquodale, and O. De Schutter, with A. Lambe, *The Third Pillar: Access to Judicial Remedies for Human Rights Violations by Transnational Business* (ICAR, CORE, and ECCJ, 2013).

[48] *Aguinda v. Texaco* [1996] S.D.N.Y., 945 F. Supp 625; *Aguinda v. Texaco* [2001] S.D.N.Y. No. 93 Civ 7527. See discussion in T. Lambooy, A. Argyrou, and M. Varner, 'An Analysis and Practical Application of the Guiding Principles on Providing Remedies with Special Reference to Case Studies Related to Oil Companies' in S. Deva and D. Bilchitz (eds), *Human Rights Obligations of Business: Beyond Corporate Responsibility to Respect?* (Cambridge: Cambridge University Press, 2013) 329, 338–41.

[49] *Aguinda v. Texaco*, 303 F.3d 470 (S.D.N.Y. 11 March 2002).

[50] J. Miller, 'Court of Appeals Ruling Re-Ignites Possibility that Texaco will Answer for its Alleged Degradation of Ecuador's Rainforests in US Courts' (1999) *Colorado Journal of International Environmental Law and Policy Yearbook* 139.

[51] https://business-humanrights.org/en/texacochevron-lawsuits-re-ecuador.

[52] P. Prince, 'Bhopal, Bougainville and OK Tedi: Why Australia's Forum Non Conveniens Approach is Better' (1998) 47 *International and Comparative Law Quarterly* 573.

doctrine has determined the practical outcome of several cases, to the point that 'issues of jurisdiction and liability are becoming harder to separate in view of the fact that evidence of parent company control that is sufficient to establish forum jurisdiction may also be sufficient to establish the liability'.[53] The application of the *forum non conveniens* doctrine 'may amount to a denial of justice if no effective local redress is available or the plaintiffs are prevented by intimidation, corruption, civil war or cost from resorting to local courts'.[54]

Another sign of conflict of interests can be discerned in the unwillingness of the home State court to pierce the corporate veil,[55] usually depending on whether it has been proven that the parent company exercises a certain level of control over the subsidiary abroad.[56] In effect, 'the function of *forum non conveniens* is often analogous to that of the corporate veil of separate legal personalities: both doctrines are used to insulate the parent company from liability carried out abroad'.[57] In the *Amoco Cadiz* oil spill case,[58] for instance, the claim for pollution damages and clean-up costs was filed by France before the US courts, alleging that the ship owner, the vessel's manager, and the parent company were each independently negligent in the design, construction, and maintenance of the vessel.[59] The argument was received favourably by the court, which found that the parent company was 'initially involved in and controlled the design, construction and management of' the *Amoco Cadiz* and treated it 'as if it were its own'.[60] Complexity and unpredictability, however, still characterize these kind of cases, as the choice of law can vary for different aspects of the case: in the *Amoco Cadiz* case, US courts applied US law to determine the liability, and French law to determine the amount of compensation due.[61]

Besides the tendency of home State courts to favour the interests of their multinationals and rule accordingly,[62] national judges may also be concerned about affecting foreign relations between the home and host State by unilaterally imposing liability on a multinational that was allowed to enter and operate in the host State.[63] This concern is exemplified by a case before US courts regarding the operation

---

[53] P. Muchlinski, 'The Bhopal Case: Controlling Ultrahazardous Industrial Activities by Foreign Investors' (1987) 50 *Modern Law Review* 545, 580.
[54] P. Birnie, A. Boyle, and C. Redgwell, *International Law and the Environment*, 3rd edn (Oxford: Oxford University Press, 2009) 309.
[55] Scovazzi (n. 15) 395.
[56] Palmer (n. 16) 12.
[57] M. J. Rogge, 'Towards Transnational Corporate Accountability in the Global Economy: Challenging the Doctrine of Forum Non Conveniens in In Re: Union Carbide, Alfaro, Sequihua, and Aguinda' (2001) 36 *Texas International Law Journal* 299, 300.
[58] For the full account of the case from the parent company's point of view, R. Jarashow, 'The Lessons for Multinationals of the Amoco Cadiz' (1986) *Energy Law* 789.
[59] Ibid. 791.
[60] *Amoco Cadiz*, District Court of Chicago, 18 April 1984, (1984) 2 Lloyds Rep. 304.
[61] Birnie et al. (n. 54) 312.
[62] Muchlinski (n. 53) 580.
[63] Khokhryakova (n. 37) 490.

of UK and Australian multinational mining companies causing environmental damage on the island of Bougainville, in Papua New Guinea, which was dismissed at the request of the US State Department on grounds of the political question doctrine.[64]

A further difficulty lies in the high standard of proof required by home State courts in terms of the factual basis of the claims, considering that most of the information is usually in the hands of the multinationals or of a host State unwilling to cooperate.[65] Issues of enforcement of judgments are equally relevant in the case of home and host State litigation: the order by the home State court to clean up a contaminated site in the host State may be difficult to monitor or enforce.[66]

Clearly, foreign direct liability is extremely expensive and time-consuming, for which victims may not have the resources. The transnational character and complexity of the cases involving a multinational often cause considerable delays in the hearing of the merits, which implies considerable delays in compensation,[67] in the few cases in which compensation is eventually awarded.

1.2.1 Application of international law by national courts

Home State case law may, in principle, contribute to the identification of a growing body of international law applicable to the environmental disasters caused by multinationals' operations. This has mainly been attempted in a limited number of jurisdictions.[68]

Lawsuits advocating the application of international standards to the irresponsible environmental conduct of multinationals have been traditionally filed in the US, under the Alien Tort Claim Act (ATCA).[69] The Act allows US district courts to have 'original jurisdiction of any civil action by an alien for a tort only, committed in violation of the law of nations or a treaty of the United States'.[70] This has led to 'the largest body of domestic jurisprudence regarding corporate responsibility for violations of international law'.[71] ATCA litigation 'can be used to illustrate

---

[64] N. L. Bridgeman, 'Human Rights Litigation under the ATCA as a Proxy for Environmental Claims' (2003) 6 *Yale Human Rights and Development Law Journal* 1, 2 and in n. 142, where it quotes *Sarei v. Rio Tinto Plc.*, 1204: 'the court to conclude that the United States' interests are aligned, or at least not inconsistent, with those of Papua New Guinea, in a way that suggests it would be appropriate to refrain from exercising jurisdiction in this case'.

[65] Zia-Zarifi (n. 44) 122.

[66] This was the reason why, in 2003, a US court dismissed the *Bhopal* case: Khokhryakova (n. 37) 492. *Bano v. Union Carbide Corat*, No. 99 Civ. 11329 (JFK) (S.D.N.Y., March 18, 2003); *Bano v. Union Carbide Corat*, No. 03–7416 (S.D.N.Y., March 17, 2004).

[67] Muchlinski (n. 53) 581.

[68] Palmer (n. 16) 11. M. D. Goldhaber, 'Corporate Human Rights Litigation in Non-US Courts: A Comparative Scorecard' (2013) 3 *University of California Irvine Law Review* 127.

[69] 28 U.S.C. §1350 (1993). For a discussion from an international law perspective, M. Karavias, *Corporate Obligations under International Law* (Oxford: Oxford University Press, 2013) 106–11.

[70] For an introduction to ATCA and its recent evolution, Zia-Zarifi (n. 44) 88–93.

[71] Report of the Special Representative of the Secretary-General on the Issue of Human Rights and Transnational Corporations and other Business Enterprises, John Ruggie, Clarifying the Concepts of 'Sphere of influence' and 'Complicity' (2008) UN Doc. A/HRC/8/16, para. 29.

the conceptual problems involved in bringing a human rights claim against a corporation'.[72] ATCA litigation had a 'limelight effect' in bringing issues of corporate accountability to the fore and a 'leverage effect' in enhancing victims' bargaining position and leading to out-of-court settlements.[73] But of thirty-six ATCA cases involving companies (on environmental and other corporate misconduct) before 2006, twenty were dismissed, three settled, and none decided in favour of the plaintiffs.[74] This is due to the limited international environmental law bases that can be invoked in the US and a more recent, restrictive interpretation of this recourse.

Given that the US is not party to any international treaty channelling liability to private actors responsible for environmental damage and has ratified only a restricted number of international environmental treaties in general,[75] most environmental cases have alleged violations of international *customary* law.[76] Several plaintiffs have thus based their allegations on the due diligence obligation to prevent transboundary pollution, according to the formulation of Principle 21 of the Stockholm Declaration,[77] which is a well-established international customary norm.[78] Nevertheless, US courts did not seem sympathetic to this argument. In 1991, for instance, a US court dismissed the case against a US corporation regarding an unauthorized shipment of hazardous waste for lack of subject-matter jurisdiction, since it did not find that customary international law was at stake. It rather found that Stockholm Principle 21

> [r]efer[s] only in a general sense to the responsibility of nations to insure that activities within their jurisdiction do not cause damage to the environment beyond their borders.[79]

---

[72] P. Muchlinski, 'Corporate Social Responsibility' in P. Muchlinski, F. Ortino, and C. Schreuer (eds), *The Oxford Handbook of International Investment Law* (Oxford: Oxford University Press, 2008) 637, 674.

[73] S. Deva, *Regulating Corporate Human Rights Violations: Humanizing Business* (Abingdon, Routledge: 2012) 74.

[74] Interim Report of the Special Representative of the Secretary-General on the issue of Human Rights and Transnational Corporations and other Business Enterprises (2006) UN Doc. E/CN.4/2006/97, para. 62.

[75] Khokhryakova (n. 37) 465.

[76] L. Lambert, 'At the Crossroads of Environmental and Human Rights Standards: Aguinda v. Texaco Inc: Using the Alien Tort Claims Act to Hold Multinational Corporate Violators of International Laws Accountable in U.S. Courts' (2000) 10 *Journal of Transnational Law & Policy* 109, 120.

[77] 'Declaration of the United Nations Conference on the Human Environment' (16 June 1972) UN Doc. A/CONF.48/14/Rev.1. Principle 21 reads as follows: 'States have, in accordance with the Charter of the United Nations and the principles of international law, the sovereign right to exploit their own resources pursuant to their own environmental policies, and the responsibility to ensure that activities within their jurisdiction or control do not cause damage to the environment of other States or of areas beyond the limits of national jurisdiction' (hereinafter, Principle 21).

[78] ICJ, *Gabčíkovo-Nagymaros Project* (Hungary-Slovakia), Judgment (25 September 1997), para. 53.

[79] *Amlon Metals, Inc. v. FMC Corat*, 775 F. Supat 668, 669 (S.D.N.Y. 1991). A. Rosencranz and R. Campbell, 'Foreign Environmental and Human Rights Suits against U.S. Corporations in U.S. Courts' (1999) 18 *Stanford Environmental Law Journal* 145, 155–56. But see *Aguinda v. Texaco*, No. 93 Civ 7527 (VLB), 1994 U.S. Dist. (S.D.N.Y. Apr. 11, 1994) 22–23 and comments by Cohan (n. 19) 162.

Another argument based on customary international law was brought before US courts. Plaintiffs alleged the violation of a 'customary obligation to avoid causing long-term, widespread and severe environmental damage that prejudices the health or survival of a population, or that deprives a people of its means of subsistence,'[80] in light of the prohibition of this type of environmental harm under the law of war which was considered of international concern regardless of whether State action was involved.[81] The respective decisions did not take note of this argument, however.

In other ATCA cases, arguments were based on principles of international environmental law. In the *Beanal v. Freeport-McMoran* case, the repeated dumping of massive quantities of toxic mine tailings into local river ways in Indonesia by a US multinational mining company[82] led the leader of the Amungme indigenous tribe, Beanal, to allege the violation of the precautionary, polluter-pays, and proximity principles by the company.[83] The court rejected these arguments, holding that the invoked environmental principles were not customary, because there was no 'universal consensus in the international community as to their binding status'.[84] In addition, it was held that even if the principles were customary, they did not apply to private actors, but only to States.[85] The court expanded on its decision during the appeal, in the following terms:

> The principles merely refer to a general sense of environmental responsibility and state abstract rights and liberties devoid of articulable or discernable standards and regulations to identify practices that constitute international environmental abuses or torts ... federal courts should exercise *extreme caution when adjudicating environmental claims under international law to ensure that environmental policies of the United States do not displace environmental policies of other governments*. Furthermore, the argument to abstain from interfering in a sovereign's environmental practices carries persuasive force especially when the alleged environmental torts and abuses occur within the sovereign's borders and do not affect neighboring countries.[86]

---

[80] For an overview of the lawsuit from the viewpoint of *amicus curiae* Earthrights, <http://www.earthrights.org/bhopal/index.shtml>.

[81] See also *Amici Curiae* Brief presented by Earthrights International, Kiss, Shelton, and Anaya among others in the *Flores v. Southern Peru Copper Corp.* case (3 December 2002) https://earthrights.org/publication/amicus-brief-in-flores-v-southern-peru-copper-corporation/; *Amici Curiae* Brief by Earthrights International in the *Texaco* case (November 2001) http://www.earthrights.org/legaldocs/jota_v._texaco_and_aguida_v._texaco.html; *Amici Curiae* Brief by Sierra Club and Earthrights International in the *Beanal v. Freeport McMoran* case (13 November 1998) <http://www.earthrights.org/legaldocs/beanal_v._freeport_mcmoran.html>.

[82] For a full account of the case, Khokhryakova (n. 37).

[83] Ibid. 472.

[84] *Beanal v. Freeport-McMoRan, Inc.*, 969 F. Supat 362 (E.D. La. 1997) (No. 96–1474).

[85] Khokhryakova (n. 37) 116. *Beanal v. Freeport-McMoRan, Inc.*, 969 F. Supat 362 (E.D. La. 1997) (No. 96–1474) 383–84.

[86] *Beanal v. Freeport-McMoRan, Inc.*, 197 F.3d 161, 166–67 (5th Cir. 1999) 167 (emphasis added). Unger (n. 17) 646.

This extract typifies the 'restrictive view of international environmental law' under ATCA.[87] As the above statement was not discussed further or supported by any citation other than previous jurisprudence, certain American scholars did not consider the decision a valid precedent.[88] But subsequent judgments under ATCA made express reference to these findings to dismiss other environmental cases.[89]

Overall, US judges have appeared reluctant or even suspicious as to the application of international environmental law under ATCA,[90] much more so than those based on human rights violations.[91] This may be motivated by the uncertainty about their legal status,[92] leading to the conclusion that '[US] courts do not yet believe that international environmental law has achieved the level of universality and specificity for supporting ATCA jurisdiction'.[93] Nevertheless, ATCA continues to be the subject of attention by legal scholars and human rights activists around the world, including from the perspective of protecting the rights of indigenous peoples in conjunction with the protection of the environment.[94]

The 2013 *Kiobel* decision of the US Supreme Court[95] has significantly limited opportunities to eventually develop national practice on universal civil jurisdiction.[96] The *Kiobel* decision underscored a presumption against extraterritorial application to avoid interferences with foreign policy,[97] pointing towards a more restrictive approach to direct foreign liability on the basis of customary international law in the future. It has been argued, however, that the *Kiobel* decision does not necessarily close the door to suits against US[98] corporations on the basis of 'federal common

---

[87] Zia-Zarifi (n. 44) 117.
[88] Ibid; Unger (n. 17) 645.
[89] *Flores v. Southern Peru Copper Corp.*, 22 and n. 43, where it stated that 'documents [presented by the plaintiffs] are insufficiently relevant or weighty to warrant discussion in the circumstances of the present case'.
[90] R. Herz, 'Litigating Environmental Abuses under the Alien Tort Claims Act: A Practical Assessment' (2000) 40 *Virginia Journal of International Law Association* 545, 572, where the author refers to 'the judiciary's general mistrust of international law'. Birnie et al. (n. 54) 327.
[91] In *Doe v. Unocal*, 963 F. Supat 880 (C.D. Cal. 1997), the court concluded that a corporation could be held liable as a State actor if jointly engaged in violations of international law with the host government, and admitted that, for certain violations, multinationals could be held liable even without being a State actor, but focused exclusively on the human rights aspects of the case and not on the inter-linked environmental ones. For a full account of the case, J. L. Peters, 'Human Rights and the Environment: The Unocal Litigation' (1998) *Colorado Journal of International Environmental Law and Policy Yearbook* 199. See also Khokhryakova (n. 37).
[92] Ward (n. 41) 110–11.
[93] Zia-Zarifi (n. 44) 114. See also E, Duruigbo, *Multinational Corporations and International Law: Accountability and Compliance Issues in the Petroleum Industry* (Ardlee, NY: Transnational Publishers, 2003) 184.
[94] J. Gilbert, 'Corporate Accountability and Indigenous Peoples: Prospects and Limitations of the US Alien Tort Claims Act' (2012) 19 *International Journal on Minority and Group Rights* 25, 47.
[95] *Esther Kiobel v. Royal Dutch Petroleum Co*, 133 S. Ct. 1659 (2013).
[96] D. Stewart and I. Wuerth, 'Kiobel v. Royal Dutch Petroleum Co.: The Supreme Court and the Alien Tort Statute' (2013) 107 *American Journal of International Law* 601, 621.
[97] Ibid. 606–08; see also J. Ku, 'Kiobel and the Surprising Death of Universal Jurisdiction under the Alien Tort Statute' (2013) 107 *American Journal of International Law* 835.
[98] A. Chander, 'Unshackling Foreign Corporations: Kiobel's Unexpected Legacy' 2013) 107 *American Journal of International Law* 829. See also A. Grear and B. H. Weston, 'The Betrayal of Human

law, some of which is derived, in part, from customary international law'.[99] The Supreme Court confirmed a 2004 cautious indication that ATCA claims must 'rest on a norm of international character accepted by the civilized world and defined with a specificity comparable to the features of the 18th-century paradigms' such as piracy.[100] This was seen by commentators as a 'continuing, seemingly visceral resistance to treating modern international law in both treaty and customary form as law of the US ... with results that are incompatible with the long-term interests of the United States in furthering the rule of law among States'.[101] It was further seen as disregarding 'contemporary "affirmative" forms of substantive law for resolving communal problems, like environmental degradation and egregious human rights violations'.[102] The decision has even been interpreted as excluding altogether international environmental law as actionable norms under the Statute.[103] Effectively, US courts' limited engagement with and conservative understanding of international law precludes arguments based on the progressive development of international environmental law,[104] including on the basis of international soft law with a view to holding 'decision-makers to take into account the interests of a greater proportion of the relevant stakeholders—including the interests of foreign stakeholders'.[105]

Paradoxically,[106] however, while the continued relevance of US courts for corporate (environmental) accountability is in doubt, national courts in the UK[107] and the Netherlands[108] are playing an increasing role, on the basis of national tort law or criminal law (and therefore not international law). This trend is emerging from the overcoming of the *forum non conveniens* barrier under EU law.[109] But it

---

Rights and the Urgency of Universal Corporate Accountability: Reflections on a Post-*Kiobel* Lawscape' (2015) 15 *Human Rights Law Review* 21.

[99] Stewart and Wuerth (n. 96) 609 and 620; on the relevance of the decision for customary international law, see ibid. 618–20.

[100] *Sosa v. Alvarez-Machain*, 542 U.S. 692 (2004) 725, 731–32, as discussed in Stewart and Wuerth (n. 96) 604–05.

[101] R. Steinhardt, 'Kiobel and the Weakening of Precedent: A Long Walk for a Short Drink' (2013) 107 *American Journal of International Law* 841, 845.

[102] Ibid.

[103] Birnie et al. (n. 54) 327, fn. 306.

[104] Generally on different national courts' approaches to international law, O. K. Fauchald and A. Nollkaemper, *The Practice of International and National Courts and the (De-)Fragmentation of International Law* (Oxford: Hart Publishing, 2012); and A. Nollkaemper and A. Reinisch (eds), *International Law in Domestic Courts: A Casebook* (Oxford: Oxford University Press, 2018).

[105] E. Benvenisti and G. Downs, *Between Fragmentation and Democracy: The Role of National and International Courts* (Cambridge: Cambridge University Press, 2017) 109 and 12.

[106] C. Kaeb and D. Scheffer, 'The Paradox of *Kiobel* in Europe' (2013) 107 *American Journal of International Law* 852.

[107] R. Meeran, 'Access to Remedy: The United Kingdom experience of MNC Tort Litigation for Human Rights Violations' in Deva and Bilchitz (n. 48) 387.

[108] R. McCorquodale, 'Waving Not Drowning: Kiobel Outside the United States' (2013) 107 *American Journal of International Law* 846.

[109] Council Regulation (EC) No. 44/2001 of 22 December 2000 on Jurisdiction and the Recognition and Enforcement of Judgments in Civil and Commercial Matters [2001] OJ L12/1, Art. 2(1); Case

is encountering opposition from governments:[110] both the US and the UK have taken measures that undermine access to justice (limiting the potential for corporate abuse victims to seek redress in US courts, and limiting legal fees for lawyers bringing human rights claims that would be borne by the opposing party).[111]

It can be concluded that recourse to national law and transnational litigation for holding corporations to account in light of international law remains a highly complex and experimental area of legal practice that has evolved into a burgeoning area of scholarship of its own right. This is set to continue to grow in importance also in connection with the expanding phenomenon of climate litigation.[112] This book cannot do justice to the extent and depth of the current debate. Rather, it limits itself to underscoring the importance of this area of practice and research as a background to the development, and an alternative to the application, of international standards that are examined in detail in the following chapters. More research is needed to better understand mutual influences among transnational litigation and international standards, as well as transnational contractual practices that seek to avoid the shortcomings identified in transnational litigation.[113]

2 The limits of international law

International law does not, in principle, envisage a special role for private companies, but rather provides for States to enact the necessary legislation to direct and control the conduct of these actors in their territory and under their jurisdiction.[114] International law could thus be relevant in an inter-State dispute over one State's failure to regulate and monitor adequately private companies under its control, under the international law on State responsibility. In addition, international environmental law includes regimes for civil liability that aim to specifically target

---

C-128/01, *Owusu v. Jackson* [2005] ECR I-553; and Council Regulation (EC) No. 864/2007 of 11 July 2007 on the Law Applicable to Non-Contractual Obligations [2007] OJ L11/40, Art. 4(1).

[110] The governments of the UK and the Netherlands held that foreign direct liability claims should not be based on international law, as it cannot be violated directly by private companies, in submitting their views to the US Supreme Court in the *Kiobel* case, revealing divergent agendas between executives and judiciary in these countries, as highlighted by Meeran (n. 107) 379; and McCorquodale (n. 108) 849.

[111] A. Mehra, 'Always in All Ways: Ensuring Business Respect for Human Rights' in C. Rodríguez-Garavito (ed.), *Business and Human Rights: Beyond the End of the Beginning* (Cambridge: Cambridge University Press, 2017) 138, 141.

[112] Eg Business and Human Rights Resource Centre, Turning up the Heat: Corporate Legal Accountability for Climate Change (2018), https://www.business-humanrights.org/sites/default/files/CLA_AB_2018_Full.pdf.

[113] N. Affolder, 'Square Pegs and Round Holes? Environmental Rights and the Private Sector' in B. Boer (ed.), *Environmental Law Dimensions of Human Rights* (Oxford: Oxford University Press, 2015) 11, 13 and 17–21.

[114] A. Kiss and D. Shelton, *International Environmental Law*, 3rd edn (New York: Transnational Publishers, 2004) 76.

certain operators. International regimes for criminal responsibility could also target the private sector. All these international approaches, however, are characterized by significant drawbacks, as will be discussed in the following sub-sections. This serves to justify the focus of this book on international environmental standards for corporate accountability and responsibility, as an alternative and complementary way of addressing the environmentally irresponsible conduct of multinationals and other companies at a point in time when States seem unable or unwilling to use traditional international law instruments to directly address corporate conduct.

This section will also investigate the link between international environmental law and other branches of public international law, such as international human rights law and international investment law. On the one hand, the search for an international system of corporate environmental accountability will be contrasted with the international protection of foreign investment, in as far as multinationals are concerned. On the other hand, actual and potential synergies between international legal instruments and processes for human rights protection and those for environmental protection will be explored, particularly in light of the exponential growth of international human rights practice concerning corporate accountability of the last decade.

2.1 International law on State responsibility

A traditional solution under international law that has been considered to hold multinationals and other companies accountable for environmental damage is the international law on State responsibility. This is a realm, however, in which 'almost nothing is certain'.[115] As State responsibility is the consequence of violations of international norms committed by State organs, one can argue that State responsibility can exist when a State instructed, directed, or controlled an entity,[116] such as a private company, that violated international environmental norms. Such a hypothesis may only cover a minority of cases of environmentally irresponsible conduct of private enterprises worldwide. It could, however, still be significant in cases in which private entities carry out functions traditionally discharged by the State,

---

[115] R. Higgins, *Problems and Processes. International Law and How We Use it* (Oxford: Clarendon Press, 1994) 146. For a discussion of international law on State responsibility from an environmental perspective, see M. Fitzmaurice, 'Liability and Compensation' in J. Viñuales (ed.), *The Rio Declaration on Environment and Development: A Commentary* (Oxford: Oxford University Press, 2015) 351, 351–59.

[116] Art. 8, ILC 'Articles on the Responsibility of States for Internationally Wrongful Acts', Report of the International Law Commission (2001) UN Doc. A/56/10, Ch. V. annex to General Assembly Res. 56/83 (12 December 2001), and corrected UN Doc. A/56/49(Vol. I)/Corr.4.

such as the provision of water.[117] It could be relevant if corporate activities result in less affordable or worse-quality goods and services that are dependent on natural resources and that are necessary for the enjoyment of basic economic, social, and cultural rights.[118] Other authors suggest that national governments should bear responsibility for actions of private companies abroad that have received foreign aid or export credit guarantees, on the basis of complicity.[119]

Alternatively, the attribution of private conduct to a State for the purpose of invoking that State's international responsibility could be arguably based on the State's failure to exercise the due diligence required by international norms in preventing or punishing certain conduct by the private company in its territory.[120] In this case, the international law of State responsibility is said to apply to the host State in the event of transboundary environmental harm caused by private entities operating within its territory.[121] In addition, State responsibility can arguably be applied to home States for the damage caused by their multinationals abroad, on the basis of a breach of due diligence over the parent company.[122] In this case, the transboundary element of the environmental damage would consist in the export of hazardous substances or technologies.[123] In both instances, it is necessary to prove a 'double due diligence standard', namely, that the company failed to exercise due diligence in carrying out its activities and that the State omitted to exercise due diligence in overseeing the activities of the company.[124]

Other authors suggest that State responsibility should function as a residual complement to civil liability and insurance regimes for environmental damage.[125] An operator fully complying with applicable domestic rules, standards, and government controls may be exempted from liability in case of environmental damage,[126] so claims for damages should be brought against the State.[127] These authors, therefore, affirm that a dual system would combine civil liability under domestic law,

---

[117] A. McBeth, *International Economic Actors and Human Rights* (Abingdon: Routledge, 2010) 251. See also Committee on Economic, Social and Cultural Rights, General Comment No. 24 (n. 22) para. 21.

[118] Committee on Economic, Social and Cultural Rights, General Comment No. 24 (n. 22) para. 22.

[119] Lowe (n. 3) 31.

[120] Birnie et al. (n. 54) 316–26; Francioni (n. 27) 153.

[121] G. Handl, 'State Liability for Accidental Transnational Environmental Damage by Private Persons' (1980) 74 *American Journal of International Law* 525, 526–40.

[122] F. Francioni, 'Exporting Environmental Hazard Through Multinational Enterprises: Can the State of Origin be Held Responsible?' in Francioni and Scovazzi (n. 15) 275.

[123] S. C. McCaffrey, 'The Work of the International Law Commission relating to Transfrontier Environmental Harm' (1987–88) 20 *New York University Journal of International Law and Policy* 715, 723.

[124] T. Scovazzi, 'State Responsibility for Environmental Harm' (2001) 12 *Yearbook of International Environmental Law* 43, 56.

[125] Birnie et al. (n. 54) 200.

[126] F. Orrego Vicuña, 'Current Trends in Responsibility and Liability for Environmental Harm under International Law' in K. Koufa (ed), *Protection of the Environment for the New Millennium* (Athens: Sakkoulas Publications, 2002) 127, 146.

[127] A. Antypas and S. Stec, 'Towards a Liability Regime for Damages to Transboundary Waters: A New Protocol in the UNECE Region' (2003) 14 *Journal of Water Law* 185, 188.

which will generally represent the most efficient means of securing redress for transboundary environmental damage, and State responsibility as a subsidiary remedy of last resort, when private parties are not liable or are insolvent.[128] This was indeed one of the ideas behind the work of the International Law Commission (ILC) on the study 'International Liability for Injurious Consequences of Acts Not Prohibited by International Law and Protection of the Environment'.[129] State liability arises directly from harm resulting from an activity permitted under international law, irrespective of the State's fault, negligence, or unlawful conduct. Liability originates automatically from the conduct of private operators acting in its territory or under its jurisdiction, on the assumption that it would be inequitable to leave the burden of unavoidable harm to lie where it falls merely because the source State has acted with all due diligence. The consequence of the damage is that the State is to pay compensation, and the activity that caused the damage can continue. The level of compensation is determined by negotiation, according to an equitable, rather than full, compensation standard. It could be counter-argued, however, that State liability is not widely supported at the international level nor is liability for any type of activity located within the territory of a State in the performance of which no State officials or agents are involved.[130] Another criticism is that non-performance of private entities' due diligence cannot easily be attributed to the State as conduct justifying attachment of liability.[131] In response to these critiques and as a reaction to the continuing reluctance of States to proceed with the topic, the ILC decided in 1997 to separate its articles on liability from those on prevention of environmental harm, and to postpone work on the former.[132] In effect, the text adopted by the ILC on prevention of transboundary harm from hazardous activities[133] envisages obligations of prevention and compensation on the State, not the operator.[134] On the other hand, one of eight draft principles on the allocation of loss in the case of transboundary harm arising out of hazardous activities, adopted by the Commission in 2006, calls upon States to impose liability on the operator.[135] Such decision has been considered 'against all logic', after the ILC

---

[128] Birnie et al. (n. 54) 282; Orrego Vicuña (n. 126) 146.
[129] R. Pisillo Mazzeschi, 'Le Nazioni Unite e la codificazione della responsabilità per danno ambientale' (1996) *Rivista Giuridica Dell' Ambiente* 371; and ILC, 'First Report on the Legal Regime for Allocation of Loss in case of Transboundary Harm arising out of Hazardous Activities' (2003) UN Doc. A/CN.4/531.
[130] ILC (n. 129) 4.
[131] Ibid. Contra C. Tomuschat, 'International Liability for Injurious Consequences Arising out of Acts Not Prohibited by International Law: The Work of the International Law Commission' in Francioni and Scovazzi (n. 15) 37, 44–45.
[132] Birnie et al. (n. 54) 190. ILC (n. 129) 17–18.
[133] ILC, 'Draft Articles on Prevention of Transboundary Harm from Hazardous Activities' (2001) UN Doc. A/56/10.
[134] ILC, 'Draft Principles on the Allocation of Loss in the case of Transboundary Harm arising out of Hazardous Activities' (2006) UN Doc. A/61/10, ch. V, paras 51–67.
[135] A. Nollkaemper, 'Responsibility of Transnational Corporations in International Environmental Law: Three Perspectives' in G. Winter (ed.), *Multilevel Governance of Global Environmental*

work had emphasized the lawfulness of activities and the possible implication that prevention of harm is not an absolute duty.[136]

During the discussions on State liability within the ILC, developing countries expressed their concern that multinationals lacked any duty to notify their home States of all the risks involved in the export of hazardous technology or to manage their operations with the same standards of safety and accountability as were applicable in the country of origin. They reiterated the argument that a duty might be placed on the State of origin to ensure that multinationals' export of hazardous technologies conform to international standards, and to accept a share in the allocation of loss resulting from any accident causing transboundary harm. The issue of the effective home or host State control over multinationals seems the most controversial point for the purpose of establishing international liability.[137] This is due to the recognition of the difficulty in exercising effective State control over multinationals, particularly in the case of developing countries, because of multinationals' 'financial power and the sole custody of knowledge on advanced science and technology'.[138]

One could also envisage a more complex scenario where both the home and the host State could incur independently joint responsibility for different breaches of their international law obligations to regulate foreign corporations operating in their own territories and to control their corporations operating abroad, respectively.[139] Or it could be possible for them to share international responsibility when the home and host State established a joint consortium through which they both empowered a company to exercise governmental authority.[140] There is no international or national case law on either scenario.[141]

Even if the resort to State responsibility could be successfully argued in the event of corporate environmental harm, several additional limits would undermine its effectiveness. First of all, the affected country has full discretion in deciding whether to bring the case against another State, thus leaving to foreign policy considerations the decision to seek clean-up costs and redress for victims.[142] Victims would thus be subject to the goodwill of States and, in any event, subject to long waits before compensation—a situation which would lead to great uncertainty for victims and possibly inequitable distribution of compensation.[143] Furthermore, in

Change: Perspectives from Science, Sociology and the Law (Cambridge: Cambridge University Press, 2006) 179.

[136] Higgins (n. 115) 164.
[137] ILC, 'Summary Record of the 2019th Meeting' (6 July 1987) UN Doc. A/CN.4/SR.2019.
[138] ILC (n. 116) 11.
[139] Karavias (n. 69) 99.
[140] Ibid.
[141] Ibid.
[142] A. Boyle, 'Making the Polluter Pay? Alternatives to State Responsibility in the Allocation of Transboundary Environmental Costs' in Francioni and Scovazzi (n. 15) 363, 364.
[143] Antypas and Stec (n. 127) 188.

the specific case of environmental damage, it may be particularly difficult to establish State responsibility, when the legal status or content of the invoked environmental rule is uncertain.[144] Uncertainty surrounding liability standards, the type of environmental damage that is recoverable, and the role of equitable balancing, means that the outcome of any claim remains inherently unpredictable.[145]

Most importantly, international practice has shown the unwillingness of States to remedy environmental damage through the traditional rules of State responsibility. A very small percentage of international environmental accidents has given rise to such claims.[146] For example, in the *Sandoz* case, when a multinational operating in Switzerland caused a widespread mercury spill into the Rhine, the Swiss government offered to restore the damaged ecosystem and pay compensation to the French government, without acknowledging its international responsibility.[147] None of the downstream States sought other remedies from Switzerland for a breach of international law either, even though Switzerland's failures to prevent transboundary environmental harm or to inform other affected countries in a timely manner were quite evident.[148] Characteristically, States are hesitant in adding detailed norms on State responsibility.[149] International practice has, therefore, relied on a sort of 'soft responsibility': States pay compensation for damage caused, avoiding or deliberately excluding admissions of responsibility at the interState level.[150]

It has also been argued that a multinational that is aiding and abetting the host State's violation of international human rights law could incur 'derivative responsibility' due to the causal connection with the State's international responsibility.[151] This would depend on the multinationals being aware that the State conduct would most likely contribute to a human rights violation (deriving such knowledge from publicly available information such as international or domestic

---

[144] J. Brunnée, 'Of Sense and Sensibility: Reflections on International Liability Regimes as Tools for Environmental Protection' (2004) 53 *International and Comparative Law Quarterly* 351, 354. See also G. Doeker and T. Gehring, 'Private or International Liability for Transnational Environmental Damage— The Precedent of Conventional Liability Regimes' (1990) 2 *Journal of Environmental Law* 1.

[145] Birnie et al. (n. 54) 199.

[146] Kiss and Shelton (n. 114) 611.

[147] A. Kiss, '"Tchernobale" ou la Pollution Accidentelle du Rhin par les Produits Chimiques' (1987) 33 *Annuaire Français de Droit International* 719; P-M. Dupuy, 'L' état et la réparation des dommages catastrophiques' in Francioni and Scovazzi (n. 15) 125; and A. Schwabach, 'The Sandoz Spill: The Failure of International Law to Protect the Rhine from Pollution' (1989) 16 *Ecology Law Quarterly* 443, 452 and 466.

[148] H. U. Jessurun d'Oliveira, 'The Sandoz Blaze: The Damage and the Public and Private Liabilities' in Francioni and Scovazzi (n. 15) 429, 439; A. Boos-Hersberger, 'Transboundary Water Pollution and State Responsibility: The Sandoz Spill' (1997) 4 *Annual Survey of International and Comparative Law* 103, 119; and D. F. McClatchey, 'Chernobyl and Sandoz One Decade Later: The Evolution of State Responsibility for International Disasters' (1996) 251 *Georgia Journal of International and Comparative Law* 659.

[149] A. Nollkaemper and I. Plakokefalos (eds), *The Practice of Shared Responsibility in International Law* (Cambridge: Cambridge University Press, 2017).

[150] Kiss and Shelton (n. 114) 617.

[151] Ibid. 104.

cases, NGO reports, communications from local communities) and significantly contribute to the violation.[152] Such a situation could involve a multinational providing technological, logistical, or financial support to the State, such as making possible mining operations in violation of the human rights of local population.[153] But such a hypothesis on derivative responsibility under international law for multinationals is necessarily premised on the argument that multinationals are directly bound by international human rights obligations,[154] which remains a matter of contention.

2.2 International regimes on civil liability for environmental damage: *en impasse*?

International environmental law includes several civil liability regimes targeting the private operator for environmental damage,[155] having led to the development of a 'web of related liability regimes' in the field of oil pollution, transport of hazardous goods by land and sea, transboundary movements of hazardous wastes, nuclear energy generation, maritime activity and human activity in Antarctica.[156] These treaties impose liability on operators.[157] They provide for the international harmonization of minimum standards of liability in national law, in specific instances where the environmental responsibility of the private sector is considered paramount. This approach in international law aims to deter harmful acts and remedy environmental damage by transferring the question from the inter-State level to interpersonal level, from public to private international law.[158] In practice, it seeks to prevent resort to the international law of State responsibility.[159] While it has been argued that these treaties 'directly address' corporations by specifying obligations of conduct upon them,[160] they still operate through domestic law to reach private operators.[161]

---

[152] Ibid.
[153] Ibid. 103.
[154] Ibid. 102.
[155] L. Bergkamp, *Liability and the Environment: Private and Public Law Aspects of Civil Liability for Environmental Harm in an International Context* (The Hague: Kluwer Law International, 2001); Francioni and Scovazzi (n. 15); M-L. Larsson, *The Law of Environmental Damage: Liability and Reparation* (The Hague: Kluwer Law International, 1999).
[156] Antypas and Stec (n. 127) 185.
[157] Nollkaemper (n. 135) 189.
[158] Kiss and Shelton (n. 114) 225–41.
[159] P-M. Dupuy, *La responsabilité international des états pour les domages d'origine technologique et industrielle* (Paris: Editions Pedone, 1976).
[160] N. Jägers, *Corporate Human Rights Obligations: In Search of Accountability* (Cambridge: Intersentia, 2002) 32; and S. Ratner, 'Business' in D. Bodansky, J. Brunnee, and E. Hey (eds), *The Oxford Handbook of International Environmental Law* (Oxford: Oxford University Press, 2007) 807, 813–15.
[161] Karavias (n. 69) 14–15.

Generally civil liability regimes in international environmental law opt for strict limited liability of the operator in specific sectors of environmental protection,[162] with State responsibility remaining as a residual option.[163] This approach entails channelling liability to the polluter (operator or owner), irrespective of his/her fault, on the assumption that the party with the most effective control of the risk at the time of the accident should be primarily liable.[164] Strict limited liability is generally coupled with the provision of additional funding sources to meet claimed damage. Additional funding is derived from public funds of State budgets, or from a common pool of funds created by contributions either from operators of the same type of dangerous activities or from entities for whose direct benefit the dangerous activity is carried out.[165]

Existing international environmental liability regimes are sector-specific, limited to specialized international schemes for ultra-hazardous activities.[166] Being usually characterized by a narrow scope,[167] they offer a piecemeal solution to environmental harm caused by the private sector.[168] In addition, they may not provide sufficient incentive to the operator to take strict measures of prevention or to meet all the legitimate demands of innocent victims for reparation in case of injuries,[169] thus only implementing in part the polluter-pays principle.[170] Most importantly, the low rate of ratification and lack of entry into force of several civil liability treaties highlights States' reluctance to commit themselves to consequences for breach of international obligations or damage,[171] because of the

---

[162] Orrego Vicuña (n. 126) 144. Examples are: International Convention on Civil Liability for Oil Pollution Damage (Brussels, 29 November 1969); International Convention on Civil Liability for Bunker Oil Pollution Damage (London, 23 May 2001); Vienna Convention on Civil Liability for Nuclear Damage (Vienna, 21 May 1963); and Protocol on Civil Liability and Compensation for Damage caused by the Transboundary effects of Industrial Accidents on Transboundary Waters (Kiev, 21 May 2003). The Protocol on Liability and Compensation for Damage resulting from Transboundary Movements of Hazardous Wastes and Their Disposal (Basel, 10 December 1999), provides for both strict, but limited liability (applying to the person notifying the export until the disposer has taken possession of the wastes) and fault-based liability.

[163] ILC (n. 116) 41; Orrego Vicuña (n. 126) 142.

[164] ILC (n. 116) 39.

[165] International Convention on the Establishment of an International Fund for Compensation for Oil Pollution Damage (Brussels, 18 December 1971).

[166] Ibid. 281.

[167] A case in point is the Protocol on Liability arising from Environmental Emergencies to the Antarctic Treaty's Environmental Protocol, which only covers damage arising from the lack of prompt action in the face of environmental emergencies, although it was initially envisaged as a regime to cover damage arising from all activities taking place in Antarctica: adopted as Annex VI to the Protocol to the Antarctic Treaty on Environmental Protection (Madrid, 4 October 1991) by the 28th Antarctic Treaty Consultative Meeting in Stockholm on 14 June 2005. See in particular Arts 1, 2, and 5. See P. Vigni, 'A Liability Regime for Antarctica' (2005) 15 *Italian Yearbook of International Law* 217. For a more general overview, see Fitzmaurice (n. 115) 359–68.

[168] Fitzmaurice (n. 115) 379–80.

[169] ILC (n. 116) 41.

[170] Birnie et al. (n. 54) 280. P. Schwartz, 'Principle 16: Polluter-Pays Principle' in Viñuales (n. 115) 441–42 and 448–49.

[171] Eg Convention on Civil Liability for Damage resulting from Activities Dangerous to the Environment (Lugano, 21 June 1993; not in force); Protocol on Liability and Compensation for Damage Resulting from the Transboundary Movement of Hazardous Wastes and their Disposal (Basel,

financial implications that liability schemes have for public budgets and private entities, including the insurance sector.[172] It can be concluded that 'while States have significantly developed environmental rules, they have been rather reluctant to simultaneously agree on the pertinent rules on responsibility and liability'.[173] This may explain the recent turn towards an administrative approach to prevent and restore environmental harm in international rules on civil liability for environmental damage.[174]

2.3 International environmental crimes?

Another potential means of establishing individual and companies' responsibility for environmental harm under international law is defining crimes as a way of enforcing international environmental law. This would also add an incentive to refrain from harmful conduct by allowing more stringent enforcement measures or penalties to be imposed,[175] such as the seizing and forfeiting of corporations' assets to compensate victims.[176]

The 1996 draft Code of Offences Against Peace and Security of Mankind[177] of the ILC included international environmental crimes as war crimes, referring to the use of methods or means of warfare which are 'intended, or may be expected, to cause widespread long-term, and severe environmental damage to the natural environment' and acts of individuals 'who willfully cause or order the causing of widespread long-term and severe environmental damage to the natural environment'. The offence could only be committed during armed conflict, only when the methods and means of warfare were not justified by military necessity, and only when the intended environmental damage gravely prejudiced the health or survival of a population.[178]

---

10 December 1999; not in force); and Convention on Liability and Compensation for Damage in Connection with the Carriage of Hazardous and Noxious Substances by Sea (London, 3 May 1996; not in force), which has meant to be superseded by a 2010 Protocol (London, 30 April 2010; not in force).

[172] Orrego Vicuña (n. 126) 181.
[173] Ibid. 135.
[174] Nagoya–Kuala Lumpur Supplementary Protocol on Liability and Redress to the Cartagena Protocol on Biosafety (Nagoya, 15 October 2010; in force in force 5 March 2018). See R. Lefeber, 'The Legal Significance of the Nagoya–Kuala Lumpur Supplementary Protocol: The Result of a Paradigm Evolution' (Amsterdam Law School, 2012); S. Jungcurt and N. Schabus, 'Liability and Redress in the Context of the Cartagena Protocol on Biosafety' (2010) 19 *Review of European Community and International Environmental Law* 197; and E. Orlando, 'From Domestic to Global? Recent Trends in Environmental Liability from a Multi-level and Comparative Law Perspective' (2015) 24 *Review of European, Comparative and International Environmental Law* 289, 299–300.
[175] Orlando (n. 174) 284.
[176] Karavias (n. 69) 99–101 and 114.
[177] ILC, Report of the Working Group for inclusion of wilful and severe damage to the environment as a war crime' (1996) UN Doc. A/51/10, ch. II(A), paras 43–44. Sands (n. 18) 894–96.
[178] Birnie et al. (n. 54) 329–33.

The draft Code influenced the drafting of the 1998 Rome Statute of the International Criminal Court, which followed the same approach by including, among the list of enumerated offences, 'internationally launching an attack in the knowledge that such an attack will cause … widespread long-term and severe environmental damage to the natural environment which would be clearly excessive in relation to the concrete and direct overall military advantage anticipated'. [179] This, however, applies only to international armed conflicts.

The hypothesis of 'willful and severe damage to the environment' as a crime against peace and security of humankind was addressed by the ILC in one of the drafts of the Code, but was not included in the final text. No similar proposal was made at the Rome Conference.[180] The question as to whether international environmental crimes, in such restricted circumstances, can be committed by a multinational has not been addressed by the Rome Statute, which does not contemplate any jurisdiction over juridical persons.[181]

Some authors have argued that serious and widespread environmental harm is prohibited by norms of *ius cogens* providing legal standing to all States.[182] The 1980 ILC Draft Articles on State Responsibility[183] listed international crimes affecting the 'human environment' in an effort to typify an international crime in connection with environmental obligations of essential importance, such as those prohibiting massive pollution of the atmosphere or of the seas.[184] However, the final ILC codification on State responsibility in 2001 did not contain this draft provision.[185] Therefore, the idea of an international environmental crime in peacetime, within the category of crimes against humanity, has not been accepted by the international community.[186] This may explain why, when in 2014 Ecuadorian communities made a complaint to the ICC against Chevron CEO for environmental degradation and attempts to evade remediation as a crime against humanity, the ICC Prosecutor did not consider these allegations international crimes under the Court's jurisdiction.[187]

---

[179] Art. 8(2)(b)(iv), Statute of the International Criminal Court (Rome, 17 July 1998).
[180] P. Robinson, 'The Missing Crimes' in A Cassese, P. Gaeta, and J. Jones (eds), *The Rome Statute of the International Criminal Court: A Commentary* (Oxford: Oxford University Press, 2002) 497, 522–23.
[181] O. Triffterer, 'Article 1' in O Triffterer (ed.), *Commentary on the Rome Statute of the International Criminal Court* (Baden-Baden: Nomos, 1999) 58.
[182] Orrego Vicuña (n. 126) 175.
[183] ILC, 'Draft Articles on State Responsibility', Report of the International Law Commission (1980) UN Doc. A/35/10, Art. 19.3.d.
[184] ILC, 'Draft Articles on State Responsibility', Report of the International Law Commission (1976) UN Doc. A/31/10.
[185] S. Nakhjavani, 'State Responsibility for Breaches of International Environmental Law: Innovation and Renewal' in K. Koufa (ed.), *The New International Criminal Law* (Thessaloniki: Institute of International Public Law and International Relations of Thessaloniki, 2003) 1107; A. Clapham, 'The Question of Jurisdiction under International Criminal Law over Legal Persons: Lessons from the Rome Conference on an International Criminal Court' in M. T. Kamminga and S. Zia-Zarifi (eds), *Liability of Multinational Corporations under International Law* (The Hague: Kluwer Law International, 2000) 139.
[186] Birnie et al. (n. 54) 331–33.
[187] https://www.business-humanrights.org/en/texacochevron-lawsuits-re-ecuador.

More generally the Rome Statute does not include corporate crimes, although at least

> The protracted debates leading to the adoption of the Statute stand as testament to the renewed significance attached to international criminal law as an appropriate and effective means of curbing the involvement of corporate entities in the commission of crimes under international law.[188]

In sum, there are currently no corporate 'crimes under international law' (ie directly punishable under international law without the intermediary of domestic law)[189] including in relation to the environment. That said, a 2015 Policy Paper providing guidance on how the ICC Office of the Prosecutor exercises its discretion in the selection and prioritization of cases, concerns 'international crimes' that are found in domestic law on the basis of international treaties obliging States to criminalize certain corporate conduct.[190] In relation to cases not selected for investigation or prosecution, the Prosecutor's Office is expected to seek to cooperate and provide assistance to States, upon request, with respect to conduct which constitutes a serious crime under national law, such as the illegal exploitation of natural resources, land grabbing, or the destruction of the environment, in light of the goal of the Statute to combat impunity and prevent the recurrence of violence by combining the activities of the Court and national jurisdictions.[191]

It remains unclear at the time of writing to what extent these guidelines will lead to a greater role for the ICC in environmental matters, by focusing on international crimes under national law (allowing the ICC to support national prosecution of multinationals, possibly in the form of complicity[192]). As was already noted in 2007, 'there is growing potential for companies to be held liable for international crimes—with responsibility imposed under domestic law but reflecting international standards of individual responsibility'.[193] Some international treaties require States to impose liability on companies for their involvement in relation to corruption, organized crime, and financing of terrorism.[194] The Malabo Protocol

---

[188] Karavias (n. 69) 99.

[189] Ibid. 60–61 and 101–03.

[190] ICC Office of the Prosecutor, Policy Paper on case selection and prioritisation, 15 September 2015, https://www.icc-cpi.int/Pages/item.aspx?name=policy-paper-on-case-selection-and-prioritisation, para. 40. N. Bernaz, 'An Analysis of the ICC Office of the Prosecutor's Policy Paper on Case Selection and Prioritization from the Perspective of Business and Human Rights' (2017) 15 *Journal of International Criminal Justice* 527.

[191] ICC Office of the Prosecutor (n. 190), para. 7, based on ICC Statute, Art. 93(10).

[192] De Schutter (n. 15) 59; Karavias (n. 69) 103–11. See also A. Mistura, 'Is There Space for Environmental Crimes under International Criminal Law? The Impact of the Office of the Prosecutor Policy Paper on Case Selection and Prioritization on the Current Legal Framework' (2018) 43 *Columbia Journal of Environmental Law* 181.

[193] This view was supposed by J. Ruggie, 'Business and Human Rights: The Evolving International Agenda' (2007) 101 *American Journal of International Law* 819, 830 (see generally 830–32).

[194] Convention against Corruption (New York, 31 October 2003, in force 14 December 2005) Art. 26; Convention against Transnational Organized Crime (New York, 15 November 2000, in force 29

to the African Court of Justice and Human Rights makes corporations criminally liable for certain international crimes, including trafficking of hazardous waste and illicit exploitation of natural resources,[195] but it has not attracted any ratification yet.[196] The practice remains uneven and 'criminal punishment of business involvement in such crimes is rare, as is the imposition of proportional civil sanctions against corporations'.[197]

2.4 Balancing the international protection of foreign investment

Several attempts at ensuring corporate accountability are directed at multinational companies, in consideration of the protection offered to these companies by international investment law, which is not balanced by corresponding duties at the international level.[198] International investment law[199] will be taken into account in this book in as much as it relates specifically to foreign direct investment—the 'transfer of tangible or intangible assets from one country to another for the purpose of their use in that country to generate wealth under the total or partial control of the owner of the assets'.[200] In other words, this should be distinguished from investment undertaken by financial intermediaries, which is increasingly addressed through socially responsible investment instruments[201] and is not addressed in this book. The discussion on international law and foreign direct investment will serve to highlight the general tendency to liberalization,[202] the resulting international rights of multinationals and some contradictions.

September 2003); and International Convention for the Suppression of Financing of Terrorism (New York, 9 December 1999, in force 10 April 2002).

[195] Protocol on Amendments to the Protocol on the Statute of the African Court of Justice and Human Rights (Malabo, 27 June 2014, not in force) Arts 22 and 46C. See D. Cassell and A. Ramasastry, 'White Paper: Options for a Treaty on Business and Human Rights' (2016) 6 *Notre Dame Journal of International and Comparative Law* 1, 27 and 36–37; and O. Abe and A. Ordor, 'Addressing Human Rights Concerns in the Extractive Resource Industry in Sub-Saharan Africa using the Lens of Article 46(c) of the Malabo Protocol' (2018) 11 *Law and Development Review* 843.
[196] Status of signatures and ratifications as of 20 May 2019: https://au.int/sites/default/files/treaties/36398-sl-PROTOCOL%20ON%20AMENDMENTS%20TO%20THE%20PROTOCOL%20ON%20THE%20STATUTE%20OF%20THE%20AFRICAN%20COURT%20OF%20JUSTICE%20AND%20HUMAN%20RIGHTS.pdf.
[197] Cassell and Ramasastry (n. 195) at 1.
[198] Sornarajah (n 4) 172; J. Ebbesson, 'Transboundary Corporate Responsibility in Environmental Matters: Fragments and Foundations for a Future Framework' in Winter (n. 135) 200, at 201.
[199] Muchlinski et al. (n. 72).
[200] Sornarajah (n. 4) 9. Accordingly, this study will not take into account the international law that has been developed to extend protection also to *portfolio* investment, ie the capital flows created through stock exchanges.
[201] J. Viñuales, 'Green Investment after Rio 2012' (2014) 16 *International Community Law Review* 153, 157. See B. J. Richardson, *Socially Responsible Investment Law: Regulating the Unseen Polluters* (Oxford: Oxford University Press, 2008).
[202] P.-M. Dupuy, *Droit International Public* (Paris: Dalloz, 2004) 680–85. See also J Viñuales, 'Foreign Direct Investment: International Investment Law and Natural Resource Governance' in E. Morgera and K. Kulovesi (eds), *International Law and Natural Resources* (Cambridge: Cambridge University

International investment law has built on the customary international law on the protection of aliens' property and its gradual extension from tangible assets to other investors' rights.[203] This has limited the sovereignty of host States over their natural resources, and enlarged the sphere of corporate interests protected at the international level. Such limitation to host States' discretion in admitting and conditioning the entry of foreign investors is significantly strengthened by the mushrooming of bilateral investment treaties (BITs)[204] setting out the rules according to which investment made by the nationals of the two States parties in each other's territory will be protected.[205] In addition, several regional free trade agreements include provisions on foreign investment.[206] These instruments tend to be drafted in favour of foreign investors, although more recent ones also address concerns about preserving the regulatory function of the State in areas such as environmental protection.[207] The actual impact of these more recent provisions, however, remains doubtful as international tribunals tend to read down their effects, emphasizing the function of these treaties to protect investment.[208]

One of the most prominent features of the international protection of foreign investment is private actors' direct resort to international dispute settlement, which further strengthens the position of multinationals as opposed to other business ventures. The 1965 Washington Convention[209] established the International Centre for Settlement of Investment Disputes (ICSID) and created an obligation to submit disputes regarding foreign investment to international arbitration, rather than leaving it to the parties to decide the appropriate tribunal. The impact of this Convention increased significantly in the 1990s, when a sudden proliferation of BITs referred to ICSID arbitration.[210] As a result, private investors can file a case before an international tribunal not only for breach of State contract, but also for breach of a BIT concluded between the host and home State.[211]

ICSID decisions are particularly relevant for this study as they focus on whether controls instituted by the host State on environmental grounds can be regarded as compensable takings.[212] As highlighted by Viñuales, these disputes for the large

Press, 2016) 26 and F. Ortino and N. M. Tabari, 'International Dispute Settlement: The Settlement of Investment Disputes concerning Natural Resources—Applicable Law and Standards of Review' in Morgera and Kulovesi (ibid.) 496.

[203] For a historic overview of this development, Sornarajah (n. 4) 19–28 and 36–46.
[204] For a detailed discussion on BITs, Muchlinski (n. 5) 617 and ch. 17; and also Sornarajah (n. 4) ch. 5.
[205] Sornarajah (n. 4) 172–224.
[206] Sornarajah (n. 10) 53.
[207] Sornarajah (n. 4) 225–27.
[208] L. E. Peterson, *Bilateral Investment Treaties and Development Policy-Making* (Winnipeg: International Institute for Sustainable Development, 2004) 23.
[209] Convention on the Settlement of Investment Disputes between States and Nationals of Other States (Washington, 18 March 1965).
[210] Sornarajah (n. 10) 167.
[211] Dupuy (n. 202) 685.
[212] Sornarajah (n. 4) 299.

part favour investors (in more than 70 per cent of the cases on jurisdiction and 60 per cent on merits).[213] The practice of international investment arbitration has 'played an unbalancing role by overemphasizing the protection of investors over the authority of host State and public interest' (which is often not aligned with interests of investors and host State).[214] In *Metalclad Corporation v. United Mexican States*, for instance, the host State's environmental protection regulation was considered an indirect expropriation because it limited the investors' reasonably-to-be-expected economic benefits.[215] As a result, host States are confronted with the prospects of costly arbitrations, and potentially onerous damage claims by private companies. Consequently, host States may exercise greater caution in their law-making, as investment arbitral tribunals may be particularly insensitive to internationally protected environmental values through national law. In the *Compañía del Desarrollo de Santa Elena S.A. v. Republic of Costa Rica* case,[216] the arbitral tribunal held that the justification of the State's action under international environmental law, namely the protection of a site rich in biodiversity, was not relevant in deciding the amount to be paid to foreign investors negatively impacted by a lawful expropriation. In other words, environmental protection objectives, which justified the expropriation and were supported by applicable international norms, did not have a bearing on the quantification of compensation.[217]

---

[213] Viñuales (n. 202) 33–34.
[214] Ibid. 42.
[215] ICSID, *Metalclad Corporation v. United Mexican States*, Case No. ARB(AF)/97/1, Award (30 August 2000), (2001) 40 *ILM* 35. The facts concerned a US multinational willing to operate a hazardous waste landfill in Mexico, for which the relevant operating permits had been obtained from the Mexican federal government, but the constitution permit had been refused by the local municipality on ecological grounds, namely concerns as to negative environmental impacts on the site, and the local population. Subsequently, the site on which the facility was located was declared a natural protected area by decree. The arbitral tribunal held that the State, and the municipal authorities, had undermined the federally authorized investment by unexpectedly refusing an unknown municipal permit, and by placing the area in a newly created ecological protection zone. Thus, the ecological decree, by itself, was considered to be tantamount to expropriation by barring forever the operation of the landfill. It embodied a 'covert or incidental interference with the use of property which has the effect of depriving the owner, in whole or in significant part, of the use or reasonably-to-be-expected economic benefit of property even if not necessarily to the obvious benefit of the host State'. It is particularly interesting to note that the tribunal did not investigate as to the reasons for the ecological decree.
[216] ICSID, *Compañía del Desarrollo de Santa Elena S.A. v. Republic of Costa Rica*, Case No. ARB/96/1, Final Award (17 February 2000), (2000) 39 *ILM* 1317.
[217] ICSID, *Compañía del Desarrollo de Santa Elena S.A. v. Republic of Costa Rica*, Case No. ARB/96/1, Final Award (17 February 2000), (2000) 39 *ILM* 1317, paras 71–72 (hereinafter, the *Santa Elena* case). The facts regarded an American multinational that purchased land for the construction of a holiday resort in the virgin dry forest of Costa Rica. Three years after the purchase, the host government expropriated the property for the purpose of protecting biodiversity by adding the area to an adjacent national park. The parties to the dispute agreed that the government act was a lawful expropriation and the question before the ICSID tribunal was the determination of the amount of compensation, which logically encompassed the question of determining the methodology for valuing environmental resources, such as the biodiversity included in the area of tropical dry forest concerned. Costa Rica alleged that the expropriation had been undertaken in accordance with its international obligations to preserve 'the unique ecological site'. Sands (n. 18) 1069–70.

In the *S.D. Meyers* case,²¹⁸ the arbitral tribunal recognized that genuine environmental measures, based on international environmental agreements, may prevail over foreign investors' interests, on the condition that the host State proves it selected the least investment-detrimental measure for the protection of the environment.²¹⁹ In this respect, it should be considered that different environmental measures have different costs, and choosing the least detrimental to foreign investors may well be too expensive an option for certain governments. Scholars suggested that environmental takings, based on international environmental law, should be considered by an arbitral tribunal against investors' liability for environmental harm, with a view to reducing the amount of compensation payable, or requiring multinationals to pay compensation in excess of the value of the taking when the harm is severe.²²⁰

Reliance by the host State on broadly framed international environmental obligations remains vulnerable to challenges on grounds of proportionality or due process.²²¹ This is clearly demonstrated by Chevron's successful international investment arbitration against Ecuador in the Texaco legal saga mentioned earlier. Ecuador was found to be in violation of a US-Ecuador BIT for unduly influencing the judiciary to condemn Chevron for environmental damages to the tune of US$9.51 billion. The international investment arbitration tribunal condemned Ecuador to pay USD$112 million in compensation to Chevron.²²² Nonetheless, foreign investors are arguably increasingly expected to include the monitoring of national developments aimed at implementing international environmental rules as part of their assessment of regulatory risk.²²³ In *Chmatura v. Canada*, for

---

²¹⁸ NAFTA Arbitration under UNCITRAL Arbitration Rules, *S. D. Myers Inc. v. Government of Canada*, Partial Award (17 November 2000).

²¹⁹ The case involved a ban on exports of hazardous waste imposed by Canada, on the basis of significant danger to the environment, and the obligations under the Basel Convention on Transboundary Movements of Hazardous Wastes (Basel, 22 March 1989). A US corporation alleged, inter alia, that the ban constituted a form of discrimination against foreign operators that could not access waste disposal facilities in Canada, notwithstanding the actual geographical proximity to the facility, particularly for US companies located along the borders. The arbitral tribunal held that, although the measure was officially justified on environmental grounds, the underlying legitimate objective could have been achieved with another measure that would have been more consistent with the obligations of investment protection. See also discussion in Z. Douglas, 'The Enforcement of Environmental Norms in Investment Treaty Arbitration' in P.-M. Dupuy and J. Viñuales (eds), *Harnessing Foreign Investment to Promote Environmental Protection: Incentives and Safeguards* (Cambridge: Cambridge University Press, 2013) 415.

²²⁰ Sornarajah (n. 4) 472.

²²¹ J. Viñuales, 'The Environmental Regulation of Foreign Investment Schemes under International Law' in Dupuy and Viñuales (n. 219) 273, 309 and 311.

²²² https://business-humanrights.org/en/texacochevron-lawsuits-re-ecuador. Permanent Court of Arbitration, Chevron and Texaco v Ecuador, Second Partial Award on Track II (30 August 2018). See S. Joseph, 'Protracted Lawfare: The Tale of Chevron Texaco in the Amazon' (2012) 3 *Journal of Human Rights and the Environment* 70; and N. Cely, 'Balancing Profit and Environmental Sustainability in Ecuador: Lessons Learned from the Chevron Case' (2014) *Duke Environmental Law & Policy Forum*, 353.

²²³ Viñuales (n. 221) 299–300.

instance, an investment tribunal upheld a targeted environmental measure[224] by reference to relevant international environmental obligations.[225]

Overall, the imbalance between the international rights of multinationals and the absence of duties to protect the environment or other interests of host States in return[226] remains a matter of concern in international law.

As aptly put by Miles,

> International investment law continues to reflect imperialistic conceptualizations of the environment in two central ways—i) the non-engagement of international investment law with the impact of investor activity on the local communities and the environment of the host state; and ii) the framing of environmental regulation as a violation of investment treaties.[227]

2.5 Synergies with international human rights law

The international accountability of multinationals has been increasingly explored in the realm of international human rights law.[228] Human rights have become the dominant frame for the international debate on corporate accountability, as crystallized in the inter-governmental endorsement of the UN Guiding Principles on Business and Human Rights. This development, combined with significant advances in the understanding of the relationship between international human rights and international environmental law,[229] provides for a critical field of research for corporate environmental accountability in international law. Interestingly, human rights have generally been a 'late arrival' in the context of international corporate accountability standards,[230] compared with environmental ones. Along similar lines, there are only exceptional cases in which human rights treaties have provided for the harmonization of domestic rules to ensure liability of private companies.[231]

---

[224] Ibid. 303.
[225] UNCITRAL Ad Hoc Tribunal, *Chematura Corp v Government of Canada*, Award (2 August 2010) para. 266.
[226] S. Maljean-Dubois and V. Richard, 'The Applicability of International Environmental Law to Private Enterprises' in Dupuy and Viñuales (n. 219) 69.
[227] K. Miles, *The Origins of International Investment Law* (Cambridge: Cambridge University Press, 2013) 210.
[228] Kamminga and Zia-Zarifi (n. 185); International Council on Human Rights Policy (n. 23); T. Weiler, 'Balancing Human Rights and Investor Protection: A New Approach for a Different Legal Order' (2004) 27 *Boston College International and Comparative Law Review* 429.
[229] As captured in the work undertaken by former UN Special Rapporteur on Human Rights and the Environment John Knox since 2012, discussed in Ch. 4: for an overview, http://www.ohchr.org/EN/Issues/Environment/SREnvironment/Pages/SRenvironmentIndex.aspx.
[230] While human rights were included in the ILO Tripartite Declaration of Principles concerning Multinational Enterprises and Social Policy (1978, 17 ILM 422), they were only included in the OECD Guidelines for Multinational Enterprises (discussed in Ch. 3) in 2000: see discussion in Deva (n. 73) 7–9.
[231] Optional Protocol to the Convention on the Rights of the Child on the Sale of Children and Child Pornography (New York, 25 May 2000, in force 18 January 2002) Art. 3(5).

The factual connection between the environment and human rights in relation to corporate accountability needs to be discussed first.[232] A survey conducted by the UN Special Representative on Business and Human Rights indicated that nearly a third of cases of alleged environmental harm had corresponding impacts on human rights. The connection between the right to health, life, adequate food and housing, minority rights to culture, as well as the right to benefit from scientific progress; and environmental concerns were raised with respect to all business sectors.[233] As discussed above, human rights violations have often been alleged before national courts when corporate environmental damage is the result of gross negligence or deliberate indifference and caused severe, long-lasting, and widespread harm on people.[234] This has been particularly the case of environmental degradation caused by multinational companies in areas traditionally occupied by indigenous peoples and local communities,[235] such as the case of the environmental damage and human rights violations arising from Texaco/Chevron's oil exploration in Ecuador.[236] The arguments regarding the existence of an international prohibition on causing intra-pollution put forward before US courts under the ATCA were also at the borderline between international environmental and human rights law. In addition, other cases alleged unsuccessfully that serious human rights abuses linked to environmentally damaging natural resource development amounted to cultural genocide partly caused by environmental degradation.[237]

Corporate environmental harm has also emerged in international human rights case law,[238] mainly in an indirect way. In effect, international human rights case

---

[232] D. Kinley and J. Tadaki, 'From Talk to Walk: The Emergence of Human Rights Responsibilities for Corporations at International Law' (2003–04) 44 *Virginia Journal of International Law* 931, 987–92.

[233] Report of the Special Representative of the Secretary-General on the issue of Human Rights and Transnational Corporations and Other Business Enterprises, Corporations and Human Rights: A Survey of the Scope and Patterns of Alleged Corporate-related Human Rights Abuse (2008) UN Doc. A/HRC/8/5/Add.2, para. 27.

[234] A. Sinden, 'Power and Responsibility: Why Human Rights Should Address Corporate Environmental Wrongs' in D. McBarnet, A. Voiculescu, and T. Campbell (eds), *The New Corporate Accountability: Corporate Social Responsibility and the Law* (Cambridge: Cambridge University Press, 2007) 728, 744. For an analysis of relevant case law, see H. Osofsky, 'Learning from Environmental Justice: A New Model for International Environmental Rights' (2005) 24 *Stanford Environmental Law Journal* 71. Generally on the legal questions arising from corporate environmental harm impacting on indigenous peoples, see G. Foster, 'Foreign Investment and Indigenous Peoples: Options for Promoting Equilibrium between Economic Development and Indigenous Rights' (2011–12) 33 *Michigan Journal of International Law* 627.

[235] Report of the Special Rapporteur on the Situation of Human Rights and Fundamental Freedoms of Indigenous People (2009) UN Doc. A/HRC/12/34, 19–20.

[236] Inter-American Commission of Human Rights, 'Report on the Situation of Human Rights in Ecuador' (24 April 1997) OEA/ser. L/V/II.96, doc10 rev1.

[237] Eg Khokhryakova (n. 37) 472 and 475 and H. M. Osofsky, 'Environmental Human Rights under the Alien Tort Statute: Redress for Indigenous Victims of Multinational Corporations' (1997) 20 *Suffolk Transnational Law Review* 335, 354.

[238] International human rights case law that has an environmental dimension is now quite extensive: eg R. Pavoni, 'Environmental Jurisprudence of the European and Inter-American Courts of Human Rights: Comparative Insights' in Boer (n. 113) 69 and A. Boyle, 'Human Rights and the Environment: Where Next?' in Boer (n. 113) 201.

law has provided an avenue to hold host States accountable for their inability or unwillingness to control private companies' environmental conduct, particularly when the life, health, and culture of indigenous and tribal peoples were negatively affected. In the seminal *Awas Tingni* case, for instance, the Inter-American Court of Human Rights looked into the effects of a logging concession to a Korean multinational in Nicaragua, which led to the violation of the human rights of indigenous communities that traditionally occupied the area concerned through a communal form of land tenure.[239] The filing of the case before the Inter-American Court created such political pressure that the logging concession was revoked.[240] In its second environmental case, the African Commission on Human and People's Rights condemned Kenya for its opening of the *Endorois* land to ruby mining activities that would have impeded the right of these tribal peoples to access water.[241] This resulted in the mining company abandoning the project.[242]

While international human rights monitoring bodies have not indicated that companies themselves can breach directly international human rights norms, they have increasingly noted their role in the context of human rights violations. In the 1990s, the Inter-American Commission of Human Rights investigated the impacts of Texaco/Chevron's oil exploitation in Ecuador[243] and concluded, in an unprecedented statement, '*Both the State and the companies* conducting oil exploration activities are responsible for these anomalies, and *both should be responsible for correcting them.* It is the duty of the State to ensure that they are corrected',[244] including on the basis of international environmental law instruments, such as the Stockholm and Rio Declarations and the Convention on Biological Diversity.[245] Another case in point is the Belize Report, in which the Inter-American Commission expressly stated that the direct cause of the damage was the activity of the multinational, and implicitly noted its partial responsibility together with the State.[246] This was also the case for the recommendations of the African Commission on Human and Peoples' Rights on Shell's environmental damage in Nigeria.[247]

---

[239] S. J. Anaya and C. Grossman, 'The Case of Awas Tingni v Nicaragua: A New Step in the International Law of Indigenous People' (2002) 19 *Arizona Journal of International and Comparative Law* 1.
[240] Ibid. 899.
[241] African Commission on Human and Peoples' Rights, 'Centre for Minority Rights Development (Kenya) and Minority Rights Group International on Behalf of Endorois Welfare Council v Kenya' (2009) Communication 276/03.
[242] See F. Francioni, 'Natural Resources and Human Rights' in Morgera and Kulovesi (n. 202) 66, 74.
[243] A. Fabra, 'Indigenous Peoples, Environmental Degradation and Human Rights: a Case Study' in A. Boyle and M. Anderson (eds), *Human Rights Approaches to Environmental Protection* (Oxford: Clarendon Press, 1996) 245.
[244] Inter-American Commission of Human Rights, Communiqué with Preliminary Findings 24/94 (Quito, 11 November 1994). Inter-American Commission of Human Rights, 'Report on the Situation of Human Rights in Ecuador' (24 April 1997) OEA/ser. L/V/II.96, doc10 rev1 (Ecuador Report).
[245] Ecuador Report, Ch. VIII.
[246] Inter-American Court of Human Rights, *Maya Indigenous Communities of the Toledo District v. Belize*, Report 96/03, Case 12.053, judgment (24 October 2003) Ch. 6.
[247] African Commission on Human and Peoples' Rights, 'The Social and Economic Rights Action Centre and the Centre for Economic and Social Rights/Nigeria' (2001) Communication 155/96, paras 52–55.

A more notable case was the 2015 decision of Inter-American Court on Human Rights in the *Case of Kaliña and Lokono Peoples v Suriname*. The Court cited the UN Framework on Business and Human Rights in noting the role of private companies in causing adverse impacts on the environment and indigenous peoples' rights from mining activities. The Court underscored businesses' responsibility to respect indigenous and tribal peoples' human rights and called upon them to 'pay special attention when such rights are violated'.[248] This was reiterated in the Inter-American Court's Advisory Opinion on Human Rights and the Environment in 2017.[249] The Court then focused on the role of the State in regulating, monitoring, preventing, punishing, and ensuring redress from corporate activities leading to human rights violations.[250]

2.5.1 Legal arguments

International human rights treaties have varying membership and are generally far from reaching universality. As opposed to international environmental law, they tend not to specify the scope of States' duties to control companies.[251] Nonetheless, international human rights bodies have clarified by way of interpretation that States have positive obligations to protect human rights in the relationships between individuals and private entities, so that host States that are party to relevant international human rights treaties have an international obligation to regulate corporate conduct within their jurisdiction.[252] Specifically, host States are 'expected to take all measures that could reasonably be taken, in accordance with international law, to prevent private actors from adopting conduct that may lead to human rights violations'. In addition, they have to provide for access to remedies because their international responsibility would be engaged when violations could have been prevented without incurring in an unreasonable burden for the State.[253] Horizontality in international human rights law has substantiated a wealth of case law concerning sub-standard corporate environmental conduct.[254] As aptly observed by Karavias, this

---

[248] Inter-American Court on Human Rights (IACtHR), *Case of Kaliña and Lokono Peoples v Suriname*, case 12.639, judgment (Merits, Reparations and Costs: 25 November 2015) paras 223 and 225.

[249] IACtHR, *Medio Ambiente y Derechos Humanos*, Oc-23/17, Opinión Consultiva (15 November 2017) para. 155.

[250] Ibid. para. 224.

[251] Cassell and Ramasastry (n. 195) 16, noting that ILO Conventions do so but are focused on labour rights.

[252] Eg Human Rights Committee, 'General Comment No. 31, Nature of the General Legal Obligation Imposed on States Parties to the Covenant', CCPR/C/21/Rev.1/Add.13 (26 May 2004), para. 8 and Committee on Economic, Social and Cultural Rights, 'General Comment No. 12 (1999): The Right to Adequate Food (Art 11)', UN Doc. E/C.12/1999/5, para. 15. See, inter alia, Karavias (n. 69) 30–59.

[253] De Schutter (n. 13) 44.

[254] Eg ECtHR, *Lopez Ostra v. Spain*, App. No. 16798/90 (1994); ECtHR, *Onereyldiz v. Turkey*, App. No. 36022/97 (2003); ECtHR, *International Federation for Human Rights v. Greece*, App. No. 72/2011 (2013); *Pueblo Indígena Kichwa de Sarayaku v. Ecuador*, case 12.465, provisional measures order (6 July 2004); Human Rights Committee, *Lubicon Band v. Canada*, Comm. No. 167/1984 (1990).

[c]orporate conduct has been recognized as a source of 'interference' with the enjoyment of human rights. But, in no case has a human rights treaty body accepted to go a step further and recognize corporations themselves as addressees of international norms.[255]

As a result, the relevant obligations for corporations operate at the domestic level: it is still the State that is obliged under international law 'to adopt legislation, to change its administrative practices, to investigate and to punish violations of human rights' caused by corporate actors.[256] In addition, international human rights case law has clarified that States cannot escape international responsibility by delegating obligations to private bodies, including through privatization.[257] As Ruggie observed, '[t]he increasing focus on protection against corporate abuse by the UN treaty bodies and regional mechanisms indicates a growing concern that States either do not fully understand or are not always able or willing to fulfill this duty'.[258]

The human rights obligations of States vis-à-vis corporations and other business entities should be understood in conjunction with the clarification provided by former UN Special Rapporteur on Human Rights and the Environment John Knox on States' duty to regulate corporations and companies' responsibility to respect environmental human rights.[259] States' procedural human rights obligations include the duty to provide for impact assessment, public participation in environmental decision-making, and access to effective remedies. States' substantive obligations include the establishment of legal and institutional frameworks to protect against environmental harm to human rights; and heightened procedural and substantive duties with respect to groups in vulnerable situations, such as women, children, and indigenous peoples.

In addition, home States are also responsible for regulating the activity of corporations under their jurisdiction (if these companies are registered under its laws, have their principal place of business under the state's jurisdiction, or have located their main administrative centre on the state's territory) even when they operate abroad,[260] if they are able to influence them through legal or political means in

---

[255] Karavias (n. 69) 44.
[256] Ibid. 44 and 59 (footnotes omitted in the citation).
[257] *Costello-Roberts v. UK* (1990) para. 27.
[258] Ruggie (n 193) 830.
[259] UN Independent Expert on Human Rights and the Environment John Knox, 'Transnational Corporations and Environmental Harm', statement at the side-event on Human Rights and Transnational Corporations (11 March 2014) 2.
[260] Committee on Economic, Social and Cultural Rights, 'General Comment No. 14 (2000): The Right to the Highest Attainable Standard of Health (Art. 12 of the International Covenant on Economic, Social and Cultural Rights)', E/C.12/ 2000/4 (2000) para. 39; Committee on Economic, Social and Cultural Rights, 'General Comment No. 15 (2002): The Right to Water (Arts. 11 and 12 of the International Covenant on Economic, Social and Cultural Rights)', E/C.12/2002/11 (26 November 2002) para. 31; Committee on Economic, Social and Cultural Rights, 'Statement on the Obligations of States Parties regarding the Corporate Sector and Economic, Social and Cultural rights' E/C.12/

accordance with international law.[261] They are responsible also when they operate outside territorial jurisdiction on the basis of extraterritorial human rights obligations (corporations established under the laws of another State that are managed, controlled, or owned by persons having the nationality of the first State or having their main place of business administration on the territory of that State[262]). Extraterritorial obligations are however not recognized by all States.[263,264]

The relevance of these international human rights arguments for the environment has been clarified by the Committee on Economic, Social and Cultural Rights. The Committee indicated that the customary international law rule on transboundary environmental damage has been interpreted as extending to human rights violations. On that basis, it pointed to a State's extraterritorial obligations to control activities of corporations domiciled in its territory or jurisdiction with a view to influencing their conduct outside their territory,[265] especially when the remedies available to victims before the domestic courts of the State where the harm occurs are unavailable or ineffective.[266] The Committee indicated that States also have obligations to take reasonable measures to prevent human rights violations associated with extractives. They also have international responsibility even if other causes have contributed to the occurrence of the violation, and even if the State had not foreseen a violation that was reasonably foreseeable.[267] State obligations of international cooperation extend to cross-border cooperation between enforcement agencies and judicial bodies to ensure access to remedies in transnational cases.[268] This implies an obligation to remove substantive, procedural, and practical barriers to remedies, by establishing parent company or group liability regimes, providing legal aid, enabling class actions and public interest litigation, facilitating access to information, and collection and use of evidence abroad.[269]

2011/1 (20 May 2011) para. 5; Maastricht Principles on the Extraterritorial Obligations of States in the Area of Economic, Social and Cultural Rights, adopted in Maastricht on 28 September 2011; ICJ, *Legal Consequences of the Construction of a Wall in the Occupied Palestinian Territory*, Advisory Opinion (9 July 2004) para. 109) and *Armed Activities on the Territory of the Congo* (Democratic Republic of the Congo v Uganda), Judgment (19 December 2005), paras. 178–80 and 216–17. De Schutter (n 13) at 45. This jurisprudence has been captured in Committee on Economic, Social and Cultural Rights, General Comment No. 24 (n 22), particularly paras 27–28.

[261] De Schutter (n. 13) 45.
[262] Ibid. 46.
[263] Eg Committee on the Elimination of Racial Discrimination, Concluding Observations: Canada, (2012) UN Doc. CERD/C/CAN/CO/19-20, 4.
[264] Mapping Report of the Independent Expert on the issue of human rights obligations relating to the enjoyment of a safe, clean, healthy and sustainable environment, John H. Knox (2013) UN Doc. A/HRC/25/53.
[265] Committee on Economic, Social and Cultural Rights, General Comment No. 24 (n. 22), section II, paras 27–28, making reference to HRC, Guiding Principles on Extreme Poverty and Human Rights: Res. 21/11, para. 92.
[266] Ibid. para. 30.
[267] Ibid. para. 32.
[268] Ibid. para. 34.
[269] Ibid. para. 44.

From a conceptual viewpoint, the use of human rights law and approaches to address corporate environmental damage facilitates tackling the power imbalances between corporations, governments, and communities, which emerge when traditional legal remedies will not be sufficient to redress the damage.[270] It has been argued, for instance, that when corporations exercise 'ultimate authority' on individuals, they should be treated as duty bearers under human rights law. This usually occurs when States fail to regulate private actors because of weak government and corruption; or when corporations have so much power over government that they essentially control State decision-making.[271] In addition, international human rights law allows international scrutiny of State behaviour in situations beyond the reach of international environmental law, which is when environmental damage is not transboundary or does not have global impacts on human rights.[272] Nonetheless, neither system has 'proposed a systematic structure for approaching environmental harm to humans'.[273]

As Cotula argued, while both international human rights and investment law set minimum standards and judicial review mechanisms with regards to the exercise of State sovereignty over natural resources, they are characterized by different historical trajectories, philosophical and conceptual approaches, and different standards of protection.[274] International investment law provides stronger protection to multinationals than international human rights law does to victims of corporate abuses, both in terms of substantive standards and in terms of accessibility and enforceability of remedies.[275] For one thing, access by foreign investors to international arbitration does not require or is interpreted as not requiring exhaustion of local remedies, which gives foreign investors a clear advantage over victims of corporate abuses who can have access to the international level via human rights redress mechanisms only after having exhausted local remedies.[276] In addition, multinational companies sometimes also benefit from the protection of international human rights law: human rights standards on access to justice have in fact been invoked by multinational companies against States in arbitrations based on bilateral investment treaties,[277] and breaches of bilateral

---

[270] Sinden (n. 234) 731–32 and 734.
[271] Ibid. 741.
[272] Osofsky (n. 234) 75–76.
[273] Ibid. 76.
[274] L. Cotula, *Human Rights, Natural Resource and Investment Law in a Globalized World: Shades of Grey in the Shadow of the Law* (Abingdon: Routledge, 2012) 39 and 65–78.
[275] Ibid.
[276] Viñuales (n. 201) 44.
[277] International Centre for the Settlement of Investment Disputes, *Mondev International Ltd. v. USA*, Case ARB/(AF)/99/2, Award (11 October 2002) para. 144, as reported by A. Savaresi, 'The International Human Rights Implications of the Nagoya Protocol' in E. Morgera, M. Buck, and E. Tsioumani (eds), *The 2010 Nagoya Protocol on Access and Benefit-sharing in Perspective: Implications for International Law and Implementation Challenges* (The Hague: Martinus Nijhoff, 2012) 53, 72.

investment treaties have been brought before human rights bodies, on similar grounds.[278]

While these conceptual linkages have been sufficiently addressed in the literature, little academic attention has yet been devoted to the usefulness of international environmental law in addressing human rights-related concerns about corporate conduct. Concepts developed under international environmental law, including re-elaborated as international standards of corporate environmental accountability, have been increasingly taken up in the development of international standards on business responsibility to respect human rights. The UN Framework on Business and Human Rights, for instance, is built on a due diligence process implying concepts and approaches[279] that have been developed and/or significantly experimented with in the environmental sphere, notably: (i) impact assessment; (ii) stakeholder involvement in decision-making; and (iii) life-cycle management.[280]

2.6 The status of multinational companies in international law

The question of multinationals' accountability on the international plane is related to the question of their legal personality.[281] A significant part of legal scholarship acknowledges the need for some form of limited legal recognition of the presence of multinationals in international affairs in order to cope better with the problems they create,[282] and their influence on the international law-making process.[283] The 'long-standing scholarly arguments, however, over whether corporations could be "subjects" of international law ... impeded conceptual thinking on ... the attribution of direct legal responsibility to corporations'.[284]

---

[278] L. Peterson, *Human Rights and Bilateral Investment Treaties. Mapping the Role of Human Rights Law within Investor-State Arbitration* (Rights & Democracy, 2009), cited in Savaresi (n. 277) 72.

[279] Sinden (n. 234) 14.

[280] E Morgera, *Expert Report Corporate Responsibility to Respect Human Rights in the Environmental Sphere*, European Commission-funded project 'Study of the Legal Framework on Human Rights and the Environment Applicable to European Enterprises Operating outside the European Union', May 2010, 12 (on file with author).

[281] N. Jagers, 'The Legal Status of the Multinational Corporation under International Law' in M. K. Addo (ed.), *Human Rights Standards and the Responsibility of Transnational Corporations* (The Hague: Kluwer Law International, 1999) 259, 261. S. Ratner, 'Business' in Bodansky, Brunnee, and Hey (n. 160) 807, 811–13.

[282] A. A. Fatouros, 'Looking for an International Legal Framework for Transnational Corporations' in A. A. Fatouros (ed.), *Transnational Corporations: The International Legal Framework* (London: Routledge, 1994) 1, 18.

[283] A. Alkoby, 'Non-State Actors and the Legitimacy of International Environmental Law' (2003) 3 *Non-State Actors and International Law* 23.

[284] Report of the Special Representative of the Secretary-General on the issue of Human Rights and Transnational Corporations and Other Business Enterprises: Mapping International Standards of Responsibility and Accountability for Corporate Acts (2007) UN Doc. A/HRC/4/35, para. 20.

Traditionally, only States are considered subjects of international law,[285] whereas multinationals are not recognized as independent subjects despite their international economic and political power, in many instances dwarfing that of States. In accordance with this traditional view, international law encompasses rights and duties of States and international organizations, while multinationals remain under the sovereignty of the States in which they operate. Although the opinion that multinationals do not have personality under international law has often been used as a reason against the development of rules addressing multinationals, this has not prevented the development of a treaty establishing multinationals' right to resort to international dispute settlement under international investment law.[286]

A way of recognizing multinationals' role in international relations is to consider them as significant *actors*,[287] indispensable interlocutors to States.[288] Alternatively, Higgins suggested defining multinationals as *participants*, rather than subjects, in a system of international law seen as a decision-making process.[289] It appears difficult to further define 'actor' or 'participant' in strict legal terms,[290] although this approach is useful in grasping the reality of the development of international law as a process. It is also helpful to underscore that the 'conservative' concepts of 'subjects, and objects of international law' have provided 'an intellectual prison of our own choosing' that is often seen as 'an unalterable constraint'.[291]

Another approach would be that of recognizing the status of multinationals as members of the international community, together with individuals.[292] On that basis, it could be argued that customary norms, being binding on the whole of the international community[293] or on the whole of the subjects of the international legal order,[294] could also bind multinational

---

[285] L. Oppenheim, *International Law—A Treatise*, 4th edn (London: Longmans, Green and Co Ltd, 1928) 19.
[286] M. Sornarajah, *The International Law on Foreign Investment* (Cambridge: Cambridge University Press, 2004) 171.
[287] Indeed, the UN Group of Eminent Persons in 1974 concluded that 'multinational corporations are important actors on the world stage', in Report of the Group of Eminent Persons, 'The Impact of Multinational Corporations on the Development Process and on International Relations' (1974) UN Doc. E/5500/Add.1.
[288] Hosein (n. 24) 308.
[289] Higgins (n. 115) 48–55. This view was supported by Ruggie (n 193) 824.
[290] P-M. Dupuy, 'Sur les rapports entre sujets et "acteurs" en droit international contemporain' in L. Chand Vohrah (ed.), *Man's Inhumanity to Man: Essays on International Law in Honour of Antonio Cassese* (The Hague: Kluwer Law International, 2003) 261.
[291] Higgins (n. 115) 49–50.
[292] D. Thurer, 'The Emergence of Non-governmental Organizations and Transnational Enterprises in International Law and the Changing Role of the State' in R. Hofmann and N. Geissler (eds), *Non-State Actors as New Subjects of International Law* (Berlin: Duncker & Humblot, 1999) 54. Although according to some doctrine, the international community is itself not yet a subject of international law (C. Tomuschat, 'International Law: Ensuring the Survival of Mankind on the Eve of a New Century' (1999) 281 *Recueil des cours* 9, 78).
[293] P. Sands, *International Environmental Law. Emerging Trends and Implications for Transnational Corporations* (New York: UN, 1993) xvii.
[294] P-M. Dupuy, *Droit International Public* (Paris: Dalloz, 2004) 319.

companies.²⁹⁵ Even if there is no international rule opposing the creation of international custom regulating directly corporate conduct, however, it remains a widely held view that no customary rules of such nature have emerged in international human rights and criminal law.²⁹⁶ This is compounded by the difficulty of convincingly making the case for the existence of relevant customary norms of international environmental law. So, this line of reasoning represents a limited ground for advancing the debate.²⁹⁷

Alternatively, it has also been suggested that multinationals should be defined as 'entities *sui generis*', whose treatment and the treatment of whose actions in international law needs to be approached on a pragmatic, case-by-case basis to reflect the functions they perform.²⁹⁸ In turn, Pierre-Marie Dupuy persuasively argued that multinationals have a 'limited and functional legal personality' under international law, in accordance with their international rights and obligations,²⁹⁹ by analogy with the recognition by the International Court of Justice (ICJ) of such characteristics for international organizations.³⁰⁰ International rights for multinationals can be identified in their ability to conclude international contracts with States, and have access to international alternative dispute resolution mechanisms.³⁰¹ These 'are conducted in a manner that is practically indistinguishable from inter-State arbitrations' and whose awards 'are commonly cited alongside inter-State awards as authorities on propositions of international law'.³⁰² In addition, multinationals have direct obligations and rights under certain internationalized functional contracts, such as those of deep-seabed mineral prospectors with the International Seabed Authority.³⁰³ In those cases, multinationals' international legal personality is 'coterminous with the scope of the obligations imposed upon

---

[295] P. Dumberry, 'L'Entreprise, sujet de droit international? Retour sur la question à la lumière des développements récents du droit international des investissements' (2004) 108 *Revue Générale de Droit International Public* 103, 110; and N. Jagers, 'The Legal Status of the Multinational Corporation under International Law' in M. K. Addo (ed.), *Human Rights Standards and the Responsibility of Transnational Corporations* (The Hague: Kluwer Law International, 1999) 259, 264.

[296] Karavias (n. 69) 69, 74–79, and 114–15; This view was supported by Ruggie (n 193) 832.

[297] See ATCA cases in which the courts rejected the argument that multinationals are subject to international law, or that certain international environmental rules are customary as in *Amlon Metals, Inc. v. FMC Corp.*, 775 F. Sup 668, 669 (S.D.N.Y. 1991); also Birnie et al. (n. 54) 327.

[298] Lowe (n. 3) 25; and J. Alvarez, 'Are Corporations 'Subjects' of International Law?' (2011) 9 *Santa Clara Journal of International Law* 1.

[299] P.-M. Dupuy, *L'unité de l'ordre juridique international* (Leiden: Martinus Nijhoff Publishers, 2003) 102–18. This view was also supported by Ruggie (n. 193) 827.

[300] ICJ, 'Reparations for Injuries Suffered in the Service of the United Nations', Advisory Opinion (11 April 1949).

[301] Jagers (n. 281) 267.

[302] Lowe (n. 3) 23.

[303] Eg Contract for Exploration ISBA 6/A/18, Annexes 3–4 and United Nations Convention on the Law of the Sea (UNCLOS) (Montego Bay, 10 December 1992, in force 16 November 1994) Arts 187(c) and 188(2)(a). The responsibility of private operators under these contracts amounts to an internationally wrongful act and can be sanctioned with countermeasures under international law (suspension or termination of the contract), and corporations have standing before an international dispute settlement body: according to Karavias (n. 69) 155–59.

them by States', including in terms of duration of these obligations in case these arise from contracts.[304]

International human rights law is an area where the question of the international legal personality of multinationals has been most studied. On the one hand, private companies are recognized as holders of the international human rights to fair trial, privacy, and freedom of expression, by the European Court of Human Rights,[305] where they have a right to petition the Court.[306] Multinationals themselves have relied on international human rights law also in international investment dispute settlement.[307] On the other hand, the letter and the purpose of international human rights documents arguably suggests that multinationals are the subject of international obligations,[308] because 'everyone' is a duty-bearer,[309] But international human rights law has essentially been developed with natural persons in mind, and therefore does not easily fit the reality of legal persons.[310]

Overall, it can be concluded that, 'at this stage in the development of international law the classification of corporations is a matter of choice'.[311] In addition, 'much of the debate on international legal personality of transnational corporations ... is rather abstract and may be of little help in an actual understanding of the form and scope of corporate accountability'.[312]

The continuing lack of an agreed, authoritative definition of multinational companies attests to the additional difficulties not only of classifying, but also of identifying multinationals, due to their continual state of change, and being subject to changing political attitudes and policy approaches.[313] In the earlier attempts to regulate the conduct of the private sector at the international level, during the

---

[304] M. Karavias, 'Shared Responsibility and Multinational Enterprises' (2015) 62 *Netherlands International Law Review* 91; see also Karavias (n. 69) 6–10.

[305] Protocol to the (European) Convention for the Protection of Human Rights and Fundamental Freedoms (Paris, 20 March 1952, in force 18 May 1954) Art. 1; and M. Emberland, *The Human Rights of Companies* (Oxford: Oxford University Press, 2006).

[306] (European) Convention for the Protection of Human Rights and Fundamental Freedoms (Rome, 4 November 1950, in force 3 September 1953) Art. 34. See discussion in Karavias (n. 69) 180–87.

[307] P.-M. Dupuy and J. Viñuales, 'Human Rights and Investment Disciplines: Integration in Progress' in M Bungenberg, J. Griebel, S. Hobe, and A. Reinisch (eds), *International Investment Law: A Handbook* (Oxford: Hart Publishing, 2015) 1739.

[308] S. Ratner, 'Corporations and Human Rights: A Theory of Legal Responsibility' (2001–02) 111 *Yale Law Journal* 488.

[309] Universal Declaration of Human Rights, UNGA Res. 3/217 (1948), preamble and Art. 29.

[310] Karavias (n. 69) 11–15 and 74–81.

[311] Lowe (n. 3) 26. On multinationals as 'addressees' of international law, M. Iovane, 'Soggetti privati, società civile e tutela internazionale dell'ambiente' in A. Del Vecchio and A. Dal Ri Jr (eds), *Il diritto internazionale dell'ambiente dopo il vertice di Johannesburg* (Napoli: Editoriale Scientifica, 2005) 133, 171–182.

[312] Nollkaemper (n. 135) 186.

[313] 'The essence of the multinational corporation is that it has no coherent existence as a legal entity; it is a political and economic fact which expresses itself in a bewildering variety of legal forms and devices', according to C. W. Jenks, 'Multinational Entities in the Law of Nations' in W. Friedmann, L. Henkin, and O. Lissitzyn (eds), *Essays in Honor of Philip C. Jessup* (New York: Columbia University Press, 1972) 70, 80; C. D. Wallace, *The Multinational Enterprise and Legal Control* (The Hague: Martinus Nijhoff Publishers, 2002) 118.

1970s, the UN draft Code of Conduct on Transnational Corporations[314] referred to groups of companies under a single home State owner, focusing on their common system of decision-making and a link between various enterprises that allowed some to exercise significant influence over others, as well as sharing knowledge, resources, and responsibilities over the others.[315] The definition in the OECD Guidelines for Multinational Corporations similarly emphasizes the large structure of the business entities with activities in more than one country, and more than one owner in more than one home State, and the link that allows for coordination of their operations.[316] In legal literature, reference is made to their most salient characteristics, such as dimension, possession of scientific-technological innovation and know-how, international management, and the dichotomy between economic unity among, and legal diversity between, subsidiaries.[317] Other commentators, however, decided against the need to specifically define them.[318] In effect, as highlighted by the OECD,

> International business has experienced far-reaching structural change... With the rise of service and knowledge-intensive industries and the expansion of the Internet economy, service and technology enterprises are playing an increasingly important role in the international marketplace. Large enterprises still account for a major share of international investment, and there is a trend toward large-scale international mergers. At the same time, foreign investment by

---

[314] Discussed in Ch. 3.

[315] Draft Code of Conduct on Transnational Corporations, UNCTC, 'Proposed Text of the Draft Code of Conduct on Transnational Corporations' (1990) UN Doc. E/1990/94, para. 1(a), which reads: 'Enterprises, irrespective of their country of origin and their ownership, including private, public or mixed, comprising entities in two or more countries, regardless of the legal form and fields of activity of these entities, which operate under a system of decision-making, permitting coherent policies and a common strategy through one or more decision-making centres, in which the entities are so linked, by ownership or otherwise, that one or more of them may be able to exercise a significant influence over the activities of the others and, in particular, to share knowledge, resources and responsibilities with the others.'

[316] OECD Guidelines for Multinational Corporations (31 October 2001) DAFFE/IME/WPG(2000)15/FINAL, Section1.3, which reads: '[Multinational enterprises] usually comprise companies or other entities established in more than one country and so linked that they may coordinate their operations in various ways. While one or more of these entities may be able to exercise a significant influence over the activities of others, their degree of autonomy within the enterprise may vary widely from one multinational enterprise to another. Ownership may be private, state or mixed. The Guidelines are addressed to all the entities within the multinational enterprise (parent companies and/or local entities).' OECD, *Guidelines on Multinational Enterprises* (Paris: OECD Publishing, 2011) para. 4, adds that 'According to the actual distribution of responsibilities among them, the different entities are expected to co-operate and to assist one another to facilitate observance of the *Guidelines*.' The OECD Guidelines are discussed in Ch. 3.

[317] Francioni (n. 27) 13–16.

[318] C. Wells and J. Elias, 'Catching the Conscience of the King: Corporate Players on the International Stage' in P. Alston (ed.), *Non-State Actors and Human Rights* (Oxford: Oxford University Press, 2005) 141, 148–50; Kamminga and Zia-Zarifi (n. 185); and J. Ebbesson, 'Transboundary Corporate Responsibility in Environmental Matters: Fragments and Foundations for a Future Framework' in Winter (n. 135) 200, who refers to 'transboundary economic organizations'.

small- and medium-sized enterprises has also increased and these enterprises now play a significant role on the international scene. Multinational enterprises, like their domestic counterparts, have evolved to encompass a broader range of business arrangements and organisational forms. Strategic alliances and closer relations with suppliers and contractors tend to blur the boundaries of the enterprise.[319]

The OECD Guidelines, therefore, consider a definition of multinationals unnecessary,[320] due also to the diversification of multinationals into manufacturing, domestic market development, and services, as well as the emergence of multinationals based in developing countries,[321] and the varying degree of autonomy within entities within a multinational.[322]

In addition, the need to address other business entities has been increasingly emphasized internationally. First, adhering countries to the OECD Guidelines are to encourage also small- and medium-sized enterprises to observe the Guidelines.[323] Second, the supply chain is addressed: governments are to 'encourage, where practicable, business partners, including suppliers and sub-contractors, to apply principles' of corporate accountability.[324] The more detailed guidance under the OECD has focused on supply and value chains, leading to more specific standards of corporate environmental responsibility.[325]

Within the UN, attention has been focused both on the 'transnational corporation',[326] but also to 'other business enterprises':

> any business entity, regardless of the international or domestic nature of its activities, including a transnational corporation, contractor, subcontractor, supplier, licensee or distributor; the corporate, partnership, or other legal form used to establish the business entity; and the nature of the ownership of the entity.[327]

---

[319] OECD Guidelines for Multinational Enterprises (2011) Preface, para. 2.
[320] Ibid. ch. I, para. 4.
[321] Ibid. Preface, para. 3.
[322] Ibid. ch. I, para. 4.
[323] Ibid. ch. I, para. 6.
[324] Ibid. ch. II, para. 13. See also Committee on Economic, Social and Cultural Rights, General Comment No. 24 (n. 22) para. 33.
[325] See Ch. 5.
[326] 'An economic entity operating in more than one country or a cluster of economic entities operating in two or more countries—whatever their legal form, whether in their home country or country of activity, and whether taken individually or collectively.'
[327] UNCHR Sub-Commission on the Promotion and Protection of Human Rights, 'Norms on the Responsibilities of Transnational Corporations and Other Business Enterprises with regard to Human Rights' (26 August 2003) UN Doc. E/CN.4/Sub.2/2003/12/Rev.2, para. H(20); and Report of the Special Representative of the Secretary-General on the issue of Human Rights and Transnational Corporations and Other Business Enterprises: Mapping International Standards of Responsibility and Accountability for Corporate Acts (2007) UN Doc. A/HRC/4/35, para. 3 (see Ch. 4).

This is in recognition of the fact that all businesses are essential competitors in the global market, and that drawing distinctions based on size or localization of activities could prove difficult, given the plethora of diverse control structures, and forms of ownerships.[328] In addition, locally owned private companies, which are less monitored than multinationals, may resort to the 'worst safety and environmental practices'.[329] Some assert that multinationals generally have a better record in relation to environmental concerns than local enterprises in developing countries.[330] For all these reasons, the UN Guiding Principles on Business and Human Rights make clear that business responsibility applies to 'all enterprises regardless of their size, sector, operational context, ownership and structure... [although] the scale and complexity of the means through which enterprises meet that responsibility may vary according to these factors and with the severity of the enterprise's adverse human rights impacts'.[331] And thus they did not make reference to control, influence, or coordination of activities.[332]

In 2017, the UN Committee on Economic, Social and Cultural Rights also stressed that States' obligations to ensure corporate responsibility concern 'all activities of business entities, whether they operate transnationally or whether their activities are purely domestic, whether fully privately owned or State-owned, regardless of size, sector, location, ownership and structure'.[333] As discussions continue on sphere of influence,[334] linkages and leverage among different enterprises

---

[328] D. Weissbrodt and M. Kruger, 'Norms on the Responsibilities of Transnational Corporations and Other Business Enterprises with regard to Human Rights' (2003) 97 *American Journal of International Law* 901, 910.

[329] W. Lepwowski, 'The Disaster at Bhopal—Chemical Safety in the Third World' in C. Pearson (ed.), *Multinational Corporations, Environment, and the Third World* (Durham: Duke University Press, 1987) 240, 246.

[330] R. J. Fowler, 'International Environmental Standards for Transnational Corporations' (1995) 25 *Environmental Law Review* 1, 13; and P. Muchlinski, 'Human Rights, Social Responsibility and the Regulation of International Business: The Development of International Standards by Intergovernmental Organizations' (2003) 3 *Non-State Actors and International Law* 23, 136, where the author favours avoiding the risk of an inadequate definition.

[331] UN Guiding Principles, Principle 14. See also controversy over a footnote in the HRC Resolution on the negotiations of a legally binding instrument on 'transnational corporations and other business entities', which expressly excluded 'local business registered in terms of relevant domestic law' (HRC Res. 26/9 (2014) para. 9) and discussion in Cassell and Ramasastry (n. 195) 40–41, on the basis of John Ruggie's criticisms expressed in 'Quo Vadis? Unsolicited Advice to Business and Human Rights Treaty Sponsors' (2014), Institute for Human Rights and Business, accessible at https://www.ihrb.org/other/treaty-on-business-human-rights/quo-vadis-unsolicited-advice-to-business-and-human-rights-treaty-sponsors. See also C. Lopez and B. Shea, 'Negotiating a Treaty on Business and Human Rights: A Review of the First Intergovernmental Session' (2015) 1 *Business and Human Rights Journal* 111, 111–14.

[332] Muchlinski (n. 72) 658.

[333] Committee on Economic, Social and Cultural Rights, General Comment No. 24 (n. 22) section II, para. 3.

[334] Office of the High Commissioner for Human Rights, United Nations Global Compact, E-Learning, Module 2, https://www.unglobalcompact.org/library/3; as discussed in Report of the Special Representative (n. 71) paras 7–8.

along the supply/value chain,[335] and complicity,[336] as well as on the role of small- and medium-sized enterprises,[337] this study will investigate the concept of corporate accountability and responsibility as referring generally to the private sector, focusing, where necessary, on the challenges and consequences for multinationals in particular.[338]

3. Concluding remarks

The prolonged and still ongoing international debate on corporate accountability and responsibility is a stark illustration of the limitations of national and international law in effectively regulating and controlling the impacts of corporate activities on the environment and on human rights, because of tensions among different bodies of international law. Multinationals benefit from the protection of international investment law and from gaps in international criminal and civil liability regimes with respect to environmentally damaging corporate conduct.[339] International environmental law is characterized even more by open-ended standards of protection and softer enforcement mechanisms.[340] This translates, at the local level, to stronger protection for large-scale, and foreign, operators to the detriment of local actors, particularly indigenous peoples and local communities, with little negotiating power and significant vulnerability to environmental degradation in the context of natural resource development.[341]

While practice and scholarship at the intersection of international human rights law and international investment law has been increasing, there has been limited cross-fertilization of the human rights and the environment linkages for business and human rights. There is still limited reflection, therefore, on how the combined reading of international human rights law and international environment law can contribute to make headway between the two areas of law with the result that much remains to be clarified with a view to contributing to the ongoing treaty

---

[335] S. Michalowski, 'Due Diligence and Complicity: A Relationship in Need of Clarification' in Deva and Bilchitz (n. 48), 193; and F. Wettstein, 'Making Noise about Silent Complicity: The Moral Inconsistency of the "Protect, Respect and Remedy" Framework' in Deva and Bilchitz (n. 48) 243.

[336] UN Global Compact (http://www.unglobalcompact.org), Principle 2; Ruggie (n. 71) paras 26–72.

[337] Report of the Working Group on the issue of human rights and transnational corporations and other business enterprises on opportunities for small- and medium-sized enterprises in the implementation of the Guiding Principles on Business and Human Rights (2017) UN Doc. A/HRC/35/32.

[338] While bearing in mind that 'the issue of the scope of enterprises to be covered by [a potential new] treaty [on business and human rights] is far from resolved ... This is likely to remain one of the stickiest issues in the process': Lopez and Shea (n. 331) 114.

[339] Birnie et al. (n. 54) 326–29.

[340] See generally F. Francioni, 'Environment' in A. Cassese (ed.), *Realizing Utopia: The Future of International Law* (Oxford: Oxford University Press, 2012) 443.

[341] Cotula (n. 274) 104, 129, and 151. See also Miles (n. 227) and P. Simons, 'International Law's Invisible Hand and the Future of Corporate Accountability for Violations of Human Rights' (2012) 3 *Journal of Human Rights and the Environment* 5.

negotiations on business and human rights, or supporting national legislative and judicial developments.

The following chapters will thus assess to what extent the emergence of international standards on corporate environmental accountability and responsibility represent the capacity of international law to renew itself, over time and in many subtle ways, to address new challenges by forging synergies across, and tapping into the relative strengths of, international human rights and environmental law respectively. The following chapters will thus ascertain to what extent international human rights law instruments and practices have contributed to advance international standards for corporate environmental accountability and responsibility. Equally they will assess to what extent environmental standards have contributed to advance the international framework on business and human rights more generally.

3
The Emergence of International Standards

This chapter[1] analyses the varied international standard-setting attempts to address the responsible conduct of multinational corporations, and of business in general, with reference to the protection of the environment. The UN has supported a series of initiatives over time: the ill-fated draft Code of Conduct on Transnational Corporations, the ongoing UN Global Compact, the now shelved UN norms on the Responsibilities of Transnational Corporations and Other Business Enterprises with regard to Human Rights, the influential UN Framework on Business and Human Rights and its Guiding Principles, and the ongoing negotiations of a legally binding instrument on business and human rights. In response to varying political undercurrents, these developments have been characterized by different conceptual approaches: international regulation, partnership with business, and a human rights-based approach. The chapter relates these developments to long-standing initiatives under the aegis of the Organization for Economic Cooperation and Development (OECD) and the International Finance Corporation (IFC), that have also evolved over time in parallel, and increasingly in response to, UN initiatives.

First, the chapter will provide a short theoretical discussion of the role of standards, as opposed to rules and principles, in the progressive development of international law. The conceptual and legal relevance, and the legacy for current debates of each initiative, independently of whether it was successful or not, will be assessed. This aims to underline an increasing normative convergence among the respective international standards on corporate accountability and responsibility in as far as the environment is concerned. Second, the chapter reflects upon how human rights, which are a latecomer in the debate on corporate accountability, have become the dominant frame at the international level.[2] This reflection will lead to an assessment of the extent to which current human rights-based approaches have built upon the earlier consolidation of international corporate

---

[1] This chapter builds on: E. Morgera, 'The UN and Corporate Environmental Responsibility: Between International Regulation and Partnerships' (2006) 15 *Review of European Community and International Environmental Law* 93; E. Morgera, 'An Environmental Outlook on the OECD Guidelines for Multinational Enterprises: Comparative Advantages, Legitimacy and Outstanding Questions in the Lead-up to the 2006 Review' (2006) 18 *Georgetown International Environmental Law Review* 751; and E. Morgera, 'From Corporate Social Responsibility to Accountability Mechanisms' in P.-M. Dupuy and J. Viñuales (eds), *Harnessing Foreign Investment to Promote Environmental Protection: Incentives and Safeguards* (Cambridge: Cambridge University Press, 2013) 321.
[2] C. Rodríguez-Garavito, 'Conclusions' in C. Rodríguez-Garavito (ed.), *Business and Human Rights: Beyond the End of the Beginning* (Cambridge: Cambridge University Press, 2017) 186, 188.

environmental accountability standards and the extent to which they contribute to further detailing these standards. Third, the chapter will foreshadow how sectoral approaches to international standard-setting have developed on the basis of more general international standard-setting initiatives at the intersection of human rights and the environment.

1 International standards and the sources of international law

While controversy continues as to the potential sources of international law that may be applicable to private companies,[3] and as to how companies' liability might be triggered and enforced through the application of international law,[4] in the face of States' continued resistance to using international treaties to create direct obligations for corporations,[5] a more promising line of inquiry has focused on whether international environmental law principles are directly applicable to companies. A 1991 resolution of the UN Economic and Social Council (ECOSOC) already refers to the observance by multinationals of international environmental principles, particularly the polluter-pays principle, prevention, and precaution.[6] Principles are considered 'potentially applicable to all members of the international community across the range of the activities they carry out or authorize and in respect of the protection of all aspects of the environment'.[7] Ong underlined the importance of prevention, the polluter-pays principle, and precaution for corporate governance (the internal regulation of companies).[8] Environmental integration has further been highlighted as the legal basis for environmental interests to be included within a corporate governance regime.[9] The international standard-setting initiatives discussed later in this chapter, such as the UN Global Compact,[10] the

---

[3] The limited relevance of international treaties has already been discussed in Ch. 2.
[4] M. Karavias, *Corporate Obligations under International Law* (Oxford: Oxford University Press, 2013) 11–16.
[5] See Ch. 2; and P. Birnie, A. Boyle, and C. Redgwell, *International Law and the Environment*, 3rd edn (Oxford: Oxford University Press, 2009) 327; and from an international human rights perspective, see Karavias (n. 4) 17. The current negotiations on an international legally binding instrument on business and human rights do not foresee the creation of international obligations immediately binding on companies (as discussed at the end of this chapter, Section 7).
[6] ECOSOC Res. 1991/55 (26 July 1991) paras 28(c) and (i).
[7] P. Sands, *International Environmental Law. Emerging Trends and Implications for Transnational Corporations* (New York: UN, 1993) 231.
[8] D. Ong, 'The Impact of Environmental Law on Corporate Governance: International and Comparative Perspectives' (2001) 12 *European Journal of International Law* 685, 693–98. Similar principles were singled out by J. Ebbesson, 'Transboundary Corporate Responsibility in Environmental Matters: Fragments and Foundations for a Future Framework' in G. Winter (ed.), *Multilevel Governance of Global Environmental Change: Perspectives from Science, Sociology and the Law* (Cambridge: Cambridge University Press, 2006) 200, 208.
[9] P-M. Dupuy, 'Soft Law and the International Law of the Environment' (1991) 12 *Michigan International Law Journal* 420.
[10] http://www.unglobalcompact.org.

OECD Guidelines for Multinational Enterprises,[11] and the UN Norms on the Responsibility of Transnational Corporations and Other Business Enterprises,[12] also made reference to international environmental law principles.[13] These sources are also framed in inter-State terms, however, but have proven able to translate into benchmarks for corporate conduct.[14]

In effect, among the calls for 'international legal *obligations* for companies'[15] or '*norms* and *rules* promoting democratic accountability for transnational environmental harm',[16] legal *principles, norms, guidelines*, or *responsibilities* of private companies in relation to international law,[17] the term 'standard' is used most often,[18] although no definition or specification as to its legal status is provided.[19] As De

---

[11] OECD, *Guidelines for Multinational Enterprises* (Paris: OECD Publishing, 2011); see Ch. 4.

[12] UNCHR Sub-Commission, 'Norms on the Responsibilities of Transnational Corporations and Other Business Enterprises with regard to Human Rights' (26 August 2003) UN Doc. E/CN.4/Sub.2/2003/12/Rev.2 (UN Norms). See Ch. 4.

[13] 'The applicability of international legal principles to acts by companies is a rapidly evolving subject', according to M. Robinson, 'Commentary on the Interim Report of the Special Representative on Business and Human Rights' (2006) <http://www.business-humanrights.org/Links/Repository/246742>; Ch. 5.

[14] A. Nollkaemper, 'Responsibility of Transnational Corporations in International Environmental Law: Three Perspectives' in Winter (n. 8) 179, 185. See Chs. 4–5.

[15] The International Council on Human Rights Policy, *Beyond Voluntarism: Human Rights and the Developing International Legal Obligations for Companies* (Versoix: International Council on Human Rights Policy, 2002) 2. C. Wells and J. Elias, 'Catching the Conscience of the King: Corporate Players on the International Stage' in P. Alston (ed.), *Non-State Actors and Human Rights* (Oxford: Oxford University Press, 2005) 141, 170.

[16] M. Mason, *The New Accountability: Environmental Responsibility Across Borders* (London: Earthscan, 2005) 3 and 174.

[17] It is significant, in this respect, to consider the different titles successively considered for the work of the Sub-Commission on the Promotion and Protection of Human Rights with regard to transnational corporations and other business entities: UNCHR Sub-Commission on the Promotion and Protection of Human Rights, '*Principles* related to the Human Rights Conduct of Companies' (2000) UN Doc. E/CN.4/Sub.2/2000/WG.2/WP.1; 'Draft Universal Human Rights *Guidelines* for Companies' (2001) UN Doc. E/CN.4/Sub.2/2001/WG.2/WP.1/Add.1; 'Principles and *Responsibilities* for Transnational Corporations and Other Business Enterprises with Commentary on the Principles' (2002) UN Doc. E/CN.4/Sub.2/2002/XX/Add.2; and finally '*Norms* on the Responsibilities of Transnational Corporations and Other Business Enterprises with regard to Human Rights' (26 August 2003) UN Doc. E/CN.4/Sub.2/2003/12/Rev.2 (emphasis added).

[18] P. Muchlinski, 'Human Rights, Social Responsibility and the Regulation of International Business: The Development of International Standards by Intergovernmental Organizations' (2003) 3 *Non-State Actors and International Law* 123, 130; UN Special Representative on Human Rights and Business Enterprises, 'Guiding Principles on Business and Human Rights to implement the UN Protect, Respect and Remedy Framework' (2011) UN Doc. A/HRC/17/31, adopted by the Human Rights Council in Res. 17/4 (6 July 2011); Committee on Economic, Social and Cultural Rights, General Comment No. 24 on State Obligations under the International Covenant on Economic, Social and Cultural Rights in the Context of Business Activities, section (2017) UN Doc. E/C.12/GC/24, para. 5.

[19] UNCTC, 'Transnational Corporations and Issues Relating to the Environment—Report of the Secretary General' (1990) UN Doc. E/C.10/1990/10, 13, eg, reads as follows: 'guidelines taking the form of environmental principles should incorporate existing standards and recommendations ... an intergovernmentally recognized format would contribute to ... the articulation of acceptable international practices and standards for transnational corporations'. See also the allegations by victims of environmental damage and international non-governmental organizations (NGOs) in Brief for Plaintiffs, *Aguinda v. Texaco Inc.*, 1994 WL 142006 (S.D.N.Y. 1994) (No. 93–7527) 27. Finally, see P. Kohona, 'Implementing Global Environmental Standards: Is the Non-State Sector a Reluctant Convert or an Eager Devotee?' (2003–04) 11 *Asian Yearbook of International Law* 69, 88; The International Council on Human Rights Policy (n. 15) 5; and UNCHR Sub-Commission on the Promotion and Protection of

Schutter observed, the variability of States' obligations under international human rights law, which is due to States being party to different international human rights treaties, also substantiates the need for standards that 'provide an international level playing field based on the minimum requirements of international human rights law'.[20]

Along similar lines, Lowe considers international standards needed to 'moderate' the application of broad international principles upon non-State actors such as private companies that are expected to act as partners with governments in the implementation of international law.[21] While the traditional catalogue of the sources of international law does not include standards,[22] these provide a much-needed 'translation'[23] of international environmental law principles into normative benchmarks of conduct applicable to the private sector, which are flexible enough to adapt from case to case and from one area to another of corporate activity. These standards are identified on the basis of their normative and practical usefulness in defining acceptable/unacceptable conduct with reference to the protection of the environment and sustainable development according to values defined and protected by traditional sources of international law.[24] The idea of standards that could be accepted through inter-governmental negotiations and be based on internationally agreed-upon instruments already emerged in a 1991 report of the UN Secretary-General to the Commission on Transnational Corporations.[25] In the same years, the first legal study on international environmental law and its consequences for private companies, in particular transnational corporations, was commissioned by the UN Department of Economic and Social Development to Philippe Sands. In the final report, entitled *Emerging Trends and Implications for Transnational Corporations in International Environmental Law*,[26] Sands concluded that 'taken as a whole, the developments identified suggest that certain minimum international standards of environmental protection have emerged which

---

Human Rights, 'Report of the 3rd Session of the Working Group' (2001) UN Doc. E/CN.4/Sub.2/2001/9, para. 24.

[20] O. de Schutter, 'Towards Corporate Accountability for Human and Environmental Rights Abuses', discussion paper for the European Coalition for Corporate Justice (April 2007) 2.

[21] V. Lowe, 'Corporations as International Actors and International Law Makers' (2004) 13 *Italian Yearbook of International Law* 23, 25 and 27.

[22] ICJ Statute, Art. 38.

[23] According to Nollkaemper (n. 14), 185, 'Because the main principles of international environmental law are written for public rather than private entities, they need to be "translated" to the private sector'.

[24] Indeed, this was also the intention expressed in the early 1990s within the UN, when it was recommended that 'environmental conventions, standards and guidelines can help to achieve an international consensus on minimum standards of corporate environmental behaviour', in UNCTC, 'Transnational Corporations and Sustainable Development: Recommendations of the Executive Director' (1991) UN Doc. E/C.10/1992/2.

[25] ECOSOC, 'Report of Secretary-General: Transnational corporations and Issues relating to the Environment' (1991) UN Doc. E/C.10/1991/3.

[26] Sands (n. 7).

could be adopted by transnational corporations as the basis for their global activities'.²⁷ Sands therefore indicated, at a time when international environmental law was fast developing but far from the level of sophistication that we know today, that international environmental standards relevant for multinationals could already be identified and considered applicable directly to private companies, if adopted voluntarily by companies themselves. Encouraging private companies to do so was premised on the negative implications of the changing international regulatory environment for companies' production costs and processes, foreign investment decisions, disclosure requirements, marketing practices, and corporate liabilities.²⁸ The specific international environmental standards identified by Sands' 1992 study as relevant for business were: sustainable use of natural resources, environmental impact assessments, and disclosure of information to citizens and international authorities.²⁹

In light of the clear resistance of some sectors of the international community to acknowledge the existence/emergence or promote the definition of companies' *obligations* in international law,³⁰ this section will explore the legal status of 'standards' under international law within the broader category of primary rules defined by Hart.³¹ This understanding will then serve as the lens through which to analyse the growing practice of addressing matters related to corporate environmental accountability and responsibility in the context of international organizations.

1.1 The distinctive nature of legal standards

In the first instance, standards will be distinguished from rules and principles. Rules *stricto sensu* provide an 'objective limitation of what is permitted or of what is protected',³² or as Pound put it, 'a precept attaching a definite detailed consequence to a definite detailed state of facts'.³³ As opposed to rules, standards are characterized by their lack of 'a sufficient normative content', without denying their legal character.³⁴ According to Hart, standards imply the idea of a 'level or model

---

²⁷ Ibid. 37.
²⁸ Ibid.
²⁹ Ibid, where Sands also identifies other trends, such as emissions in the atmosphere and in the marine environment, and waste management, which have direct implications for business but are more related to regulatory action by the State.
³⁰ The International Council on Human Rights Policy (n. 15) 156.
³¹ H. Hart, *The Concept of Law* (Oxford: Clarendon Press, 1994).
³² Union Académique Internationale, *Dictionnaire de la terminologie du droit international* (Paris: Librairie du Recueil Sirey, 1960) 581, citing P. Roubier, *Théorie générale du droit: Histoire des doctrines juridiques et philosophie des valeurs sociales* (Paris: Dalloz, 1951).
³³ R. Pound, *Social Control through Law* (New Haven: Yale University Press, 1942) 45.
³⁴ J. Salmon, *Dictionnaire de Droit International Public* (Bruxelles: Bruylant/AUF, 2001) 1049; A. Sanhoury, *Les restrictions contractuelles à la liberté individuelle de travail dans la jurisprudence anglaise. Contribution à l'étude comparative de la règle de droit et du standard juridique* (Paris: Marcel Giard, 1925); and M. Stati, *Le standard juridique* (DPhil thesis, Paris, 1927).

to which to conform and with reference to which one can evaluate or critically appraise certain behaviour'.[35] In other words, they provide a legal benchmark allowing an appreciation of the conduct of individuals based on a model.[36] Pound, along the same lines, defines standards as 'measures of conduct prescribed by law from which one departs at his peril of answering for resulting damage'.[37] Dworkin considers standards a 'consideration of justice or fairness', a goal to be reached.[38]

Standards involve an idea of reasonableness, of what is acceptable conduct in the circumstances, thus functioning as a model against which to evaluate certain behaviours. The most common examples of standards are due care, fair conduct,[39] or fair and equitable treatment.[40] In order to define what is reasonable under the circumstances, standards require a balancing technique: 'when the sphere to be controlled is such that it is impossible to identify a class of specific actions to be uniformly done or forborne and to make the subject of a simple rule, yet the ranges of circumstances varies but covers familiar features of common experience', a common judgment weighs up and strikes 'a balance between the social claims which arise in various unanticipated forms'.[41] Legal standards, therefore, have a 'normative character, but their content and object are only partially normative, making reference to elements beyond law such as social custom or human reasonability', namely the ideas of normality, average or common practice.[42] Standards 'enter the realm of law' when they are used as the 'yardstick for correct behavior'.[43]

It follows that legal standards are usually imprecise and vague, making reference to undetermined types of behaviour, whose actual content depends on the legal operators that apply them in concrete cases.[44] Their strength actually lies in such generality and abstraction, which allow for their application in different circumstances.[45] The legal character of standards rests on their prescriptive purpose whose normative threshold can only be reached through the concrete application on a case-by-case basis.[46] Thus, standards can be characterized as an 'intermediary class of norms'[47] that practice operationalizes in those instances in which it would

---

[35] These elements are suggested by Hart (n. 31) 32, cited by Salmon (n. 34) 1049.
[36] Union Académique Internationale (n. 32) 581.
[37] Pound (n. 33) 44–49.
[38] R. Dworkin, 'Is Law a System of Rules?' in R. Dworkin (ed.), *The Philosophy of Law* (Oxford: Oxford University Press, 1977) 38, 43.
[39] Pound (n. 33) 48.
[40] For an overview of legal standards in the fields of intentional investment law, see: P. Daillier and A. Pellet, *Droit International Public* (Paris: LGDJ, 1999) 1065; P. Juillard, 'L'évolution des sources du droit des investissements' (1994) 250 *Recueils de Cours* 133.
[41] Hart (n. 31) 132.
[42] Cercle de Sociologie et Nomologie Juridiques, *Dictionnaire encyclopédique de théorie et de sociologie du droit* (Paris: Librairie Générale de Droit et de Jurisprudence, 1993) 581.
[43] C. Tomuschat, 'International Law: Ensuring the Survival of Mankind on the Eve of a New Century' (1999) 281 *Recueil des cours* 9, 352.
[44] Salmon (n. 34) 1049.
[45] Ibid.
[46] Ibid. 1050.
[47] P. Weil, 'Le droit international en quête de son identité. Cours général de droit international public' (1992) 237 *Recueil des Cours* 203, 214.

be 'unreasonable to attempt to formulate a definition of reasonable'[48] *ex ante*. In sum, standards are a legal notion with an indeterminate or variable content.[49]

The idea of reasonableness underlying standards could serve to capture the expectations voiced by the international civil society that international environmental law is relevant to assess the conduct of private companies around the world. It chimes with John Ruggie's observation that 'standards [of corporate accountability and responsibility] are in the process of being socially construed'[50] by the international community. More generally, legal standards embody a social element, which can derive from the participation of different actors in their formation.[51] The underlying reasonable expectations of a community is based on experience or on moral sentiment.[52] Standards encapsulate 'normative expectations and pave the way for the consolidation of patterns of behaviour'.[53]

Standards are particularly useful when facing temporal gaps in which the legal system is not yet ready to regulate emerging problems, and interested parties 'find solutions inspired by good faith and common sense'.[54] Such can be the specific case of normative gaps due to the relation between international law-making and State sovereignty,[55] which is exactly the reason for lack of agreement at the intergovernmental level on international obligations on corporate responsibility.[56]

In a way, legal standards favour the normative power of international organizations in bending the conditions of classic 'access to normativity', 'accelerating the evolution of international law with the hope to overcome States' resistance or the inertia of the traditional mechanisms of law-making'.[57] It should also be noted that legal standards may have non-legal functions that can support the realization of human rights, namely by contributing to actual recognition, public discussion,

---

[48] Pound (n. 33) 48.
[49] Cercle de Sociologie et Nomologie Juridiques (n. 42) 581.
[50] Interim Report of the Special Representative of the Secretary-General on the issue of Human Rights and Transnational Corporations and other Business Enterprises' (2006) UN Doc. E/CN.4/2006/97 (hereinafter, Special Representative's Interim Report) para. 54.
[51] Lowe (n. 21) 25.
[52] Pound (n. 33) 80; see references to expectations in UN Guiding Principles, Principle 11 and Commentary; and Committee on Economic, Social and Cultural Rights, General Comment No. 24 on State Obligations under the International Covenant on Economic, Social and Cultural Rights in the Context of Business Activities, section (2017) UN Doc. E/C.12/GC/24, para. 5.
[53] L. Boisson de Chazournes, 'Policy Guidance and Compliance: The World Bank Operational Standards' in D. Shelton (ed.), *Commitment and Compliance—The Role of Non-Binding Norms in the International Legal System* (Oxford: Oxford University Press, 2000) 281, 301.
[54] Weil (n. 47) 206.
[55] Ibid.
[56] See the opposition of the State members of the UN Commission on Human Rights to the UN Norms on the Responsibility of Transnational Corporations, discussed in the next chapter.
[57] Weil (n. 47) 240. For a discussion of the movements towards law in the context of corporate social responsibility (CSR) debates, see L. Catá Backer, 'Rights and Accountability in Development ("RAID") d Das Air and Global Witness v Afrimex: Small Steps towards an Autonomous Transnational Legal System for the Regulation of Multinational Corporations' (2009) 10 *Melbourne Journal of International Law* 258, 265–66; and K. Buhmann, 'Public Regulators and CSR: The "Social Licence to Operate" in Recent United Nations Instruments on Business and Human Rights and the Juridificaiton of CSR' (2016) 136 *Journal of Business Ethics* 699.

and education that may be more effective than legal approaches in changing behaviour. As such, standards provide tools of communication, advocacy, exposure, and informed public discussion that may back effective human rights claims without necessarily resort to legal coercion.[58]

The above discussion has referred to *legal* standards, which should thus be differentiated from *technical standards*. The latter have been created in the field of international environmental law through technical appendices to multilateral environmental treaties.[59] Legal standards are, therefore, different from the so-called product or process standards, which may still be based on international environmental law. Basically the latter refer to setting quantitative or qualitative emission or discharge limits for pollution activities or specific procedural steps for environmental auditing, accounting, and environmental management programmes.[60] Technical standards are also those developed by the International Standards Organization, the central body for negotiating and promoting technical industry standards.[61]

As opposed to technical standards, legal standards referred to in the present study are based on international environmental principles and treaty provisions (normative core) and represent the growing expectation as to the acceptable conduct of business, due to its '*relation to* and *position in* society'.[62] Legal standards are also different from *operational standards*, which embody an international organization's internal instructions to its staff, although these can evolve to be considered normative benchmarks to assess an organization's activities.[63]

The flexibility of legal standards fits well with the idea of international law as a process, a varied system of formal and informal law-making directed towards the attainment of certain declared values.[64] As such, international law is made up of a variety of phenomena, including claims and counterclaims, State practice, and

---

[58] A. Sen, 'Human Rights and the Limits of Law' (2005–06) 27 *Cardozo Law Review* 2913, 2920–21.

[59] P. Contini and P. H. Sand, 'Methods to Expedite Environmental Protection: International Ecostandards' (1972) 66 *American Journal of International Law* 37, 41, where the authors argue that 'technical standards (usually appended to the basic treaty in the form of annexes or schedules) provide detailed rules and codes of practice, drafted by technicians or scientists rather than diplomats or lawyers, and periodically revised by a designated international body'. P-M. Dupuy, *La responsabilité internationale des états pour les dommages d'origine technologique et industrielle* (Paris: Pedone, 1976) 272–4, where the author elaborated on eco-standards in relation to international State responsibility. Technical 'environmental protections standards' are also discussed by C. Pearson, 'Environmental Standards, Industrial Relocation and Pollution Havens' in C. Pearson (ed.), *Multinational Corporations, Environment, and the Third World* (Durham: Duke University Press, 1987) 113.

[60] As advocated by R. J. Fowler, 'International Environmental Standards for Transnational Corporations' (1995) 25 *Environmental Law Review* 1, 18–25.

[61] V. Haufler, *A Public Role for the Private Sector* (Washington DC: Carnegie Endowment for International Peace, 2001) 36–37.

[62] S. Deva, *Regulating Corporate Human Rights Violations: Humanizing Business* (Abingdon, Routledge: 2012) 150 (emphasis in the original).

[63] Boisson de Chazournes (n. 53) 282–84.

[64] Juillard (n. 40) 131; R. Higgins, *Problems and Processes. International Law and How We Use it* (Oxford: Clarendon Press, 1994) vi; J. Pauwelyn, R. Wessel, and J. Wouters (eds), *Informal International Lawmaking* (Oxford: Oxford University Press, 2012).

decisions by a variety of authorized decision-makers.⁶⁵ Seeing international law as a process may pragmatically assist in explaining the emergence of legal standards at a time when international obligations have not formally or completely emerged. According to Higgins, substantial non-compliance over a period of time implies that the concerned norms begin to lose their normative character, because the legal obligation no longer reflects community expectations that claim requirements of behaviour.⁶⁶ *A contrariis* it can be argued that legal standards backed up by a growing community expectation are gradually increasing their normative character, thus acquiring binding character in the measure in which they are accepted and function as such,⁶⁷ on the basis of what 'the actors (most often States, but not necessarily only States) believe normative in their relations with each other'.⁶⁸

From a different perspective, the emergence of international standards can be ascribed to the idea of the 'objectivization' of international law. As articulated by Dupuy, that is the prevalence of the content, the substance (*unité materielle*) of international law over its form (*unité formelle*). The substantive core of international law is based on the priority of moral imperatives for the coordinated management of a universal public order that includes also non-State actors, whereas its form concerns the origin of international law as the expression of the will of States about their legal obligations.⁶⁹ Thus, the flexibility and the social and fairness components of international legal standards reflect the dynamics of the international legal system in its substance, which is characterized by the incorporation of ethics into law, particularly through the work of the UN. This has been seen as an expression of certain political and ideological choices that at certain points of history evolve from moral potential rules to new normative concepts.⁷⁰

It should also be clarified that these standards are not part of 'transnational law', which was defined by Jessup as 'the law that regulates actions or events that transcend national frontiers', thus including both civil and criminal aspects, both public and private international law, and both public and private national law.⁷¹ As will be argued more in detail with reference to international environmental law, the legal standards mentioned in this study are essentially drawn from international law. The emergence of these standards shows how public international law is being accepted as the 'yardstick' that should guide the conduct not only of States,⁷² but also of other actors. The 'collective wisdom' and 'basic values' contained in international law are considered capable of 'indicating the right direction for new answers to

---

⁶⁵ Higgins (n. 64) 10.
⁶⁶ Ibid. 19.
⁶⁷ Hart (n. 31) 235.
⁶⁸ Higgins (n. 64) 18. See also J. Brunnée and S. J. Toope, *Legitimacy and Legality in International Law* (Cambridge: Cambridge University Press, 2010).
⁶⁹ Dupuy (n. 9) 399.
⁷⁰ Ibid. 209.
⁷¹ P. Jessup, *Transnational Law* (New Haven: Yale University Press, 1956) 2.
⁷² As argued by Tomuschat (n. 43) 26.

new problems'[73] and as the 'common regime setting binding standards for humankind as a whole'.[74] In the same direction, this study argues that legal standards are the translation of the basic values that underpin inter-State obligations and principles in international law into an operative benchmark for measuring the environmental performance of business enterprises. That said, these international standards emerge from a variety of mutual interactions between international law and other legal orders, that draw on the practice of non-State actors, particularly international organizations, international networks of experts, international civil society, bilateral donors, indigenous peoples, and local communities and the private sector.[75]

In sum, in the absence of (settled) international environmental norms directly binding upon private companies or multinational corporations in particular,[76] this chapter will assess to what extent international legal standards are emerging as a bridge between the traditional, State-centred approach in international environmental law and the possibility of qualifying the private sector's conduct according to international environmental law objectives and principles.[77] Do international environmental legal standards allow for the determination of the acceptability of certain corporate behaviour on the basis of international expectations, on a case-by-case basis? Do these standards usefully describe the reasonable conduct of business, so as to fill with content the abstract idea of due diligence for business responsibility to respect human rights with internationally recognized values and approaches for the protection of the environment?

1.2 International standards as soft law

Soft law is the expression used to define law whose normativity or legal character is ambiguous,[78] with the understanding that normativity is not necessarily based on an obligatory character or justiciability.[79] As Georges Abi-Saab so aptly described, soft law allows the exploration of new areas for the expansion of law, by articulating

---

[73] Ibid. 28.
[74] Ibid. 29.
[75] Rather, the emergence of international standards can be linked to global environmental law: E. Morgera, 'Bilateralism at the Service of Community Interests? Non-judicial Enforcement of Global Public Goods in the Context of Global Environmental Law' (2012) 23 *European Journal of International Law* 743; and K. Kulovesi, M. Mehling, and E. Morgera, 'Global Environmental Law: Context and Theory, Challenge and Promise' (2019) 8 *Transnsational Environmental Law* 405.
[76] Special Representative's Interim Report (n. 50) para. 64.
[77] Contra Nollkaemper (n. 14) 183, where he asserts '[corporate] responsibility has nothing to do with international law. It is neither based on the violation of norms that according to the sources of international law are binding on transnational corporations, nor are the consequences of a violation of standards of conduct in any way determined by international law.'
[78] G. Abi-Saab, 'Cours général de droit international public' (1987) 207 *Recueil des cours* 9, 206.
[79] Ibid. 208.

a common interest or value and defining guidelines that States are encouraged to further in normative elaboration.[80] At the same time, soft law represents the recognition by the international community of the need for a new legal rule, providing some provisional measures for the protection of a future legal interest by influencing the way in which the existing law is applied.[81]

International environmental law itself has been developed to a significant extent on the basis of soft law.[82] Soft law is carefully negotiated and drafted. It contains at least an element of good faith commitment by States, thereby influencing their practice and the progressive development of international law.[83] Although the support of States members of the international organizations under the aegis of which these instruments of soft law have been adopted do not express an *opinio juris* (the conviction to the effect that the conduct at stake is required or permitted as a matter of law), but rather a political commitment, States are no longer in a position to raise objections against the general orientation indicated in these documents.[84]

Soft law addresses not only States, but also other members of the international community such as individuals and corporations.[85] It can thus provide a pragmatic (interim) response to the uncertainty as to the legal status of corporations under international law.[86] The flexibility of soft law ensures the continuous adaptation to the changing conditions in which private companies operate. It enables a follow-up process to monitor not only State practice, but also companies' practices.[87] Thus, this study will assess whether the role of soft law is to provide 'an answer to the demands of international civil society that action be taken while preserving to political elites the freedom to curtail their obligations',[88] with 'the necessary flexibility to enable the international community to progress and address problems new to international cooperation.'[89]

---

[80] Ibid. 210.
[81] Ibid. 210–11.
[82] A. Kiss, 'The Environment and Natural Resources. Commentary and Conclusion' in Shelton (n. 53) 223; and P. Sands, J. Peel, A. Fabra, and R. MacKenzie, *Principles of International Environmental Law*, 4th edn (Cambridge: Cambridge University Press, 2018) 116–19.
[83] Birnie et al. (n. 5) 25–26. A. Boyle and C. Chinkin, *The Making of International Law* (Oxford: Oxford University Press, 2007) 211–29.
[84] Tomuschat (n. 43) 352.
[85] Sands (n. 7) 124; and S. Ratner, 'Business' in D. Bodansky, J. Brunnée, and E. Hey, *The Oxford Handbook of International Environmental Law* (Oxford: Oxford University Press, 2007) 807, 815.
[86] Discussed in Ch. 2, Section 2.6.
[87] K. P. Sauvant and V. Aranda, 'The International Legal Framework for Transnational Corporations' in A. A. Fatouros (ed.), *Transnational Corporations: The International Legal Framework* (London: Routledge, 1994) 83, 109–10.
[88] C. Chinkin, 'Normative Development in the International Legal System' in D. Shelton (ed.), *Commitment and Compliance—The Role of Non-Binding Norms in the International Legal System* (Oxford: Oxford University Press, 2000) 21, 41.
[89] Kiss (n. 82) 239.

Many soft-law initiatives in the field of corporate accountability have been developed by international organizations, NGOs, and the private sector, in a 'beyond-State' process of standard-setting.[90] This has effectively 'downplay[ed] the role of States as the broker of standards' on the assumption that States' *de facto* consent is already embodied in the underpinning treaties and soft-law instruments used as basis for standard-setting.[91] In examining specific international standard-setting initiatives, the following sections will distinguish between documents negotiated and approved by national delegations on the one hand, and international experts' documents on the other. The latter, in the absence of any inter-governmental endorsement, enjoy a residual legitimacy, by reflecting primarily the experts' contribution to the rationalization and clarification of international norms.[92]

The significance of the international (albeit soft) law character of these standards[93] lies in providing a uniform and legitimate benchmark, instead of the plethora of different criteria currently adopted by disparate initiatives. Uniformity contributes to the avoidance of a situation in which different actors adopt different standards leading to a situation of uncertainty that is detrimental to victims, governments, and companies themselves. In addition, these standards assure a certain degree of legitimacy, because they translate international environmental law that can count on the consent or endorsement of the international community.

This chapter therefore investigates the making of international standards that are based on, but separate from, international environmental law principles and treaties. International standards provide an additional and immediate way of contributing to other international efforts, without assuming that other solutions cannot be developed by the international community to address the shortcomings of traditional legal approaches. As soft law, they contribute to the making of international law.[94]

---

[90] This is indeed the main finding of D. Coleman, 'The United Nations and Transnational Corporations: From an Inter-Nation to a "Beyond-State" Model of Engagement' (2003) 17 *Global Society* 339. See also Catá Backer (n. 57) 265.

[91] Coleman (n. 90) 340–41.

[92] P.-M. Dupuy, 'Formation of Customary International Law and General Principles' in Bodansky et al. (n. 85) 449. This was a critical consideration in the elaboration of the 2016 FAO-OECD Guidance on Responsible Agricultural Supply Chains: see FAO-OECD, International Standards considered in the OECD-FAO Guidance for Responsible Agricultural Supply Chains (undated) 1, which reads 'The standards meet the following three criteria established by the multi-stakeholder Advisory Group that led the consultation process to develop the Guidance: (i) they have been negotiated and/or endorsed through an inter-governmental process; (ii) they are relevant to agricultural supply chains; and (iii) they target in particular the business/investor community': http://mneguidelines.oecd.org/OECD-FAO-Guidance_International-Standards.pdf.

[93] Special Representative's Interim Report (n. 50) para. 53, where he also highlighted that the weakness of most international initiatives on corporate social responsibility is the fact that they choose their own definitions and standards, rarely based on internationally agreed standards.

[94] A. Boyle and C. Chinkin, *The Making of International Law* (Oxford: OUP, 2009) 211–29.

1.3 The functions of international standards

Once international standards have been identified, the next logical question is whether and how these standards can be put into practice. Standards may operate in different ways, and each can potentially make a distinctive contribution to corporate environmental accountability and responsibility. From the viewpoint of victims and international NGOs, standards provide a 'template ... that [is] intended to serve as common substantive reference points' for advocacy and litigation, as well as for third-party benchmarking exercises.[95]

Standards can also serve to clarify States' obligations to develop and enforce legislation, and provide access to justice, to ensure that businesses exercise due diligence.[96] Standards can influence judicial practice.[97] They can inform national law-making, providing the basis upon which States may decide to hold corporations directly responsible by extraterritorial application of domestic law or as the basis for establishing some form of international jurisdiction.[98]

From an international investment law perspective, these standards could be integrated in international investment treaty-making (a reconceptualized bilateral investment treaty model) and dispute resolution (as interpretative tools), thereby potentially 'reorient[ing] the sole focus on investor protection that currently dominates international investment law'.[99] This may be facilitated by greater openness and accountability of international arbitration,[100] with a view to moving away from a 'narrow, asocial perception of investors' legitimate expectations concentrated on the conduct of the host country alone'.[101] For instance, standards of corporate environmental accountability and responsibility could contribute to delineate the

---

[95] For instance, the Global Reporting Initiative's standardized reporting developed by an NGO-led coalition including also companies, academics, and accounting firms, was designed explicitly to complement the UN Global Compact (discussed in Section 3): C. Metcalf, 'Corporate Social Responsibility as Global Public Law: Third Party Rankings as Regulation by Information' (2010–11) 28 *Pace Environmental Law Review* 145, 148 and 154, who ultimately notes insufficient empirical research to determine whether this is an effective approach.

[96] Draft General Comment on State Obligations under the ICESCR in the context of Business Activities, UN Doc. E/C.12/60/R.1, paras 17–21 (2016) and Committee on Economic, Social and Cultural Rights, General Comment No. 24 (n. 18); Office of the High Commissioner for Human Rights, Report to the Human Rights Council: Improving accountability and access to remedy for victims of business-related human rights abuse (2016) UN Doc. A/HRC/32/19, Annex, paras 1.5–6 and 12.3–4, calling upon States to develop domestic public and private law regimes that 'communicate clearly the *standards* of management and supervision *expected*' of corporate entities for impacts associated with or arising from group operations and within their supply chains (emphasis added).

[97] Birnie et al. (n. 5) 327.

[98] Special Representative's Interim Report (n. 50) para. 65.

[99] K. Miles, *The Origins of International Investment Law* (Cambridge: Cambridge University Press, 2013) 224–25 and 238.

[100] P. Muchlinski, 'Corporate Social Responsibility' in P. Muchlinski, F. Ortino, and C. Schreuer (eds), *The Oxford Handbook of International Investment Law* (Oxford: Oxford University Press, 2008) 637, 683. On the topic, L. Cotula, 'Expropriation Clauses and Environmental Regulation: Diffusion of Law in the Era of Investment Treaties' (2015) 24 *Review of European Community and International Environmental Law* 278. As discussed in Ch. 2, Section 2.4.

[101] Muchlinski (n. 100) 683.

'fair and equitable treatment' that host States owe to foreign investors, to determine the poor judgment of an investor and its objectionable conduct as a defense for host States in international investment disputes.[102] States could also include in their agreement with investors an obligation for the latter to respect international corporate environmental accountability standards with communities, determining goals and minimum parameters to be respected in the investor–community agreement.[103] This would allow governments to monitor and enforce possible violations of investor–community contracts, including by sanctioning them with the termination of State–investor agreements.[104]

An aspect that is particularly promising but has yet to receive sufficient attention in practice and scholarship is the use of corporate environmental standards in 'internationalized functional contracts' between international organizations and corporations, akin to those concluded by the International Seabed Authority and the World Bank, which could allow standards to turn into international obligations upon companies subject to international responsibility and amenable to be brought before international dispute settlement bodies.[105]

From the viewpoint of corporations, international standards have a significant and growing commercial relevance. International standards for corporate environmental accountability may enhance the process of project review by expanding the substantive criteria applicable to risk assessment and creating additional layers of corporate compliance beyond national law and possibly also beyond international treaties to which the host State is a party.[106] The increasing number of direct commitments of private companies to key provisions or goals of multilateral environmental agreements, and their direct involvement in international standard-setting on corporate environmental accountability[107] helps companies in anticipating and preparing for future legal developments and improve their image with consumers.[108] They can also influence the behaviour of private companies in their voluntary efforts. Arguably, ignoring global standards would be 'contrary to

---

[102] P. Muchlinski, 'Implementing the New UN Corporate Human Rights Framework: Implications for Corporate Law, Governance, and Regulation' (2012) 22 *Business Ethics Quarterly* 145, 172–73 drawing from M. Sornarajah, 'The Fair and Equitable Standard of Treatment: Whose Fairness? Whose Equity?' in F. Ortino, L' Liberti, A. Sheppard, and H. Warner (eds), *Investment Treaty Law, Current Issues II* (London: British Institute of International and Comparative Law, 2007) and P. Muchlinski, 'Caveat Investor? The Relevance of the Conduct of the Investor under the Fair and Equitable Treatment Standard' (2006) 55 *International and Comparative Law Quarterly* 527.

[103] Albeit to the extent allowed by the State's bilateral investment treaties: L. Cotula and K. Tienhaara, 'Reconfiguring Investment Contracts to Promote Sustainable Development' (2013) 2011–12 *Yearbook of International Investment Law and Policy* 281, 303 and 294; and E. Morgera, 'Under the Radar: Fair and Equitable Benefit-sharing and the Human Rights of Indigenous Peoples and Local Communities connected to Natural Resources' (2019) 23 *International Journal of Human Rights* 1098, 1120.

[104] Cotula and Tienhaara (n. 103) 303 and 293.

[105] Karavias (n. 4) 116–62.

[106] A. Meyerstein, 'Global Adversarial Legalism: The Private Regulation of FDI as a Species of Global Administrative Law' in M. Audit and S. Schill (eds), *Transnational Law of Public Contracts* (Brussels: Bruylant, 2016) 799.

[107] N. Affolder, 'The Market for Treaties', 11 *Chicago Journal of International Law* (2010) 159, 186.

[108] Sands (n. 7).

the requirement of due diligence under the UN Guiding Principles'.[109] As put by Miles, 'the interplay of actors, instruments and differing forms of CSR implementation is also leading to the internalization of a CRS rationale within the business community—in other words, the normalization or mainstreaming of CSR within the private sector', as well as 'gradually altering the cultural environment in which transnational business is conduct'.[110] International standards may also inform criteria of reasonableness at the domestic level, in company law (with regard to a broad understanding of shareholders' interests or 'enlightened shareholder value') or tort law.[111] They can also guide commercial lawyers in their capacity as 'wise counsellors' to companies that are interested in engaging in collaborative and capacity-building approaches with subcontractors, rather than including 'boilerplate language' in the contracts and engage in top-down audits of their suppliers,[112]

The following sections will, therefore, investigate the conceptual, normative, and operational contribution of the development and implementation of international standards for corporate environmental accountability and responsibility, as part of the 'work in progress', rather than an 'established and fully functioning system of, international regulation of private corporate conduct.'[113]

2 Attempts at international regulation: the UN draft Code of Conduct on Transnational Corporations

Since the 1970s, relevant discussions within the UN system have focused on multinationals' cross-border activities, their status as major international economic actors, and the consequent difficulty for individual States to regulate them effectively.[114] The first major initiative within the UN in the field of corporate responsibility arose, against the backdrop of decolonization, from early discussions initiated by the Group of Developing Countries and China (G-77), in the UN General Assembly[115] on the question of the international regulation of multinationals.

---

[109] R. McCorquodale, 'Waving Not Drowning: Kiobel Outside the United States' (2013) 107 *American Journal of International Law* 846, 848.
[110] Miles (n. 99) 226 and 231.
[111] See also their relevance in domestic law: Muchlinski, 'Implementing the New UN Corporate Human Rights Framework' (n. 102) 157–60.
[112] J. Ruggie and J. Sherman, 'Adding Human Rights Punch to the New *Lex Mercatoria*: The Impact of the UN Guiding Principles on Business and Human Rights on Commercial Legal Practice' (2015) 6 *Journal of International Dispute Settlement* 455. See also D. Baumann-Pauly, 'Bridging Theory and Practice through Immersion: Innovations for Teaching Business and Human Rights at Business Schools' (2018) 3 *Business and Human Rights Journal* 139.
[113] Muchlinski, 'Caveat Investor' (n. 102) 681.
[114] S. K. B. Asante, 'The Concept of Good Corporate Citizen in International Business' in A. A. Fatouros (ed.), *Transnational Corporations: The International Legal Framework* (London: Routledge, 1994) 169.
[115] J. M. Kline, 'Business Codes of Conduct in a Global Political Economy' in O. F. Williams (ed.), *Global Codes of Conduct: An Idea Whose Time Has Come* (Notre Dame, Ind: University of Notre

The General Assembly provided a forum in which developing countries were using their numerical advantage and their relatively strong bargaining power[116] for the adoption of resolutions on the principle of permanent sovereignty over natural resources.[117] The principle was particularly significant at a time when most foreign direct investment was natural resources-related.[118] The concerns of the G-77 with regards to multinationals were mainly based on the inaccessibility of full information on these companies, their international mobility, size, and resources, which prevented arm's-length bargaining, and their ability to call upon the home State for protection.[119]

Against this background, the G-77 led the United Nations Economic and Social Council (ECOSOC), in 1972, to acknowledge the lack of an international policy on, or regulatory mechanism for, multinationals; and establish a Group of Eminent Persons to observe, analyse, and discuss issues related to transnational corporations.[120] Such a decision has been interpreted as an explicit assumption of responsibility to deal with multinationals-related issues at the international level.[121] In 1974, the Report of the Eminent Persons' Group[122] recommended the elaboration by the UN of a code on multinationals. The recommendation was accepted by ECOSOC, which created a permanent body, the UN Commission on Transnational Corporations (UNCTC),[123] with the mandate to: monitor multinationals' activities and report on developments in international investment activities; provide developing countries with expertise and advice in their dealings with multinationals; and draft proposals for *normative frameworks* governing multinationals' activities. The last task was consistently given the highest priority in the agenda of the UNCTC.[124] A Working Group charged with the drafting of a UN

Dame Press, 2000) 39, 43; K. P. Sauvant, 'The Negotiations of the United Nations Code of Conduct on Transnational Corporations: Experience and Lessons Learned' (2015) 16 *Journal of World Investment and Trade* 11.

[116] This was also due to the oil crisis in the 1970s: Sauvant and Aranda (n. 87) 89.
[117] 'Permanent Sovereignty over Natural Resources' UNGA Res. 1803 (XVII) (14 December 1962).
[118] Sauvant and Aranda (n. 87) 90.
[119] P. Muchlinski, 'Attempts to Extend the Accountability of Transnational Corporations: The Role of UNCTAD' in M. T. Kamminga and S. Zia-Zarifi (eds), *Liability of Multinational Corporations under International Law*' (The Hague: Kluwer Law International, 2000) 97, 99.
[120] ECOSOC Res. 1721 (LIII) (28 July 1972) (adopted unanimously).
[121] A. Beghè Loreti, 'L'elaborazione di un codice di condotta delle società multinazionali ad opera delle Nazioni Unite' (1979) 2 *Il diritto comunitario e degli scambi internazionali* 262, 267; and R. J. Waldmann, *Regulating International Business through Codes of Conduct* (Washington DC: American Enterprise Institute for Public Policy Research, 1980) 70.
[122] ECOSOC, 'Effects of Transnational Corporations on Development and International Relations' (1974) UN Doc. E/5500/Rev.1/ST/ESA/6, 55.
[123] ECOSOC Res. 1913(LVII) (5 December 1974).
[124] M. Hansen, 'Environmental Regulation of Transnational Corporations' in P. Utting (ed.), *The Greening of Business in Developing Countries* (London: Zed Books in association with UNRISD, 2002) 158, 161; S. J. Rubin, 'Transnational Corporations and International Codes of Conduct: a Study of the Relationship between International Legal Cooperation and Economic Development' (1994–95) 10 *American University Journal of International Law and Policy* 1275, 1282; S. Coonrod, 'The United

draft Code of Conduct on Transnational Corporations began work in 1977. The first draft was presented in 1982 and negotiations on it lasted until 1992.[125]

The draft Code represented the first attempt at a universal and complete instrument on multinationals, both because of its global scope and of its comprehensive subject-matter.[126] It was initially agreed that it would reflect, to some degree, existing regulatory agreements or other relevant instruments under development in other international fora.[127] According to developing country proponents, the UN draft Code was to deal only with the regulation of multinationals' activities.[128] However, in 1980, a compromise was reached to have two sections in the draft. One was to focus on regulating multinationals' activities, providing rules of conduct directly applying to them. The other was to concentrate on their treatment (ie their protection), providing rules of conduct applying to capital-importing countries.[129] This decision was meant to strike a balance between the rights and the responsibilities of multinationals and of governments in a single document.[130] Thus, the objective of the draft Code was two-fold: to contribute to ensuring a stable, predictable, and transparent framework for the strengthening of international investments; and to help minimize the negative effects of multinationals, while promoting their contribution to development efforts of host States.[131] The first section, on the activities of multinationals, covered, inter alia: respect for national sovereignty, adherence to the economic and development goals of host States, respect for human rights, non-interference with the host countries' internal affairs, abstention from corrupt practices, employment conditions, and consumer and environmental protection. Its aim was not to oppose the establishment of multinationals in developing countries, but rather to require their regulation to ensure their contribution to development.[132] The second section, on the treatment of multinationals, focused on compensation for nationalization, jurisdiction, and dispute settlement.

While fundamental disagreement persisted on the second part of the code (regarding the protection of foreign direct investment),[133] substantial agreement was

Nations Code of Conduct for Transnational Corporations' (1977) 18 *Harvard International Law Journal* 273, 273.

[125] The latest text of the draft Code dates back to 1990: UNCTC, 'Proposed Text of the Draft Code of Conduct on Transnational Corporations' (12 June 1990) UN Doc. E/1990/94 (hereinafter, UN draft Code of Conduct).
[126] Beghè Loreti (n. 121) 269; P. Hansen and V. Aranda, 'An Emerging International Framework for Transnational Corporations' (1990) 14 *Fordham International Law Journal* 881, 886; and Coonrod (n. 124) 274.
[127] Rubin (n. 124) 1284.
[128] F. Francioni, 'International Codes of Conduct for Multinational Enterprises: An Alternative Approach' (1977) 3 *The Italian Yearbook of International Law* 143, 161.
[129] ECOSOC Res. 60 (24 July 1980); Muchlinski (n. 119) 100.
[130] Sauvant and Aranda (n. 87) 105.
[131] W. Sprote, 'Negotiations on a United Nations Code of Conduct on Transnational Corporations' (1990) 33 *German Yearbook of International Law* 331.
[132] Muchlinski (n. 119) 100.
[133] Hansen and Aranda (n. 126) 887; Sprote (n. 131) 341.

already reached on the first part (containing the environmental protection section) by 1981.[134] The remaining disagreement, however, led to the collapse of the negotiations in 1992, since the draft Code was discussed as a package deal.[135] The following sections will explore the environmental content of the draft Code, and its legacy.

2.1 Environmental content

The question of the legal nature of the draft Code was from the start a contentious issue, so much so that the Working Group decided to postpone it to a subsequent phase of the negotiations.[136] As a result, the language of the draft Code was vague and exhortatory.[137] Nonetheless, its most significant contribution was the unprecedented attribution to the international community of the task of developing a set of international general standards on multinationals' expected conduct.[138] Although still containing the words 'shall/should', reflecting disagreement as to the legal effects desired,[139] the fact that agreement could be reached on the wording of its environmental protection section shows how this issue was capable of attracting broader consensus. In particular, the draft Code prescribes that multinationals should carry out their activities with 'due regard to relevant international *standards*',[140] with a view to taking steps to protect the environment and, where damaged, to restore it.[141] The environmental provisions of the draft Code were drafted in a sufficiently flexible manner, thus permitting the adoption of different national implementing measures.[142] Shelton identified an inherent tension between the draft Code requirement of non-interference with the internal affairs of the host State, and adherence to international environmental standards that the host States may have not accepted.[143]

---

[134] A. A. Fatouros, 'Looking for an International Legal Framework for Transnational Corporations' in Fatouros (n. 87) 1, 9; and Sauvant and Aranda (n. 87) 102.
[135] Sprote (n. 131) 339.
[136] T. Treves, 'Nazioni Unite e imprese multinazionali' (1978) 14 *Rivista di diritto internazionale privato e processuale* 900.
[137] Beghè Loreti (n. 121) 265; and Waldmann (n. 121) 84.
[138] Coonrod (n. 124) 296; Beghè Loreti (n. 121) 536; and F. Nelli Feroci, 'Società multinazionali: verso un codice di condotta' (1978) 33 *La comunità internazionale* 325.
[139] D. T. Hamilton, 'Regulation of Corporations under International Environmental Law: Preserving the Global Environment' (1989) *Proceedings of the Annual Conference of the Canadian Council of International Law* 72, 85.
[140] UN Code of Conduct, para. 41 (emphasis added); Fatouros (n. 134) 22.
[141] UN Code of Conduct, para. 41.
[142] C. Pearson, 'An Environmental Code of Conduct for Multinational Companies?' in S. Rubin and T. Graham (eds), *Environment and Trade* (New Jersey: Allendheld Osman and Co, 1982) 154, 155.
[143] D. Shelton, 'The Utility and Limits of Codes of Conduct for the Protection of the Environment' in A. Kiss, D. Shelton, and K. Ishibashi, *Economic Globalization and Compliance with International Environmental Agreements* (The Hague: Kluwer Law International, 2003) 211, 213.

The draft Code further required multinationals supply to the competent authorities the host States of all relevant information concerning products, processes, and services. The detailed list of required information is considered to be one of the main contributions of the draft Code to the definition of corporate environmental accountability,[144] and remains a critical aspect of successive UN initiatives to clarify international standards for corporate environmental accountability.[145] Finally, the draft Code expected multinational companies to cooperate not only with national governments, but also with international organizations, for the protection of the environment.[146]

In addition to supporting the Code negotiations, the UNCTC engaged in further regulatory activities in the field of corporate environmental accountability. In its preparations for the 1992 Rio Conference on Environment and Development, the UNCTC elaborated a set of recommendations for large industrial enterprises and sustainable development, for possible inclusion in the drafting of Agenda 21,[147] noting that clear environmental guidelines and coordinated international, regional, and national policies were required for supporting corporate efforts in global environmental management.[148] These criteria, however, failed to be adopted at the Rio Summit.[149]

The UNCTC was eventually relocated to the United Nations Conference on Trade and Development (UNCTAD), in Geneva, in 1993, as UNCTAD's Division on Investment, Technology and Enterprise Development. The result of this relocation was to place the responsibility for multinationals-related issues in the part of the UN system directly responsible for economic development, and to base it in Geneva, which also hosts the headquarters of the World Trade Organization (WTO).[150] UNCTAD has continued work on multinationals, focusing in particular on the economic development aspect of the corporate social accountability agenda, advising, for example, on how to ensure the creation by multinationals of additional employment opportunities in the host country, linkages with local suppliers, and technology transfer to local business.[151] From an environmental

---

[144] Pearson (n. 142) 154.
[145] See Ch. 4, Section 2.4.
[146] UN Code of Conduct, para. 43.
[147] UNCTC, *Criteria for Sustainable Development Management* (1991), reproduced in UNCTC, 'Transnational Corporations and Sustainable Development: Recommendations of the Executive Director' (1991) UN Doc. E/CN.10/1992/2. See H. Gleckman, 'Transnational Corporations' Strategic Responses to "Sustainable Development"' in H. O. Bergenses, G. Parmann. and Ø. B. Thommessen (eds), *Green Globe Yearbook of International Cooperation on Environment and Development* (Oxford: Oxford University Press, 1995) 93, 95; Sauvant and Aranda (n. 87) 108; and Hansen and Aranda (n. 126) 88.
[148] Hansen (n. 124), 162.
[149] Utting (n. 124) 2–3. See Ch. 1.
[150] Muchlinski (n. 119) 105.
[151] L. Odenthal's contribution in United Nations Research Institute for Social Development (UNRISD), 'Corporate Social Responsibility and Development: Towards a New Agenda: Summaries of Presentations' (Geneva, 17–18 November 2003) 92. For a discussion on policy options to increase multinationals' contributions to development, UNCTAD, *World Investment Report 2003: FDI Policies for Development: National and International Perspectives* (New York: UN, 2003).

perspective, UNCTAD has kept under evaluation the self-regulation instruments put in place by industries against the relevant provisions of Agenda 21.[152] In 2004, UNCTAD's contribution was formally endorsed by the member States of the Conference, which conferred for the first time an explicit mandate on 'corporate social responsibility' (CSR).[153] In 2008, UNCTAD was tasked to identify best practices for maximizing the development impact of corporate activities.[154] Since 2011, UNCTAD has been co-organizing annual Interagency Roundtables on CSR to bring together experts from international organizations, including the UN Environment Programme, to explore current topics in CSR, share experiences, and identify opportunities for collaboration.[155] In addition, UNCTAD's 2015 Investment Policy Framework for Sustainable Development provides guidance for developing national investment policies and designing international investment agreements that support sustainable development, including by calling on governments to promote corporate accountability standard-setting, monitor compliance with them, and possibly enshrine them in national legislation to provide them with legally binding force.[156]

2.2 Legacy

Understanding the failure of the draft Code implies a further analysis of the historical and ideological background to its negotiation. The discussions in the 1970s were characterized by two major contexts: the Cold War and the process of decolonization.[157] The contraposition between the capitalist and non-capitalist blocks, as well as the North/South divide, polarized the debate on multinationals around two main positions: either the protection of foreign investors against undue restrictions by host governments, or host States' need to protect their own interests and freedom of action with regard to the impact of multinationals.[158] At the national level, this second attitude was reflected in developing countries' widespread practice of establishing regulatory frameworks which directly targeted multinationals by restricting their market shares, imports and profit repatriations, technology transfer, and domestic participation in investment projects.[159]

---

[152] UNCTAD, 'Self Regulation of Environmental Management: Guidelines set by World Industry Associations for their Members' Firms' (1996) UN Doc. UNCTAD/DTCI/29; and UNCTAD, 'Self Regulation of Environmental Management—Guidelines set by World Industry Associations for their Members' Firms: an Update 1996–2003' (2003) UN Doc. UNCTAD/ DITE/IPC/2003/3.
[153] UNCTAD, 'Sao Paulo Consensus' (2004) UN Doc. TD/410, paras 45, 49, and 89.
[154] Accra Accord, 2008, para.152.
[155] http://www.csrroundtable.org/.
[156] Investment Policy Framework for Sustainable Development, UN Doc. UNCTAD/DIAE/PBC/2015/5, Principle 9, at 35.
[157] Muchlinski (n. 119) 99 and 110.
[158] Fatouros (n. 134) 17.
[159] Hansen (n. 124) 161.

The debate on multinationals within the UN was further linked to that of the New International Economic Order (NIEO),[160] an attempt at radically restructuring the global economic system by prioritizing the objective of development. Within the NIEO framework, the growing expansion of multinationals was interpreted by the newly independent States as a continuation of the colonial ties in economic terms, which could threaten their political independence and developmental process.[161] As a consequence, the right to self-determination was affirmed to encompass also the right of the State to control the activities of multinationals operating within its territory, on the understanding that attainment of economic independence is a necessary aspect of political sovereignty.[162] The NIEO provided the context for the concept of national sovereignty over natural resources to support the self-determination of states and of peoples to decide about the economic, social, and cultural aspects of human development.[163] In both cases, the NIEO called for international cooperation on the basis of need and for shifting away from legal techniques that serve to perpetrate economic domination by a minority of States.[164] The question of the regulation of multinationals was thus entangled with that of national sovereignty over natural resources and the highly controversial expropriation debate,[165] which eventually led the negotiations on the draft Code to turn into a 'shouting match'.[166]

By the late 1980s, the historic and ideological background to the drafting of the Code was further complicated by several changes, which—combined—led to the concluding phase of the negotiations. Due to an acute shortfall in foreign direct investment in developing countries and the debt crisis, the main purpose of the debate shifted from the control of the potentially adverse impacts of multinationals to the question of how to best reintegrate developing countries into the world economy, ensuring inflows of new investment capital.[167] This was reflected

---

[160] UNGA Res. 3201 'Declaration on the Establishment of a New International Economic Order' (6 September 1974); and UNGA Res. 3202 'Programme of Action for the Establishment of a New International Economic Order' (6 September 1974).
[161] See Hansen and Aranda (n. 126) 885; Muchlinski (n. 119) 99; Hansen (n. 124) 160.
[162] Muchlinski (n. 119) 99.
[163] M. Salmon, 'From NIEO to Now and the Unfinishable Story of Economic Justice' (2013) 62 *International and Comparative Law Quarterly* 31.
[164] C. Rossi, *Equity and International Law: A Legal Realist Approach to International Decision-Making* (The Hague: Martinus Nijhoff, 1993) 200–01.
[165] S. J. Rubin, 'Reflections Concerning the United Nations Commission on Transnational Corporations' (1976) 70 *American Journal of International Law* 73, 79. For an overview of the debate on expropriation within the negotiations, P. Robinson, 'The Question of a Reference to International Obligations in the United Nations Code of Conduct on Transnational Corporations' (1986) UN Doc. ST/CTC/SER.A/1; and D. Vagts, 'The Question of a Reference to International Obligations in the United Nations Code of Conduct on Transnational Corporations: A Different View' (1986) UN Doc. ST/CTC/SER.A/2.
[166] Rubin (n. 165) 1276.
[167] P. Utting, 'UN-Business Partnerships: Whose Agenda Counts?' (Paper presented at seminar 'Partnerships for Development or Privatization of the Multilateral System', Oslo, Norway, 8 December 2000) 2; and Muchlinski (n. 119) 103.

in a gradual reformulation of the draft Code closer to that preferred by capital-exporting States. Other factors also contributed to the suspension of the negotiations in 1992,[168] such as the overly ambitious goal of universality for the draft Code,[169] the persistent disagreement about its legal status,[170] along with the opposition by multinationals themselves to possible binding standards,[171] and the limited participation in the drafting process of non-State actors, and particularly of the business community.[172] In the 1990s, wider concerns about the role of the private sector in the attainment of sustainable development have characterized the relevant debate within the UN, on the assumption that globalization is 'forging new relationships between business and society, which demand the application of ethical standards of conduct by business'.[173]

The NIEO has thus formally disappeared from the international agenda, its project of overhauling the international economic order having been abandoned following the creation of the World Trade Organization.[174] However, the discourses on equitable globalization and the principle of sustainable development have been seen as 'direct reminders' of the NIEO's call for equity among states[175] and for a rights-based approach to development.[176] To a still significant extent, the NIEO has thus evolved into a general approach to the making of international environmental law aimed at solidarity and cooperation to the benefit of the least-favoured countries.[177] And it has been enriched by the recognition of cultural diversity among and within States, resulting in the protection of the rights of marginalized individuals and communities over natural resources in order to protect their cultural identity and livelihoods.[178] As a result, national sovereignty over natural resources has been progressively qualified by duties and responsibilities towards other States and towards communities[179] (including communities outside States'

---

[168] Muchlinski (n. 119) 115.
[169] Francioni (n. 128) 160; and Asante (n. 114) 173, pointing specifically at the treatment part of the code.
[170] F. Calder and M. Culverwell, *Following up the WSSD Commitments on Corporate Responsibility & Accountability* (London: Royal Institute of International Affairs, 2004) 15.
[171] D. Weissbrodt, 'The Beginning of a Sessional Working Group on Transnational Corporations within the UN Sub-Commission on Prevention of Discrimination and Protection of Minorities' in Kamminga and Zia-Zarifi (n. 119) 119, 127.
[172] S. Prakash Seti, 'Gaps in Research, Formulation, Implementation and Effectiveness, Measurement of International Codes of Conduct' in Williams (n. 115) 117, 120; contra Asante (n. 114) 190, where the author asserted the need for full participation of representatives of the business community in the deliberations of the Commission.
[173] Shelton (n. 143) 211.
[174] Francioni, 'Equity' in R. Wolfrum (ed.), *Max Planck Encyclopedia of Public International Law* (Oxford: Oxford University Press, online edition, 2010) 632, para. 21.
[175] E. Tourme-Jouannet, *What Is a Fair International Society? International Law between Development and Recognition* (Oxford: Hart Publishing, 2013) 37, 86–87.
[176] Salmon (n. 163) 49.
[177] Eg S. Maljean-Dubois, 'Justice et société internationale: l'équité dans le droit international de l'environnement' in A. Michelot (ed.), *Equité et environnement* (Brussels: Lancier, 2012) 355, 358–59.
[178] Tourme-Jouannet (n. 175) 121, 149.
[179] F. Lenzerini, 'Sovereignty Revisited: International Law and Parallel Sovereignty of Indigenous Peoples' (2006) 42 *Texas International Law Journal* 155.

own borders[180]), which finds resonance in the most recent developments related to corporate accountability.

Although the UN draft Code of Conduct was never approved, it left a legacy for corporate environmental accountability in international law. With regard to its impact on the UN, undeniably its failure had 'substantial psychological and political implications'[181] that have been reflected in the new strategies adopted within the UN to contribute to tackle the issue of corporate accountability, such as the partnership approach of the UN Global Compact and the human rights-based approach.

Certainly, the draft Code's failure showed the lack of political will of negotiating States to have an international instrument regulating foreign direct investment and multinationals' responsibility, particularly due to the changed political and economic background to the negotiations. This was further exemplified in the failed negotiations of a Multilateral Agreement on Investment within the OECD in 1998.[182] Nonetheless, one should not underestimate the 'impressive achievement of the UNCTC', namely the wide measure of consensus reached over the first part of the draft (on the activities of transnationals) which constituted a quite comprehensive elaboration of the expectations on acceptable corporate conduct.[183] As it appears less controversial now than it did in the 1970s and 1980s, the draft seems sufficiently broad in subject-matter to encompass many issues of the contemporary international agenda on corporate responsibility and accountability.[184]

3 Subsequent practice of the UN in the 1990s: the partnership approach

By the late 1990s, the UN aimed at ensuring further understanding of multinationals' activities and their impacts on development, in order to facilitate access of developing countries to foreign direct investment.[185] With the recognition of the potentially positive role of the private sector in the global efforts towards sustainable development,[186] a new trend of promoting UN–business partnerships developed to become an 'integral part' of the work of the UN,[187] and increasingly

---

[180] E. Benvenisti, 'Sovereigns as Trustees of Humanity: On the Accountability of State to Foreign Stakeholders' (2013) 107 *American Journal of International Law* 295.
[181] Rubin (n. 124) 1289.
[182] W. Crane, 'Corporations Swallowing Nations: The OECD and the Multilateral Agreement on Investment' (1998) 9 *Colorado Journal of International Environmental Law and Policy* 429, 429.
[183] Asante (n. 114) 172–73.
[184] Muchlinski (n. 119) 115.
[185] Ibid.
[186] Agenda 21 (12 August 1992) UN Doc. A/CONF.151/26/Rev.1 vol 1, Annex II, Ch. 30.
[187] UNGA, 'Report of the Secretary-General: Enhanced Cooperation between the United Nations and all Relevant Partners, in particular the Private Sector' (2003) UN Doc. A/58/227. For a detailed analysis of the UN–private sector partnerships, A. Zammit, *Development at Risk. Rethinking UN-Business Partnerships* (Geneva: UNRISD, 2003).

relevant for the environmental sector.[188] This is the result of a shift in discussions on multinationals from concerns over expropriation[189] to concerns over globalization.[190] Due to the development aid crisis, the debt crisis, and the shortfall in investment towards developing countries, a re-evaluation of benefits of foreign direct investment took place, with greater competition among developing countries to attract multinationals.[191] This was accompanied by increasing privatization, a growing number of bilateral investment agreements, and international action aiming at the establishment of new structures for investors' protection through the World Bank and the World Trade Organization.[192] The idea of partnerships is also responsive to a multi-stakeholder approach in the definition and implementation of international environmental standards for corporate accountability, as part of a changed system of international governance increasingly involving non-State actors, both the private sector and the NGO community, in the shaping and implementation of international law.[193] Within this, attention was increasingly focusing on the whole private sector, and no longer multinationals alone.[194]

A study by the United Nations Research Institute for Social Development (UNRISD)[195] identified two main purposes of UN partnerships. On the one hand, they represented an attempt by the UN to regain political relevance by welcoming non-State actors in international deliberative fora and project implementation.[196] Partnerships provided the UN with a means of mobilizing resources, and tapping the technology, competencies, creativity, and global reach of the business community for development purposes.[197] This second aspect was specifically linked to the financial crisis that the UN underwent particularly in the 1990s.[198] The UNRISD study also points to some of the weaknesses of this approach, namely the political and material limitations of the UN in systematically screening companies with which they start partnerships. It highlighted how the different agendas of the different actors involved in the partnership may render it difficult to contribute significantly to the goals of the UN. This would be the case of companies willing to enhance their competitiveness through a fairly minimalist agenda of corporate

---

[188] The most notable, although controversial, outcome of WSSD was 'Type II Partnerships', namely opportunities for the private sector to engage actively in the process through multistake-holder involvement, as an alternative to Type I (formal) commitments <http://www.un.org/esa/sustdev/ partnerships/partnerships.htm>, as highlighted by Calder and Culverwell (n. 170) 18 and 47–8.
[189] Fatouros (n. 134) 12.
[190] Rubin (n. 124) 1277.
[191] Hansen (n. 124) 164.
[192] Muchlinski (n. 119) 104; see also Ch. 2.
[193] For further reading on this point, M. Bettati and P-M. Dupuy (eds), *Les O.N.G. et le droit international* (Paris: Economica, 1986); and V. Haufler, *A Public Role for the Private Sector* (Washington DC: Carnegie Endowment for International Peace, 2001).
[194] Ch. 3.
[195] Utting (n. 124) 3.
[196] Ibid. 4.
[197] Ibid. 3.
[198] Ibid. 6–7.

accountability, by improving their reputation and image through their association with the UN.[199] Some commentators have thus underscored that partnerships may permit the 'smuggling' of a business agenda into the UN.[200] Other authors, conversely, consider partnerships as an indispensable step in the enhancement of international cooperation, which is much needed for the attainment of goals that are 'too big a job for governments alone'.[201] Against this background, the following sections focus on the most prominent partnership of the UN with the private sector—the UN Global Compact—because of its international standard-setting role.

3.1 The UN Global Compact

The highest-profile example of UN partnerships with the private sector is the Global Compact.[202] It was launched by former UN Secretary-General Kofi Annan to respond to the lack of an international framework to assist companies in the development and promotion of global value-based management.[203] In January 1999 Annan addressed the World Economic Forum,[204] challenging 'world business leaders to help build the social and environmental pillars required to sustain the new global economy, on the basis of shared values and principles'.[205] The initiative was subsequently officially launched in July 2000, within ECOSOC.[206] Almost 10,000 companies in over 160 countries participate in the Global Compact.[207] But reportedly 'growth in membership has been relatively moderate in recent years' and the Compact lacks 'a strategic vision for increased engagement of private companies'.[208]

The UN Global Compact has been widely publicized and criticized,[209] due to its innovative approach according to which 'confrontation' with the business

---

[199] Ibid. 5.
[200] K. Bruno and J. Karliner, 'The UN's Global Compact, Corporate Accountability and the Johannesburg Earth Summit' (2002) 45 *Development* 33–34.
[201] B. King, 'The UN Global Compact: Responsibility for Human Rights, Labour Relations, and the Environment in Developing Nations' (2001) 34 *Cornell International Law Journal* 481, 483.
[202] Bruno and Karliner (n. 200) 34.
[203] UN Global Compact Office, 'United Nations Guide to the Global Compact: A Practical Understanding of the Vision and the Nine Principles' (undated) <http://www.unglobal compact.org/irj/servlet/prt/portal/prtroot/com.sapportals.km.docs/ungc_html_content/Public_ Documents/gcguide.pdf> 4 (hereinafter, United Nations Guide to the Global Compact).
[204] UN Press Release, 'Secretary-General Proposes Global Compact on Human Rights, Labour, Environment in Address to World Economic Forum in Davos' (1 February 1999) UN Doc. SG/SM/6881 <http://www.un.org/News/Press/docs/1999/19990201.sgsm6881.html>.
[205] United Nations Guide to the Global Compact, 4.
[206] Ibid.
[207] See UN Global Compact, 'Participants' <https://www.unglobalcompact.org/what-is-gc/participants>.
[208] UN Joint Inspection Unit, 'The UN System-private sector partnership in the context of the 2013 Agenda for Sustainable Development' (2017) UN Doc. JIU/REP/2017/8, para. 181.
[209] For an overview of opinions on the Global Compact, M. Shaughnessy, 'The United Nations Global Compact and the Continuing Debate about the Effectiveness of Corporate Voluntary Codes of Conduct' (2000) *Colorado Journal of International Environmental Law and Policy Yearbook* 156; W.

community was replaced with 'cooperation'.[210] Its main aim is to build collaborative relations with the private sector, on the basis of internationally agreed principles of good corporate citizenship (human rights, labour standards, environmental sustainability, and anti-corruption).[211] This section will discuss the innovative strategy of the UN Global Compact, and its legal significance as 'the world's largest corporate social responsibility initiative'.[212]

The scope of the UN Global Compact is to encourage the private sector to commit its support to the ten principles, expecting companies to integrate them into their core business operations, and pursuing activities that advance implementation of the principles, and other UN-related objectives, such as the Millennium Development Goals (MDGs) first[213] and the Sustainable Development Goals after 2015.[214] Adhering companies are further expected to post on the Global Compact website, at least once a year, a report of the concrete steps taken, and lessons learnt on any of the principles. Under these conditions, business enterprises are free to publicize their participation in the UN Global Compact.[215] This is supposed to provide the best incentives for companies to adhere. In addition, engagement by the private sector also includes the commitment to work in a transparent and accountable manner, particularly to be prepared to respond to NGO observations and critiques on the Compact website.[216] One of the Global Compact's main features is thus multi-stakeholder involvement, through the encouragement of the 'spotlight effect' by voluntary monitoring undertaken by NGOs and the media.[217]

The Global Compact does not address or refer specifically to multinationals, but is open to all business entities, without distinction. Opinions on the Global Compact are quite divided. Environmental activists characterize the Global Compact as an ideal 'greenwash' instrument arguing that in the run-up to the WSSD,[218] several corporations expressed their commitment to environmental principles to improve their public image, without undertaking any significant implementation.[219] Conversely, business considered that the Global Compact renders redundant the adoption of other international (possibly binding) documents

---

H. Meyer and S. Boyka, 'Human Rights, the UN Global Compact, and Global Governance' (2001) 34 *Cornell International Law Journal* 501; and E. Duruigbo, *Multinational Corporations and International Law: Accountability and Compliance Issues in the Petroleum Industry* (Ardlee, NY: Transnational Publishers, 2003) 150–3.

[210] Bruno and Karliner (n. 200) 34.
[211] Ibid.
[212] Special Representative's Interim Report (n. 50) para. 40.
[213] UNDP, *Millennium Development Goals Report 2015* (New York: UN, 2015).
[214] https://www.unglobalcompact.org/sdgs.
[215] Shelton (n. 143) 216.
[216] United Nations Guide to the Global Compact, 9.
[217] Meyer and Boyka (n. 209) 504.
[218] Ch. 2.
[219] O. Hoedeman, 'Rio + 10 and the Greenwash of Corporate Globalization' (2002) 45 *Development* 39–40.

on corporate accountability.[220] The legal significance of the Global Compact itself, however, requires further reflection, as discussed below.

3.1.1 Legal significance

The UN qualifies the Global Compact as a 'voluntary corporate citizenship initiative based on a learning approach'.[221] Companies are free to adhere to any of the ten principles through a letter of intent. The 'opt-in' approach[222] of the UN Global Compact and its being a UN Secretariat-driven process could be understood as an institutional reaction within the UN system to the failure of the UN draft Code of Conduct inter-governmental negotiations.[223] Particularly in consideration of the alleged lack of involvement of the private sector in the Code negotiations, the UN Global Compact sought to integrate multinationals as participants in the shaping and maintenance of an international framework on corporate accountability.[224]

Regret has been expressed with regard to the flexibility for companies to 'pick and choose' among the ten principles.[225] No further formal requirements are in place,[226] except for the posting on the website of the reports.[227] The UN Global Compact makes it clear that it is not a substitute for effective action by governments nor does it supplant other voluntary initiatives. It is further specified that it does not endorse the companies participating in the initiative.[228] The initiative is, rather, a platform designed to promote institutional learning, through transparency, dialogue with stakeholders, and dissemination of best practices. In addition, the lack of specificity of the principles has been considered as an impediment to effective implementation: while it aims to adapt the Compact to different business cultures,[229] it allows for varying degrees of stringency in its application.[230] The Global Compact should thus be assessed on the basis of its track record in providing a venue for 'accumulated experience—through trial, error and social

---

[220] Ibid. 41; Bruno and Karliner (n. 200) 34; Utting (n. 124) 8; Judith Richter's contribution in UNRISD (n. 151) 77. The same argument has also been used by the International Chamber of Commerce (ICC) against a formal endorsement of the Norms on the Responsibilities of Transnational Corporations and Other Business Enterprises with regard to Human Rights': ICC and International Organization of Employers (IOE), 'Joint views of the IOE and ICC on the draft norms on the responsibilities of transnational corporations and other business enterprises with regard to human rights' (22 July 2003).
[221] United Nations Guide to the Global Compact, 4.
[222] As defined by Meyer and Boyka (n. 209) 502.
[223] As confirmed by D. Coleman, 'The United Nations and Transnational Corporations: From an Inter-Nation to a "Beyond-State" Model of Engagement' (2003) 17 *Global Society* 339, 350.
[224] Meyer and Boyka (n. 209) 510.
[225] Utting (n. 124) 2.
[226] This is highlighted by Shelton (n. 143) 216.
[227] United Nations Guide to the Global Compact, 7.
[228] Ibid. 4.
[229] Calder and Culverwell (n. 170) 37.
[230] Shaughnessy (n. 209) 164; L. A. Mowery, 'Earth Rights, Human Rights: Can International Environmental Human Rights Affect Corporate Accountability?' (2002) 13 *Fordham Environmental Law Journal* 343, 363; and M. Gjølberg and R. Audun, 'The UN Global Compact—A Contribution to Sustainable Development?' (University of Oslo Working Paper n.1/05, 2005).

vetting—to gradually fill the blanks'.[231] As discussed below, its relevance should also be assessed on the basis of its contribution to further international standard-setting on corporate environmental accountability and responsibility.[232]

The learning approach has been lauded for its potential to reach through dialogue to 'broader, consensus-based definitions of what constitutes good practices ... which will become a standard of reference source' through transparency, advocacy, and competition.[233] The approach also has the potential to 'lead gradually to a desire for greater codification benchmarking and moving from "good" to best "practice"', with 'laggards [having] a harder time opposing actual achievements by their peers than a priori standard'.[234]

Two other aspects of the Global Compact are, however, relevant from a legal perspective: the origin of the standards and the existence of a follow-up mechanism. Like the UN draft Code, the ten principles are based on pre-existing, internationally agreed UN documents, namely: the Universal Declaration of Human Rights;[235] the International Labour Organization's (ILO's) Declaration on Fundamental Principles and Rights at Work;[236] the Rio Declaration on Environment and Development;[237] and the UN Convention against Corruption.[238] The relevance of the UN Global Compact for international environmental law therefore consists in the underlying assumption that international environmental law principles can be directly applied to multinationals, particularly the precautionary principle.[239] To that extent, it can be argued that the Global Compact is 'built on a theoretical contradiction in terms of its true nature ... in effect it tries to regulate, using the disguise of voluntary self-regulation'.[240]

As opposed to the UN draft Code of Conduct, the UN Global Compact is an autonomous initiative of the Secretary-General. In time, however, the Global Compact received an inter-governmental endorsement through General Assembly resolutions.[241] So the question of the lack of its inter-governmentally agreed mandate was raised.[242] Evidence of inter-governmental backing can

---

[231] J Ruggie, 'Theory and Practice of Learning Networks: Corporate Social Responsibility and the Global Compact' (2002) 5 *Journal of Corporate Citizenship* 26, 32.
[232] Section 3.1.2.
[233] Ruggie (n. 231) 32.
[234] Ibid. 33.
[235] UNGA Res. 217A(III) (10 December 1948).
[236] 86th Session of the General Conference of the International Labour Organization (Geneva, 19 June 1998).
[237] 'Rio Declaration on Environment and Development' (13 June 1992) UN Doc. A/ CONF.151/6/Rev.1 (Rio Declaration).
[238] UNGA Res. 58/4 (31 October 2003). United Nations Guide to the Global Compact, 7.
[239] Utting (n. 124) 1.
[240] Deva (n. 62) 97.
[241] UNGA Res. 62/211 'Towards Global Partnership' (2007) para. 9 and 64/223 'Towards Global Partnership' (2009) para. 13.
[242] See the Joint Inspection Unit, United Nations Corporate Partnerships: The role and functioning of the Global Compact, UN Doc. JIU/REP/2010/9 (2010) paras 13–18 and recommendation 1; and 'A response from the Global Compact Office' 24 March 2011, at 2.

now found in the periodic General Assembly Resolution 'Towards Global Partnership', which routinely refers to 'strengthening the capacity of the United Nations to partner strategically with the private sector, ... to advance United Nations values and responsible business practices within the United Nations system and among the global business community'.[243] The UN General Assembly also regularly encourages and urges all companies to adopt principles for responsible business, such as respecting the principles of the United Nations Global Compact, by translating them into operational corporate policies, codes of conduct and management, monitoring and reporting systems.[244] More recently, the UN Joint Inspection Unit has recommended more inter-governmental involvement in the Compact's governance structure, emphasizing how the mandate identified by the General Assembly still needs to be 'framed, translated and positioned within the ... wider context of the UN System'.[245]

Overall, the Global Compact can be considered as an advancement in the direct application of international norms to multinationals by shaping global discourse, global governance methodology, and cultural expectations.[246] In time it has become 'more sophisticated' in the interpretation of its principles, the guidance it provides to companies, and the reporting requirements.[247] Its key weaknesses, however, remain the lack of a gatekeeping function to screen participants[248] or review substantively their reporting and adherence to the principles: it relies on a global database to identify potential concerns and makes enquires with local Global Compact networks.[249] Even if 'Integrity Measures' were introduced in 2005 to monitor companies' compliance with the reporting requirements and allow the submission of complaints about 'systematic or egregious abuses' of the aims and principles of the Compact to the Global Compact Office,[250] the procedure is not a compliance-based initiative, but essentially aims to safeguard the reputation and integrity of the Global Compact.[251]

---

[243] UNGA Res. 70/224 (2016) para. 24 preambular.
[244] Ibid. paras 7 and 12, preambular para. 7.
[245] UN Joint Inspection Unit (n. 242), Recommendation 8 and para. 174.
[246] Miles (n. 99) 249.
[247] P. Simons and A. Macklin, *The Governance Gap: Extractive Industries, Human Rights and the Home State Advantage* (Abingdon: Routledge, 2014) 114.
[248] UN Joint Inspection Unit, 'United Nations Corporate Partnerships: The Role and Functioning of the Global Compact' (2010) UN Doc. JIU/REP/2010/9, paras 63 and 14, and comments by Simons and Macklin (n. 247) 116–17.
[249] Simons and Macklin (n. 247) 117.
[250] UN Global Compact Office, 'Note on Integrity Measures' (26 November 2007).
[251] U. Wynhoven and M. Stausberg, 'The United Nations Global Compact's Governance Framework and Integrity Measures' in A. Rasche and G. Kell (eds), *The United Nations Global Compact: Achievements, Trends and Challenges* (Cambridge: Cambridge University Press, 2010) 251, 262–63. See discussion in Ch. 4, Section 5.

3.1.2 Environmental content

From an environmental perspective, the Global Compact is significant for the emergence of international standards for corporate environmental accountability implying the relevance, if not direct applicability, of international environmental principles to private enterprises.[252] The Global Compact has thus been referred to in the context of international advice on corporate environmental accountability through due diligence to respect human rights: this is the case of UN Special Rapporteur on Toxics, for instance.[253]

As opposed to its principles on human rights, the UN Global Compact makes reference only implicitly to the international framework for environmental protection of the environment. Its most prominent feature is the application of the precautionary approach to adhering companies.[254] In this respect, the Guide to the UN Global Compact cautiously mentions that the principle is accepted in the EU and forms 'part of international environmental law'.[255] The Guide further emphasizes that the principle entails that businesses should take the most cost-effective, early action to prevent the occurrence of irreversible environmental damage. To this end, companies are expected to carry out assessments of their environmental impacts and environmental risks, invest in sustainable production methods and research, and develop environmentally-friendly products.[256]

In addition, the UN Global Compact encourages businesses to undertake initiatives to promote greater environmental responsibility.[257] The Guide elaborates on environmentally sound business practices encompassing: resource productivity, cleaner production, corporate governance, and multi-stakeholder dialogue.[258] Finally, the Global Compact expects adhering companies to encourage the development and diffusion of environmentally-friendly technologies.[259] These are defined in the Guide to the UN Global Compact by express reference to Agenda 21, thus including technologies that allow for limited pollution, protection of the environment, sustainable use of natural resources, and reduction or reuse of waste.[260]

While, per se, the Global Compact environmental principles may be too vague to provide adequate guidance to companies,[261] they have provided a basis upon which the Global Compact has developed more specific guidance over time,

---

[252] Utting (n. 167) 1; contra, affirming that the Global Compact is 'devoid of legal normativity', see Karavias (n. 4) 103.
[253] Report of the Special Rapporteur on the human rights obligations related to environmentally sound management and disposal of hazardous substances and waste, Calin Georgescu (2012) UN Doc. A/HRC/21/48, paras 50 and 70.
[254] The Global Compact, Principle 7.
[255] UN Guide to the Global Compact, 52.
[256] Ibid. 54.
[257] Global Compact, Principle 8.
[258] UN Guide to the Global Compact, 58.
[259] Global Compact, Principle 9.
[260] UN Guide to the Global Compact, 64.
[261] Deva (n. 62) 97.

engaging in two types of activities. First, the Global Compact Office has partnered with the secretariat of multilateral environmental agreements to engage companies in reflection and action on specific environmental challenges. These activities exemplify a thematic or sectoral approach (climate change, biodiversity, water), focused on targets and company policies, reporting, and stakeholder engagement, along the supply chain. Second, the Global Compact has produced guidance documents on international standards of particular relevance for the natural resource sector, such as on indigenous peoples' rights,[262] bringing together different international advice from the International Finance Corporation, Inter-American Court of Human Rights, and African Commission on Human and Peoples' Rights cases.[263]

4 The human rights-based approach

Almost at the same time as the development of the UN Global Compact, the former UN Commission on Human Rights (UNCHR) started work on corporate accountability. Until 2006, the UNCHR was the UN body, composed of the representatives of fifty-three member States, that was mandated to examine, monitor, and publicly report either on human rights situations in specific countries or on major phenomena of human rights violations worldwide. Its subsidiary body—the UN Sub-Commission on the Promotion and Protection of Human Rights, which was in turn composed of twenty-six independent human rights experts acting in their personal capacity as the Commission's 'think tank',[264] developed the Norms on the Responsibility of Transnational Corporations and Other Business Enterprises with regard to Human Rights,[265] which were rejected by member States in 2003, as discussed below.

Following this initiative, the UNCHR nominated a Special Representative of the Secretary-General to continue to investigate the issue of corporate responsibility and accountability from a human rights perspective,[266] with a view to identifying and clarifying standards of corporate responsibility and accountability for multinationals and other business, and elaborating on the role of States in effectively regulating and adjudicating on multinationals, including through international

---

[262] Global Compact Office, *The Business Reference Guide to the UN Declaration on the Rights of Indigenous Peoples* (United Nation Global Compact Office, 2013).
[263] Ch. 4.
[264] On the relationship between Sub-Commission and the Commission in relation to the Norms, Simon Walker's contribution in UNRISD (n. 151) 83. The mandate of the Sub-Commission is detailed in UNCHR Res. 2003/59 (24 April 2003) and Res. 2004/60 (20 April 2004).
[265] UNCHR Sub-Commission on the Promotion and Protection of Human Rights, 'Norms on the Responsibilities of Transnational Corporations and Other Business Enterprises with regard to Human Rights' (26 August 2003) UN Doc. E/CN.4/Sub.2/2003/12/Rev.2 (UN Norms).
[266] UNGA Res. 60/251 (3 April 2006) and HRC Res. 8/7 (18 June 2008).

cooperation. While the self-declared regulatory approach of the Sub-Commission seems closer to that of the UN draft Code, the conclusions of the UN Special Representative have been framed much more cautiously on the state of international law and on the need for action by the UN—although, as will be discussed, the actual conceptual approach of the two initiatives is similar in many ways. This cautious approach, however, has allowed for the gathering of political support for the UN Framework on Business and Human Rights and its Guiding Principles, which represent the only inter-governmentally endorsed UN instruments on corporate accountability and responsibility, and as such are now shaping the gamut of international human rights processes under the UN. It has been argued that the Guiding Principles have generated 'a shift in the dynamic' towards 'greater understanding' and a focus on implementation, as opposed to polarized debates on the relevance of human rights for business.[267] This has led to an 'unprecedented point of engagement'.[268]

The human rights-based approach may present some advantages in pushing the international agenda on corporate environmental accountability and responsibility forward. On the one hand, the notion of applying international law to non-State actors has been developed in the field of human rights, on the basis of an interpretation of the preamble of the Universal Declaration of Human Rights,[269] referring to the responsibility of both governments and 'other organs of society' to respect the fundamental rights of individuals.[270] Secondly, the human rights machinery brings in a 'claims and responsibility' approach, which typically empowers citizens to complain directly for breaches of international law.[271] Finally, this approach may prove beneficial in increasing the credibility of corporate accountability.[272] Denouncing corporate misconduct as a human rights matter may immediately convey the opprobrium of society and raise the prospects that the conduct will be of international concern,[273] gathering political momentum, bringing in new allies from human rights advocates.[274] From an environmental viewpoint, however, this

---

[267] L. Bickford, 'What Next for Business and Human Rights?' in Rodríguez-Garavito (n. 2) 150, 153.
[268] B. Meyersfeld, 'Committing the Crime of Poverty: The Next Phase of the Business and Human Rights Debate' in Rodríguez-Garavito (n. 2) 173, 177.
[269] GA Res. 217 A (III), 10 December 1948.
[270] UNCHR Sub-Commission, 'Principles related to the Human Rights Conduct of Companies, working paper prepared by D. Weissbrodt' (2000) UN Doc. E/CN.4/Sub.2/2000/ WG.2/WP.1, para. 12; The International Council on Human Rights Policy (n. 15) 56. Contra Interim Report of the Special Representative of the Secretary-General on the issue of Human Rights and Transnational Corporations and other Business Enterprises' (2006) UN Doc. E/CN.4/2006/97. See Ch. 2, Section 2.5.
[271] Interview with Simon Walker, Officer, UN High Commissioner's Office for Human Rights (Geneva, 19 July 2004).
[272] D. Geron, 'Human Rights and Transnational Corporations: Beyond UN Norms?' (summary of discussions at the International Law Programme Discussion Group of the Chatham House, London, 21 October 2004).
[273] Ibid. 18; M. Anderson, 'Public Interest Perspectives on the Bhopal Case: Tort, Crime or Violation of Human Rights?' in D. Robinson and J. Dunkley (eds), *Public Interest Perspectives in Environmental Law* (London: Wiley Chancery, 1995) 154.
[274] The International Council on Human Rights Policy (n. 15) 15.

approach does not seem to lead to radically different substantive solutions. As will be discussed in more detail below, the corporate environmental accountability standards identified by this initiative tend to converge with those identified by other international organizations at different points in time. That said, the human rights-based approach has placed more emphasis on grievance mechanisms, and has some strategic advantages.

4.1 The Norms on the Responsibilities of Transnational Corporations and Other Business Enterprises with regard to Human Rights

The UNCHR Sub-Commission first required a report on the issue of human rights and multinationals in 1997.[275] From 1998–2004, the Sub-Commission established a Working Group to examine the working methods and activities of multinationals,[276] with a view to examining the effects of multinationals on human rights and investment agreements' compatibility with human rights.[277] As early as 1999, when setting its agenda, the Working Group decided to prepare a draft code of conduct for companies. The final document, entitled 'Norms on the Responsibilities of Transnational Corporations and Other Business Enterprises with regard to Human Rights', was approved at the technical level by the Sub-Commission in August 2003. The Sub-Commission and its working group, acting in their members' individual capacity, undertook broad consultations with stakeholders on the matter, including public dissemination of previous drafts and collection of comments,[278] outside the constraints of inter-governmental negotiations.[279] The Norms also took into consideration best practices in corporate accountability, with a particular view to business organizations' and NGOs' codes and guidelines on the matter.[280]

---

[275] UNCHR Sub-Commission Res. 1997/11 (22 August 1997).
[276] UNCHR Sub-Commission's Res. 1998/8 (20 August 1998); UNCHR Sub-Commission, 'Compte rendu analytique de la 25ᵉ séance' (available only in French) (31 August 2001) UN Doc. E/CN.4/Sub.2/2001/SR.25.
[277] For a full account of the drafting of the Norms, D. Weissbrodt and M. Kruger, 'Norms on the Responsibilities of Transnational Corporations and Other Business Enterprises with regard to Human Rights' (2003) 97 *American Journal of International Law* 901, 904. Weissbrodt was one of the experts on the Working Group.
[278] Sub-Commission's Resolution 2002/8 (14 August 2002): 'The relationship between the enjoyment of economic, social and cultural rights and the right to development, and the working methods and activities of transnational corporations' (14 August 2002); C. F. Hillemanns, 'UN Norms on the Responsibility of Transnational Corporations and Other Business Enterprises with regard to Human Rights' (2003) 4 *German Law Journal* 1065, 1069; and Weissbrodt and Kruger (n. 277) 905.
[279] C. Garsten, 'The UN—Soft and Hard: Regulating Social Accountability for Global Business' (paper for the conference 'Organizing the World: Rules and Rule-Setting among Organizations', 13–15 October 2005, Stockholm) 10.
[280] Weissbrodt and Kruger (n. 277) 912. For the list of source materials of the Norms, UNCHR Sub-Commission, 'Proposed Draft Human Rights Code of Conduct for Companies with source materials' (25 May 2000) UN Doc. E/CN.4/Sub.2/2000/WC.2/WAT1/Add.1.

Unlike the UN draft Code of Conduct, the Norms not only addressed multinationals, but also 'other' business enterprises. They were expected to be applied by all businesses. Unlike the UN Global Compact, however, which applies to all business companies regardless of their size, the Norms paid special attention to multinationals, and other business enterprises which, although not transnational in character, have relationships with multinationals, and have activities that produce delocalized impacts, or which involve violations of the right to security.[281] It was expressly acknowledged, however, that multinationals raise the greatest international concerns and are the least susceptible to national regulations,[282] thus leading to a system of 'relative application' in the Norms. Accordingly, the degree of responsibility incumbent on a particular company was considered dependent on its sphere of activity and influence.

4.1.1 Legal significance

The Norms enjoyed a level of *expert legitimacy* based on the adoption by the Sub-Commission, but lacked *political* legitimization, which could have derived from the adoption by the Commission.[283] When the Norms were submitted to the UN Commission for consideration and adoption, however, the Commission merely 'took note' of them and 'expressed its appreciation' for the work of the Sub-Commission.[284] The Commission further underlined that the Norms had 'not been requested by the Commission and, as a draft proposal, had no legal standing, and that the Sub-Commission should not perform any monitoring function in this regard'.[285] The member States of the Commission therefore took great care to highlight that the Norms had been developed at the sole initiative of the Sub-Commission. They remain a document representing the opinion of experts but lacking the political endorsement of States.

Turning to their intention, the Norms[286] were drafted as a comprehensive 'restatement of international legal principles applicable to business',[287] covering: human rights, labour law, humanitarian law, environmental and consumer protection, and anti-corruption law. They purported to reflect, interpret,

---

[281] UN Norms, Section I 'Definitions', para. 21; Hillemanns (n. 278) 1069.
[282] Weissbrodt and Kruger (n. 277) 910.
[283] Walker (n. 264) 85. On the lack of international legal implications, D. Kinley and R. Chambers, 'The UN Human Rights Norms for Corporations: The Private Implications of Public International Law' (2006) 6 *Human Rights Law Review* 447, 482–88.
[284] UNCHR Decision 2004/116 (20 April 2004).
[285] Ibid. para. C. This is particularly significant when compared with UNCHR Sub-Commission Res. 2003/16 (13 August 2003), which explicitly sought to create an initial implementation procedure for the Norms through the Sub-Commission's consideration of information from NGOs, business, and individuals. Weissbrodt and Kruger (n. 277).
[286] T. Rathgeber, 'UN Norms on the Responsibilities of Transnational Corporations' (Friedrich-Ebert-Stiftung Occasional Geneva Papers n. 22, 2006), who claims that the Norms have a 'systemizing function' and are 'a benchmark for negotiations on a future standard'.
[287] Weissbrodt and Kruger (n. 277) 327.

and elaborate primarily upon legally binding treaties and non-binding guidelines adopted by the vast majority of States and international organizations. A commentator highlighted the 'hybrid nature' of the Norms, as they were considered at the same time recommendations and clarification of States' obligations and identification of the need to further develop direct corporate obligations.[288] In addition, 'imposing the full range of duties on [multinationals] directly under international law by definition reduces the discretionary space of individual governments within the scope of those duties ... [it] may further undermine domestic political incentives to make governments more responsive and responsible to their own citizenry ... [and] the rights of vulnerable groups are not well served' in the 'endless strategic games and legal wrangling on the part of governments and companies alike'.[289] It was further noted that the UN Norms included 'substantive provisions [going] beyond a conventional human rights-based agenda and belong[ing] more to a general corporate social responsibility code' such as fair business, marketing, and advertising practices.[290]

The Norms aimed to provide the first comprehensive set of international human rights standards directly applicable to multinationals,[291] thereby seeking to mark an important step in applying international law directly to business enterprises as non-State actors.[292] In addition, the Norms were envisaged as an evolving document that did not endeavour to freeze standards by drawing on past drafting efforts and present practices, but rather encourage further evolution.[293] Like the UN draft Code of Conduct, the value of the Norms rested on their universality, ie in their broad subject-matter, and in their general approach based on international principles to be applied wherever companies operate.[294] The intention of the drafters was thus for the Norms to constitute a 'non-voluntary initiative'[295] on corporate accountability, as evidenced by their 'self-consciously normative' tone,[296] and the clear and measurable drafting.[297] The drafters, therefore, intended to differentiate this initiative from the voluntary approach of the UN Global Compact,[298] arguing that the Norms' legal authority derived mainly from the sources of the principles,

---

[288] N. Rosemann, 'The UN Norms on Corporate Human Rights Responsibilities: An Innovating Instrument to Strengthen Business' Human Rights Performance' (Friedrich-Ebert-Stiftung Occasional Geneva Papers n. 20, 2005).
[289] J. Ruggie, 'Business and Human Rights: The Evolving International Agenda' (2007) 101 *American Journal of International Law* 819, 826.
[290] Muchlinski (n. 100) 660–61.
[291] Hillemanns (n. 287) 1065.
[292] Weissbrodt and Kruger (n. 286) 907; Kinley and Chambers (n. 292) 464.
[293] Weissbrodt and Kruger (n. 286) 912.
[294] Amnesty International, *The UN Human Rights Norms for Business: Towards Legal Accountability* (London: Amnesty International Publications, 2004) 13 and 15.
[295] Weissbrodt and Kruger (n. 286) 903; A. King, *The United Nations Human Rights Norms for Business and the UN Global Compact* (2004) <http://www.kingzollinger.ch/pdf/UN% 20Norms.pdf>.
[296] Amnesty International (n. 303) 6.
[297] King (n. 210) 2.
[298] Hillemanns (n. 287) 1080.

particularly those embodied in treaty law or crystallized in customary international law.[299] The text was accompanied by a Commentary, as a 'useful interpretation and elaboration tool'[300] in order to provide detailed clarification for each of the principles.[301]

As opposed to the draft Code of Conduct, the Norms devoted considerable room to suggested means of implementation, distinguishing between the roles of different actors. Business entities were first expected to adopt, disseminate, and implement their own internal rules of operation in compliance with the Norms. They were further encouraged to apply them in their relationships with subcontractors. Secondly, they were expected to report annually on the incorporation of the Norms into all their business dealings. In doing so, private companies would make their responsibility known to the general public, thus further legitimizing and institutionalizing it.[302] Thirdly, a provision suggested that business should provide 'adequate, effective, and prompt reparation' to all persons, entities, and communities that have been adversely affected by their failure to comply with the Norms.[303] This provision was later regarded by the UN Special Representative on Transnational Corporations as 'highly contentious and largely symbolic'.[304]

With regard to action at the UN level, the Norms envisaged periodic monitoring of their implementation, in a transparent and inclusive way, by an existing or new UN body, that could also receive complaints from stakeholders about specific companies' violations of the Norms. In other words, the Norms sought to extend classic international human rights monitoring and enforcement mechanisms to non-State entities.[305] However, the Commission's 2004 decision made it crystal clear that the Sub-Commission should not perform any monitoring function.[306] Furthermore, the Norms could have been used by the UN human rights treaty bodies for the creation of additional reporting requirements for States, as well as a benchmark for procurement requirements for the UN and its specialized agencies.[307] The Norms were thus noteworthy in suggesting that other actors, in addition to States and corporations, could contribute to their implementation, thereby supporting the UN and non-State actors in using them to assess business practice.[308] They omitted to

---

[299] Weissbrodt and Kruger (n. 286) 913.
[300] Ibid. 906.
[301] Ibid. 905.
[302] Ibid. 916.
[303] UN Norms, Section H, para. 18; Hillemanns (n. 287) 1078; Weissbrodt and Kruger (n. 286) 913.
[304] Special Representative's Interim Report (n. 56) para. 59. Nollkaemper (n. 14) 197, considers this part of the UN Norms 'confusing'.
[305] Kinley and Chambers (n. 292) 452.
[306] UNCHR Decision 2004/116 (20 April 2004) para. C.
[307] Weissbrodt and Kruger (n. 286) 917.
[308] Muchlinski (n. 100) 679.

refer to the possible role of the UN Global Compact in monitoring the Norms' implementation.[309]

With regard to States, it was recommended to them to consider the Norms in adopting general comments and legislation on corporate accountability,[310] although no established process for incorporating the Norms into national legal systems was suggested.[311]

4.1.2 Environmental content

The Norms[312] required 'accordance with national laws, regulations, administrative practices and policies of the countries in which multinationals operate' in relation to environmental protection, as well as 'accordance with relevant international agreements, principles, objectives, responsibilities and standards' on the environment, human rights, public health, safety, bioethics, and the precautionary principle'. The preamble highlighted the obligation for multinationals and other business enterprises to respect 'generally recognised responsibility and norms contained in UN treaties and other international instruments', such as the Convention on Biological Diversity (CBD)[313] the Rio Declaration, the Plan of Implementation of the World Summit on Sustainable Development,[314] and the Millennium Declaration.[315] In addition, multinationals' activities were expected to be conducted 'in a manner contributing to the wider goal of sustainable development'.[316]

The operational section on environmental protection of the Norms was framed in obligatory terms and required business to conduct its activities 'in a manner contributing to the wider goal of sustainable development'.[317] The preamble would arguably guide the interpretation of the reference to the relevant international instruments: at a minimum, companies would be expected to respect the standards and principles embodied, for example, in the Convention on Biodiversity and the Rio Declaration. It was noted how the insertion of the precautionary principle constituted an unprecedented step in human rights law.[318]

The Commentary to the Norms called for: respect of the right to a clean and healthy environment, respect of the concerns for intergenerational equity, and

---

[309] S. Deva, 'UN's Human Rights Norms for Transnational Corporations and Other Business Enterprises: An Imperfect Step in the Right Direction?' (2004) 10 *ILSA Journal of International and Comparative Law* 493, 515.
[310] Hillemanns (n. 278) 1070.
[311] Calder and Culverwell (n. 170) 41.
[312] Section G, para. 14.
[313] Convention on Biological Diversity (Rio de Janeiro, 5 June 1992, in force 29 December 1993). See Ch. 4.
[314] WSSD, Johannesburg Plan of Implementation (4 July 2002) UN Doc. A/CONF.199/20, Resolution 2 (WSSD Plan of Implementation).
[315] UNGA Res. 55/2 (8 September 2000).
[316] Ibid. Section G, para.14.
[317] UN Norms, Section G, para.14.
[318] Walker (n. 264) 83.

respect of 'internationally recognized *standards*' on air, and water pollution, land use, biodiversity, and hazardous waste.[319] Secondly, the Commentary expressed the expectation that companies would be responsible for the environmental and human health impacts of all their activities. Thirdly, business enterprises are to assess the environmental impacts of their activities on a periodic basis, in order to ensure that the burden of the negative environmental consequences does not fall on vulnerable racial, ethnic, and socio-economic groups. The reports of such assessments are required to be circulated in a timely and accessible manner to the UN Environment Programme, ILO, and other international bodies, to the national governments of the host and home countries, and to other affected groups. In addition, the reports should be accessible to the general public.[320] Fourthly, it expected companies to respect the prevention and precautionary principles, and to take appropriate steps to reduce the risk of accidents and damage to the environment, by adopting best management practices, and technologies.[321] Finally, the Commentary indicated the expectation for business to ensure effective means of collecting the remains of products or services for recycling, reuse or other environmentally responsible disposal.[322]

4.1.3 Legacy

The adoption of the Norms by the Sub-Commission elicited intense reactions. Among civil society, the International Chamber of Commerce immediately stressed the undesirability of the Norms,[323] arguing that they would undermine the spirit of the UN's new cooperation strategy with business underpinning the UN Global Compact.[324] On the other hand, Amnesty International, among other NGOs, welcomed the Norms, which, in their view, provided guidance and leadership for setting a stronger international framework for corporate accountability.[325] In particular, Amnesty International also advocated for the UN Global Compact to formally indicate that the Norms were an authoritative guide to its principles and for the OECD to indicate that the Norms were to be used as a reference for understanding the scope of the OECD Guidelines.[326] None of this followed, but support for 'hardening' the Norms had come from the Special Rapporteur on Toxics and Human Rights.[327]

---

[319] UN Norms, Section G, Commentary, (a) (emphasis added).
[320] Ibid. (b) and (c).
[321] Ibid. (e) and (g).
[322] Ibid. (f).
[323] ICC and IOE (n. 220).
[324] Utting (n. 124).
[325] Amnesty International (n. 294) 13 and 15.
[326] Ibid. 14 and 16.
[327] UNCHR, 'Report of the Special Rapporteur on the *Adverse Effects of the Illicit Movement and Dumping of Toxic and Dangerous Products and Wastes on the Enjoyment of Human Rights*' (2003) UN Doc. E/CN.4/2004/46/ Add. 2, para. 118.

The majority of States did not favour the formal adoption of the Norms, because of their shift away from voluntary approaches, the duplication of existing initiatives, and the misstatement of international law embodied in the recognition of legal obligations on business.[328] Such criticism, however, appears misplaced. It should be noted from the outset that the Norms asserted that the primary responsibility for human rights protection is that of national governments, and that companies are not requested to replace governments in such a task.[329] Whereas the Norms did not intend to create new obligations for governments in relation to human rights,[330] they aimed to provide for an allocation of responsibility between governments and business.[331]

Scholars were rather critical of the Norms' effort to 'enlist [multinations] as agents of international law implementation, even against States that have either refused to ratify certain international instruments or that have objected to the gloss advancement by international institutions'.[332] In addition, it was pointed out that they did not recognize the limits of national company law, whereby contracts incorporating the Norms 'would be voided as exceeding the authority of the [multinations] board'.[333] For this reason, Ruggie involved corporate lawyers in his consultations leading to the development of the Guiding Principles.[334] Other commentators have also criticized the Norms for implying that all human rights may be relevant to corporate conduct, including human rights that corporations cannot logically infringe and positive duties to promote and fulfil human rights which could only be envisaged in limited cases such as the privatization of certain State services.[335] Ruggie considered the Norms' *ex ante* identification of rights relevant for companies as an 'inherently fruitless exercise' compared with a determination on a case-by-case basis of relevant rights[336] and without taking into account the complexities of global value chains.[337] The Norms were further criticized for failing to delimit the relevance of human rights to persons under multinationals' factual control.[338]

---

[328] All submissions on the Norms are available at <http://www.ohchr.org/english/issues/globalization/business/reportbusiness.htm>; and UNCHR, 'Report of the United Nations High Commissioner on Human Rights on the Responsibility of Transnational Corporations and Related Business Enterprises with regard to Human Rights' (15 February 2005) UN Doc. E/CN.4/2005/91, para. 20 (hereinafter, 'High Commissioner's report'). See also Karavias (n. 4) 77–78.
[329] UN Norms, para. A, 'General Obligations'; Weissbrodt and Kruger (n. 277) 911. Kinley and Chambers (n. 283) 481.
[330] Weissbrodt and Kruger (n. 277) 912.
[331] Ibid. 915; and Amnesty International (n. 294) 7.
[332] L. Catá Backer, 'Multinational Corporations, Transnational Law: The United Nations' Norms on the Responsibilities of Transnational Corporations as a Harbinger of Corporate Social Responsibility in International Law' (2005–06) 37 *Columbia Human Rights Law Review* 287, 292.
[333] Ibid. 360.
[334] Ruggie and Sherman (n. 112).
[335] Karavias (n. 4) 165–66 and 168–70.
[336] Ruggie (n. 289) 825.
[337] Ibid. 823.
[338] Karavias (n. 4) 174.

Despite their political rejection, the Norms for a time provided a benchmark that clarified society's expectations and put pressure on businesses.[339] Certain NGOs engaged in road-testing the Norms.[340] But after the inter-governmental support for the UN Framework on Business and Human Rights, the UN Norms have been rapidly set aside. Nevertheless, they provide certain conceptual insights that remain relevant today and were confirmed, implicitly, by the UN Framework on Business and Human Rights, as will be highlighted in the following sections.

4.2 The UN Framework and Guiding Principles on Business and Human Rights

The end of the debate on the future of the Norms did not prevent the continuation of discussions on corporate accountability. In 2005, the UN Commission on Human Rights considered a recommendation from the UN High Commissioner for Human Rights to act expeditiously to define and clarify the human rights responsibilities of business, and to discuss further the possibility of establishing a UN statement of universal human rights standards applicable to business.[341] The decision was presented as a cross-regional initiative,[342] with the objectives of achieving progress on the issue of human rights and business within the UN Commission, and gathering a broad-based consensus. This showed how most States were unwilling to allow corporate accountability to slip off the UN agenda, although many were reluctant to politically endorse the UN Norms.[343] Although the 2005 decision did not mention explicitly the UN Norms, it mandated the Special Representative also to clarify the implications of the concepts of 'complicity' and 'sphere of influence', which were controversial concepts in the text of the Norms.[344]

---

[339] Hillemanns (n. 278) 1080; see also Kinley and Chambers (n. 283) 461–62.
[340] Walker (n. 264) 105, the 'road mapping' by the Business Leaders' Initiative on Human Rights, a 2003–09 programme for business leaders committed to integrating concern for human rights into their work, also on the basis of the Norms: High Commissioner's report, para. 22.
[341] UNCHR Res. 2005/69 (20 April 2005). States in favour of the decision (forty-nine in total) were: Argentina, Armenia, Bhutan, Brazil, Canada, China, Congo, Costa Rica, Cuba, Dominican Republic, Ecuador, Egypt, Eritrea, Ethiopia, Finland, France, Gabon, Germany, Guatemala, Guinea, Honduras, Hungary, India, Indonesia, Ireland, Italy, Japan, Kenya, Malaysia, Mauritania, Mexico, Nepal, Netherlands, Nigeria, Pakistan, Paraguay, Peru, Qatar, Republic of Korea, Romania, Russian Federation, Saudi Arabia, Sri Lanka, Sudan, Swaziland, Togo, Ukraine, United Kingdom, and Zimbabwe. The three States against were: Australia, South Africa, and the United States. Burkina Faso abstained.
[342] The initial proponents were: Russian Federation, India, Nigeria, UN, and Argentina. Other sponsors included: Austria, Belgium, Canada, Croatia, Chile, Cyprus, Czech Republic, Denmark, Estonia, Ethiopia, Finland, France, Germany, Greece, Guatemala, Hungary, Ireland, Italy, Latvia, Lithuania, Luxembourg, Malta, Mexico, Netherlands, Norway, Poland, Portugal, Romania, Slovakia, Slovenia, Spain, Switzerland, and Sweden (UNCHR, Draft Decision on Human Rights and Transnational Corporations and Other Business Enterprises' (2005) UN Doc. E/ CN.4/2005/L.87).
[343] This view was supposed by Ruggie (n. 289) 821.
[344] Kinley and Chambers (n. 283) 467–72.

In 2006, the first interim report by the Special Representative dealt a blow to the UN Norms, which were considered the origin of a stalemate on this issue.[345] Specifically, the Special Representative opposed the legal authority advanced by the Norms, largely disagreeing with the Norms' premise on the existence of binding obligations on corporations under existing State-based human rights instruments, the proposed allocation of human rights responsibilities between States and companies, and the concept of 'sphere of influence'.[346] Commentators, however, have considered it a false dichotomy to distinguish the UN Norms as an attempt to prevent and redress corporate human rights violations from the encouragement of corporations' positive contributions to development.[347] Some scholars have therefore identified the UN Norms' continued relevance lies in providing 'a template on which to base any future initiatives',[348] and 'a useful framework to guide corporate human rights impact assessments'.[349] The following chapter will demonstrate to what extent the UN Norms find resonance in current work undertaken by UN Special Rapporteurs.

UN Special Representative John Ruggie, who had already been involved in the development of the UN Global Compact,[350] focused on companies' responsibility vis-à-vis human rights in terms of prevailing societal expectation around 'no harm' and 'due diligence'.[351] Interestingly, the latter concept had already been put forward in the UN Norms, but was presented in the UN Framework in a more politically acceptable context that explicitly distanced itself from the conceptual approach of the UN Norms. While 'do no harm' represents a substantive standard, the second pillar is mainly focused on procedural dimensions (due diligence), as a 'benchmark against which other social actors judge the human rights impacts of companies'[352] —which is the concept of 'accountability' as defined in this study.[353] As opposed to singling out specific thematic areas where concerns had already been expressed by the international community, however, the UN Framework indicated that the scope of corporate responsibility to respect human rights is defined on a case-by-case basis by the actual and potential human rights impacts generated by business, in line with the International Bill of Rights.[354] As such, the UN

---

[345] Special Representative's Interim Report (n. 50) para. 55.
[346] Ibid. paras 59–69.
[347] D. Augenstein and D. Kinley, 'Beyond the 100 Acre Wood: In which International Human Rights Law Finds New Ways to Tame Global Corporate Power' (2015) 19 *International Journal of Human Rights* 828, 831.
[348] Miles (n. 99) 230.
[349] Muchlinski (n. 100) 658.
[350] Harvard Kennedy School, 'John Ruggie' < https://www.google.co.uk/webhp?sourceid=chrome-instant&ion=1&espv=2&ie=UTF-8#q=john%20ruggie> accessed 27 February 2016.
[351] UN Framework for Business and Human Rights, paras 25 and 58.
[352] Ibid.
[353] Ch. 2.
[354] Report of the Special Representative of the Secretary-General on the Issue of Human Rights and Transnational Corporations and Other Business Enterprises, 'Business and Human Rights: Towards Operationalizing the "Protect, Respect and Remedy" Framework' (2009) UN Doc. A/HRC/11/13, at 15.

Framework avoids mentioning specifically environmental and human rights concerns about business conduct in the natural resource sector. Rather, the proposed 'common conceptual and policy framework' is expected to be further elaborated and taken up by relevant social actors.[355]

As a result of this more appeasing and less specific approach,[356] the UN Framework elicited inter-governmental support in 2008,[357] when the Human Rights Council recognized the need to operationalize the Framework.[358] Although States remained divided as to the need for international legal instruments on corporate responsibility and accountability,[359] they agreed in 2008 to renew the Special Representative's mandate with a view to further elaborating the scope and content of corporate responsibility. In particular, they highlighted the need for providing concrete guidance to business and other stakeholders in this regard, exploring options, and making recommendations for better access to effective remedies, and conducting multi-stakeholder consultations on ways and means to operationalize the Framework.[360] The resulting Guiding Principles on Business and Human Rights were adopted by the Human Rights Council in 2011,[361] which, according to Ruggie, was 'the first time the UN adopted a set of standards on the subject of business and human rights ... that governments did not negotiate themselves', in the face of the stagnation of 'traditional forms of international legalization and negotiation through universal consensus-based institutions'.[362]

4.2.1 Conceptual and normative contributions

The main normative contribution of the UN Framework was to confirm that companies are expected to go beyond the level of respect for the international obligations of host States as enshrined in their national laws.[363] The Guiding Principles

---

[355] Ibid. para. 107.
[356] S. Deva, 'Treating Human Rights Lightly: A Critique of the Normative Foundations of the SRSG's Framework and Guiding Principles' in S. Deva and D. Bilchitz (eds), *Human Rights Obligations of Business: Beyond Corporate Responsibility to Respect?* (Cambridge: Cambridge University Press, 2013) 86.
[357] UN Framework for Business and Human Rights.
[358] Human Rights Council Res. 8/7 (18 June 2008) para. 2.
[359] Compare the statement by the EU stressing the lack of legal obligations embedded in the term 'corporate responsibility', and the statement by South Africa calling for a coherent, comprehensive legal instrument to cover the existing gap in international law concerning private companies (in HRC, Press release 'Human Rights Council adopts 13 Resolutions, appoints 13 new mandate holders and extends eight mandates' (18 June 2008).
[360] Human Rights Council Res. 8/7 (18 June 2008).
[361] Human Rights Council Res. 17/4 (6 July 2011).
[362] J. Ruggie, 'Global Governance and "New Governance Theory": Lessons from Business and Human Rights' (2014) 20 *Global Governance* 5, 5–6.
[363] See a discussion of the background to this point in Ruggie (n. 289) 834, indicating that this formulation was initially offered, as a response to his request for inputs, from leading international business associations: International Organisation of Employers, International Chamber of Commerce, and Business and Industry Advisory Committee to the OECD, Business and Human Rights: The Role of Business in Weak Governance Zones, para. 15 (Dec. 2006), available at <http:llwww.business-humanrights.org/Updates/Archive/SpecialRepPapers>.

further clarified that there is a 'global standard of expected conduct for all business enterprises wherever they operate', that exists independently of States' abilities and willingness to fulfil their human rights obligations. Such global standard operates 'over and above compliance with national laws and regulations protecting human rights', basically requiring business entities to take adequate measures to prevent, mitigate, and remediate adverse human rights impacts.[364] Political acceptability was ensured by placing these considerations as the second of three pillars: the duty of the State to protect against human rights abuses by third parties, including business; the corporate 'responsibility' to respect human rights; and the need for greater access to effective remedies.[365]

Under the second pillar, due diligence aims to: avoid causing or contributing to adverse human rights impacts through companies' own initiatives; and seek to prevent or mitigate adverse human rights impacts that are directly linked to their operations, products, or services by their business relationships, even if a business entity has not contributed to the impacts.[366] This is the same effort to look beyond multinationals through supply chains and other business relations. Under the third pillar—access to remedies—the Special Representative recognized not only the role of States but also the role of grievance mechanisms to be developed by private companies themselves,[367] as long as they are geared towards redressing imbalances in information and expertise, and enabling effective dialogue with affected stakeholders.[368]

The UN Guiding Principles further clarify that the human rights due diligence process entails: (i) assessing actual and potential impacts with 'meaningful consultations' with potentially affected groups and other stakeholders at regular intervals; (ii) integrating the assessment findings in internal decision-making, budget allocation, and oversight processes; (iii) acting upon those findings; (iv) tracking responses (including by drawing on feedback from affected stakeholders); and (v) communicating how impacts are addressed to right-holders in a manner that is sufficient for stakeholders to evaluate the adequacy of the company's response.[369] Companies are expected to prioritize the prevention and mitigation of most severe impacts or those that a delayed response would make irremediable.[370]

---

[364] UN Special Representative on Human Rights and Business Enterprises, 'Guiding Principles on Business and Human Rights to implement the UN Protect, Respect and Remedy Framework' (2011) UN Doc. A/HRC/17/31, para. 11 (the Guiding Principles were adopted by the Human Rights Council by Resolution 17/4 (2011); see also Office of the UN High Commissioner on Human Rights press release, 'New Guiding Principles on Business and human rights endorsed by the UN Human Rights Council', 16 June 2011.
[365] The UN Framework was 'welcomed' by consensus by the Human Rights Council and the need for its operationalization was recognized: HRC Res. 8/7 (2008) para. 2.
[366] UN Guiding Principles, Principle 13.
[367] Ibid. paras 93–95.
[368] Ibid. para. 95.
[369] Ibid. para. 17-21.
[370] Ibid. para. 24.

Following this overview, this section will discuss the key conceptual innovations of the Framework and its Guiding Principles, the importance of inter-governmental support, and the criticisms voiced in the human rights literature.

Writing in his academic capacity, Ruggie underscored that the main contribution of the Framework and its Guiding Principles was 'generating the beginnings of a new global regulator dynamic ... [which] consciously reflected on and was informed by the reasons for past failures'.[371] It has also been noted that the Framework takes a 'complex, interactive and nuanced' approach that goes beyond self-regulation due to the interaction of the three pillars, reflecting an 'inextricably intertwined and not mutually exclusive' relationship between self-regulation and (domestic) mandatory regulation.[372] In addition, the intuition of the UN Framework is that of focusing attention on expanding the scope of routine corporate assessments of enterprise-wide risk, that tend to 'aggregate, rather than atomize, risks across the corporate groups and functions', thereby disregarding the question of separate legal personality for the purposes of enterprise risk management.[373] Furthermore, the reference to due diligence also benefitted from the notion being 'well-known to companies'.[374] This has also had the effect of gathering interest and support from the legal profession and CSR consultants in their client advisory role.[375] Ruggie concluded that he had successfully provided the 'parameters and perimeters of business and human rights as an international policy domain' where international legal instruments provide 'carefully crafted precision tools' for the evolution of the international agenda.[376]

While undoubtedly a political success, the UN Framework and its Guiding Principles have raised a host of criticisms from international human rights scholars and practitioners. In particular, it has been lamented that the emphasis on 'impacts', rather than 'violations', of human rights in the UN Framework points to 'a shift from a legal to a managerial conception of the responsibility of business' that responds better to corporate lobbies' interest than to the long-standing demands of victims.[377] Other scholars have also pointed out that the UN Framework failed to show 'sensitivity towards the way in which emerging [international] norms crystallize over time into hard law'[378] by misrepresenting the 'dynamic relationship

---

[371] J. Ruggie, 'Hierarchy or Ecosystem? Regulating Human Rights Risks of Multinational Enterprises' in Rodríguez-Garavito (n. 2) 46, 61.
[372] Muchlinski (n. 102) 150.
[373] Ruggie (n. 362) 14.
[374] Deva (n. 62) 108.
[375] Ibid. 14–15, referring to the formal endorsement of the Guiding Principles by the American Bar Association http://www.abanow.org/2012/01/2012mml09 and ISO26000 chapter on human rights modelled after the Guiding Principles.
[376] Ruggie (n. 362) 7–8.
[377] Deva (n. 356) 78.
[378] D. Bilchitz, 'A Chasm between "is" and "ought"? A Critique of the Normative Foundations of the SRSG's Framework and the Guiding Principles' in Deva and Bilchitz (n. 356), 107; and Deva (n. 62) 117 and 125.

between international and domestic law'.³⁷⁹ Another reason for criticism was the exclusive focus on avoiding negative impacts on human rights, rather than also on the positive contribution of business to the realization of human rights.³⁸⁰ Another shortcoming of the UN Framework has been identified in the lack of guidance to companies on how to address 'human rights dilemmas of conflicting requirements' in which a decision to avoid the risk of violating one human rights may inevitably lead to causing the violation of other human rights of apparently equal severity or irremediable character.³⁸¹ The Framework has been further criticized for falling short of proposing how to overcome legal barriers to hold corporations legally accountable at the national level, such as the *forum non conveniens* doctrine and the corporate veil.³⁸² The Guiding Principles are considered 'under-inclusive' of international human rights obligations, whereas the draft UN Norms had reasonably incorporated existing international human rights obligations relevant to business activity'.³⁸³ It has been argued that corporations already have certain legally binding human rights obligations and these obligations are not limited to the 'respect' category, or to the International Bill of Human Rights.³⁸⁴

More fundamentally, it has been argued that the Framework and its Guiding Principles 'ignore the critical elements of a *human rights approach* to social change ... empowerment, participation and accountability', by considering a possible new human rights treaty as an extreme and antiquated regulatory option and by preventing rightholders themselves to 'shift dynamics in decision-making towards human rights protection in locally responsive ways'. ³⁸⁵ Ultimately, to gain political legitimacy, the UN Framework has 'steered clear of employing concepts cognate to international human rights law'³⁸⁶ in a concerted effort to avoid the impression that companies are assimilated to States in terms of human rights protection.

With regard to the first pillar, it has been argued that the Special Representative missed an opportunity to emphasize State extraterritorial obligations vis-à-vis the victims of corporate abuse, including States' obligations to take reasonable and appropriate measures to secure the victim's rights.³⁸⁷ So, for instance, the

---

³⁷⁹ Deva (n. 62) 112.
³⁸⁰ Bilchitz (n. 378) 107; and Deva (n. 62) 117 and 125.
³⁸¹ K. Buhmann, 'Damned if you Do, Damned if You Don't? The Lundbeck Case of Pntobarbital, the Guiding Principles on Business and Human Rights, and Competing Human Rights Responsibilities' (2012) 40 *Journal of Law, Medicine and Ethics* 206, with specific regard to UN Guiding Principle 24.
³⁸² Deva (n. 62) 113.
³⁸³ Rodríguez-Garavito (n. 2) 33–34.
³⁸⁴ S. Deva, 'Business and Human Rights: Time to Move Beyond the "Present"?' in Rodríguez-Garavito (n. 2) 62, 63–64.
³⁸⁵ T Melish, 'Putting "Human Rights" back into the UN Guiding Principles on Business and Human Rights: Shifting Frames and Embedding Participation Rights' in Rodríguez-Garavito (n. 2) 76, 76–78 and 83 (emphasis in the original).
³⁸⁶ Karavias (n. 4) 83 (and more generally at 81–83).
³⁸⁷ D. Augenstein and D. Kinley, 'When Human Rights 'Responsibilities' become 'Duties': The Extra-Territorial Obligations of States that Bind Corporations. Human Rights Obligations of

Guiding Principles do not account for the role of States in preventing companies from violating the right to water of individuals and communities in other countries by taking legal or political steps to influence companies.[388] This can also be considered a way to fulfil States' responsibilities to engage in international assistance and cooperation in the realization of relevant international human rights treaties,[389] including at the intersection of human rights and environmental protection.[390] Furthermore, the UN Guiding Principles have fallen short of critiquing the protection of multinationals in international investment law, ignoring the power imbalances not only in the negotiations of bilateral investment agreements but also in host States' technical and financial support to home States/developing countries on regulatory reform that supports multinationals.[391]

4.2.2 Legacy: the Working Group on Business and Human Rights

It is undeniable that the UN Framework has become the quintessential international reference with regard to corporate accountability: it has influenced the most recent review of the OECD Guidelines and other international standards,[392] as well as the practice of international monitoring and complaints bodies.[393] At the very least, the UN Framework and Guiding Principles have helped move from a polarized debate to a shared understanding that has allowed attention to be shifted to implementation.[394] From an institutional perspective, for instance, the inter-governmental endorsement of the UN Guiding Principles has led to a light-touch follow-up development. This section will thus reflect on the legacy of the Framework in the context of the 2011 decision by the Human Rights Council to

---

Business: Beyond the Corporate Responsibility to Respect?' in Deva and Bilchitz (n. 356) 271, 285–94; Rodríguez-Garavito (n. 2) 33.

[388] Augenstein and Kinley (n. 387) 289–90, based on CESCR, 'General Comment No. 15: The Right to Water' (20 January 2003) UN Doc. E/C.12/2002/11, para. 33.

[389] Augenstein and Kinley (n. 347) 841, with regard to: CESCR, para. 3, and CRC, para. 41; and UN Charter Art. 56.

[390] Augenstein and Kinley (n. 347) 842; in reference to, eg, CERD, 'Concluding Observations: Australia', CERD/C/AUS/CO/15-17 (13 September 2010) para. 13. Report of the Special Rapporteur on the Issue of Human Rights and the Environment John Knox: Framework Principles on Human Rights and the Environment (2017) UN Doc. A/HRC/34/49, para. 70.

[391] P. Simons, 'International Law's Invisible Hand and the Future of Corporate Accountability for Violations of Human Rights' (2012) 3 *Journal of Human Rights and the Environment* 5, 19. See Ch. 2.

[392] Update of the Guidelines on a Principle-based Approach to the Cooperation between the United Nations and the Business Sector, undertaken in order to ensure their full alignment with the Guiding Principles on Business and Human Rights: Implementing the United Nations 'Protect, Respect and Remedy' Framework (https://business.un.org/en/documents/5292). See Ch. 4.

[393] Morgera, 'From Corporate Social Responsibility to Accountability Mechanisms' (n. 1). See, eg, Council of Europe, Recommendation CM/Rec(2016)3.

[394] Bickford (n. 267) 153.

establish a Working Group on the issue of human rights and transnational corporations and other business enterprises.[395]

The mandate of the Working Group includes: to promote the effective and comprehensive dissemination and implementation of the Guiding Principles; and to identify, exchange, and promote good practices and lessons learned on their implementation. In addition, it is to make recommendations on the basis of information from governments, transnational corporations and other business enterprises, national human rights institutions, civil society, and rights-holders; and cooperate with other relevant special procedures of the Human Rights Council, relevant UN and other international bodies, the treaty bodies and regional human rights organizations.[396] Arguably, the Working Group was meant to exercise pressure from the bottom up on companies to continually improve the protection of human rights, but doubts were raised about its ability to do so in the absence of civil society as participants in norm creation, revision, monitoring, and enforcement.[397]

In most respects, the Working Group's mandate is facilitative and supportive, seeking to promote capacity-building around the Guiding Principles. It also foresees that the Working Group, upon request, will provide advice and recommendations regarding the development of domestic legislation and policies relating to business and human rights. The same facilitative approach can also be detected in the task of developing a regular dialogue with governments and all relevant actors, including relevant United Nations bodies, as well as transnational corporations and other business enterprises, national human rights institutions, representatives of indigenous peoples, civil society organizations, and other regional and subregional international organizations. But the Working Group has arguably taken a narrow interpretation of its mandate, focusing on disseminating the Guiding Principles, as opposed to addressing more complex questions such as the need for regulation and effective remedy.[398] So it will be discussed here in the context of its contributions to international standard setting.[399]

The main contribution of the Working Group has been tracking and supporting the development, including through the development of guidance for, national action plans on business and human rights.[400] National Action Plans, which were requested in 2011 by the EU and in 2014 by the Human Rights Council, have been considered a 'new governance' tool, in the EU law

---

[395] HRC resolutions 17/4 (2011) and 26/22 (2014).
[396] The mandate was renewed until 2020. HRC res. 35/7 (2017).
[397] Rodríguez-Garavito (n. 2) 23.
[398] C. Rodríguez-Garavito, 'Business and Human Rights: Beyond the End of the Beginning' in Rodríguez-Garavito (n. 2) 11, 20–21.
[399] Its role in monitoring and compliance is briefly discussed in Ch. 5, in comparison with the role of UN Special Rapporteurs.
[400] HRC res. 26/22 (2014).

sense,[401] to promote convergence in State practice on a topic on which there is no consensus for legislative development.[402] National Action Plans, however, have so far paid little attention to access to legal remedies for victims and they have not been fully transparent as a process.[403] Nevertheless, they appear to have the potential to provide 'raw data' for the evaluation of different options for a new treaty on corporate responsibility, as well as lay the ground for cross-government coordination and dialogue as part of an iterative process of learning and improvement.[404]

In addition, the Working Group's mandate refers specifically to the need to continue to make recommendations at the national, regional, and international levels for enhancing access to effective remedies,[405] including in conflict areas, which is overlooked in other international corporate environmental accountability standards. Notwithstanding the status of a UN special procedure of the Human Rights Council, which has been 'traditionally interpreted as privileging engagement with victims of human rights violations', the Working Group did not prioritize the concerns emerging from individual complaints or ensure participation of communities and local organizations.[406] The Working Group, however, has responded to critiques, including more civil society in its meetings (albeit without privileging organizations that represent victims).[407] It has also taken a more critical approach to National Action Plans, requiring that their baseline assessments not only list relevant existing policies and laws, but also assess their effectiveness on all the three pillars, on the basis of more detailed metrics to measure business impact on human rights.[408]

Overall, it is yet unclear if the Working Group will be able to live up to the expectations of civil society and scholars that it will 'incorporate the highest human rights standards available in its work', and make up for the lack of consultations on the Guiding Principles with people living in poverty and in rural areas.[409] Concerns have also been raised about the need to ensure the

---

[401] Eg G. de Burca and J. Scott, *Law and New Governance in the EU and the US* (Portland: Hart Publishing, 2006).

[402] European Commission, 'A Renewed EU Strategy 2011–14 for Corporate Social Responsibility' COM(2011)681 final (25 October 2011) and HRC Res. 26/22 (2015). See discussion in C. Methven O'Brien, A. Mehra, S. Blackwell, and C. Poulsen-Hansen, 'National Action Plans: Current Status and Future Prospects for a New Business and Human Rights Governance Tool' (2015) 1 *Business and Human Rights Journal* 117, 117–18.

[403] Methven O'Brien et al (ibid), 122 and 124.

[404] Ibid. 124 –26. See also H. Cantú Rivera, 'National Action Plans on Business and Human Rights: Progress or Mirage?' (2019) 4 *Business and Human Rights Journal* 201.

[405] Report of the Working Group on the issue of human rights and transnational corporations and other business enterprises (2017) UN Doc. A/72/162.

[406] Rodríguez-Garavito (n. 398) 28.

[407] Ibid. 30.

[408] Rodríguez-Garavito (n. 398) 42.

[409] Meyersfeld (n. 268) 176–80.

impartiality and independence of the Working Group's members,[410] particularly in light of the criticism that governments and business may represent the same interests.[411]

4.2.3 Environmental relevance?

As opposed to the Norms, the UN Framework on Business and Human Rights and its Guiding Principles do not identify specific environmental standards that are relevant for the private sector, leaving that to a case-by-case identification. They thus did not address the challenge for companies to identify relevant international standards.[412] This appears even more surprising as all previous UN initiatives had an environmental component that was largely convergent. Even at times when the focus shifted from regulating multinationals to facilitating foreign direct investment, broad consensus emerged that it is appropriate and desirable to develop standards to guide or direct multinationals' conduct when environmental risks were at stake.[413]

Instead, the Special Representative stressed the importance for the Framework of international policy coherence,[414] particularly with specific regard to 'prevailing social norms ... that have acquired near-universal recognition by all stakeholders'.[415] He made no attempt, however, to seek or acknowledge synergies between the UN Framework and relevant widely ratified international environmental agreements in the specific case of natural resource exploitation[416]—an area in which serious corporate abuses of human rights have been documented. Nonetheless, the Special Representative developed the procedural aspect of human rights due diligence process on concepts and approaches[417] that have been developed and experimented in the environmental sphere, notably: (i) impact

---

[410] J. Kweitel, 'Regulatory Environment on Business and Human Rights: Paths at the International Level and Ideas about the Roles of Civil Society Groups' in Rodríguez-Garavito (n. 2) 160, 165–66.
[411] Meyersfeld (n. 268) 176–80.
[412] Deva (n. 62) 11.
[413] R. J. Fowler, 'International Environmental Standards for Transnational Corporations' (1995) 25 *Environmental Law Review* 1, 3.
[414] Report of the Special Representative of the Secretary-General on the issue of human rights and transnational corporations and other business enterprises, Business and Human Rights: Further steps toward the operationalisation of the 'protect, respect and remedy' framework, (2010) UN Doc. A/HRC/14/27, para. 52.
[415] Ibid. 13.
[416] The UN Representative indicated that the scope of corporate responsibility to respect human rights is defined by the actual and potential human rights impacts generated by business, which can be identified on the basis of an authoritative list of internationally recognized rights including the 'International Bill of Rights', Conventions of the International Labour Organisation (ILO) and, depending on circumstances, also human rights instruments concerning specifically indigenous peoples and other vulnerable groups: Report of the Special Representative of the Secretary-General on the issue of human rights and transnational corporations and other business enterprises, 'Business and human rights: Towards operationalising the "Protect, Respect and Remedy" Framework' (2009) UN Doc. A/HRC/11/13, 15.
[417] Ibid. 14.

assessment; (ii) stakeholder involvement in decision-making; and (iii) life-cycle management.[418] Equally, the UN Guiding Principles continue the self-referential trend of the UN Framework, with no specific reference to the relevance of multilateral environmental agreements. No reference was made to specific rights of indigenous peoples either, which provide one of the most vivid connections between human rights to environmental protection discourses.[419]

Nevertheless, the Working Group on Business and Human Rights has occasionally indicated the 'need to better delineate roles, responsibilities and appropriate accountability systems' for both States and business enterprises with regard to specific environmental issues. This has been the case of water and sanitation, agricultural investment, climate justice,[420] environmental crimes, and cross-border cooperation for access to remedies, [421] and the need to better integrate human rights in environmental impact assessments.[422] In its guidance for National Action Plans on business and human rights, the Working Group made a passing reference to 'protecting and respecting environmental and natural resource rights, including land acquisition and tenure and property rights'.[423] The Working Group also addressed to some extent matters of corporate environmental accountability in its thematic report on indigenous rights.[424] Furthermore, some country reports made reference to environmental issues,[425] and occasionally the Working Group has recommended directly to companies to ensure greater focus on safety and

---

[418] E. Morgera, Expert Report Corporate Responsibility to Respect Human Rights in the Environmental Sphere, European Commission-funded project 'Study of The Legal Framework on Human Rights and the Environment Applicable to European Enterprises Operating outside the European Union', May 2010, at 12: http://www.law.ed.ac.uk/euenterpriseslf/documents/files/CSREnvironment.pdf.

[419] E Morgera, 'Environmental Accountability of Multinational Corporations: Benefit-sharing as a Bridge between Human Rights and the Environment' in B. Boer (ed.), *Human Rights and the Environment* (Oxford: Oxford University Press, 2015) 37.

[420] Report of the Working Group on the issue of human rights and transnational corporations and other business enterprises (2015) UN Doc. A/HRC/29/28, para. 89.

[421] Best practices and how to improve on the effectiveness of cross-border cooperation between States with respect to law enforcement on the issue of business and human rights: Study of the Working Group on the issue of human rights and transnational corporations and other business enterprises—Note by the Secretariat (2017) UN Doc. A/HRC/35/33, paras 42–70. See Ch. 2.

[422] Report of the Working Group on the issue of human rights and transnational corporations and other business enterprises: 'Addressing the human rights impacts of agro-industrial operations on indigenous and local communities: State duties and responsibilities of business enterprises' (2016) UN Doc. A/71/291, para. 86.

[423] Report of the Working Group on the issue of human rights and transnational corporations and other business enterprises: National Action Plans on Business and Human Rights (2014) UN Doc. A/69/263, para. 81. Note that the UN Global Compact also published a guidance document: 'Guidance for Global Compact Local Networks on National Action Plans on Business and Human Rights' (2015).

[424] Report of the Working Group on the issue of human rights and transnational corporations and other business enterprises (2016) UN Doc. A/71/291; see also Ch. 4.

[425] Eg Report of the Working Group on the issue of human rights and transnational corporations and other business enterprises on its visit to the Republic of Korea—Note by the Secretariat (2017) UN Doc. A/HRC/35/32/Add.1, paras 20–21, 44–62; Report of the Working Group on the issue of human rights and transnational corporations and other business enterprises on the Asia Forum on Business and Human Rights (2016) UN Doc. A/HRC/32/45/Add.2, paras 47, 60–63.

contingency plans, particularly companies operating mines and infrastructure development projects, with regard to 'international guidance documents such as the United Nations Environment Programme Guidance for the Mining Industry in Raising Awareness and Preparedness for Emergencies at Local Level.'[426]

The mismatch between the work of the UN Special Representative on Business and Human Rights and international initiatives contributing to defining corporate environmental accountability standards was picked up by former UN Rapporteur on indigenous peoples' rights, James Anaya,[427] who fleshed out due diligence standards on the basis of the UN Declaration on the Rights of Indigenous Peoples (UNDRIP)[428] and the Convention on Biological Diversity.[429] On that basis, the UN Framework on Business and Human Rights and its Guiding Principles were referred to in the 2018 UN Framework Principles on Human Rights and the Environment.[430] Other UN Special Rapporteurs have followed suit, contributing to a more sectoral development of due diligence at the intersection of human rights and the environment.[431] This is the case of UN Special Rapporteur on Toxics[432] and the UN Special Rapporteur on the Right to Food.[433] These considerations help further translate all human rights recognized in international law into standards for companies, which could feed into the ongoing negotiations of a legally binding instrument on business and human rights, as discussed below. They have also reported on sector-specific developments on corporate responsibility discussed in the next chapter.

The UN Framework and Guiding Principles on Business and Human Rights also had an impact on pre-existing international initiatives on corporate environmental accountability, such as the OECD Guidelines and Performance Standards of the International Finance Corporation (IFC), which had been developed in parallel with the UN initiatives discussed so far.

---

[426] Report of the Working Group on the issue of human rights and transnational corporations and other business enterprises on its mission to Brazil (2016) UN Doc. A/HRC/32/45/Add.1, paras 21–33 and 71(g). See also recommendation to companies to 'take a more active role in addressing concerns about social and environmental impacts of their operations' in the Working Group's statement at the end of visit to Peru by the United Nations Working Group on Business and Human Rights (July 2017): http://www.ohchr.org/EN/NewsEvents/Pages/DisplayNews.aspx?NewsID=21888&LangID=E.
[427] Anaya started addressing corporate environmental accountability issues in 2009 (A/HRC/12/34, Section E); and expanded upon this preliminary guidance by devoting the substantive section of his 2010 annual report to corporate accountability (UN Doc. A/HRC/15/37 (2010), Section III).
[428] UN Declaration on the Rights of Indigenous Peoples, UNGA Res. 61/295 (13 September 2007).
[429] Morgera (n. 419) 37–68. Discussed in Ch. 4, Section 3.1.
[430] UN Doc. A/HRC/37/58 (2018), para. 22.
[431] Summary Report of Expert Roundtable on Elements of a Possible Binding International Instrument on Business and Human Rights: University of Notre Dame London Gateway, 16 May 2017 (11 July 2017) 6.
[432] Report of the Special Rapporteur on the implications for human rights of the environmentally sound management and disposal of hazardous substances and wastes, Başkut Tuncak (2015) UN Doc. A/HRC/30/40, paras 80–101. Discussed in Ch. 4.
[433] Report of the Special Rapporteur on the right to food, O. De Schutter, Final report: The transformative potential of the right to food (2014) UN Doc. A/HRC/25/57. Discussed in Ch. 4.

5 The OECD Guidelines for Multinational Enterprises

At the height of the discussion on a draft Code of Conduct on Transnational Corporations within the UN,[434] arguably in an effort to create a stalemate in that process,[435] the OECD first approved its Guidelines for Multinational Enterprises[436] in 1976. This section will discuss the key differences characterizing the OECD as an international forum on corporate accountability, the different approach taken at the OECD compared to the draft UN Code of Conduct, and the continued relevance of the OECD Guidelines after the endorsement of the UN Framework on Business and Human Rights.

The OECD was created in 1961 with the understanding that 'the economically more advanced nations should co-operate in assisting to the best of their ability the countries in process of economic development' and in the recognition 'that the further expansion of world trade is one of the most important factors favouring the economic development of countries and the improvement of international economic relations'.[437] It aims to achieve the highest sustainable economic growth and employment and a rising standard of living in member countries, while maintaining financial stability, and thus contributing to the development of the world economy, through the expansion of world trade on a multilateral, non-discriminatory basis in accordance with international obligations.[438] It groups major capital-exporting States.

The early success of its activities on corporate accountability can be explained in light of two factors. The first was the significantly limited membership of like-minded countries, as opposed to the United Nations.[439] Some viewed the birth of the OECD Guidelines as the developed countries' strategy to create their own framework for multinationals' activities, in order to reinforce their negotiating position at the multilateral level, in particular in the negotiations for the UN Code.[440] Others went further to identify the desire on the part of OECD countries

---

[434] J. Huner, 'The Multilateral Agreement on Investment and the Review of the OECD Guidelines for Multinational Enterprises' in Kamminga and Zia-Zarifi (n. 119) 197, 197–98.

[435] J. Salzman 'Decentralized Administrative Law in the Organization for Economic Cooperation and Development (2005) 68 *Law and Contemporary Problems* 189, 276.

[436] OECD, 'Guidelines for Multinational Corporations' (31 October 2001) OECD Doc. DAFFE/IME/WPG(2000)15/FINAL. For an initial appraisal, see A. Levi, 'Il Codice OCSE Sulle Imprese Multinazionali' (1982) *Giurisprudenza Commerciale* 326.

[437] Convention on the Organisation for Economic Co-operation and Development (Paris, 14 December 1960, in force 30 September 1961), preamble.

[438] Ibid. Art. 1.

[439] Originally there were twenty member States and there are currently thirty-five: Australia, Austria, Belgium, Canada, Chile, the Czech Republic, Denmark, Estonia, Finland, France, Germany, Greece, Hungary, Iceland, Ireland, Israel, Italy, Japan, Korea, Latvia, Luxembourg, Mexico, the Netherlands, New Zealand, Norway, Poland, Portugal, the Slovak Republic, Slovenia, Spain, Sweden, Switzerland, Turkey, the United Kingdom, and the United States <http://www.oecd.org/document/1/0,2340,en_2649_201185_1889402_1_1_1_1,00.html>.

[440] Sauvant and Aranda (n. 87) 99.

to pre-empt stricter regulation under the UN Code.[441] Another significant difference with the draft UN Code was that the OECD opted for the traditional view that governments were more powerful than multinationals, thus assuming a pre-existing balance. Conversely, developing countries in the UN were voicing their concerns about the growing power of multinationals, which was considered in some instances to be overwhelming the host countries' capacity for control.[442] The second was the extensive involvement of business and labour organizations, through the Advisory Committees of Business and of Labour Federations.[443] Their participatory drafting process arguably contributed to 'prevent misunderstandings and build an atmosphere of confidence and predictability between business, labour and governments' within the OECD.[444]

5.1 Conceptual approach and legal significance

The OECD Guidelines were adopted as part of the Declaration on International Investment and Multinational Enterprises,[445] which was designed to improve the international investment climate and to strengthen the basis for mutual confidence between enterprises and the society in which they operate. As opposed to the draft UN Code which focused both on the regulation of multinationals' activities and their protection from the unlawful conduct of capital-importing countries, the OECD Guidelines were drafted solely as governmental recommendations formulated to directly address multinationals operating in adhering countries.

Until States' support for the UN Framework on Business and Human Rights, the OECD Guidelines were the only inter-governmentally endorsed corporate accountability instrument featuring a comprehensive subject-matter and supported by an explicit commitment for States to ensure acceptable corporate conduct.[446] Forty-eight major home States, including non-OECD members, have adhered to the Guidelines.[447] The more recent history of the OECD Guidelines is characterized by normative alignment with the UN Framework, but they have remained

---

[441] The International Council on Human Rights Policy (n. 15) 101.
[442] A. A. Fatouros, 'The OECD Guidelines in a Globalizing World' (17 February 1999) OECD Doc. DAFFE/IME/RD(99)3, 7.
[443] Huner (n. 434) 201.
[444] J. Karl, 'The OECD Guidelines for Multinational Enterprises' in M. K. Addo (ed.), *Human Rights Standards and the Responsibility of Transnational Corporations* (The Hague: Kluwer Law International, 1999) 259, 89–90.
[445] OECD, 'The OECD Declaration and Decisions on International Investment and Multinational Enterprises: Basic Texts' (9 November 2000) OECD Doc. DAFFE/IME (2000) 20 (most recent version).
[446] The OECD Guidelines were negotiated and approved by national delegations, as highlighted in UNCHR Decision 2004/116; Office of the High Commissioner for Human Rights and Global Compact Office, 'Consultation on Business and Human Rights—Summary of Discussions' (22 October 2004).
[447] See OECD, 'National Contact Points' < http://www.oecd.org/investment/mne/ncps.htm> accessed 1 August 2018.

influential in their own right as they provide a more detailed international reference. The Guidelines further translated the concept of business due diligence of the UN Framework as the process through which enterprises can identify, prevent, mitigate, and account for how they address their actual and potential adverse impacts as an integral part of business decision-making and risk management systems. The process aims to avoid causing or contributing to adverse impacts on matters covered by the Guidelines, through multinationals' own activities, and address such impacts when they occur. In other words, due diligence can be included within broader enterprise risk management systems, provided that it goes beyond simply identifying and managing material risks to the enterprise itself, to include the risks of adverse impacts related to matters covered by the Guidelines. Potential impacts are to be addressed through prevention or mitigation, while actual impacts are to be addressed through remediation.[448]

The OECD Guidelines have been praised by some scholars for contributing to providing 'a common frame of reference [in] assisting multinationals to ensure that their operations are compatible with expectations by host countries'[449] and for legitimizing the social sanctions performed by non-State actors against irresponsible companies, such as boycotts, and general advocacy campaigns.[450] The Guidelines can also be seen as a tool for interpreting the meaning, and guiding the application, of other international instruments and domestic laws.[451] Other commentators, however, have expressed concern over the vagueness of the Guidelines, which fail to offer any immediate basis for a possible agreement to develop international obligations on the subject.[452]

With regard to their legal strength, it is significant to connect the evolution of the Guidelines with the collapse of the negotiations within the OECD of a binding Multilateral Agreement on Investment (MAI).[453] The MAI had been proposed as a comprehensive legally binding agreement covering all aspects of investment protection, together with an independent dispute settlement mechanism. As in the case of the draft UN Code of Conduct, States could not agree on the international standards for the protection of foreign direct investment,[454] which contributed to

---

[448] Para. 14. More practical information on business due diligence can also be found in the 2018 OECD Due Diligence Guidance on Responsible Business Conduct: see comments by C. Shavin, 'Unlocking the Potential of the New OECD Due Diligence Guidance on Responsible Business Conduct' (2019) 4 *Business and Human Rights Journal* 139.

[449] Karl (n. 455) 90.

[450] N. Tru, 'Les codes de conduite: un bilan' (1992) 96 *Revue Générale de Droit International Public* 45, 54.

[451] The International Council for Human Rights Policy (n. 15) 68.

[452] Francioni (n. 128) 157.

[453] P. van der Gaag, 'OECD Guidelines for Multinational Enterprises: Corporate Accountability in a Liberalised Economy?' (November 2004) <http://www.oecdwatch.org/docs/ paper%20NC%20IUCN.pdf>.

[454] M. Sornarajah, *The International Law on Foreign Investment* (Cambridge: Cambridge University Press, 2004) 293.

the collapse of negotiations in late 1998.[455] As a result, instead of being included in the MAI, the Guidelines were significantly revised in 2000.[456] They expressly stated their applicability to the operations of multinationals and all their entities,[457] in adhering countries and abroad.[458] They also stressed that all business entities, not just multinationals, were subject to the same expectations of good corporate conduct.[459]

A posteriori, it has been argued that the OECD Guidelines represented a 'kind of regulatory gesture', which avoided legal sanctions against multinationals [460] but 'reflected firm expectations'.[461] The Guidelines may thus have arguably achieved 'hard-law effects by developing behavioral norms from *within* the corporate culture'.[462] Interestingly, in their most recent version, the Guidelines acknowledge that on some matters they reflect binding international law and that multinationals should honour the Guidelines even if this does not lead to a violation of national law,[463] anticipating the clarifications of the UN Framework on Business and Human Rights. In addition, the Guidelines underscore that 'in countries where domestic laws and regulations conflict with the principles and standards of the Guidelines, enterprises should seek ways to honour such principles and standards to the fullest extent which does not place them in violation of domestic law'.[464]

Their authoritativeness is also demonstrated by the successive development of sectoral guidance in the mining, textile, agriculture sectors,[465] further translating treaties and international guidance into substantive standards of corporate environmental accountability and responsibility.[466]

---

[455] Huner (n. 434) 203. J. Salzman, 'The Organization for Economic Cooperation and Development's Role in International Law' (2011) 43 *The George Washington International Law Review* 255, 266–72, argued that the OECD Secretariat focused on a straightforward technical harmonization exercise, and lacked of experience in managing highly politically contentious negotiations.
[456] S. Tully, 'The 2000 Review of the OECD Guidelines for Multinational Enterprises' (2001) 50 *International and Comparative Law Quarterly* 394.
[457] OECD Guidelines, ch. II, paras 10, 11; OECD, 'Roundtable on Corporate Responsibility: Encouraging the Positive Contribution of Business to Environment through the OECD Guidelines for Multinational Enterprises' (Background Report, June 2004) 7.
[458] OECD Guidelines, ch. I, para. 2.
[459] Ibid.
[460] G. Schuler, 'Effective Governance through Decentralized Soft Implementation: The OECD Guidelines for Multinational Enterprises' (2008) 9 *German Law Journal* 1753, 1757.
[461] R. Geiger, 'Coherence in Shaping the Rules for International Business: Actors, Instruments and Implementation' (2011) 43 *The George Washington International Law Review* 295, 303.
[462] R. Valsan and D. Holloway, 'MNE Guidelines' in E. Morgera, G. Marín Durán, and A. Boyle (eds), *Study on the Standard-setting Role and Legal Acquis of the OECD* (2013, unpublished, on file with author).
[463] Preface, para. 1. See Deva (n. 62) 85.
[464] OECD Guidelines, I.2.
[465] OECD Due Diligence Guidance for Responsible Supply Chains of Minerals from Conflict-Affected and High-Risk Areas (Paris: OECD, 2013); and OECD-FAO Guidance on Responsible Agricultural Supply Chains (Paris: OECD, 2015). Discussed in Ch. 4.
[466] As discussed in Ch. 4-5.

Although the OECD Guidelines themselves are a voluntary initiative, they include an 'implementation procedure'[467] that is based on one formal obligation for adhering countries to set up national contact points (NCPs).[468] In effect, the implementation procedure is considered the 'most visible sign of adhering governments' commitment to the Guidelines'.[469] As it is based on a legally binding act of the OECD (a Council Decision), it has been argued that this obligation may give rise to international responsibility for the State failing to create an NCP or to further the effectiveness of the Guidelines and international cooperation, although it is difficult to imagine which international or national body would make such an attribution in a particular case.[470] In addition, they have also made an impact at the national level: certain countries linked access to external trade assistance and export credit to the absence of findings against companies by the OECD National Contact Points.[471]

5.2 Environmental content

The Guidelines have been through various phases of evolution in their environmental content. Following the Union Carbide industrial accident in Bhopal,[472] notwithstanding opposition by business representatives,[473] a chapter on environmental protection was added to the Guidelines in 1991.[474] Another significant historical turning point for the Guidelines was their 2000 review,[475] which took place just after the collapse of the negotiations of the Multilateral Agreement on Investment, as international NGOs voiced concerns about the lack of provisions on labour and the environment in the proposed MAI.[476] The Guidelines' environmental provision was significantly strengthened, in order to reflect the Rio

---

[467] OECD, 'Implementation of the OECD Guidelines for Multinational Enterprises: Implementation Procedures' (2000) <http://www.oecd.org/document/43/0,2340,en_2649_34889_2074731_1_1_1_1,00.html>.
[468] Huner (n. 434) 200.
[469] OECD Secretary-General, May 2004.
[470] S. Robinson, 'International Obligations State Responsibility and Judicial Review under the OECD Guidelines for Multinational Enterprises Regime' (2014) 30 *Utrecht Journal of International and European Law* 68.
[471] R. Cirlig, 'Business and Human Rights: From Soft Law to Hard Law?' (2016) 6 *Juridical Tribune* 228, 243.
[472] V. Nanda and B. Bailey, 'Challenges for International Environmental Law—Seveso, Bhopal, Chernobyl, the Rhine and Beyond' (1988) 21 *Law and Technology* 1.
[473] Huner (n. 434) 201.
[474] However, in 1985 the OECD Committee on International Investment and Multilateral Enterprises (CIME) had issued a clarification on environmental matters ('Clarification to the Reference to Environmental Policies in the Guidelines for Multinational Enterprises, reprinted in OECD' in OECD, *OECD and the Environment* (Paris: OECD, 1986) 191).
[475] J. Murray, 'A New Phase in the Regulation of Multinational Enterprises: The Role of the OECD' (2001) 30 *International Law Journal* 255.
[476] Crane (n. 182) 429.

Declaration on Environment and Development[477] and Agenda 21[478] and to respond to the calls for the improvement of internal environmental management systems and for greater disclosure of environmental information. The objective of sustainable development, and general language on human rights, was also introduced in the Guidelines at this time,[479] along with a requirement for public disclosure of information on companies' social, ethical, and environmental policies for multinationals as a whole.[480]

The 2000 Review and the discussions on corporate accountability at the 2002 World Summit on Sustainable Development (WSSD) revived environmental NGOs' interest in the OECD Guidelines, particularly after the failure of the NGO proposal at WSSD to initiate negotiations on an international legally binding instrument on corporate liability.[481] The text of the OECD Guidelines contains a specific and quite detailed chapter on the environment, but also includes several other sections directly relevant to the environmentally sound conduct of business. The Preface lists among the objectives: 'to enhance the contribution to sustainable development made by multinational enterprises',[482] and stresses that the common aim of adhering governments is to encourage multinationals' positive contributions to economic, environmental, and social progress while minimizing the difficulties to which their various operations may give rise.[483] Under the General Principles, enterprises should fully take into account established policies in the countries in which they operate, consider the views of other stakeholders, and contribute to economic, social, and environmental progress with a view to achieving sustainable development.[484] Multinationals should also refrain from seeking or accepting exemptions not contemplated in the statutory or regulatory framework related to environmental incentives or other issues.[485]

The Environment Chapter of the Guidelines refers to general standards of environmental protection and to a list of specific tools for corporate environmental accountability, with a view to broadly reflecting the principles and objectives contained in the Rio Declaration and Agenda 21, while also taking into account the Aarhus Convention on Access to Information, Public Participation in Decision-making and Access to Justice in Environmental Matters.[486] Besides stating the

---

[477] 'Rio Declaration on Environment and Development' (13 June 1992) UN Doc. A/CONF.151/6/Rev.1. See Ch. 1.
[478] 'Agenda 21' (13 June 1992) UN Doc. A/CONF.151/6/Rev.1; Huner (n. 434) 204. See Ch. 1.
[479] OECD Guidelines, para. II.2. See comments by Deva (n. 62) 80–81.
[480] OECD Guidelines, III.5.a.
[481] Friends of the Earth, 'Towards Binding Corporate Accountability' (Position paper for the WSSD, January 2002). See Ch. 1, Section 3.1.
[482] OECD Guidelines, Preface, paras 1, 6.
[483] Ibid. para. 10.
[484] Ibid. II.A.1.
[485] Ibid. II.A.5.
[486] Ibid. para. 60; Convention on Access to Information, Public Participation in Decision-Making and Access to Justice in Environmental Matters (Aarhus Convention) (Aarhus, 25 June 1998, in force 30 October 2001).

obvious fact that multinationals must respect the national laws of the host country, the chapeau significantly, albeit in soft language, recommends a general consideration of international instruments and objectives.[487] In addition, the paragraph calls for 'due account' of environmental protection, public health and safety, and sustainable development objectives.[488] Most of the chapeau, therefore, refers to supranational standards for the protection of the environment. With a pragmatic approach, the following, more detailed provisions list a series of tools for corporate environmental accountability: environmental management systems, communication and stakeholder involvement, life-cycle assessment and environmental impact assessments, education and training of employees, and contribution to public policies.[489] Certain elements also serve to delineate substantive dimensions, such as risk prevention and mitigation, and continuous improvement of corporate environmental performance. The most recent version also contributes to corporate social responsibility with substantive standards on climate change, biodiversity, and resource efficiency.[490]

The most recent revision of the OECD Guidelines, in 2011, aimed, inter alia, to reflect the key normative innovations of the UN Framework on Business and Human Rights in terms of risk-based due diligence.[491] While the Guidelines themselves make no explicit link between the new provisions on human rights and their chapter on the environment, these additions also have relevance for business due diligence to respect the interface of human rights and the environment, as highlighted by former UN Special Rapporteur John Knox.[492]

The OECD Guidelines also elaborated on the extent to which their addressees extend beyond multinational corporations. They expressed the expectation that companies would also seek to prevent or mitigate an adverse impact where they had not contributed to that impact, if the impact is nevertheless directly linked to their operations, products, or services by a business relationship. Consequently, multinationals are to encourage, where practicable, business partners, including suppliers and sub-contractors, to apply principles of responsible business conduct compatible with the Guidelines.[493] Multinationals are also expected to seek ways to prevent or mitigate adverse human rights impacts that are directly linked to their business operations, products, or services by a business relationship, even if they do not contribute to those impacts.[494]

The new human rights chapter of the 2011 OECD Guidelines, therefore, signals that 'corporate respect for human rights is no longer exclusively anchored in host

---

[487] OECD Guidelines, Ch. VI.
[488] Ibid.
[489] Ibid. Ch. V, paras 1–8.
[490] Discussed in Ch. 4.
[491] OECD Guidelines, II.10-13. See Deva (n. 62) 86.
[492] See Ch. 2.
[493] OECD Guidelines, II.A.10-14.
[494] Ibid. IV.1-3 and 6.

States' international obligations, but in international recognized human rights, irrespective of the country or specific context of [multinationals'] operations'.[495] It spells out that multinationals' respect for internationally recognized human rights of those affected by their activities[496] means they should avoid infringing on the human rights of others and should address adverse human rights impacts with which they are involved. It also entails engaging with relevant stakeholders to provide meaningful opportunities for their views to be taken into account in relation to planning and decision making for projects or other activities that may significantly impact local communities.[497] It further entails providing for, or cooperating through legitimate processes in, the remediation of adverse human rights impacts where they identify that they have caused or contributed to these impacts.[498]

5.3 Legacy

Overall, the Guidelines' continued influence builds on certain defining characteristic of the OECD that make it a distinctive player in international law-making more generally. As already mentioned, the OECD benefits from international law-making forum shopping, as its members privilege a forum that is characterized by a commitment to economic liberalization and an 'explicit economic perspective on policy issues'.[499] As a result, the OECD Guidelines are 'a useful mechanism to influence OECD member countries and their corporations through surveillance and peer pressure, as well as adverse publicity'.[500] In addition, however, the OECD is a forum for transnational problem-solving that strategically combines a high-power research and networking organization for the collection of data, trend monitoring, economic forecasting, and development of policy options.[501] The OECD thus engages in 'conditional agenda setting' that is developed through regular meetings of global networks of state agencies and experts, that 'exercise influence on policy development challenges and strategic analysis of their resolution', thereby framing issues for future consideration, including in other fora with broader membership.[502] For these reasons, the OECD continues to serve as a proactive forum that has relevance also beyond its membership as a result of widely acknowledged cutting-edge normative work.

---

[495] L. Liberti, 'OECD 50th Anniversary: The Updated OECD Guidelines for Multinational Enterprises and the New OECD Recommendation on Due Diligence Guidance for Conflict-Free Mineral Supply Chains' (2012) 13 *Business Law International* 35, 45.
[496] OECD Guidelines, II.A.2.
[497] Ibid. II.A.10-14.
[498] Ibid. IV.1-3 and 6.
[499] Ibid. 274–75.
[500] Salzman (n. 455) 265.
[501] Ibid. 256.
[502] Ibid. 272–76.

The 2011 version of the OECD Guidelines has been considered 'the first example of how the due diligence and supply chain provisions of the [UN Guiding Principles] ... can be further translated into operational terms in a specific context' and has led to a 'first example of [a] new demand-driven proactive agenda'.[503] In effect, on the basis of the 2011 Guidelines, the OECD has developed a series of sectoral guides that follow the same approach: a five-step due diligence framework; a model policy for companies based on a common set of inter-governmental expectations, suggested measures for risk mitigation and indicators for measuring improvement, and specific recommendations tailored to the challenges associated with specific supply chains.[504] This is the case of the OECD Due Diligence Guidance for Responsible Supply Chains of Minerals from Conflict-Affected and High-Risk Areas, which support the 'progressive improvement of responsible sourcing practices through constructive engagement with suppliers'.[505] The OECD then partnered with the UN Food and Agriculture Organization (FAO) in developing guidance to help enterprises observe standards of responsible business conduct in the agricultural supply chain, following the structure of the Due Diligence Guidance for Minerals but also integrating FAO international standards, such as the Principles for Responsible Investment in Agriculture and Food Systems,[506] and the Voluntary Guidelines on the Responsible Governance of Tenure of Land, Fisheries and Forests in the Context of National Food Security.[507] In 2017, the OECD also developed a due diligence guidance for responsible supply chain management in the garment and footwear sector.[508] All these examples of human rights-based, sector-specific guidance include detailed environmental standards (discussed in the next chapter). They have translated a broader range of inter-governmental standards into benchmarks for corporate conduct, using a coherent approach based on the UN understanding of the relevance of human rights for business and OECD's understanding of corporate governance. They have been considered as a useful source of inspiration for national legislative initiatives,[509] as well as a 'standard of public interest which may affect national courts' decisions'.[510]

The OECD has therefore taken on an explicit role in supporting the implementation of the UN Guiding Principles, and in cooperating with the UN Global

---

[503] Ibid. 38–39.
[504] Ibid. 41.
[505] OECD Due Diligence Guidance for Responsible Supply Chains of Minerals from Conflict-Affected and High-Risk Areas (Paris: OECD, 2013).
[506] Committee on Food Security (CFS), Principles for Responsible Investment in Agriculture and Food Systems (2014).
[507] Food and Agriculture Organization (FAO), Voluntary Guidelines on the Responsible Governance of Tenure of Land, Fisheries and Forests in the Context of National Food Security (VGGT), UN Doc. CL 144/9 (C 2013/20) (2012), Appendix D.
[508] OECD Due Diligence Guidance for Responsible Supply Chains in the Garment and Footwear Sector (Paris: OECD, 2017) 156–57.
[509] Liberti (n. 495) 43.
[510] Birnie et al. (n. 5) 328.

Compact,[511] while driving the agenda for sector-specific guidance to corporations. This has been understood as an attempt by the OECD to remain relevant in the face of more politically successful developments at the UN. It is also seen as a testament to the capacity of the OECD to evolve and adapt 'to the growing needs of a global marketplace'.[512]

6 The Performance Standards of the International Finance Corporation

The International Finance Corporation (IFC)[513] is the largest multilateral source of financing for private sector projects in the developing world.[514] This section will briefly introduce the IFC and the relevance of its Performance Standards from an international environmental law perspective. It will then discuss how the Standards are aligned with the environmental content of the UN and OECD instruments discussed in this chapter, and how they have evolved in response to the UN Framework on Business and Human Rights. The section will conclude with a reflection about the broader trend-setting relevance of the IFC Standards.

6.1 The IFC

The IFC is the private-sector arm of the World Bank family.[515] Established in 1956, its functions also include assisting private companies in the developing world to mobilize financing in international financial markets, and providing advice and technical assistance to business and governments. Its mission is to promote private-sector investment in developing countries, which will reduce poverty and improve people's lives.[516] In this light, the IFC can be described as an institution 'at the

---

[511] Catá Backer (n. 57) 266.
[512] A. Santner, 'A Soft Law Mechanism for Corporate Responsibility: How the Updated OECD Guidelines for Multinational Enterprises Promote Business for the Future' (2011) 43 *The George Washington International Law Review* 375, 376 and 380.
[513] Articles of Agreement of the IFC (20 July 1956, as amended by resolutions effective 21 September 1961 and 1 September 1965); C. Mates, 'Project Finance in Emerging Markets: the Role of the International Finance Corporation' (2004) 18 *The Transnational Lawyer* 165.
[514] IFC, *IFC in Brief* (undated) <http://www.ifc.org/ifcext/about.nsf/Content/IFC_in_Brief> 3. Note that the IFC provides both direct and indirect investments: in the latter case, the Performance Standards apply to financial intermediaries rather than to private companies carrying out projects in developing countries. See B. Richardson, 'Financing Sustainability: The New Transnational Governance of Socially Responsible Investment' (2008) 17 *Yearbook of International Environmental Law* 73.
[515] A. Kiss and D. Shelton, *International Environmental Law*, 3rd edn (New York: Transnational Publishers, 2004) 157–58.
[516] D. L. Khairallah, 'International Finance Corporation' in R. Blanpain (ed.), *International Encyclopaedia of Laws* (Intergovernmental Organizations—Suppl. 12) (The Hague: Kluwer Law International, 2002).

crossroads of the public and private sectors', as it is a public-sector institution committed to working with the private sector, sharing private-sector risks in making loans and equity investments without government guarantee of repayment.[517]

Although the IFC coordinates its activities with other institutions in the World Bank Group, it generally operates independently as it has its own legal and financial autonomy with its own Articles of Agreement, share capital, management, and staff. Such separation is motivated by the fact that the IFC focuses on generating profits from its investment and does not offer grants like the World Bank does; and it does not work directly with governments.[518] Nonetheless, there remain certain links between the Corporation and the Bank. First, the Bank safeguard policies,[519] although drafted for public-sector projects, are deemed to apply by default to IFC-funded projects with the private sector when there are gaps in the IFC's own policies and standards. Second, the Bank and IFC often cooperate when operating in the same country, thus in some instances the procedures of both organizations apply to a single project.[520] Third, the president of the World Bank Group also serves as the IFC president.

Although the IFC was established in the late 1950s, it was only in 1990 that it first addressed the environment-related impacts of its projects, subjecting IFC projects to an environmental review process to ensure their consistency with 'the spirit and the intent of the appropriate [World] Bank guidelines and policies'.[521] The vague formulation and the fact that the World Bank Guidelines were drafted with reference to financial support to governments rather than private companies left significant room for interpretation and led to limited impacts on enhancing the environmental performance of IFC-funded projects.[522] In 1993, the IFC reformulated this position, stating instead 'IFC projects must comply with appropriate World Bank environmental policies and guidelines'.[523] This formulation also failed to determine which World Bank policies were considered appropriate in the IFC sphere of action.[524] Criticisms were also voiced because the IFC environmental

---

[517] C. Lee, 'International Finance Corporation: Financing Environmentally and Socially Sustainable Private Investment' in S. Schlemmer-Schulte and K. Tung (eds), *Liber Amicorum Ibrahim F.I. Shihata* (The Hague: Kluwer Law International, 2001) 469–70.

[518] B. Saper, 'The International Finance Corporation's Compliance Advisor/Ombudsman (CAO): An Examination of the Accountability and Effectiveness from a Global Administrative Law Perspective' (2011) 44 *NYU Journal of International Law and Policy* 1280, 1283 and 1285.

[519] Boisson de Chazournes (n. 53) 297–302.

[520] As in the case of the Chad/Cameroon Pipeline and the Bujagali Hydropower Project in Uganda. Kiss and Shelton (n. 515) 156; and G. Hernández Uriz, 'The Application of the World Bank Standards to the Oil Industry: Can the World Bank Group Promote Corporate Responsibility?' (2002) 28 *Brooklyn Journal of International Law* 77.

[521] IFC, *Procedure for Environmental Review of IFC Projects*, Purpose of Review, para. 1, in effect from March 1990 to December 1992.

[522] Lee (n. 517) 477.

[523] IFC, 'Environmental Analysis and Review of International Finance Corporation Projects, Procedure for Environmental Review of the International Finance Corporation' (8 September 1993).

[524] This was the case of a Pangue hydroelectric project in Chile, for which the IFC asserted that the World Bank's policy on Dams and Reservoirs did not apply. Lee (n. 517) 477.

review process occurred at a late stage of project development, did not require consultations with local communities and affected groups, and did not make the environmental assessment available for review and comment.[525]

Following increasing public attention and disapproval of IFC-funded projects' environmental performance in the late 1990s,[526] the IFC undertook to pay greater attention to incorporating environmental requirements in its legal documents, differentiating its procedures and requirements, and strengthening public consultation and disclosure.[527] Thus, in 1998 the Corporation adopted nine of the ten World Bank's policies as its own Safeguard Policies, and released its Pollution Prevention and Abatement Handbook,[528] which sought to apply to the private sector the principles of sustainable development, cleaner production processes, and pollution prevention.[529] A 2003 review of its environmental policy and guidelines concluded that the system was weak, lacked specific objectives and an effective monitoring system, and was poorly integrated into the IFC's core business,[530] not being able to ensure in a comprehensive manner that IFC-funded projects were environmentally sound.[531]

The IFC Board approved renewed policy and standards for environmental sustainability in February 2006. One of the novelties of the 2006 documents was a clear separation between the environment-related roles and responsibilities of the Corporation itself, on the one hand, and of its clients, ie private companies, on the other. The Policy on Social and Environmental Sustainability[532] illustrated the Corporation's commitment, roles, and responsibilities, including that of reviewing projects proposed for direct financing against the Performance Standards,[533] while the Performance Standards detailed the role and responsibilities of private enterprises that receive funding from the IFC. The IFC Performance Standards were revised in 2011 in parallel with the OECD Guidelines with a view to incorporating the main normative innovations of the UN Framework and its Guiding Principles on Business and Human Rights.[534]

---

[525] Kiss and Shelton (n. 515) 245.
[526] Lee (n. 517) 475.
[527] Ibid. 479–81.
[528] (1998) <http://www.ifc.org/ifcext/enviro.nsf/Content/PPAH>. The Handbook provides pollution and abatement measures and emissions levels that are normally acceptable to the IFC, subject to project-specific analysis in the environmental assessment.
[529] Lee (n. 517) fn. 33.
[530] CAO, *A Review of IFC's Safeguard Policies* (January 2003) 7.
[531] I. Bowles, A. Rosenfels, C. Kormos, C. Reining, J. Nations, and T. Ankersen, 'The Environmental Impact of the International Finance Corporation Lending and Proposals for Reform: A Case Study of Conservation and Oil Development in the Guatemalan Petén' (1999) 29 *Environmental Law* 103.
[532] IFC, *Policy on Social and Environmental Sustainability* (30 April 2006) <http://www.ifc.org/sustainability>.
[533] IFC, *Performance Standards on Social and Environmental Sustainability*, adopted by the IFC Board on 21 February 2006, with implementation starting on 30 April 2006 (hereinafter, IFC 2006 Performance Standards).
[534] Note that the UN Special Representative on Business and Human Rights that elaborated the UN Framework participated in both reviews: Report of the Special Representative (n. 414) para. 13.

6.2 The IFC environmental standards

The IFC environmental standards clearly identify the responsibility of the private sector on the basis of international environmental principles, multilateral environmental agreements and other international environmental law materials,[535] as well as of formalized dialogue with business and NGO representatives.[536] On the whole, the IFC Performance Standards mostly converge with other international initiatives on corporate accountability, such as the UN Norms, the UN Global Compact, and the OECD Guidelines in the choice of minimum standards based on international environmental principles, with the notable exception of precaution. They go beyond these initiatives by also spelling out international standards on the basis of multilateral environmental agreements.

The explicit reference to the UN Framework Convention on Climate Change,[537] the Convention on Biodiversity, the Basel Convention on Transboundary Movements of Hazardous Waste,[538] the World Heritage Convention,[539] the Convention on Long-range Transboundary Air Pollution,[540] the Stockholm Convention on Persistent Organic Pollutants,[541] and the Montreal Protocol on Substances that Deplete the Ozone Layer[542] may offer opportunities for fostering the implementation of multilateral environmental agreements directly through the responsible conduct of the private sector. In referring to these multilateral environmental treaties, the IFC took care to specify that these references are 'intended to acknowledge the international consensus and support on these instruments, but not to create client obligations to comply with these agreements, as these agreements rest with signatory States and not with business'.[543] The Corporation noted that the client's responsibility is to meet the requirements of the IFC Performance Standards.[544] Nonetheless, the alignment of the IFC Performance Standards with

---

[535] As suggested in OECD, 'Key Messages' (OECD Workshop on Multilateral Environmental Agreements and the Private Sector, Helsinki, 16–17 June 2005).
[536] D. Bradlow and A. Naudé Fourie, 'The Operational Policies of the World Bank and the International Finance Corporation: Creating Law-Making and Law-Governed Institutions?' (2013) 10 *International Organizations Law Review* 3, 24–26.
[537] United Nations Framework Convention on Climate Change (New York, 9 May 1992, in force 21 March 1994).
[538] Convention on the Control of Transboundary Movements of Hazardous Wastes and Their Disposal (Basel Convention) (Basel, 22 March 1989, in force 24 May 1992).
[539] Convention for the Protection of the World Cultural and Natural Heritage (World Heritage Convention) (Paris, 16 November 1972, in force 17 December 1975).
[540] Convention on Long-range Transboundary Air Pollution (Geneva, 13 November 1979, in force 16 March 1983).
[541] Stockholm Convention on Persistent Organic Pollutants (Stockholm, 22 May 2002, in force 17 May 2004).
[542] Montreal Protocol on Substances that Deplete the Ozone Layer (Montreal, 16 September 1987, in force 1 January 1989).
[543] IFC, 'Policy and Performance Standards on Social and Environmental Sustainability and Policy on Disclosure of Information: IFC Responses to Stakeholder Comments and Rationale for Key Policy Changes' (22 September 2006) 9.
[544] Ibid.

other documents agreed at the international level can arguably contribute to the credibility and legitimacy of these initiatives in the eyes of international civil society.[545]

The IFC Standards further contribute to raise the profile (and, if incorporated in the loan agreements, the legal status) of soft-law instruments and promote compliance with them,[546] such as the FAO Code of Conduct on Pesticides.[547] The latter had already attracted the attention of international lawyers interested in applicability to private companies, as it 'is divided roughly equally between commitments for governments and commitments for industry'.[548]

There are several environmental dimensions to the IFC Performance Standards, as they comprise: a general, cross-cutting requirement for environmental self-assessment and management system (Performance Standard 1); a series of more specific environmental standards (Performance Standard 3 on resource efficiency and pollution prevention, and Performance Standard 4 on biodiversity conservation and sustainable management of living natural resources), and other thematic standards that may concern the environment, such as Performance Standard 7 on indigenous peoples and Performance Standard 8 on cultural heritage.[549] Furthermore, the IFC considers climate change and water, in addition to human rights and gender, as cross-cutting topics that are addressed across multiple Performance Standards.[550]

As opposed to the OECD Guidelines review, however, since 2011 the IFC has significantly strengthened its approach to community consultations, linking the need for companies to conduct 'informed consultation' with a specific and express (albeit qualified) requirement for prior informed consent. The 2011 review also expanded on substantive standards of corporate environmental responsibility, with more extensive standards on climate change, resource efficiency, and biodiversity, including the introduction of resource efficiency for energy, water, and inputs; an increased emphasis on energy efficiency and greenhouse gas (GHG) measurement; accountability for historical pollution; and a new duty of care for hazardous waste disposal. This is in line with the IFC Policy on Social and Environmental

---

[545] The World Wide Fund for Nature (WWF) (A. Durbin, S. Herz, D. Hunter, and J. Peck), 'Shaping the Future of Sustainable Finance: Moving from Paper Promises to Performance' (January 2006) http://www.wwf.org.uk/researcher/issues/companiesandfinance/index.asp 15. Furthermore, the IFC CAO also highlighted in its review of the 1998 environmental safeguard policies that explicit mention of international agreements, norms and standards may give 'helpful context and reference points' (CAO, n. 523, at 37.) See also comments by A. McBeth, *International Economic Actors and Human Rights* (Abingdon, Routledge: 2010) 208.
[546] Boisson de Chazournes (n. 53) 297.
[547] FAO, The International Code of Conduct on the Distribution and Use of Pesticides (revised version adopted by the 123rd Session of the FAO Council in November 2002).
[548] Ratner (n. 85) 815.
[549] The other Performance Standards focus on: labour and working conditions; community health, safety, and security; and land acquisition and involuntary resettlement (Performance Standards 2, 4 and 5). Due to the focus of this study, these standards will not be analysed.
[550] Overview of IFC Performance Standards (2012) para. 4.

Standards, which targets the IFC itself, acknowledged the need to support the private sector's contribution to climate change mitigation and adaptation, building the capacity of the private sector in relation to climate change, biodiversity, and resource efficiency, as well as to limit its impacts on ecosystem services,[551] and to reflect a human rights due diligence approach across its sustainability principles.[552]

It has been concluded that 'the IFC has not only chosen to integrate evolving standards developed in other intergovernmental forums, but decided to take the lead in developing environmental standards applicable to its private-sector clients'.[553] In the *Pulp Mills* case, for instance, the International Court of Justice (ICJ) considered the fact that the IFC decision to fund a project after having assessed compliance with multilateral environmental agreements referred in its Performance Standards, even those that are not applicable in Latin America.[554]

6.3 Operational distinctiveness and broader trend-setting value

The IFC Standards are intended to apply throughout the life of an investment.[555] They are meant to provide 'guidance' to clients on how to identify risks and impacts, and are designed to 'help avoid, mitigate and manage risks and impacts as a way of doing business in a sustainable way'.[556]

Because of the degree of international personality of international financial institutions, these are subject to duties under international law, thereby including international environmental law. Any failure to comply with international environmental obligations may entail their international responsibility as well as liability for damages.[557] The incorporation of such standards as conditions into loan agreements can make such international environmental standards for corporate

---

[551] Which are defined at para. 2 of 2012 IFC Performance Standard 6, 'Biodiversity Conservation and Sustainable Management of Living Natural Resources', as the 'benefits that people, including businesses, derive from ecosystem services'. The definition is clearly based on the Millennium Ecosystem Assessment, a global scientific process that facilitated inter-governmental endorsement of the term 'ecosystem services': The Millennium Ecosystem Assessment, Ecosystems and Human Well-Being: Synthesis (2005), <http://www.maweb.org/en/index.aspx>. See Ch. 1.

[552] 2012 IFC Policy on Social and Environmental Sustainability, http://www.ifc.org/ifcext/policyreview.nsf/Content/SustainabilityPolicy, paras 10–11 and 15.

[553] M. Langer, 'Key Instruments of Private Environmental Finance: Funds, Project Finance and Market Mechanisms' in Dupuy and Viñuales (n. 1) 131, 159.

[554] Birnie et al. (n. 5) 81.

[555] Overview of IFC Performance Standards (2012) para. 2.

[556] Ibid. para 1.

[557] P. Sands and J. Peel, with A. Fabra and R. MacKenzie, *Principles of International Environmental Law*, 4th edn (Cambridge: Cambridge University Press, 2018) 669. Indeed, major concerns for the severe negative environmental impacts caused by projects funded by international financial institutions are continuously being raised by environmental NGOs: For instance, 'IDB President Admits Serious Problems in Spill-Prone Amazon Pipeline', press release by Amazon Watch and Environmental Defence (3 April 2006) <http://www.amazonwatch.org/newsroom/view_news.php?id=1134>. See generally A. Rigo Suerda, 'The Law Applicable to the Activities of International Development Banks' (2004) 308 *Recueil des Cours* 1, 123–27.

accountability contractually binding on private companies. As opposed to the loan agreements between the World Bank and borrower governments that fall under the domain of the international law of treaties, the loan agreements of the IFC with private companies are usually concluded under the law of New York or English law,[558] and thus may not be enforceable under international law.[559] That said, investment contracts can avoid mentioning IFC standards or undermine them by placing restrictions preventing the host State from using domestic law to require investors to comply with their IFC standards on the basis of the agreement with the IFC or an Equator Bank.[560]

The relevance of the IFC Standards is broader than that. They have also set a trend for other international financial institutions, notably in the area of public participation[561] and commercial banks.[562] The Equator Principles are the best-known example,[563] but together with other socially responsible initiatives they are arguably 'a modest, niche sector of the financial economy only occasionally influencing the environmental practice of companies'[564] In addition, all OECD export credit agencies claim that they apply the IFC standards through the non-binding Common Approaches agreement,[565] thereby facilitating access to capital markets because the IFC due diligence procedure reduces credit and capital risks.[566] The IFC has also started to control its financial intermediaries by imposing

---

[558] Private correspondence with IFC staff, dated 17 October 2006 (on file with author).

[559] Boisson de Chazournes (n. 53) 290. The actual operationalization of these standards by the IFC will be discussed in more detail in Ch. 5.

[560] S. Leader, 'Human Rights, Risks and New Strategies for Global Investment' (2006) 9 *Journal of International Economic Law* 657, 671.

[561] D. Bradlow and M. Chapman, 'Public Participation and the Private Sector: The Role of Multilateral Development Banks and the Evolving Legal Standards' (2011) 4 *Erasmus Law Review* 91, 92 and 95.

[562] This is the notable case of the Equator Principles, which were last reviewed in 2013 following the latest review of the IFC Performance Standards: http://www.equator-principles.com/. C. Wright, 'The Equator Principles' in T. Hale and D. Held (eds), *Handbook of Transnational Governance* (Cambridge: Polity Press, 2011) 229. And this is clearly an intention of the IFC itself: R. Kyte, Director of the IFC Environmental and Social Development Department, 'The New IFC Standards' (2006) 12 *CSR Asia Weekly* (15 March) 13; L. Ahearn, 'Environmental Procedures and Standards in International Transactions: Multilateral Models and Private Lending Practices' (1999) 27 *International Business Lawyer* 419.

[563] B. Richardson, 'Financial Markets and Socially Responsible Investing' in B. Sjåfjell and B. Richardson (eds), *Company Law and Sustainability: Legal Barriers and Opportunities* (Cambridge: Cambridge University Press, 2015) 226, 263–67. See also B. Richardson, 'Socially Responsible Investing through Voluntary Codes' in Dupuy and Viñuales (n. 1) 383, 412–41; Wright (n. 562) 230–34; D. Ong, 'From "International" to "Transnational" Environmental Law? A Legal Assessment of the Contribution of the "Equator Principles" to International Environmental Law' (2010) 79 *Nordic Journal of International Law* 35; D. Ong, 'Public Accountability for Private International Financing of Natural Resource Development Projects: The un Rule of Law Initiative and the Equator Principles' (2016) 85 *Nordic Journal of International Law* 201.

[564] Richardson, 'Financial Markets' (n. 563) 273.

[565] OECD, Recommendation of the Council on Common Approaches for Officially Supported Export Credits and Environmental and Social Due Diligence (TAD/ECG/(2015)5, 28 June 2012); Simons and Mackling (n. 247) 132.

[566] Langer (n. 553) 161.

136 THE EMERGENCE OF INTERNATIONAL STANDARDS

a review procedure on their activities, if the project they finance with the IFC support may have environmental and social impacts.[567]

Overall, the IFC has been 'largely underestimated' in its leading standard-setting role and in reaching out beyond its initial sphere of influence,[568] including making an impact on the further development of international law.[569]

7 Preliminary conclusions and their relevance for a new treaty on business and human rights

The initiatives within the UN in the field of corporate environmental accountability and responsibility have been continuous and multifaceted. The UN draft Code of Conduct and the UN Norms faced significant opposition from capital-exporting States. And even in the case of the seemingly voluntary UN Global Compact, inter-governmental support has been an issue, notwithstanding the fact that this initiative drew on inter-governmentally approved sources such as the Rio Declaration on Environment and Development, and provided a strong indication of companies' acceptance of international environmental law principles.

The UN Framework and Guiding Principles on Business and Human Rights are the only UN instrument that has received inter-governmental support, demonstrating that the UN can provide a forum for discussing corporate accountability and responsibility with the broadest possible involvement of States[570] (arguably equalizing bargaining powers among them[571]) thanks to its 'obvious role' in framing the debate in human rights terms.[572] The imprimatur of the UN has had the expected legitimizing effect on the international search for corporate environmental accountability and responsibility standards.[573] Although conceptually the understanding of the relevance of international law for business is not so different under the UN Framework and its Guiding Principles and under the rejected UN Norms, the Framework's political endorsement has immediately proved influential on the OECD Guidelines and IFC Performance Standards. And even though the UN Framework on Business and Human Rights and its Guiding Principles have not made specific reference to the environment, other international processes that have built upon them have made explicit how the human-rights based approach can be integrated into corporate environmental responsibility and accountability

---

[567] Ibid. 163.
[568] Ibid. 165.
[569] Bradlow and Naudé Fourie (n. 536) 6–7.
[570] Coonrod (n. 124) 303.
[571] Ibid. 305; B. Kjellén, 'The Desertification Convention: Towards Creating a Multilateral Framework for Coping with Global Threats' in M. Rolén, H. Sjöberg, and U. Svedin (eds), *International Governance on Environmental Issues* (Dordrecht: Kluwer Academic Publishers, 1997) 77.
[572] King (n. 201) 481.
[573] Coonrod (n. 124) 305; Amnesty International (n. 294) 15; and Gleckman (n. 147) 100.

standards, as well as contributing to their implementation. The development of sector-specific standards by the OECD and IFC, and the normative clarifications offered by UN Special Rapporteurs, as discussed in the next chapter, will further demonstrate this point.

Regardless of the varying political success and normative differences among all the international initiatives discussed in this chapter, international standards on corporate environmental accountability have emerged coherently on the basis of parallel work under the UN in the field of environmental protection.[574] The UN draft Code, the UN Norms, the UN Global Compact, the OECD Guidelines, and the IFC Performance Standards have all been based on the international environmental principles enshrined in the Rio Declaration on the Environment and Development, and some of them have also made reference to the UN Convention on Biological Diversity and other multilateral environmental treaties. International environmental principles have clearly served as a basis for translating the international community's expectation about acceptable business conduct with regard to the environment: information disclosure, impact assessments and consultation, prevention, and precaution.[575] The 2011 parallel review of the OECD Guidelines and the IFC Standards, which was mainly motivated by the need to align with the UN Framework on Business and Human Rights, has led to further convergence in international standard-setting.[576] The resulting normative coherence makes it difficult for governments or business to credibly make the argument that 'there is no fundamentally clear set of minimal demands' in this connection.[577] Instead, international standards have been progressively linked to growing interest in supply-chain responsibility and external monitoring of corporate conduct.[578]

What remains to be seen is whether such normative coherence will provide a sufficient basis for the negotiations of a new international treaty on business and human rights,[579] or an excuse not to proceed with it. To what extent will a new treaty effectively tackle the often inextricable links between environmental degradation and human rights violations[580] in the natural resource sector? These links have already

---

[574] As already anticipated in UNCTAD, *World Investment Report 1999: Foreign Direct Investment and the Challenge of Development* (Geneva: UN, 1999) 367–69 and Coonrod (n. 124) 303.

[575] Miles (n. 99) 227; J. Zerk, 'Corporate Liability for Gross Human Rights Abuses: Towards a Fairer and More Effective System of Domestic Law Remedies', report prepared for the Office of the High Commissioner for Human Rights (2012) 262–77; J. Viñuales, *Foreign Investment and the Environment in International Law* (Cambridge: Cambridge University Press, 2012) 67.

[576] Morgera, 'From Corporate Social Responsibility to Accountability Mechanisms' (n. 1) 321.

[577] Bickford (n. 267) 153.

[578] Zerk (n. 575) 262–77.

[579] Draft Report of the Open-ended Intergovernmental Working Group on Transnational Corporations and Other Business Enterprises With Respect to Human Rights (10 July 2015) available at <http://www.ohchr.org/EN/HRBodies/HRC/WGTransCorp/Session1/Pages/Draftreport.aspx> accessed 27 February 2016, paras 37 and 47.

[580] A. Sinden, 'Power and Responsibility: Why Human Rights Should Address Corporate Environmental Wrongs' in D. McBarnet, A. Voiculescu, and T. Campbell (eds), *The New Corporate Accountability: Corporate Social Responsibility and the Law* (Cambridge: Cambridge University Press, 2007) 728; E. Morgera, 'Human Rights Dimensions of Corporate Environmental Accountability' in

been well documented and discussed in international environmental law processes, and in the preparation of the UN Framework on Business and Human Rights.[581] They have also emerged in the debate on a new treaty,[582] notably in relation to the right to water[583] and multilateral environmental agreements as potential sources of inspiration.[584] But references to environmental dimensions of the treaty remain controversial.[585] On the whole, it seems more likely that a new treaty will clarify States' obligations to exercise control over business, through domestic legal liability deriving from business responsibility to respect human rights[586] and through an extraterritorial duty to regulate corporations and facilitate access to justice.[587] The treaty could also specify obligations and reinforce compliance mechanisms, and open existing international human rights remedy and participation mechanisms for civil society.[588] The opportunity for the treaty to provide 'institutional mechanisms to facilitate empowered participation by affected individuals and civil society'[589] could change significantly the current international landscape of international corporate accountability and responsibility initiatives.[590]

P-M. Dupuy, E-U. Petersmann, and F. Francioni (eds), *Human Rights, Investment Law and Investor-State Arbitration* (Oxford: Oxford University Press, 2009) 511.

[581] Morgera (n. 576); and D. Bilchitz and S. Deva, 'The Human Rights Obligations of Business: A Critical Framework for the Future' in Deva and Bilchitz (n. 356) 1.

[582] The issue has been raised in the first session of the working group on business and human rights: see the Draft Report of the Open-ended Intergovernmental Working Group on Transnational Corporations and Other Business Enterprises With Respect to Human Rights (n. 579), paras 21, 26–28, and 31. At the time of writing the most recent negotiating text is Open-ended intergovernmental working group on transnational corporations and other business enterprises with respect to human rights Chairmanship Revised Draft 16.7.2019 Legally Binding Instrument To Regulate, In International Human Rights Law, The Activities Of Transnational Corporations And Other Business Enterprises and Draft report on the fifth session of the open-ended intergovernmental working group on transnational corporations and other business enterprises with respect to human rights available at https://www.ohchr.org/EN/HRBodies/HRC/WGTransCorp/Pages/IGWGOnTNC.aspx (5 November 2019). See P. Hood and J. Hughes-Jennet, 'UN Working Group Publishes Revised Draft Business and Human Rights Treaty: Commentary on Scope, Prevention and Legal Liability' (26 July 2019).

[583] Report on the second session of the open-ended intergovernmental working group on transnational corporations and other business enterprises with respect to human rights (2017) UN Doc. A/HRC/34/47, paras 11, 36, 100.

[584] Ibid. paras 50, 97–98.

[585] Draft report of the fifth session (n. 582) paras 35, 51, and 65.

[586] Improving Accountability and Access to Remedy for Business and Human Rights Abuses: A submission from the Office of the United Nations High Commissioner for Human Rights (OHCHR) on the Revised Draft of the legally binding instrument to regulate, in international human rights law, the activities of transnational corporations and other business enterprises (8 October 2019) 5–6.

[587] Particularly through mutual legal assistance across borders: O. De Schutter, 'Towards a New Treaty on Business and Human Rights' (2016) 1 *Business and Human Rights Journal* 41 53, 55. Report on the second session (n. 583) para. 9.

[588] Rodríguez-Garavito (n. 407) 33.

[589] Ibid. 40.

[590] It has been observed that although there are conflicting research findings on the importance of an international treaty for improved human rights conditions, there is convergence in the importance of civil society advocacy and demands for human rights implementation: C. Vargas, 'A Treaty on Business and Human Rights? A Recurring Debate in a New Governance Landscape' in Rodríguez-Garavito (n. 2) 111, 115.

As the possibility for the treaty to create international obligations directly binding on corporations, address their status in international law, and establish an international dispute settlement for corporate violations,[591] appears remote at the time of writing, the treaty could still include 'more expressive commitments' to the existing international standards.[592] And it could contribute to make them more responsive to local needs through an institutional process for engaging the full range of stakeholders, including those most affected by corporate conduct.[593] This would contribute to filling a critical gap in international standard-setting initiatives so far, which is sustained engagement with victims[594] and right-holders 'before harm occurs, and in continual monitoring, agenda-setting, awareness raising and review processes'.[595] It has been underscored that so far regional and local organizations that have direct experience of supporting victims of corporate human rights abuses linked to environmental degradation have not yet had sufficient voice[596] in the process of learning from, assessing, or developing standards and their monitoring mechanisms discussed in the next chapters. This approach would contribute to make a new treaty 'a component of a broader toolkit' comprising also local political organization and litigation, sectoral multi-stakeholder standard-setting initiatives, further elaboration of UN treaty bodies' recommendations on States' extraterritorial obligations and domestic regulation.[597] In effect, even if a new treaty is adopted, the remaining instruments and approaches are largely expected to continue to be explored.

---

[591] Report on the second session (n. 583) paras 19–20, 23.
[592] Expressiveness could serve to clearly and publicly manifest a commitment to principles that provide an 'agreed operational modality' that goes above and beyond existing obligations and resonate with lived the experience of right-holders, carefully avoiding shopping lists and over-specification: Melish (n. 385) 92–93.
[593] Ibid.
[594] OHCHR (n. 586) 2–3.
[595] Melish (n. 385) 84–85 and 88 (emphasis in the original).
[596] Rodríguez-Garavito (n. 398) 37.
[597] Ibid. 38. This is also reflected in Draft report on the fifth session (n. 582) para. 2. See further S. Blackwell and N. Vander Meulen, 'Two Roads Converged: The Mutual Complementarity of a Binding Business and Human Rights Treaty and National Action Plans on Business and Human Rights' (2016) 6 *Notre Dame Journal of International and Comparative Law* 51.

4
Assessing the Convergence of International Standards on Corporate Environmental Accountability

This and the following chapter will carry out a critical analysis of the international standards on corporate environmental accountability and responsibility by relying on the normative advances made under the Convention on Biological Diversity (CBD).[1] The reason is three-fold. First, under this treaty 196 Parties have achieved consensus on a variety of standards addressed to the private sector in the achievement of global environmental objectives.[2] Second, this consensus guidance has been recognized as relevant to interpret the human rights of indigenous peoples by different international human rights bodies, thereby contributing to show how international corporate accountability and responsiblity standards are increasingly emerging at the intersection of international environmental law and international human rights law. Third, these CBD standards have been relied upon to develop sector-specific standards[3] under the more general international initiatives on corporate environmental accountability and responsibility discussed in the previous chapter.

A brief explanation of the developments related to private-sector involvement under the CBD will precede the standard-by-standard discussion at the core of this chapter and the next. The degree of normative convergence will be assessed first

---

[1] Convention on Biological Diversity (CBD) (Rio de Janeiro, 5 June 1992, in force 29 December 1993). The point was made initially in E. Morgera and E. Tsioumani, 'Yesterday, Today and Tomorrow: Looking Afresh at the Convention on Biological Diversity' (2011) 21 *Yearbook of International Environmental Law* 3–40, 24. Contra L. Siegele and H. Ward, 'Corporate Social Responsibility: A Step towards Stronger Involvement of Business in MEA Implementation?' (2007) 16 *Review of European Community and International Environmental Law* 135.

[2] It should be recalled (as discussed in Ch. 3) that the preamble of the UN Norms (UNCHR Sub-Commission, 'Norms on the Responsibilities of Transnational Corporations and Other Business Enterprises with regard to Human Rights' (26 August 2003) UN Doc. E/CN.4/Sub.2/2003/12/Rev.2) refers to: the CBD; International Convention on Civil Liability for Oil Pollution Damage (Brussels, 29 November 1969); Convention on Civil Liability for Damage resulting from Activities Dangerous to the Environment (Lugano, 21 June 1993, not in force); UNGA Res. 41/128 'Declaration on the Right to Development' (4 December 1986); 'Rio Declaration on Environment and Development' (13 June 1992) UN Doc. A/CONF.151/6/Rev.1 (Rio Declaration); and WSSD, 'Johannesburg Plan of Implementation' (4 July 2002) UN Doc. A/CONF.199/20, Res. 2 (WSSD Plan of Implementation).

[3] D. Santillo and P. Johnston, 'Ethical Standards and Principles of Sustainability' in M. K. Addo (ed.), *Human Rights Standards and the Responsibility of Transnational Corporations* (The Hague: Kluwer Law International, 1999) 351, stressed the need to better define sectoral standards.

across the general standards discussed in the previous chapter, and contrasted with the advice elaborated by UN Special Rapporteurs relying on various international human rights materials and inter-governmentally approved guidance under the CBD. This analysis will show that, on the one hand, principles of international environmental law have been initially translated as corporate environmental accountability standards, but over time have also been specified more substantively into corporate environmental responsibility standards.[4] On the other hand, the more recent cross-fertilization of international biodiversity law and international human rights law has led to the emergence of self-standing substantial standards of corporate environmental responsibility, particularly in as far as the human rights of indigenous peoples to their territories, lands, natural resources, and traditional knowledge are concerned. Other international standards of corporate environmental responsibility have also emerged with regard to protected areas and the sustainable use of natural resources. Corporate environmental responsibility standards will be discussed in the next chapter.

1 The Convention on Biodiversity and the private sector

The Convention on Biological Diversity (CBD) aims at the conservation of the variability of living organisms[5] and their interactions, and the sustainable use of living natural resources, encompassing genetic resources and associated traditional knowledge. It also concerns non-living resources that form part of ecosystems,[6] and the use of non-living natural resources that may affect biodiversity conservation and sustainable use. Its subject-matter is thus remarkably wide, and its membership is virtually global (196 Parties, with the notable absence of the United States). At the crossroads of environmental protection and development,[7] the CBD supports a balance between conservation and sustainable use rather than a blanket preference for conservation.[8] For instance, the CBD has addressed biodiversity concerns arising from climate change mitigation and adaptation measures.[9] More

---

[4] See Ch. 1, Section 4.
[5] The definition of biodiversity is provided in CBD Art. 2 as 'the variability among living organisms from all sources including, inter alia, terrestrial, marine and other aquatic ecosystems and the ecological complexes of which they are part; this includes diversity within species, between species and of ecosystems'.
[6] See the definition of ecosystems under CBD Art. 2.
[7] L. Glowka et al., *A Guide to the Convention on Biological Diversity* (Gland, IUCN: 1994); C. Tinker, 'A New Breed of Treaty: The United Nations Convention on Biological Diversity' (1995) 12 *Pace Environmental Law Review* 191.
[8] S. Johnston, 'The Convention on Biological Diversity: The Next Phase' (1997) 6 *Review of European Community and International Environmental Law* 219.
[9] E. Morgera, 'Against All Odds: The Contribution of the Convention on Biological Diversity to International Human Rights Law' in D. Alland et al. (eds), *Unity and Diversity of International Law: Essays in Honour of Professor Pierre-Marie Dupuy* (Leiden: Martinus Nijhoff Publishers, 2014) 983.

generally, the CBD has provided an innovative and flexible framework for accommodating developed and developing countries' concerns and capacities[10] and for encouraging partnerships between national and local authorities, local and indigenous communities, and the private sector.[11]

The open-ended and heavily qualified rules contained in the CBD, however, have been criticized for their vagueness and for their soft-law nature,[12] despite being contained in a formally legally binding instrument.[13] It has also been considered an ineffective and fragmented process that has had little impact on State practice, making instead a continuous attempt to expand its subject-matter without fully achieving or systematically assessing progress on previously agreed commitments.[14] These weaknesses can also be considered the strength of the regime, however, if one considers that the consensus decisions of the CBD's Conference of the Parties (COP)[15] have provided subsequent agreement on the interpretation[16] of relevant CBD rules[17] in light of intervening legal, scientific, and technological developments in different sectors. As a result, CBD COP decisions have expanded upon the scope and content of the Convention, well beyond the expectations of its drafters, by way of interpretation or documentation of good practices. The CBD COP's normative activity is thus testimony to an intense, evolving, and creative interpretation of the convention by the international community,[18] including a certain degree of openness to inputs from indigenous peoples' and local communities' representatives.[19] That said, such consensus has come at a price: CBD COP

---

[10] D. McGraw, 'The CBD: Key Characteristics and Implications for Development' (2002) 11 *Review of European Community and International Environmental Law* 17.

[11] L. Kimball, 'Institutional Linkages between the Convention on Biological Diversity and Other International Conventions' (1997) 6 *Review of European Community and International Environmental Law* 239.

[12] M. Chandler, 'The Biodiversity Convention: Selected Issues of Interest to the International Lawyer' (1993) 4 *Colorado Journal of International Environmental Law* 141. Note that P. Birnie, A. Boyle, and C. Redgwell, *International Law and the Environment*, 3rd edn (Oxford: Oxford University Press, 2009) 617, argue that it is necessary to 'look more to the implementation process than the textual analysis of the Convention's provisions in order to measure its contribution to the conservation of biodiversity'.

[13] A. Boyle and C. Chinkin, *The Making of International Law* (Oxford: Oxford University Press, 2007) 220–22.

[14] McGraw (n. 10) 23.

[15] J. Brunnée, 'COP-ing with Consent: Law-Making under Multilateral Environmental Agreements' (2002) 15 *Leiden Journal of International Law* 1.

[16] Convention on the Law of the Treaties (Vienna, 23 May 1969, in force 27 January 1980), Art. 31(3)(b): First and Second Report on Subsequent Agreements and Subsequent Practice in Relation to Treaty Interpretation, UN Doc. A/Cn.4/660 (2013) and UN Doc. A/CN.4/671 (2014).

[17] Morgera and Tsioumani (n. 1) 3.

[18] For a discussion of the significant evolution of the interpretation of the CBD references to benefit sharing, see E. Morgera and E. Tsioumani, 'The Evolution of Benefit-Sharing: Linking Biodiversity and Community Livelihoods' (2010) 15 *Review of European Community and International Environmental Law* 150.

[19] Under the CBD Working Group on Art. 8(j) (traditional knowledge), the fullest possible participation of indigenous and local communities is ensured in all Working Group meetings, including in contact groups, by welcoming community representatives as Friends of the Co-Chairs, Friends of the Bureau and Co-Chairs of contact groups; without prejudice to the applicable rules of procedure of the Conference of the Parties establishing that representatives duly nominated by parties are to conduct the business of CBD meetings so that any text proposal by indigenous and local communities'

decisions, similarly to the text of the Convention itself, also suffer from heavily qualified language,[20] which has allowed for a very wide margin of discretion for States in their interpretation and implementation. In addition, guidance on certain concepts or issues is often dispersed in a myriad of CBD decisions, which have not been subject to any significant monitoring or compliance process.[21]

The relevance of the Convention on Biological Diversity from a human rights perspective was confirmed in the 2017 report of the UN Special Rapporteur on Human Rights and the Environment.[22] For the first time, CBD obligations have been authoritatively assessed as a matter of international human rights law, based on the unequivocal understanding that the full enjoyment of everyone's human rights to life, health, food, and water depend on healthy ecosystems and their benefits to people.[23] On the one hand, the report served to underscore that procedural dimensions of biodiversity conservation and sustainable use[24] are not just a matter of mere good governance,[25] but a matter of international human rights law. This means that human rights obligations limit the discretion of CBD parties in their interpretation and implementation of otherwise open-ended treaty language. In addition, Special Rapporteur Knox clarified that there are substantive human rights law obligations that serve to clarify the limits of State discretion in pursuing the CBD objectives relating to biodiversity conservation and sustainable use.[26] At the domestic level, in authorizing any activity, either conservation or use, CBD parties are to ensure that no unjustified, foreseeable infringements of human rights may arise from the decision.[27] This is based both on potential public interventions that may infringe biodiversity-dependent human rights and on States' obligation to prevent business entities from violating these rights.[28] In other words, implementing the CBD obligations in a mutually supportive way with international human rights law clarifies that States must develop laws and institutions that effectively 'regulate harm to biodiversity from private actors as well as government entities' in a

---

representatives must be supported by at least one party. Conference of the Parties to the Convention on Biodiversity, *Report of the Seventh Meeting of the Ad Hoc Open-Ended Working Group on Article 8(j) and Related Provisions of the Convention on Biological Diversity* (2011) UN Doc. UNEP/CBD/COP/11/7, para. 20.

[20] Morgera and Tsioumani (n. 1) 3.
[21] Ibid. 23–25.
[22] Report of the UN Special Rapporteur on the Issue of Human Rights Obligations Relating to the Enjoyment of a Safe, Clean, Healthy and Sustainable Environment: Biodiversity, UN Doc. A/HRC/34/49 (19 January 2017). This paragraph builds on E. Morgera, 'Dawn of a New Day? The Evolving Relationship between the Convention on Biological Diversity and International Human Rights Law' (2018) 54 *Wake Forest Law Review* 101.
[23] Knox (n. 22) para. 5.
[24] Ibid. para. 67.
[25] E. Brown Weiss and A. Sornarajah, 'Good Governance' in R. Wolfrum (ed.), *Max Planck Encyclopedia of Public International Law* (Oxford: Oxford University Press, 2012).
[26] Knox (n. 22) para. 34.
[27] Ibid.
[28] Ibid. paras 33–34.

way that is 'non-retrogressive and non-discriminatory'.[29] Furthermore, John Knox confirmed the relevance of certain CBD COP decisions for the second pillar of the UN Framework on Business and Human Rights—business respect of human rights in the context of extractives and conservation,[30] as discussed below.

1.1 The extent to which the CBD has addressed corporate environmental accountability and responsibility

The text of the Convention on Biological Diversity explicitly addresses the private sector with regard to the sustainable use of biodiversity components (Article 10(e)): accordingly, the Convention commits State Parties to encouraging cooperation between government authorities and the private sector in developing methods for the sustainable use of biological resources. Furthermore, the Convention refers to the private sector in relation to access to and transfer of technology[31] and implicitly with regard to incentive measures.[32] Against this background, in 2005, explicit discussions among State Parties began on various tools for facilitating the private sector engagement in biodiversity-related issues.[33] In line with the practice of other international organizations, the CBD Secretariat proposed translating the goals and objectives of the Convention into a set of clear *standards*, as a critical step in facilitating the integration of biodiversity considerations into business policies and practices.[34] Several consultations of the CBD Secretariat with the private sector[35] highlighted that at least certain sectors of the business community felt the need for further guidance on good practice, in particular on how industry should cooperate with indigenous peoples and local communities to apply the principle of prior informed consent.[36] Participating companies further noted the need to compile

---

[29] Ibid. para. 69.

[30] Ibid. paras 33 and 72.

[31] CBD Art. 16(4) reads: 'Each Contracting Party shall take legislative, administrative or policy measures, as appropriate, with the aim that the private sector facilitates access to, joint development and transfer of technology referred to in paragraph 1 above for the benefit of both governmental institutions and the private sector of developing countries and in this regard shall abide by the obligations included in paragraphs 1, 2 and 3 above.'

[32] CBD Art. 11.

[33] This was initially discussed in September 2005 at the first meeting of the Ad Hoc Open-Ended Working Group on Review of Implementation (Montreal, Canada, 5–9 September 2005). Executive Secretary of the CBD, 'Private Sector Engagement in the Implementation of the Convention' (2005) UN Doc. UNEP/CBD/WG-RI/1/8, para. 3

[34] Executive Secretary of the CBD, 'Private Sector Engagement in the Implementation of the Convention' (2005) UN Doc. UNEP/CBD/WG-RI/1/8. Also in other fora, academics and practitioners agreed on the importance of developing standards for facilitating private-sector engagement in biodiversity-related issues. OECD, 'Key Messages' (OECD Workshop on Multilateral Environmental Agreements and the Private Sector, Helsinki, 16–17 June 2005).

[35] CBD, 'Report of the Business and the 2010 Biodiversity Challenge Meeting' (2005) UN Doc. UNEP/CBD/WG-RI/1/INF/5; CBD, 'Report of the Second Business and the 2010 Biodiversity Challenge Meeting' (2005) UN Doc. UNEP/CBD/COP/8/INF/11.

[36] CBD, 'Report of the Second Business and the 2010 Biodiversity Challenge Meeting' (n. 35) 6.

biodiversity standards and criteria (both general and sector-specific) and align them with the CBD goals and objectives, to be integrated in good practice guidance and measures,[37] with a view to setting priorities for biodiversity conservation and management for business.[38] Participating companies further called for guidance on incorporating biodiversity into environmental impact assessments.[39] In response to these calls, the COP adopted in 2006 its first decision on private sector engagement,[40] emphasizing that stakeholder involvement in the implementation of the Convention and achievement of the 2010 target is in addition to the 'primary' responsibility of States.[41] It also highlighted the need to enhance both voluntary and regulatory means for the private sector to support the implementation of the Convention objectives.[42] It thus identified 'internationally agreed *standards* on activities that impact biodiversity' as one of the mechanisms to facilitate the private sector's contribution to the Convention implementation and achievement of the 2010 target.[43] Successive decisions on the private sector have not, however, in and of themselves, advanced standard-setting on corporate accountability. But they have eventually led to the establishment of a Global Partnership for Business and Biodiversity,[44] which is a network to enhance the understanding of the role of business in the realization of the CBD objectives. In addition, more recent decisions on biodiversity mainstreaming have continued consideration of the need for international standards for the business sector, making reference to the UN Global Compact and addressing specific sectors, such as agriculture, forestry, fisheries, tourism, infrastructure, energy, mining, manufacturing, and processing sectors.[45] The biodiversity mainstreaming agenda has led to the establishment of an Informal

---

[37] Ibid. 11 and 17–18.
[38] Ibid. 7.
[39] On the basis of the CBD, Voluntary Guidelines on Biodiversity-inclusive Environmental Impact Assessment' (2006) CBD Dec VIII/28 (Annex), that are targeted to governments.
[40] CBD, COP Decision VIII/11 'Private Sector Engagement' (2006). Many decisions adopted at the 8th meeting of the Conference of the Parties, in addition to Decision VIII/17, also explicitly referred to business. In Decisions 1, 3, 4, 5, 6, 8, 10, 11, 12, 20, 25, and 27 adopted at the 8th meeting of the Conference of the Parties, reference is made to 'business', 'business/private sector groups', 'business sector', 'developers', 'economic activities', 'industry', 'key economic sectors', 'operators', 'private decisions', 'private entities', 'private sector', 'private sector agencies'. A number of economic sectors are also referred to, including agriculture (Decisions VIII/1, VIII/6, VIII/8, VIII/9), animal breeding industry (VIII/27), energy (VIII/9), fisheries (VIII/1, VIII/6, VIII/8, VIII/9), forestry (VIII/1, VIII/6, VIII/8, VIII/9), financial institutions (VIII/1, VIII/5, VIII/8, VIII/9), infrastructure development (VIII/1), mining (VIII/1, VIII/8, VIII/9), shipment organizations (VIII/27), and tourism (VIII/1, VIII/8, VIII/9). The decisions cover, inter alia, business engagement and partnerships; the development and promotion of best practices; resource mobilization; incentives, market creation, and certification; awareness raising; and business participation in Convention processes (as reported in CBD, 'Note on Cooperation with the other Conventions, International Organizations and Initiatives and Engagement of Stakeholders, Addendum: Engagement of Business' (2008) UN Doc. UNEP/CBD/COP/9/21/Add.1).
[41] CBD, COP Decision VIII/11, preambular para. 2.
[42] Ibid., preambular para. 3. For a discussion on standards and international environmental law, see Ch. 3, Section 1.
[43] CBD, COP Decision VIII/11, preambular para. 9(d) (emphasis added).
[44] CBD COP Decision XII/10 (2014).
[45] CBD, COP Decision XIII/3 (2016) and CBD Art. 6(b).

Advisory Group on Mainstreaming of Biodiversity to support the development of a long-term approach to this area of work,[46] but it is too early to say whether this new body will engage in standard-setting.

Up to now, therefore, the development of standards under the explicit label of engagement with the private sector under the CBD has been limited. But, as opposed to elaborating standards that are solely addressed to private companies, the most promising approach under the Convention has instead been developing guidelines that are addressed to a variety of actors (governments, but also private developers, development funders, etc), which have the potential to act as international standards for corporate environmental accountability and responsibility.[47] While these guidelines shy away from clearly drawing a line between State obligations and business responsibility, they have provided more detailed approaches upon which private companies can draw, than those discussed in the previous chapter. These guidelines have received the endorsement of the CBD's virtually universal membership.

This chapter will argue that there are several other CBD COP decisions and guidelines that are relevant to better understand international standards on corporate environmental accountability and responsibility, beyond those already identified by international human rights bodies, such as: the CBD Akwé: Kon Guidelines on socio-cultural and environmental impact assessments for developments in sacred sites and on lands and waters traditionally occupied or used by indigenous peoples and local communities;[48] the Addis Ababa Principles and Guidelines for the Sustainable Use of Biodiversity;[49] the International Guidelines on Biodiversity and Tourism Development;[50] the Tkarihwaié:ri Code of Ethical Conduct to Ensure Respect for the Cultural and Intellectual Heritage of Indigenous and Local Communities;[51] and the Mo'otz kuxta Voluntary Guidelines on consent and benefit-sharing from the use of traditional knowledge of indigenous peoples and local communities.[52]

---

[46] CBD, COP Decision XIV/3 (2018), para. 18.
[47] CBD, 'Report of the Business and the 2010 Biodiversity Challenge Meeting' (n. 29).
[48] CBD Decision VII/16F, 'Akwé: Kon Voluntary Guidelines for the Conduct of Cultural, Environmental and Social Impact Assessment regarding Developments Proposed to Take Place on, or which are Likely to Impact on, Sacred Sites and on Lands and Waters Traditionally Occupied or Used by Indigenous and Local Communities, in Article 8(j) and related provisions' (2004).
[49] CBD Decision VII/12 (2004), Annex II.
[50] CBD Decision V/25 (2000).
[51] CBD, Tkarihwaié:ri Code of Ethical Conduct to Ensure Respect for the Cultural and Intellectual Heritage of Indigenous and Local Communities, CBD Decision X/42 (2010).
[52] The Mo'otz Kuxtal Voluntary Guidelines for the development of mechanisms, legislation or other appropriate initiatives to ensure the 'prior and informed consent', 'free, prior and informed consent', or 'approval and involvement', depending on national circumstances, of indigenous peoples and local communities for accessing their knowledge, innovations, and practices, for fair and equitable sharing of benefits arising from the use of their knowledge, innovations, and practices relevant for the conservation and sustainable use of biological diversity, and for reporting and preventing unlawful appropriation of traditional knowledge, CBD Dec. XIII/18 (2016).

2 International standards on corporate environmental accountability

The following sections will provide an in-depth assessment of the degree of normative convergence of international standards on corporate accountability at the intersection of international environmental law and human rights, relying on CBD decisions. Standards based on international environmental law principles will be examined: their translation into procedural standards of corporate environmental accountability will be discussed, drawing the necessary distinctions between what is requested internationally from States and what are the emerging normative benchmarks for private companies. The extent to which these international standards on corporate accountability have also been developed into substantive standards of corporate environmental responsibility will be interrogated.

2.1 Environmental integration

The principle of environmental integration is one of the building blocks of the international efforts for the protection of the environment and is considered an essential element of sustainable development.[53] It implies that countries and international organizations commit to integrate environmental considerations into economic development or sectoral policies. The principle of environmental integration, although initially conceived with regard to national development planning,[54] has served as a strong basis for the concept of corporate environmental accountability. It has been translated into the general expectation that business enterprises take into account environmental concerns within their corporate decision-making process. As such, it provides a precondition for other corporate environmental accountability standards, such as prevention and precaution, and is contingent upon the standards related to environmental information, consultation, and grievance mechanisms.

This standard implies the explicit consideration of environmental impacts of corporate activities at the boardroom level, so that any negative impact would be identified, rectified, and prevented from occurring.[55] While private companies are bound by national environmental laws to this effect in the case of major developments, in light of this international standard they are also reasonably expected

---

[53] P. Sands and J. Peel, with A. Fabra and R. MacKenzie, *Principles of International Environmental Law*, 4th edn (Cambridge: Cambridge University Press, 2018) 215–17; and V. Barral, 'The Principle of Sustainable Development' in L. Krämer and E. Orlando (eds), *Principles of Environmental Law* (Cheltenham: Edward Elgar, 2018) 103, 108 and 111.
[54] Rio Declaration, Principle 4.
[55] D. Ong, 'The Impact of Environmental Law on Corporate Governance: International and Comparative Perspectives' (2001) 12 *European Journal of International Law* 685, 695.

to go beyond the specific implementation and enforcement capacity in a State to integrate environmental concerns in all their operations on an ongoing basis. Assessing in practice whether a company has fully or properly taken into account environmental considerations in its operations may be difficult, although egregious disregard of serious environmental consequences could be more easily identified on a case-by-case basis. The two main standards that translate environmental integration for companies are impact assessment and environmental management systems.

The IFC Performance Standard explains at the outset how assessment of environmental impacts, and the adoption of an environmental management system provide 'the umbrella policy' for managing all other performance standards—in other words, the central planning tool that acts as the backbone for the implementation of more specific standards.[56] This is based on earlier experience in IFC-funded projects where a weak environmental impact assessment (either compiled after the beginning of the project, or not broad enough in scope, or carried out by a client lacking sufficient capacity) had undermined the effectiveness and impact of all performance standards.[57] In effect, the 2006 version of the Performance Standard already stressed the relevance of impact assessments and environmental management systems also for the purposes of community engagement, disclosure of information, and prevention (discussed below). This supports the idea that companies should take a proactive approach in continuously searching for opportunities to add environmental value to their investment.[58] The following sub-sections will discuss environmental impact assessments and environmental management in turn.

2.1.1 (Self-)assessment of environmental impacts

Environmental impact assessments (EIAs), which were already in use in the 1970s, are now a well-established international and domestic legal technique for States to integrate environmental concerns into socio-economic development and decision-making.[59] Internationally, EIAs are considered to include, at a minimum: scientific evidence, effective consideration of possible impacts on the environment, and communication to authorities of the findings.[60] So they entail the identification, assessment and evaluation of potential adverse impacts in a 'scientifically rigorous, transparent and participatory' manner, [61] with the last requirement entailing 'a

---

[56] The Compliance Advisor/Ombudsman (CAO) of the IFC, *A Review of IFC's Safeguard Policies* (January 2003) 7 and 9.
[57] Ibid. 30.
[58] M. Warner, *The New International Benchmark Standards for Environmental and Social Performance of the Private Sector in Developing Countries: Will it Raise or Lower the Bar?* (London: Overseas Development Institute, 2006) 2.
[59] Sands et al (n. 53) 601–22; and A. Kiss and D. Shelton, *International Environmental Law*, 3rd edn (New York: Transnational Publishers, 2004) 236–44.
[60] P-M. Dupuy, *Droit International Public* (Paris: Dalloz, 2004) 109.
[61] N. Craik, 'Environmental Impact Assessment' in Krämer and Orlando (n 53) 195.

dialogue or, at a minimum, ... a response that demonstrates some account of the views expressed'.[62] The International Court of Justice (ICJ) considered EIAs of potential transboundary impacts a customary rule of international law, and left the determination of its precise requirements to the State's discretion.[63] It has been argued that at least two additional components of impact assessments are required by general international law—cumulative impact assessments and post-project monitoring.[64] Furthermore, international human rights processes have been quite consistent in establishing that prior, comprehensive environmental and sociocultural impact assessments be carried out as a safeguard for indigenous and tribal peoples' rights over their natural resources (discussed below).[65]

Most national laws around the world require EIAs, although they are usually confined to major developments that are likely to have significant negative impacts on the environment. Thus national legislation typically sets thresholds below which an EIA is not required, as international law requires States to put in place a 'reasoned process for the determination of the significance [of potential harm] that accounts for the contextual nature of the determination'.[66] That said, significance vis-à-vis biodiversity and climate change is difficult to determine because of the cumulative and highly diffuse nature of the sources of impacts.[67] While the precise contents of EIAs are determined in national legislation, not all exemptions and exclusions in national law would serve to relieve the State of its international obligations.[68]

In most national laws, the responsibility to carry out the EIA is placed on private developers.[69] In contrast to national laws, the international standard of corporate environmental accountability on impact assessment is not triggered by a particular threshold of risk, so companies are expected as a matter of practice to assess environmental impacts in all their activities on an ongoing basis. The standard can therefore refer to additional impact assessments than those required by national legislation (self-assessments), but it can also emphasize higher expectations on how business entities carry out assessments required by national legislation. The

---

[62] Ibid. 205.
[63] ICJ, *Pulp Mills on the River Uruguay (Argentina v Uruguay)*, Judgment (20 April 2010) para. 205.
[64] N. Craik, 'Principle 17: Environmental Impact Assessment' in J. Viñuales (ed.), *The Rio Declaration on Environment and Development: A Commentary* (Oxford: Oxford University Press, 2015) 451.
[65] See Ch. 5, Section 1.1.
[66] Craik (n. 61) 199–200, on the basis of ICJ, *Construction of a Road Case (Nicaragua v Costa Rica)* (merit) Judgment (16 December 2015) para. 154.
[67] Craik (n. 61) 205. Notably CBD State Parties adopted specific guidelines to ensure systematic integration of biodiversity concerns in EIAs, including in consideration of the specific challenges raised by marine biodiversity: CBD COP Decision VIII/28 (2008) Voluntary Guidelines on Biodiversity-inclusive Impact Assessments and Decision XI/18 B (2012), Voluntary Guidelines for the Consideration of Biodiversity in Environmental Impact Assessments and Strategic Environmental Assessments in Marine and Coastal Areas (contained in (2012) UN Doc. UNEP/CBD/COP/11/23).
[68] Craik (n. 61) 202, based on ICJ, *Construction of a Road Case* (n. 66) para. 157 and Separate Reasons of Judge Donoghue, para. 15.
[69] UNEP, *Assessing Environmental Impacts—A Global Review of Legislation* (Nairobi: UN, 2018).

standard entails that the private sector assesses, on a periodic basis, the possible impacts on the environment of all its activities, on the basis of scientific evidence and communication with likely affected communities. It further requires companies to take such an assessment into account in deciding whether to carry out, or continue to carry out, such activities or not, and if so with which cautions. A self-assessment of environmental impacts, leading to the adoption of an environmental management system is called for by the UN Norms on the Responsibility of Transnational Corporations, the OECD Guidelines, and the IFC Performance Standards.[70] The UN Global Compact refers to such an assessment of environmental risks and impacts in the context of the precautionary principle. The assessment of impacts was also a key tool singled out by the UN Special Representative on Business and Human Rights, which is broadly in line with the human rights-based approach found in the UN Norms.[71] Accordingly, business enterprises are to assess the environmental impacts of their activities on a periodic basis, in order to ensure that the burden of the negative environmental consequences does not fall on vulnerable racial, ethnic, and socio-economic groups.[72]

The OECD Guidelines define a 'life-cycle assessment' as a tool for systematic evaluation of the environmental aspects of a product or service through all stages of its life-cycle—that is, when the raw material is extracted, manufactured, transported, used, recycled, and disposed of.[73] This is reinforced in the OECD-FAO Guidance for Responsible Agricultural Supply Chains,[74] which contain an EIA requirement for continuously assessing and addressing in decision-making the actual and potential impacts of companies' operations, processes, goods and services over their full life-cycle with a view to avoiding or, when unavoidable, mitigating any adverse impacts. Life-cycle approaches are considered to reflect an emerging international principle on sustainable production and consumption, which provides 'a normative orientation for the strategy decisions of private companies and their business models'.[75] It is considered one of the ways to implement sustainable use (discussed below) by identifying and balancing conflicting targets at the operational level.[76] It calls for the assessment of environmental impacts 'from raw materials over the production process until final disposal', with particular emphasis

---

[70] Ch, 3, Sections 2.1, 5.2, and 6.2.
[71] Ch. 3, Section 4.2.3.
[72] D. Weissbrodt and M. Kruger, 'Human Rights Responsibilities of Business as Non-State Actors' in P. Alston (ed.), *Non-State Actors and Human Rights* (Oxford: Oxford University Press, 2005) 315, 343.
[73] OECD, *Guidelines on Multinational Enterprises* (2011), VI.3.
[74] OECD-FAO, Guidance for Responsible Agricultural Supply Chains (Paris: OECD, 2015). For a commentary, M. Brunori, 'Recomposing the mosaic of responsible business conduct along the agricultural supply chain: the FAO-OECD Guidance' BENELEX Blog post (March 2016), https://benelexblog.wordpress.com/2016/03/16/recomposing-the-mosaic-of-responsible-business-conduct-along-the-agricultural-supply-chain-the-fao-oecd-guidance/, last visited 19 November 2019.
[75] M. Führ and J. Schenten, 'Sustainable Production and Consumption' in Krämer and Orlando (n. 53) 125, 126.
[76] Ibid. 128.

on hazardous and toxic materials and waste management at the consumer's end.[77] Life-cycle approaches are considered conducive to learning systems, with permanent feedback and evaluation loops to draw on the 'full potential for (disruptive) innovation'.[78]

The IFC 2012 Performance Standards, in turn, call for a case-by-case determination of the scope of the risks and impacts that is consistent with 'good international industry practice', calling for 'full-scale' assessments, 'limited or focused' assessments or 'straightforward application of environmental siting, pollution standards, design criteria, or construction standards'.[79] Previously the IFC had required the consideration of multilateral environmental treaties in project environmental analyses 'where relevant and feasible, with a view to minimizing possible adverse impacts on global environmental quality'.[80] The 2012 version instead refers more restrictively to 'laws implementing host country obligations under international law' and 'under some circumstances, clients may also subscribe to other international recognized standards' as part of the development of an overarching policy defining the environmental and social objectives and principles guiding the project.[81] What this language implies is that the IFC's more explicit reliance on multilateral environmental treaties has come at the cost of excluding the relevance of environmental treaties that are not joined only by the home country, or that address other standards that have not been specifically translated into the IFC Standards themselves.

2.1.1.1 Cumulative impacts

As mentioned above, a key element of international EIA obligations is the assessment of cumulative impacts, which encompass 'the incremental impact of an activity in the light of past, present and reasonably foreseeable future actions'.[82] This is not systematically reflected in the international standards on corporate environmental accountability. For instance, the OECD Guidelines have been criticized for not including a specific requirement to consider cumulative environmental impacts.[83] This had also been the case for the IFC in its 1998 EIA Safeguard Policy,[84]

---

[77] Ibid. 131.
[78] Ibid. 135 and 131.
[79] IFC 2012 Performance Standard 1, para. 7.
[80] IFC, 'Guidance Note: Checklist of Potential Issues for an Environmental Assessment' (December 1998) 42.
[81] IFC 2012 Performance Standard 1, para. 6.
[82] Craik (n. 61) 202.
[83] OECDWatch statement on the update of the OECD Guidelines for Multinational Enterprises: Improved content and scope, but procedural shortcomings remain (25 May 2011); and Amnesty International, 'The 2010–11 Update of the OECD Guidelines for Multinational Enterprises has come to an end: the OECD must now turn into effective implementation' (23 May 2011).
[84] IFC, Environmental Impact Assessment Safeguard Policy (OP 4.01) (October 1998) <http://www.ifc.org/ifcext/enviro.nsf/Content/Safeguardpolicies>.

which lacked reference to assessing cumulative effects[85] and integration with social impacts.[86] As a response, already in 2006, the IFC had indicated the EIA standard extends to cumulative impacts and possible global impacts through consideration of applicable multilateral environmental agreements, in particular the CBD.[87] To that end, the 2006 Standards had introduced the concept of the project's 'area of influence'.[88] This encompassed not only the primary project site, related facilities controlled or developed by the client, and associated facilities, but also areas potentially impacted by cumulative impacts from further planned development related to the project, or even areas potentially affected by impacts from unplanned but predictable developments caused by the project that may occur later or in a different location.[89] The client was also expected to address risks and impacts deriving from third parties, in a manner proportionate to the client's control and influence over the third party.[90] This at least partially answered the WWF's proposal to require clients to exercise leadership in their sphere of influence, to require environmental management from their suppliers, and to exercise due diligence to ensure that inputs purchased or received from third parties do not violate their own environmental policies.[91] This requirement was clarified in 2012, with specific reference to the purchase of primary production of food, fibre, and other commodities from regions where there is a known risk of significant conversion of natural and/or critical habitats.[92] In these instances, the company is expected to adopt a system of evaluation of suppliers and ongoing verification practices, including 'where possible, require[ing] actions to shift the client's primary supply chain over time to suppliers that can demonstrate that they are not significantly adversely impacting these areas'.[93] In addition, under the 2012 Performance Standard the project's area of influence also includes indirect impacts on biodiversity or ecosystem services upon which affected communities' livelihoods are dependent,[94] which is linked to the expansion of the community consultation requirements discussed below.[95] The

---

[85] Whose importance is underlined by Principle 5 of the CBD Addis Ababa Principles and Guidelines (n. 49).
[86] CAO (n. 56) 30. This is also supported by the CBD Voluntary Guidelines on Biodiversity-Inclusive Environmental Impact Assessment, CBD COP Decision VIII/28 (2008) 10.
[87] IFC, 'Performance Standards on Social and Environmental Sustainability' (30 April 2006) <http://www.ifc.org/sustainability> (IFC Performance Standards): Performance Standard 1, para. 5; and Performance Standard 6, para. 4.
[88] IFC, 'Policy and Performance Standards on Social and Environmental Sustainability and Policy on Disclosure of Information: IFC Responses to Stakeholder Comments and Rationale for Key Policy Changes' (22 September 2006) 10.
[89] 2006 Performance Standard 1, para. 5; 2012 Performance Standard 1, para. 9.
[90] 2006 Performance Standard 1, para. 6; 2012 Performance Standard 1, para. 8.
[91] WWF (A. Durbin, S. Herz, D. Hunter, and J. Peck), *Shaping the Future of Sustainable Finance: Moving from Paper Promises to Performance* (January 2006) 68.
[92] IFC 2012 Performance Standard 1, para. 10 and Performance Standard 6, para. 30.
[93] IFC 2012 Performance Standard 6, para. 30.
[94] IFC 2012 Performance Standard 1, para. 8.
[95] IFC 2012 Performance Standard 1, para. 8, fn. 16, which refers to 'cumulative impacts generally recognised as important on the basis of scientific concerns and/or concerns of affected communities'.

2012 version further refers to 'cumulative, regional, sectoral or strategic environmental assessments where relevant',[96] which could be related to concerns raised under the CBD, such as target species and ecosystems,[97] areas that are adjacent to touristic spots or ecosystems of importance for tourism,[98] or to indigenous peoples' land claims, or long-term implications of resource development on community interests.[99]

2.1.1.2 Outcomes

The principal outcome of the (self-)assessment of environmental impacts is the production of information that will be used by the company itself for its environmental management purposes (as discussed below). According to scholars, an international requirement for (self-)assessment of environmental impacts can compel private companies' management to pay greater attention to environmental performance and contribute to the transfer of valuable information on environmental control technology and costs.[100] There is, however, also the expectation that the information should be shared outside the company. Very early concerns were voiced at the UN, and encapsulated in the draft UN Code of Conduct that transnational companies cooperate not only with national governments, but also with international organizations, for the protection of the environment.[101] According to the UN Norms, the reports of (self-)assessments are expected to be circulated in a timely and accessible manner to the UN Environment Programme, the International Labour Organization, and other international bodies, to the national governments of the host and home countries, and to other affected groups. In addition, the Norms suggested that these reports be accessible to the general public.[102]

Besides the procedural dimension related to the production and sharing of environmental information (further discussed below as a self-standing standard of corporate environmental accountability), the most complex question regarding the (self-)assessment of environmental impacts is whether a specific substantive approach should arise from this exercise, and whether a profound re-thinking of proposed activities should be also engendered. In inter-State relations, an identification of alternative can be considered 'desirable, but not a necessary required element', although alternatives 'play a critical role in providing a basis by

---

[96] IFC 2012 Performance Standard 1, para. 11.
[97] CBD Addis Ababa Principles and Guidelines (n 49), Principle 5, Operational Guidelines. See Ch. 5, Section 3.
[98] CBD Biodiversity and Tourism Guidelines (n 50), para. 44.
[99] E. Morgera, 'Under the Radar: Fair and Equitable Benefit-sharing and the Human Rights of Indigenous Peoples and Local Communities connected to Natural Resources' (2019) 23 *International Journal of Human Rights* 1098, 1112. See Ch. 5, Section 1.
[100] C. Pearson, 'Environmental Standards, Industrial Relocation and Pollution Havens' in C. Pearson (ed.), *Multinational Corporations, Environment, and the Third World* (Durham: Duke University Press, 1987) 113, 128. On the standard on information disclosure, see Section 2.4 below.
[101] UN Code of Conduct, para. 43.
[102] Commentary to the UN Norms, (b) and (c).

which to assess proposed activities'.[103] The IFC, however, does not require that among possible alternatives a no-project scenario is taken into account.[104] The CBD Akwé: Kon Guidelines, on the other hand, specifically call on development proponents to include in their impact assessments options for no-action alternatives.[105] The analysis of alternatives in environmental assessments has been considered essential to demonstrate good faith at the interim stages, not just at the stage of the final decision, as well as the meaningful character of consultations in the absence of clear quantitative standards to assess the acceptability of impacts.[106] This is particularly the case when indigenous peoples' human rights may be at stake and the developer may not be able to show that mitigation measures correspond to the preferred alternatives put forward by indigenous peoples or local communities.[107]

2.1.1.3 Links with consultation

Business and human rights scholars have raised concerns about limiting human rights impact assessments only to high-risk circumstances and the lack of guidance on how to integrate human rights into impact assessments.[108] The OECD Due Diligence Guidance for Responsible Supply Chains of Minerals from Conflict-Affected and High-Risk Areas[109] suggest involving on-the-ground personnel and stakeholders in conducting transparent social, environmental, and human rights impact assessments,[110] with preliminary field research related to the environment through interviews with relevant individuals working for the enterprise or with other enterprises operating in the region.[111] Document-based understanding of context includes environmental baselines/impact assessments, which can provide information on air and water quality, water availability and sources, soil conditions, climate, rainfall, and status of flora and fauna.[112] The IFC Standard further specifies that the assessment should take into account the differing values of biodiversity for affected communities, and consider threats ranging from 'habitat loss, degradation

---

[103] Craik (n. 61) 201.

[104] IFC Responses to Stakeholders (n. 88) 11, where the IFC argues that in the case of private sector projects, 'it would be more productive for the assessment to consider how the project should be implemented to avoid or minimize impacts, rather than whether the project should happen at all ... [whereas] it is for IFC to decide whether to finance a project or not, based on the client's assessment of risks and impacts.'

[105] CBD Akwé: Kon Guidelines (n 48), para. 21.

[106] N. Craik, H. Gardner, and D. McCarthy, 'Indigenous—Corporate Private Governance and Legitimacy: Lessons Learned from Impact and Benefit Agreements' (2017) 52 *Resources Policy* 379.

[107] Ibid. See Ch. 5, Section 1.1.

[108] P. Simons and A. Macklin, *The Governance Gap: Extractive Industries, Human Rights and the Home State Advantage* (Abingdon, Routledge: 2014) 133–34.

[109] OECD Due Diligence Guidance for Responsible Supply Chains of Minerals from Conflict-Affected and High-Risk Areas (Paris: OECD, 2013).

[110] Ibid. 30.

[111] Ibid. 36.

[112] Ibid. 37, table 1.

and fragmentation, invasive alien species, overexploitation, hydrological change, nutrient loading and pollution'.[113]

The CBD Guidelines on Biodiversity and Tourism Development provide another useful reference linking (self-)assessment of environmental impacts with consultation processes. They call on those promoting tourism developments to undertake the following steps: identify the various stakeholders (which should be read as 'right-holders' in light of the UN Framework on Business and Human Rights) involved in or potentially affected by the proposed project,[114] assess the potential impacts of the proposals, provide information on these potential impacts through a notification process,[115] undertaking and funding necessary studies,[116] and involve indigenous peoples and local communities in the assessment.[117]

As these standards reflect the fact that participation of potentially affected stakeholders is a widely accepted and essential element of environmental assessment,[118] they face similar challenges in their implementation. Notably, the general effectiveness of environmental assessments 'as procedural measures generating environmentally sound and just outcomes in socio-ecological systems characterized by uncertainty and normative disagreement' remains 'an open question, notwithstanding over forty years of practice across the globe'.[119]

2.1.2 Environmental management system

(Self-)assessment of environmental impacts are a precondition for companies to elaborate an environmental management system. These serve to ensure that the outcome of (self-)assessments is followed by the identification of practical implications for corporate management. Environmental management systems may serve to control both direct and indirect environmental impacts of enterprise activities over the long term, and address pollution control and resource management.[120]

The OECD Guidelines elaborate on environmental management systems and contingency plans as the internal framework necessary to control a company's environmental impacts and integrate environmental considerations into business operations.[121] In addition to contributing to the realization of corporate

---

[113] IFC 2012 Performance Standard 6, paras 6–7, in response to IFC CAO (n 56) 31 and WWF (n. 91) 41. See Ch. 5, Section 3.
[114] CBD, Guidelines on Biodiversity and Tourism (n 50), para. 20(a)ii.
[115] Ibid. para. 36.
[116] Ibid. para. 38.
[117] Ibid. para. 39.
[118] Rio Declaration, Principles 10 and 22; International Law Commission, 'Draft Articles on Prevention of Transboundary Harm from Hazardous Activities' (2001) UN Doc. A/56/10, art. 13; Independent Expert on Environment and Human Rights, John Knox, Mapping Report on the Issue of Human Rights Obligations Relating to the Enjoyment of a Safe, Clean, Healthy and Sustainable Environment, (2013) UN Doc. A/HRC/25/53, para. 78; *generally* Craik (n. 52) and J. Holder, *Environmental Assessment: The Regulation of Decision-Making* (Oxford: Oxford University Press, 2004) ch. 6.
[119] Craik (n. 64) 443.
[120] OECD Guidelines, Commentary, 30.
[121] Ibid. 29.

environmental accountability standards based on prevention and precaution (discussed below), environmental management systems allow companies to engage in a process of continual improvement of their environmental performance,[122] essentially though the collection and evaluation of information and monitoring of measurable environmental objectives and targets, without setting absolute performance standards.[123] This aims at allowing companies to tackle 'both a business responsibility and a business opportunity' through a systematic approach to continual improvement.[124]

The IFC also considers environmental management systems as the basis for both mitigation and proactive performance enhancement by companies, by defining measurable outcomes and estimating resources, allocating responsibility for implementation and being responsive to changes in project circumstances.[125] These systems also provide a practical way for companies to assess whether they are employing the 'best practical means' or 'best available technology' with regard to their environmental performance. A standard for private companies' best practices can be considered part and parcel of the broader idea of environmental management systems.[126]

Another important feature of environmental management systems is its support for disclosure of information and community engagement.[127] The IFC has detailed these through the requirement for private companies to establish, as part of the environmental management system, mechanisms for external reporting on implementation,[128] ongoing consultation with potentially affected communities,[129] and a grievance mechanism.[130] These requirements were meant to respond to civil society's calls for enhancing transparency, compliance, and accountability in environmental management systems.[131]

2.1.2.1 Substantive dimensions

Environmental management system have been further detailed in specific sectors, blurring the lines between procedural and substantive standards. This has

---

[122] OECD, 'Roundtable on Corporate Responsibility: Encouraging the positive contribution of business to environment through the OECD Guidelines for Multinational Enterprises: Summary of the Roundtable Discussion' (16 June 2004) <http://www.oecd.org/document/1/0,2340,en_2649_34889_31711425_1_1_1_1,00.html> 4.
[123] UNCTAD, *Environment* (Geneva: UN, 2001) 56.
[124] OECD Guidelines, para. 61.
[125] IFC 2006 Performance Standard 1, paras 13–15; 2012 Performance Standard 1, paras 13–16.
[126] Ong (n. 55) 693–98; J. Ebbesson, 'Transboundary Corporate Responsibility in Environmental Matters: Fragments and Foundations for a Future Framework' in G. Winter (ed.), *Multilevel Governance of Global Environmental Change: Perspectives from Science, Sociology and the Law* (Cambridge: Cambridge University Press, 2006) 200, 219; and Commentary to UN Norms, Section (g).
[127] Discussed at Sections 2.4–2.5.
[128] IFC 2006 Performance Standard 1, para. 16.
[129] IFC 2006 Performance Standard 1, para. 19.
[130] IFC 2006 Performance Standard 1, paras 16 and 23.
[131] WWF (n. 91) 7.

been particularly the case with regard to freshwater and climate change, under the Global Compact and the IFC Performance Standards.

With regard to water management, the Global Compact 'CEO Water Mandate'[132] calls upon companies to collect data on internal water performance and the condition of the basins in which the company operates. Data generated is used to identify water-related business risks and opportunities and negative impacts; and define and refine corporate water policy, strategies, and performance targets that drive performance improvements and address risks and negative impacts; implement water strategies and policies throughout the company and across the company's value chain. The policies and targets are in turn used to monitor progress and changes in performance and basin conditions; communicate progress and strategies externally; and engage with stakeholders in the company's continuous improvement by means of corporate water disclosure. While these specific steps are procedural, the Global Compact has also provided substantive guidance to integrate water sustainable use concerns in light of relevant international human rights law.[133]

Similarly, the Global Compact 'Caring for Climate' initiative contains a commitment for companies to improve continuously energy efficiency and reduce their carbon footprint of products, services, and processes; set voluntary targets for doing so; and report publicly and annually on the achievement of those targets. This is accompanied by building significant capacity within their organizations to understand fully the implications of climate change for business and to develop a coherent business strategy for minimizing risks and identifying opportunities.[134] In addition, the initiative refers to responsible engagement in the development of policies and measures for a low-carbon and climate-resilient economy. The initiative also foresees that companies will work with other enterprises and along value chains to set standards to reduce climate risks and assist with adaptation to climate change,[135] thereby pointing at opportunities for self-regulation and contributions to State regulation. As part of the general requirement for environmental management systems, IFC Performance Standard 3 also focuses on climate change, expressing the expectation that companies will consider alternatives to reduce their greenhouse gas (GHG) emissions during project design and operation, including renewables or low-carbon energy sources, sustainable land use practices, and reduction of gas flaring.[136]

---

[132] http://ceowatermandate.org/
[133] *The Human Right to Water: Emerging Corporate Practice and Stakeholder Expectations* (United Nation Global Compact Office, 2010).
[134] 2013 The Guide for Responsible Corporate Engagement in Climate Policy.
[135] https://www.unglobalcompact.org/docs/news_events/8.1/caring_for_climate.pdf; https://www.unglobalcompact.org/take-action/action/climate
[136] IFC 2012 Performance Standard 3, para. 7.

2.2 Prevention

The prevention principle calls for States' due diligence to avoid conduct that is harmful to the environment,[137] by reducing, limiting, or controlling activities that may cause or constitute a risk of environmental damage.[138] According to the Rio Declaration, this implies States' obligation to prevent damage to the environment within their own jurisdiction, by means of appropriate regulatory, administrative, and other measures.[139] It can also mean that action should be taken at an early stage and before the damage has occurred, by prohibiting activities that cause or may cause damage to the environment in violation of standards established under international law.[140] Prevention encompasses both proactive and anticipatory approaches, including the positive obligation of risk anticipation to protect the environment as a whole and harm mitigation, although the latter should not be used as an 'excuse to deliberately act on environmental harm in a belated manner'.[141] Among States, relevant obligations are triggered by foreseen harm of a certain magnitude and of an imminent or urgent nature: generally 'significant harm' that does not equate necessarily to 'serious' or 'substantial' and that needs to be determined on a case-by-case basis through an integrated evaluation of risks in light of the ecosystem approach.[142] Prevention thus calls for a 'degree of care [that] should be appropriate and proportional to the level of risk that the harm represents', which may increase over time as science and technology advance[143] (with the ecosystem approach providing for an integrated and adaptive process to that end).[144] With regard to its territorial scope, States are called upon to prevent environmental damage of a transboundary nature, in areas beyond national jurisdiction, as well as in the domestic context if international human rights law may be violated as a result of the environmental harm.[145]

As one of the *raisons d'être* of international environmental law, prevention is also a fundamental component of international standards on corporate environmental accountability. It chimes with the idea of 'no harm' under the IFC and the second pillar of the UN Framework on Business and Human Rights.[146] Applied

---

[137] Dupuy (n. 60) 105; and Kiss and Shelton (n. 59).
[138] Sands et al (n 53) 200–03.
[139] Rio Declaration, Principle 11.
[140] Sands et al (n 53) 200–03. 'Declaration of the United Nations Conference on the Human Environment' (16 June 1972) UN Doc. A/CONF.48/14/Rev.1 (Stockholm Declaration), Principles 6, 7, 15, 18, and 24.
[141] L. A. Duvic-Paoli, 'Principle of Prevention' in Krämer and Orlando (n. 53) 161, 161 and 167.
[142] Ibid. 165–66.
[143] Ibid. 167–68.
[144] E. Morgera, 'The Ecosystem Approach and the Precautionary Principle' in E. Morgera and J. Razzaque (eds), *Encyclopedia of Environmental Law: Biodiversity and Nature Protection Law* (Cheltenham: Edward Elgar, 2017) 70.
[145] Duvic-Paoli (n. 141) 169–70.
[146] Ch. 3, Sections 4.2.1 and 6.2.

to the private sector, a standard based on prevention complements the need for private companies to take into account the possible environmental impacts of the companies' activities on the environment. It expects private companies to take active steps, including the suspension of certain activities, when this is necessary to prevent otherwise certain or likely damage to internationally protected environmental resources.[147] Wherever avoidance of environmental damage is not possible, damage control and minimization should be undertaken by the company to limit adverse impacts on the environment.

The practical translation of the prevention principle into a corporate accountability standard operated by the OECD Guidelines implies that companies should put in place contingency plans for preventing, mitigating, and controlling serious environmental and health damage from their operations, including accidents and emergencies, as well as mechanisms for immediate reporting to competent authorities.[148] Again, the idea behind this provision is that of a cycle for emergency management, in which multinationals should evaluate the likelihood that an accident will occur, be prepared through emergency planning, land-use planning, and risk communication, and limit the adverse consequences to human health, the environment, and private property in the event of an accident.[149] In this respect, the OECD has further elaborated on this tool by adopting the Guiding Principles for Chemical Accident, Prevention, Preparedness and Response,[150] which assign primary responsibility for the safety of installations handling chemicals and hazardous substances to owners and operators.[151]

The IFC 2012 Standard, in turn, refers to a mitigation hierarchy, whereby companies are to anticipate and avoid, or, where this is not possible, minimize and compensate or offset residual impacts to the environment, as well as workers and affected communities.[152] This is also seen as necessary for businesses to avoid infringing human rights and to address adverse human rights impacts that they may cause or contribute to.[153] The 2012 version includes the idea of the mitigation hierarchy in environmental management systems, as far as 'technically and financially feasible' so as to take into account commercial availability and other commercial considerations such as incremental and maintenance costs.[154] The IFC Standards thus set certain limits to this general approach, by qualifying it with reference to technical and financial feasibility and cost-effectiveness in the context of

---

[147] Ong (n. 55) 105.
[148] OECD Guidelines, Ch. V, para. 5.
[149] OECD, Roundtable on Corporate Responsibility: Encouraging the Positive Contribution of Business to Environment through the OECD Guidelines for Multinational Enterprises. Background Report (June 2004), 69.
[150] OECD, 'Guiding Principles for Chemical Accident Prevention, Preparedness and Response' (2003) <http://www2.oecd.org/guidingprinciples/>.
[151] OECD, 2004 Roundtable Background Report (n. 149) 76.
[152] IFC 2012 Performance Standard 1, objectives.
[153] Ibid. para. 3.
[154] Ibid. para. 14 and fn. 20.

a project that relies on commercially available skills and resources, with a view to integrating 'cleaner production' into product design and production processes.[155] Technical feasibility is understood on the basis of commercially available skills, equipment, and materials, taking into account prevailing local factors.[156] Cost-effectiveness refers to the capital and operational costs and financial benefits of the measure considered over the life of the measure.[157] 'Good international industry practice' is defined as the exercise of professional skill, diligence, prudence, and foresight that would reasonably be expected from skilled and experienced professionals engaged in the same type of undertaking under the same or similar circumstances globally or regionally.[158] Private companies are expected to refer to an 'internationally recognized source' when evaluating and selecting resource efficiency and pollution prevention and control techniques, including the IFC Environmental, Health and Safety Guidelines,[159] unless host country regulations are more stringent.[160]

The IFC Standard also spells out provisions for environmental and social action plans, as well as emergency preparedness and response, and monitoring and review to be established in cooperation with affected communities.[161] It calls upon companies to involve external experts only when there are potentially significant adverse impacts or technically complex issues involved in the assessment.[162] This should be read in light of guidance provided by international human rights bodies, which stress the need for independent expertise when the rights of indigenous peoples and local communities are at stake.[163] The UN Special Rapporteur on Toxics, for instance, recommended routinely monitoring for associated toxic substances at mine sites, as well as in nearby sources of drinking water or aquatic habitat, when hazardous substances that can contaminate water are used, such as cyanide and hydro-fracking solutions.[164]

In addition, the objectives of the IFC Standard encompass: promoting 'more sustainable' use of resources, including water and energy; and reducing project-level GHG emissions.[165] More specifically, the Performance Standard requires companies to apply, during the whole project life-cycle, technologies and practices that are 'best suited to avoid, or where not feasible, to minimize or reduce adverse

---

[155] IFC 2006 Performance Standard 3, para. 1; 2012 Performance Standard 3, paras 4 and 6.
[156] IFC 2012 Performance Standard 3, fn. 3.
[157] Ibid. fn. 5.
[158] IFC 2012 Performance Standard 1, fn. 10.
[159] These are technical reference documents that address IFC's expectations regarding the industrial pollution management performance of its projects, and are currently under review (<http://www.ifc.org/ifcext/policyreview.nsf/Content/EHSGuidelinesUpdate#How>).
[160] IFC 2012 Performance Standard 3, para. 5.
[161] Ibid. paras 16 and 20–24.
[162] Ibid. para. 19.
[163] See Ch. 5, Section 1.1.
[164] Report of the Special Rapporteur on the human rights obligations related to environmentally sound management and disposal of hazardous substances and waste, Calin Georgescu (2012) UN Doc. A/HRC/21/48, paras 50 and 70.
[165] IFC 2012 Performance Standard 3, objectives.

impacts on human health and the environment', and that are tailored to the project, in light of the risk and impact assessment, and consistent with 'good international industry practice'.[166] Translation of the prevention principle into a standard based on best practices and technologies is echoed in the UN Global Compact[167] and the UN Norms,[168] as a complement to the standard on environmental management systems[169] that can underpin substantive standards on sustainable use.[170]

2.2.1 Substantive dimensions
More recently, prevention has also inspired the development of substantive standards of corporate environmental responsibility in specific thematic areas, such as freshwater, chemicals, waste, and climate change.

The 2012 version of IFC Standards, for instance, contains a substantive standard on water consumption, which appears in line with similar developments under the UN Global Compact. It focuses on projects that are 'potentially significant consumer[s] of water', and calls for adopting measures to avoid or reduce water usage to avoid adverse impacts on others, including the use of alternative water supplies, water consumption offsets to reduce the total demand for water resources to within the available supply, and the evaluation of alternative project locations.[171] Concerns have been raised about the fact that this Standard does not explicitly refer to its significance vis-à-vis the human rights to health and water,[172] without safeguards or exceptions developed in the human rights field.[173] The OECD Due Diligence Guidance for Responsible Supply Chains in the Garment and Footwear Sector, in turn, draws from the OECD Principles on Water Governance and the Global Compact's CEO Water Mandate,[174] to emphasize the need to employ best available technologies to promote water efficiency and/or reduce dependence on freshwater, including through investment in water-saving equipment and water reuse and reduction in water usage.[175] The guidance also notes that

---

[166] Ibid.
[167] Principle 10 of the UN Global Compact expects adhering companies to encourage the development and diffusion of environmentally-friendly technologies, which are defined in the Guide to the UN Global Compact as including technologies that allow for limited pollution, protection of the environment, sustainable use of natural resources, and reduction or reuse of waste. UN Global Compact Office, 'United Nations Guide to the Global Compact: A Practical Understanding of the Vision and the Nine Principles' (2012) < https://www.unglobalcompact.org/library/318 > (Guide to the UN Global Compact) 64.
[168] Commentary to the UN Norms, (e) and (g).
[169] See Section 2.1.2.
[170] See Ch. 5, Section 3.
[171] IFC 2012 Performance Standard 3, para. 9.
[172] P. Simons and A. Macklin, *The Governance Gap: Extractive Industries, Human Rights and the Home State Advantage* (Abingdon, Routledge: 2014) 135.
[173] A. McBeth, *International Economic Actors and Human Rights* (Abingdon: Routledge, 2010) 218.
[174] OECD Due Diligence Guidance for Responsible Supply Chains in the Garment and Footwear Sector (Paris: OECD, 2018) 167.
[175] Ibid. 164. On best available technologies, the Guidance also relies on the integrated pollution and prevention control instruments at EU level: Ibid. 167.

when considering expansions, enterprises should consider ways to address net increase in water demand and, generally, direct sourcing to regions that are not water-stressed.[176]

The translation of the prevention principle into standards of waste minimization featured in the UN Norms:[177] they expressed the expectation that private companies ensure effective means of collecting the remains of products or services for recycling, reuse, or other environmentally responsible disposal.[178] The IFC Performance Standard on pollution prevention refers to the Basel Convention on the Control of Transboundary Movement of Hazardous Wastes,[179] and the London Convention on the Prevention of Marine Pollution by Dumping of Wastes or Other Matters,[180] to develop project-level requirements on wastes and other hazardous materials.[181] As a result, IFC Performance Standard 3 requires: avoiding, or where that is not feasible, minimizing, waste generation; recovering and reusing waste; or treating, destroying, and disposing of it in an environmentally sound manner.[182] The OECD-FAO Guidance for Responsible Agricultural Supply Chains, in turn, encapsulates the specific expectation that companies avoid or reduce the generation of hazardous and non-hazardous waste, substituting or reducing the use of toxic substances, and enhancing the productive use or ensuring a safe disposal of waste.[183] Reducing, minimizing, and preventing pollution and waste is also underscored in the CBD Guidelines on Tourism.[184] This can be seen as a reflection of an emerging principle of extended producer responsibility, where the producer is responsible for the post-consumer phase in the life-cycle, by establishing a link between product design and waste phase.[185] Prevention is thus translated as placing the responsibility to address waste management on the 'actors that have the most influence on the system'.[186]

The IFC, furthermore, contains a detailed Performance Standard on pollution prevention, which translates into a project-level approach a series of international standards related to pollution, climate change, resource efficiency with particular emphasis on water use, and safe use of chemicals.[187] The Convention

---

[176] Ibid.
[177] CBD Sustainable Use Principles, Principle 12.
[178] Commentary to the UN Norms, (f).
[179] Convention on the Control of Transboundary Movements of Hazardous Wastes and Their Disposal (Basel Convention) (Basel, 22 March 1989, in force 24 May 1992), already referred to in 2006 IFC Performance Standard 3, para. 5.
[180] Convention on the Prevention of Marine Pollution by Dumping of Wastes and Other Matter (London, 29 December 1972, in force 30 August 1975), a reference to which had been suggested by WWF with regard to the 2006 version: WWF (n. 91) 57.
[181] IFC 2012 Performance Standard 3, para. 12 and fn. 15.
[182] Ibid. para. 12.
[183] OECD-FAO Guidance for Responsible Agricultural Supply Chains, 29.
[184] CBD Biodiversity and Tourism Guidelines (n 50), para. 44.
[185] C. Dalhammar, 'Extended Producer Responsibility' in Krämer and Orlando (n. 53) 208.
[186] Ibid. 215.
[187] 2012 IFC Performance Standard 3, para. 2.

on Long-range Transboundary Air Pollution[188] is a reference in avoiding or minimizing the release of pollutants in different media (air, water, and land), and controlling the intensity or load of their release, in routine, non-routine, or accidental circumstances with the potential for local, regional, and transboundary impacts.[189] Companies are further subject to the prohibition to purchase, store, manufacture, use, or trade in products classified as extremely hazardous or highly hazardous by the World Health Organization (WHO).[190] Furthermore, Performance Standard 3 requires companies' environmentally responsible conduct in relation to integrated pest management in accordance with the FAO International Code of Conduct on the Distribution and Use of Pesticides.[191] Although stakeholders requested the IFC to refer to pollution transfer and release registers, which are referred to in OECD Guidelines,[192] these instruments have not been considered by the IFC as an appropriate requirement for the private sector, because they necessitate collaboration with multiple parties which is beyond the control of a private company, and also because they may be detrimental to clients' competitiveness.[193]

In addition, the OECD Due Diligence Guidance for Responsible Supply Chains in the Garment and Footwear Sector[194] also contains a section on hazardous chemicals, with a combination of procedural and substantive standards. The Guidance calls on companies to identify which harmful, hazardous, or restricted chemicals are in use in the sub-sector, identify higher-risk stages in its own operation, higher-risk countries due to inadequate regulation or enforcement, and develop an inventory of chemicals.[195] As part of the corrective action plan, a company is expected to stop using banned chemicals, implement best available techniques, and develop a chemical management plan for safe storage, labelling, and protection.[196]

While these specifications provide a significant level of additional detail to international standards of prevention, they do not take into account particular concerns for sectors of society that are most vulnerable to the negative impacts of substandard chemicals management. The UN Special Rapporteur on Toxics thus developed in 2012 a series of specific recommendations on business responsibility with regard to the need to respect the human rights of the child. He indicated that companies should identify, prevent, and mitigate children's exposure to toxics through the companies' own activities, products, or business relationships, including global supply chains and other international relationships; and use

---

[188] Geneva, 13 November 1979, in force 16 March 1983.
[189] IFC 2006 Performance Standard 3, para. 4; 2012 Performance Standard 3, para. 10 and fn 10.
[190] 2012 IFC Performance Standard 3, paras 9, 12, and 17.
[191] IFC 2006 Performance Standard 3, paras 12–15; and 2012 Performance Standard 3, para. 16.
[192] OECD Guidelines, Ch. 5.
[193] IFC Responses to Stakeholders (n. 88) 19.
[194] OECD Due Diligence Guidance for Responsible Supply Chains in the Garment and Footwear Sector (Paris: OECD, 2018).
[195] Ibid. 158–59.
[196] Ibid. 160.

available safer alternatives to mitigate human rights impacts or actively invest in the development and adoption of safer alternatives and mitigation measures.[197]

A variety of substantive dimensions have emerged with regard to climate change. The 2012 IFC Standards foresee that 'the commercial feasibility of the project is to be less of a consideration than the prevention of negative impacts of a project'.[198] IFC Performance Standard 3 sets a threshold of emissions (25.000 tonnes Co2 equivalent per year) above which clients are expected to quantify and monitor direct and indirect emissions annually, in accordance with internationally recognized methodologies, such as those provided by the International Panel on Climate Change (IPCC).[199] This builds on an innovation of the 2006 revision,[200] that responded to suggestions made by the IFC's own Compliance, Advisor/Ombudsman[201] and international environmental non-governmental organizations (NGOs).[202] In comparison, the OECD Guidelines mainly refer to climate change in more general terms, with regard to continually seeking to improve corporate environmental performance, at the level of the enterprise and, where appropriate, of its supply chain, focusing on sustainable consumption rather than sustainable production. In effect, the OECD Guidelines encourage consumers' reduction of GHG emissions, by expecting companies to provide accurate information on their products.[203] The OECD Guidelines further refer to climate change in encouraging disclosure or communication practices in 'areas where reporting standards are still evolving' such as GHG emissions.[204] An approach based on best available technologies and precaution, in turn, can be found in the OECD-FAO Guidance for Responsible Agricultural Supply Chains with regard to GHG reduction,[205] along with energy efficiency measures, energy conservation measures, and reduction in the size of packaging, or reusable or recyclable packaging, and the design of durable products.[206] The section on climate change is also notable for building upon the sustainable consumption-related provisions in the OECD Guidelines chapter on the environment, by

---

[197] Report of the Special Rapporteur on the implications for human rights of the environmentally sound management and disposal of hazardous substances and wastes (2016) UN Doc. A/HRC/33/41, Section 4. Compare with: Committee on the Rights of the Child, General comment No. 16 on State obligations regarding the impact of the business sector on children's rights (2013) UN Doc. CRC/C/GC/16, section III. C. See also P. Gerber, J Kyriakasis, and K. O'Byrne, 'General Comment 16 on State Obligations regarding the Impact of the Business Sector on Children's rights: What is its Standing, Meaning and Effect?' (2013) 14 *Melbourne Journal of International Law* 93.
[198] A. Adeyemi, 'Changing the Face of Sustainable Development in Developing Countries: The Role of the International Finance Corporation' (2014) 16 *Environmental Law Review* 91, 98.
[199] IFC 2012 Performance Standard 3, para. 8 and fn 9.
[200] IFC 2006 Performance Standard 3, paras 10–11.
[201] CAO (n. 56) 37. The role of CAO is discussed in detail in Ch. 6, Section 3.
[202] WWF (n. 91) 30–33.
[203] OECD Guidelines, Chapter V, para. 6(b)–(c).
[204] OECD Guidelines, Commentary, para. 33.
[205] OECD Garment and Footwear Due Diligence Guidance, 169–70.
[206] Ibid. 170–71.

recommending that companies increase customer awareness on behaviour that reduces emissions.[207]

2.3 Precaution

According to the Rio Declaration formulation, precaution implies that States should not use the lack of scientific certainty as a reason for postponing cost-effective measures to prevent environmental degradation, where there are threats of serious or irreversible damage.[208] While 'there is no single formulation' of the precautionary principle in international law with regard to the risk triggers and how early and how stringent measures should be taken, precaution is often understood as calling for a cost-benefit analysis and a provisional approach that is re-evaluated over time with a view to support learning.[209] The importance of precaution for States' due diligence with respect to the human-rights-and-the-environment nexus has also been underscored by the Inter-American Court of Human Rights.[210] Several inter-governmental organizations and environmental NGOs[211] have relied on the precautionary principle/approach to define the concept of corporate environmental accountability. Some of its implications for States, however, cannot be applied to the business sector. One case in point is the need for activities and substances that may be harmful to the environment to be regulated and possibly prohibited, even if no conclusive or overwhelming evidence is available as to the harm or likely harm to the environment.[212] This has, nonetheless, had the 'most profound effect' on companies: arguably precaution has significantly altered the processes by which new products and technologies are developed and exploited, and increasingly limited the admissibility of activities recognized as being potentially hazardous, as opposed to waiting until actual harm has occurred or is proved to be imminent.[213]

As opposed to applicable national legal requirements, a precautionary standard of corporate environmental accountability may require companies to act carefully and with foresight when taking decisions concerning activities that may have adverse impacts on the environment.[214] More specifically, it may prevent companies

---

[207] Ibid. 171.
[208] Rio Declaration, Principle 15; Kiss and Shelton (n. 59) 206.
[209] J. Wiener, 'Precautionary Principle' in Krämer and Orlando (n. 53) 174, 177–79 and 182.
[210] Inter-American Court of Human Rights, *Medio Ambiente y Derechos Humanos*, Oc-23/17, Opinión Consultiva (15 November 2017) paras 180–81.
[211] A. Khokhryakova, 'Beanal v. Freeport-Mcmoran, Inc.: Liability of a Private Actor for an International Environmental Tort under the Alien Tort Claims Act' (1998) 9 *Colorado Journal of International Environmental Law* 463.
[212] Ibid.
[213] P. Sands, *International Environmental Law. Emerging Trends and Implications for Transnational Corporations* (New York: UN, 1993) 27.
[214] Paraphrasing Sands et al (n 53) 222.

from using a certain level of scientific certainty as an excuse for carrying out activities potentially dangerous for the environment. In addition, this standard may imply a shift of the burden of proof, thus requiring that a company wishing to carry out an activity will have to prove that such activity will not cause harm to the environment.[215] In all these instances, it will depend on a case-by-case determination of the cost-effective measures that a company can take, and the level of scientific uncertainty and of environmental threat or likely harm at stake.

A corporate environmental accountability standard based on precaution can be found in almost all recent international initiatives discussed in the previous chapter. The UN Global Compact's[216] Guide cautiously mentions that the precautionary principle is accepted in the EU and forms 'part of international environmental law'.[217] The inclusion of precaution in the UN Norms[218] was considered an unprecedented step in human rights law.[219] While precaution is also included in the OECD Guidelines, it is, however, conspicuously missing from the IFC Performance Standards, which is surprising considering the reliance by the IFC on the Convention of Biological Diversity and its extensive standards on sustainable use. In comparison, the CBD Addis Ababa Principles on Sustainable Use are based on precaution, aiming to avoid or minimize adverse impacts on ecosystem services, structures, and functions, as well as other components of ecosystems.[220] Nonetheless, ecosystem services are addressed in the IFC Performance Standards.

The Guide to the UN Global Compact translates the precautionary principle for businesses as the expectation that companies will take the most cost-effective, early action to prevent the occurrence of irreversible environmental damage, on the basis of the (self-)assessment of environmental impacts. The application of this standard is expected to result in companies investing in sustainable production methods and research, and developing environmentally-friendly products.[221] In a different formulation, the OECD Guidelines intend to use the precautionary approach to prevent multinationals from delaying action to prevent or minimize *serious* environmental damage (also taking into account human health and safety) in the absence of full scientific certainty, as long as such action entails *cost-effective* measures and is consistent with the scientific and technical understanding of risks.[222] Both refer to cost-effective measures, but the UN Global Compact links the standard to irreversible environmental damage, while the OECD Guidelines set

---

[215] Ibid.
[216] The UN Global Compact, Principle 7.
[217] UN Guide to the Global Compact, 52.
[218] Ibid. Section G, para. 14.
[219] Simon Walker's contribution in United Nations Research Institute for Social Development (UNRISD), 'Corporate Social Responsibility and Development: Towards a New Agenda: Summaries of Presentations' (Geneva, 17–18 November 2003) 83.
[220] CBD Sustainable Use Principles, Principle 5.
[221] UN Guide to the Global Compact, 54.
[222] OECD Guidelines for Multinational Enterprises, Ch. V, para. 4.

a lower threshold by referring to serious harm. Whereas the UN Global Compact emphasizes the role of private companies in taking action, the OECD Guidelines express in negative terms that companies should not delay precautionary action. Along similar lines, the CBD Akwé: Kon Guidelines provide that, where there is a threat of significant reduction or loss of biodiversity and particularly with respect to mitigation measures associated with development, lack of full scientific certainty should not be used as a reason for postponing measures to avoid or minimize such a threat.[223]

An important part of the Commentary to the OECD Guidelines is devoted to precaution, stressing that although several instruments already adopted by adhering countries enunciate a precautionary approach, including Rio Principle 15, none of these instruments is explicitly addressed to enterprises but 'business involvement is implicit in all of them'.[224] Accordingly, the Guidelines do not intend 'to reinterpret any existing instruments or to create new commitments or precedents on the part of governments—they are intended only to recommend how the precautionary approach should be implemented at the level of enterprises'.[225] Companies should act affirmatively as soon as possible to avoid serious or irreversible environmental damage resulting from their activities. Recognizing the need for flexibility in its application, based on the specific context in which the approach is carried out, the Commentary also stresses that governments 'determine the basic framework in this field, and have the responsibility to periodically consult with stakeholders on the most appropriate ways forward'.[226]

The OECD Guidelines have provided a forum for businesses and others to reflect on the challenges posed by precaution as a matter of corporate environmental accountability. In that context, companies underscored the challenge to apply a truly precautionary approach, when traditionally it is the role of regulators to apply precaution and interpret what constitutes acceptable risk, subject to a consultative process with the public.[227] Because of the absence of a single, internationally accepted interpretation of the precautionary approach,[228] participants considered it 'essential' that countries institute and enforce appropriate laws that specify scientific approaches and citizens' risk tolerance, in order to guide multinationals' operations.[229] This lack of clarity currently appears in many sector-specific standards for risk management in relation to chemicals, hazardous waste, air pollution, ozone depletion, climate change, and biodiversity.[230] The OECD suggested that risk analysis relating to food safety and consumer protection, which has been operationally

---

[223] Ibid. para. 61.
[224] Ibid. para. 37.
[225] Ibid. paras 37 and 39.
[226] Ibid.
[227] OECD, 2004 Roundtable Summary of Discussions (n 122) 9.
[228] Ibid.
[229] Ibid. 8–9.
[230] Ibid. 63.

defined in international standards by the Codex Alimentarius Commission, is also relevant for environmental risk analysis.[231] The 2011 version of the Guidelines' Commentary thus goes to great lengths in confirming that 'no existing instrument is completely adequate for expressing this recommendation.'[232]

Perhaps for the same reasons, the IFC Performance Standards fall short in aligning themselves with other international corporate environmental accountability standards as they do not mention explicitly, nor even imply, in any of its new standards, the precautionary approach. This is largely evident with reference to hazardous substances and chemicals management, invasive alien species,[233] and fishing activities, where international instruments consider this approach a cornerstone. While the 2006 version indicated that the assessment should be based on 'current information' and 'appropriate baseline data',[234] the 2012 version makes reference to 'recent environmental and social baseline data at an appropriate level of detail', adding specific reference also to GHG emissions, risks associated with a changing climate and adaptation opportunities, and potential transboundary effects.[235] Neither, however, mentioned the consequences of lack of scientific certainty about possible risks or impacts on the private company's assessment of environmental risks and their management. Such a shortcoming was already highlighted by WWF, according to which IFC projects that have the potential for disproportionate and irreversible impacts should not be funded, at least until more certainty about such impacts can be achieved,[236] instead of privileging an approach based on mitigation.[237]

2.4 Disclosure of environmental information

Disclosure of environmental information is considered the basis of the private-sector cooperation with local and other authorities, particularly for compliance with the prevention standard.[238] As early as 1989, UN reports prioritized corporate environmental information disclosure as an 'essential element for the

---

[231] Ibid. 59.
[232] OECD Guidelines for Multinational Enterprises, para. 69. This chimes with Sands et al (n 78) 222: 'There is no clear and uniform understanding of the meaning of the precautionary principle among States and other members of the international community.'
[233] Discussed in Ch. 5, Section 3.
[234] IFC 2006 Performance Standard 1, para. 4.
[235] IFC 2012 Performance Standard 1, para. 16.
[236] WWF (n. 91) 67.
[237] WWF, *Guidelines for Investment in Operations that Impact Forests* (September 2003) <http://www.forestandtradeasia.org/files/WWF%20FOrest%20Investment%20Guideline.pdf> 3.
[238] D. Partan, 'The Duty to Inform in International Environmental Law' (1988) 6 *Boston University International Law Journal* 43, 80, highlights that the objective of the duty to inform is to facilitate the reduction or mitigation of consequences of environmental risks.

implementation of sustainable development'.[239] At the same time, commentators drew attention to the growing body of policy recommendations on transnational disclosure of information on hazardous products and processes.[240] Several cases of environmental damage led to aggravated consequences because of the lack of timely disclosure of information to public authorities and affected communities.[241] For instance, in the case of the Bhopal disaster, the company did not send out an immediate alarm when the gas escaped, did not take any steps to communicate to public authorities or the local communities the consequences of exposure to leaked gas produced by the reaction, nor did they give information on the medical steps to be taken in the aftermath of the disaster.[242] Also the consequences of the Seveso dioxin release were significantly worsened by the late disclosure of information by the company.[243]

Against this background, activists and scholars have advocated that information held by private companies should be disclosed when a key public interest such as the environment is at risk.[244] This is justified by practical reasons, namely it is argued that companies are well capable of providing timely response information, are likely to possess the most updated information on specific technologies, and are best placed to transmit such information between countries.[245] It should also be noted that this standard is extremely dependent for its normative definition upon case-by-case application, requiring specification as to who should receive the information, the time of information disclosure, the kind of information expected, and the limitations to such standard.[246]

The fundamental character of the standard on disclosure of information for the concept of corporate environmental accountability was already evident in the 1990 UN draft Code of Conduct.[247] The UN Global Compact considers disclosure of information a necessary component of companies' multi-stakeholder dialogue.[248] The UN Norms, the OECD Guidelines, and the IFC Performance Standards link

---

[239] UNCTC, 'Ongoing and Future Research: Transnational Corporations and Issues Relating to the Environment—Report of the Secretary General' (1989) UN Doc. E/C.10/1989/12, 12–13, where it was recommended developing an internationally accepted list of basic environmental data items that should be disclosed on a regular basis by individual firms.

[240] H. Gleckman, 'Proposed Requirements for Transnational Corporations to Disclose Information on Product and Process Hazards' (1988) 6 *Boston University International Law Journal* 89.

[241] R. T. Ako, 'Issues on Environmental Human Rights and Corporate Social Responsibility in the Niger Delta' (2005) 15 *Lesotho Law Journal* 1.

[242] The International Council on Human Rights Policy, *Beyond Voluntarism: Human Rights and the Developing International Legal Obligations for Companies* (Versoix: International Council on Human Rights Policy, 2002) 13.

[243] UNCTC, 'Environmental Aspects of the Activities of Transnational Corporations: A Survey' (1985) UN Doc. ST/CTC/55, 93.

[244] International Council (n. 242) 41.

[245] Gleckman (n. 240) 90.

[246] Ibid. 89.

[247] UNCTC, 'Proposed Text of the Draft Code of Conduct on Transnational Corporations' (1990) UN Doc. E/1990/94 (UN Draft Code of Conduct) para. 42.

[248] Guide to the UN Global Compact, 58.

the environmental integration standard with disclosure of information.[249] Beyond an overarching shared understanding of the importance of ensuring access to information, however, international standards vary in determining what kind of information should be provided to whom and in what ways.

2.4.1 Recipients of information

With regard to addressees, the UN Norms indicated that information should be provided not only to the government of the State in which activities are taking place, but also to the State of incorporation, to relevant international organizations, and to the public at large.[250] According to the CBD Guidelines on Tourism Development, both the developer and the operator are required to notify designated government authorities of any failures to comply with conditions attached to an approval.[251] In case of risk of transboundary environmental pollution or other catastrophic environmental harm, cooperation may extend to regional and international bodies.[252] The OECD Guidelines, in contrast, only provide for limited cooperation with national authorities in charge of environmental protection through the provisions of environmental information.[253] These omissions may reflect the OECD's view that the main driver for corporate environmental accountability is national legislation, usually motivated by major accidents,[254] and that the existence of criminal or financial responsibility for non-compliance with environmental norms creates a disincentive for companies to find and report environmental problems on a voluntary and proactive basis.[255]

The IFC Standards underscore the private sector's primary responsibility for disclosing information to the public.[256] According to the CBD Guidelines on Tourism Development, both the developer and the operator are required to report periodically to designated authorities and to the public on compliance.[257] In addition, both the OECD Guidelines and the OECD-FAO Guidance for Responsible Agricultural Supply Chains point to business responsibility to share information with 'potentially affected communities'.[258] The UN Special Rapporteur on Toxics indicated that companies are expected to communicate to the public relevant

---

[249] Commentary to the UN Norms, (b) and (c); and IFC Performance Standard 1.
[250] UN Norms, Section G, Commentary, (b) and (c).
[251] CBD Biodiversity and Tourism Guidelines (n 50), para. 60.
[252] Ibid. para. 47.
[253] M. Bekhechi, 'International Investment and Environmental Protection: Notes on the Environmental Conditions of Investments in the Oil and Mining Sectors' in The International Bureau of the Permanent Court of Arbitration, *International Investments and Protection of the Environment. The Role of Dispute Resolution Mechanisms* (The Hague: Kluwer Law International, 2001) 73, 77–78.
[254] OECD, 2004 Roundtable Background Report (n. 149) 70.
[255] Ibid. 35.
[256] IFC Responses to Stakeholders (n. 88) 32.
[257] CBD Biodiversity and Tourism Guidelines (n 50), paras 67 and 71.
[258] OECD Guidelines, para. 35; and the OECD-FAO Guidance for Responsible Agricultural Supply Chains, 25.

information about hazardous substances in their supply chains and products in a user-friendly format; and publish information in the languages of linguistic minorities and indigenous peoples, paying special attention to providing information to those most at risk.[259]

The OECD Guidelines also provide insights into the links between providing information to consumers and the role for companies in sustainable consumption. The Guidelines call upon companies to promote higher levels of awareness among customers of the environmental implications of using the products and services of the enterprise, including by providing accurate information on their products (eg on GHG emissions, biodiversity, resource efficiency, or other environmental issues). This should be read in conjunction with the chapter on consumer protection, which calls for providing accurate, verifiable, and clear information that is sufficient to enable consumers to make informed decisions, including information on the prices and, where appropriate, content, safe use, environmental attributes, maintenance, storage, and disposal of goods and services. Where feasible this information should be provided in a manner that facilitates consumers' ability to compare products.[260] The Guidelines further call upon companies to support efforts to promote consumer education in areas that relate to their business activities, with the aim of, inter alia, improving consumers' ability to better understand the environmental impact of their decisions,[261] for example on the basis of information on the energy efficiency and the degree of recyclability of products and, in the case of food products, information on agricultural practices.[262]

2.4.2 Types of information

With regard to the kind of information to be shared, the draft UN Code of Conduct emphasized the need for multinational companies to supply host countries' competent authorities with all relevant information concerning products, processes, and services, including: their characteristics, other activities including experimental uses and related aspects which may harm the environment, the measures and costs necessary to avoid or at least to mitigate their harmful effects; as well as prohibitions, restrictions, warnings, and other public regulatory measures imposed in other countries on grounds of protection of the environment on these products, processes, and services.[263] The detailed list of required information was

---

[259] Report of the Special Rapporteur on the implications for human rights of the environmentally sound management and disposal of hazardous substances and wastes, Başkut Tuncak (2015) UN Doc. A/HRC/30/40, para. 101(c)(vi–vii), (vii), (iii), (iv). On standards specifically focused on indigenous peoples' rights, see Ch. 5, Section 1.
[260] OECD Guidelines, VIII.2.
[261] Ibid. VIII.5.
[262] Ibid. para. 85. International standards specifically related to the agri-business sector are discussed in more detail at Section 3.6 in Ch 5.
[263] UN draft Code, para. 42.

considered to be one of the main contributions of the draft Code to the definition of corporate environmental accountability.[264]

The OECD Guidelines include a generic expectation for multinationals' disclosure policies to include foreseeable risk factors,[265] which arguably include environmental risks. In addition, companies are expected to disclose 'policies and other codes of conduct to which they subscribe, as well as their performance in relation to these statements and codes',[266] which implies environmental commitments. According to the Commentary, this should be seen as 'a second set of disclosure or communication practices in areas where reporting standards are still evolving', as opposed to more standard corporate governance transparency standards. The evolving standards that relate to the environment include 'greenhouse gas emissions, as the scope of their monitoring is expanding to cover direct and indirect, current and future, corporate and product emissions' or biodiversity.[267] In addition, enterprises are explicitly encouraged to apply high-quality standards for non-financial information, including environmental reporting where such standards exist.[268] An annual audit should be conducted by an independent, competent, and qualified auditor in order to provide an external and objective assurance to the board and shareholders that the financial statements fairly represent the financial position and performance of the enterprise in all material respects.[269] The Commentary to the Guidelines further notes that non-financial information 'may pertain to entities that extend beyond those covered in the enterprise's financial accounts', such as subcontractors, suppliers, or joint venture partners, which may be particularly appropriate to monitor the transfer of environmentally harmful activities to partners.[270] The OECD-FAO Guidance for Responsible Agricultural Supply Chains specifically refers to timely and accurate information related to foreseeable risk factors and response to particular environmental, social, and human rights impacts to potentially affected communities, at all stages of the investment cycle, as well as the provision of accurate, verifiable, and clear information that is sufficient to enable consumers to make informed decisions.[271]

---

[264] Pearson (n. 100) 154.
[265] OECD Guidelines, III.2.f.
[266] Ibid. III.3.b–c.
[267] Ibid. para. 33.
[268] Ibid. III.4.
[269] Ibid.
[270] Ibid. para. 33.
[271] OECD-FAO Guidance for Responsible Agricultural Supply Chains, para. 25 and fnn. 22–23, referring to OECD Guidelines, II.10, VI.3, III.1–3, VI.2.a, and VIII.2; Food and Agriculture Organization (FAO), Voluntary Guidelines on the Responsible Governance of Tenure of Land, Fisheries and Forests in the Context of National Food Security (VGGT), (2012) UN Doc. CL 144/9 (C 2013/20), Appendix D (VGGT) para. 12.10; UN Guiding Principles on Business and Human Rights, paras 17 and 21; CBD, Art. 14; CBD Akwé: Kon Guidelines (n 48); IFC Performance Standard 1, paras 5, 8–10, and 29; Convention on Access to Information, Public Participation in Decision-Making and Access to Justice in Environmental Matters (Aarhus Convention) (Aarhus, 25 June 1998, in force 30 October 2001) Art. 5. See Annex A, 1.1 and 1.3.

The IFC had received a plethora of critiques about vague information disclosure requirements, which were depending on the extent of the potential environmental and social impacts, at an 'appropriate' stage. As a result, disclosure practices varied widely among projects, resulting in difficult access to project information, insufficient details in available environmental information, and the inappropriate extension of business confidentiality concerns to the social and environmental dimensions of the project.[272] In response, the 2006 Standard marked a step forward in requiring: disclosure of key information at the beginning of the project; inclusion of the action plan among the documents to be made accessible to the public; and ensuring that such disclosure continues beyond the planning stage, in order to address the whole implementation of the action plan and issues raised by affected communities during the whole project life-cycle. Strengthening the links with consultation, the 2012 version added to the list of information to be disclosed risks and potential impacts on communities and relevant elements of the management programme, and the envisaged stakeholder engagement process.[273] The IFC does not go as far as setting indicative timelines for disclosure of information.[274]

CBD decisions and international human rights guidance have provided detailed guidance in some areas. According to the CBD Guidelines on Tourism Development, for instance, periodic reports should be provided on compliance with conditions set out in approvals, and on the conditions of biodiversity and the environment in relation to tourism facilities and activities for which they are responsible, such as ensuring respect for endangered species, prevention of introduction of alien species, and access to genetic resources.[275] With particular regard to risks concerning the human rights of the child, the Special Rapporteur on Toxics called upon companies to generate and disclose information related to the risks of exposure and on the intrinsic hazards of industrial substances, pesticides, and food additives that they manufacture and sell. Businesses are thus expected to communicate publicly and objectively measures taken to mitigate potential childhood exposures; and ensure that health and safety information about the potential hazards of industrial chemicals and pesticides to children is made accessible to regulators and businesses down the supply or value chain.[276]

2.4.3 Degree of disclosure

Most international standards do not address in detail the question of the degree of disclosure of information. In the specific sector of toxic substances, however, where 'virtually every industry and business sector is linked to the production,

---

[272] CAO (n. 56) 27.
[273] IFC 2012 Performance Standard 1, para. 29.
[274] IFC, 'Response to the Compliance Advisor/Ombudsman Review on IFC Policy and Performance Standards on Social and Environmental Sustainability' (22 September 2005) 5.
[275] CBD Guidelines on Tourism Development (n 50), paras 67 and 71.
[276] Report of the Special Rapporteur on Toxics (n. 197) para. 111.

use, release or disposal of hazardous substances and wastes up and down the value chain',[277] the UN Special Rapporteur on Toxics recommended that businesses be guided by the principle of full disclosure. He thus considered companies to be allowed secrecy only when the necessity and legitimacy of confidentiality are proved, upon exhaustively listing information or types of information that is not publicly accessible but provided to governments, including the reason for non-disclosure. In addition, the Special Rapporteur called on companies to recognize the right of access to information and avoid using the privilege of confidential business information to shield health and safety information on the hazardous substances used and produced, and to which humans and wildlife may be exposed, such as chemicals dispersants and hydro-fracking solutions.[278]

With regard to business responsibility to respect indigenous peoples' human rights,[279] the UN Special Rapporteur on Indigenous Peoples' Rights indicated that due diligence implies that companies facilitate indigenous peoples' full access to information about potential financial benefits, including when this information is considered proprietary (in which case, it should be shared on a confidential basis).[280]

2.5 Consultation with potentially affected communities

Both in relation to the (self-)assessments of environmental impacts and environmental management systems, all the international standards discussed in the previous chapter refer to the need for the private sector to facilitate participation of potentially affected communities in companies' decision-making processes. This is a specification, with a narrower scope, of the general principle of public participation in decision-making that can be found in the Rio Declaration on Environment and Development.[281] Expectations around communities' involvement by the private sector have become clearer as the inter-linkages between environment and human rights have emphasized cases where expected or likely environmental impacts may also negatively affect the enjoyment of local communities' and indigenous peoples' rights to their traditional lifestyle, cultural practices, lands, and natural resources.[282] The question of effective and genuine participation, where communities can have some influence on the outcome, is tightly linked to prior access to sufficient and comprehensible information discussed above and access

---

[277] Report of the Special Rapporteur on Toxics (n. 259) para. 80.
[278] Ibid. para. 101(c)(vi)–(vii), (vii), (iii), (iv).
[279] Discussed in Ch. 5, Section 1.
[280] UN Special Rapporteur on Indigenous Peoples' Rights Anaya, Study on Extractive Industries and Indigenous Peoples (2013) UN Doc. A/HRC/24/41, para. 62.
[281] Rio Declaration, Principle 10.
[282] Morgera (n. 99).

to grievance mechanisms discussed in Section 2.6. Benefits arising to companies from community involvement are generally identified as enhanced quality of prior assessments, higher-quality information feeding into better decision-making, and solutions to mitigation and contingency planning that are more appropriate to local circumstances.

The UN Global Compact invites companies more generally to hold multi-stakeholder dialogues, without providing further specifications.[283] The Global Compact's framework on biodiversity and ecosystem services, however, introduces the concept of ecosystem linkages at the landscape level, to support integrated planning along the value chain. This serves to emphasize the need for companies to respect land and land-use rights of local stakeholders, safeguard livelihoods of local communities that are natural resource-dependent, and involve them in decision-making, in order to advance common goals and ensure that environmental as well as social needs are met.[284]

Carefully avoiding human rights language, the 2011 review of the OECD Guidelines stressed stakeholder engagement as an interactive and two-way process based on good faith for the planning and decision-making concerning projects or activities 'that may significantly impact local communities', such as those involving the intensive use of land and water, as well as disclosure of climate change and biodiversity-specific information.[285] These recent revisions, however, have been criticized by civil society for their lack of explicit reference to free prior informed consent in the consultations with indigenous peoples.[286] The OECD-FAO Guidance for Responsible Agricultural Supply Chains, in contrast, referred not only to good faith, but also effective and meaningful, consultations with communities through their own representative institutions before initiating any operations, as well as during and at the end of operations.[287]

With regard to the International Finance Corporation, a significant evolution has taken place along the various reviews of the standards in this connection. The 1998 safeguard policies mentioned exclusively indigenous peoples. The successive version referred to affected communities,[288] thereby including local communities that are not recognized or do not self-identify as indigenous,

---

[283] Guide to the UN Global Compact, 58. See Ch. 5.
[284] UN Global Compact and the International Union for Conservation of Nature (IUCN), A Framework for Corporate Action on Biodiversity and Ecosystem Services (UN, 2012) 12.
[285] OECD Council, 'OECD Council, 'OECD Guidelines for Multinational Enterprises: Update 2011—Note by the Secretary-General', OECD doc. C(2011)59 (3 May 2011), Appendix II, para. II. A.14; OECD Council, 'OECD Guidelines for Multinational Enterprises: Update 2011—Commentaries', OECD Doc. C(2011) 59/ADD1, 3 May 2011, paras 25 and 33.
[286] Discussed in detail in Ch. 5, Section 1.2.
[287] OECD-FAO Guidance for Responsible Agricultural Supply Chains, 26.
[288] IFC 2012 Performance Standard 1, para. 26.

but exclusively with respect to potential risks that could severely affect their health.[289] The 2012 version, instead, calls upon clients to identify individuals and groups that may be 'directly and differently or disproportionately affected by their project because of their disadvantaged or vulnerable status', including because of their 'dependence on unique natural resources'.[290] It substituted the term 'stakeholder engagement' with 'community engagement' with a view to broadening the constituencies to be engaged, although the language on the scope and purpose of the engagement is similar and it 'remains unclear who is meant to determine the scope of engagement that is initially required'.[291] There is in effect no mention of human rights holders.[292] In addition, the most recent version of the IFC Performance Standards indicates that companies are to 'consider' involving representatives of affected communities in monitoring the effectiveness of their environmental management programs only 'where appropriate',[293] thus leaving a considerable margin of discretion to individual business entities. This is coupled with the creation of an 'external communications system' that will allow IFC clients to screen, assess, and reply to communications from stakeholders with a view to continually improving their management system. The system is in turn subject to the requirement for a 'stakeholder engagement framework' where the exact location of the project is unknown but the project is nonetheless reasonably expected to have significant impacts on local communities. More detailed indications regarding dissemination of information are provided when communities may be affected by risks of adverse impacts of the project, with the significant specification that when stakeholder consultations are the responsibility of the host government, the company is expected to conduct a complementary process if the government-led engagement does not meet the IFC Performance Standards.[294] While the general standards on consultation remain quite different in their detail, more coherent, higher standards of due diligence apply to indigenous peoples, as will be discussed in the next chapter.[295]

---

[289] In a case of water contamination with gold mine waste. See S. Langdon, *Peru's Yanacocha Gold Mine: The IFC's Midas Touch?* (September 2000) <http://www.ciel.org/Ifi/ifccaseperu.html>.
[290] IFC 2012 Performance Standard 1, para. 12 and fn. 18.
[291] D. Bradlow and M. Chapman, 'Public Participation and the Private Sector: The Role of Multilateral Development Banks and the Evolving Legal Standards' (2011) 4 *Erasmus Law Review* 91, 98.
[292] Including with regard to non-indigenous local/traditional communities: Report of the Special Rapporteur on the Issue of Human Rights and the Environment John Knox: Framework Principles on Human Rights and the Environment (2018) UN Doc. A/HRC/37/59, paras 9 and 47–48; and E. Morgera, 'A reflection on benefit-sharing as a Framework Principle on Human Rights and the Environment proposed by UN Special Rapporteur John Knox (Part II: Right-holders and duty-bearers)' BENELEX Blog post (April 2018), https://benelexblog.wordpress.com/.
[293] IFC 2012 Performance Standard 1, 'Assessment and Management of Social and Environmental Risks and Impacts', para. 21.
[294] IFC 2012 Performance Standard 1, paras 26, 30–31, and 38.
[295] Ch. 5, Section 1.

2.6 Grievance

As discussed in the previous chapter, the UN Framework on Business and Human Rights addresses private companies in its third pillar on access to remedies, noting the need for companies to set up a grievance mechanism. More specifically, according to the UN Guiding Principles, enterprises 'should establish or participate in ... legitimate, transparent, predictable, equitable, and right-compatible grievance mechanisms' that are directly accessible to individuals and communities that may directly be affected by their business operations, with a view to both supporting the identification of adverse impacts and systematic problems, and remedying adverse impacts.[296]

A project-level grievance mechanism can support both risk mitigation as part of the (self)-assessment of environmental impacts, and as a system to monitor implementation and effectiveness on the basis of information disclosure and stakeholder consultation, thereby also supporting the continuous improvement efforts of the company.[297] A grievance mechanism can provide the company with access to additional information about the project's external environment that can serve to identify and address shortcomings in its environmental management systems.[298] Company grievance systems also benefit from the results of impact self-assessment, as the outcomes can help to determine the likely complexity of future grievances and consequently the nature and amount of resources needed for implementation, including a variety of third parties, given the complexity of environmental impacts.[299] Company-level grievance mechanisms can also serve to identify complexities around the State responsibility to respect human rights and protect the environment, and business responsibility.[300]

The OECD Guidelines inserted reference to grievance mechanisms as part of their new section on human rights due diligence in 2011. Instead of right-compatible grievance, they refer, however, to 'compatibility with the Guidelines'.[301] They stress that company-level grievance mechanisms 'are based on dialogue and engagement with a view to seeking agreed solutions', could be administered by an enterprise in collaboration with other stakeholders, and can support continuous learning. They add that not only should these mechanisms not preclude access to

---

[296] IFC 2012 Performance Standard 1, paras 29 and 31.
[297] IFC, Addressing Grievances from Project-Affected Communities: Good Practice Note (2009), also on the Global Compact website at: https://www.unglobalcompact.org/library/38.
[298] Ibid. 6.
[299] Ibid. 7.
[300] Ibid. 21.
[301] 2011 OECD Guidelines, Commentary, para. 46.

judicial or non-judicial grievance mechanisms, but they also should not preclude access to the National Contact Points.[302]

The IFC Standards have undergone a significant evolution along the various reviews of the standards in this connection. The 1998 safeguard policies only provided that the private company should engage affected people in dialogue and take their concerns into account during the project preparation and implementation,[303] which, according to commentators, led to environmentally catastrophic projects.[304] The 2006 version, instead, contained the expectation that companies would respond to communities' concerns, and establish a grievance mechanism to receive and facilitate resolution of communities' complaints on its environmental performance. With quite some detail, the standard required that the mechanism be understandable, transparent, culturally appropriate, readily accessible, and free of charge. The 2012 version also added that it should 'not impede access to judicial or administrative remedies'.[305]

While none of the international standards discussed in the previous chapter make an explicit connection between grievance mechanisms, human rights, and the environment, this can be considered implicit.[306] Even when environmental grievances do not specifically mention human rights, they may nonetheless raise human rights implications, such as negative impacts on the human right to health or food.[307] Accordingly, information and independent expertise in human rights and the environment should be ensured in the context of grievance mechanisms, including from academic institutions (or professional associations) and international/regional organizations with a local presence.[308] Finally, it should be noted that CBD sources tend not to address this issue. The exception is the Akwé: Kon Guidelines on socio-cultural and environmental impact assessments, which call upon development proponents to establish a review and appeal process, in which parties should ensure the full participation of affected indigenous peoples and local communities.[309]

---

[302] Ibid.

[303] C. Lee, 'International Finance Corporation: Financing Environmentally and Socially Sustainable Private Investment' in S. Schlemmer-Schulte and K. Tung (eds), *Liber Amicorum Ibrahim F.I. Shihata* (The Hague: Kluwer Law International, 2001) 469, 473.

[304] I. Bowles, A. Rosenfels, C. Kormos, C. Reining, J. Nations, and T. Ankersen, 'The Environmental Impact of the International Finance Corporation Lending and Proposals for Reform: A Case Study of Conservation and Oil Development in the Guatemalan Petén' (1999) 29 *Environmental Law* 103.

[305] IFC 2006 Performance Standard 1, para. 23; IFC 2012 Performance Standard 1, para. 35.

[306] UN Framework Principles on Human Rights and the Environment (n. 292) paras 22 and 35.

[307] Harvard Kennedy School of Government's Corporate Social Responsibility Initiative, Rights-compatible Grievance Mechanisms: A Guidance Tool for Companies and their Stakeholders, 2008, on the UN Global Compact website: https://www.unglobalcompact.org/library/57, 7.

[308] Ibid. 17.

[309] Akwé: Kon Guidelines (n 48), para. 22.

3 Preliminary conclusions

International standard-setting initiatives on corporate environmental accountability have been increasingly characterized by a significant degree of normative convergence.[310] This is a trend that has accelerated and became more explicit since the early 2010s, and that can be ascribed to the increasingly clear interface between international biodiversity law and international human rights.

Environmental integration for companies is consistently translated as impact assessment and environmental management systems. In contrast to national laws, the former is not triggered by a particular threshold of risk, so companies are expected as a matter of practice to assess environmental impacts in all their activities on an ongoing basis, including when those are not required by national legislation (self-assessments). This also serves to emphasize higher expectations on how business entities carry out assessments required by national legislation. That said, divergences remains with regard to the need to address cumulative impacts (although some progress can be noted in that connection with regard to the attention paid to supply chains and areas of influence). In addition, the identification of alternatives for proposed projects, including a no-project alternative, remains unclear in international standards of corporate environmental accountability. Standards based on prevention are also common, but the difference lies in the details, with the OECD focusing on contingency planning for emergency management and the IFC taking a broader approach to mitigation hierarchy, which also includes offsetting. Corporate environmental accountability standards based on precaution are present in all instruments discussed in the previous chapter, with the exception of the IFC. Both the UN Global Compact and the OECD Guidelines refer to cost-effective measures, but the Global Compact links the standard to irreversible environmental damage, while the OECD Guidelines set a lower threshold by referring to serious harm. Along similar lines, corporate environmental accountability standards based on access to information are widespread, but they vary in determining what kind of information should be provided to whom and in what ways. Useful clarifications have been provided by the UN Special Rapporteur on Toxics, who has also emphasized the need for business due diligence to integrate specific concerns for vulnerable groups, notably children. Corporate environmental accountability standards focused on consultation and grievance mechanisms are also common, and tend to avoid explicit reference to human rights, even if they have been introduced or reinforced on the basis of the UN Framework and Guiding Principles on Business and Human Rights.

---

[310] E Morgera, 'From Corporate Social Responsibility to Accountability Mechanisms' in P.-M. Dupuy and J. Viñuales (eds), *Harnessing Foreign Investment to Promote Environmental Protection: Incentives and Safeguards* (Cambridge: Cambridge University Press, 2013) 321.

On the whole, while there is a significant degree of convergence among all standards of corporate environmental accountability, remaining divergence points to particularly controversial concepts in international law, such as precaution or the justiciability of environmental human rights. In addition, substantive dimensions of these international standards have started to emerge for some international corporate environmental accountability standards and have quickly reached a significant level of detail.[311] In the context of environmental management systems, for instance, more substantive standards have emerged with regard to freshwater and climate change targets. The international standard on prevention has particularly lent itself to developing substantive dimensions in relation to freshwater, chemicals, waste, and climate change. This confirms the recommendation by former UN Special Rapporteur on Human Rights and the Environment, John Knox, that more work is necessary to clarify the responsibilities of businesses in relation to human rights and the environment, including how the nexus between human rights and the environment relates to gender and other types of discrimination.[312] In effect, as also exemplified by the normative work of the UN Special Rapporteur on Toxics, international standards on business due diligence need to further develop in order to take into account specific groups of right-holders, such as children. As will be discussed in the next chapter, progress has been made specifically with regard to indigenous peoples in this connection. In addition, as will be discussed in Chapter 6, means of monitoring and implementation of international standards on corporate environmental accountability and responsibility have served to ensure coherence among these standards and fill gaps in specific cases.

---

[311] Contra S. Deva, 'UN's Human Rights Norms for Transnational Corporations and Other Business Enterprises: An Imperfect Step in the Right Direction?' (2004) 10 *ILSA Journal of International and Comparative Law* 493, 509, where the author argues that international standards are 'generally so vague and general that it is quite easy to comply with their words without adhering to their spirit'.

[312] UN Framework Principles on Human Rights and the Environment (n. 292) para. 18.

5
Assessing the Convergence of International Standards on Corporate Environmental Responsibility

Substantive human rights law obligations serve to clarify the limits of State discretion in pursuing the objectives of the Convention on Biological Diversity (CBD).[1] At the domestic level, in authorizing any activity, either biodiversity conservation or use, CBD Parties are to ensure that no unjustified, foreseeable infringements of human rights may arise from the decision.[2] This also implies States' obligation to prevent business entities from violating these rights.[3] In other words, implementing the CBD obligations in a mutually supportive way with international human rights law entails that States must develop laws and institutions that effectively 'regulate harm to biodiversity from private actors' in a way that is 'non-retrogressive and non-discriminatory'.[4] These clarifications of the relationship between international biodiversity law and international human rights law are quite recent[5] and provide a basis to better understand the emergence of substantive international standards of corporate environmental responsibility in relation to indigenous peoples' rights to territories, land, and natural resources. They also serve to understand the emergence of substantive standards on protected areas and the sustainable use of natural resources.

1 Indigenous peoples and local communities

Through successive decisions, CBD Parties have made significant conceptual and normative contributions to clarify the content of business due diligence to respect

---

[1] E. Morgera, 'Under the Radar: Fair and Equitable Benefit-sharing and the Human Rights of Indigenous Peoples and Local Communities connected to Natural Resources' (2019) 23 *International Journal of Human Rights* 1098. Convention on Biological Diversity (CBD) (Rio de Janeiro, 5 June 1992, in force 29 December 1993).

[2] Report of the UN Special Rapporteur on the Issue of Human Rights Obligations Relating to the Enjoyment of a Safe, Clean, Healthy and Sustainable Environment: Biodiversity, UN Doc. A/HRC/34/49 (19 January 2017) para. 34.

[3] Ibid. paras 33–34.

[4] Ibid. para. 69.

[5] E. Morgera, 'Dawn of a New Day? The Evolving Relationship between the Convention on Biological Diversity and International Human Rights Law' (2018) 54 *Wake Forest Law Review* 101.

the human rights[6] of indigenous peoples' rights to natural resources but also for other local communities in the context of the ecosystem approach.[7] These contributions have been recognized by some of the international standard-setting initiatives on corporate accountability discussed in Chapter 3, notably the UN Norms, the IFC Performance Standards, and the activity of UN Special Rapporteurs. These developments, however, may be surprising as the Convention is not seen as a forward-looking treaty from a human rights standpoint. Its text does not include the word 'right'.[8] Both the Convention and decisions of the CBD Conference of Parties (COP) until 2014 have referred to 'indigenous and local communities', because State Parties could not find consensus on utilizing the more human rights-cognizant expression 'indigenous peoples'.[9] It was only in 2014 that the CBD COP decided to change the terminology, with Parties going to great lengths to indicate that the reference to 'indigenous peoples and local communities' in future CBD COP decisions had no implication from the perspective of treaty interpretation (either as subsequent agreement or subsequent practice),[10] with a view to pre-empting limitations to States' discretion in developing national legislation.[11]

There is indeed some scope for concern about the position of certain CBD Parties vis-à-vis human rights:[12] the CBD has provided a forum in which States'

---

[6] This was also expanded upon in E. Morgera, 'Benefit-Sharing as a Bridge between Human Rights and the Environment and Human Rights Accountability of Multinational Corporations' in B. Boer (ed.), *Environmental Law Dimensions of Human Rights* (Oxford: Oxford University Press, 2015) 37; E. Morgera, 'From Corporate Social Responsibility to Accountability Mechanisms' in P.-M. Dupuy and J. Viñuales (eds), *Harnessing Foreign Investment to Promote Environmental Protection: Incentives and Safeguards* (Cambridge: Cambridge University Press, 2013) 321.

[7] Principles of the Ecosystem approach, in Ecosystem approach (CBD Decision V/6, 22 June 2000), Annex B and Refinement and Elaboration of the Ecosystem Approach, Based on Assessment of Experience of Parties in Implementation, in Ecosystem approach (CBD Decision VII/11, 13 April 2004) Annex I.

[8] P. Birnie, A. Boyle, and C. Redgwell, *International Law and the Environment*, 3rd edn (Oxford: Oxford University Press, 2009) 627.

[9] Notwithstanding repeated recommendations to do so from the UN Permanent Forum on Indigenous Issues: see, eg, *Report of the Tenth Session of the UN Permanent Forum on Indigenous Issues* (UNPFII), (2011) UN Doc. E/2011/43-E/C.19/2011/14, paras 26–27.

[10] COP CBD Dec. XII/12 (2014), F, para. 2(c) (with reference to Convention on the Law of the Treaties (Vienna, 23 May 1969, in force 27 January 1980) (VCLT) Art. 31(3)(a) and (b) or special meaning as provided for in VCLT Art. 31(4)). This is without prejudice to the interpretation or application of the Convention in accordance with VCLT Art. 31(3)(c).

[11] This has been clarified in a footnote (fn. 2) to a successive CBD decision, namely The Mo'otz Kuxtal Voluntary Guidelines for the development of mechanisms, legislation, or other appropriate initiatives to ensure the 'prior and informed consent', 'free, prior and informed consent', or 'approval and involvement', depending on national circumstances, of indigenous peoples and local communities for accessing their knowledge, innovations, and practices, for fair and equitable sharing of benefits arising from the use of their knowledge, innovations, and practices relevant for the conservation and sustainable use of biological diversity, and for reporting and preventing unlawful appropriation of traditional knowledge: CBD Dec. XIII/18 (2016).

[12] For instance, the more significant CBD provision from a human rights perspective (Art. 8(j) on traditional knowledge) is heavily qualified, notably by a clause 'subjecting' it to 'national law'. Subjecting compliance with international law as expressed in the CBD to national law was considered unusual at the time of the Convention's adoption but the terminology has shifted over time in the development of soft law under the CBD. This type of reference to national law seems to point to the negotiators' intention to preserve the legal relationship between a State and the indigenous peoples within its territory

reticence on certain human rights questions has emerged.[13] Negotiations under the CBD, for instance, highlighted continued opposition to the right to 'prior informed consent' of indigenous peoples[14] and tepid language merely 'noting'[15] the relevance of the UN Declaration on the Rights of Indigenous Peoples,[16] notwithstanding its intervening universal endorsement.[17] And yet, even in the face of continued reluctance by some CBD Parties to use explicit human rights language,[18] international human rights bodies have recognized that the CBD COP normative activity has contributed to clarify the application of indigenous peoples' human rights in the context of the technicalities of environmental decision-making and management processes, including for the purposes of business due diligence.[19]

The most notable case is represented by the CBD Akwé: Kon Guidelines on socio-cultural and environmental impact assessments (EIAs) for developments in sacred sites and on lands and waters traditionally occupied or used by indigenous peoples and local communities.[20] These guidelines have been used more and more often in different contexts to assess whether private companies' conduct is acceptable in light of international human rights standards. CBD Parties themselves have encouraged business entities to monitor and assess impacts on biodiversity and ecosystem services, to develop and apply processes and production methods that

---

based on pre-existing, but possibly also future, national law. L. Glowka et al., *A Guide to the Convention on Biological Diversity* (Gland: IUCN, 1994) 48–49.

[13] Indigenous peoples' representatives and the UN Special Rapporteur on Indigenous Peoples' Rights, lamented that negotiations of a new legally binding protocol under the CBD did not sufficiently respect indigenous peoples' rights: Report of the Special Rapporteur on the Rights of Indigenous Peoples to the General Assembly, (2012) UN Doc. A/67/301, para. 58.

[14] Resulting in the adoption of the ambiguous expression 'prior informed consent or approval and involvement' in Nagoya Protocol on Access to Genetic Resources and the Fair and Equitable Sharing of Benefits Arising from Their Utilization to the Convention on Biological Diversity (Nagoya, 29 October 2010, in force 12 October 2014) Art. 7. Note that the UN Permanent Forum on Indigenous Issues noted that the term 'consultation' cannot replace or undermine the right of indigenous peoples to prior informed consent: UNPFII (n. 9) para. 36

[15] Nagoya Protocol, preambular recital 26.

[16] UN Declaration on the Rights of Indigenous Peoples (UN General Assembly Resolution 61/295, 13 September 2007).

[17] The adoption of the Declaration by the General Assembly was initially opposed by Australia, Canada, the US, and New Zealand. All these countries reversed their position by 2010 (See UN Office of the High Commissioner for Human Rights, press release 'Indigenous rights declaration endorsed by States' (23 December 2010) at http://www.ohchr.org/EN/NewsEvents/Pages/Indigenousrightsdeclarationendorsed.aspx.

[18] E. Morgera, 'Against All Odds: The Contribution of the Convention on Biological Diversity to International Human Rights Law' in D. Alland et al. (eds), *Unity and Diversity of International Law: Essays in Honour of Professor Pierre-Marie Dupuy* (Leiden: Martinus Nijhoff Publishers, 2014) 983, 983.

[19] See generally Morgera (n. 1).

[20] CBD Decision VII/16F, 'Akwé: Kon Voluntary Guidelines for the Conduct of Cultural, Environmental and Social Impact Assessment regarding Developments Proposed to Take Place on, or which are Likely to Impact on, Sacred Sites and on Lands and Waters Traditionally Occupied or Used by Indigenous and Local Communities, in Article 8(j) and related provisions' (2004).

minimize or avoid negative impacts on biodiversity, and 'take into account, as appropriate, the Akwé: Kon Guidelines'.[21]

The work of the former UN Special Rapporteur on Indigenous Peoples' Rights, James Anaya, on extractive industries is particularly illuminating in this respect:[22] Anaya emphasized that social and environmental impact studies should be conducted according to the CBD Akwé: Kon Guidelines.[23] Anaya also devoted significant attention to fair and equitable benefit-sharing—an international legal concept that has been subject to significant development under the CBD.[24] Similarly, the UN Expert Mechanism on the Rights of Indigenous Peoples, in 2010, stressed the link between prior informed consent, benefit-sharing, and mitigation measures in the context of large-scale natural resource extraction on indigenous peoples' territories or the creation of national parks, and forest and game reserves,[25] referring to the CBD work programme on protected areas as a helpful reference for the purposes of business due diligence.[26] In turn, the International Finance Corporation's 2012 Performance Sustainability Standards relied on the CBD and the legal concept of benefit-sharing, as a key link between free prior informed consent and due diligence.[27] The normative work under the CBD has further been drawn upon by the implementation procedure of the OECD Guidelines for Multinational Enterprises, including to complement and operationalize the UN Framework on Business and Human Rights.[28]

As a result, international legal materials consistently pointed to the applicability of environmental impact (self-)assessment, free prior informed consent (FPIC), and fair and equitable benefit-sharing to business enterprises in the natural resource sector,[29] albeit to different extents.[30] These specialized standards are intertwined with the substantive human rights of indigenous peoples.[31] Prior to applying these standards, Anaya recommended that companies identify, fully

---

[21] CBD Decision X/21, 'Business Engagement' (2010) para. 2(b)–(c).
[22] Report of the Special Rapporteur on the Situation of Human Rights and Fundamental Freedoms of Indigenous People, James Anaya (2009) UN Doc. A/HRC/12/34, Section E.
[23] Ibid. paras 73–74.
[24] E. Morgera, 'The Need for an International Legal Concept of Fair and Equitable Benefit-Sharing' (2016) 27 *European Journal of International Law* 353.
[25] UN Expert Mechanism on the Rights of Indigenous Peoples, Follow-up Report on Indigenous Peoples and the Right to Participate in Decision-making with a Focus on Extractive Industries (2012) UN Doc. A/HRC/21/52, para. 37.
[26] The CBD work programme on protected areas (CBD Decision VII/28 (2004), Annex) was referred to by the Expert Mechanism on the Rights of Indigenous Peoples, Progress Report on the Study on Indigenous Peoples and the Right to Participate in Decision-making (2010) UN Doc. A/HRC/15/35, para. 37.
[27] Ch. 3, Section 6.2.
[28] Ch. 6, Section 2.3. OECD, *Guidelines on Multinational Enterprises* (Paris: OECD Publishing, 2011), introduced in Ch. 3, Section 5 of this book.
[29] Morgera (n. 1) 1120–23.
[30] S. Seck, 'Indigenous Rights, Environmental Rights, or Stakeholder Engagement? Comparing IFC and OECD Approaches to the Implementation of the Business Responsibility to Respect Human Rights' (2016) 12 *McGill Journal of International Sustainable Development Law and Practice* 57.
[31] Eg IFC 2012 Performance Standard 7: Guidance Note, 9.24; Morgera (n. 1) fn. 201.

incorporate, and make operative the norms concerning the rights of indigenous peoples within every aspect of the work carried out within or in close proximity to indigenous lands. In this connection, assessments are also expected to take into account indigenous peoples' and local communities' rights over lands and waters traditionally occupied or used by them and associated biodiversity.[32] As part of their due diligence, companies should avoid endorsing or contributing to any act or omission on the part of the State amounting to a failure to adequately consult with the affected indigenous community before proceeding with a project.[33] For their part, States still have to comply with their international human rights obligations when delegating to companies the execution of impact assessments and FPIC processes, considering the power imbalances and indigenous peoples' lack of access to technical information about proposed projects.[34]

Different international standards, however, have not all referred to all the triggers for applying specialized standards to business due diligence. Former UN Special Rapporteur Knox identified as triggers, first, the use of indigenous peoples' and traditional communities' traditional knowledge; and second, the extraction or other activities (including conservation) in relation to territories, lands, or resources (including genetic resources) that are traditionally owned, occupied, or used by indigenous peoples and traditional communities. The latter includes lands to which they have had access for their subsistence and traditional activities, and may not have formal recognition of property rights or delimitation and demarcation of boundaries.[35] Along similar lines, the OECD-FAO Guidance for Responsible Agricultural Supply Chains refers to operations involving indigenous peoples' lands, resources, and knowledge.[36] The IFC 2012 Standards identify as triggers: potential relocation of indigenous peoples, impacts on lands and natural resources subject to traditional ownership or under customary use, and projects proposing to use cultural resources for commercial purposes.[37] These are only partly overlapping with those identified by Knox, because the reference to traditional knowledge is limited to commercial use.[38] And while the IFC Standards make explicit reference to relocation in line with the UN Declaration on the Rights

---

[32] CBD Akwé: Kon Guidelines (n. 20), para. 57.
[33] Report of the Special Rapporteur Anaya A/HRC/12/34 (n. 22) Section E.
[34] Seck (n. 30) 392.
[35] Report of the Special Rapporteur on the Issue of Human Rights and the Environment John Knox: Framework Principles on Human Rights and the Environment (2018) UN Doc. A/HRC/37/59, paras 53 and 48. See comments in E. Morgera, 'A reflection on benefit-sharing as a Framework Principle on Human Rights and the Environment proposed by UN Special Rapporteur John Knox (Part I)' BENELEX Blog post (April 2018), https://benelexblog.wordpress.com/.
[36] OECD-FAO Guidance for Responsible Agricultural Supply Chains (Paris: OECD, 2016) para. 53 and fnn. 19–21 referring to CBD Akwé: Kon Guidelines (n. 20), para. 46 and IFC Performance Standard 7, paras 18–20.
[37] IFC 2012 Performance Standard 1, para. 35.
[38] Nagoya Protocol, Art. 8(a); E. Morgera, E. Tsioumani, and M. Buck, *Unraveling the Nagoya Protocol: Commentary on the Protocol on Access and Benefit-Sharing to the Convention on Biological Diversity* (Leiden: Martinus Nijhoff, 2014) 179–84.

of Indigenous Peoples (UNDRIP),[39] they have not included projects adjacent to indigenous peoples' lands and when waste or hazardous materials are stored in their lands, which UNDRIP also singles out.[40] The IFC Standards further emphasize that FPIC and benefit-sharing are envisaged where the business entity 'intends to utilise natural resources that are central to the identity and livelihoods of indigenous peoples and their use exacerbates livelihood risk'.[41] This should be understood in line with the concept of physical and cultural survival discussed by the Inter-American Court of Human Rights:[42] either proposed development projects or conservation initiatives concern natural resources that are *traditionally used* by indigenous and tribal peoples; or the extraction of natural resources (notably minerals) that are not traditionally used by indigenous peoples is likely to affect other natural resources that are.[43] This is in line with ILO monitoring bodies' view that not only projects implemented in traditional lands, but also those having an impact on communities' life require a heightened level of protection.[44] The African Commission, in turn, underscored the need to protect natural resources found on or under indigenous land, rather than only those resources the extraction of which may have a negative impact on the group indirectly.[45] As coherent international guidance from a human rights perspective would be helpful to feed into the development of corporate responsibility standards, it has been underlined with concern that the UN Working Group on Business and Human Rights did not mention any cases in which international law required FPIC.[46]

It should also be preliminarily noted that while most attention in the following section will be concentrated on indigenous peoples, these triggers can apply also to a category of less clear status in international human rights law—local/traditional communities.[47] This term could apply to a variety of groups benefiting from the

---

[39] UNGA Res. 61/295 (13 September 2007).

[40] P. Simons and A. Macklin, *The Governance Gap: Extractive Industries, Human Rights and the Home State Advantage* (Abingdon: Routledge, 2014) 135 based on Amnesty International, 'Public Statement a Missed Opportunity to Better Protect the Rights of those Affected by Business related Human Rights Abuses' (2011).

[41] IFC 2012 Performance Standard 1, para. 18.

[42] Inter-American Court of Human Rights, *Case of the Saramaka People v. Suriname*, Judgment (Interpretation of the Judgment on Preliminary Objections, Merits, Reparations and Costs), 12 August 2008, paras 122–23; P. Thornberry, *Indigenous Peoples and Human Rights* 352 (Manchester: Manchester University Press, 2002) 282.

[43] *Saramaka (Merits)* paras 155–58.

[44] S. Errico, 'The Controversial Issue of Natural Resources: Balancing States' Sovereignty with Indigenous Peoples' Rights' in S. Allen and A. Xanthaki (eds), *Reflections on the UN Declaration on the Rights of Indigenous Peoples* (Oxford: Hart Publishing, 2011) 348.

[45] G. Pentassuglia, 'Indigenous Groups and the Developing Jurisprudence of the African Commission on Human and Peoples' Rights: Some Reflections' (2010) 3 *UCL Human Rights Rev*iew 150, 160.

[46] C. Rodríguez-Garavito, 'Business and Human Rights: Beyond the End of the Beginning' in C. Rodríguez-Garavito (ed.), *Business and Human Rights: Beyond the End of the Beginning* (Cambridge: Cambridge University Press, 2017) 11, 20.

[47] Eg Special Rapporteur De Schutter, Interim Report (2012) UN Doc. A/67/268, para. 39; ECOWAS, Directive on the Harmonization of Guiding Principles and Policies in the mining Sector (2009); UN-REDD Programme, 'Guidelines on Free, Prior and Informed Consent' (2013) 11–12; and Roundtable on Sustainable Biofuels, Principles and Criteria (2012): see Morgera, Tsioumani, and Buck (n. 38) 40;

protection of human rights of general application (such as those related to property, subsistence, and culture),[48] which may be negatively affected by interferences with these communities' customary relations with land and natural resources,[49] such as traditional farmers[50] and small-scale fishing communities.[51] Under the CBD, these groups are singled out because of their *ecosystem stewardship*,[52] which hinges on the intrinsic connection between these communities' knowledge and their natural resources—in other words, the development and transmission of traditional knowledge *through* the management of traditionally used natural resources.[53] Such knowledge is thus embodied in *traditional lifestyles*[54] that are inextricably linked to natural resources, shared cultural identity and customary rules.[55] This resonates with the understanding, under international human rights law, of the traditional use of natural resources as 'part of a way of life'.[56] Former UN Special Rapporteur Knox underscored local communities' comparable vulnerability to those of indigenous peoples due to their similarly close relationship with territories, and the fact that local communities equally 'depend directly on nature for their material needs and cultural life' without self-identifying as indigenous peoples.[57] In other

---

and L. Cotula and K. Tienhaara, 'Reconfiguring Investment Contracts to Promote Sustainable Development' (2013) 2011–12 *Yearbook of International Law on Investment and Policy* 281, 301 and 303.

[48] A. Bessa, 'Traditional Local Communities in International Law' (PhD dissertation, European University Institute, 2013).
[49] O. De Schutter, 'The Emerging Human Right to Land' (2010) 12 *International Community Law Review* 303, 324–25, 319.
[50] International Treaty on Plant Genetic Resources for Food and Agriculture (Rome, 3 November 2001, in force 29 June 2004) Art. 9.2; Food and Agriculture Organization (FAO), Voluntary Guidelines on the Responsible Governance of Tenure of Land, Fisheries and Forests in the Context of National Food Security (VGGT) (2012) UN Doc. CL 144/9 (C 2013/20), Appendix D (VGGT) Art. 8.6; and UN Declaration on the Rights of Peasants and Other People Working in Rural Areas, UN General Assembly Resolution 73/165 (2019). For a discussion, see E. Tsioumani, 'Beyond Access and Benefit-sharing: Lessons from the Law and Governance of Agricultural Biodiversity' (2018) *Journal of World Intellectual Property* 1.
[51] FAO, Voluntary Guidelines for Securing Sustainable Small-scale Fisheries in the Context of Food Security and Poverty Eradication (2013) para. 5.1.
[52] Principles of the Ecosystem Approach, Decision V/6 (2000) para. 9, and CBD Decision VII/11 (2004), Annex I, annotations to rationale to Principle 4. This appears to be reflected in the General Assembly, Strategic Framework for the period 2012–13 (UN Doc. A/65/6/Rev.1) para. 11(24)(b) and for 2014–15 (UN Doc. A/67/6 (prog. 11)) para. 11(16). See discussion in E. Morgera, 'Ecosystem and Precautionary Approach' in E. Morgera and J. Razzaque (eds), *Encyclopedia of Environmental Law: Biodiversity and Nature Protection Law* (Cheltenham: Edward Elgar, 2017) 70.
[53] In the light of the placement of CBD Art. 8(j) in the context of *in situ conservation* (CBD Art. 8). J. Gibson, 'Community Rights to Culture: The UN Declaration on the Rights of Indigenous Peoples' in Allen and Xanthaki (n. 44) 434, 434–35.
[54] On the basis of the wording of CBD Art. 8(j): see definition of traditional knowledge in Akwé: Kon Guidelines (n. 20).
[55] See generally B. Tobin, *Indigenous Peoples, Customary Law and Human Rights: Why Living Law Matters* (Abingdon: Routledge, 2014).
[56] Thornberry (n. 42) 334 and 353.
[57] UN Framework Principles on Human Rights and the Environment, paras 48 and 9. See E. Morgera, 'A reflection on benefit-sharing as a Framework Principle on Human Rights and the Environment proposed by UN Special Rapporteur John Knox (Part II: Right-holders and duty-bearers)' BENELEX Blog post (April 2018), https://benelexblog.wordpress.com/.

words, the emerging 'rights of ecologically concerned non-indigenous local communities'[58] are increasingly being expected to be integrated in business due diligence through impact assessments, FPIC, and benefit-sharing.

1.1 Environmental and socio-cultural impact (self-)assessment

The Global Compact developed specific guidance on business responsibility to respect indigenous peoples' rights,[59] which translates into an expectation for business to 'first recognize that indigenous peoples' relationship to land and natural resources may not align with non-indigenous concepts of property'.[60] This chimes with former UN Special Rapporteur Anaya's proposal that companies identify prior to commencing their activities all matters related to the basic human rights of indigenous peoples with a view to taking them into account when their activities are carried out.[61] This underscores a risk in relying on host States' domestic frameworks as their spiritual connection to land that is not technically, under the law of the relevant country, considered to be a form of ownership. The Guidance, therefore, indicated that indigenous peoples themselves should identify what activities may or may not impact this right, and their views in this regard should be sought and incorporated by companies into impact assessments and project planning.[62] In that connection, reference is made to the CBD's Akwé: Kon Guidelines, as well as the UN Voluntary Guidelines on the Responsible Governance of Tenure of Land, Fisheries and Forests in the Context of National Food Security.[63]

The UN Working Group on Business and Human Rights has taken a more limited approach, without reference to benefit-sharing or the integration of indigenous methodologies. It recommended that business enterprises should ensure

---

[58] S. Seck, 'Transnational Corporations and Extractive Industries' in S. Alam, S. Atapattu, C. Gonzalez, and J. Razzaque (eds), *International Environmental Law and the Global South* (Cambridge: Cambridge University Press, 2015) 380, 392. See also Pentassuglia (n. 45) 157, and generally and C. Doyle and J. Gilbert, 'Indigenous Peoples and Globalization: From "Development Aggression" to "Self-Determined Development"' (2008/9) 7 *European Yearbook of Minority Issues* 219.

[59] Global Compact Office, *The Business Reference Guide to the UN Declaration on the Rights of Indigenous Peoples* (United Nations Global Compact Office, 2013).

[60] Ibid. 66.

[61] Special Rapporteur Anaya, Report on the situation of human rights and fundamental freedoms of indigenous people (2010) UN Doc. A/HRC/15/37, para. 46. This has been confirmed in IACtHR, *Kichwa*, para. 300; IACtHR, *Kaliña and Lokono*, para. 214; and Committee on the Elimination of Racial Discrimination (CERD), Concluding observations on the combined thirteenth to fifteenth periodic reports of Suriname (2015) UN Doc. CERD/C/SUR/CO/13-15, para. 26.

[62] Global Compact Office (n. 59) 66.

[63] Ibid.

that impact assessment processes provide for an evidence-based and gender-disaggregated review of socio-anthropological issues pertaining to any adverse impacts on indigenous peoples living in areas affected by a project, differentiating impacts on possibly vulnerable groups and paying particular attention to any operations in the territories and lands of indigenous peoples.[64]

International human rights processes have indicated that prior impact assessments provide information necessary for indigenous peoples to decide whether to provide FPIC or not. The Inter-American Court has consistently indicated that these assessments should aim at ensuring that permitted levels of impact do not negate the physical or cultural survival of the members of indigenous peoples, and that indigenous peoples are aware of possible risks, including environmental and health ones, so that they can weigh up whether to accept proposed developments voluntarily and with full knowledge.[65] The Akwé: Kon Guidelines clarify that negative impacts could include potential damage to ways of life, livelihoods, well-being, and traditional knowledge.[66] The breadth of the assessment, as a result, ranges from cultural elements such as belief systems, languages, and customs,[67] to systems of natural resource use, the maintenance of genetic diversity through indigenous customary management, the exercise of customary laws regarding land tenure and distribution of resources and benefits,[68] food, and health.[69] It also includes community well-being, vitality and viability (employment levels and opportunities, welfare, education, and availability and standards of housing, infrastructure, services).[70] It further extends to transgenerational aspects, such as opportunities for elders to pass on their knowledge to youth.[71]

Respect for indigenous traditions and cultures[72] in impact assessments further implies integrating indigenous peoples' and local communities' expertise, methodologies, and procedures.[73] This, in turn, may contribute to realizing indigenous peoples' right to participate in public affairs,[74] which points to the public dimension

---

[64] Report of the Working Group on Business and Human Rights on the issue of human rights and transnational corporations and other business enterprises (2016) UN Doc. A/71/291.
[65] IACtHR, *Case of the Saramaka People v. Suriname*, Judgment (Preliminary Objections, Merits, Reparations and Costs: 28 November 2007) para. 133; IACtHR, *Kichwa Indigenous Communitiy of Sarayaku v Ecuador*, Judgment (Merits and Reparations: 27 June 2012) para. 205; IACtHR, *Case of Kaliña and Lokono Peoples v Suriname*, Judgment (Merits, Reparations and Costs: 25 November 2015) para. 214.
[66] Akwé: Kon Guidelines (n. 20), para. 36.
[67] Ibid. para. 6(f).
[68] Ibid. paras 24 and 27–28, 34.
[69] Ibid. para. 42.
[70] Ibid. para. 6(d).
[71] Ibid. para. 49.
[72] IACtHR, *Saramaka People v. Suriname*, Judgment (Interpretation of the Judgment on Preliminary Objections, Merits, Reparations and Costs: 12 August 2008) para. 41; IACtHR, *Kichwa*, para. 206; IACtHR, *Kaliña and Lokono*, para. 215; also citing Rio Declaration, Principle 10.
[73] Akwé: Kon Guidelines (n. 20), para. 64.
[74] IACtHR, *Kaliña and Lokono*, paras 197 and 202–03.

of these exercises even if they are fully run by private actors. Another inter-linked dimension of this international standard is that these assessments should not be limited to identifying negative impacts on indigenous peoples and local communities, but also potential positive impacts upon them: the Akwé: Kon Guidelines call for addressing fair and equitable benefit-sharing[75] during prior impact assessments.[76] It can therefore be argued that while impact assessments are generally understood as geared towards *damage prevention* or *damage control*,[77] they should also identify, in an integrated fashion environmental, economic, and socio-cultural benefits.[78] The CBD Akwé: Kon Guidelines require that consideration of benefit-sharing starts significantly early on in the process—as early as the screening and scoping phases of assessments.[79] This is to be achieved through collaborative procedures and methodologies aimed at ensuring the full involvement of indigenous peoples and local communities.[80] As a result, following the Akwé: Kon Guidelines arguably implies moving away from a technical damage-control approach, shifting to collaboratively identifying and understanding also opportunities for positive impacts according to indigenous peoples' and local communities' worldviews.[81] These worldviews would then determine the scope of the assessment.[82]

International human rights processes have also underscored that prior impact assessments should be prepared by an independent, technically qualified entity with 'active participation of indigenous communities concerned'.[83] The Akwé: Kon Guidelines further recommend establishing processes for recording indigenous communities' views also when they are unable to attend public meetings because of remoteness or poor health, and not just in written form.[84] Governments are expected to provide adequate human, financial, technical, and legal resources to support indigenous expertise, proportionally to the scale of the proposed development.[85] In addition, the Akwé: Kon Guidelines recommend involving indigenous communities in the financial auditing processes of the development to ensure that the resources invested are used effectively.[86] Furthermore, companies are expected

---

[75] Discussed as a self-standing standard at Section 3.1.2.
[76] Akwé: Kon Guidelines (n. 20), para. 40.
[77] N. Craik, 'Biodiversity-inclusive Impact Assessment' in Morgera and Razzaque (n. 52), 431, argues that consideration of biodiversity concerns more generally expands the range of issues and values to be included in environmental assessments. See also C. Doyle, *Indigenous Peoples, Title to Territory, Rights and Resources: The Transformative Role of Free, Prior and Informed Consent* (Abingdon: Routledge, 2015) 94.
[78] Akwé: Kon Guidelines (n. 20), para. 23; Morgera (n. 1) 1110.
[79] Akwé: Kon Guidelines (n. 20), Forward, and paras 3, and 13–14.
[80] Ibid. paras 64 and 15–16.
[81] Ibid. para. 37.
[82] N. Craik, 'Process and Reconciliation: Integrating the Duty to Consult with Environmental Assessment' (2016) 52 *Osgoode Hall Law Journal* 1, 28–29; Morgera (n. 1) 1121.
[83] IACtHR, *Kichwa*, para. 300; IACtHR, *Kaliña and Lokono*, para. 214; CERD (n. 61), para. 26.
[84] Akwé: Kon Guidelines (n. 20), para. 17.
[85] Ibid. paras 18, 64–66, 70.
[86] Ibid. para. 46.

to negotiate an agreement with indigenous peoples or a local community that traditionally occupies certain sites, to cover the procedural aspects of assessment, including options for no-action alternatives; setting out rights, duties, and responsibilities of all parties; and addressing measures to prevent or mitigate any negative impacts of the proposed development.[87]

To ensure the full and effective participation and involvement of indigenous peoples and local communities in screening, scoping, and development planning exercises,[88] the Akwé: Kon Guidelines further suggest appointing community representatives on bodies advising on the screening and scoping phases, and ensuring that communities are consulted on the assessment process, and involved in the establishment of the terms of reference for conducting the assessment.[89] Furthermore, participatory models of community engagement should be used for conducting assessments, including in decision-making, while the proponent is expected to provide 'regular feedback to affected communities throughout the impact assessment and development processes'.[90] To support such involvement, developers are further expected to engage local experts 'at the earliest opportunity'.[91] The usefulness of these clarifications in the CBD Akwé: Kon Guidelines was recognized by the OECD-FAO Guidance for Responsible Agricultural Supply Chains[92] and the OECD Due Diligence Guidance for Responsible Supply Chains of Minerals from Conflict-Affected and High-Risk Areas.[93]

That said, the actual suitability of EIAs in different countries to effectively and respectfully integrate traditional knowledge with 'scientific knowledge',[94] remains to be explored. In addition, evidence confirms that EIAs may not provide a culturally appropriate and open space for understanding the worldviews of indigenous peoples, due to embedded tendencies to privilege mainstream views of development.[95] This is demonstrated by indigenous peoples' preference for indigenous assessments that are fully based on indigenous laws and legal traditions.[96]

---

[87] Ibid. para. 21. See Sections 1.2.4 and 1.3.3 later in this chapter.
[88] Ibid. para. 3(a).
[89] Ibid. para. 14.
[90] Ibid. para. 15.
[91] Ibid. para. 16.
[92] OECD-FAO Guidance on Responsible Agricultural Supply Chains, para. 25 and fn. 21. See discussion at Section 3.1.
[93] OECD Due Diligence Guidance for Responsible Supply Chains of Minerals from Conflict-Affected and High-Risk Areas (Paris: OECD, 2013) 35, fn. 2.
[94] S. Vermeylen, G. Martin, and R. Clift, 'Intellectual Property, Rights Systems and the Assemblage of Local Knowledge Systems' (2008) 15 *International Journal of. Cultural Property Rights* 201.
[95] C. Laude, *A Tale of Two Reconciliations in Environmental Planning: The Right to Say No to Development and the Enticement of a 'Politics of Recognition'*, presentation at Decolonizing the Academy conference, University of Edinburgh (26 February 2016).
[96] N. Schabus, 'Traditional Knowledge' in Morgera and Razzaque (n. 52) 264.

1.2 Free prior informed consent

Although it is commonly considered a relatively recent international legal concept,[97] free prior informed consent has been claimed as a key concept originating in indigenous peoples' own legal traditions and relations with other peoples.[98] The exact content of this requirement for States remains a matter of contention. It is explicitly mentioned in the UN Declaration on the Rights of Indigenous Peoples (UNDRIP)[99] and the ILO Convention concerning Indigenous and Tribal Peoples in Independent Countries,[100] and considered implicit in other international human rights treaties such as the Convention on the Elimination of All Forms of Racial Discrimination.[101] It is also included in more limited terms in the text of the Convention on Biological Diversity[102] and decisions adopted under it.

FPIC encounters varied degrees of recognition among States,[103] which is also apparent under the CBD.[104] Notably, although some CBD instruments such as the Akwé: Kon Guidelines refer to 'prior informed consent',[105] more recent instruments[106] refer to 'prior informed consent or approval and involvement' reflecting the reluctance by some CBD Parties to fully endorse the standards enshrined in UNDRIP. According to proponent countries, the expression 'approval and involvement' was introduced in order to allow for a greater degree of flexibility in implementation at the national level,[107] in the light of different domestic legal arrangements concerning the relations between governments and indigenous

---

[97] Eg UN Expert Mechanism, Final report of the study on indigenous peoples and the right to participate in decision-making (2011) UN Doc. A/HRC/18/42, para. 63, criticized by Doyle (n. 77) 15 and 5.

[98] *See* generally Doyle (n. 77) 15.

[99] United Nations Declaration on the Rights of Indigenous Peoples, UN General Assembly Resolution 61/295 (13 September 2007).

[100] International Labour Organization's (ILO) Convention no. 169 Concerning Indigenous and Tribal Peoples in Independent Countries (27 June 1989, in force 5 September 1991).

[101] International Convention on the Elimination of All Forms of Racial Discrimination (New York, 7 March 1966, in force 4 January 1969).

[102] CBD Art. 8(j).

[103] J. Gilbert and C. Doyle, 'A New Dawn over the Land: Shedding Light on Collective Ownership and Consent' in Allen and Xanthaki (n. 44) 325.

[104] Morgera, Tsioumani, and Buck (n. 38) 145–56.

[105] Akwé: Kon Guidelines (n. 20), paras 29, 52–53, and 60, refer consistently only to 'prior informed consent'.

[106] Nagoya Protocol Art. 6(2), with 'approval and involvement' being found in the wording of CBD Art. 8(j); CBD, Bonn Guidelines on Access to Genetic Resources and Fair and Equitable Sharing of the Benefits Arising out of Their Utilization, CBD Decision VI/24 (2002) Annex, para. 31; and CBD Decision V/16, para. 5. For an indication of continued diverge of views on utilizing UNDRIP language in the context of the CBD, see C. Benson et al., *'Summary of the Seventh Meeting of the Working Group on Article 8(j)'* (2011) 9:557 *ENB* 5–6; and B. Antonich et al., 'Summary of the Eighth Meeting of the Working Group on Article 8(j) and 17th Meeting of the Subsidiary Body on Scientific, Technical and Technological Advice of the Convention on Biological Diversity' (2013) 9:611 *ENB* 4, 6–7, and 20.

[107] G. Burton, 'Implementation of the Nagoya Protocol in JUSCANZ Countries: The Unlikely Lot' in E. Morgera, M. Buck, and E. Tsioumani (eds), *The 2010 Nagoya Protocol on Access and Benefit-Sharing in Perspective: Implications for International Law and National Implementation* (The Hague: Martinus Nijhoff, 2013) 295, 318–19.

peoples within their territories.¹⁰⁸ It can be hypothesized that these differences mainly concern the ways and degree to which the FPIC process is determined and controlled by indigenous communities.¹⁰⁹ Several commentators have suggested that CBD Parties can consider the two expressions as having essentially the same meaning in practice,¹¹⁰ that is, an effective guarantee to protect human rights connected to natural resources by empowering communities to genuinely *influence* decisions that affect their interests,¹¹¹ not merely a right to be *involved* in such processes.¹¹² CBD Parties have indicated that it would be 'not practical to propose a "one-size-fits-all" approach' instead of 'taking into account national and local circumstances of the indigenous peoples and local communities concerned'.¹¹³ Another explanation could be that those governments that made a declaration on the UN Declaration on the Rights of Indigenous Peoples wish to protect room for manoeuvre at the national level in regulating their relationships with indigenous peoples.¹¹⁴

The dividing line between the general principle of international law on effective consultation and FPIC obligations is, in effect, not clear-cut. The Inter-American Court has emphasized the need for 'special and differentiated' consultation processes when the interests of indigenous and tribal peoples are about to be affected,¹¹⁵ with the public interest test set at a higher threshold because the physical and cultural survival of indigenous and tribal peoples is at stake.¹¹⁶ In other words, FPIC goes beyond a more general right to consultation with the public, as a matter of *intensity* of the duty that is intertwined with substantive aspects.¹¹⁷ It has been

---

¹⁰⁸ 'Joint submission Grand Council of the Crees (Eeyou Istchee)' 133–36, and comments by A. Savaresi, 'The International Human Rights Implications of the Nagoya Protocol' in Morgera, Buck, and Tsioumani (n. 107) 53, 69.
¹⁰⁹ UN Special Rapporteur on Indigenous Peoples' Rights Anaya, Study on Extractive Industries and Indigenous Peoples (2013) UN Doc. A/HRC/24/41, paras 26–36.
¹¹⁰ Eg Singh Nijar, *The Nagoya Protocol on Access and Benefit Sharing: An Analysis* (2011); Report of the Special Rapporteur on indigenous peoples' rights James Anaya (2012) UN Doc. A/67/301, paras 92 and 61, where the Special Rapporteur specifically expresses the 'hopeful expectation' that the provisions of the Nagoya Protocol will be implemented 'in harmony with' UNDRIP.
¹¹¹ Doyle (n. 77) 154; Thornberry (n. 42) 349.
¹¹² Expert Mechanism on the Rights of Indigenous Peoples, *Advice No. 2, Indigenous peoples and the right to participate in decision-making* (2011) para. 1, emphasis added. See also M. Århén, *Indigenous Peoples in the International Legal System* (Oxford: Oxford University Press, 2016) 141.
¹¹³ CBD Mo' otz Kuxtal Guidelines (n. 11), para. 9.
¹¹⁴ Morgera (n. 1) 1106.
¹¹⁵ IACtHR, *Kichwa*, paras 165–66.
¹¹⁶ Ibid.; see also African Commission on Human and Peoples' Rights (Afr. Comm.), *Centre for Minority Rights Development (Kenya) and Minority Rights Group International on behalf of Endorois Welfare Council v Kenya* (4 February 2010) Case 276/2003, para. 212. Compare with K. Gover, 'Settler-State Political Theory, "CANZUS" and the UN Declaration on the Rights of Indigenous Peoples' (2015) 26 *European Journal of International Law* 345.
¹¹⁷ See contra, the argument that the right to consultation is procedural, whereas FPIC as a core element of the internal aspect of the right to self-determination is substantive (the right to effectively determine the material outcome of decision-making process): see Århén (n. 112) 135–38. The present author is rather persuaded that procedural and substantive dimensions are intertwined in consultation as well as in FPIC, impact assessment, and benefit-sharing: Morgera (n. 1) 1106–07.

argued that FPIC should guarantee a 'distinguishable voice' for indigenous and tribal peoples within a pluralistic and democratic society in light of their right to decide their own development priorities.[118]

These divergences of interpretation among States are reflected in international standards of corporate environmental responsibility. The IFC 2006 version failed to align itself with international standards on indigenous peoples' rights. It required private companies undertaking projects with significant adverse impacts on local communities to put in place 'free, prior and informed *consultations* and facilitate their informed *participation*'.[119] The IFC at the time referred to its Board of Directors' decision not to mention the international standard expression 'prior informed consent' without providing further details.[120] The 2012 Standard marks a departure for the IFC and provides for the need for companies to conduct 'informed consultation' with a specific and express (albeit qualified) requirement for prior informed consent. The latter has been hailed as 'a watershed moment in international development history', considering significant pressure applied by civil society to achieve this change.[121] In comparison, the UN Working Group on Business and Human Rights has been criticized for not distinguishing consultation from consent.[122] FPIC is not specifically mentioned in the OECD Guidelines, but could be considered implied in an oblique reference to UNDRIP in the Guidelines Commentary.[123] The OECD-FAO Guidance for Responsible Agricultural Supply Chains makes reference to the IFC Performance Standards: accordingly, consent should be 'consistent with achieving the ends of [UNDRIP] and with due regard for particular positions and understanding of individual states'.[124] Against this backdrop, the following elements of FPIC have been translated for the private sector under the CBD and international human rights processes: the meaning of consent and the need for appropriate representation, iterative and culturally appropriate modalities, and documentation.

---

[118] In light of ILO Convention 169, Art. 7(1): A. Fuentes, 'Judicial Interpretation and Indigenous Peoples' Rights to Lands, Participation and Consultation. The Inter-American Court of Human Rights' Approach' (2015) 23 *International Journal of Minority and Group Rights* 39, 74–76 and 79.

[119] IFC 2006 Performance Standard 1, para. 22 (emphasis added).

[120] IFC, 'Policy and Performance Standards on Social and Environmental Sustainability and Policy on Disclosure of Information: IFC Responses to Stakeholder Comments and Rationale for Key Policy Changes' (22 September 2006) 5, where it reads 'we note that this proposal was already considered and rejected during the discussions on the World Bank group's management response'; and at 29 where it reads 'the World Bank group concluded that the process of free, prior and informed consultations leading to broad community support would be more appropriate for the bank group'.

[121] S. Baker, 'Why the IFC's Free, Prior and Informed Consent Policy Does Not Matter (Yet) to Indigenous Communities Affected by Development Projects' (2012–13) 30 *Wisconsin International Law Journal* 668, 669 and 679.

[122] Rodríguez-Garavito (n. 46) 20.

[123] OECD Guidelines, para. 40.

[124] OECD–FAO Guidance for Responsible Agricultural Supply Chains, 98.

1.2.1 Meaning of consent

The IFC translated the concept of prior informed consent for private companies as a good-faith negotiation with culturally appropriate institutions representing indigenous peoples' communities, with a view to reaching an agreement that is seen as legitimate by the majority within the community.[125] This is more specific and less top-down than the recommendation of the UN Working Group on Business and Human Rights, that companies consult indigenous peoples and focus on dialogue as a means to address and resolve grievances; and engage regularly and directly with men and women in the communities in order to inform them as to the way their lifestyles, livelihoods, and human rights may be affected.[126]

The IFC further indicated that 'consent does not necessarily require unanimity and may be achieved even when individuals and sub-groups explicitly disagree'.[127] This is in line with the understanding of FPIC proposed by the Human Rights Council[128] and commended by the UN independent expert on the promotion of a democratic and equitable international order, who, however, cautioned against overlooking minority viewpoints.[129]

In addition, former UN Special Rapporteur on indigenous peoples' rights James Anaya clarified that FPIC does not provide indigenous peoples with a veto power when the State acts legitimately and faithfully in the public interest. But rather it 'establishes the need to frame consultation procedures in order to make every effort to build consensus on the part of all concerned' that is seen as legitimate by the community[130] and is in line with customary legal traditions.[131] Thus, consensus-driven consultation processes should not only address measures to mitigate or compensate for adverse impacts of projects, but also explore and arrive at means of equitable benefit-sharing in a spirit of true partnership.[132]

While it is difficult to anticipate in the abstract when indigenous communities may say yes to a proposed development, particular difficulties may arise in situations where ownership over natural resources is not clarified in domestic frameworks, or when consultations with communities in this regard are inconclusive. The Mo' otz Kuxtal Guidelines clarify that the understanding of 'consent' includes the right *not* to grant consent, and only allows the *temporary* use of traditional

---

[125] IFC 2012 Performance Standard 7, para. 15.
[126] Report of the Working Group on the issue of human rights and transnational corporations and other business enterprises: Business-related impacts on the rights of indigenous peoples (2013) UN Doc. A/68/279, paras 31 and 56.
[127] IFC 2012 Performance Standard 7, para. 12.
[128] Human Rights Council Res. 17/4, para. 11 (2011).
[129] Report of the Independent Expert on the promotion of a democratic and equitable international order (2017) UN Doc. A/HRC/36/40, paras 62–63.
[130] Special Rapporteur Anaya, A/HRC/12/34 (n. 22) para. 53.
[131] Which are considered premised on principles of good faith, justice, friendship, and solidarity, as a notion that affirms and protects the rights of both parties and clarify their duties towards one another: Doyle (n. 77) 41.
[132] Special Rapporteur Anaya's report, UN Doc. A/HRC/12/34 (n. 22) paras 48 and 53.

knowledge for the purpose for which it was granted, unless otherwise and mutually agreed.[133] As has been argued elsewhere, the link between self-assessment of impacts and fair and equitable benefit-sharing may also serve to clarify when indigenous peoples may be entitled to say no to a private company.[134] If the proposed activity is likely to affect traditionally owned or used resources, or has the potential to negatively impact on traditionally used resources threatening the community's cultural and physical survival, the lack of early, genuine, and culturally appropriate identification and discussion of benefits according to their worldviews justifies the withholding of consent in and of itself. Withholding consent can also be justified if the dialogue on benefits has not had any impact on the final outcome, in the absence of sufficient reasons to justify such an outcome.[135]

1.2.2 Appropriate representation

Another complexity concerns the need to ensure that consent is given by the legitimate representatives of the peoples or communities concerned.[136] International human rights materials emphasize the need to take into account indigenous peoples' and local communities' 'self-chosen and autonomously managed'[137] decision-making mechanisms.[138] Accordingly, States are responsible to ensure the genuine involvement of legitimate representatives of indigenous peoples and the true nature of consent in the context of customary institutions, taking into account that consent may be withdrawn at a later stage.[139] But, as underscored by the Guidance to the UN Global Compact, 'the practical role of governments in ensuring compliance with FPIC varies by country, and many governments are still in the early stages of working out how to best comply with international FPIC standards.'[140] This creates added risks for companies to ensure respect for indigenous peoples' rights as part of their due diligence.

The IFC CAO issued guidance, based on its practical experience, including principles and strategies to support companies in tackling issues around representation. The principles stressed self-identification of group representatives, the need for each party to feel reasonably assured that the representatives of the other party are credible and legitimate, consideration of gender equity in representation structures, and, where possible, consideration of other factors such age, culture, geography, level of impact, positions and opinions, political views, education, language,

---

[133] CBD Mo'otz Kuxtal Guidelines (n. 11), para. 7(b).
[134] Morgera (n. 1) 1114–15.
[135] Ibid. See also ILA, Report on the Rights of Indigenous Peoples (2010).
[136] UN Permanent Forum on Indigenous Issues: see, eg, *Report of the Tenth Session of the UN Permanent Forum on Indigenous Issues* (2011) UN Doc. E/2011/43-E/C.19/2011/14.
[137] Doyle (n. 77) 16.
[138] Ibid. 154; Thornberry (n. 42) 349.
[139] Ibid.
[140] Global Compact Office (n. 59) 25. See also Global Compact's Good Practice Note on Free Prior Informed Consent (UN, 2014).

or religion; and the need to understand, agree upon, and clearly define and document consent.[141] They also mentioned the responsibility of representatives to keep their constituents informed throughout the dispute resolution process, including how their inputs are weighed and acted upon; and the need to adapt to changes in representation over time.[142] One of the key challenges, which is relevant to all standards discussed in this section, is addressing limitations in a representative's capacity (in resources, organization and coordination, information, and technical knowledge) and related power imbalances.[143] The IFC suggests in this connection that companies take into account communities' capacities, provide them opportunities to assess risks and impacts, and enable them to access legal advice.[144]

1.2.3 Iterative and culturally appropriate modalities

The 2012 version of the IFC Performance Standards emphasize the ongoing nature of the consultation process, which is in line with guidance in international human rights law and international biodiversity law.[145] It underscores the need for direct exchanges of views with communities on matters that affect them, as well as with regard to benefit-sharing measures,[146] with particular attention to gender equality issues.[147] In addition, the IFC Performance Standards clarify that all consultations should be free from external manipulation, interference, coercion, or intimidation; enabling meaningful participation, 'where applicable',[148] which appears to be below international standards.[149] In addition, the IFC Standard recommends documenting consent, using the language of preference of affected communities.[150] This is followed up through ongoing reporting to affected communities on issues identified through consultation or grievances, including updates on mitigation measures and actions.[151]

Although the IFC Standards are aligned with international guidance on the need for culturally appropriate approaches to FPIC processes,[152] mismatches between assumptions and decision-making modalities between the developer and communities with regard to contracts are significant and may prove 'insurmountable'.[153] Scholars have expressed concern that the IFC may still appear to suggest that

---

[141] CAO, 'Reflections from the Practice of Dispute Resolution No 2: Representation' (CAO, undated) 4.
[142] Ibid. 5.
[143] Ibid. 6.
[144] IFC 2012 Performance Standard 7: Guidance Note 7, at 8; see Baker (n. 121) 690.
[145] This mainly relates to consultations with indigenous peoples: Ch. 5, Section 1.
[146] See Ch. 5, Section 1.3.
[147] IFC 2012 Performance Standard 1, para. 31.
[148] Ibid, para. 30.
[149] See discussion of triggers for this standard in Section 1 of this chapter.
[150] IFC 2012 Performance Standard 1, para. 30.
[151] Ibid. para. 36.
[152] IFC 2012 Performance Standard 7: Guidance Note 7, at 8.
[153] Baker (n. 121) 702.

'project approval may be obtained prior to obtaining FPIC'.[154] In effect, whether the IFC's understanding of FPIC will make a difference depends on effective opportunities for communities to 'affect in any meaningful way the social and environmental risks' of large projects. At the stage of engagement with the company, considerable investment has already occurred and meaningful and broad discursive space needs to be found between the developers' interest in risk management and communities' aspirations for self-determination, which can then lead to the conclusion of legally enforceable contract[155] to ensure respect of the human rights of communities.

One of the increasingly common features across international instruments on corporate environmental responsibility in this connection is the understanding of FPIC as a continuous process, rather than a one-off exercise,[156] which 'should underpin and be an integral part of developing a relationship'.[157] Bringing together the IFC Standards and the findings of the Inter-American Court of Human Rights and African Commission, the Guidance to the UN Global Compact indicated that FPIC 'is an on-going process that should be maintained throughout the life cycle of planning, researching, developing, implementing, and executing a project through regular engagement with affected indigenous peoples'.[158] Along similar lines, the FAO-OECD Guidance for Responsible Agricultural Supply Chains refers to the process of seeking PIC as an 'iterative rather than one-off discussion' based on 'continuous dialogue',[159] with a view to mitigating impacts in a manner that reflects communities' aspirations and priorities.[160] This appears aligned with international human rights sources underscoring the need to seek FPIC at all stages of development projects or conservation initiatives, whenever there is a possible impact on communities' traditional life[161] from the inception to the final authorization and implementation of proposed activities.[162] The CBD Mo' otz Kuxtal Guidelines, which were inter-governmentally adopted after incorporating considerable inputs from indigenous representatives,[163] indicated that FPIC should be understood as a *continual* process building mutually beneficial, *ongoing* arrangements to 'build trust, good relations, mutual understanding, intercultural spaces, knowledge exchanges, create new knowledge and reconciliation'.[164]

---

[154] Ibid. 694.
[155] Ibid. 671–72 and 686–88.
[156] Morgera (n. 1) 1105.
[157] CBD Mo' otz Kuxtal Guidelines (n. 11), para. 8.
[158] Global Compact Office (n. 59) 26.
[159] OECD-FAO Guidance for Responsible Agricultural Supply Chains, 80.
[160] Ibid. 94.
[161] IACtHR, *Kaliña and Lokono*, Joint Concurring Opinion of Judges Sierra Porto and Ferrer MacGregor Poisot, para. 14; UNPFII (n. 26), particularly para. 34.
[162] IACtHR, *Kaliña and Lokono*, Joint Concurring Opinion of Judges Sierra Porto and Ferrer MacGregor Poisot, para. 14.
[163] Morgera (n. 5) 114.
[164] CBD Mo' otz Kuxtal Guidelines (n. 11), para. 8.

Another increasingly common feature across international guidance is the linkage between cultural appropriateness and the timing of the FPIC process. In the context of international human rights processes, FPIC has been interpreted as entailing that consent should be given freely, without coercion, intimidation, or manipulation, including by allowing sufficient time for internal discussion within the community.[165] The IFC indicated that FPIC should also allow for sufficient time for consensus-building and for communities to develop responses to project issues that impact upon their lives and livelihoods, as well as for sufficient time for the developer to address communities' concerns and suggestions on project design and implementation.[166] The CBD 2014 Mo' otz Kuxtal Guidelines underscore the need for FPIC to be free from 'expectations or timelines that are externally imposed',[167] and rather take into account communities' time requirements.[168]

The degree and modalities of information-sharing during the FPIC process also have a bearing on cultural appropriateness. International human rights bodies have also clarified that FPIC should be based on an understanding of the full range of issues and implications entailed by the activity or decision in question, with a view to providing indigenous peoples with 'full and objective information about all aspects of the project that will affect them, including the impact of the project on their lives and environment'.[169] The UN Working Group on Business and Human Rights recommended paying due attention to the various methods of informing and consulting indigenous peoples that may be required owing to their distinct cultures and languages.[170] The CBD Mo' otz Kuxtal Guidelines have provided more detail on the need for adequate and balanced information from a variety of sources that is made available in indigenous or local languages using terms understood by indigenous peoples and local communities, and including safeguards to ensure that all parties to an agreement have the same understanding of the information and terms provided.[171]

1.2.4 Documentation and community protocols

The requirement to document the FPIC process can have significant substantive dimensions, including in terms of defining 'what would constitute consent' from the viewpoint of communities.[172] While most examples are soft in nature (such as

---

[165] IACtHR, *Kichwa*, para. 18.
[166] IFC Performance Standard 7: Guidance Note 7, at 8.
[167] CBD Mo' otz Kuxtal Guidelines (n. 11), para. 14.
[168] Ibid. para. 7(b).
[169] IACtHR, *Saramaka (Merits)* para. 134; and A. Fodella, 'Indigenous Peoples, the Environment, and International Jurisprudence' in N. Boschiero, T. Scovazzi, C. Pitea, and C. Ragni (eds), *International Courts and the Development of International Law: Essays in Honour of Tullio Treves* (The Hague: TMC Asser Press, 2013) 356 and 360.
[170] Report of the Working Group on the issue of human rights and transnational corporations and other business enterprises: Business-related impacts on the rights of indigenous peoples (2013) UN Doc. A/68/279, paras 31 and 56.
[171] CBD Mo' otz Kuxtal Guidelines (n. 11), para. 17(c)(iii).
[172] Baker (n. 121) 695–99; IFC Guidance Note 7, at 9.

memoranda of understanding, letter of intent, and joint statement of principles), using a legally binding contract or at least tying violations of communities' requirements to a default under the primary loan agreement can provide firmer evidence of good-faith engagement on the part of the company.[173]

While the OECD Guidelines do not necessarily prescribe an agreement in written form, they call for agreement with indigenous peoples on what constitutes appropriate consent and a consultation process, on the basis of communities' customary laws and practices, with their own freely chosen representatives.[174] The OECD-FAO Guidance for Responsible Agricultural Supply Chains refers to the need to document and implement agreements resulting from consultations, including by establishing a process by which community views and concerns can be properly recorded. While written statements may be preferred, community members' views could also be recorded on video or audio tape, or any other appropriate way, subject to the consent of communities.[175]

Other written materials can support the process of seeking FPIC from the outset, rather than towards the end of the process. To facilitate the understanding of customary laws, as well as community values and beliefs, as the first step in seeking FPIC, recent CBD Guidelines devoted significant attention to 'community protocols'. Supporting a bottom-up approach, community protocols are a written document developed through a community consultation to outline its core ecological, cultural, and spiritual values and customary laws, based on which the community provides clear terms and conditions to regulate access to their knowledge and resources.[176] These protocols may allow a community to prepare in advance for any negotiations with private developers, rather than entering into such negotiations in an ad hoc manner, potentially also preventing internal conflicts. Compliance with community protocols remains voluntary, unless it is secured through national legislation or contractual means.[177]

Community protocols have become a recurring feature under the CBD, as they are expected to 'cover a broad array of expressions, articulations, rules and practices generated by communities to set out how they expect other stakeholders to engage with them. They may reference customary as well as national or international laws to affirm indigenous peoples' and local communities' rights to be approached according to a certain set of standards.'[178] The 2014 Mo' otz Kuxtal Guidelines clarify the role of community protocols as being to:

---

[173] Baker (n. 121) 699.
[174] Ibid. 97.
[175] OECD-FAO Guidance for Responsible Agricultural Supply Chains, 51.
[176] E. Morgera and E. Tsioumani, 'The Evolution of Benefit-Sharing: Linking Biodiversity and Community Livelihoods' (2010) 15 *Review of European Community and International Environmental Law* 150, 157–58.
[177] Morgera and Tsioumani (n. 176) 157–58.
[178] CBD Mo' otz Kuxtal Guidelines (n. 11), para. 19.

provide communities an opportunity to focus on their development aspirations vis-a-vis their rights and to articulate for themselves and for users their understanding of their bio-cultural heritage and therefore on what basis they will engage with a variety of stakeholders. By considering the interconnections of their land rights, current socio-economic situation, environmental concerns, customary laws and traditional knowledge, communities are better placed to determine for themselves how to negotiate with a variety of actors.[179]

In other words, these documents not only better prepare communities to interact with private developers, but they also better prepare private developers to engage respectfully and appropriately with communities. Community protocols can thus help to shape interactions around FPIC and benefit-sharing in line with communities' worldviews, including by clarifying what communities are not willing to compromise on, how they expect outsiders to respect their decision-making processes, and what kind of benefits communities themselves would consider.[180] An empirical study on community protocols, however, has identified common challenges with regard to community protocols across four different regions (Europe, Africa, Latin America, and Asia) and five different sectors (traditional medicine, protected area management, extractives, traditional pastoralism, and traditional agriculture). First, this study underscored that communities' needs and practices change over time, which may not necessarily be accurately reflected in existing community protocols. Therefore, community protocols need to be considered a basis for opening a dialogue, as opposed to a fixed basis for negotiation, as communities may not always have the capacity and resources to update protocols over time. Second, the development and update of community protocols require time, resources and often external support[181] (including legal assistance to better understand relevant international and national legal regimes)[182] that may not necessarily be available to communities, or may bring about the risk that external actors may influence or impose certain expectations on communities.[183] Private companies, therefore, need to exercise caution in expecting communities to have protocols in place that can support the FPIC process, and should not rely on community protocols that have been developed for other specific purposes. With these cautions in mind, becoming familiar with existing community protocols should be considered part of business due diligence to respect the human rights of specific indigenous peoples.

---

[179] Ibid.
[180] L. Parks, 'Challenging Power from the Bottom Up? Community Protocols, Benefit-sharing and the Challenge of Dominant Discourses' (2018) 88 *Geoforum* 87.
[181] Ibid.
[182] Morgera and Tsioumani (n. 176) 157–58.
[183] L. Parks and E. Morgera, 'The Need for an Interdisciplinary Approach to Norm Diffusion: The Case of Fair and Equitable Benefit-sharing' (2015) 24 *Review of European, Comparative and International Environmental Law* 353, 361.

1.3 Fair and equitable benefit-sharing

Fair and equitable benefit-sharing is considered a subset of the general principle of international law of equity.[184] It is also seen as a component of sustainable development, as a corollary of inter- and intra-generational equity.[185] Similarly to States' benefit-sharing obligations, former UN Special Rapporteur Anaya emphasized that companies should consider benefit-sharing as independent of compensation measures,[186] as a tool to create genuinely equal partnerships with indigenous peoples with a view to strengthening their capacity to establish and pursue their own development priorities and enhancing their own decision-making mechanisms and institutions.[187] Anaya argued that business due diligence would imply that companies set up specific benefit-sharing mechanisms, based on international standards.[188] This implies moving away from an exclusive focus on damage prevention to a proactive and collaborative identification of benefit-sharing opportunities according to indigenous peoples' worldviews.[189] To that end, Anaya envisaged that, if indigenous peoples themselves do not wish or are unable to initiate resource extraction, they are entitled to participate in project decision-making *and* share in their profits through an agreement with outside companies (for instance, through a minority ownership interest in the extractive operations).[190] This points to the usefulness of benefit-sharing arrangements that at the same time provide enhanced participation opportunities and income generation for indigenous peoples, illustrating the interconnectedness of procedural and substantive standards.

In accordance with the 2012 version of the IFC Standards, private companies are called upon to put in place benefit-sharing by taking into account indigenous peoples' laws, institutions, and customs.[191] Benefit-sharing does not feature in the OECD Guidelines or in the UN Global Compact, but sectoral guidance produced

---

[184] Francioni, 'Equity' in R. Wolfrum (ed.), *Max Planck Encyclopedia of Public International Law* (Oxford: Oxford University Press, online edition, 2010) para. 21; and E. Morgera, 'Fair and Equitable Benefit-Sharing' in L. Krämer and E. Orlando (eds), *Principles of Environmental Law* (Cheltenham: Edward Elgar, 2018) 323, 330–31.

[185] V. Barral, 'The Principle of Sustainable Development' in Krämer and Orlando (n. 184) 103, 108.

[186] Special Rapporteur Anaya, A/HRC/15/37 (n. 61), paras 89–91.

[187] Special Rapporteur Anaya, Report on the rights of indigenous peoples (2011) UN Doc. A/HRC/66/288, para. 102 ; and UN Special Rapporteur Anaya, Progress report on extractive industries (2012) UN Doc. A/HRC/21/47, paras 52 and 62.

[188] Special Rapporteur Anaya, A/HRC/15/37 (n. 61), paras 76–80.

[189] UN Expert Mechanism, Advice no. 4: Follow-up report on indigenous peoples and the right to participate in decision-making, with a focus on extractive industries (2012) UN Doc. A/HRC/21/55, para. 39(h) and implicitly UK National Contact Point, Final Statement on the Complaint from Survival International against Vedanta Resources plc, at http://www.oecd.org/investment/mne/43884129.pdf, para. 73 (2009).

[190] Special Rapporteur Anaya, A/HRC/24/41 (n. 109) para. 75. These points have been reiterated by the African Commission's Working Group on Extractive Industries, Environment and Human Rights Violations in Africa, Final Communiqué on the National Dialogue on the Rights of Indigenous Peoples and Extractive Industries, from 7–8 October 2019, Nairobi, Kenya.

[191] IFC 2012 Performance Standard 7, para. 19.

under these two general instruments has included it. The Global Compact guidance on business responsibility to respect indigenous peoples' rights refers to transparent benefit-sharing and cautions against providing financial or other benefits in exchange for investment rights without first acquiring FPIC. It further calls for sharing benefits based on regular, annual reviews of the activity and profitability.[192] In turn, the OECD-FAO Guidance for Responsible Agricultural Supply Chains makes benefit-sharing part of a broader commitment to ensure that operations are in line with the development priorities and social objectives of the host government.[193] One challenge for companies, however, is when government priorities are at odds with indigenous peoples' and local communities' development priorities, creating a very complex setting for companies to respect this international standard.

The CBD Mo' otz Kuxtal Guidelines emphasize that, in line with the understanding of FPIC discussed above,[194] benefit-sharing is equally about partnership building through establishing mutually agreed terms, rather than a top-down and/or unilateral flow of benefits. In addition, they indicate that 'benefits should, as far as possible, be shared in understandable and culturally appropriate formats, with a view to building enduring relationships, promoting intercultural exchanges, knowledge and technology transfer, synergies, complementarity and respect'.[195] Furthermore, the Mo' otz Kuxtal Guidelines draw attention to the role of benefit-sharing in supporting cultural reproduction, by stating that 'benefit-sharing could include a way of recognizing and strengthening the contribution of indigenous peoples and local communities to the conservation and sustainable use of biological diversity, including by supporting the intergenerational transmission of traditional knowledge'.[196]

The following sections will discuss to what extent international standards have clarified the kind of benefits to be shared, necessary cautions (based on previous negative experiences in the private sector), and the challenges of relying on business-community benefit-sharing agreements.

1.3.1 Kinds of benefits

Former UN Special Rapporteur Anaya indicated that business enterprises should regard benefit-sharing '*as a means of complying with a right*, and not as a charitable award or favour granted by the company in order to secure social support for the project or minimize potential conflicts'.[197] He underscored the need to go beyond the usual model of natural resource extraction, whereby the initial plans

---

[192] Global Compact Office (n. 59) 70.
[193] OECD-FAO Guidance for Responsible Agricultural Supply Chains, 26.
[194] Section 1.2.3.
[195] CBD Mo' otz Kuxtal Guidelines (n. 11), para. 23.
[196] Ibid. para. 13.
[197] Special Rapporteur Anaya, A/HRC/15/37 (n. 61) para. 79.

for exploration and extraction of natural resources are developed by a corporation, with some involvement by the State, but little or no involvement of the affected indigenous community, with the result that indigenous peoples are 'at best being offered benefits in the form of jobs or community development projects that typically pale in economic value in comparison to the profits gained by the corporation'.[198]

Similar to guidance emerging in international human rights law, the CBD Mo' otz Kuxtal Guidelines underscore that benefit-sharing 'may vary depending upon the type of benefits, the specific conditions and national legislation ..., the content of the mutually agreed terms and the stakeholders involved' and benefit-sharing mechanisms 'should be flexible' and determined on a case-by-case basis.[199] A wider choice of benefits could allow for taking into account communities' needs, values, and priorities on a case-by-case basis, as required under international human rights law, on the basis of a finer-grained understanding of opportunities within natural resource governance. Equally, however, the menu of benefits reveals the limitation of international biodiversity law: in the absence of specific procedural guarantees and indications of the minimum level of protection, benefit-sharing could be used to impose certain views of development upon indigenous peoples and local communities that could endanger their cultural or physical survival. In effect, business-community benefit-sharing models can be far from clearly beneficial towards indigenous peoples, as they may involve unfair pricing and indebtedness.[200]

The OECD-FAO Guidance for Responsible Agricultural Supply Chains refers to promoting fair and equitable sharing of monetary and non-monetary benefits with affected communities on mutually agreed terms, in accordance with international treaties, where applicable for parties to such treaties, for example, when using genetic resources for food and agriculture.[201] This is an implicit reference to the CBD Nagoya Protocol on Access to Genetic Resources and Benefit-sharing and the International Treaty on Plant Genetic Resources for Food and Agriculture. The OECD-FAO Guidance makes no reference, however, to the need to respond to indigenous peoples' views and preferences in this connection. It calls upon companies to strive to identify opportunities for development benefits, such as through: the creation of local forward and backward linkages and of local jobs with safe working environments; the diversification of income-generating opportunities; capacity development; local procurement; technology transfer; improvements in local infrastructure; better access to credit and markets, particularly for small and medium-sized businesses; payments for environmental services; allocation of revenue; or the creation of trust funds.[202] These are largely based on CBD

---

[198] Special Rapporteur Anaya, A/HRC/21/47 (n. 187) paras 68, 74, and 76.
[199] Mo' otz Kuxtal Guidelines (n. 11), para. 24.
[200] Cotula and Tienhaara (n. 47) 293.
[201] OECD-FAO Guidance for Responsible Agricultural Supply Chains, 26.
[202] Ibid. 53.

sources on monetary benefit-sharing, including not only profit-sharing through trust funds, but also licences with preferential terms, job creation for communities (which find resonance in the *Endorois* decision of the African Commission[203]), and payments for ecosystem services.[204] In addition, CBD Parties have identified benefits that support indigenous peoples' own economic activities, such as: fostering local enterprises, participating in others' enterprises and projects, offering direct investment opportunities, facilitating access to markets, and supporting the diversification of income-generating (economic) opportunities for small and medium-sized businesses.[205]

According to the IFC Standards, benefits may include culturally appropriate improvement of communities' standard of living and livelihoods and the long-term sustainability of the natural resources on which they depend.[206] The IFC further clarified that benefits associated with the natural resource use that 'may be collective in nature rather than directly oriented towards individuals and households', taking into account the ecological context.[207] With specific regard to involuntary resettlement, IFC clients are expected to implement measures to ensure, for communities with natural resource-based livelihoods, the continued access to affected resources or alternative resources with equivalent livelihood-earning potential and accessibility. With regard to continued access, according to the CBD Akwé: Kon Guidelines, proponents of development and associated personnel should respect the cultural sensitivities and needs of indigenous peoples and local communities for privacy, especially with regard to important ritual ceremonies, and also ensure that their activities do not interfere with daily routines and other activities of such communities.[208] With regard to alternative resources, it should be noted that international human rights sources have not made reference to this but only referred to the need for continued access, because equivalent livelihood-earning potential may not provide for cultural appropriateness and may threaten the cultural survival of certain communities. This points to the need to distinguish more clearly under the IFC Performance Standards between the international standards of benefit-sharing and requirements of compensation, which is discussed later in this chapter.[209]

Further types of benefits have been identified under the CBD to *improve and consolidate* the conditions under which indigenous peoples' and local communities'

---

[203] African Commission, *Endorois*, para. 297.
[204] Akwé: Kon Guidelines (n. 20) para. 46. See M. Menton and A. Bennett, 'PES: Payments for Ecosystem Services and Poverty Alleviation?' and I. Porras and N. Asquith, 'Scaling-up Conditional Transfers for Environmental Protection and Poverty Alleviation' in K. Schreckenberg et al. (eds), *Ecosystem Services and Poverty Alleviation: Trade-offs and Governance* (London: Routledge, 2018) 189 and 204 respectively.
[205] CBD, Guidelines on Biodiversity and Tourism, Decision V/25 (2000) paras 22–23, 43.
[206] Ibid. paras 12–13.
[207] IFC 2012 Performance Standard 5: Land Acquisition and Involuntary Resettlement, para. 26.
[208] Akwé: Kon Guidelines (n. 20), para. 33.
[209] See Section 1.3.2 below.

ecosystem stewards and traditional knowledge holders develop and maintain their practices. These benefits include information sharing, capacity building, scientific cooperation, or assistance in diversifying management capacities,[210] as well as the incorporation of traditional knowledge in environmental and socio-cultural impact assessments[211] and in natural resource management planning.[212] The last two options could be explored in the context of the substantive dimensions related of the standards on impact (self-)assessments[213] and environmental management systems,[214] having to do with the integration of indigenous peoples in project management itself, rather than as outside beneficiaries.

1.3.2 Cautions

Benefit-sharing arrangements, however, can be used in disruptive and damaging ways. The Inter-American Court, for instance, has noted that discussions on benefit-sharing can take the form of 'attempts to undermine social cohesion of affected communities by bribing community leaders or establishing parallel leaders, or by negotiating with individual members of the community. It thus considered these practices contrary to international standards,'[215] in responding to evidence that benefit-sharing may be offered in exchange for obtaining consent.[216] The Inter-American Court further noted that the mere offer of money and different economic benefits to obtain consent, without the State monitoring the dialogue between outsiders and indigenous peoples, encourages a climate of disrespect.[217]

There are also concerns about potential inequities when benefits are shared within communities. The Mo'otz Kuxtal Guidelines note that 'benefit-sharing should be fair and equitable within and among relevant groups, taking into account relevant community-level procedures, and as appropriate gender and age/intergenerational considerations'. The Akwé: Kon Guidelines also provide significant words of caution on the risks of elite capture[218] associated with benefit-sharing: they draw

---

[210] Principles of the Ecosystem Approach (n. 7), para. 9; CBD expanded work programme on forest biodiversity, Decision VI/22 (2002) at goal 5, objective 1, activities; CBD work programme on mountain biodiversity, CBD decision VII/27 (2004), Annex, para. 1.3.7; Akwé: Kon Guidelines (n. 20), paras 40 and 46; Addis Ababa Guidelines, CBD Decision VII/12 (2004), Annex II, rationale to Principle 4; CBD, Bonn Guidelines on Access to Genetic Resources and Benefit-Sharing (n. 106), para. 50.

[211] Akwé: Kon Guidelines (n. 20), para. 56.

[212] Addis Ababa Guidelines (n. 210), operational guidelines to Principle 4; and CBD work programme on forest biodiversity, para. 34. See also Agenda 21 (1992) UN Doc. A/CONF.151/26/Rev.1 vol. 1, Annex II, para. 15(4)(g) and Johannesburg Plan of Implementation (2002) UN Doc. A/CONF.199/20, Res. 2, para. 44(j).

[213] Section 2.1.1 in Ch 4.

[214] Section 2.1.2 in Ch 4.

[215] IACtHR, *Kichwa*, para. 186.

[216] Ibid. para. 194.

[217] Ibid. paras 193–94.

[218] P. Keenan, Business, *'Human Rights, and Communities: The Problem of Community Contest in Development'* Illinois Public Law Research Paper No. 14-18 (2013), at http://ssrn.com/abstract=2353493.

attention to the 'affected community and its people as a whole' so as to ensure that 'particular individuals or groups are not unjustly advantaged or disadvantaged to the detriment of the community as a result of the development'.[219]

In addition, business enterprises themselves have noted the challenge that national regulatory frameworks on benefit-sharing are insufficient.[220] In effect, there is more developed national legislation on EIAs and on FPIC than on benefit-sharing.[221] National legal frameworks could, for instance, require that companies share benefits with all community members, rather than only those directly participating in joint ventures, through different stages of the project cycle.[222] Furthermore, national legal frameworks could determine the extent to which developers will be held responsible for monitoring project impacts, disseminating information, and using it to inform periodic reviews of benefit-sharing agreements in light of international standards of best practice.[223]

Finally, the distinction between benefit-sharing and compensation can be difficult to draw in practice and can be abused. Such distinction is not clear, in effect, in existing standards, which is notably the case of the IFC Standards.[224] The Global Compact guidance on business responsibility to respect indigenous peoples' rights focuses on compensation, indicating that businesses are expected to ensure that population increases caused by business activity do not strain natural resources, and do not otherwise disrupt the way of life for indigenous peoples, including their access to food, water, medicinal plants, animals, and other resources.[225] In addition, business are further expected to provide compensation and restitution for damages inflicted upon the territory, land, and resources of indigenous peoples and the rehabilitation of degraded environments caused by any existing or historic activities that did not obtain FPIC. Businesses are also to ensure that the allocated budget from activities covers all costs associated with closure and restoration and include sufficient funds to provide for potential future liabilities. The OECD-FAO Guidance on Responsible Agricultural Supply Chains, on the other hand, clarifies that benefit-sharing is separate (and may be additional) to compensation for unavoidable adverse impacts.[226]

---

[219] CBD Akwé: Kon Guidelines (n. 20), para. 51.
[220] Special Rapporteur Anaya, Extractive industries operating within or near indigenous territories (2011) UN Doc. A/HRC/18/35, para. 49.
[221] P. Marchegiani, E. Morgera, and L. Parks, 'Indigenous Peoples' Rights to Natural Resources in Argentina: The Challenges of Impact Assessment, Consent and Fair and Equitable Benefit-sharing in Cases of Lithium Mining (2019) 24 *International Journal of Human Rights* 224.
[222] C. Filer, 'The Development Forum in Papua New Guinea: Evaluating Outcomes for Local Communities' in M. Langton and J. Longbottom (eds), *Community Futures, Legal Architecture: Foundations for Indigenous Peoples in the Global Mining Boom* (Abingdon: Routledge, 2012) 145, 158.
[223] Ibid.
[224] IFC 2012 Performance Standard 5, para. 9; as discussed earlier, in Section 1.3.
[225] Ibid.
[226] OECD-FAO Guidance, 52.

To clarify the distinction, former UN Special Rapporteur Anaya suggested that benefit-sharing may make up for *broader, historical inequities* that have determined the situation in which the specific material and immaterial damage has arisen.[227] These observations may support an argument whereby benefit-sharing is understood as a proactive tool for the full realization of human rights connected to natural resources in light of communities' worldviews. Benefit-sharing can thus arguably be distinguished from compensation that is expected to make up for lost control over resources and income-generation opportunities.[228] Benefit-sharing combines instead *new* opportunities of income generation and *continued*, or possibly enhanced, control over the use of the lands and resources affected by the development.[229] At the very least, the distinction rests on the fact that compensation derives from and is commensurate to a violation of the right to natural resources, whereas benefit-sharing is independent of any violation of their rights.[230]

1.3.3 Business-community agreements

The use of contractual tools for incorporating benefit-sharing agreements between companies and indigenous peoples, which is generally expected in the form for 'mutually agreed' benefits, as referred by both human rights bodies and CBD Parties,[231] is also fraught with complexities. These agreements may also contain the written documentation of FPIC discussed earlier.[232] Contractual negotiations may in principle function as a dialogic partnership-building process between private companies and communities for a contextual application of benefit-sharing. But there have been well-documented, unequal negotiating powers, as well as information and capacity asymmetries.[233] These concerns are compounded by objective difficulties in reconciling communities' customary law within dominant legal systems,[234] including in connection with dispute resolution. In principle, benefit-sharing contracts may provide an opportunity to 'co-author' the terms of

---

[227] Special Rapporteur Anaya, A/HRC/24/41 (n. 109) para. 76.
[228] F. Lenzerini, 'Reparations for Indigenous Peoples in International and Comparative Law: An Introduction' in F. Lenzerini (ed.), *Reparations for Indigenous Peoples: International and Comparative Perspectives* (Oxford: Oxford University Press, 2008) 3, 13–14. See also D. Shelton, 'Reparations for Indigenous Peoples: The Present Value of Past Wrongs' in Lenzerini (ibid.) 47, 60–61 and 66–69.
[229] E. Morgera, 'The Need for an International Legal Concept of Fair and Equitable Benefit-Sharing' (2016) 27 *European Journal of International Law* 353, on the basis of Special Rapporteur Anaya, A/HRC/21/47 (n. 187) paras 68, 74, and 76 and A/HRC/24/41 (n. 109) para. 75.
[230] Morgera (n. 1) 1115–17.
[231] IACtHR, *Kaliña and Lokono*, paras 227–29 and 159. For a discussion, A. Lucas, 'Participatory Rights and Strategic Litigation: Benefits Forcing and Endowment Protection in Canadian Natural Resource Development' in L. Barrera-Hernandez, B. Barton, L. Godden, A. Lucas, and A. Rønne (eds), *Sharing the Costs and Benefits of Energy and Resource Activity* (Oxford: Oxford University Press, 2016) 339.
[232] Section 1.2.3 above.
[233] Morgera (n. 1) 1105.
[234] For a reflection on the challenges of legal pluralism in the context of benefit-sharing from bioprospecting, S. Vermeylen, 'The Nagoya Protocol and Customary Law: The Paradox of Narratives in the Law' (2013) 9 *Law Environment & Development Journal* 185.

cooperation between companies and indigenous peoples.[235] Contracts may incorporate community worldviews as principles of interpretation, and/or as elements determining the fairness and equity in benefit-sharing.[236] They may also incorporate reference to international human rights standards[237] to substantiate contractual obligations to respect community worldviews. The incorporation of different worldviews in contractual arrangements faces several practical challenges deriving from the limited opportunities for full and effective community engagement in contractual negotiations and likely clashing with the developer's commercial demands for expediency and cost-effectiveness.[238] A further layer of complexity arises from confidentiality clauses in benefit-sharing agreements, which limits cross-community communication of lessons learnt in negotiating benefit-sharing.[239] These fundamental challenges add to significant technical difficulties in accounting, calculating benefits, and ensuring environmental sustainability, that require significant administrative capacity.

A recent analysis in the Canadian context has underscored that despite their private law nature, business-community benefit-sharing contracts are meant to secure public benefits, as an indirect means for the governments to comply with international and constitutional obligations towards indigenous peoples.[240] This justifies a role for the State in the negotiations of business-community agreement. From the government perspective, these contracts incorporate the findings of impact assessments, as well as providing for follow-up and monitoring obligations mandated by national law.[241] Special Rapporteur Anaya underlined that 'the State remains ultimately responsible for any inadequacy in the consultation or negotiation procedures and therefore should employ measures to oversee and evaluate the procedures and their outcomes, and especially to mitigate against power imbalances between the companies and the indigenous peoples with which they negotiate'.[242] To this end, domestic legislation is needed to ensure that benefit-sharing serves as a 'limit to contractual autonomy', on the basis of international human rights law.[243] In addition, consultations carried out directly by private companies with indigenous peoples should be supervised by the State.[244] States are also to

---

[235] N. Craik, H. Gardner, and D. McCarthy, 'Indigenous—Corporate Private Governance and Legitimacy: Lessons Learned from Impact and Benefit Agreements' (2017) 52 *Resources Policy* 379, 386.
[236] K. Carpenter and A. Riley, 'Indigenous Peoples and the Jurisgenerative Moment in Human Rights' (2014) 102 *California Law Review* 173.
[237] Cotula and Tienhaara (n. 47) 302.
[238] Craik et al. (n. 235) 384.
[239] K. Caine and N. Krogman, 'Powerful or Just Plain Power-Full? A Power Analysis of Impact and Benefit Agreements in Canada's North' (2010) 23 *Organization & Environment* 76. See also M. Langton, 'The Resource Curse Compared: Australian Aboriginal Participation in the Resource Extraction Industry and Distribution of Impacts' in Langton and Longbottom (n. 222) 23, 29 and 38.
[240] See generally Craik et al. (n. 235).
[241] Ibid. 383.
[242] Special Rapporteur Anaya, A/HRC/24/41 (n. 109) para. 62.
[243] Francioni (n. 184) 3, paras 23–24 and 27.
[244] Ibid.

verify that benefit-sharing agreements with extractive industries are crafted on the basis of full respect for indigenous peoples' rights.[245] On the ground, some evidence points to substantive positive impacts of government's participation in negotiations between communities and companies.[246] But it may be particularly complex for companies to respect international and national standards, if communities themselves do not wish to involve the government out of concern that the contract may become a source of external control (including on the distribution of benefits within the community).[247] More generally, communities could find themselves in an adversarial relationship with the government, as different State entities may have a vested interest in the negotiations. One approach to address these concerns would be relying on national human rights ombudsmen as semi-independent government entities that can mediate and facilitate negotiations between private companies and communities, including by signalling when proposals may be undermining existing human rights.[248]

Even more complexity surrounds community negotiations with private operators that are foreign investors. These negotiations may be constrained by the terms of an investor-State contract, which may limit the types of benefits to be made available, such as local employment and local business opportunities.[249] States could include in their agreement with investors an obligation for the latter to conclude a benefit-sharing agreement with communities, determining goals and minimum parameters below which the investor-community agreement cannot go.[250] This would allow the government to monitor and enforce possible violations of the investor-community benefit-sharing contract, including by sanctioning the violation of key terms of benefit-sharing contracts with the termination of State-investor agreements.[251]

Overall, the use of private and/or public instruments for encapsulating mutually agreed benefit-sharing remains a matter for further study in international environmental, human rights, and investment law. Much remains to be understood about the actual room for communities' worldviews to be expressed, understood, and realized within contractual, investment, and corporate legal tools and structures.[252] More research is also required on the necessary oversight of benefit-sharing agreements, including with regard to integrating in such scrutiny also indigenous procedural and substantive standards.[253]

---

[245] Ibid. paras 88 and 92.
[246] Langton (n. 239) 32.
[247] Craik et al. (n. 235) 385.
[248] See generally Marchegiani et al. (n. 221).
[249] Cotula and Tienhaara (n. 47) 292.
[250] Albeit to the extent allowed by the State's bilateral investment treaties: ibid. 303 and 294.
[251] Ibid. 303 and 293.
[252] Ibid. 293.
[253] C. Kamphuis, 'Contesting Indigenous-Industry Agreements in Latin America' in D. Newman and I. Odumosu-Ayanu (eds), *The Law and Politics of Indigenous-Industry Agreements* (London: Routledge, 2019).

2 Protected areas

The establishment of protected areas or other areas for the conservation of habitats, ecosystems, or certain species both on land and at sea is one of the most basic techniques for environmental protection.[254] Such techniques have been widely used at the international level, with the Ramsar Convention on Wetlands of International Importance[255] and the World Heritage Convention[256] being the pioneers in this respect. A substantive standard of corporate environmental responsibility is based upon the international identification and protection of particular sites, for their environmental and cultural characteristics. It entails that business respects at least areas where the international community has recognized a global value and the need for international cooperation, avoiding undermining the purpose for which protected areas have been created.[257]

This is not a common standard across the corporate accountability initiatives discussed in the previous chapter, however: the IFC Performance Standards are the exception in this connection. Two Performance Standards are relevant here: Performance Standard 8 on cultural heritage and Performance Standard 6 on biodiversity.

2.1 Natural and cultural heritage

IFC Performance Standard 8 is purportedly based on the World Heritage Convention, and aims to guide clients on how to protect irreplaceable cultural heritage in the course of their operations.[258] Under the World Heritage Convention, listed World Heritage 'natural' sites include areas that constitute the habitat of threatened species of animals of outstanding universal value from the point of view of science or conservation.[259] Cases of corporate environmentally irresponsible conduct addressed by the World Heritage Committee have demonstrated how cultural and natural heritage are often interlinked and how

---

[254] See, eg, A. Gillispie, *Protected Areas and International Law* (Leiden: Martinus Nijhoff, 2007); and A. Cliquet and H. Schoukens, 'Terrestrial Areas Protection' in Morgera and Razzaque (n. 52) 110.
[255] A. Kiss and D. Shelton, *International Environmental Law*, 3rd edn (New York: Transnational Publishers, 2004) 377–80.
[256] Ibid. 380–87.
[257] Earthwatch Institute, IUCN, and World Business Council for Sustainable Development, 'Business and Biodiversity: The Handbook for Corporate Action' (2002) <http://www.wbcsd.ch/DocRoot/ob3ZstqTvcmXQVtEtMxh/20020819_biodiversity.pdf> 25.
[258] IFC 2012 Performance Standard 8, para. 1.
[259] Convention for the Protection of the World Cultural and Natural Heritage (World Heritage Convention) (Paris, 16 November 1972, in force 17 December 1975) Art. 2. See, eg, M. Bowman, P. Davies and C. Redgwell, *Lyster's International Wildlife Law*, 2nd edn (Cambridge: Cambridge University Press, 2010) 451–82; and F. Francioni (ed.), *The World Heritage Convention: A Commentary* (Oxford: Oxford University Press, 2008).

important the protection of one is to the protection of the other.[260] The Standard is relevant from an environmental and human rights perspective for two reasons: it targets unique natural features, such as sacred groves, rocks, lakes, and watercourses; and it is also concerned with traditional knowledge.[261] It is therefore closely linked with the international standards specific to indigenous peoples and local communities.[262]

Specifically, the IFC standard objectives include not only the protection of cultural heritage from adverse impacts of project activities, but also supporting its preservation and the equitable sharing of benefits from the use of cultural heritage in business activities.[263] Thus, this is another instance in which the IFC expects companies to make a positive contribution rather than limiting themselves to 'do no harm' . In addition, the standard applies to all kinds of cultural heritage, regardless of whether it has been legally protected or previously disturbed.[264] This should be read in conjunction with the biodiversity standards related to protected areas, and could be interpreted as an additional standard that applies when cultural heritage is not included in a World Heritage Site, for example.

Performance Standard 8 expects companies to identify and protect cultural heritage by 'undertaking internationally recognized practices for protection, field-based study and documentation'.[265] There is no specific reference, however, to which international law sources could serve this purpose directly, but rather to the national law implementing the host country's obligations under the World Heritage Convention.[266] The CBD Akwé: Kon Guidelines provide further detail, indicating that, in the event that sites or objects of potential heritage significance are uncovered during earthworks associated with a development, all activities in and around the area of discovery should cease until a proper archaeological or heritage assessment has been completed.[267] Businesses are expected to site and design projects in order to avoid significant damage to cultural heritage, and not to diminish the chances of discovering cultural heritage products until an assessment by a competent specialist indicates what type of action to take.[268] Furthermore, the company is expected to consult with affected communities who use or have used within living memory cultural heritage for long-standing cultural purposes.[269]

---

[260] Eg Report of the Mission to the Kakadu National Park, Australia, 26 October–1 November 1998 (1998) UN Doc. WHC-98/CONF.203/INF.18.
[261] 2012 Performance Standard 8, para. 3.
[262] Section 1 above.
[263] IFC 2006 Performance Standard 8, Objectives; 2012 Performance Standard 8, Objectives. This is discussed in Section 3.1.1.
[264] IFC 2006 Performance Standard 8, para. 3; 2012 Performance Standard 8, para. 5.
[265] IFC 2006 Performance Standard 8, para. 6; 2012 Performance Standard 8, para. 8.
[266] IFC 2012 Performance Standard 8, para. 6.
[267] CBD Akwé: Kon Guidelines (n. 20), para. 26.
[268] Ibid. para. 5.
[269] See Section 3.1.

This has a two-fold purpose: first, to identify cultural heritage of importance, which calls for additional responsibility for the company; and second to incorporate into the client's decision-making process communities' views.[270] Neither the 2006 or 2012 version requested that companies obtain the prior informed consent of these communities, which is instead a requirement under international biodiversity law and international human rights law.[271] In the case of conservation measures, FPIC, benefit-sharing, and indigenous peoples' effective participation in management and monitoring of traditional territories, including continued access and use that are compatible with environmental protection, are required under international human rights law.[272]

The IFC Standard is more stringent when it relates to critical cultural heritage, as in the case of critical habitats for biodiversity protection in light of consultations with communities. Critical heritage also includes heritage situated in legally protected areas and internationally recognized ones.[273] In these circumstances, the company is required not to significantly alter, damage, or remove the cultural heritage. In exceptional circumstances, when the project may significantly damage critical cultural heritage and its loss may endanger the cultural or economic survival of communities that use such heritage for longstanding cultural purposes, the company will also conduct good faith negotiations and ensure the informed participation of affected communities, and mitigate other impacts on critical heritage appropriately, also with the informed participation of communities.[274] The 2012 version also expects companies to allow continued access to the cultural site or provide an alternative access route, subject to overriding health, safety, and security considerations,[275] which is an important consideration emerging from regional human rights case law.[276]

The CBD Guidelines on Biodiversity and Tourism Development, in turn, suggest[277] controlling impacts of major tourist flows, reducing impacts of activities outside tourism areas on adjacent and other ecosystems of importance for tourism, contributing to the conservation of biodiversity, and conserving landscapes and heritage.[278]

---

[270] IFC 2006 Performance Standard 8, paras. 9 and 6; 2012 Performance Standard 8, para. 9.
[271] Morgera (n. 1) 1102. See Section 1 above.
[272] See African Commission, *Endorois*, paras 81, 156, 173, 249 and Recommendation 1(b); and IACtHR, *Kaliña and Lokono* paras 98, 138–39, 159, and 197; and Special Rapporteur Anaya, Cases examined by the Special Rapporteur (June 2009–July 2010), (2010) UN Doc. A/HRC/15/37/Add.1, paras 257–67; and Report of the Special Rapporteur Anaya to the General Assembly (2016) UN Doc. A/71/229, paras 74 and 80.
[273] IFC 2012 Performance Standard 8, para. 13.
[274] IFC 2006 Performance Standard 8, para. 9; 2012 Performance Standard 8, para. 14.
[275] IFC 2012 Performance Standard 8, para. 10.
[276] See sources at n. 272.
[277] CBD Biodiversity and Tourism Guidelines (n. 208), para. 44.
[278] Ibid. para. 49.

2.2 Natural areas

IFC Performance Standard 6 focuses on legally protected areas and internationally recognized areas, and refers exclusively to proposed projects located within such sites, but does not provide for cases in which the project is located in an adjacent area. Cases of IFC-funded projects conducted in the vicinity of protected areas with severe environmental adverse effects spilling into the protected sites have already been documented.[279] This shortcoming may be compensated by other IFC Standards on sustainable use: the IFC 2012 version clarifies that biodiversity standards apply, on the basis of the impact (self-)assessment, to projects located in certain habitats, projects that may potentially impact on or are dependent on ecosystem services over which the company has management control or significant influence; or projects that include the production of living natural resources.[280] The most recent version also introduced more specific requirements for biodiversity offsets, plantations and natural forests, management of renewable natural resources, and supply chains.[281]

The 2012 version refers to two international treaties, the World Heritage Convention and the Ramsar Convention on Wetlands of International Importance, as well as the UNESCO Man and Biosphere Reserves,[282] which is a global network of national parks rather than a treaty.[283] Ramsar sites are listed under the Convention on the basis of their international significance in terms of 'ecology, botany, zoology, limnology or hydrology'.[284] State Parties must promote the protection of the fundamental ecological functions of wetlands as regulators of water regimes and as habitats supporting a characteristic flora and fauna, especially migratory birds.[285] It requires IFC clients to act only with legal permission, in a manner consistent with government-recognized protected-area management plans. Businesses also have to consult with sponsors, managers, and local communities, and implement additional programmes to promote and enhance conservation aims and effective management of the area.[286]

Even if the CBD programme on protected areas is explicitly addressed to State Parties, it contains guidance that has been considered relevant also for business, on how to respect indigenous peoples' and local communities' rights in the context

---

[279] F. Wing Solis, *Panama's Corredor Sur: Turning the Bay of Panama into a 'Faecal Swamp'* (September 2000) < https://www.ciel.org/Publications/IFCCSPanama.pdf >.
[280] IFC 2012 Performance Standard 6, paras 4–5.
[281] Section 3.3 below.
[282] IFC 2012 Performance Standard 6, fn. 17.
[283] On biosphere reserves, see Gillispie (n. 254) 12–13.
[284] Ramsar Convention on Wetlands of International Importance (Ramsar Convention) (Ramsar, 2 February 1971, in force 21 December 1975) Art. 2(2). See, eg, Bowman, Davies, and Redgwell (n. 259) 403–50.
[285] Ramsar Convention, preamble and Arts 3–4.
[286] Ibid. 6, para. 20.

of protected areas, which has become an issue of increasing concern internationally.[287] The CBD programme on protected areas points to the role of business in assessing the economic and socio-cultural costs, benefits, and impacts arising from the establishment and maintenance of protected areas, particularly for indigenous peoples and local communities, to avoid and mitigate negative impacts, and, where appropriate, to compensate costs and equitably share benefits in accordance with national legislation. In addition, businesses can be expected to use social and economic benefits generated by protected areas for poverty reduction, consistent with protected-area management objectives. Furthermore, companies operating in protected areas should engage indigenous peoples and local communities and relevant stakeholders in participatory planning, management, governance, and monitoring of protected areas, in line with the ecosystem approach[288] and these communities' rights under national legislation and applicable international obligations. In addition, businesses are to identify barriers preventing adequate participation, provide resources for the involvement of indigenous peoples and local communities, and support the development of their capacities to establish and manage protected areas. In 2018 CBD Parties adopted further guidance on equitable management of protected areas, such as ensuring gender equality and legitimate representation of indigenous peoples and local communities, including in the establishment, governance, planning, monitoring, and reporting of protected and conserved areas on their traditional territories (lands and waters);[289] setting up appropriate procedures and mechanisms for the effective participation of and/or coordination with other stakeholders; transparency and accountability; procedures and mechanisms for fair dispute or conflict resolution; and a monitoring system that covers governance issues, including impacts on the well-being of indigenous peoples and local communities,[290] which is mainly procedural. The inter-governmental consensus achieved under the CBD on indigenous and community conserved areas is particularly instructive in this connection,[291] starting from the need to recognize, respect, and support community-based approaches to conservation and the

---

[287] Eg Report of the Special Rapporteur on the rights of indigenous peoples—Conservation measures and their impact on indigenous peoples' rights (2016) UN Doc. A/71/229.
[288] CBD COP Decision VII/28 (2006) paras 2.1, 2.1.4, and 2.15.
[289] Ibid. where the Conference of the Parties 'notes that the establishment, management and monitoring of protected areas should take place with the full and effective participation of, and full respect for the rights of, indigenous and local communities consistent with national law and applicable international obligations'.
[290] CBD COP Decision XIV/8 (2018) Annex II Voluntary Guidance on Effective Governance Models for Management of Protected Areas, Including Equity, Taking into Account Work Being Undertaken under Article 8(j) and Related Provisions: B. Voluntary guidance on effective and equitable governance models.
[291] See generally H. Jonas, 'Indigenous Peoples' and Community Conserved Territories and Areas (ICCAs): Evolution in International Biodiversity Law' in Morgera and Razzaque (n. 52) 145.

integration of communities in governance and management arrangements,[292] which can provide more substantive guidance to business entities.

3 Sustainable use of natural resources

The concept of sustainable development is one of the foundations of the international agenda on corporate environmental accountability and responsibility. The CBD defines sustainable use as 'the use of components of biological diversity in a way and at a rate that does not lead to the long-term decline of biological diversity, thereby maintaining its potential to meet the needs and aspirations of present and future generations'.[293] Interestingly, the Convention expressly calls for private-sector involvement in ensuring the sustainable use of biodiversity components.[294] In the relations among States, however, sustainable use is 'highly contextualized and has no single fixed meaning', but it can be considered a customary international rule in as far as living natural resources are concerned.[295] It is also widely understood as incorporating the idea that use is in principle not precluded but needs to take into account sustainability over time so the 'rate or extent of utilization permitted will vary depending on the status of the resource and the demands upon it at a particular time', including in light of the precautionary principle/approach.[296]

Both the UN Norms on the Responsibility of Transnational Corporations and the OECD Guidelines for Multinational Enterprises expect private companies to operate in a manner contributing to the objective of sustainable development. Only few standards, however, clarify what the private sector should be expected to do substantively to preserve natural resources for the benefit of future generations[297] or at least to use natural resources at levels that are sustainable, thus allowing for the recovery of species currently depleted, and internationally protected, for example, or for the natural reproduction cycle of others. The CBD Addis Ababa Principles for Sustainable Use can provide some detailed guidance, as they set a framework for advising as to how the private sector should avoid leading to the long-term decline of biodiversity.[298] Under the principle of adaptive management, standards potentially applicable to the private sector include: ensuring that for particular uses adaptive management schemes are in place; responding quickly

---

[292] CBD Decisions X/31/B (2010) para. 31, XII/19 (2014) para. 4(f) and X/33 (2010) para. 8(i) in relation to climate change (which are addressed to 'other/relevant organizations'); and XII/5 (2014) para. 11 (which is addressed to 'relevant stakeholders').
[293] CBD Art. 2.
[294] CBD Art. 10(e) reads as follows: 'Encourage cooperation between its governmental authorities and its private sector in developing methods for sustainable use of biological resources.'
[295] C. Redgwell, 'Sustainable Use of Natural Resources' in Krämer and Orlando (n. 184) 115.
[296] Ibid. 121. On precaution as a standard of corporate environmental accountability, see Ch. 4, Section 2.3.
[297] Barral (n. 185) 103.
[298] CBD Sustainable Use Principles, Principle 1.

to unsustainable practices; and designing monitoring systems on a temporal scale sufficient to ensure that information about the status of the resource and ecosystems is available to inform management decisions for the conservation of the resource. Other principles potentially applicable to business entities in the Addis Ababa Principles include ensuring the compatibility of spatial and temporal scale of management with ecological and socio-economic scales of use and its impacts, enabling full public participation in preparation of management plans to better ensure ecological and socioeconomic sustainability;[299] optimizing benefits from users,[300] and involving local stakeholders to equitably share monetary and non-monetary benefits with them for their efforts.[301]

The following sub-sections will explore the extent to which international standards have clarified the expected conduct of private companies with regard to: threatened or endangered species, sustainable production, ecosystem services, invasive alien species, habitats, and sustainable agri-business.

3.1 Threatened or endangered species

Threatened or endangered species have been identified, listed, and periodically reviewed by the international community through certain international agreements, such as the Convention on International Trade in Endangered Species (CITES)[302] and the Convention on Migratory Species.[303] Although private companies can quite easily identify species that are globally relevant according to the decisions and recommendations under these international treaties, as well as through communication with national authorities, the actual standard of conduct may, however, be very difficult to strictly define in practice.[304]

The IFC addresses business responsibility vis-à-vis critically endangered or endemic species in relation to critical habitats, which are considered of high biodiversity value also because of globally significant concentrations of migratory species and highly threatened or unique ecosystems.[305] Accordingly, companies are not

---

[299] Ibid. Principle 7.
[300] Ibid. Principle 11.
[301] Ibid. Principle 12.
[302] Convention on International Trade in Endangered Species of Wild Fauna and Flora (Washington, 3 March 1973, in force 1 July 1975). See generally, Bowman, David, and Redgwell (n. 259) 483–534; and E. Techera, 'Species-based Conservation' in Morgera and Razzaque (n. 52) 97.
[303] Convention on the Conservation of Migratory Species of Wild Animals (Bonn, 23 June 1979, in force 1 November 1983). See generally, Bowman, David, and Redgwell (n. 259) 535–84; and Techera (n. 302).
[304] United Nations Convention on the Law of the Sea (UNCLOS) (Montego Bay, 10 December 1992, in force 16 November 1994) Arts 61(3), 62(1), 119(1)(a), and 150(b), eg, refers to several standards: maximum sustainable yield, optimum utilization, and rational management. See, eg, D. Diz, 'Marine Biodiversity: Unravelling the Intricacies of Global Frameworks and Applicable Concepts' in Morgera and Razzaque (n. 52) 123.
[305] IFC 2012 Performance Standard 8, para. 16.

supposed to implement any project activity only if three conditions are met. First, there are no measurable adverse impacts on biodiversity values and ecological processes. Second, the project does not lead to a net reduction in global or national population of endangered species over a reasonable period of time. Third, there is a robust, appropriate long-term biodiversity monitoring and evaluation programme in the environmental management systems.[306] Similar to the 2006 version, this seems to presume that only in critical habitats, but not in natural ones, is there a risk for irreversible damage or irreplaceable biodiversity loss, and the definition of critical habitats relies on international standards, although not on relevant international environmental agreements. Reference is made instead to the endangered species listed in the International Union for Conservation of Nature (IUCN) Red List of Threatened Species.[307] It remains unclear why the Performance Standard does not make reference to international treaties that list endangered species, in addition to the IUCN Red List. The World Wide Fund for Nature (WWF), for instance, had suggested excluding from financing projects that could lead to trading species listed as endangered under CITES Appendix I.[308]

3.2 Sustainable production

The 2011 review of the OECD Guidelines considered 'exploring and assessing ways to improve environmental performance' with reference to emission reduction, efficient resource use, the management of toxic substances, and the conservation of biodiversity.[309] Regrettably, this addition was not addressed in the commentary to the Guidelines. Nevertheless, the environment chapter of the OECD Guidelines refers to sustainable production as the development and provision of products or services that: have no undue environmental impacts; are safe in their intended use; are efficient in their consumption of energy and natural resources; and can be reused, recycled, or disposed of safely.[310] The same standard also incorporates a requirement related to climate change, in that products should 'reduce greenhouse gas emissions'.[311] These add to procedural standards for companies to explore and

---

[306] 2012 Performance Standard 6, para. 17.
[307] The main purpose of the IUCN Red List is to catalogue and highlight those taxa that are facing a higher risk of global extinction (ie those listed as Critically Endangered, Endangered and Vulnerable). Since 1997, the Red List has been prepared jointly by IUCN and UN Environment Programme-World Conservation Monitoring Centre.
[308] WWF (A. Durbin, S. Herz, D. Hunter, and J. Peck), *Shaping the Future of Sustainable Finance: Moving from Paper Promises to Performance* (January 2006) 42.
[309] OECD Council, 'OECD Guidelines Update 2011—Note by the Secretary-General', Appendix II, para. II.A.10; and OECD Guidelines, ch. VI, para. 6.d.
[310] See Ch. 4, Section 2.2.
[311] OECD Guidelines, ch. VI, para. 4(c).

assess ways of improving the environmental performance of the enterprise over the longer term, for instance by developing strategies for emission reduction, efficient resource utilization and recycling, substitution or reduction of use of toxic substances, or strategies on biodiversity.[312] These could contribute to address some of the causes of biodiversity loss.

The IFC has also included standards on sustainable use, which have been subject to evolution. In accordance with the objectives of the Convention on Biological Diversity,[313] the 2006 version made reference also to sustainable natural resources management, based on the principle of sustainable development (defined as supporting the adoption of practices that integrate conservation needs and development priorities).[314] The IFC translated the concept of sustainable development as 'the use, development and protection of resources in a way or at a rate that enables people and communities to provide for their present social, economic, and cultural well-being while also sustaining the potential of those resources to meet the reasonably foreseeable needs of future generations and safeguarding the life-supporting capacity of the air, water, and soil ecosystems'.[315]

The IFC Performance Standard then targets companies engaged in primary production of living natural resources (including forestry, agriculture, animal husbandry, fisheries, and aquaculture), particularly in the absence of appropriate and applicable global, regional, or national standards.[316] Additional requirements include: committing to applying international industry operating principles and good management practices and available technology; actively engaging and supporting the development of national standards, for the definition and demonstration of sustainable practices; and (as was the case in the previous version of the Standards) committing to achieving certification.[317] In the case of multi-stakeholders' schemes based on international environmental law principles, this may well be a practical solution to adapt the standards to different industry sectors. Certification, however, has been the object of sustained criticism for their weak implementation and monitoring.[318] Reliance on private certification schemes along a complex supply chain has also been considered 'a cause for concern' because of the potential for rent-seeking behaviour by certification scheme operators.[319] Finally,

---

[312] Ibid. para. 4(d).
[313] 2006 Performance Standard 6, para. 1; 2012 Performance Standard 6, para. 1.
[314] 2006 Performance Standard 6, para. 1 and Objectives.
[315] IFC Performance Standard 6, fn. 7.
[316] 2012 Performance Standard 6, para. 26.
[317] Ibid. paras 26 and 29–30.
[318] K. Bourdreaux and S. Schang, 'Threats of, and Responses to, Agribusiness Land Acquisitions' (2019) 4 *Business and Human Rights Journal* 365, 369.
[319] J. Lin, 'Governing Biofuels: A Principal-Agent Analysis of the European Union Biofuels Certification Regime and the Clean Development Mechanism' (2012) 24 *Journal of Environmental Law* 43.

private companies are also expected to prefer suppliers that can demonstrate they are not significantly impacting on natural or critical habitats.[320]

3.3 Ecosystem services

The 2012 version of the IFC Performance Standards also added an objective on the maintenance of ecosystem services.[321] These are also included in the Performance Standard on community health,[322] calling upon business enterprises to determine likely adverse impacts on ecosystem services, and systematically identify priority ecosystem services (either those having adverse impacts on affected communities or those on which the project will be directly dependent for its operations) in a participatory process. These are aimed at avoiding negative impacts, or minimizing them and implementing measures to increase the operations' resource efficiency,[323] including in connection with community health, relocation, indigenous peoples, and cultural heritage.[324]

As a substantive dimension of the international standards on environmental management systems,[325] the Global Compact, in 2012, produced a framework for developing, implementing, and disclosing policies and practices on biodiversity and ecosystem services that are integrated into corporate sustainability strategies, responding to the Millennium Ecosystem Assessment.[326] Accordingly, the framework identified first relevant procedural standards, such as identifying and valuing the company's dependencies, as well as its direct and indirect impacts on biodiversity and ecosystem services. In addition, it expects companies to adopt an integrated reporting approach that shows impacts and dependency as an integral part of company operational and financial performance at different levels. The framework also calls for monitoring, evaluating, and reporting on biodiversity impacts using relevant biodiversity and ecosystem service impact indicators, and establish a review mechanism to build these results into company strategy and overall corporate sustainability. On a more substantive note, the framework further supports companies in extending the strategy along the supply chain by integrating requirements to safeguard biodiversity and ecosystem services in sourcing schemes and provide support to suppliers, especially micro, small, and medium-sized operators.[327]

---

[320] IFC 2012 Performance Standard 6. para. 31.
[321] 2012 Performance Standard 6, Objectives and paras 2–3. On the concept of ecosystem services, see Ch. 1, Section 1.
[322] 2012 Performance Standard 4, para. 8.
[323] Ibid. paras 24–25.
[324] Ibid. para. 25, with reference to Performance Standards 4–5 and 7–8.
[325] Ch. 4, Section 2.1.2.
[326] See Ch. 1.
[327] UN Global Compact and IUCN, *A Framework for Corporate Action on Biodiversity and Ecosystem Services* (2012) https://www.unglobalcompact.org/library/139

3.4 Invasive alien species

In the sphere of biodiversity protection, prevention standards of a substantive nature imply the avoidance of the risk of irreversible biodiversity loss. More developed prevention standards have emerged with regard to invasive alien species, which is addressed by the CBD Tourism Guidelines[328] and is also expected from private companies receiving funding from the IFC. The IFC requires that companies 'seek to avoid', 'as a matter of priority', impacts on biodiversity and ecosystem services, by adopting adaptive management practices so that the implementation of mitigation and management measures are responsive to changing conditions and the results of monitoring throughout the project's life-cycle,[329] which is arguably a translation of the CBD ecosystem approach.[330] Accordingly, IFC clients should not intentionally introduce new alien species, unless in accordance with existing regulatory frameworks and subject to risk assessment to determine the potential for invasive behaviour.[331] The 2012 version clarifies that companies must also implement measures to avoid potential accidental or unintended introductions, and exercise due diligence in not spreading invasive alien species to areas in which they have not been established. In addition, clients are expected to take measures 'as practicable' to eradicate these species from natural habitats over which they have management control.[332] The CBD Guiding Principles for the Prevention, Introduction and Mitigation of Impacts of Alien Species that Threaten Ecosystems, Habitats or Species also call for taking into account risks for unintentional introduction of alien species in environmental impact assessments.[333] The OECD–FAO Guidance for Responsible Agricultural Supply Chains, more laconically, calls upon agri-business to minimize the spread of invasive alien species.[334]

3.5 Habitats

With reference to the private sector's impacts on habitats, IFC Performance Standard 6 differentiates between modified habitats, natural habitats, and critical habitats. In the first instance—modified habitats, including agricultural land and

---

[328] Ibid., para. 67.
[329] IFC 2012 Performance Standard 6, para. 7.
[330] See generally Morgera (n. 52). On international standards on cultural heritage, see Section 3.2 above.
[331] IFC 2006 Performance Standard 6, paras 12–13; 2012 Performance Standard 6, para. 22.
[332] IFC 2012 Performance Standard 6, para. 23.
[333] CBD Guiding Principles for the Prevention, Introduction and Mitigation of Impacts of Alien Species that Threaten Ecosystems, Habitats or Species, Decision VI/23 (2002), Guiding Principle 11. See generally S. Burgiel, 'Invasive Alien Species' in Morgera and Razzaque (n. 52) 283. On EIAs, see Ch. 4, Section 2.1.1.
[334] OECD–FAO Guidance for Responsible Agricultural Supply Chains, 66.

forest plantations, that still have significant biodiversity value[335]—under the 2006 version, companies were expected to 'exercise care' to minimize any conversion or degradation of modified habitats, but also to identify opportunities to enhance habitats and preserve biodiversity as part of their operations, albeit depending on the nature and scale of the project.[336] This was a case in which the IFC Performance Standards not only aimed at environmental damage avoidance or control, but also encouraged the private sector to make an active contribution to environmental protection. The 2012 version, instead, has strengthened the requirement for minimizing impacts, but only added the implementation of mitigation measures.[337]

In the second case—natural habitats—the Standard allows for significant conversion or degradation to occur. In effect, the CAO had raised concerns that the 2006 Standards did not include the principle that projects should be sited on land that has already been converted, or the requirement to minimize unavoidable impacts or degradation of natural habitats rather than merely mitigate them.[338] As a result, the 2012 Standard sets the following conditions: there are no viable alternatives within the region, consultation has established stakeholders' and affected communities' view on the extent of conversion and degradation, and mitigation is designed to achieve no net biodiversity loss such as set-asides, biological corridors, ecosystem restoration, or biodiversity offsets.[339] Set-aside areas are excluded from development and targeted for conservation enhancement measures, and should be identified by their 'high conservation value' based on internationally recognized guidelines.[340]

The 2012 version also included a set of safeguards around biodiversity offsets, as part of the mitigation hierarchy:[341] they are to be designed and implemented to achieve 'measurable conservation outcomes', be reasonably expected to result in 'no net loss' and preferably in a 'net gain of biodiversity' (which is required for critical habitats), and adhere in their design to the 'like-for-like or better' principle, as well as being carried out by external experts on the basis of best available information and current practices.[342] The Global Compact's framework for developing, implementing, and disclosing policies and practices on biodiversity and ecosystem services that are integrated into corporate sustainability strategies, identifies the following steps: companies are to avoid, minimize, and rehabilitate negative impacts and then offset any unavoidable residual biodiversity losses, prioritizing implementation on sites of high biodiversity value; and encourage the adoption of this approach throughout the supply chain, with a view to achieving a net positive

---

[335] Ibid. paras 11–12.
[336] IFC 2006 Performance Standard 6, para. 6.
[337] Ibid., para. 12.
[338] CAO (n. 141) para. 49. No reply in IFC response (n. 120) 5.
[339] IFC 2012 Standard 6, paras 14–15.
[340] Ibid. para. 14 and fn. 10.
[341] This was discussed in relation to the standard of prevention in Ch. 4, Section 2.2.
[342] IFC 2012 Performance Standard 6, para. 10.

impact or at the minimum no net loss of biodiversity.³⁴³ Although offsets remain controversial under the CBD,³⁴⁴ former UN Special Rapporteur on Human Rights and the Environment Knox cautioned against 'reject[ing] the concept [of offsets] entirely' as properly employed, offsets 'can help to fulfil the duties and responsibilities of States and corporations to protect and respect the human rights of those most directly affected by the commercial exploitation of natural resources'.³⁴⁵

3.6 Sustainable agri-business

The more specific international guidance on the role of agri-business provides a good example of a sectoral approach to sustainable use that brings together, contextualizes, and further details standards of corporate environmental accountability and responsibility. At the same time, it illustrates unsettled views on certain substantive benchmarks. The OECD-FAO Guidance for Responsible Agricultural Supply Chains, for instance, provides a more specific translation of the prevention standards,³⁴⁶ calling upon agri-business to reduce food loss and waste, promote recycling, control and minimize the spread of invasive alien species,³⁴⁷ and enhance the productive use of waste and/or by-products. It also calls for implementing technically and financially feasible and cost-effective measures for improving efficiency in energy consumption; and taking measures, as appropriate, to reduce and/or remove greenhouse gas (GHG) emissions.³⁴⁸ In addition, it spells out sustainable use standards in terms of 'good agricultural practices', such as: maintaining or improving soil fertility and avoiding soil erosion; increasing the resilience of agriculture and food systems, the supporting habitats, and related livelihoods to the effects of climate change through adaptation measures;³⁴⁹ and selecting the most appropriate production system to enhance resource use efficiency while preserving the future availability of current resources, such as water and agricultural inputs and outputs.³⁵⁰

As agri-business has surpassed extractives as the sector 'most often implicated in killings of land and environmental defenders' due to land tenure-related conflicts,³⁵¹ and also because of environmental and human rights impacts arising from

---

³⁴³ UN Global Compact and IUCN, *A Framework for Corporate Action on Biodiversity and Ecosystem Services* (2012), < https://www.unglobalcompact.org/library/139> Last visited 22 December 2019.
³⁴⁴ Eg World Bank and Profor, *Biodiversity Offsets: A User Guide* (2016) < https://www.cbd.int/financial/doc/wb-offsetguide2016.pdf> last visited on 22 December 2019.
³⁴⁵ Report of the Special Rapporteur on the issue of human rights obligations relating to the enjoyment of a safe, clean, healthy, and sustainable environment, on his visit to Madagascar, (2017) UN Doc. A/HRC/34/49/Add.1, paras 43–45.
³⁴⁶ See Ch. 4, Section 2.2.
³⁴⁷ See Section 3.4 above.
³⁴⁸ OECD-FAO Guidance for Responsible Agricultural Supply Chains, 66 and fnn 84–89.
³⁴⁹ Ibid.
³⁵⁰ Ibid.
³⁵¹ Bourdreaux and Schang (n. 318) 366.

the use of pesticides,[352] further guidance has emerged from international human rights processes. Former UN Special Rapporteur on the Right to Food Olivier De Schutter has pointed out the need to prevent negative impacts on small-scale farmers[353] and to support agro-ecological forms of production (ie sustainable, knowledge-intensive modes of production that rely on on-farm fertility generation and pest management rather than on external inputs).[354] He opposed highly input-intensive modes of production that rely on external inputs such as improved varieties of seeds and chemical fertilizers that increase dependency and undermine sustainable practices such as biological control, composting, poly-cropping, or agroforestry.[355] These recommendations go well beyond the reference to good agricultural practices in the OECD-FAO Guidance.

4 Preliminary conclusions

Substantive international standards of corporate environmental responsibility have started to emerge and have quickly reached a significant level of detail,[356] particularly in the context of sectoral approaches. With regard to substantive standards to ensure business respect of indigenous peoples' human rights, the Convention on Biological Diversity has provided a global good-practice reference with its Akwé: Kon Guidelines on socio-cultural and environmental impact assessments, which have been extensively used to fill gaps across international standards of corporate environmental accountability and responsibility. Nevertheless, more clarity is still needed on the interface of prior (self-)assessments, FPIC, and fair and equitable benefit-sharing as iterative and culturally appropriate processes. And this is in addition to practical challenges in ensuring that companies' (self-)assessment practices do not preclude communities from expressing their views in ways that effectively influence the decision-making process.

While FPIC is increasingly required, divergences of interpretation among States are reflected in international standards of corporate environmental responsibility

---

[352] D. Strouss, 'Bringing Pesticide Injury Cases to US Courts: The Challenges of Transnational Litigation' (2019) 4 *Business and Human Rights Journal* 337; and UN Special Rapporteur on the Right to Food Hilal Elver (in collaboration with UN Special Rapporteur on Toxics), Report on the Effects of pesticides on the right to food (2017) UN Doc. A/HRC/34/48.

[353] UN Special Rapporteur on the Right to Food, Olivier De Schutter, Final Report: The Transformative Potential of the Right to Food (2014) UN Doc. A/HRC/25/57, 27.

[354] UN Special Rapporteur on the Right to Food, Olivier De Schutter, Report on agroecology and the right to food (2011) UN Doc. A/HRC/16/49.

[355] UN Special Rapporteur on the Right to Food, Olivier De Schutter, Report to the General Assembly: Human Rights Criteria for Making Contract Farming and Other Business Models Inclusive of Small-scale Farmers (2011) UN Doc. A/66/262, paras 54, 25, and 31.

[356] Contra S. Deva, 'UN's Human Rights Norms for Transnational Corporations and Other Business Enterprises: An Imperfect Step in the Right Direction?' (2004) 10 *ILSA Journal of International and Comparative Law* 493, 509, where the author argues that international standards are 'generally so vague and general that it is quite easy to comply with their words without adhering to their spirit'.

with regard to the nature of consent, the need for appropriate representation for indigenous peoples and other communities, and the need to provide documentation of consent. Standards converge on the need for culturally appropriate processes. But divergences can be detected with regard to the degree and modalities of information-sharing, the timing of the FPIC process, and the implications of its iterative nature. An international standard on benefit-sharing has also increasingly emerged, but much remains to be clarified about the kind of benefits to be shared and the safeguards to be put in place to avoid top-down and bad-faith practices that have resulted in disruptive and damaging impacts on communities. Finally, a great challenge surrounds the roles of companies in taking into account the limited capacities of indigenous peoples and local communities to engage in negotiations and put in place concrete measures to enhance communities' capacities, with a view to making EIAs, FPIC, and benefit-sharing a genuine process of partnership-building.

A substantive standard of corporate environmental responsibility based upon the international identification and protection of particular sites, for their environmental and cultural characteristics, is still not common despite the ease of identifying relevant benchmarks in international environmental treaties. The IFC Performance Standards remain the exception in this context. With regard to the sustainable use of natural resources, few standards have clarified what the private sector should be expected to do substantively to use natural resources at levels that allow for the recovery of species currently depleted, and internationally protected, for example, or for the natural reproduction cycle of others. Nevertheless, more international guidance is becoming available to address specifically threatened or endangered species, sustainable production, ecosystem services, invasive alien species, habitats, and sustainable agri-business.

While there is a significant degree of convergence among all these standards, continuing divergence points to particularly controversial concepts in international law remain, such as free prior informed consent, biodiversity offsets, or agro-ecology, to name a few examples. These are also several thematic areas where substantive standards of corporate environmental responsibility could be much more detailed, such as in the case of climate change,[357] the use

---

[357] UN Special Rapporteur on Human Rights and the Environment David Boyd, Report 'Safe Climate' (2019) UN Doc. A/74/161, para. 72, identified as the 'five main responsibilities of business related to climate change ... to reduce greenhouse gas emissions from their own activities and their subsidiaries; reduce greenhouse gas emissions from their products and services; minimize greenhouse gas emissions from their suppliers; publicly disclose their emissions, climate vulnerability and the risk of stranded assets; and ensure that people affected by business-related human rights violations have access to effective remedies' (citing Expert Group on Climate Obligations of Enterprises, *Principles on Climate Obligations of Enterprises: Legal Perspectives for Global Challenges* (Expert Group on Climate Obligations of Enterprises, 2018). Note that contrary to his 2007 report on biodiversity, which contained specific references to business responsibility to respect human rights and biodiversity, there was no reference to business responsibility in in the 2006 report on climate change of former UN Special Rapporteur on Human Rights and the Environment John Knox (2006) UN Doc. A/HRC/31/52.

of traditional knowledge of indigenous peoples, farmers, and local communities,[358] and the transfer of technologies.[359] Furthermore, standards have been mainly conceived in relation to land, so ocean-related conservation and sustainable use remain so far unaddressed explicitly by existing international guidance.

---

[358] See generally E. Morgera, 'Fair and Equitable Benefit-sharing at the Crossroads of the Human Right to Science and International Biodiversity Law' (2015) 4 *Laws* 803, 819–26 and Report of the UN Special Rapporteur in the field of cultural rights: the right to enjoy the benefits of scientific progress and its applications (2012) UN Doc. A/HRC/20/26.

[359] Global Compact, Principle 9; OECD Guidelines, ch. IX; and OECD-FAO Guidance for Responsible Agricultural Supply Chains, 29. See also, generally, Morgera (n. 358) 817–19 and Special Rapporteur on cultural rights (n. 358).

6
International Oversight

International initiatives on corporate environmental accountability and responsibility have not limited themselves to standard-setting, but have also put in place mechanisms to monitor corporate conduct, exercise some degree of oversight on the implementation of international standards, and/or consider complaints from members of the public. Even the UN Global Compact, which was 'not designed, nor does it have the mandate or resources, to monitor or measure participants' performance',[1] has developed a procedure to handle 'credible allegations of systematic or egregious abuse of [its] overall aims and principles'.[2] The UN Framework on Business and Human Rights and its Guiding Principles are in turn subject to a follow-up mechanism under the Working Group on Business and Human Rights.[3] By far the most well-established procedure can be found under the OECD Guidelines,[4] which is based on the creation of national contact points (NCPs) in adhering countries, handling inquiries ('specific instances') at the national level.[5] Under the International Finance Corporation (IFC), inclusion of environmental conditions in loan agreements by the IFC allows the use of contractual enforcement approaches, while an independent Ombudsman is available to receive complaints from affected communities and individuals. In addition, UN Special Rapporteurs on human rights increasingly address specific instances of corporate disregard for international standards in their country visits.

This chapter will assess the evolving mandate and practices of the international initiatives on corporate environmental accountability and responsibility discussed in the previous chapters, with a view to drawing comparative observations about the functions they perform. The chapter will first place international oversight approaches in the context of the academic debate on compliance. It will focus on analysing the practice of the best-developed initiatives (the OECD implementation procedure and the IFC Ombudsman) and then contrast them with more incipient

---

[1] UN Global Compact, 'Note on Integrity Measures' (12 April 2010) available at <https://www.unglobalcompact.org/docs/about_the_gc/Integrity_measures/Integrity_Measures_Note_EN.pdf> accessed 27 February 2016, 1.
[2] Ibid. On the origins of the procedure, see K. Norwrot, 'The New Governance Structure of the Global Compact: Transforming a "Learning Network" into a Federalized and Parlamentarized Transnational Regulatory Regime' (2005) 47 *Essays in Transnational Economic Law* 24–30.
[3] HRC Res. 17/4 (2011) para. 6.
[4] The Implementation Procedure of the OECD Guidelines for Multinational Enterprises is included in Part II of the OECD Guidelines, Section 1.
[5] OECD Guidelines, Section 2.

initiatives, such as the country visits by UN Special Rapporteurs and the integrity measures under the UN Global Compact. The aim of the analysis is to understand the contribution of these processes not only to the implementation of international standards in a particular context, but also to further international standard-setting itself.

1 Tools for compliance?

International oversight initiatives may serve to bring to light instances of substandard corporate conduct in the natural resource sector and potentially to proactively manage possible conflicts among different stakeholders through an independent mechanism for assessing facts and facilitating the identification of constructive solutions. These mechanisms may provide a readily available, inexpensive, and impartial avenue for individuals, communities, and civil society groups to have their complaints against private companies heard, going beyond the hurdles and bias that may be experienced in accessing justice at the national level.[6] From a practical perspective, oversight may be also helpful in documenting the instances in which private companies respect international standards of corporate environmental accountability and responsibility. On the one hand, the evidence gathered by these international mechanisms can support the claims of affected communities and civil society, lending them more weight in processes with public authorities and private companies. On the other hand, these mechanisms may respond to requests from private companies to have allegations against them assessed and managed by an independent entity through fact-finding and good offices, thereby helping to prevent conflicts from escalating. And although these monitoring activities result only in non-binding recommendations to companies or even only to the State in which they operate, a systematic assessment of the environmental conduct of enterprises, based on internationally recognized standards, may arguably put sufficient pressure on individual companies to stop harmful conduct or offer compensation to victims.

From an international law-making perspective, these mechanisms may offer concrete opportunities to test the suitability of corporate environmental accountability and responsibility standards, further clarifying the conditions for their applicability to private companies in different contexts. These initiatives can also contribute to ensure their coherent application of international standards notwithstanding their different origin. In addition, these initiatives may assess the suitability and completeness of international standards in the context of specific cases, identifying gaps and potentially filling them. In that context, these international

---

[6] Discussed in Ch. 2, Section 1.2.1.

initiatives can also contribute to ensuring normative coherence among different sets of international standards, including to further the cross-fertilization between international human rights law and international biodiversity law on business responsibility to respect the human rights of indigenous peoples.[7] Consolidated quasi-jurisprudence from these monitoring efforts may facilitate the progressive development of public international law, and influence successive proceedings at the international and national level, to clarify an evolving system of shared responsibilities between States and non-State actors.[8] Furthermore, international oversight mechanisms may be valuable in gathering evidence to back up ongoing inter-governmental negotiations on the strengthening of the legal status of minimum standards of corporate environmental accountability and responsibility.[9] Establishing facts may facilitate a shift in public opinion towards demanding greater accountability of multinationals and other business enterprises through international law.[10]

The existence of implementation mechanisms established at the international level is a factor upon which the effectiveness of legal tools, whether binding or not, depends,[11] given that their normative core is clarified through case-by-case application. Returning to Hart's legal theory and his concept of secondary rules as rules that confer powers, be they public or private, to determine in various ways the incidence of primary rules or to control their operations, it seems that the concept of rules of adjudication[12] may be useful in explaining the implementation of legal standards for corporate environmental accountability and responsibility. In a broad sense, rules of adjudication can encompass, particularly in international law, all means to enforce or but also facilitate the effective implementation of primary rules. According to Hart, rules of adjudication specify ways in which to determine conclusively the violation of primary rules.[13] They are intended as a 'remedy to the inefficiency of diffused social pressure', and thus empower individuals to make authoritative determinations as to whether on a particular occasion a primary rule has been breached.[14] In the words of Abi-Saab, 'norms of adjudication concern the practical application of primary rules to concrete situations'.[15] Rules of

---

[7] See Ch. 5, Section 1.
[8] N. Rosemann, 'The UN Norms on Corporate Human Rights Responsibilities: An Innovating Instrument to Strengthen Business' Human Rights Performance' (Friedrich-Ebert-Stiftung, Occasional Geneva Papers no. 20, 2005) 32.
[9] Discussed in Ch. 3, Section 7.
[10] C. Wells and J. Elias, 'Catching the Conscience of the King: Corporate Players on the International Stage' in P. Alston (ed.), *Non-State Actors and Human Rights* (Oxford: Oxford University Press, 2005) 141, 173.
[11] As highlighted by C. Tomuschat, 'International Law: Ensuring the Survival of Mankind on the Eve of a New Century' (1999) 281 *Recueil des cours* 9, 353.
[12] H. L. A. Hart, *The Concept of Law* (Oxford: Clarendon Press, 1994) 81.
[13] Ibid. 94.
[14] Ibid. 97.
[15] G. Abi-Saab, 'Cours général de droit international public' (1987) 207 *Recueil des cours* 9, 115.

adjudication can also be described as a 'technique to secure routine compliance with norms of behaviour', with a view to securing values.[16] Taking into account the specificities of standards as primary rules, means beyond traditional enforcement mechanisms could rely on international standards for corporate environmental accountability as the benchmark for determining the legitimacy of the conduct of multinational corporations and other business enterprises, and facilitate in a practical way the effective implementation of international environmental law principles and of the objectives of multilateral environmental agreements by the private sector.[17] The operationalization of international standards of corporate environmental accountability and responsibility thus depends on process-oriented approaches with multiple components: information, communication, consultation, technical assistance, and stakeholder empowerment.[18]

Before turning to the analysis of the practice of existing oversight processes, it seems necessary to make a preliminary distinction between several concepts related to the means to ensure the effectiveness of multilateral environmental agreements and norms. Shihata proposed to differentiate 'implementation' *stricto sensu*, which describes all the actions required to carry out States' commitments resulting from the agreements, from 'enforcement', which refers to measures jointly or unilaterally adopted by competent authorities to ensure the respect for such international commitments, if they are not honoured in practice. He then pointed to other 'less structured' or 'indirect' forms of enforcement such as international networks for the diffusion of information, verification, and monitoring that ensure 'compliance', understood as the actual respect of substantive requirements of the agreements in the actual behaviour of those concerned.[19] The last category can be usefully applied to private companies, and not only to States. Tools for compliance will thus be assessed, bearing in mind the lack of adequate remedies before an international forum for claims by individuals against multinational corporations.[20] Better understanding, from a doctrinal and empirical perspective, of the role of international monitoring and complaints mechanisms in testing international standards of corporate environmental accountability and responsibility providing constructive approaches, if not remedies, for corporate substandard conduct may provide important insights for the ongoing negotiations of a new international

---

[16] R. Higgins, *Problems and Processes. International Law and How We Use it* (Oxford: Clarendon Press, 1994) 1.
[17] I. Shihata, 'Implementation, Enforcement and Compliance with International Environmental Agreements—Practical Suggestions in light of the World Bank's Experience' (1996–97) 9 *Georgetown International Environmental Law Review* 37.
[18] Ibid. 45.
[19] Ibid. 37: these definitions have been elaborated by Shihata with specific reference to States.
[20] J. Ebbesson, 'Transboundary Corporate Responsibility in Environmental Matters: Fragments and Foundations for a Future Framework' in G. Winter (ed.), *Multilevel Governance of Global Environmental Change: Perspectives from Science, Sociology and the Law* (Cambridge: Cambridge University Press, 2006) 200, 215. See discussion in Ch. 2.

treaty on business and human rights, which is mainly expected to enhance access to justice for victims.[21]

2 The implementation procedure of the OECD Guidelines

The OECD Guidelines' 'implementation procedure'[22] is based on one formal obligation for adhering countries to set up national contact points (NCPs).[23] State discretion is quite broad in fulfilling this obligation as long as the NCP structure allows it to operate in accordance with 'core criteria of visibility, accessibility, transparency and accountability', according to the Guidelines' Procedural Guidance.[24] NCPs are charged with promoting the Guidelines at the national level, encouraging their observance in the national context, ensuring that they are well known and understood by the national business community, and gathering information on national experience. Most importantly, NCPs handle inquiries ('specific instances'),[25] which are basically a means for any 'interested party' to draw the NCP's attention to a company's alleged non-observance of the Guidelines.[26] NCPs make an initial assessment of the issue and then offer their services as mediators. If the conflict is not resolved, it can be referred to the OECD Committee on International Investment and Multilateral Enterprises (Investment Committee),[27] where non-binding decisions are taken by consensus. In the vast majority of cases, however, the onus of attempting to resolve specific instances and ensuring the effectiveness of the Guidelines rests largely upon NCPs.[28]

The Investment Committee comprises all OECD members and observers. Although it is ultimately responsible for their interpretation of the OECD Guidelines,[29] its involvement in the implementation procedure remains rather

---

[21] Draft Report of the Open-ended Intergovernmental Working Group on Transnational Corporations and Other Business Enterprises With Respect to Human Rights (10 July 2015) available at <http://www.ohchr.org/EN/HRBodies/HRC/WGTransCorp/Session1/Pages/Draftreport.aspx> accessed 27 February 2016, paras 4 and 19. See discussed in Ch. 3, Section 7.

[22] OECD, 'Implementation of the OECD Guidelines for Multinational Enterprises: Implementation Procedures' (2000) <http://www.oecd.org/document/43/0,2340,en_2649_34889_2074731_1_1_1_1,00.html>.

[23] J. Huner, 'The Multilateral Agreement on Investment and the Review of the OECD Guidelines for Multinational Enterprises' in M. T. Kamminga and S. Zia-Zarifi (eds), *Liability of Multinational Corporations under International Law*' (The Hague: Kluwer Law International, 2000) 197, 200.

[24] OECD, Council Decision of the Council on the OECD Guidelines for Multinational Enterprises (2000) OECD doc. C(2000)96/FINAL, 4.

[25] Ibid.

[26] P. van der Gaag, 'OECD Guidelines for Multinational Enterprises: Corporate Accountability in a Liberalised Economy?' (November 2004) <http://www.oecdwatch.org/docs/paper%20NC%20IUCN.pdf>, 3.

[27] Ibid.

[28] J. Karl, 'The OECD Guidelines for Multinational Enterprises' in M. Addo (ed.), *Human Rights Standards and the Responsibility of Transnational Corporations* (The Hague: Kluwer Law International, 1999) 89, 92–95.

[29] Ibid.

exceptional and guarded.[30] NCPs report annually to the Investment Committee, which also responds to requests from adhering countries on specific or general aspects of the Guidelines, organizes exchange of views on related matters, and issues clarifications (providing additional information about whether and how the Guidelines apply to a particular business situation, without assessing the appropriateness of that enterprise's conduct). Furthermore the Investment Committee reviews the Guidelines and related procedural decisions to ensure their relevance and effectiveness, and reports to the OECD Council.[31]

The OECD implementation procedure is considered the result of 'multi-level cooperation and ... centralized soft mediation-based implementation' that provides assurances of 'impartial problem-solving capacity' on politically sensitive issues and exchange of views and expertise with other organizations.[32] It has further been noted that the OECD implementation procedure has been used for some time in regions where there is resistance to engage in litigation against corporations.[33] It has also been observed that NCPs can play a 'quasi-judicial role' applying both soft and hard law, with considerable leeway in determining burdens of proof, particularly when multinationals operate in countries with weak or absent governments and are therefore expected to assume public-law expectations.[34] Non-governmental organizations (NGOs) argue that NCPs' statements could become a source of useful precedents on acceptable business behaviour.[35] In addition, NGOs file complaints before an NCP as a means of gaining direct access to companies and to publicize the results of complaint procedures as part of a broader strategy for putting pressure on, or creative incentives for, multinationals.[36]

The following sub-sections will discuss, in turn: the evolution of the procedure, including as a result of influence from other international corporate environmental accountability processes; the various outcomes of this procedure, including further normative convergence among different sets of international standards; and institutional cooperation, notably with the UN Security Council.

---

[30] G. Schuler, 'Effective Governance through Decentralized Soft Implementation: The OECD Guidelines for Multinational Enterprises' (2008) 9 *German Law Journal* 1753, 1773.

[31] P. Acconci, 'The Promotion of Responsible Business Conduct and the New Text of the OECD Guidelines for Multinational Enterprises' (2001) 2 *Journal of World Investment* 123, 140–41.

[32] Schuler (n. 30) 1755–56 and 1758.

[33] J. Wouters and C. Ryngaert, 'Litigation for Overseas Corporate Human Rights Abuses in the European Union: The Challenge of Jurisdiction' (2008–09) 40 *George Washington International Law Review* 939—although this paper pre-dates the developments discussed in Ch. 2, Section 1.2.1.

[34] L. Catá Backer, 'Rights and Accountability in Development (RAID) v Das Air and Global Witness v Afrimex: Small Steps towards an Autonomous Transnational Legal System for the Regulation of Multinational Corporations' (2009) 10 *Melbourne Journal of International Law* 258, 287, 291, and 303.

[35] The International Council on Human Rights Policy, *Beyond Voluntarism: Human Rights and the Developing International Legal Obligations for Companies* (Versoix: International Council on Human Rights Policy, 2002) 101.

[36] F. Calder and M. Culverwell, *Following up the WSSD Commitments on Corporate Responsibility & Accountability* (London: Royal Institute of International Affairs, 2004) 28.

2.1 Evolution of the procedure

Criticisms about the implementation mechanism of the Guidelines,[37] including by the UN Special Representative on Business and Human Rights,[38] have to some extent been addressed through successive reviews of the implementation procedure. This section will first discuss more detailed criticism of the implementation procedure, and then assess to what extent this has been taken into account in the 2011 review of the Guidelines.

During the 2000 review of the OECD Guidelines, NGOs expressed their disappointment with the weak implementation mechanism and the variability in NCPs' willingness and capacities to play a proactive and preventive role.[39] Other critiques concerned: the lack of independent verification of whether companies follow the Guidelines, the confidentiality rule applied in the 'best interests' of the implementation of the Guidelines, and the failure by NCPs to issue statements and make recommendations when no agreement can be achieved between the parties concerned.[40] Other observers stressed that the implementation mechanism relied too heavily on private companies' cooperation, did not provide effective remedies, and often did not identify publicly concerned companies.[41] Difficulty in gathering official information on specific instances regarding the environmentally sound conduct of multinationals in or from OECD adhering countries arose from the practice of not using companies' names in official OECD documents and the uneven practice by NCPs of publishing their statements on their websites makes it complicated to match information on the same cases as reported by NGOs.

High variation in procedures, timelines, and final outcomes of the NCPs were underscored with concern over time. Some NCPs were proactive in gathering additional information, facilitating a constructive dialogue between companies and NGOs, and ensuring the Guidelines had an impact on the ground, whereas others have been said to use the lack of 'investment nexus' (discussed below)[42] as an easy

---

[37] Friends of the Earth, 'OECD Guidelines for Multinational Enterprises' (undated) <http://www.foe.org/oecdguidelines/> accessed 27 February 2016, 6; OECD, 'Roundtable on Corporate Responsibility: Encouraging the Positive Contribution of Business to Environment through the OECD Guidelines for Multinational Enterprises. Background Report' (June 2004) <http://www.oecd.org/document/1/0,2340,en_2649_34889_31711425_1_1_1,00.html> accessed 27 February 2016, 12 (hereinafter, OECD 2004 Roundtable Background Report); UNCTAD, 'Disclosure of the Impact of Corporations on Society: Current Trends and Issues' (2003) UN Doc. TD/B/COM.2/ISAR/20, 6; V. Nilsson, 'The OECD Guidelines for Multinational Corporations in Practice' (Paper Presented at the OECD Global Forum on International Investment—Investment for Development: Forging New Partnerships, 19–21 October 2004) <http://www.oecd.org/dataoecd/6/61/33807212.pdf> accessed 27 February 2016.
[38] Report of the Special Representative of the Secretary-General on the Issue of Human Rights and Transnational Corporations and Other Business Enterprises, John Ruggie: Protect, Respect and Remedy: A Framework for Business and Human Rights (2008) UN Doc. A/HRC/8/5, para. 98.
[39] Friends of the Earth (n. 37) 6; OECD 2004 Roundtable Background Report (n. 37) 12.
[40] Ibid.; UNCTAD, 'Disclosure of the Impact of Corporations on Society: Current Trends and Issues' (15 August 2003) UN Doc. TD/B/COM.2/ISAR/20, 6; and Nilsson (n. 37).
[41] The International Council on Human Rights Policy (n. 35) 117.
[42] Section 2.5 in this chapter.

excuse not to start investigations on certain specific instances.[43] The UN Special Representative on Business and Human Rights had recommended that NCPs have clear timeframes for the commencement and completion of the process, and public reports of outcomes.[44] The UN Special Representative further questioned the avoidance of conflict of interests when NCPs are hosted by national government structures, the adequacy of their resources to undertake investigations, missed opportunities for peer learning across NCPs, and the adequacy of assurances provided to aggrieved parties.[45] Nevertheless, Ruggie, in his personal capacity, argued that human rights complaints fare better in the NCP process than in other types of complaints.[46]

In response, the 2011 review resulted in spelling out principles for NCP 'functional equivalence' (accessibility, transparency, predictability, impartiality, accountability, efficiency, and timeliness), while leaving adhering governments flexibility in their set-up, as long as NCPs are enabled to operate in an impartial manner while maintaining an adequate level of accountability to the adhering government.[47] The 2011 review also called for the systematic publication of the outcomes of the NCP procedure and detailed their minimum content: NCP statements should describe the issue raised and the reasons for the NCP decision, and state recommendations on the implementation of the Guidelines 'as appropriate'.[48] As a result, NCPs are now required to publish a statement in situations where they decide not to consider an issue further, a report when parties reach an agreement, and a statement when parties fail to reach an agreement. But there is still no requirement to publicize a complaint when it has been filed or the name of the parties, or to keep parties informed about the case or publish an initial assessment, except when the NCP decides that the issue raised does not merit further consideration.[49] The new version also includes suggested timelines: three months for the initial assessment of instances and three months for issuing a statement of report following the conclusion of the procedure, with a view to concluding the whole

---

[43] Van der Gaag (n. 26) 5.
[44] UN Protect, Respect and Remedy Framework (n. 38) para. 98.
[45] J. Ruggie, 'Keynote Presentation by the Special Representative of the UN Secretary-General on Business and Human Rights to the Annual Meeting of National Contact Points of the Organization for Economic Cooperation and Development' (Paris, 24 June 2008) <http://www.reports-and-materials.org/Ruggie-presentation-OECD-Natl-Contact-Points-24-Jun-2008.doc>.
[46] J. Ruggie and T. Nelson, 'Human Rights and the OECD Guidelines for Multinational Enterprises: Normative Innovations and Implementation Challenges' (2015) *The Brown Journal of World Affairs* 22; J. Ruggie 'Hierarchy or Ecosystem? Regulating Human Rights Risks of Multinational Enterprises in C. Rodríguez-Garavito (ed.), *Business and Human Rights: Beyond the End of the Beginning* (Cambridge: Cambridge University Press, 2017) 46, 49.
[47] OECD Guidelines Update 2011—Note by the Secretary-General, Appendix III, section 1 A and C. The 'Procedural Guidance' and its Commentary are included in Part II of the OECD Guidelines; OECD Guidelines Update 2011—Commentaries, para. 9.
[48] OECD Guidelines Note by the Secretary-General, Appendix III, section I.C, para. 3.
[49] P. Simons and A. Macklin, *The Governance Gap: Extractive Industries, Human Rights and the Home State Advantage* (Abingdon: Routledge, 2014) 108; OECD Procedural Guidance, 70.

procedure in twelve months.⁵⁰ But it allows discretion to extend these timelines if circumstances warrant it. One such circumstance can be the case of an activity in non-adhering countries, which would occur in the majority of cases.⁵¹

The 2011 review was thus seen to have 'missed the opportunity to make the compliance mechanism more accessible, more independent, and more effective in pressuring corporate actors to respect human rights in their transnational operations'.⁵² The 2011 review was criticized for not requiring NCPs to identify breaches of the Guidelines and set out consequences for companies' failure to engage in the implementation procedure, as well as to monitor and follow up on their recommendations.⁵³ The lack of requirement for NCPs to come to a decision on breaches of the OECD Guidelines in cases where the parties fail to reach an agreement is considered a barrier to NCPs playing a quasi-judicial role.⁵⁴ And even when instances are concluded with the identification of a breach of the Guidelines, according to the NGO, OECDWatch, 'the vast majority of OECD Guidelines cases have unfortunately not led to any significant improvement in the respective company's behaviour or the situation that led to the complaint'.⁵⁵

2.2 Variation in outcomes

Instances to date have concerned different parts of the environmental recommendations of the Guidelines, often focusing on prior (self-)assessment of environmental and human rights impacts of projects and their communication to the affected communities.⁵⁶ In this section, the varied outcomes of the NCP process will be discussed with a view to assessing how the international standards discussed in the previous chapters can be applied in specific contexts. The outcomes generally range from mediation leading to a joint statement between the parties to findings of a breach of the Guidelines with specific recommendations on information and consultation, possibly leading to the institutionalization of local platforms for dialogue. Even in cases where NCPs find that there is no violation of the Guidelines, some instances can result in recommendations to seek higher standards of stakeholder engagement.

Following mediation by the UK NCP, an agreement was reached between the World Wide Fund for Nature (WWF) and an extractive company about the

---

⁵⁰ OECD Guidelines Update 2011—Commentaries, para. 40.
⁵¹ Ibid. 109, and Commentary on Procedural Guidance, 83.
⁵² Simons and Macklin (n. 49) 113.
⁵³ Ibid.
⁵⁴ Ibid. 111.
⁵⁵ Ibid. 109 and OECDWatch, '10 Years On: Assessing the Contribution of the OECD Guidelines for Multinational Enterprises to Responsible Business Conduct' (2010) https://www.oecdwatch.org/wp-content/uploads/sites/8/2010/06/OECD-Watch-10-Years-On.pdf.
⁵⁶ Discussed in Ch. 4, Sections 2.1.1 and 2.4–2.5.

suspension of activities in an internationally protected area,[57] the Virunga National Park in the Democratic Republic of Congo (DRC). The outcome included specific commitments to both procedural and substantive standards. The company committed not to undertake or commission any exploratory or other drilling within the park unless the UN Educational, Scientific and Cultural Organization (UNESCO) and the DRC government agreed that such activities were not incompatible with its World Heritage status. The company's statement also went beyond the specific case at hand, by including a commitment not to conduct any operations in any other World Heritage site, and seek to ensure that any current or future operations in buffer zones adjacent to World Heritage sites, as defined by national governments and UNESCO, do not jeopardize the outstanding universal value for which these sites are listed. The company further confirmed that when undertaking environmental impact assessments (EIAs) and human rights due diligence, the processes will be in full compliance with international standards and industry best practice, including appropriate levels of community consultation and engagement on the basis of publicly available documents.[58]

Another successful mediation was achieved by the Norwegian NCP, leading to a joint statement from the parties in which a fish farming company acknowledged it had not taken a precautionary approach in meeting social and environmental challenges and accepted responsibility for its subsidiaries' activities . In the statement, the company committed to strive for excellence on environmental initiatives in its industry, including by contributing to the development and use of environmentally friendly technology, taking a more structured approach to the exchange of knowledge and best practice between companies in the group regardless of business location, and further developing its efforts to minimize the risk of inflicting serious environmental damage on their surroundings. In addition, the company committed to seek to enter into mutually beneficial agreements with indigenous peoples in all areas where their rights were affected by fish farming operations.[59] In the joint statement, all the parties also recognized the benefits that arose from the company's research into fish disease and the new insights of relevance for the whole sector to better prevent fish diseases.[60] These commitments, therefore, provide a contextual application of the substantive standard related to sustainable use.[61]

On occasion, the finding of a breach of the OECD Guidelines leads the NCP to support the creation of a local institution to facilitate dialogue among parties.

---

[57] See discussion of relevant standards in Ch. 5, Section 2.
[58] UK NCP, Final statement following agreement reached in a complaint from WWF International against SOCO International plc, 2014.
[59] Joint Statement by Cermaq ASA, Norwegian Society for the Conservation of Nature/Friends of the Earth Norway and Forum for Environment and Development (2011).
[60] Ibid.
[61] See discussion of relevant standards in Ch. 5, Section 3.

The 2001 case on Canadian and Swiss copper mining in Zambia[62] was submitted to the Canadian NCP by Oxfam Canada alleging a violation of the Guidelines on, inter alia, communication and consultation with communities on environmental, health, and safety policies linked to the impending removal of local farmers from the company-owned land.[63] The Canadian NCP facilitated communications between the company's headquarters in Canada, the Canadian office of Oxfam, and operations in Zambia. The parties reached a resolution 'after the company met with groups from the affected communities and worked out an approach whereby the farmers could continue to use the land, at least for the short term'.[64] The Canadian NCP[65] encouraged the company to maintain an open line of communication with Oxfam and other groups concerned about the welfare of the people affected by the operations of the Zambian mining company.[66] This resulted in the establishment of a land task force committee by the company, the local government, and local NGOs, with the mandate to, inter alia, protect the environment, provide information to the public on land and environmental issues, and resolve any land disputes at the local level.[67] This provided a co-developed permanent structure for implementing procedural standards of corporate environmental accountability.[68]

In other instances, even where no breach was found, the NCP still included recommendations to improve the implementation of procedural standards related to stakeholder engagement. An example is a case submitted in 2004 concerning a dam project by Electricité de France (EDF)[69] based on a concession agreement with the Laos government.[70] A coalition of NGOs[71] alleged, inter alia, that EDF had failed to identify, respond to, and consider the environmental impacts of the project, due to lack of baseline data necessary to address the environmental, health, and social impacts, and to anticipate changes before the project commenced.[72] The complaint also highlighted uncertainty regarding the project's impact on endemic and nationally threatened species, and regarding the increased pressure on timber resources due to clear-cuts already carried out in the reservoir area.[73] In addition,

---

[62] J. Smith, 'Public Summary of the Report of an International NGO Training and Strategy Seminar on the OECD Guidelines for Multinationals: A Tool to Combat Violations of Environmental and Workers' Rights?' (2003) <http://www.milieudefensie.nl/foenl/publications/oesdtraining_eng.pdf>.
[63] OECDWatch (n. 55) 12.
[64] Government of Canada, 'Annual Report 2002: Canada's National Contact Point for the OECD Guidelines for Multinational Enterprises' (2002) http://www.ncp-pcn.gc.ca/annual_2002-en.asp#implementation.
[65] Ibid.
[66] Ibid.
[67] Friends of the Earth (n. 37) 17.
[68] See discussion of relevant standards in Ch. 4, Section 2.
[69] The EDF Group is an integrated energy company made up of a network of different companies. Its head office is in Paris, France.
[70] 'Complaint from Proyecto Gato, Amis de la Terre, CRBM, World Rainforest Movement, Finnish Asiatic Society, and International Rivers Network' (10 February 2005) http://www.reports-and-materials.org/Proyecto-Gato-and-Amis-de-la-Terre-press-release-EDF-10-Feb-2005.doc.
[71] Ibid.
[72] Ibid. 2.
[73] Ibid. 3. See Section 3.1 in Ch 5.

the complaint stressed that EDF only provided limited information about the project and its impact to communities, and did not allow community members to participate in the decision-making process.[74] The NCP concluded in 2005[75] that no breach of the Guidelines could be attributed to EDF.[76] The conclusion seemed to be based on two considerations. First, the company had signed an agreement on social responsibility going above what was requested by the OECD Guidelines. Second, the NCP considered that the host State had a weak legal and regulatory system. On that basis, it recommended that companies do their utmost to implement the internationally acknowledged best practices that they follow in their own country on the construction site and for the people affected by their activity.[77] Thus, the NCP recommended that EDF remain involved in implementing compensatory measures to affected communities, together with the Laotian national authorities.[78]

Recommendations on procedural standards were also formulated by the UK NCP in a case where no breach of the Guidelines was found. In a case concerning an aluminium smelter in Mozambique, the NCP considered the company's environmental management approach appropriate 'after having analysed each allegation in detail'.[79] Nevertheless, it encouraged the companies

'to build upon their existing procedures for engagement with local communities and be forthcoming in disclosing to interested parties (particularly the affected communities and their representatives) information on projects that may have an impact on the environment and the health and safety of the communities affected by the smelter'.[80]

In yet another case, the Norway NCP did not find any grounds for concluding that a company had failed to comply with the Guidelines, but still encouraged it to work in a manner that more clearly promoted indigenous peoples' rights and the implementation of the Guidelines. It noted for instance that the actual implementation of the consultations process could have been better facilitated, to foster mutual trust with a view to obtaining the Saami village's consent. The NCPs also noted that the company went above and beyond the Guidelines by covering parts of the Saami village's outlays and travel expenses in connection with participation in consultation, underscoring that this may be necessary in order to achieve

---

[74] Ibid. 4–5. See Sections 2.4–2.5 in Ch 4.
[75] French NCP, 'Recommendations intended for EDF and its Partners with Regard to the Implementation of the "Nam Theun 2" Project in Laos' (1 April 2005) http://www.reports-and-materials.org/French-NCP-Nam-Theun-2-recommendations-1-April-2005.doc.
[76] Ibid.
[77] Ibid.
[78] Ibid.
[79] B. Maheandiran, 'Calling for Clarity: How Uncertainty Undermines the Legitimacy of the Dispute Resolution System under the OECD Guidelines for Multinational Enterprises' (2015) 20 *Harvard Negotiation Law Review* 205, 224.
[80] UK NCP, Final statement by the UK National Contact Point for the OECD Guidelines for Multinational Enterprises: Complaint from Justiça Ambiental et al. against BHP Billiton PLC (on Mozal SARL) in Mozambique, 13 September 2012.

genuine consultations during which indigenous groups are given an opportunity to promote and safeguard their rights.[81] Furthermore, the NCPs considered that consultations are a continuing process that must be upheld and adapted so that new circumstances are also addressed, for example, when it subsequently emerged that the impacts of the wind power development were greater than originally expected. All these specifications are in line with the international human rights law and international biodiversity law guidance on free prior informed consent (FPIC) as an ongoing process.[82] The NCP also remarked that the company, being aware of indigenous groups' vulnerability to more adverse impacts than assumed in the licence application, 'could have shown even more willingness to implement mitigating measures and adapt the scope of the project to a level where agreement could be reached, prior to the legal process and without waiting for decisions to be made by the court system'.[83] While the NCP did not explicitly refer to the standard of fair and equitable benefit-sharing (as opposed to compensation),[84] it arguably made an implicit reference to the usefulness of community protocols in the situation:[85] it remarked that 'it would have benefited the process if the Saami village had prepared a well thought-through plan for its use of the area. It would also have been beneficial if a coordinated process had been developed between indigenous groups in the regions for how to deal with development project'.[86] The NCP recommended hiring an independent third party to assist in the consultation process and joint mapping of the impact of the project and/or monitoring of existing agreements, noting international expectations captured in 'A Good Practice Note', which has received support from the UN Global Compact's Human Rights and Labour Working Group.[87]

Follow-up reports to NCP statements provide insights into the effectiveness of the NCP's role in the actual relations between companies, governments, and affected communities. They also shed further light on the practical conditions for the applicability of international standards on corporate environmental accountability and responsibility. In an instance involving negative impacts from mining operations on communities' access to water, the UK NCP found no indication of a systematic methodology to engage with the wider community on an ongoing basis, and no evidence of a documented strategy or process for raising and addressing grievances. It also found lack of detail on what information was shared with the communities on the company's environmental and social impacts and what expectations communities could have from staff. Besides underscoring non-compliance

---

[81] See discussion of relevant standards in Ch. 5, Section 1.
[82] See discussion of relevant standards in Ch. 5, Section 1.2.
[83] Norway NCP, Jijnjevaerie Saami Village vs. Statkraft AS: Final Statement (2016).
[84] See discussion in Ch. 5, Section 1.3.
[85] See discussion in Ch. 5, Section 1.2.2.
[86] Norway NCP (n. 83).
[87] Ibid.

with procedural standards, the NCP also delved into the substantive aspects of communities' access to water from a human rights perspective. It documented that even if both parties to the complaint recognized that clean water was supplied to the community free of charge, the original NCP recommendation had emphasized the need for continued and unrestricted access in recognition of the human right to water. The NCP therefore indicated that the issue of a permanent water supply was only partially resolved and remained an outstanding obligation. The NCP further noted that notwithstanding recognition of the importance of communities' input in the development process, the company did not address the community's lack of the experience in fulfilling this role or the support it required to successfully engage with other parties in an overall resolution process, such as the maintenance of the already established water facilities. The NCP also noted lack of progress in the development of a joint monitoring approach.[88]

Overall, the role of the OECD implementation procedure ranges from documenting cases of companies' non-compliance with the OECD Guidelines and proactively managing their relations with affected communities, to clarifying how international standards apply in specific circumstances and filling gaps in the OECD Guidelines by relying on other sources of international standards of corporate environmental accountability and responsibility.

2.3 Promoting normative coherence

Although NCPs have made uneven references to international standards for corporate accountability other than the OECD Guidelines, the UK NCP set a precedent in 2009, pointing to another significant function of the OECD compliance procedure—contributing to normative coherence among international standards on corporate environmental accountability and responsibility. The UK NCP addressed a complaint brought to its attention by Survival International, a UK-based NGO, against Vedanta, a UK-registered mining company operating directly or through subsidiaries in India. The instance concerned the company's use of forest land for bauxite mining near Lanjigarh and its failure to consult with an indigenous group affected by its operations, the Dongria Kondh. The NCP found, mostly on the basis of evidence from the complainant (as Vedanta did not engage fully in the procedure and its own investigations), that Vedanta had failed to put in place an adequate and timely consultation mechanism to engage fully with the Dongria Kondh. Accordingly, the NCP declared non-compliance with the OECD Guidelines sections on engaging in adequate and timely communication and consultation with the communities directly affected by the environmental policies

---

[88] UK NCP, Follow up statement after recommendations in complaint from RAID against ENRC (2018).

of the enterprise and by their implementation. It further found that Vedanta did not respect the rights and freedoms of the Dongria Kondh in a manner consistent with India's commitments under various international instruments, including the Convention on Biological Diversity (CBD)[89] and the UN Declaration on the Rights of Indigenous Peoples (UNDRIP).[90]

Specifically, the NCP used the CBD Akwé: Kon Guidelines on environmental and socio-cultural impact assessments[91] to interpret the OECD Guidelines' provisions on consultations on environmental impacts,[92] to determine that Vedanta did not employ the local language or means of communication other than written form for consultations with communities with very high rate of illiteracy. It also found that the environmental impact assessment that had been carried out, although including an analysis of the 'socio-economic environment' of the study area, did not address the impact of the mine on the community.[93] The NCP concluded that the company did not carry out adequate or timely consultations about the potential environmental impact of the construction of the mine on them.[94]

The NCP thus recommended that Vedanta engage in consultations with the indigenous group on access to the project-affected area, ways to secure communities' traditional livelihoods, and alternative arrangements (other than resettlement) for the affected families according to the process outlined in the CBD Akwé: Kon Guidelines. At a minimum, the NCP expected Vedanta to advertise the consultation in a language and form that could be easily understood by the Dongria Kondh, thereby ensuring the participation of the maximum number of their representatives in the consultation.[95] Interestingly, the NCP also underlined that in carrying out a human rights impact assessment, as suggested by the UN Framework on Business and Human Rights, the Akwé: Kon Guidelines could be used as a point of reference, particularly for carrying out indigenous groups' impact assessments.[96]

The follow-up statement by the NCP, however, provided a mixed picture, with the NGO claiming that no change in the company's conduct could be detected. In turn, Vedanta reported on specific action being undertaken following

---

[89] Convention on Biological Diversity (CBD) (Rio de Janeiro, 5 June 1992, in force 29 December 1993).
[90] UN General Assembly Res. 61/295 (13 September 2007).
[91] CBD Decision VII/16F, 'Akwé: Kon Voluntary Guidelines for the Conduct of Cultural, Environmental and Social Impact Assessment regarding Developments Proposed to Take Place on, or which are Likely to Impact on, Sacred Sites and on Lands and Waters Traditionally Occupied or Used by Indigenous and Local Communities, in Article 8(j) and related provisions' (2004).
[92] UK NCP, Final Statement on the Complaint from Survival International against Vedanta Resources plc, 25 September 2009, paras 44–46, at http://www.berr.gov.uk/files/file53117.doc.
[93] Ibid. para. 57.
[94] Ibid. paras 65 and 67.
[95] Ibid. paras 73–74.
[96] Ibid. para. 79.

consultations with affected communities, and no comment provided by the NCP.[97] Nevertheless, the case shows how the OECD Guidelines implementation procedure can significantly point to companies' shortcomings vis-à-vis international environmental standards, as well as leading to coherent interpretation and application of different international sources of corporate environmental accountability standards. To the latter end, the NCP proposed filling a gap in the UN Framework on Business and Human Rights through CBD guidelines.[98]

2.4 Inter-institutional cooperation

Another interesting function of the OECD implementation procedure is that it can lead to inter-institutional cooperation, including with the UN System. The most notable case concerns the UN Security Council addressing private companies operating in situations of conflict[99] in relation to the illegal exploitation of natural resources in the Democratic Republic of Congo.[100] The UN Security Council directly addressed the conduct of multinationals at the international level, and through an international process, namely the establishment of an international, independent fact-finding body ('experts group') to conduct field visits, and investigate directly the irresponsible conduct of, among others, private companies.

An annex to the experts' report listed individuals, States, and *companies* whose international violations had been documented by the expert group.[101] Listed companies had either been involved in natural resources exploitation in a way directly linked to the funding of the conflict (Annex I), or were responsible for failing to ensure that their commercial links did not contribute to funding and perpetuating the conflict (Annex III). The experts used the OECD Guidelines as a benchmark in assessing the conduct of companies so that these were included in Annex III of their report because of an apparent breach of the OECD Guidelines.[102] Although the report of the experts group did not primarily address the environmental provisions of the OECD Guidelines, it highlighted other specific environmental misconduct,

---

[97] Follow up to Final Statement by the UK National Contact Point for the OECD Guidelines for Multinational Enterprises: Complaint from Survival International against Vedanta Resources plc (12 March 2010).

[98] E. Morgera, 'From Corporate Social Responsibility to Accountability Mechanisms' in P.-M. Dupuy and J. Viñuales (eds), *Harnessing Foreign Investment to Promote Environmental Protection: Incentives and Safeguards* (Cambridge: Cambridge University Press, 2013) 321.

[99] The International Council on Human Rights Policy (n. 35) 145–47.

[100] UN Security Council, 'Presidential Statement on the situation concerning the Democratic Republic of the Congo' (19 December 2001) UN Doc. S/PRST/2001/139; UN Security Council Res. 1457/2003 (24 January 2003) and UN Security Council Res. 1499/2003 (13 August 2003).

[101] UN Security Council, 'Final Report of the Panel of Experts on the Illegal Exploitation of Natural Resources and Other Forms of Wealth of the Democratic Republic of Congo' (16 October 2002) UN Doc. S/2002/1146, Annex (2002 Experts' Report).

[102] UN Security Council, 'Letter dated 23 October 2003 from the Secretary-General addressed to the President of the Security Council', para. 12.

namely how the exploitation of natural resources in DRC entailed illegal logging and trade in endangered species illegally taken from protected areas.[103] During the investigations, the experts communicated with the OECD Committee on International Investment and Multilateral Enterprises, thus developing a modus operandi according to which the experts would hand over to OECD NCPs' information on companies for further follow-up in their jurisdiction.

The publication of the report in October 2002 raised much media attention and several companies acknowledged their own responsibility, in particular with reference to supply chains for raw materials. Besides its impact in terms of international public pressure, the initiative also comprised a follow-up procedure. For a company to be delisted, it needed to 'achieve a resolution of the issue' through dialogue with the experts group, on the assumption that higher standards of corporate behaviour by foreign companies could play a major role in improving the situation in the Democratic Republic of Congo.[104] Where it was not possible to reach a resolution, the experts referred the relevant governments for follow-up under their jurisdiction, in the form of monitoring of compliance with resolutions or further/updating investigation.

In September 2003, the OECD Committee requested the Security Council, expressing access to the information justifying the experts group's conclusions on OECD-based enterprises' roles in DRC to support adhering governments' cooperation on the Guidelines implementation.[105] However, at its December 2003 session, the OECD Committee noted the need for improving cooperation with the UN Security Council,[106] as no exchange of information had taken place. Some NCPs reported that they had been in contact with enterprises named in Annex III of the 2002 Experts' Report, while others mentioned that they had approached the experts group by various means, asking for information. The experts group was invited to the next Committee meeting in April 2004, to meet with NCPs in the countries involved.[107] Eventually, NGOs noted that only a few NCPs initiated any inquiries in response to the UN Security Council Report.[108] Several instances were

---

[103] 2002 Experts' Report (n. 101) 33. An NGO report also indicated severe air and water pollution due to radioactive materials originating from illegal uranium mining sites: RAID, 'Unanswered Questions: Companies, Conflict and the Democratic Republic of Congo' (May 2004) <http://www.unites.uqam.ca/grama/pdf/RAID-DRC_Ex-Summary.pdf> 63.

[104] UN Security Council, 'Letter dated 2002/10/15 from the Secretary-General addressed to the President of the Security Council: addendum' (20 June 2003) UN Doc. S/2002/1146/Add.1; and UN Security Council, 'Final Report of the Panel of Experts on the Illegal Exploitation of Natural Resources and Other Forms of Wealth of the Democratic Republic of Congo' (2003) UN Doc. S/2003/1027 (2003 Experts' Report).

[105] 'Letter from Marinus W. Sikkel, Chair of CIME, to Mahmoud Kassem, Chairman of the UN Panel of Experts on DRC' (26 September 2003), reprinted in OECD 2004 Report by the Chair, 46 (Annex 4).

[106] 'Letter from Donald Johnston, OECD Secretary-General, to Kofi Annan, UN Secretary-General' (9 January 2004), reprinted in OECD 2004 Report by the Chair, 48 (Annex 4).

[107] Smith (n. 62) 10.

[108] OECD, '2004 Annual meeting of the National Contact Points. Report by the Chair' (2004) <http://www.oecd.org/dataoecd/5/36/33734844.pdf> 4–5.

concluded because the NCP indicated that the UN Panel report did not specify sufficiently the grounds on which a company had been listed.[109] One exception was the Israel NCP, which reported that, following an enquiry, the company stopped illegitimate sourcing from DRC.[110]

In another follow-up instance, information was supplied to an NCP on the condition that it was to remain confidential and could only be disclosed to the companies involved or as part of a criminal prosecution. This prevented the NCP from assessing a related, independent NGO complaint in conjunction with the UN Panel allegations. Although the UN Panel reached a resolution with the company, the NCP stressed to the private company concerned the need to contribute to economic, social, and environmental progress with a view to achieving sustainable development in the countries in which it operates. The NCP, however, did not succeed in facilitating a constructive dialogue between the NGO and the company, or in mediating an agreed settlement between the parties.[111]

Overall, although this example shows that the NCP drew on UN work 'well before the UN Guiding Principles', setting the stage for the 2011 review,[112] the high-profile opportunity for cooperation between the UN and the OECD remained a largely unrealized potential.

2.5 Continued challenges

Confidentiality and a sufficient nexus to the OECD Guidelines have been recurrent challenges in the OECD implementation procedure. The degree of confidentiality proposed by the Canadian NCP, for instance, led an NGO to pull out of a facilitated dialogue on mining operations in Ecuador by a Canadian company that had allegedly failed in communicating to the public and its employees environmental, health, and safety impacts and in consulting with the communities on environmental, health, and safety policies.[113] Commentators have concluded that NCPs can only play a meaningful role when they do not assign undue emphasis to confidentiality, effectively preventing complainants from fully engaging in the process.[114]

---

[109] Belgium NCP, 'Press release on Speciality Metals Company' (undated) <http://economie.fgov.be/organization_market/oecd_guidelines/pdf/SMC_fr.pdf>; France NCP, 'DRC/SDV Transami, as reported in OECD, '2007 Annual meeting of the National Contact Points: Report by the Chair' (2007) <http://www.oecd.org/dataoecd/5/36/33734844.pdf>; UK National Contact Point Statement on allegations against De Beers' (undated) <http://www.csr.gov.uk/oecddoc/file23459.pdf>.

[110] As reported in OECD (n. 105).

[111] UK NCP, 'Statement on allegations against Oryx Natural Resources' (June 2005) <http://www.csr.gov.uk/oecddoc/file23454.pdf>.

[112] Ruggie and Nelson (n. 46) 5.

[113] Canadian NCP, 'Statement Concerning Ascendant Copper Corporation in Ecuador' (undated) <http://www.ncp-pcn.gc.ca/ncpanual-en.asp>. See discussion of relevant standards in Ch. 4, Section 2.4.

[114] Maheandiran (n. 79) 236.

Until the 2011 review, several cases were also hindered by the need to establish an investment nexus. In a 2003 case,[115] two NGOs asked the Swedish NCP to assess two mining companies' operations in Ghana in relation to the human rights and environmental provisions of the OECD Guidelines. The NCP concluded that, although environmental and social problems existed, the roles played by the two companies were limited, and they did not fail to comply with the Guidelines.[116] At the same time, the NCP found that the companies' on-site personnel did not have adequate knowledge of their responsibilities under the Guidelines,[117] and encouraged the multinational to take into account its actual ability of influencing a business partner in the host country.[118] Other cases had not been accepted by NCPs due to the question of business relations,[119] but this barrier was removed by the 2011 review of the OECD Guidelines, so trade and finance activities of multinationals also fall under the scope of NCPs' activities.[120]

On the basis of the 2011 review extending coverage to the supply chain, the number of instances before NCPs involving manufacturing, in addition to extractives, has increased.[121] The Norwegian NCP in 2013 indicated, drawing on the UN Guiding Principles on Business and Human Rights and a letter from the UN Office of the High Commissioner for Human Rights, that the OECD Guidelines apply to minority shareholders.[122] To provide another example, in 2011, the French NCP provided its good offices in a specific instance concerning foreign investors associated with a palm oil producer that allegedly diminished the availability of natural resources, did not adequately treat water and prevent air pollution, and failed to prevent other negative environmental impacts. The NCP considered that the investors were not exercising all possible influence on their trading partners, even if they had taken positive steps towards improving the producer's

---

[115] OECD (n. 104), at 43.
[116] RAID and SOMO, 'OECDWatch Review of National Contact Points for the OECD Guidelines for the period June 2003–June 2004 and Update of NCP cases filed by NGOs' (August 2004) <www.corporate-accountability.org/docs/OW_2004_Review.pdf>, 11 (statement from the Swedish National Contact Point for OECD Guidelines with reference to specific instances received concerning Atlas Copco and Sandvik).
[117] Ibid.
[118] OECD, 'Guidelines for Multinational Corporations' (31 October 2001) DAFFE/IME/WPG(2000)15/FINAL (OECD Guidelines), Ch II, para. 10, which states that enterprises should '[e]ncourage, where practicable, business partners, including suppliers and sub-contractors, to apply principles of corporate conduct compatible with the Guidelines'.
[119] The instances are against: TotalFinaElf (Germany), submitted in 2002 by Greenpeace Germany on alleged pollution in Russia; West LB (Germany), submitted in 2003 by Greenpeace Germany on the financing of a pipeline to be built in Ecuador; Chemie Pharmacie Holland, submitted in 2003 by FOE Netherlands on human rights violations in the Democratic Republic of Congo; and Australia and New Zealand Banking Group (Australia), submitted in 2006 on forestry activities in Papua New Guinea (Australian NCP Statement (28 May 2008) <http://www.ausncp.gov.au/content/docs/366_415_ANZ%20Statement.pdf>).
[120] R. Geiger, 'Coherence in Shaping the Rules of International Business: Actors, Instruments and Implementation' (2011) 43 *George Washington International Law Review* 295, at 305.
[121] Ruggie and Nelson (n. 46) 115 and 118.
[122] Ibid. 119, fn. 55.

environmental performance, including by supporting the producer in proceeding with international certification. With support from the NCP, the parties involved jointly drew a roadmap to be implemented by the producer to prevent pollution, collaborate with local authorities in detecting pollution-related illnesses and compensate affected communities for medical expenses.[123] The action plan further called on the producer to: facilitate access to drinkable water, education, and electricity for affected communities; support village plantations and harvesting; recruit local workers for its own plantations; and ease the dialogue with local communicates to address land issues. The parties also agreed to report on the implementation of the action plan to the NCP and to select an independent organization to monitor its implementation and ensure stakeholder involvement.[124] These could be considered elements of a benefit-sharing agreement, but it remains to be seen to what extent communities have been able to co-identify these benefits.[125]

The main source of disappointment, however, remains the discrepancy across NCPs' practices. Scholars have therefore underscored as the main source of concern the divergence in whether different NCPs carry out a thorough examination of facts and include in their statement an assessment of whether or not the company has breached the OECD Guidelines.[126] It has been argued that NCPs can provide 'significant insights into the relationship between foreign investment and environmental protection'[127] only when, as a matter of practice, they go beyond the mediation phase (which is not the case for the Canadian, Swiss, and US NCPs, for instance).[128] Furthermore, the US, Mexican, and Australian NCPs do not engage in the investigation of an instance if the company declines to participate in the dialogue and mediation, which has been considered at odds with the primary function of NCPs to further the effectiveness of the Guidelines.[129] All in all, notwithstanding all the evolution in the process, 'considerable divergence continues to exist among NCPs on their roles and powers regarding individual complaints'.[130]

Given the disparate results of complaints submitted to NCPs on environmental matters, the NCPs' actual impact on improving corporate environmental accountability and responsibility remains an open question.[131] The track record of

---

[123] French NCP, Report SOCAPALM, 3 June 2013, available at http://www.tresor.economie.gouv.fr/File/397319 (in English). OECD-FAO, Guidance for Responsible Agricultural Supply Chains (Paris: OECD, 2015) Lessons Learnt, 15.
[124] French NCP (n. 123).
[125] See discussion of relevant standards in Ch. 4, Section 3.1.3.
[126] J. C. Ochoa Sanchez, 'The Roles and Powers of the OECD National Contact Points Regarding Complaints on an Alleged Breach of the OECD Guidelines for Multinational Enterprises by a Transnational Corporation' (2015) 84 *Nordic Journal of International Law* 89, 97.
[127] J. Viñuales, *Foreign Investment and the Environment in International Law* (Cambridge: Cambridge University Press, 2012) 76.
[128] Maheandiran (n. 79) 230.
[129] Ibid. 102–03.
[130] Ibid. 126.
[131] P. Feeney, 'Making Companies Accountable' (NGO Report on Implementation of the OECD Guidelines for Multinational Enterprises by National Contact Points, October 2002) <http://www.oecd.org/dataoecd/16/37/2965489.pdf>; RAID and SOMO (n. 116); Van der Gaag (n. 26) 5.

corporate compliance with NCP decisions remains to be studied empirically more systematically: in the Vedanta case (discussed above),[132] the company refused to fully engage in the complaint process including in the sponsored professional conciliation or mediation, and it appealed against the decision of the relevant minister to prevent the development of the mining project.[133]

3 Compliance under the IFC

The mission and functions of the IFC place this organization in a unique position to contribute to clarifying international standards on corporate environmental accountability and responsibility at the international level and to the monitoring of their implementation. The IFC's funding to private companies allows the Corporation to influence how major development projects are designed and implemented in developing countries in respect of minimum international environmental standards. Specifically, both in the pre-project approval and in the post-fund disbursement phases, the IFC is able to directly assess the conduct and performance of private companies, and request or suggest remedial action.

Unlike all the other international corporate environmental accountability initiatives discussed in this book, the IFC is the only one that can make international environmental standards contractually binding on private companies as conditions in loan agreements,[134] monitoring their application, and even sanctioning their violation through the suspension or withdrawal of previously approved financing. In addition, it has established a complaint mechanism that can provide an additional layer of oversight through the examination of complaints by affected individuals and groups.

While the IFC remains still relatively little-studied, it has been considered capable of application and enforcement of its own international standards.[135] In addition, the Compliance Advisor/Ombudsman (CAO) has been seen as a source of more expansive interpretation of international standards.[136] As a result, the IFC has been perceived as being capable of contributing to the hardening of international standards and the creation of precedents in their application.[137] The role of the CAO is also significant because in its Ombudsman role, it can contribute to

---

[132] Section 1.3.
[133] Simons and Macklin (n. 49) 92.
[134] CAO, *A Review of International Finance Corporation's Safeguard Policies* (January 2003) <www.cao-ombudsman.org/html-english/documents/ReviewofIFCSPsfinalreportenglish   04-03-03.pdf> (hereinafter, IFC CAO 2003 Review).
[135] D. Bradlow and A. Naudé Fourie, 'The Operational Policies of the World Bank and the International Finance Corporation: Creating Law-Making and Law-Governed Institutions?' (2013) 10 *International Organizations Law Review* 3, 59.
[136] Ibid. 41 and 43.
[137] Ibid. 61.

new standard-setting, by drawing from international obligations and implementation of practical human rights-based approaches in its mediation activities.[138] In addition, based on its project-specific experience, it can investigate systemic problems in its Advisor function and provide recommendations to the IFC,[139] making reference to international norms for the IFC to take into account.[140] The following sub-sections will discuss, in turn, the role of the IFC itself in applying and monitoring the implementation of international environmental standards (and the assessment of its effectiveness by the CAO in its Compliance and Advisor functions); and the role of the CAO to assess the application of these standards on the basis of complaints from victims in its Ombudsman function.

3.1 Contract-related procedures

The IFC can ensure that private companies comply with its environmental standards, in two stages: at the stage of selection and review of projects, prior to allocating funding to private companies; and at the stage of monitoring of companies' operations, through the Environmental and Social Review Procedure, once funds have been disbursed.[141]

During the project approval phase, the IFC reviews its clients' assessment of environmental risks and possible impacts of the project; assists them in developing measures to avoid, minimize, mitigate, or compensate for environmental impacts; categorizes projects to specify IFC's institutional requirements to disclose to the public project-specific information; and support the identification of opportunities to improve environmental outcomes. According to the Policy, the IFC seeks to ensure that the projects it finances are operated in an environmentally sustainable manner. The environmental review of a proposed project is 'an important factor', but not a condition, in the IFC's decision to finance a project. The basic benchmark for determining the environmental sustainability of projects is determined in the negative, that is, the avoidance of negative impacts on the environment and local communities, or at least their reduction, mitigation, and appropriate compensation.[142]

In the project appraisal phase, the IFC carries out a review of the impact assessment and possibly makes suggestions for the environmental management plan, while also encouraging disclosure of information and ensuring public

---

[138] B. Saper, 'The International Finance Corporation's Compliance Advisor/Ombudsman (CAO): An Examination of Accountability and Effectiveness from a Global Administrative Law Perspective' (2011–12) 44 *NYU Journal of International Law & Policy* 1279, 1300.
[139] Ibid. 1297.
[140] Ibid. 1306.
[141] IFC, *Environmental and Social Review Procedure* (1 January 2012).
[142] Ibid. 4–8.

involvement. One of the crucial elements of the review is its determination of the scope of the environmental conditions applied to the IFC financing.[143] In a way, the IFC is, therefore, aiming at damage control or avoidance, which could be considered in line with the 'no harm' approach of UN Framework on Business and Human Rights and the international law principle of prevention.[144] As a result, the Corporation could stipulate prior conditions with respect to the entry into force of the loan agreement or the disbursement of the loan upon compliance with certain environmental standards, or include a covenant committing the client to execute specific measures by a certain date[145] in accordance with the environmental management plan.

After disbursing the funding, the IFC is expected to supervise the clients' environmental performance and bring clients back into compliance or exercise remedies as appropriate.[146] Another responsibility of the IFC is to help the project sponsor select technologies that meet environmental standards and are energy- and cost-efficient.[147] Attention should be drawn in particular to the possibility of making a site visit by the IFC staff.[148] This can provide the most direct opportunity to assess the environmental impacts of the project, the use of appropriate technologies, compliance with loan conditions and the environmental plan, as well as the participation of affected communities on the ground. However, due to budget and human resource constraints, only a fraction of projects receive a visit from the IFC staff. In some of the environmentally harmful projects funded by the IFC in the past, the lack of site visits was considered by environmental activists to be one of the missed opportunities to exercise pressure on improving environmental performance by the companies and devise mitigation measures through an inclusive process.[149]

In this second phase, following site visits and other forms of monitoring that reveal clients' poor compliance with environmental standards and conditions, the IFC is in a position to make recommendations on remedial action and improvements in performance. It may suggest modifications to the environmental management system and draw together with the client a timetable for improved

---

[143] Ibid. 9.
[144] Section 2.2 in Ch 4.
[145] L. Boisson de Chazournes, 'Policy Guidance and Compliance: The World Bank Operational Standards' in D. Shelton (ed.), *Commitment and Compliance—The Role of Non-Binding Norms in the International Legal System* (Oxford: Oxford University Press, 2000) 281, 290.
[146] IFC Policy on Social and Environmental Sustainability (2012) para. 24.
[147] C. Lee, 'International Finance Corporation: Financing Environmentally and Socially Sustainable Private Investment' in S. Schlemmer-Schulte and K. Tung (eds), *Liber Amicorum Ibrahim F.I. Shihata* (The Hague: Kluwer Law International, 2001) 469, 473.
[148] IFC Policy on Social and Environmental Sustainability (2012) para. 28.
[149] J. Hay, 'Pangue Hydroelectric Project (Chile): An Independent Review of the International Finance Corporation's Compliance with Applicable World Bank Group Environmental and Social Requirements' (1997), cited by CIEL, 'Analysis of IFC's role and Impact' (September 2000) <http://www.ciel.org/Ifi/ifccaseanalysis.html>.

compliance. In case of persistent substandard conduct, the IFC is also in a position to suspend or withdraw a loan for breach of the loan agreement.

The Corporation could equally ensure a systematic inclusion and disclosure of environmental conditions in its loan agreement, to allow NGOs and local communities to identify corporate environmentally irresponsible conduct. Indeed, the IFC could allow communities to monitor the project, given its limited resources for field visits.[150] Another important measure is the requirement to conduct postproject evaluations, to assess the ultimate environmental aspects of funded projects and identify lessons learnt for similar projects on the basis of the performance standards involved.[151]

In cases of non-compliance, the IFC could request from the company measurable progress against time-bound action plans in the next semi-annual or annual review[152] and may even suspend its funding to a project. A possible withdrawal of IFC funds, however, seems less appropriate, since it would result in the IFC's exit from the project and in the termination of its oversight role.[153] Thus, the Corporation should ensure that this 'sanctional aspect'[154] of its involvement in project development is fully taken into consideration by private companies and used as a deterrent against substandard environmental performance.

The IFC could further start including in its loan agreements provisions for continued monitoring of environmental performance in case of prepayment of the loans by the private company, to avoid the risk of companies escaping its control at an early stage of the project life-cycle. Finally, the Corporation could enforce the client's commitments even after the completion of the project and full disbursement of the loan, by declaring the client's default in performing its obligations under the agreement and, where the client does not take any action, this could accelerate the maturity of the loan or affect future relations with the IFC.[155]

Against this background, the following sub-sections will discuss the CAO's assessments over time of the IFC's practice in applying its own standards, including

---

[150] Eg the case in which it contracted an NGO for an environmental appraisal of the project (IFC commissioned the NGO Flora and Fauna International to investigate illegal logging in Liberia when considering financing a project in the same area; reported by G. Saul, 'Liberian Agricultural Project: Can't See the People for the Trees' (September 2000) <http://www.ciel.org/Ifi/ifccaseliberia.html>.

[151] Boisson de Chazournes (n. 144) 291.

[152] WWF, 'Guidelines for Investment in Operations that Impact Forests' (September 2003) <http://www.forestandtradeasia.org/files/WWF%20FOrest%20Investment%20Guideline.pdf> 11.

[153] Boisson de Chazournes (n. 144) 291, also observed that in the case of the World Bank loans to governments, an interruption of the contractual relationship impedes 'the continuation of a dialogue that may find ways to correct the non-complying situation'.

[154] So defined by I. Shihata, 'Implementation, Enforcement and Compliance with International Environmental Agreements—Practical Suggestions in Light of the World Bank's Experience' (1996–97) 9 *Georgetown International Environmental Law Review* 37, 48.

[155] I. Shihata, 'The World Bank and the Environment: A Legal Perspective' in A. Parra, F. Tschofen, M. Stevens, and S. Schlemmer-Schulte (eds), *The World Bank in a Changing World* (Boston: M. Nijhoff, 1995) 135, 154.

recent insights into the application of the 2012 standards on biodiversity and ecosystem services.

3.1.1 Internal assessment

It was in the aftermath of an independent review of an IFC-funded project in Chile in 1997 that the need for an independent compliance mechanism for the IFC was identified. The independent review concluded: 'there is no indication at this time that IFC has in place the necessary institutional operating system or clarity in its policy and procedural mandate to manage complex projects in a manner that complies consistently with World Bank Group environmental requirements'.[156] As a consequence, the CAO was established to provide the IFC with policy and process advice on environmental and social performance (Advisor function), and conduct environmental and social audits and reviews as an aid to institution learning (Compliance function).[157] The degree of independence of the CAO is, however, subject to debate,[158] although the selection process of the Vice President that serves as CAO has been considered extraordinarily independent, with interviews being conducted by civil society and private sector representatives, and a recommendation being made directly to the President of the World Bank Group, not through IFC management.[159]

In 2003, the CAO's review concluded that the IFC environmental standards were having 'some positive effects', at the same time cautioning that the necessary systems to guide implementation and interpretation of such standards were lax or absent.[160] Indeed, NGOs had been very active in documenting the environmental damage caused by IFC-funded projects, showing how major projects that purportedly complied with IFC environmental safeguard policies did not achieve the minimum environmentally sound practices and impacts expected. Several drawbacks had been highlighted in the literature as possible causes of the poor environmental record of IFC-funded projects in the past. Some underscored the fact that the IFC applied different standards of compliance to different clients, depending on their sense of the company's commitment to environmental issues.[161] Others noted that EIAs were often inadequate, when IFC funding was sought at a late stage in the project development.[162] The IFC replied to these criticisms in 2006, noting that it evaluated the client's willingness or ability to

---

[156] Ibid.
[157] The CAO role in addressing complaints will be discussed in detail in Section 3.2 in this chapter.
[158] A. McBeth, *International Economic Actors and Human Rights* (Abingdon: Routledge, 2010) 215.
[159] CAO, 'CAO at 10' (CAO, 2010) 4–6.
[160] CAO, *A Review of International Finance Corporation's Safeguard Policies* (January 2003) http://www.cao-ombudsman.org/html-english/documents/ReviewofIFCSPsfinalreportenglish04-03-03.pdf 21.
[161] Ibid. 26.
[162] Ibid. 7.

take remedial action to meet IFC requirements also at a later stage of the project development.[163]

The CAO also raised other concerns, such as on the selection of clients, particularly on the need to assess a proven commitment to positive environmental outcomes and for specific assessment of the client's capacity at the pre-appraisal stage.[164] In 2006, the IFC pledged to have put in place systems to review clients' past practice, noting, however, that assessing client commitment is a 'business judgement call'.[165] Another critique centred on the role of the IFC to engage government authorities and strengthen their capacity[166] to hold companies accountable. In addition, continued concerns were raised about a conflict of interests between the World Bank's public lending operations and the IFC's private loans, as the World Bank was pressing a government for restructuring certain economic sectors to the benefit of the private sector financed by the IFC.[167]

From a corporate environmental accountability perspective, the CAO identified as one of the most serious drawbacks in the past implementation activity of the IFC its limited practice in including environmental conditions systematically in its loan agreements[168] and in not making such conditions publicly available.[169] It suggested, therefore, that similarly to the World Bank and other private banks, the IFC should consider suspending loans or withdrawing from projects whose environmental performance presented unacceptable risks to the Corporation.[170] Another significant flaw in past implementation occurred when a company decided to prepay its loans to the IFC, thus effectively precluding the Corporation from any further involvement in the project, including its ability to monitor and oversee the environmental performance of its loans.[171] Environmental NGOs proposed as a possible solution to this situation that the agreement between the IFC and the private company could state that the loan is contingent upon the client's commitment to continue, after the IFC funding, environmental assessment procedures, and

---

[163] IFC, 'Response to the Compliance Advisor/Ombudsman Review on IFC Policy and Performance Standards on Social and Environmental Sustainability' (22 September 2005) (IFC Response to CAO Review), 3.
[164] CAO (n. 159) 8.
[165] IFC Response (n. 162).
[166] CAO (n. 159) 51.
[167] L. Pottinger, 'Uganda's Bujagali Dam: A Case Study in Corporate Welfare' (September 2000) <http://www.ciel.org/Ifi/ifccaseuganda.html>. 'The World Bank's public sector arm is pressuring the Ugandan government to restructure its energy sector to ensure the smooth functioning of the private sector. The IFC is supporting a major project that stands to directly benefit from World Bank-sponsored reforms' through the construction of large-scale dams.
[168] CAO (n. 159) 48.
[169] I. Bowles, A. Rosenfels, C. Kormos, C. Reining, J. Nations, and T. Ankersen, 'The Environmental Impact of the International Finance Corporation Lending and Proposals for Reform: A Case Study of Conservation and Oil Development in the Guatemalan Petén' (1999) 29 *Environmental Law* 103, 115.
[170] CAO (n. 155) 52.
[171] Bowles et al. (n. 168) 105.

maintain insurance coverage and other measures agreed with the IFC in addition to requirements under domestic law.[172]

Another shortcoming in past implementation was limited public participation in the environmental assessment and management of IFC projects. Public consultations occurred too late to affect the project design, because private companies did not facilitate stakeholders' understanding of the project, and their ability to express concerns. Furthermore, companies allowed insufficient time for processing the information, providing thorough feedback, and did not sustain public participation efforts after the project approval.[173] Given the fundamental role of affected communities in monitoring the project and their direct interest in ensuring its environmental sustainability, it was suggested that the IFC should recognize communities' greater role in monitoring and supervising IFC-funded projects, with specific supervision protocols being developed for certain categories of projects.[174] During the 2006 review, the IFC considered this option but decided, with a quite restrictive approach, that this could be decided on a project-by-project basis depending on the interest and capacity of communities involved.[175] Concerns about the categorization of projects continued to be raised by the CAO in successive audit reports.[176]

In the context of a complaint for a project in Chile, which the CAO agreed to consider notwithstanding the Corporation's exit from the project,[177] the CAO very openly criticized the 'decree of secrecy and the tentative approach to disclosure ... which hampered the ability of affected communities and internal constituencies of the IFC to understand the project'.[178] The CAO further argued that given the conditions of the loan agreement, the exit of the IFC should have taken place with its independent verification of the fulfilment of the loan conditions.[179] According to the IFC's interpretation that the agreement was still valid until all of its conditions were fulfilled, the CAO requested the IFC to revisit its decision not to undertake any further external reviews of the project, to disclose the details of the agreement relating to environmental and social conditions, and to press the private company to disclose the results of monitoring and supervision in relation to downstream impacts.[180]

In 2010, the CAO continued to underscore in its advisory work the generalized need to improve the IFC's practices relating to consultation and disclosure of

---

[172] Ibid. 127.
[173] CAO (n. 159) 27.
[174] Ibid. 52.
[175] Ibid. 3.
[176] *Indonesia Wilmar Group 01 West Kalimantan* (Complaint filed 1 July 2007), Compliance Advisor Ombudsman, Audit Report (19 June 2011) para. 2.8.3); discussed by Bradlow and Naudé Fourie (n. 135) 49.
[177] CAO, Assessment Report in relation to a complaint against IFC's investment in ENDESA Pangue SA, Chile (May 2003).
[178] Ibid. 4.
[179] Ibid. 5.
[180] Ibid. 6–7.

information as local stakeholders appear to be unaware of the IFC's support to projects and the requirement for 'broad community support' is limited to 'a very small number of the most sensitive projects in the [IFC's] portfolio'.[181] In addition, the CAO identified cases in which the IFC interpreted 'too narrowly' its policies, even in cases where there was full awareness of significant environmental and social concerns in certain sectors such as palm oil plantations.[182] The case led to the setting up of a panel of experts to audit the IFC, on the basis of which (and also due to resulting pressure from international civil society) the President of the World Bank placed a moratorium on IFC investments in the sector and carried out a global review of the sector.[183]

Other cases have led to the CAO underscoring the need for more disclosure of information on environmental performance that can impact on affected communities' livelihoods, including the outcomes of monitoring and supervision activities in relation to downstream impacts.[184] Furthermore, the CAO called attention to the IFC's responsibilities in assessing more systematically the adequacy of clients' capacity at pre-investment stage so as to identify specific requirements to enhance environmental and social capacity where needed; and to risks arising from well-known deficiencies or contradictions in the national legal framework applicable to the proposed project.[185]

In some instances, the CAO's review focused on specific substantive matters related to the environmental dimensions of projects: for example, in one case it considered insufficient the IFC's narrow assessment of water availability only vis-à-vis the client's own operational needs, as opposed to the sustainability of the aquifer and impacts on vulnerable users.[186] Since 2010, the IFC has responded to CAO's advisory notes finding by finding, providing explanations of follow-up action and its rationale where the IFC is in agreement with the CAO's assessment.[187] Generally, concerns remain about the lack of timeliness of information disclosure to communities by the IFC, usually following the conduct of 'significant preliminary planning work'.[188] Once the IFC has committed to fund a project, it becomes very difficult and costly to withdraw its support, so a suggestion has been made to

---

[181] Ibid. 64.

[182] *Indonesia Wilmar Group 01 West Kalimantan* (Complaint filed 1 July 2007), Compliance Advisor Ombudsman, Appraisal Report I (September 2008); discussed by Bradlow and Naudé Fourie (n. 135) 33–35 and 43.

[183] Saper (n. 138) 1312.

[184] *Chile Empresa Electrica Pangue SA 02 Upper Bio-Bio Watershed* (Complant filed 1 July 2002), Compliance Advisor Ombudsman, Assessment Report (May 2003) 17; discussed by Bradlow and Naudé Fourie (n. 135) 44.

[185] *Bolivia Comsur V-01 Bosque Chiquitano* (Complaint filed 1 June 2003), Compliance Advisor Ombudsman, Audit Report (June 2004); discussed by Bradlow and Naudé Fourie (n. 135) 50.

[186] *Peru Agrokasa-01/Ica* (Complaint filed 2 June 2009), CAO, Audit Report (22 February 2011) para. 4.1.1); discussed by Bradlow and Naudé Fourie (n. 135) 53.

[187] Saper (n. 138) 1317.

[188] Ibid. 1319.

widely publicize the IFC's initial consideration of projects to allow potentially affected communities to provide inputs into the process at a sufficiently early stage of decision-making within the IFC.[189] Disclosure of subsequent environmental and social assessment and monitoring documentation is also a shortcoming, as is local language information on project environmental and social risks and impacts.[190]

All in all, the CAO's advisory and compliance roles, and its own efforts to improve its effectiveness, should be assessed against the background of the IFC's immunity to national courts' jurisdiction,[191] which is increasingly challenged—including on the basis of CAO's findings.[192] This should also be contextualized with other World Bank activities, such as the Doing Business model, which support fiscal and regulatory practices that have detrimental effects on the environment and on human rights.[193] The UN Independent Expert on the promotion of a democratic and equitable international order thus suggested that CAO recommendations are publicized, and its reports include explicit reference to negative impacts on human rights on the basis of recommendations from human rights treaty bodies and special procedure mandate holders.[194] The UN Independent Expert also advocated that the IFC waive institutional immunity when gross violations of human rights have occurred.[195]

Empirical research is limited on how the IFC management and staff apply the operational policies, as 'technical compliance' based on narrow interpretations of policies could nevertheless lead to 'problematic results.'[196] More research should also be carried out to assess the evolution of the CAO's relationship with the IFC, in order to better understand the impact of the CAO's recommendations on the functioning of the Corporation, including how direct recommendations to private companies are treated by the IFC President.

3.1.1.1 Implementation of biodiversity standards

A 2019 compliance investigation underscored the IFC's shortcomings in implementing the 2012 Performance Standard on biodiversity,[197] providing a host of considerations in relation to the integration of biodiversity concerns in impact assessments, the consideration of high biodiversity value and nationally protected areas, as well as ecosystem services.

---

[189] Ibid. 1320 and 1324.
[190] Ibid. 1320.
[191] Ibid. 1322.
[192] Report of the Independent Expert on the promotion of a democratic and equitable international order, (2017) UN Doc. A/HRC/36/40, paras 55–57.
[193] Ibid. paras 50–54.
[194] Whose relevance for corporate international environmental accountability and responsibility standard-setting is discussed in Ch. 4.
[195] Report of the Independent Expert on the promotion of a democratic and equitable international order (n. 191) para. 91(k) and (o).
[196] Bradlow and Naudé Fourie (n. 135) 27–28 and 31.
[197] Discussed in Ch. 4, Sections 3.2–3.3.

The CAO found that the IFC at the pre-investment phase overlooked gaps in the prospective client's assessment of risks for engendered and endemic species, as well as cumulative impacts on freshwater systems.[198] The CAO, however, remarked that while the IFC did not require the client to remedy these gaps in assessment, it requested the retention of a biodiversity expert to design and manage the implementation of a biodiversity monitoring programme.[199] This led to biodiversity concerns being addressed during project implementation on the basis of additional biodiversity studies and a biodiversity monitoring programme. In addition, the CAO found that the IFC took adequate steps to assure itself that the client managed risks in relation to the protection and conservation of biodiversity in compliance with the requirements for critical habitat.

With regard to standards related to an area of high biodiversity value, the CAO looked into whether the project had ensured environmental flows (the quantity and quality of water flows allocated to sustain riverine ecosystems), in accordance with the IFC's own good practice methodology.[200] It observed that the minimum environmental flow described in the environmental assessment was prescribed without assessing the adequacy of the proposed environmental flow regime or alternative flow scenarios. But the CAO also noted that the complexity and challenges of validating the environmental flow, and the IFC's recommendation to the client to adopt an adaptive management framework as part of the monitoring of biodiversity impacts. Considering ongoing monitoring results did not point to measurable adverse impacts, the CAO found that the IFC's supervision of the environmental flow issue was adequate.[201]

Another important finding was the location of the development within a national park (not its core zone, but its sustainable use, recreational, and traditional use zones).[202] This had not been mentioned or noticed at the pre-investment stage, thus no relevant IFC requirements, or the need to respect Albanian law on protected areas, had been triggered, even if the client had obtained necessary permits. The CAO therefore recommended ongoing supervision to ensure that the client activities respect the park management plan (which had been developed a couple of years after the start of the project and of which the client was unaware at the time of the CAO's involvement).[203] The client's consultation with protected area stakeholders was also to be ensured.[204]

---

[198] CAO, 2019 Annual Report, https://cao-ar19.org/, 18.
[199] CAO, Compliance Investigation Report (IFC Investment in Enso Albania, complaint 01), 25 June 2018, 15.
[200] IFC Good Practice Handbook, Environmental Flows for Hydropower Projects, February 2018—https://goo.gl/nVD85b.
[201] CAO, Compliance Investigation Report: IFC Investment in enso Albania, Complaint 1 (2018) 21.
[202] Ibid. 24.
[203] Ibid. 28.
[204] Ibid. 24.

In addition, in this case the CAO also investigated how the IFC applied its standards on ecosystem services, notably cultural services that could have been negatively impacted by the ecotourism project, and that the client was expected to analyse in the context of the project's areas of influence, and co-defined in consultation with affected stakeholders.[205] The national park's management plan emphasized the development of low-impact tourism and recreational activities, as well as the need for stakeholder engagement and resourcing challenges to the realization of the national park's conservation objectives the differing values attached. The CAO therefore considered that the IFC did not ensure that the client took measures to minimize, mitigate, and/or offset project impacts on the touristic value of the area, and did not ensure adequate stakeholder consultation. At the pre-investment review stage, therefore, the CAO noted the need for the IFC to carry out further analysis of risks and impacts related to ecosystem services (including impacts on the area's visual and touristic appeal). Even if the IFC's supervision had captured impacts on ecosystem services related to ecotourism and the broader touristic value of the area, the IFC had not ensured that the client's consultation and disclosure requirements were met in relation to assessments carried out during supervision.[206]

3.2 Ombudsman function of the CAO

Having examined the role of the IFC itself to apply its Performance Standards to private companies, this section examines the role of the CAO in its Ombudsman function to serve as an independent oversight authority that receives complaints directly from affected communities through a flexible problem-solving approach aimed at enhancing the environmental outcomes of IFC-funded projects. The section will discuss the role of the Ombudsman and the evolution of its practices, with the following sub-sections focusing on the various outcomes that can result from the Ombudsman's involvement and comparing them with those arising from the OECD Implementation Procedure discussed earlier. In addition, another subsection will focus specifically on the insights that the Ombudsman's activities have provided to better understand practical challenges in implementing international standards on fair and equitable benefit-sharing.

As opposed to the other two functions of CAO, the Ombudsman interacts directly with private companies and looks into their conduct, as well as that of the IFC. Outcomes of the Ombudsman's cases are made publicly available. Issues that cannot be resolved by the Ombudsman can be referred to the CAO in its Compliance and Advisor functions. Lessons learnt from the Ombudsman's cases are also used to inform more generally the other two roles of CAO.

---

[205] See discussion in Ch. 4, Section 3.2.
[206] CAO (n. 198) 22–23.

According to one commentator, the CAO 'is meant to provide a voice to project-affected people, so that the host state, the project company and the IFC itself are not the only voices in the conversation'.[207] An additional rationale for its creation was, however, identified in the private sector's desire to create a new institution focused on problem-solving, rather than relying on the pre-existing Inspection Panel of the World Bank that was seen as more concerned with 'fault-finding'.[208]

While it has been argued that the CAO provides 'an opportunity for greater consideration of human rights obligations and the implementation of practical human rights outcomes' as a result of its emphasis on mediation,[209] the CAO itself has not yet addressed human rights in explicit terms in its mandate. In its tenth anniversary review of activities, the CAO noted that it has 'not yet conducted a robust analysis of human rights aspects of [its] caseload', although universities and think tanks have remarked that its Ombudsman work has addressed matters related to the right to an adequate standard of living, the right to health, the right to food, the right to property, and the right to life.[210] In addition, most cases involve procedural human rights (including procedural environmental human rights),[211] such as access to environmental information and consultation.[212] In its self-reflection, the CAO added that its own experience provided an indication that more 'recognizable' human rights language in IFC policies that reflects companies' own better understanding of their responsibility to respect human rights could benefit communities in understanding the role of the IFC Performance Standards and CAO in preventing harm and protecting their rights.[213]

The modus operandi of the Ombudsman includes field visits to the site of contested projects and interviews with all concerned parties: staff of the private company, local authorities, affected communities' representatives, other relevant local organizations, and IFC staff. The Ombudsman usually concludes its consideration of complaints within six months to one year from receipt. Complaints, reports of field missions, and recommendations are all published on the CAO website, together with updates on ongoing investigations.[214]

After considering complaints, the CAO formulates recommendations not only to the IFC itself on the basis of its Environmental Performance Policy, but also directly to the private company involved, albeit such recommendations will then need to be endorsed by the IFC President. The latter would transmit the CAO's recommendations to the private company and/or request the IFC to take the appropriate

---

[207] Saper (n. 138) 1288.
[208] Ibid. 1291.
[209] McBeth (n. 157) 231.
[210] CAO (n. 159) 58–59.
[211] See Ch. 4, Sections 2.4 and 2.5.
[212] CAO (n. 159) 60.
[213] Ibid. 59.
[214] http://www.cao-ombudsman.org/html-english/ombudsman.htm, where all the CAO documents cited below can be found.

action.²¹⁵ In some instances, the CAO also engages in follow-up monitoring and site visits.²¹⁶ Its assessment report is intended both as a summary of factual findings by the CAO in relation to allegations contained in the complaint, and as an assessment of the 'ripeness' of any conflict or tension for resolution or management.²¹⁷ The report can serve to identify actual substandard corporate conduct in the natural resource sector, and equally to look into whether allegations against companies are well-founded in a particular case.

After 2006, however, the CAO abandoned its practice of establishing its own findings and making its own recommendations,²¹⁸ and has focused instead on creating the conditions for more collaborative interactions between the company and stakeholders, setting out steps for establishing or strengthening dialogue,²¹⁹ or where dialogue is not favoured by the complainants, proposing to refer the case to the Compliance facility.²²⁰ This is confirmed by the fact that in recent reports the CAO explicitly cautions that it merely 'summarizes the views expressed by the various stakeholders without the intention to validate or deny any issues',²²¹ with the explicit aim of serving as a 'trusted third-party facilitator focused on collaborative problem-solving with stakeholders'.²²²

Self-reflecting on this change in 2010, the CAO indicated that this was a strategic change in direction aimed at ensuring practical effectiveness on the basis of evidence accrued in its first ten years of experience: it first noted 'confusion' among complainants about the CAO's role, next steps, and implementation of recommendations arising from the inclusion in the same report (and in the same modality of operation of the Ombudsman) of 'technical analyses and an opinion on the merits and neutral recommendations about how the parties might work together'.²²³ On that basis, the CAO considered that this prevented it in its Ombudsman capacity from facilitating the reaching of a collaborative agreement between parties, with the effect of increasing local ownership of solutions and the identification of scalable response, which was further supported by the CAO's engagement of local and regional partners as mediators and facilitators.²²⁴ The CAO itself could then arguably focus on creating a neutral space for dialogue that would

---

²¹⁵ Ibid. 4.
²¹⁶ CAO, Follow-up Assessment Report on Complaint regarding the Marlin Mining Project, Guatemala (May 2006).
²¹⁷ CAO, Assessment Report on the complaint concerning COMSUR/Don Mario Mine, Bolivia (November 2003) (hereinafter, Bolivia Assessment Report).
²¹⁸ CAO, revised Operational Guidelines (2006).
²¹⁹ See, for instance, CAO, Assessment Report of the complaint regarding the Electron Investment S.A. Pando-Monte Lirio Hydroelectric Project, Ciriqui Province, Panama, July 2010, 20–21.
²²⁰ CAO, Assessment Report to Stakeholders regarding concerns of local stakeholders about the PRONACA Farms in Santo Domingo, Ecuador, June 2011.
²²¹ CAO, Pando assessment report (n. 218) 18.
²²² CAO (n. 159) 35.
²²³ Ibid. 23 and 34.
²²⁴ Ibid. 27.

prevent a cycle of conflict, mentoring parties to ensure that the dialogue would reflect sufficiently and accurately their interests, while understanding the constraints of the dialogue process and committing to ongoing monitoring as long as parties committed to a monitoring plan with milestones.[225] On the one hand, this more recent approach has effectively stopped the CAO's factual assessments of private companies' conduct. On the other hand, it has allowed consideration of the connections between conflicts around projects and broader historical issues within a certain country, and the employment of trust-building processes through scientific assessments that respond to questions co-identified by concerned communities and addressed by independent experts co-selected by communities through a competitive process. The CAO claims that this aims at changing the 'dynamics of long-term conflicts'.[226]

Commentators argued that the CAO's mediation function provides 'an opportunity for greater consideration of human rights obligations and implementation of practical human rights outcomes'.[227] The CAO, in effect, 'is meant to provide a voice to project-affected people'.[228] This is particularly relevant as the IFC has been criticized for relying heavily on information about compliance from clients, leaving them considerable discretion, and for negotiating with them rather than applying sanctions, to bring them back into compliance. As a result, the IFC's withdrawal is rarely, if ever used, with concerns remaining about the extent of the Performance Standards' effectiveness in influencing business behaviour, given the limited track record of enforcement.[229]

The Ombudsman practice of the CAO reveals a proactive approach in interpreting the IFC's environmental standards and suggesting ways of enhancing their implementation by private companies. The fact that its decisions are publicly available and easily accessible at all stages of consideration of complaints is another positive feature of the mechanism. The move away from determining if private companies are at fault in respecting the IFC Performance Standards towards a collaborative approach to co-identifying root causes and possible ways forward has both disadvantages and advantages from the perspective of international standard-setting on corporate environmental accountability and responsibility. On the one hand, the change in practice of the Ombudsman has meant that the CAO no longer assesses private companies' compliance with the IFC Performance Standards, allowing more limited discussion of the practical application of relevant international standards. This is lamentable as the IFC Performance Standards remain the most explicit and elaborated substantive standards on corporate environmental

---

[225] Ibid. 27 and 29.
[226] Ibid. 29 and 31.
[227] Saper (n. 138) 1300.
[228] Ibid. 1288.
[229] Simons and Macklin (n. 49) 130, 132, and 137.

accountability and responsibility on the basis of the CBD,[230] and could provide important lessons learnt for other international oversight mechanisms discussed in this chapter. On the other hand, the more recent practice can allow experienting with collaborative approaches to use the international standards to better clarify the responsibility of the private sector and that of the government and of international organizations. This can allow the co-identification with communities of the root causes of complex issues and a move beyond the timeframe and scope of a particular development project to identify ways to enhance environmental protection and the respect of human rights. In that sense, the CAO can provide important lessons learnt for the contextual application of international standards.

3.2.1 Variation in outcomes
Some of the outcomes from the CAO procedure can be compared with those under the OECD implementation procedure, notably support towards a mediated agreement. In addition, the CAO has also led to the creation of local platforms for dialogue or has assessed whether private companies have undertaken appropriate prior impact (self-)assessments.[231] In addition, similarly to the OECD Guidelines NCPs, the Ombudsman, even in the absence of formal non-compliance with IFC standards, recommended that companies still build a climate of trust and understanding with local communities with regard to the environmental impacts of the project. Other outcomes range from information sharing to joint fact-finding, participatory monitoring, and establishment of grievance mechanisms.[232] This sub-section will focus on how the Ombudsman has contributed to clarify the applicability of international standards related to environmental impact assessments, disclosure of information, consultation, and benefit-sharing[233]—increasingly as part of its support for a mediated agreement between communities and companies (and occasionally the government).

With regard to implementation of international standards on EIAs, the Ombudsman pointed to insufficient methodological rigour in impact assessments that led to the provision of insufficient information for decision-making. This in turn indicated that the relevant information was not made available to the communities concerned and that environmental commitments were not developed to adequately address the 'perceived social and cultural concerns of people affected' by a river diversion.[234] In a complaint regarding a pulp mill in Uruguay,[235] the

---

[230] In addition to 2012 IFC Performance Standard 6 (discussed under Section 1 in this chapter), also 2012 IFC, Performance Standard 8: Cultural Heritage, para. 1, is 'based in part on standards set by the Convention on Biological Diversity'.
[231] See Ch. 4, Section 2.1.1.
[232] CAO (n. 158) 25.
[233] Discussed in Ch. 4, Sections 2.1.1, 2.4, 2.5, and 3.1.3.
[234] CAO, Assessment Report of the complaint regarding Allain Duhangan Hydropower Project, India (March 2005).
[235] CAO, Preliminary Assessment Report on the complaint regarding the IFC's Proposed Investment in Celulosas and Orion Projects, Uruguay (November 2005). The preliminary assessment was followed

Ombudsman underlined the lack of consideration of cumulative environmental impacts and the possible transboundary environmental effects of the project, as well as the limited public consultation process that did not involve concerned communities in Argentina. The Ombudsman regretted that there was 'not sufficient acknowledgement of the concerns and fears of communities that are local to the project'.[236] It further recommended that the impact assessment demonstrate the application of best available technology.[237] The following year, the IFC Board of Directors approved a US$170 million investment by the IFC on the basis of the positive findings of a cumulative impact study, subsequently reviewed by independent experts.[238] Nonetheless, public opposition to the project continued, both on the part of Argentinean communities and government and of environmental NGOs.[239] When the case reached the International Court of Justice (ICJ), the ICJ considered that the assessments of alternative sites produced under the aegis of the IFC paid regard to freshwater habitats, and that the consultations with affected communities in Argentina and Uruguay had been adequate.[240]

The complaint regarding a hydropower project in India provided an opportunity for the Ombudsman to formulate recommendations directly to the private company[241] that can be related to Anaya's recommendation that EIAs are carried out by independent experts.[242] The CAO recommended that the company provide for an independent study of environmental concerns, make it public, ensure the public monitoring of resulting commitments, and generally engage local communities more constructively, through the intermediation of independent facilitators or observers. The CAO further called for developing a schedule for implementation of commitments resulting from the EIA on the basis of each of the IFC performance standards.[243] In addition, the CAO provided for both the IFC and the private company to engage in quality monitoring. The IFC was requested to appoint

---

in February 2006 by an audit of the IFC's due diligence in applying its environmental standards (CAO, Audit of IFC's and MIGA's Due Diligence for two Pulp Mills in Uruguay (22 February 2006)).

[236] Ibid. 10.
[237] Ibid. 11.
[238] IFC press release, 'IFC and MIGA Board Approves Orion Pulp Mill in Uruguay: 2,500 Jobs to Be Created, No Environmental Harm' (21 November 2006) <http://www.ifc.org/ifcext/media.nsf/content/SelectedPressRelease?OpenDocument&UNID=F76F15A5FE7735918525722D005 8F472>.
[239] Press release, 'Against the Will of 300,000 local Stakeholders World Bank Board Approves Loans to Botnia' (21 November 2006) <http://www.cedha.org.ar/en/more_information/ world-bank-approves-loans-botnia.php>. In the press release, it is further argued that the IFC decision ignored the CAO recommendations, which verified that the IFC had failed to comply with its environmental and social safeguards in the project.
[240] The ICJ concluded against the existence of an imminent threat of irreparable damage to the aquatic environment of the River Uruguay or to the economic and social interests of the riparian inhabitants on the Argentine side of the river: ICJ, *Pulp Mills on the River Uruguay (Argentina v. Uruguay)* Order (13 July 2006) paras 210 and 219.
[241] CAO, Allain Duhangan Conclusion Report, India (March 2008) 7.
[242] Ch. 5, Section 1.1.
[243] CAO (n. 241) 8–9.

an independent engineer to oversee the project and report on social and environmental matters, while the company was requested to report to the IFC on a quarterly and annual basis on social, environmental, and health issues.[244] Later on, the private company sponsoring the project prepared a register of its obligations under the EIA, which was publicly available, and agreed to meet publicly with the community on a monthly basis to allow participatory verification and discussion on progress with respect to commitments made at the outset of the project planning process.[245] This provides an interesting example of international support to ensure that a procedural standard is implemented in meaningful ways that contribute to other dimensions of corporate environmental accountability.

Similar to the OECD implementation procedure, the CAO has also concluded that no breach of the Performance Standards was found but still called for enhanced business practices in consulting with affected communities.[246] The CAO has self-assessed this kind of intervention as a pragmatic balancing between documenting instances of private companies' non-compliance and identifying a long-lasting and satisfactory solution for the parties concerned.[247] In the specific case of a gold and silver mine in Guatemala, the CAO concluded that no significant environmental risk from waterways contamination would result from the project and that the EIA had adequately considered the risks and led to substantial improvements in the project design. Nonetheless, given continuing public concerns, the Ombudsman suggested stepping up an already ongoing consultation process of the private company with affected communities through participatory environmental monitoring and an analysis of Mayan customary perspectives and traditional decision-making in matters related to mining operations.[248]

Where possible, the Ombudsman prioritizes facilitating an agreement between the private sector and the complainants, which can also be considered comparable to the OECD NCPs' approach. These kind of cases may in effect provide an example in which international oversight bodies support directly the implementation of the corporate environmental responsibility standard of benefit-sharing as an ongoing process of relationship-building. Whether or not the resulting benefit-sharing approach is culturally appropriate and has been co-developed by communities, however, remains to be assessed through empirical research.[249] This was, for instance, the case with a pipeline project in Georgia,[250] which has led to the highest

---

[244] Ibid. 14.
[245] Ibid.
[246] See Ch. 4, Section 2.5.
[247] CAO (n. 159) 27.
[248] CAO, Assessment Report of a complaint in relation to the Marlin Mining Project in Guatemala (September 2005).
[249] See Ch. 5, Section 1.3.
[250] CAO, Assessment Report in relation to a complaint regarding the Baku-Tbilisi-Ceyhan (BTC) Pipeline Project, Georgia (February 2006). As of February 2008, the CAO Ombudsman has two open complaints regarding the BTC pipeline.

case workload on a single project for the CAO (thirty-two complaints accounting for nearly half of all cases assessed by CAO within its first ten years of operation).[251] As the CAO's mandate does not allow it to enter into complaints about amounts of compensation, it has been argued that it should play a role in facilitating agreements on compensation among local authorities,[252] private companies, and communities. After a series of findings about the company's fault, the CAO tried to play a more neutral role which led, in its own assessment, to an increased willingness from the company and the IFC to constructively engage in a mediation process, as well as strengthening grievance mechanisms.[253]

In the early stages of investigations into local communities' complaints regarding a company's exploitation of palm oil plantations in Indonesia, which were allegedly causing land and primary forest clearing and biodiversity destruction, the CAO facilitated consultations. It helped ensuring that the company accepted as preconditions for dialogue the freezing of its activities within the plantations, including planting, harvesting, clearing, and expansion.[254] The resulting settlement agreement provided that the company could increase the proportion of land to be allocated as smallholdings and return those lands to communities that insisted they did not wish the land to be cleared; that lands used for oil palm would be leased as community lands and revert to those communities at the end of the lease; and that the company would adopt standards in line with the multi-stakeholder Roundtable on Sustainable Palm Oil.[255] The CAO also developed a facilitation process that respected customary norms and was eventually able to facilitate the payment of compensation, as well as the adoption by the company of improved operational standards.[256] The implementation of this company–community agreement[257] was monitored in 2011 and 2013, giving the community and the company an opportunity to change who received the compensation and to assess progress in reforestation.[258]

In a case in the Philippines on the privatization of a large-scale hydroelectric facility, the CAO was able to broker formal agreements between the company, the community, and local government for benefit-sharing and land-use rights, taking into account the community's desire to address long-standing land claims and the opportunities to use the complaint as a basis for developing a shared vision for development.[259] The agreement provided for a usufruct that handed over to the local

---

[251] CAO (n. 159) 22.
[252] Ibid. 18.
[253] Ibid. 23.
[254] CAO, Preliminary Stakeholder Assessment regarding Community and Civil Society Concerns in relation to Activities of the Wilmar Group of Companies, Indonesia (November 2007).
[255] CAO (n. 159) 41.
[256] Wilmar care (CAO, n. 159), discussed by Saper (n. 138) 1311.
[257] See Ch. 4, Section 3.1.33.
[258] CAO Ombudsman's work in Sambas, Indonesia—Wilmar Group, 25 June 2014.
[259] CAO (n. 159) 53.

government the management of the residual areas of the watershed area for the common use by communities, while the company set up a 'substantial corporate social responsibility funds, and alignment of corporate programs with the indigenous people's livelihood objectives'.[260]

Another case concerned negative environmental and human rights impacts from resettlement on nomadic herders in the Gobi Desert in Mongolia, and the use of land and water, by gold and copper mining by Rio Tinto. The CAO supported the establishment of a tripartite council of herder and local government representatives focused on livelihood alternatives in the context of mining, but also solar-water pumps to address water security, and support for the transmission of traditional knowledge as a way to build a lasting partnership.[261] This was based on a series of: interim agreements on access to information, tours/inspections of the mine site for herders, joint fact-finding, and access to grazing land inside the project site; as well as independent socio-economic study of herder households over the previous decade, and an independent assessment of project impacts on the main tributary of the Undai River. The studies were conducted by independent experts jointly selected by the parties. The implementation plan that summarizes the substantive content of the agreement reached clearly distinguishes the role of the government, of the company, and of joint actions with communities in relation to re-establishing grazing systems and herder access to water and land. Accordingly, the company is charged with rehabilitating disturbed and abandoned sites for pasture, shortening time of dust generation from disturbed sites, minimizing risks of accidents in quarries, and supporting livestock grazing in areas within the fenced production sites. On water, the company is expected to provide collective compensation for constructing new wells that would align with the customary livelihood practices of the community and their concerns for impacts on wildlife, fund studies on water reserves under pastures, and hand over boreholes for local herders' pastoral water supply needs. Furthermore, it is expected to replace outsourced monitoring with local monitoring programmes that are sensitive to herding practices and based on joint methodologies and genuine engagement, revise the grievance mechanism in light of feedback from communities, and widely publicize the changes arising from this process. The implementation plan also includes a sustainable livelihood programme, including life skills training, access to markets and creation of supply chains, fodder plantations, creating artificial water collection points, and supporting the connection of herders' deep wells with renewables, etc.[262] The final joint statements, based on monitoring activities over 2017–18 expressed satisfaction with the trust and cooperation between parties.[263]

---

[260] CAO, Ambuklao-Binga Complaint, Conclusion report, 2009.
[261] CAO 2019 Annual Report (n. 197) 12.
[262] CAO, Complaint Resolution Agreement, May 2017.
[263] TPC Joint Statement, 28–29November 2018; and CAO Communique—Mongolia OT Closure—March 2019.

This is an interesting case in which a benefit-sharing agreement supported by an international oversight body provides an opportunity to enhance the implementation of procedural and substantive standards of corporate environmental accountability and responsibility.

In another case in Uganda in the context of agri-business, a UK-based forestry company was involved in alleged forced evictions and displacement in the area of timber plantations. The CAO's involvement focused on a resettlement and livelihood programme for communities with a forest company, by building the capacity of communities and company representatives to enter into a productive dialogue. On the one hand, a community cooperative was established to purchase land to resettle families and conduct small-scale farming.[264] The private company, on the other hand, undertook to provide significant financial support to the cooperative, expanding its social responsibility investment programme to meet some of the specific needs of the community, and collaborated with the cooperative to build lasting mutually beneficial relations with the community. This could be considered a form of benefit-sharing.[265] The complainants agreed to respect the company's legal rights to operate within the area, and both the company and the complainants agreed to act lawfully and to engage with each other through a joint development forum, which was created to facilitate decision-making. The CAO monitored the parties' implementation of the terms of the agreement over four years (2014–18), and appointed a community development coordinator to work with the cooperative on resettlement planning and income-generation projects. While not mediated by the CAO, this process also led to the conclusion of a memorandum of understanding whereby the government provided financial contributions towards the acquisition of land by the cooperative for resettling their members and rebuilding livelihoods.[266]

In conclusion, it is worth underlining the efforts of the CAO in ensuring a stable and fair relationship between IFC clients and local communities, even when it is threatened by misunderstandings rather than by actual substandard practices. The conciliatory approach and creation of roundtables to facilitate dialogue locally has allowed the examination of substantive environmental, social, and health issues through commissioned studies that show the value added by the CAO and also for the start of cooperation between the company and the community.[267] The CAO's approach to disclosure of information has also been considered a significant factor in helping communities understand the extent of environmental and social risks of projects, where previously, their perception had been affected by the insufficient information shared by the company.[268] In doing so, the CAO has also been

---

[264] CAO 2019 annual report (n. 197) 14.
[265] See Ch. 4, Section 3.1.3.
[266] CAO, Conclusion Report, Agri-Vie Fund-01/Kiboga, October 2018.
[267] McBeth (n. 157) 229 with reference to CAO Exit Report, regarding two complaints filed with the CAO in relation to Minera Yanacocha Cajamarca, Peru (2006).
[268] Saper (n. 138) 1309 and 1312.

able to support the start of co-developed solutions with communities, based on the information shared, and supports companies' responsiveness to community needs.[269] In not all cases, however, does CAO meet the expectations of the complainants. Following the release of the CAO assessment,[270] it has been argued that the Ombudsman underestimated the environmental harm caused by one project in terms of toxic emissions.[271] On the one hand, the CAO is seen to provide 'an opportunity for greater consideration of human rights obligations and the implementation of practical human rights outcomes as a result of its emphasis on mediation'[272] and offers an easier avenue than other complaints procedures. On the other hand, barriers remain due to local communities still being insufficiently aware of IFC and CAO and work,[273] the CAO's procedures, and the need to draft a complaint despite the limited formal requirements.[274] In addition, the CAO finds itself in a complex position in striking a balance between the identification of instances of non-compliance by companies and the opportunity to keep companies engaged in the progressive improvement of their practices.

In light of the growing number of cases dealt by the Ombudsman, the CAO could engage in a comparative analysis of its jurisprudence and its approach to the admissibility of complaints, interpretation of performance standards, and drafting recommendations.[275] More independent empirical study is needed, in addition, to understand the IFC's effectiveness: the CAO review in 2010 underscored that only 53 per cent of clients disclosed action plans to communities and none updated them on their implementation; only 53 per cent established grievance mechanisms; and 33 per cent of annual monitoring reports were found to be unsatisfactory due to insufficient information to assess the company's performance.[276] The actual impact on the ground of the CAO's cases, particularly in as far as facilitated benefit-sharing agreements is concerned, remains a matter for further empirical research.

3.2.2 Mediation and fair and equitable benefit-sharing

In a particular instance, the CAO did engage in a detailed process of documentation of lessons learnt and of impacts not only at the community level, but also at national level and on the practices of the CAO itself at the international level. The

---

[269] Ibid. 1310.
[270] CAO Assessment Report on a complaint regarding the Lukoil Overseas Project, Kazakhstan (April 2005), which focused mainly on health issues raised by the project.
[271] Letter from CrudeAccountability to CAO (12 August 2005).
[272] McBeth (n. 157) 221 and 231.
[273] 2019 CAO Annual Report (n. 197) 3.
[274] Bradlow and Naudé Fourie (n. 135) 28.
[275] This suggestion was put forward in relation to the World Bank's Inspection Panel by Boisson de Chazournes (n. 144) 296.
[276] CAO, Review of IFC's Policy and Performance Standards on Social and Environmental Sustainability and Policy of Disclosure of Information' 2010, 13–14; see comments by Simons and Macklin (n. 49) 137–38.

CAO documentation is particularly illuminating to contextualize the international standards of fair and equitable benefit-sharing.[277]

Following a series of complaints in 2000 concerning a mercury spill provoked by the largest gold mining company in Peru, the CAO supported the establishment of a permanent roundtable for facilitating multi-stakeholder dialogue and resolving issues of concern between local communities and the mining company regarding the aftermath of the spill and its long-term environmental impacts (*Mesa de Diálogo y Consenso*). The roundtable was meant to act in a proactive way, rather than being retrospective.[278] The *Mesa* eventually established itself as a formal legal entity, and succeeded in functioning both as a forum for civil society dialogue and a mechanism for providing objective, technical information on communities' concerns surrounding the company's environmental conduct (most notably, by producing a water quality and quantity assessment). It did not, however, represent a formal system of conflict resolution, and its legitimacy was not recognized by local NGOs or local authorities, possibly due to the lack of disclosure of members' direct and indirect relationships to the company's activities.[279] Having provided financial and technical support to the *Mesa* since 2001, the CAO concluded its phased withdrawal from it in March 2006, recommending the continuation of the *Mesa*'s water monitoring programme, as well as the setting up of transparent dispute resolution mechanisms.[280]

Nonetheless, the CAO continued to assess developments under the *Mesa*, culminating in the publication of three monographs assessing the impacts at different levels of four and a half years of work. In particular, from a standard-setting perspective, the CAO's assessment has unveiled the linkages between the implementation of the international standard of fair and equitable benefit-sharing[281] and perceptions of risks, mediation training, as well as the independence and transparency, and monitoring of benefit-sharing arrangements.

First of all, the CAO linked the positive impacts of the *Mesa* with a combined vision of: commitment to scientific rigour and simultaneous recognition of the value and importance of local knowledge, its own growing expertise on environmental issues, and its understanding and practice of conflict resolution.[282] It then focused on the role of the platform in dealing with different perceptions of environmental

---

[277] Ch. 5, Section 1.3.
[278] CAO, Exit Report regarding two complaints filed with the CAO in relation to Minera Yanacocha Cajamarca, Peru (February 2006).
[279] CAO, Report of the Independent Evaluation of the Mesa de Dialogo y Consenso CAO-Cajamarca, Peru (May 2005).
[280] CAO, Exit Report regarding two complaints filed with the CAO in relation to Minera Yanacocha Cajamarca, Peru (February 2006).
[281] See Ch. 4, Section 3.1.3.
[282] CAO, The Power of Dialogue—Building Consensus: History and Lessons from the Mesa de Diálogo y Consenso CAO-Cajamarca, Peru (Executive Summary), (CAO, 2007), http://www.cao-ombudsman.org/publications/documents/CAO_Monograph_ExecutiveSummary_PowerofDialogueEnglish.pdf.

risks from the project, arriving at the conclusion that the *Mesa* was successful at dealing with the environmental hazard but less able to compel the mining company to address community perceptions and emotions about the risks. It thus noted the need for distinctive processes and solutions to engage with a discrepancy between people's perceived risk (such as negative impacts to water quality and quantity; loss of land, livelihoods, and traditional way of life; and eroding social cohesion) and their perceived benefits (such as economic and educational benefits; improved standard of living; and improved infrastructure). To that end, the CAO recommended that dialogue platforms be established on the basis of a 'situation assessment' that focuses also on the history of the communities and their territories, a cultural context assessment to understand the distinctive ways that stakeholders approach conflict resolution (influence of power, rights, and interests, availability of social capital to obtain compliance with agreements), and corporate culture (its leadership, consistent messaging, and track record of compliance with community agreements).[283]

The CAO also assessed the role of mediation training to build capacity for dialogue, equipping communities with skills to give voice to the marginalized and bring about meaningful change. These skills were considered relevant for building trust and reciprocity within an iterative dialogue process that eventually evolved from a mechanism to prevent and resolve conflicts to an accountability mechanism that could assess the mine's operations and fulfilment of specific benefit-sharing commitments.[284]

Furthermore, the CAO investigated through the experience of the *Mesa* the conditions to ensure independence and transparency in benefit-sharing arrangements. It noted the importance of a careful structure of governance arrangements that can be 'viewed by the majority of stakeholders as independent, even when the company is a major contributor' and are based on full disclosure and transparency. This is coupled with co-developed selection criteria for technical experts to support fact-finding or joint problem-solving; as well as regular communication on how independence is maintained.[285] This extends to co-developing monitoring and compliance approaches with benefit-sharing agreements with a clear outline of lines of authority, incentives for all parties, and consequences of not complying. Pragmatically, the *Mesa* led to the development of a public tracking of benefit-sharing agreements and of the implementation of the recommendations arising from a water study and water monitoring program, as well as specific claims of noncompliance brought by *Mesa* members. The tracking system was eventually used by the local branch of the national government's ombudsman office and supported external monitoring. The local ombudsman made public results and

---

[283] Ibid. 5.
[284] Ibid. 7.
[285] Ibid. 8.

270 INTERNATIONAL OVERSIGHT

conclusions from its analysis of the tracking results and then met with the mining company to evaluate progress and ensure follow-through with implementation.[286] This could be considered a pragmatic approach to considering benefit-sharing as an ongoing partnership-building process,[287] that can also facilitate external oversight of the actual flows of benefits.

The *Mesa* also led in and of itself to a new benefit-sharing approach, with a view to engaging the company towards a more comprehensive development programme. As a result, the companies agreed in 2007 to allocate US45 million over the next four years for development projects in the region under the aegis of a technical commission consisting of the regional government and the municipality and under the administration of the United Nations Development Program (UNDP).[288] The funding was used for social development projects (nutrition, education, and health), roads, water conservation programmes, tourism, strengthening institutions, and capacity building, as well as for feasibility studies (about expanding the regional hospital, constructing a dam) and developing a comprehensive urban development plan. The CAO also underlined the 'pioneering independent participatory water study and the community water monitoring programmes' developed under the *Mesa* as the catalysts for a number of projects being implemented today.[289]

The *Mesa* also led to industry-wide benefit-sharing arrangements at the national level. In 2006, an agreement was reached between the government of Peru and the country's mining sector to make a voluntary payment of US$757.5 million over the next five years into an equity fund to fight poverty, malnutrition, and social exclusion in poor mining regions. The fund prioritized as beneficiaries, communities near mines, the poorest areas of mining regions, and the victims of political violence in those areas. The fund was to be co-managed by companies, beneficiary communities, and local and regional governments that would together allocate and administer the payments.[290] This shows the potential usefulness of documenting (and the need to independently research) the impacts of international oversight of corporate environmental accountability and responsibility standards across different levels.

Finally, through the assessment of the *Mesa* process, the CAO also identified lessons for its own Ombudsman role. It underscored the need for benchmarks to measure progress, the importance of developing clear exit strategies for interventions, and the challenges associated with independence and impartiality.[291] This particular instance thus shows the CAO's role in proactively managing conflicts

---

[286] Ibid. 10.
[287] See Ch. 5, Section 1.2.3.
[288] CAO (n. 281) 11.
[289] Ibid. 12.
[290] Ibid.
[291] Ibid. 14.

between companies and affected communities. First, it provided communities with a structured opportunity to be heard and supported in engaging in complex dialogue processes. Second, through that dialogue, it clarified the conditions for the applicability of international standards of corporate environmental accountability and responsibility. Third, this underscored the capacity needs of private companies to take into account broader contextual and historical factors around project-specific benefit-sharing options.

4 Human rights monitoring bodies and special procedures

When the domestic legal system of the host State is ineffective, the consideration of complaints by international human rights bodies has provided an alternative means for individuals and groups to access justice at the supranational level in egregious cases of environmental degradation.[292] These international initiatives may help to remedy human rights violations that could not be asserted at the national level, and allow individuals to act as 'guardians of the treaty'.[293] These initiatives include only to a limited extent international human rights tribunals.[294]

In an effort to move beyond the current limitations of international human rights tribunals, the African Commission has established the Working Group on Extractive Industries' Impact in Africa to formulate proposals on appropriate measures to prevent right violations.[295] The Working Group has a mandate to: undertake research on the violations of human and peoples' rights by non-State actors in Africa; gather information from all relevant sources, including governments, communities, and organizations, on violations of human rights by non-State actors in Africa; inform the African Commission on the possible liability of non-State actors for human rights violations under its protective mandate; and propose appropriate measures and activities for the prevention and reparation of violations of human rights by extractive industries in Africa. The Working Group has been focusing on the need for improved protection of human rights and the environment, including by developing effective continental mechanisms for monitoring the human rights

---

[292] A. Fabra, 'Indigenous People, Environmental Degradation and Human Rights: A Case Study' in A. Boyle and M. Anderson (eds), *Human Rights Approaches to Environmental Protection* (Oxford: Clarendon Press, 1996) 245, 262; M. Mullen de Bolívar, 'A Comparison of Protecting the Environmental Interests of Latin-American Indigenous Communities from Transnational Corporations under International Human Rights and Environmental Law' (1998) 8 *Journal of Transnational Law and Policy* 105, 148.

[293] D. Hanschel, 'Environment and Human Rights: Cooperative Means of Regime Implementation' (Mannheimer Zentrum für Europäische Sozialforschung Working Paper no. 29, 2000) 29.

[294] See Ch. 2, Section 2.5.

[295] Resolution on the Establishment of a Working Group on Extractive Industries, Environment and Human Rights Violations in Africa—148(XLVI)09; repeatedly renewed: 386 Resolution on the Renewal of the Mandate and Reconstitution of the Working Group on Extractive Industries, Environment and Human Rights Violations in Africa—ACHPR/Res.386(LXI)2017.

impact of extractive industries' activities and the development of jurisprudence on holding non-State actors accountable for human rights violations in Africa.[296] On the occasion of country visits, the Working Group made recommendations directly to business enterprises to comply with the principle of free prior informed consent[297] and to apply a human rights-based approach to development, by widely consulting indigenous peoples before developing new projects and recognizing their ownership rights over lands and territories.[298]

Extending classic international human rights monitoring and enforcement mechanisms to non-State entities, as suggested by the UN Norms on Business and Human Rights,[299] and even earlier on in the context of the draft UN Code of Conduct,[300] has a few advantages compared with other oversight mechanisms, such as the OECD National Contact Points. Some of these advantages include: being impartial and independent, instead of being established within a national government; providing transparency into both corporate and State conduct, thereby incrementally clarifying the dividing line in a context-specific and authoritative fashion, on the basis of experience in applying international standards; and being open to all States rather than just those countries adhering to the OECD Guidelines.[301] In addition, the universality of the forum could help to bring about more pressure and wider publicity.[302] But as discussed earlier,[303] the UN Working Group on Business and Human Rights played down its role to consider individual cases,[304] and has been criticized by NGOs and scholars for lacking a mandate to assess the implementation of the UN Framework as a whole, and to provide a complaint mechanism.[305] The UN Working Group, nonetheless, conducts country visits, which could allow for a soft approach to monitoring the implementation of the UN Guiding Principles on Business and Human Rights. But so far it has not taken the opportunity to play an 'autonomous', 'credible',

---

[296] https://www.achpr.org/specialmechanisms/detailmech?id=13.
[297] Working Group on Extractive Industries, Environment and Human Rights Violations in Africa, Final Communiqué on the National Dialogue on the Rights of Indigenous Peoples and Extractive Industries, 27–28 November 2018, Kampala, Uganda. See discussion in Ch. 5, Section 1.2.
[298] Working Group on Extractive Industries, Environment and Human Rights Violations in Africa, Final Communiqué on the National Dialogue on the Rights of Indigenous Peoples and Extractive Industries, from 7–8 October 2019, Nairobi, Kenya.
[299] See Ch. 3, Section 4.1. See also D. Kinley and R. Chambers, 'The UN Human Rights Norms for Corporations: The Private Implications of Public International Law' (2006) 6 *Human Rights Law Review* 447, 452; and D. Vagts, 'The UN Norms for Transnational Corporations' (2003) 16 *Leiden Journal of International Law* 795.
[300] See Ch. 3, Section 2. See also W. Sprote, 'Negotiations on a United Nations Code of Conduct on Transnational Corporations' (1990) 33 *German Yearbook of International Law* 331, 344.
[301] O. de Schutter, Towards Corporate Accountability for Human and Environmental Rights Abuses, discussion paper for the European Coalition for Corporate Justice (April 2007) 5–6 and 11.
[302] Ibid. 6.
[303] Ch. 3, Section 4.2.2.
[304] C. Rodríguez-Garavito, 'Business and Human Rights: Beyond the End of the Beginning' in Rodríguez-Garavito (n. 46) 11, 20–21.
[305] Simons and Macklin (n. 49) 39.

and 'consistent' interpretative role providing bottom-up evolutive guidance that could 'be taken up by those bodies with substantially more authority to bind' companies.[306] In addition, the UN Working Group has not provided sufficient information on relevant corporations, action taken and rate of response, so it remains unclear if individual complaints 'have provided information to Working Group that is relevant to its overall mandate and has informed the thematic choices of his post-2013 reports'.[307]

The country visits of UN Special Rapporteurs have so far provided a richer area of practice, including by complementing the work of the UN Working Group on Business and Human Rights.

4.1 Country visits by UN Special Rapporteurs

UN Special Rapporteurs have increasingly engaged in assessing whether private companies are respecting international standards of corporate environmental accountability and responsibility during their country visits. They have done so to different extents, so no coherent practice across mandate holders or within the same mandate has emerged yet. Nonetheless they have contributed to clarifying how international standards apply in a specific context, provided evidence of substandard corporate practice, and reflected on the implications for States. They have also contributed to normative coherence by relying on the standard-setting and oversight activities of other international human rights processes.

The UN Special Rapporteur on Human Rights and the Environment, for instance, has addressed questions related to corporate accountability and responsibility in a couple of field missions. As part of a visit to Mongolia, the Rapporteur recalled concerns expressed by the Committee on the Rights of the Child[308] and the Working Group on Business and Human Rights[309] about the adverse impact of mining projects on herders' human rights, including in relation to free prior informed consent and inadequate compensation for the adverse effects of the mine.[310] The Special Rapporteur's recommendations, however, were solely addressed to the government (increasing the transparency of agreements between

---

[306] L Catá Backer, 'From Guiding Principles to Interpretative Organizations: Developing a Framework for Applying the UNGPs to Disputes that Institutionalizes the Advocacy Role of Civil Society' in Rodríguez-Garavito (n. 46) 97, 104–05.
[307] Rodríguez-Garavito (n. 303) 43.
[308] Committee on the Rights of the Child, Concluding observations on the fifth periodic report of Mongolia (2017) UN Doc. CRC/C/MNG/CO/5.
[309] Report of the Working Group on the issue of human rights and transnational corporations and other business enterprises: Country visit to Mongolia (2013) UN Doc. A/HRC/23/32/Add.1.
[310] Report of the Special Rapporteur on the issue of human rights obligations relating to the enjoyment of a safe, clean, healthy and sustainable environment on his mission to Mongolia, (2018) UN Doc. A/HRC/37/58/Add.2, para. 60 and fn. 36. See Ch. 4, Section 3.1.2.

mining companies and local authorities, ensuring that the conclusions of environmental assessments are taken into account in the environmental management plans for mines, and providing for full transparency of payments by mining companies into reclamation funds, and of payments of royalties to local development funds).[311] He did not, therefore, drew upon the relevant international standards of corporate environmental accountability and responsibility.[312]

As part of a visit to Madagascar, the UN Special Rapporteur on Human Rights and the Environment commended a specific mining company for its positive environmental mitigation and redress measures. He also noted that local communities, however, indicated that the company's measures had negatively and disproportionately affected the poorest members who were most dependent on the forest and the least able to take advantage of new development opportunities. The Special Rapporteur, therefore, urged the company and the community to discuss these issues. The Special Rapporteur then addressed a general recommendation to businesses working in Madagascar, to 'ensure that in all their actions affecting local communities, from conducting mining operations to managing protected areas', they respect community members' human rights.[313]

The Special Rapporteur on Human Rights and the Environment has therefore engaged in fact-finding with regard to alleged corporate misconduct. It has done so by addressing recommendations to specific companies and to the business sector as a whole, while documenting both positive and negative corporate conduct. The country visits of the UN Special Rapporteurs on Indigenous Peoples' Rights and on Toxics have, in turn, contributed to ensuring coherence between, and filling gaps across, international standards of corporate environmental accountability and responsibility. As will be demonstrated in the following sub-sections, UN Special Rapporteurs are emerging as a significant source of guidance on how to implement these international standards in specific circumstances. On the whole, their practices remain quite inconsistent in terms of scope and depth of oversight, and it remains to be seen if transnational litigation,[314] new international standard-setting initiatives,[315] and the international negotiations on a treaty on business and human rights[316] will fully benefit from their insights in further clarifying the content of international standards, and the conditions for their implementation in particular contexts or sectors, or across levels.

---

[311] A/HRC/37/58/Add.2, para. 85(c–e). The last point relates to the benefit-sharing standard discussed in Ch. 5, Section 1.3.
[312] See Ch. 5.
[313] Report of the Special Rapporteur on the issue of human rights obligations relating to the enjoyment of a safe, clean, healthy and sustainable environment, on his visit to Madagascar, (2017) UN Doc. A/HRC/34/49/Add.1, para. 85.
[314] See Ch. 2, Section 1.2.1.
[315] See Ch. 3.
[316] See Ch. 3, Section 7.

4.1.1 UN Special Rapporteur on Indigenous Peoples' Rights

The UN Special Rapporteur on Indigenous Peoples' Rights has addressed corporate environmental accountability and responsibility issues in the context of environmental impact assessments, free prior informed consent, benefit-sharing, and compensation.[317] The contribution of this mandate-holder has been subject to evolution: from a phase of original standard-setting to one more focused on implementation of the standards. In his first report to the General Assembly, former Special Rapporteur James Anaya prioritized the task of responding on an ongoing basis to specific cases of alleged human rights violations, noting that cases hitherto brought to his attention included infringements of the right to free, prior informed consent, especially in relation to natural resource extraction and displacement or removal of indigenous communities, and denial of rights of indigenous peoples to lands and resources.[318] Accordingly, Anaya established a practice of gathering, requesting, receiving, and exchanging information from all relevant sources, notably from indigenous peoples and governments, and carrying out on-site visits to examine the issues raised with a view to providing observations and recommendations on the underlying human rights issues.

In a case concerning the Marlin mine project in Guatemala and Maya indigenous communities, for instance, Anaya focused mostly on the regulatory and administrative shortcomings of the State, but did not shy away from noting that private companies had an influence on the conflicts with indigenous peoples in that context.[319] Anaya further noted that the consultations undertaken by the company did not lead to an adequate understanding of the project impacts on the communities, did not take into account sufficiently the community concerns, and in all events should have involved the government more fully. He thus called for a new consultation process focusing on mitigation measures, reparation of damage, establishment of a formal benefit-sharing mechanism with full participation of the relevant communities, and the establishment of a complaint and conciliation mechanism.[320] In his final recommendation, Anaya confirmed that the private enterprises' faults in due diligence could not be justified by the limitations of the host State's legal framework alone.[321] He recommended that private enterprises adopt internal policies on indigenous peoples' rights and independent follow-up mechanisms, as well as permanent mechanisms for dialogue and grievance with

---

[317] Report of the Special Rapporteur on the situation of human rights and fundamental freedoms of indigenous people: Communications to and from Governments (2010) UN Doc. A/HRC/15/37/Add.1.
[318] Report of the Special Rapporteur on the situation of human rights and fundamental freedoms of indigenous people (2009) UN Doc. A/64/338, Section D.
[319] Report of the Special Rapporteur on the situation of human rights and fundamental freedoms of indigenous people: Observaciones sobre la situación de los derechos de los pueblos indígenas de Guatemala en relación con los proyectos extractivos, y otro tipo de proyectos, en sus territorios tradicionales, (2011) UN Doc. A/HRC/18/35/Add.3, para. 69.
[320] Ibid. paras 69–70.
[321] Ibid. paras 69–72.

the participation of State authorities.[322] It was in effect this monitoring activity that led Anaya to develop the guidance discussed in Chapter 5 to give greater substance to the UN Framework on Business and Human rights vis-à-vis indigenous peoples' rights. He concluded that 'in its prevailing form, the model for advancing natural resource extraction within the territories of indigenous peoples appears to run counter to the self-determination of indigenous peoples in the political, social and economic spheres'.[323]

Following the adoption of his guidance, Anaya continued to investigate the conditions for fair and equitable benefit-sharing as part of business due diligence. In the context of a visit to Peru, he differentiated social funds as models that encourage the development of social investment projects specifically intended for indigenous communities as compensation for the negative impacts of private companies from benefits in the form of 'jobs or community development projects, that typically pale in economic value in comparison to profits gained by the corporation'. He also underscored that priority should be given at the outset to an alternative model for extractive activities in indigenous territories consisting of indigenous peoples themselves controlling the extractive operations, through their own initiatives and enterprises, through partnerships with responsible non-indigenous companies, with the necessary experience and funding to launch projects and with State support to build indigenous peoples' capacity.[324] He addressed a recommendation directly to companies to ensure that indigenous peoples participate directly in the distribution of fees or royalties, or in the earnings derived from the extractive operations.[325]

The successive Special Rapporteur, Vicky Tauli Corpuz, has addressed business directly and indirectly in most of her country visit reports, in a varied manner, occasionally building upon the reports of the UN Working Group on Business and Human Rights. This served also to draw a clearer line between State obligations and business due diligence, with the latter including the expectation that private companies develop human-rights impact studies in accordance with international standards and the UN Guiding Principles on Business and Human Rights, in cooperation with indigenous peoples.[326]

---

[322] Ibid. paras 89–93.
[323] Report of the Special Rapporteur on the situation of human rights and fundamental freedoms of indigenous people, Extractive industries operating within or near indigenous territories (2011) UN Doc. A/HRC/18/35, paras 82 and 74–75.
[324] Report of the Special Rapporteur on the rights of indigenous peoples, James Anaya, The situation of indigenous peoples' rights in Peru with regard to the extractive industries (2014) UN Doc. A/HRC/27/52/Add.3, paras 59–61.
[325] Ibid. para. 72.
[326] Report of the Special Rapporteur on the rights of indigenous peoples: Visit to Ecuador (2019) UN Doc. A/HRC/42/37/Add.1, para. 118; Report of the Special Rapporteur on the rights of indigenous peoples: Visit to Mexico (2018) UN Doc. A/HRC/39/17/Add.2, para. 108; and Report of the Special Rapporteur on the rights of indigenous peoples on her visit to Guatemala (2018) UN Doc. A/HRC/39/17/Add.3, para. 103(f).

As part of a visit to Ecuador, for instance, Tauli Corpuz observed the absence of environmental rehabilitation, reparations, and adequate compensation for communities that have suffered for decades the impact of oil exploitation on their lands and territories, as in the case of the area affected by the operations of Chevron-Texaco.[327] She also provided insights into benefit-sharing practices, noting that '[i]n the absence of State services, the companies provided basic social services which involved cronyism and paternalistic practices'.[328] This is indeed one of the main pitfalls in attempting to implement the international standard on benefit-sharing.[329] During a visit to Mexico, Tauli Corpuz underscored that companies' social and environmental impact assessments were approved before consultations were carried out with indigenous peoples and did not adequately identify the real impacts that projects will have on the rights of indigenous peoples. She also reiterated the findings of an earlier mission by the Working Group on Business and Human Rights about competent authorities' limited capacity to examine these assessments and ensure proper oversight of their activities.[330] She further noted that contracts between large-scale wind power project proponents and communities were not necessarily concluded with representative authorities and had resulted in negative impacts on indigenous land tenure, the environment, traditional economic activities, and community life.[331] During a visit to Guatemala, the Special Rapporteur noted that despite having adopted a human rights policy under a co-ordinating committee of the Agricultural, Commercial, Industrial, and Financial Associations, none of the participating companies had carried out human rights impact studies before any activity affecting indigenous peoples.[332]

A whole section was devoted to business responsibility in the report of the visit to Brazil, where the Special Rapporteur highlighted the responsibility of businesses to ensure respect for indigenous peoples' rights in their sugar, soy, timber, palm oil, and minerals supply chains, to conduct adequate human rights due diligence. She also called on companies involved in mining, hydroelectric dams, transmission lines, or infrastructure projects to assess whether the State has complied with its duty to seek free prior informed consent and has guaranteed that the projects will not impact on indigenous peoples' rights. She underscored that companies, including banks, need to 'know and show' that they are not complicit in or contributing to human rights violations arising from the failure of the Brazilian authorities to adequately address indigenous peoples' environmental concerns, provide them

---

[327] The case is discussed in Ch. 2, Section 1.2.1.
[328] A/HRC/42/37/Add.1 (n. 326), para. 30.
[329] See Ch. 4, Section 3.1.3.
[330] Report of the Special Rapporteur on the rights of indigenous peoples: Visit to Mexico (2018) UN Doc. A/HRC/39/17/Add.2, para. 38, citing also the Working Group on Business and Human Rights, A/HRC/35/32/Add.2, paras 58–62.
[331] A/HRC/39/17/Add.2, para. 41. See Ch. 4, Section 3.1.3.3.
[332] Report of the Special Rapporteur on the rights of indigenous peoples on her visit to Guatemala (2018) UN Doc. A/HRC/39/17/Add.3, para. 43.

with effective remedies[333] and implement previous recommendations by the UN Working Group on Business and Human Rights.[334] Her recommendations highlighted the independent nature of companies' due diligence obligations to respect indigenous peoples' rights, including their land and consent rights, both for their own operations and for those in their supply chains. She also underscored the need to participate in meaningful remediation processes in consultation with the concerned indigenous peoples, using their leverage to prevent further rights violations and ensure appropriate remediation.[335] Companies' independent responsibility to respect indigenous peoples' rights was also underscored in her visit report to Honduras,[336] in which the Special Rapporteur noted that the Miskito community had relied on a 'biocultural [community] protocol', as recommended under the Convention on Biological Diversity,[337] as a basis for the consultations on a proposed hydrocarbon operations, which the government considered 'a basis for future consultations with indigenous peoples on mining projects'.[338]

During visits in developed countries, however, the UN Special Rapporteur did not address recommendations directly to companies, but rather to the governments. In her visit to the US, after discussing the Standing Rock case, she underscored that indigenous peoples' self-determination extends to control over their energy resources and income generated from natural resources not only to support critical government programmes, but also to reconcile the protection of their lands, waters, and sacred places with the benefit of revenue and jobs.[339] She called upon companies to make committed and meaningful efforts towards mutual understanding with indigenous peoples to meet their responsibilities under the UN Guiding Principles on Business and Human Rights.[340] Her recommendations, however, were solely addressed to the federal government to 'take appropriate measures to encourage consideration of the Guiding Principles' by all actors in any project that impacts indigenous peoples in the US with regard to environmental harm, and to 'take measures to encourage private corporations working on tribal lands to follow the Guiding Principles, including adequate consideration and provision of remediation in advance of project commencement'.[341] During her visit to Sápmi, the UN Special Rapporteur drew attention to the absence of provisions for benefit-sharing with Sami communities when mines are located on traditional Sami lands. She also noted the absence of any frameworks for dispute

---

[333] Report of the Special Rapporteur on the rights of indigenous peoples on her mission to Brazil (2016) A/HRC/33/42/Add.1, paras 77–78.
[334] Ibid. paras 105 and 107.
[335] Ibid. para. 104.
[336] Ibid. para. 99.
[337] Ch. 5, Section 1.2.2.
[338] Brazil report (n. 332) para. 54.
[339] Report of the Special Rapporteur on the rights of indigenous peoples on her mission to the United States of America (2017) UN Doc. A/HRC/36/46/Add.1, para. 76.
[340] Ibid. para. 33.
[341] Ibid. para. 88(f).

resolution between mining companies and affected Sami communities, as well as the lack of cumulative impacts across different applications for exploration and exploitation concessions,[342] although the last point had already been identified by the OECD National Contact Point.[343] She underscored that notwithstanding governments' endorsement of the UN Guiding Principles on Business and Human Rights and adoption of a national action plan for business and human rights,[344] deficient national regulatory frameworks created barriers for businesses to carry out their operations in a manner consistent with international expectations regarding the rights of indigenous peoples.[345]

Overall, the Special Rapporteur on Indigenous Peoples' Rights has developed a practical understanding of the dividing line between business due diligence and State obligations, and with that, of the opportunities and risks in complying with business respect for the human rights of indigenous peoples.

4.1.2 UN Special Rapporteur on Toxics

The UN Special Rapporteur on Toxics Başkut Tuncak has increasingly addressed private companies' responsibility to respect human rights in his country visit reports. He has done so in much more detail than any other Special Rapporteur, occasionally addressing recommendations to named companies, as well as to sectoral business organizations. On some occasions he has devoted a whole section of his report to businesses and human rights, but this is not always an indication that his recommendations would be directly addressed to business.[346] Among international standards of corporate environmental accountability and responsibility, he has focused on access to information, impact assessments particularly with regard to vulnerable groups, benefit-sharing to some extent, and remedies.

In his visit report to Denmark, he underscored the extraterritorial environmental effects of private companies' shipbreaking activities leading to the release of toxic substances in other countries where independent judicial systems are lacking.[347] He engaged in direct dialogue with specific companies, who pointed

---

[342] Report of the Special Rapporteur on the rights of indigenous peoples on the human rights situation of the Sami people in the Sápmi region of Norway, Sweden and Finland (2016) UN Doc. A/HRC/33/42/Add.3, para. 51.

[343] Ibid. para. 42 (fn. 21 referring to Norwegian National Contact Point for the OECD Guidelines for Multinational Enterprises in Jijnjevaerie Sami Village and Statkraft SCA Vind AB (SSVAB) (2016) 6.4).

[344] Ibid. para. 35.

[345] Ibid. paras 32 and 74 (reiterated in the recommendations).

[346] This is, for instance, the case of the Report of the Special Rapporteur on the implications for human rights of the environmentally sound management and disposal of hazardous substances and wastes on his mission to the United Kingdom of Great Britain and Northern Ireland (2017) UN Doc. A/HRC/36/41/Add.1, para. 67 (where he pointed to 'several cases of United Kingdom businesses failing to conduct adequate due diligence on the impacts of their activities and business relationships abroad with respect to toxic chemicals, pollution and waste', but eventually addressed recommendations only to the UK government).

[347] Report of the Special Rapporteur on the implications for human rights of the environmentally sound management and disposal of hazardous substances and wastes on his mission to Denmark and Greenland (2018) UN Doc. A/HRC/39/48/Add.2, para. 33.

to the slowness of the evolution of the international regulatory framework, which placed them at a competitive disadvantage.[348] He then contrasted their views with those of civil society, who lamented the lack of accurate environmental data necessary to confirm improvements in this sector and limited access for civil society organizations to conduct visits.[349] He also made reference to engagement of the company with the UN Working Group on Business and Human Rights.[350] He concluded by raising concerns about the lack of attention to the continued export of hazardous pesticides banned by Denmark to countries that have lower levels of protection from the adverse impacts of such pesticides on the human right to health.[351] His recommendations, however, only focused on the government's obligation to require companies to conduct human rights-related due diligence to identify, monitor, assess, and address any abuses of human rights relating to toxic substances, including in relation to international operations and throughout their supply chains.[352]

In Sierra Leone, the Special Rapporteur drew links between the implementation of international standards related to corruption and to the environment, noting that the victims of exposure to toxic chemicals resulting from highly profitable agriculture and mining activities have gone without compensation, financial or otherwise. He argued that tax avoidance resulted in situations where the costs of economic development are borne by the community while the benefits are claimed by powerful elites. He concluded that this is 'threatening the governance framework on chemicals management, environmental protection and waste management and … result[ing] in the most vulnerable, including the local community, having to pay for the adverse effects of such projects through loss of life, health and well-being'.[353] He called upon the State to develop strong anti-corruption measures to accompany cost-recovery systems and other financial measures to ensure that resources are efficiently and appropriately allocated to protect the public against exposure to toxics.[354] He also focused on the right to information and extractives, underscoring that information, particularly on health impacts, was unavailable, inaccurate, or too technical; and processes for gathering information were not reasonably accessible, including the sharing of completed evaluations of the social and environmental risk assessments of large-scale mining projects with neighbouring communities. He thus called directly on companies to take proactive measures to prevent or mitigate adverse impacts on

---

[348] Ibid. para. 38.
[349] Ibid. para. 39.
[350] Ibid. para. 42.
[351] Ibid. para. 45.
[352] Ibid. para. 81(b).
[353] Report of the Special Rapporteur on the implications for human rights of the environmentally sound management and disposal of hazardous substances and wastes on his mission to Sierra Leone (2018) UN Doc. A/HRC/39/48/Add.1.
[354] Ibid. paras 19–20.

human rights resulting in irremediable harm (such as irreversible health effects or biodiversity loss).[355]

He also contributed to clarifying the application of the benefit-sharing standards in the context of extractives in Sierra Leone. He noted inadequate guarantees of meaningfulness and fairness in the process for establishing community development agreements, with the responsibility resting primarily with the business enterprise and local chiefs. This is particularly significant in the context of political and economic power imbalances between the two parties and generally without the involvement of external expert bodies with technical expertise on the social, cultural, and economic implications of projects and without a chance of accessing remedies.[356] As a result, his country visit report included a series of recommendations addressed directly to business enterprises, such as putting into effect the UN Guiding Principles on Business and Human Rights with respect to the production, use, release, and other activities that may result in human exposure to toxic substances. He also recommended internalizing the costs of chemicals and waste management, and increasing transparency with regard to their activities and interactions. Based on his observations that children accompany their parents to farms, plantations, mines, and other workplaces with risks of exposure to toxics, he further called upon private companies to increase the protection from exposure to pesticides and other toxic chemicals for children and women of childbearing age.[357]

Direct recommendations to business can be found, in addition, in his country visit report to Germany. He called upon German chemical business enterprises to engage in capacity-building with developing countries, with a view to eliminating the manufacture/use/release of hazardous substances, including an orderly phase-out of highly hazardous pesticides globally, and transitioning to safer alternatives; and work with industry partners to develop global mechanisms to finance the cost of chemicals management at the national and/or regional levels for developing countries.[358] With specific regard to embedding the UN Guiding Principles on Business and Human Rights, he called upon business entities to ensure meaningful consultation with affected individuals and communities, paying attention to marginalized persons or those in vulnerable situations in assessing actual or potential adverse human rights impacts due to hazardous substances and wastes (paying particular attention to how human rights risks from hazardous substances and wastes affect women, children, the elderly, and men differently). He further called upon business to ensure that affected communities have timely and complete

---

[355] Ibid. para. 38.
[356] Ibid. paras 63–64.
[357] Ibid. para. 83.
[358] Report of the Special Rapporteur on the implications for human rights of the environmentally sound management and disposal of hazardous substances and wastes on his mission to Germany (2016) UN Doc. A/HRC/33/41/Add.2, para. 134.

information about proposed projects, products, or changes that may affect them and the capacity to put forward their opinions. He also recommended that the German Chemical Industry Association bring to the attention of its board allegations of any chemical company being involved in human rights abuses and take appropriate measures; and ensure all member companies embed and implement the UN Guiding Principles on Business and Human Rights.[359]

In his country visit report to Korea,[360] he included in the recommendations that businesses have a responsibility to ensure that information about hazardous substances is available and accessible, and that it functions to protect the everyone's rights.[361] He also made recommendations directly to specific companies, such as acknowledging two particular companies for their commitment to ensuring that the victims of toxic humidifier sterilizers have access to an effective remedy. He recommended that they ensured all victims are identified and receive compensation; and to put in place measures to prevent a recurrence of similar incidents, and share mistakes made and lessons learned with the global community so that other governments and businesses may avoid similar mistakes.[362] Finally, in his country visit report to Kazakhstan,[363] Başkut Tuncak recommended directly to companies that they do their utmost to provide remedies to victims, to remediate contamination caused by their activities and business relationships, and to adopt policies to minimize adverse impacts on the environment and human rights. [364]

Overall, the UN Special Rapporteur on Toxics engaged in oversight at different levels, documenting both negative and positive business conduct, and assessing the interplay between procedural and substantive standards.

5 Complaints before the UN Global Compact

Notwithstanding the emphasis on its voluntary nature, the UN Global Compact has also made efforts to improve its implementation through some degree of international oversight. Although originally there were no mechanisms for monitoring or assessing performance under the Global Compact, companies' compliance with the reporting requirement has been monitored since the introduction of 'Integrity Measures' in August 2005.

---

[359] Ibid. paras 136–37.
[360] Report of the Special Rapporteur on the implications for human rights of the environmentally sound management and disposal of hazardous substances and wastes on its mission to the Republic of Korea (2016) UN Doc. A/HRC/33/41/Add.1, para. 42.
[361] Ibid. para. 106(f).
[362] Ibid. para. 110. See also ibid. para. 109.
[363] Report of the Special Rapporteur on the implications for human rights of the environmentally sound management and disposal of hazardous substances and wastes, Başkut Tuncak: Mission to Kazakhstan (2015) UN Doc. A/HRC/30/40/Add.1, para. 52.
[364] Ibid. para. 97.

Former UN Secretary-General Kofi Annan endorsed a new governance structure for the Compact to 'improve its focus, transparency and sustained impact'.[365] Besides a new policy to protect the use of the Compact name and its logo, the most notable feature of the new governance structure is the possibility to submit complaints of 'systematic or egregious abuses' of the aims and principles of the Compact to the Global Compact Office.[366] The procedure is not a compliance-based initiative, but has the objective of assisting participants in aligning their actions with the commitments undertaken. Essentially, it aims to safeguard the reputation and integrity of the Global Compact.[367]

If a complaint is not found prima facie frivolous, the Office will forward it to the concerned company requesting written comments to be addressed to the complainant. In addition, the company is to keep the Office informed of any action to be taken to remedy the situation. The Office may also provide guidance and assistance to encourage the resolution of the situation. Among various options, the Office may also decide to refer the complaint to the Board, which comprises representatives of business, civil society, trade unions, and the United Nations, or refer the matter to one of the UN agencies that are guardians of the Global Compact for advice (such as the UN Environment Programme). Interestingly, if a company refuses to engage in the dialogue on a complaint, the Office may decide to have the company labelled as 'non-communicating' on the Compact website (as it is also now possible to do for failure to report to the Global Compact). It may further remove the company from the list of participants and indicate that fact on the website when the company is considered to be detrimental to the reputation and integrity of the Compact.[368]

Although the Compact has already listed as inactive several companies that failed to comply with the minimum requirement to report on their activities implementing its principles,[369] there is no information on complaints related to allegations of systematic or egregious abuse on the website. This was already underscored by the UN Joint Inspection Unit in 2010.[370] Information on integrity cases

---

[365] UN Global Compact Office, 'The Global Compact New Phase' (6 September 2005) <http://www.unglobalcompact.org/AboutTheGC/stages_of_development.html>.
[366] UN Global Compact Office, 'Note on Integrity Measures' (26 November 2007).
[367] U. Wynhoven and M. Stausberg, 'The United Nations Global Compact's Governance Framework and Integrity Measures' in A. Rasche and G. Kell (eds), *The United Nations Global Compact: Achievements, Trends and Challenges* (Cambridge: Cambridge University Press, 2010) 251, 262–63.
[368] Ibid.
[369] UN Global Compact Office, 'Update: Over 900 Global Compact Participants Marked "Inactive" or Delisted' (28 January 2008) <http://www.unglobalcompact.org/NewsAndEvents/news_archives/2008_01_28.html>.
[370] Joint Inspection Unit, 'United Nations Corporate Partnerships: The Role and Functioning of the Global Compact' (2010) UN Doc. JIU/REP/2010/9, paras 70–73 and Recommendation 6(d). See also UN Global Compact Office, A Response from the Global Compact Office (24 March 2011) <http://www.unglobalcompact.org/docs/news_events/9.1_news_archives/2011_03_24/gco_jiu_response.pdf> accessed 27 February 2016, 5.

is being included in the Global Compact Annual Review starting from the 2009 edition, but to date these reports have limited themselves to noting the number of cases received and handled by the Global Compact Office,[371] without providing any further information—not even with reference to the specific principles that were alleged to be seriously violated by the company. In addition, scholars have underscored the lack of publicly available statistics on how many matters have been submitted, or are deemed frivolous or not, or on the outcome of the cases, including whether participants have been expelled under the procedure.[372]

This practice can be contrasted with that of the implementation procedure of the OECD Guidelines: although until mid-2000s the OECD did not publish the names of companies involved in instances under consideration by its implementation procedure, it did provide an annual update of the status of each instance with specific reference to the guideline alleged to be non-complied. This was, however, largely considered insufficient, and OECDWatch started to independently produce quarterly updates on the filing, conclusion, or rejections of instances.[373] Publicly available documentation of complaints could, however, increase the credibility of the implementation of the Global Compact and allow for public pressure to motivate private companies towards more environmentally sound conducts. In addition, reference to other, more specific standards elaborated by other bodies such as the CBD and co-operation with relevant secretariats could serve to avoid the difficulty in applying the very general Global Compact principles. Finally, the possibility for site visits by the UN specialized agencies and bodies to the operation sites of companies accused of systematic or egregious abuses could also contribute to an international system of fact-finding, to document the actual respect by private companies of international standards for corporate environmental accountability.

Global Compact members have been listed as 'non-communicating' if they missed one deadline for reporting, 'inactive' if they missed two consecutive deadlines, and some have been permanently removed from the website after missing more than two deadlines. The quality or accuracy of reports, however, remains outside of any form of assessment. Criticism has been voiced on the lack of evaluation of the effectiveness of the initiative, together with the lack of independent monitoring of its actual implementation by adhering companies, on the part of the

---

[371] The 2010 edition of the Annual Report states that '21 separate matters alleging abuses of the Ten Principles by business entities were raised with the Global Compact Office in 2010 [of which] 3 matters were handled under the Integrity Measures dialogue facilitation mechanism' (UN Global Compact Office, 2010 Annual Report of the Global Compact (UN, 2011) 42). Similar information is provided in the 2009 edition (UN Global Compact Office, 2010 Annual Report of the Global Compact (UN, 2010) 20).

[372] Simons and Macklin (n. 49) 120–21.

[373] E. Morgera, 'An Environmental Outlook on the OECD Guidelines for Multinational Enterprises: Comparative Advantage, Legitimacy, and Outstanding Questions in the Lead-up to the 2006 Review' (2006) 18 *Georgetown International Environmental Law Review* 751, 774. The OECDWatch database can be consulted at http://oecdwatch.org/cases.

UN.³⁷⁴ Scholars have criticized the complaints procedure of the Global Compact because the outcome is neither a change of status or a referral to other bodies.³⁷⁵ It has also been criticized for not engaging in investigations, hearings, or required monitoring to check whether corporate conduct has changed or the situation has been addressed.³⁷⁶ As a result, the UN Joint Inspection Unit recommended more proactive and transparent handling of complaints and more effective mechanisms to determine the credibility of a complaint beyond the consultation with the Global Compact Board and local networks.³⁷⁷

The system has, however, been subject to progressive improvements: for instance, the category of 'inactive' has been phased out and was replaced with delisting in 2011.³⁷⁸ The commitment of the UN Secretary-General to continuing to retain the integrity and unique role of the UN Global Compact, and the importance of the integrity measures have been underscored by the UN General Assembly in its recent resolutions.³⁷⁹ So, overall, the Global Compact process has been less successful in translating business commitments into actual change than in supporting a global dialogue and a network of companies across the globe,³⁸⁰ including developing specific guidance on human rights and the environment for business.³⁸¹

6 Concluding remarks

To a significant extent, the impacts on corporate conduct of these international monitoring or complaint arrangements may provide evidence of the practical importance of the existing international soft-law instruments on corporate environmental accountability and responsibility, particularly in the face of significant constraints in access to, and limited results obtained from, national and transnational litigation.³⁸² All these initiatives, with the exception of the UN Global Compact, have engaged, to different extents, in fact-finding on corporate

---

[374] Among others, Calder and Culverwell (n. 36) 38.
[375] Viñuales (n. 127) 75.
[376] Simons and Macklin (n. 49) 120–21.
[377] UN Joint Inspection Unit, 'United Nations Corporate Partnerships: The Role and Functioning of the Global Compact' (2010) UN Doc. JIU/REP/2010/9, 17. This finding is not challenged in the more recent report of the Joint Inspection Unit discussed in Ch. 4.
[378] S. Deva, *Regulating Corporate Human Rights Violations: Humanizing Business* (Abingdon: Routledge, 2012) 84 95. See https://www.unglobalcompact.org/news/104-02-25-2011. See UN Global Compact, Integrity Measures (updated June 2016) https://www.unglobalcompact.org/docs/about_the_gc/Integrity_measures/Integrity_Measures_Note_EN.pdf.
[379] UNGA Res. 73/254 (2019) para. 17.
[380] Simons and Macklin (n. 49) 121–22.
[381] See Ch 3, Section 3.1.2.
[382] Eg R. Meeran, 'Access to Remedy: The United Kingdom Experience of MNC Tort Litigation for Human Rights Violations' in S. Deva and D. Bilchitz (eds), *Human Rights Obligations of Business: Beyond Corporate Responsibility to Respect?* (Cambridge: Cambridge University Press, 2013) 378.

substandard practice and in clarifying the conditions under which international standards can be applied in practice. The OECD NCPs and the UN Special Rapporteurs have also contributed to normative coherence and filling gaps across international standards. They have also further clarified the dividing line between business due diligence and State obligations to protect the environment and respect human rights.

The practice of different international monitoring initiatives, however, remains to be more systematically compared, with a view to revealing any limitations and lessons learnt in the application of international standards. In addition, research is needed to clarify the opportunities and challenges for genuine collaboration among different international processes in preventing and moderating conflicts over natural resources among governments, private companies, and local users.[383]

Ultimately, there is a need for better understanding, from a doctrinal and empirical perspective, of the role of international monitoring and complaints mechanisms in not only testing international standards of corporate accountability and responsibility, but also providing remedies for corporate abuses. This is particularly relevant for the ongoing negotiations of a new international treaty on business and human rights, which is mainly expected to enhance access to justice for victims.[384] In particular, the experience of the CAO of documenting its own impact on communities on the ground provides an interesting example in this connection, particularly in illuminating practical approaches in implementing international standards such as fair and equitable benefit-sharing.

The balance between pointing at instances of non-compliance with international standards and keeping companies engaged in the progressive improvement of their practices, including through supported co-development of solutions with affected communities, is a difficult one to assess without further independent empirical research. But it has the potential to engage companies, and possibly governments, in a broader dialogue with communities about pre-existing or systemic causes of marginalization in natural resource development.

---

[383] Notably in consideration of the limited outcomes discussed in Section 2.4 of this chapter.
[384] See Ch 3, Section 7.

Conclusions: Contributions and Areas for Further Research

The progressive development of international law to address corporate environmental accountability and responsibility has intensified since 2010. This has been the combined result of the inter-governmental support for the UN Framework and Guiding Principles on Business and Human Rights and the growing international recognition of the inter-dependence of human rights and the environment culminated in the 2018 UN Framework Principles on Human Rights and the Environment. These international developments have fuelled—and have been fuelled in turn by—a burgeoning scholarship and transnational practices on business and human rights. The area of transnational litigation alone has become a field of study in its own right, with sub-fields devoted, for instance, to climate litigation. Against this backdrop, this concluding section will reflect on the original contributions to academic and policy debates that this book has offered, and identify areas for further research.

The contribution of this book has been, first, to confirm that international standards on corporate environmental accountability have translated into procedural benchmarks for the private sector the general principles of international environmental law (environmental integration, prevention, and precaution), thereby contributing to clarifying businesses' due diligence to respect human rights. Another important area of international standard-setting concerns procedural environmental rights (access to information, participation in decision-making, and access to justice), which has built on insights from UN Special Rapporteurs. Furthermore, substantive standards of corporate environmental responsibility have emerged, notably in relation to how environmental management systems and prevention can contribute to the sustainable use of freshwater, the responsible management of chemicals, waste minimization, and climate change mitigation. This is also the case with increasingly substantive standards to ensure business respect for indigenous peoples' human rights to natural resources, and business due diligence in relation to biodiversity conservation and the sustainable use of natural resources. All these developments have drawn significantly from the guidance that has been adopted inter-governmentally under the Convention on Biological Diversity (CBD), often with significant input from indigenous peoples' and local communities' representatives. The cross-fertilization of international human rights law and international biodiversity law through international standard-setting has benefitted from a clearer identification under international human rights law of the minimum content of States' obligations, notably in relation to necessary procedural guarantees that tend to remain unspecified in international biodiversity law. On the other hand, international biodiversity law provides pragmatic indications on how to put human rights precepts in practice within the complex landscape of environmental regulation and natural resource development. The present analysis has also underscored that while there is a significant degree of convergence between all the standards, remaining divergence points to particularly controversial concepts in international law, such as the assessment of cumulative environmental impacts, precaution, free prior informed consent (FPIC), the distinction between benefit-sharing and compensation, and agro-ecology, to name a few examples. These are also several thematic areas where substantive standards of corporate environmental responsibility could be much more detailed, such as in the case of climate change, the use of traditional knowledge of indigenous peoples, local communities', women's and children's human rights, and the transfer of technology. In addition, the relevance and appropriateness of international standards of corporate environmental accountability and responsibility for ocean conservation and the sustainable use of marine resources remains to be assessed.[1]

Contrasted with the traditional sources of international environmental law, international standards have clarified how businesses are expected to relate to inter-State obligations, in ways that are adaptable from case to case and from one area to another of corporate activity. This explains both how States and business enterprises are expected to collaborate in the pursuance of international objectives, and how businesses are expected to go above and beyond what States require of them in their domestic legislation and practices. This is particularly relevant when businesses operate in States with poor human rights and environmental records. While there is continued opposition to consider or develop international law as directly applicable to multinational companies and other business entities, international standards represent a step forward conceptually from a traditional understanding that international law does not matter for corporations if not through the State. These standards can then back up victims' legal claims and advocacy initiatives; inform States' regulatory, implementation, and monitoring efforts; and inform judicial practice. They can also inform corporate governance reforms, guide legal advisory services to private companies, and be included in legal education. Another original finding of this book is, however, that the current scholarly and policy efforts on business and human rights have not yet ensured systematic connections with the standards of corporate environmental accountability and responsibility. It thus remains to be better understood to what extent in practice reliance on these environmental standards can contribute to more successful litigation and law-making efforts on business and human rights, at the national and international levels. While this book does not do justice to the highly complex and experimental

---

[1] One exception is the translation by the International Finance Corporation (IFC) of the international rules on ocean dumping for business: see Ch. 4, Section 2.2.1.

areas of scholarship and practice making recourse to national law and transnational litigation for holding corporations to account in light of international law, it has identified the need to contrast these areas of practice and research as an alternative to the development and application of international standards of corporate environmental accountability and responsibility. Furthermore, more research is needed to better understand mutual influences among transnational litigation and international standards, as well as transnational contractual practices that seek to avoid the shortcomings identified in transnational litigation.

The final original contribution of this book relates to the oversight mechanisms that international standard-setting initiatives on corporate environmental accountability and responsibility have set up and the different functions they perform. Regardless of the differences in approaches, structures, and coverage, all these mechanisms have the potential to further advance international standard-setting. This potential includes ensuring further coherence among different sets of international standards, as well as collecting lessons learnt in terms of their practical application in specific circumstances. In light of the growing number of cases dealt by the national contact points (NCPs) under the OECD Guidelines, and by the IFC Ombudsman, more efforts could be devoted to a comparative analysis of the quasi-jurisprudence of these bodies with a view to determining, on the one hand, the impacts on these decisions on corporate conduct and on the standard-setting of the international organizations concerned. On the other hand, this comparative exercise could shed further light on missed opportunities for transnational litigation and for international and national law-making efforts to build upon the insights gathered by these bodies. In addition, UN Special Rapporteurs are emerging as a significant source of guidance on how to implement international standards of corporate environmental accountability and responsibility in specific circumstances. It remains to be seen if transnational litigation, the international negotiations on a treaty on business and human rights, and international standard-setting initiatives will fully benefit from these insights. Even more significantly, it remains to be assessed empirically to what extent international monitoring and complaints mechanisms can provide effective approaches to prevent or provide more timely remedy to corporate abuses than traditional judicial avenues. This is particularly relevant for the ongoing negotiations of a new international treaty on business and human rights, which is mainly expected to enhance access to justice for victims.

The final area for further research that has been identified by this book relates to the need to bring together international human rights lawyers and international environmental lawyers in a dialogue with private (international) lawyers.[2] This

---

[2] See also E. Morgera and L. Gillies, 'Realizing the Objectives of Public International Environmental Law through Private Contracts: The Need for a Dialogue with Private International Law Scholars?' in D. French, V. Ruiz Abou-Nigm, and K. McCall Smith (eds), *Public and Private International Law: Strengthening Connections* (Oxford: Hart Publishing, 2018) 175.

is because often private law instruments are critical to encapsulate international standards of corporate environmental accountability and responsibility and other standards of business due diligence to respect human rights in the relationships between companies and potentially affected communities. Much remains to be understood about the actual room for communities' worldviews to be expressed, understood, and realized within contractual tools and approaches. Furthermore, more research is required on the oversight of the conclusion and implementation of business–community agreements, in addition to growing research on their impact on the ground.

Bibliography

O. Abe and A. Ordor, 'Addressing Human Rights Concerns in the Extractive Resource Industry in Sub-Saharan Africa Using the Lens of Article 46(c) of the Malabo Protocol' (2018) 11 *Law and Development Review* 843.
G. Abi-Saab, 'Cours général de droit international public' (1987) 207 *Recueil des cours* 9.
D. Abrahams, *Regulating Corporations. A Resource Guide* (Geneva: United Nations Research Institute for Social Development, 2004).
P. Acconci, 'The Promotion of Responsible Business Conduct and the New Text of the OECD Guidelines for Multinational Enterprises' (2001) 2 *Journal of World Investment* 123.
M. K. Addo (ed.), *Human Rights Standards and the Responsibility of Transnational Corporations* (The Hague: Kluwer Law International, 1999).
A. Adeyemi, 'Changing the Face of Sustainable Development in Developing Countries: The Role of the International Finance Corporation' (2014) 16 *Environmental Law Review* 91.
N. Affolder, 'The Market for Treaties' (2010) 11 *Chicago Journal of International Law* 159.
L. Ahearn, 'Environmental Procedures and Standards in International Transactions: Multilateral Models and Private Lending Practices' (1999) 27 *International Business Lawyer* 419.
R. T. Ako, 'Issues on Environmental Human Rights and Corporate Social Responsibility in the Niger Delta' (2005) 15 *Lesotho Law Journal* 1.
A. Alkoby, 'Non-State Actors and the Legitimacy of International Environmental Law' (2003) 3 *Non-State Actors and International Law* 23.
S. Allen and A. Xanthaki (eds), *Reflections on the UN Declaration on the Rights of Indigenous Peoples* (Oxford: Hart Publishing, 2011).
P. Alston, 'A Third Generation of Solidarity Rights: Progressive Development or Obfuscation of International Human Rights Law?' (1982) 29 *Netherlands International Law Review* 307.
P. Alston (ed.), *Non-State Actors and Human Rights* (Oxford: Oxford University Press, 2005).
J. Alvarez, 'Are Corporations "Subjects" of International Law?' (2011) 9 *Santa Clara Journal of International Law* 1.
J. A. Amiott, 'Environment, Equality, and Indigenous Peoples' Land Rights in the Inter-American Human Rights System: Mayagna (Sumo) Indigenous Community of Awas Tingni v. Nicaragua' (2002) 32 *Environmental Law* 873.
Amnesty International, *Clouds of Injustice: Bhopal Twenty Years On* (London: Amnesty International, 2004).
Amnesty International, *Injustice Incorporated: Corporate Abuses and the Human Right to Remedy* (London: Amnesty International, 2014).
Amnesty International, *The UN Human Rights Norms for Business: Towards Legal Accountability* (London: Amnesty International, 2004).
S. J. Anaya, *Indigenous Peoples in International Law* (Oxford: Oxford University Press, 2004).
S. J. Anaya and S. T. Crider, 'Indigenous Peoples, the Environment, and Commercial Forestry in Developing Countries: The Case of Awas Tingni, Nicaragua' (1996) 18 *Human Rights Quarterly* 345.

S. J. Anaya and C. Grossman, 'The Case of Awas Tingni v Nicaragua: a New Step in the International Law of Indigenous People' (2002) 19 *Arizona Journal of International and Comparative Law* 1.

S. J. Anaya and R. A. Williams, 'The Protection of Indigenous Peoples' Rights over the Lands and Natural Resources under the Inter-American Human Rights System' (2001) 14 *Harvard Human Rights Journal* 33.

M. Anderson, 'Transnational Corporations and Environmental Damage: Is Tort Law the Answer?' (2002) 41 *Washburn Law Journal* 399.

S. Anderson and J. Cavanagh, *Top 200: The Rise of Global Corporate Power* (Corporate Watch, 2000).

A. Anghie, B. Chimni, K. Mickelson, and O. Okafor (eds), *The Third World and International Order: Law, Politics and Globalization* (Leiden: Martinus Nijhoff Publishers, 2003).

A. Antypas and S. Stec, 'Towards a Liability Regime for Damages to Transboundary Waters: A New Protocol in the UNECE Region' (2003) 14 *Journal of Water Law* 185.

M. Århén, *Indigenous Peoples in the International Legal System* (Oxford: Oxford University Press, 2016).

J. E. Arlow, 'The Utility of ATCA and the "Law of Nations" in Environmental Torts Litigation: Jota v. Texaco, inc. and Large Scale Environmental Destruction' (2000) 7 *Wisconsin Environmental Law Journal* 93.

D. Augenstein and D. Kinley, 'Beyond the 100 Acre Wood: In Which International Human Rights Law Finds New Ways to Tame Global Corporate Power' (2015) 19 *International Journal of Human Rights* 828.

H. W. Baade, 'Legal Effects of Codes of Conduct for Multinational Enterprises' (1979) 22 *German Yearbook of International Law* 11.

S. Baker, 'Why the IFC's Free, Prior and Informed Consent Policy Does Not Matter (Yet) to Indigenous Communities Affected by Development Projects' (2012–13) 30 *Wisconsin International Law Journal* 668.

G. Banks and C. Ballard (eds), *The Ok Tedi Settlement: Issues, Outcomes and Implications* (Canberra: National Centre for Development Studies and Resource Management, 1997).

I. Bantekas, 'Corporate Social Responsibility in International Law' 22 (2004) *Boston University International Law Journal* 309.

M. Barbut, 'Improving Cooperation and Encouraging Private Investment to Strengthen MEA Implementation' (paper presented at the OECD Workshop Multilateral Environmental Agreements and the Private Sector, Helsinki, 16–17 June 2005).

M. Barelli, 'Free, Prior and Informed Consent in the Aftermath of the UN Declaration on the Rights of Indigenous Peoples: Developments and Challenges Ahead' (2012) 16 *International Journal of Human Rights* 1.

L. Barrera-Hernandez, B. Barton, L. Godden, A. Lucas, and A. Rønne (eds), *Sharing the Costs and Benefits of Energy and Resource Activity* (Oxford: Oxford University Press, 2016).

D. Baumann-Pauly, 'Bridging Theory and Practice through Immersion: Innovations for Teaching Business and Human Rights at Business Schools' (2018) 3 *Business and Human Rights Journal* 139.

A. Beghè Loreti, 'L'elaborazione di un codice di condotta delle società multinazionali ad opera delle Nazioni Unite' (1979) 2 *Il diritto comunitario e degli scambi inter-nazionali* 262.

J. Bendell, *Barricades and Boardrooms. A Contemporary History of the Corporate Accountability Movement* (Geneva: UNRISD, 2004).

J. Bendell, *Flags of Inconvenience? The Global Compact and the Future of the United Nations* (International Centre for Corporate Social Responsibility Paper no. 22, 2004).

E. Benvenisti, 'Sovereigns as Trustees of Humanity: On the Accountability of State to Foreign Stakeholders' (2013) 107 *American Journal of International Law* 295.

E. Benvenisti and G. Downs, *Between Fragmentation and Democracy: The Role of National and International Courts* (Cambridge: Cambridge University Press, 2017).

H. O. Bergenses, G. Parmann, and Ø. B. Thommessen (eds), *Green Globe Yearbook of International Cooperation on Environment and Development* (Oxford: Oxford University Press, 1995).

L. Bergkamp, *Liability and the Environment: Private and Public Law Aspects of Civil Liability for Environmental Harm in an International Context* (The Hague: Kluwer Law International, 2001).

N. Bernaz, 'An Analysis of the ICC Office of the Prosecutor's Policy Paper on Case Selection and Prioritization from the Perspective of Business and Human Rights' (2017) 15 *Journal of International Criminal Justice* 527.

M. Bettati and P-M. Dupuy (eds), *Les O.N.G. et le droit international* (Paris: Economica, 1986).

P. Birnie and A. Boyle, *International Law and the Environment*, 2nd edn (Oxford: Oxford University Press, 2002).

P. Birnie, A. Boyle, and C. Redgwell, *International Law and the Environment*, 3rd edn (Oxford: Oxford University Press, 2009).

S. Blackwell and N. Vander Meulen, 'Two Roads Converged: The Mutual Complementarity of a Binding Business and Human Rights Treaty and National Action Plans on Business and Human Rights' (2016) 6 *Notre Dame Journal of International and Comparative Law* 51.

R. Blanpain (ed.), *International Encyclopaedia of Laws* (Intergovernmental Organizations—Suppl. 12) (The Hague: Kluwer Law International, 2002).

P. Blumberg, 'Accountability of Multinational Corporations: The Barriers Presented by the Concepts of the Corporate Judicial Entity' (2001) 24 *Hastings International and Comparative Law Review* 297.

N. Bobbio, *Dalla struttura alla funzione: nuovi studi di teoria del diritto* (Milano: Edizioni di Comunità, 1977).

B. Boer (ed.), *Environmental Law Dimensions of Human Rights* (Oxford: Oxford University Press, 2015).

A. Boos-Hersberger, 'Transboundary Water Pollution and State Responsibility: The Sandoz Spill' (1997) 4 *Annual Survey of International and Comparative Law* 103.

K. Bourdreaux and S. Schang, 'Threats of, and Responses to, Agribusiness Land Acquisitions' (2019) 4 *Business and Human Rights Journal* 365.

M. Bovens, 'Analysing and Assessing Accountability: A Conceptual Framework' (2007) 13 *European Law Journal* 447–68.

I. Bowles, A. Rosenfels, C. Kormos, C. Reining, J. Nations, and T. Ankersen, 'The Environmental Impact of the International Finance Corporation Lending and Proposals for Reform: A Case Study of Conservation and Oil Development in the Guatemalan Petén' (1999) 29 *Environmental Law* 103.

M. Bowman, P. Davies, and C. Redgwell, *Lyster's International Wildlife Law*, 2nd edn (Cambridge: Cambridge University Press, 2010).

A. Boyle, 'State Responsibility and International Liability for Injurious Consequences of Acts not Prohibited by International Law: A Necessary Distinction?' (1990) 39 *International and Comparative Law Quarterly* 1.

A. Boyle and M. Anderson (eds), *Human Rights Approaches to Environmental Protection* (Oxford: Clarendon Press, 1996).

A. Boyle and C. Chinkin, *The Making of International Law* (Oxford: Oxford University Press, 2007).
D. Bradlow and A. Naudé Fourie, 'The Operational Policies of the World Bank and the International Finance Corporation: Creating Law-Making and Law-Governed Institutions?' (2013) 10 *International Organizations Law Review* 3.
D. Bradlow and M. Chapman, 'Public Participation and the Private Sector: The Role of Multilateral Development Banks and the Evolving Legal Standards' (2011) 4 *Erasmus Law Review* 91.
N. L. Bridgeman, 'Human Rights Litigation under the ATCA as a Proxy for Environmental Claims' (2003) 6 *Yale Human Rights and Development Law Journal* 1.
C. Brunch and J. Pendergrass, 'Type II Partnerships, International Law and the Commons' (2003) 15 *Georgetown International Environmental Law Review* 855.
J. Brunnée, 'COP-ing with Consent: Law-Making under Multilateral Environmental Agreements', 15 *Leiden Journal of International Law* (2002) 1.
J. Brunnée, 'Of Sense and Sensibility: Reflections on International Liability Regimes as Tools for Environmental Protection' (2004) 53 *International and Comparative Law Quarterly* 351.
J. Brunnée, D. Bodanski, and H. Hey (eds), *Handbook on International Environmental Law* (Oxford: Oxford University Press, 2007).
J. Brunnée and S. J. Toope, *Legitimacy and Legality in International Law* (Cambridge: Cambridge University Press, 2010).
K. Bruno and J. Karliner, 'The UN's Global Compact, Corporate Accountability and the Johannesburg Earth Summit' (2002) 45 *Development* 33.
K. Buhmann, 'Damned if you Do, Damned if You Don't? The Lundbeck Case of Pntobarbital, the Guiding Principles on Business and Human Rights, and Competing Human Rights Responsibilities' (2012) 40 *Journal of Law, Medicine and Ethics* 206.
K. Buhmann, 'Public Regulators and CSR: The "Social Licence to Operate" in Recent United Nations Instruments on Business and Human Rights and the Juridificaiton of CSR' (2016) 136 *Journal of Business Ethics* 699.
B. Bull, M. Bøås, and D. McNeill, 'Private Sector Influence in the Multilateral System: A Changing Structure of World Governance?' (2004) 10 *Global Governance* 481.
K. Caine and N. Krogman, 'Powerful or Just Plain Power-Full? A Power Analysis of Impact and Benefit Agreements in Canada's North' (2010) 23 *Organization & Environment* 76.
F. Calder, *Developing an Effective Follow-up Process for WSSD Partnerships: The Role of the Commission on Sustainable Development* (London: Royal Institute of International Affairs Discussion Paper, 2003).
F. Calder, *The Potential for Using the Multistakeholder Network Method to Develop and Deliver Partnerships for Implementation for the World Summit on Sustainable Development* (London: Royal Institute of International Affairs discussion paper, 2002).
F. Calder and M. Culverwell, *Following up the WSSD Commitments on Corporate Responsibility & Accountability* (London: Royal Institute of International Affairs, 2004).
The California Global Corporate Accountability Project, *Whose Business? A Handbook on Corporate Responsibility for Human Rights and the Environment* (The Nautilus Institute, Natural Heritage Institute, Human Rights Advocates, 2002) <http://www.nautilus.org/archives/cap/reports/CapHandbook.PDF>.
T. Cannon, *Corporate Responsibility: A Textbook on Business Ethics, Governance, Environment: Roles and Responsibilities* (London: Pitman Publishing, 1994).
H. Cantú Rivera, 'National Action Plans on Business and Human Rights: Progress or Mirage?' (2019) 4 *Business and Human Rights Journal* 201.

K. Carpenter and A. Riley, 'Indigenous Peoples and the Jurisgenerative Moment in Human Rights' (2014) 102 *California Law Review* 173.

D. Carreau and P. Juillard, *Droit International Economique* (Paris: Dalloz, 2003).

D. Cassell and A. Ramasastry, 'White Paper: Options for a Treaty on Business and Human Rights' (2016) 6 *Notre Dame Journal of International and Comparative Law* 1.

A. Cassese, P. Gaeta, and J. Jones, *The Rome Statute of the International Criminal Court: A Commentary* (Oxford: Oxford University Press, 2002).

L. Catá Backer, 'Multinational Corporations, Transnational Law: The United Nations' Norms on the Responsibilities of Transnational Corporations as a Harbinger of Corporate Social Responsibility in International Law (2005–06) 37 *Columbia Human Rights Law Review* 287.

L. Catá Backer, 'Rights and Accountability in Development ("RAID") d Das Air and Global Witness v Afrimex: Small Steps towards an Autonomous Transnational Legal System for the Regulation of Multinational Corporations' (2009) 10 *Melbourne Journal of International Law* 258.

N. Cely, 'Balancing Profit and Environmental Sustainability in Ecuador: Lessons Learned from the Chevron Case' (2014) *Duke Environmental Law & Policy Forum* 353.

Centre for International Environmental Law (CIEL), 'A Handbook on the Office of the Compliance Advisor/Ombudsman of the International Finance Corporation and Multilateral Investment Guarantee Agency' (2000) <http://www.ciel.org/Ifi/ifcproblemprojects.html#CAO%20Handbook>.

Cercle de Sociologie et Nomologie Juridiques, *Dictionnaire encyclopédique de théorie et de sociologie du droit* (Paris: Librairie Générale de Droit et de Jurisprudence, 1993).

A. Chander, 'Unshackling Foreign Corporations: Kiobel's Unexpected Legacy' (2013) 107 *American Journal of International Law* 829.

M. Chandler, 'The Biodiversity Convention: Selected Issues of Interest to the International Lawyer' (1993) 4 *Colorado Journal of International Environmental Law* 141.

A. Chauveau and J. Rosé, *L'entreprise responsable: Développement durable, responsabilité sociale de l'entreprise, éthique* (Paris: Éd. d'Organisation, 2003).

S. K. Chopra, 'Multinational Corporations in the Aftermath of Bhopal: the Need for a New Comprehensive Global Regime for Transnational Corporate Activity' (1994) 29 *Valparaiso University Law Review* 235.

N. Choucri (ed.), *Global Accord: Environmental Challenges and International Responses* (Cambridge, Mass: MIT Press, 1993).

R. Cirlig, 'Business and Human Rights: From Soft Law to Hard Law?' (2016) 6 *Juridical Tribune* 228.

J. A. Cohan, 'Environmental Rights of Indigenous Peoples under the Alien Tort Claims Act, the Public Trust Doctrine and Corporate Ethics, and Environmental Dispute Resolution' (2001–02) 20 *UCLA Journal of Environmental Law and Policy* 133.

D. Coleman, 'The United Nations and Transnational Corporations: From an Inter-Nation to a "Beyond-State" Model of Engagement' (2003) 17 *Global Society* 339.

Commission on the Private Sector and Development, *Unleashing Entrepreneurship: Making Business Work for the Poor* (New York: UNDP, 2004).

The Compliance Advisor/Ombudsman (CAO) of the International Finance Corporation (IFC), 'A Review of IFC's Safeguard Policies' (January 2003) <http://www.cao-ombudsman.org/html-english/documents/ReviewofIFCSPsfinalreportenglish04-03-03.pdf>.

P. Contini and P. H. Sand, 'Methods to Expedite Environmental Protection: International Ecostandards' (1972) 66 *American Journal of International Law* 37.

S. Coonrod, 'The United Nations Code of Conduct for Transnational Corporations' (1977) 18 *Harvard International Law Journal* 273.

M. C. Cordonier Segger, 'Sustainability and Corporate Accountability Regimes: Implementing the Johannesburg Summit Agenda' (2003) 12 *Review of European Community and International Environment Law* 295.

C. M. Correa and N. Kumar, *Protecting Foreign Investment. Implications of a WTO Regime and Policy Options* (London: Zed Books, 2003).

L. Cotula, 'Expropriation Clauses and Environmental Regulation: Diffusion of Law in the Era of Investment Treaties' (2015) 24 *Review of European, Comparative and International Environmental Law* 278.

L. Cotula and K. Tienhaara, 'Reconfiguring Investment Contracts to Promote Sustainable Development' (2013) 2011–12 *Yearbook of International Investment Law and Policy* 281.

N. Craik, 'Process and Reconciliation: Integrating the Duty to Consult with Environmental Assessment' (2016) 52 *Osgoode Hall Law Journal* 1.

N. Craik, H. Gardner, and D. McCarthy, 'Indigenous—Corporate Private Governance and Legitimacy: Lessons Learned from Impact and Benefit Agreements' (2017) 52 *Resources Policy* 379.

W. Crane, 'Corporations Swallowing Nations: The OECD and the Multilateral Agreement on Investment' (1998) 9 *Colorado Journal of International Environmental Law and Policy* 429.

H. Creech and T. Willard, *Virtual Exhibition E-Discussions: Working Together for Sustainable Development* (Winnipeg: International Institute for Sustainable Development, 2002).

P. Daillier and A. Pellet, *Droit International Public* (Paris: LGDJ, 1999).

G. de Burca and J. Scott, *Law and New Governance in the EU and the US* (Portland: Hart Publishing, 2006).

A. Del Vecchio and A. Dal Ri Jr (eds), *Il diritto internazionale dell'ambiente dopo il ver-tice di Johannesburg* (Napoli: Editoriale Scientifica, 2005).

B. Desai, 'The Bhopal Gas Leak Disaster Litigation: An Overview' (1994) *Asian Yearbook of International Law* 163.

O. De Schutter, 'The Right of Everyone to Enjoy the Benefits of Scientific Progress and the Right to Food: From Conflict to Complementarity' (2011) 33 *Human Rights Quarterly* 304.

O. De Schutter, 'Towards a New Treaty on Business and Human Rights' (2016) 1 *Business and Human Rights Journal* 41.

E. Desmet, Indigenous Rights Entwined With Nature Conservation (Cambridge: Intersentia, 2011).

I. Detter, *Law-Making by International Organizations* (Stockholm: Norstedt & Soners, 1965).

S. Deva, 'UN's Human Rights Norms for Transnational Corporations and Other Business Enterprises: An Imperfect Step in the Right Direction?' (2004) 10 *ILSA Journal of International and Comparative Law* 493.

S. Deva, *Regulating Corporate Human Rights Violations: Humanizing Business* (Abingdon, Routledge: 2012).

S. Deva and D. Bilchitz (eds), *Human Rights Obligations of Business: Beyond Corporate Responsibility to Respect?* (Cambridge: Cambridge University Press, 2013).

G. Doeker and T. Gehring, 'Private or International Liability for Transnational Environmental Damage—The Precedent of Conventional Liability Regimes' (1990) 2 *Journal of Environmental Law* 1.

C. Dommen, 'Claiming Environmental Rights: Some Possibilities Offered by the United Nations' Human Rights Mechanisms' (1998) 11 *Georgetown International Environmental Law Review* 1.

C. Doyle, *Indigenous Peoples, Title to Territory, Rights and Resources: The Transformative Role of Free, Prior and Informed Consent* (Abingdon: Routledge, 2015).

C. Doyle and J. Gilbert, 'Indigenous Peoples and Globalization: From "Development Aggression" to "Self-Determined Development"' (2008/9) 7 *European Yearbook of Minority Issues* 219.

P. Dumberry, 'L'Entreprise, sujet de droit international? Retour sur la question à la lumière des développements récents du droit international des investissements' (2004) 108 *Revue Générale De Droit International Public* 103.

P-M. Dupuy, *La responsabilité international des états pour les dommages d'origine technologique et industrielle* (Paris: Editions Pedone, 1976).

P-M. Dupuy, 'Soft Law and the International Law of the Environment' (1991) 12 *Michigan International Law Journal* 420.

P-M. Dupuy, *L'unité de l'ordre juridique international* (Leiden: Martinus Nijhoff Publishers, 2003).

P-M. Dupuy, *Droit International Public* (Paris: Dalloz, 2004).

P-M. Dupuy and J. Viñuales, 'Human Rights and Investment Disciplines: Integration in Progress' in M. Bungenberg, J. Griebel, S. Hobe, and A. Reinisch (eds), *International Investment Law: A Handbook* (Oxford: Hart Publishing, 2015) 1739.

E. Duruigbo, *Multinational Corporations and International Law: Accountability and Compliance Issues in the Petroleum Industry* (Ardlee, NY: Transnational Publishers, 2003).

R. Dworkin (ed.), *The Philosophy of Law* (Oxford: Oxford University Press, 1977).

Earth Negotiations Bulletin, 'Summary of the eleventh session of the United Nations Commission on Sustainable Development: 28 April–9 May 2003' (12 May 2003) <http://www.iisd.ca/vol05/enb05193e.html>.

Earth Negotiations Bulletin on the Side, 'Special Report on Selected Side Events at COP 11 & Kyoto Protocol COP/MOP 1: Events convened on Saturday, 3 December 2005' (5 December 2005) <http://www.iisd.ca/climate/cop11/enbots/enbots1706e.html>.

Earthwatch Institute, IUCN and World Business Council for Sustainable Development, 'Business and Biodiversity: The Handbook for Corporate Action' (2002) <http://www.wbcsd.ch/DocRoot/ob3ZstqTvcmXQVtEtMxh/20020819_biodiversity.pdf>.

J. P. Eaton, 'The Nigerian Tragedy, Environmental Regulation of Transnational Corporations, and the Human Right to a Healthy Environment' (1997) 15 *Boston University International Law Journal* 261.

The Ecumenical Team, 'Corporate Accountability—A Matter of Sustainable Justice: fact sheet for the WSSD' (2002) <http://www.wcc-coe.org/wcc/what/jpc/corp-account.pdf>.

A. Eide, C. Krause, and A. Rosas (eds), *Economic, Social and Cultural Rights: A Textbook* (The Hague: Kluwer Law International, 2001).

M. Emberland, *The Human Rights of Companies* (Oxford: Oxford University Press, 2006).

J. Erler, 'International Legislation' (1964) 2 *Canadian Yearbook of International Law* 153.

A. S. Farha, 'The Corporate Conscience and Environmental Issues: Responsibility of Multinational Corporations' (1990) 10 *Northwestern Journal of International Law & Business* 379.

A. A. Fatouros (ed.), *Transnational Corporations: The International Legal Framework* (London: Routledge, 1994).

A. A. Fatouros, 'The OECD Guidelines in a Globalizing World' (17 February 1999) OECD Doc. DAFFE/IME/RD(99)3.

O. K. Fauchald and A. Nollkaemper, *The Practice of International and National Courts and the (De-)Fragmentation of International Law* (Oxford: Hart Publishing, 2012).

P. Feeney, 'Making Companies Accountable: An NGO Report on Implementation of the OECD Guidelines for Multinational Enterprises by National Contact Points' (October 2002) <http://www.oecd.org/dataoecd/16/37/2965489.pdf>.

M. Fitzmaurice, D. Ong, and P. Merkouris (eds), *Research Handbook on International Environmental Law* (Cheltenham: Edward Elgar, 2010).

M. Flores, 'A Practical Approach to Allocating Environmental Liability and Stabilizing Foreign Investment in the Energy Sectors of Developing Countries' (2001) 12 *Colorado Journal of International Environmental Law and Policy* 141.

A. Fodella, 'Indigenous Peoples, the Environment, and International Jurisprudence' in N. Boschiero, T. Scovazzi, C. Pitea, and C. Ragni (eds), *International Courts and the Development of International Law: Essays in Honour of Tullio Treves* (The Hague: TMC Asser Press, 2013), 360.

A. Fonseca, 'Codici di condotta per le multinazionali' (1981) 30144 *La Civiltà Cattolica* 533.

R. J. Fowler, 'International Environmental Standards for Transnational Corporations' (1995) 25 *Environmental Law Review* 1.

F. Francioni, 'International Codes of Conduct for Multinational Enterprises: An Alternative Approach' (1977) 3 *The Italian Yearbook of International Law* 143.

F. Francioni, *Imprese multinazionali, protezione diplomatica e responsabilità internazionale* (Milano: Giuffré Editore, 1979).

F. Francioni (ed.), *The World Heritage Convention: A Commentary* (Oxford: Oxford University Press, 2008).

F. Francioni, 'Environment' in A. Cassese (ed.), *Realizing Utopia: The Future of International Law* (Oxford: Oxford University Press, 2012) 443.

F. Francioni and T. Scovazzi (eds), *International Responsibility for Environmental Harm* (London: Graham & Trotman, 1991).

C. Freeman, C. Heydenreich, and S. Lillywhite, *Guide to the OECD Guidelines for Multinational Enterprises' Complaints Procedure: Lessons from Past NGO Complaints* (OECDWatch, 2006).

W. Friedmann, L. Henkin, and O. Lissitzyn (eds), *Essays in Honor of Philip C. Jessup* (New York: Columbia University Press, 1972).

Friends of the Earth, 'Dubious Development: How the World Bank's Private Arm Fails the Poor and the Environment' (September 2000) <http://www.foe.org/camps/intl/worldbank/ ifcreport/>.

Friends of the Earth, 'Towards Binding Corporate Accountability' (Position paper for the World Summit on Sustainable Development, January 2002).

Friends of the Earth, 'OECD Guidelines for Multinational Enterprises' (undated) <http://www.foe. org/oecdguidelines/>.

Friends of the Earth Netherlands, 'Using the OECD Guidelines for Multinational Enterprises. A Critical Startkit for NGOs' (August 2002) <http://www.niza.nl/docs/200304291605312806.pdf>.

R. Geiger, 'Coherence in Shaping the Rules for International Business: Actors, Instruments and Implementation' (2011) 43 *The George Washington International Law Review* 295.

D. Geron, 'Human Rights and Transnational Corporations: Beyond UN Norms?' (summary of discussions at the International Law Programme Discussion Group of the Chatham House, London, 21 October 2004) <http://www.chathamhouse.org.uk/pdf/ research/il/ILP211004.pdf>.

P. Gerber, J. Kyriakasis, and K. O'Byrne, 'General Comment 16 on State Obligations regarding the Impact of the Business Sector on Children's rights: What is its Standing, Meaning and Effect?' (2013) 14 *Melbourne Journal of International Law* 93.

A. Gibson, 'The Real Price of Oil: Cultural Survival and the U'wa of Colombia' (2000) 34 *Colorado Journal of International Environmental Law and Policy* 139.

J. Gilbert, 'Corporate Accountability and Indigenous Peoples: Prospects and Limitations of the US Alien Tort Claims Act' (2012) 19 *International Journal on Minority and Group Rights* 25.

A. Gillispie, *Protected Areas and International Law* (Leiden: Martinus Nijhoff, 2007).

M. Gjølberg and R. Audun, 'The UN Global Compact—A Contribution to Sustainable Development?' (University of Oslo Working Paper no.1/05, 2005).

H. Gleckman, 'Proposed Requirements for Transnational Corporations to Disclose Information on Product and Process Hazards' (1988) 6 *Boston University International Law Journal* 89.

L. Glowka et al., *A Guide to the Convention on Biological Diversity* (Gland, IUCN: 1994).

M. D. Goldhaber, 'Corporate Human Rights Litigation in Non-US Courts: A Comparative Scorecard' (2013) 3 *University of California Irvine Law Review* 127.

K Gover, 'Settler-State Political Theory, 'CANZUS' and the UN Declaration on the Rights of Indigenous Peoples' (2015) 26 *European Journal of International Law* 345.

Government of Canada, 'Annual Report 2002: Canada's National Contact Point for the OECD Guidelines for Multinational Enterprises' (2002) <http://www.ncp-pcn.gc.ca/annual_2002-en.asp#implementation>.

A. Gowlland Gualtieri, 'The Environmental Accountability of the World Bank to Non-State Actors: Insights from the Inspection Panel' (2001) *British Yearbook of International Law* 213.

A. Grear and B. H. Weston, 'The Betrayal of Human Rights and the Urgency of Universal Corporate Accountability: Reflections on a Post-*Kiobel* Lawscape' (2015) 15 *Human Rights Law Review* 21.

Greenpeace, *The Bhopal Legacy: Toxic Contaminants at the Former Union Carbide Factory Site, Bhopal, India*, Technical Note 04/99 (Amsterdam: Greenpeace, 1999).

A. Grigg, 'What Are the Gains—for Business and Others—From Private Investment that Contributes to MEA Implementation?' (Paper presented at the OECD Workshop on Multilateral Environmental Agreements and the Private Sector, Helsinki, 16–17 July 2005).

S. Guitart, 'The Ramsar/DANONE Partnership: How can Private Sector Help to Implement an International Convention to Conserve Wetlands?' (Paper presented at the OECD Workshop on Multilateral Environmental Agreements and the Private Sector, Helsinki, 16–17 June 2005).

T. Hale and D. Held (eds), *Handbook of Transnational Governance* (Cambridge: Polity Press, 2011).

R. Hamann, N. Acutt, and P. Kapelus, 'Responsibility versus Accountability? Interpreting the World Summit on Sustainable Development for a Synthesis Model of Corporate Citizenship' (2003) *The Journal of Corporate Citizenship* 36.

D. T. Hamilton, 'Regulation of Corporations under International Environmental Law: Preserving the Global Environment' (1989) *Proceedings of the Annual Conference of the Canadian Council of International Law* 72.

G. Handl, 'State Liability for Accidental Transnational Environmental Damage by Private Persons' (1980) 74 *American Journal of International Law* 525.

D. Hanschel, *Environment and Human Rights: Cooperative Means of Regime Implementation* (Mannheimer Zentrum für Europäische Sozialforschung Working Paper no. 29, 2000).

P. Hansen and V. Aranda, 'An Emerging International Framework for Transnational Corporations' (1990) 14 *Fordham International Law Journal* 881.

H. L. A. Hart, *The Concept of Law* (Oxford: Clarendon Press, 1994).

J. Harrison, 'Establishing a Meaningful Human Rights Due Diligence Process for Corporations: Learning from Experience of Human Rights Impact Assessment' (2013) 31 *Impact Assessment and Project Appraisal* 107–17.

V. Haufler, *A Public Role for the Private Sector* (Washington DC: Carnegie Endowment for International Peace, 2001).

G. Hernández Uriz, 'The Application of the World Bank Standards to the Oil Industry: Can the World Bank Group Promote Corporate Responsibility?' (2002) 28 *Brooklyn Journal of International Law* 77.

G. Hernández Uriz, 'Human Rights as the Business of Business: The Application of Human Rights Standards to the Oil Industry' (DPhil thesis, European University Institute, 2005).

R. Herz, 'Litigating Environmental Abuses under the Alien Tort Claims Act: A Practical Assessment' (2000) 40 *Virginia Journal of International Law Association* 545.

R. Higgins, *Problems and Processes. International Law and How We Use it* (Oxford: Clarendon Press, 1994).

C. F. Hillemanns, 'UN Norms on the Responsibility of Transnational Corporations and Other Business Enterprises with regard to Human Rights' (2003) 4 *German Law Journal* 1065.

O. Hoedeman, 'Rio + 10 and the Greenwash of Corporate Globalization' (2002) 45 *Development* 39.

R. Hofmann and N. Geissler (eds), *Non-State Actors as New Subjects of International Law* (Berlin: Duncker & Humblot, 1999).

J. Holder, *Environmental Assessment: The Regulation of Decision-Making* (Oxford: Oxford University Press, 2004).

S. Holwick, 'Transnational Corporate Behaviour and its Disparate and Unjust Effects on the Indigenous Cultures and the Environment of Developing Nations: Jota v. Texaco, a Case Study' (2000) 11 *Colorado Journal of International Environmental Law and Policy* 183.

N. Horn (ed.), *Legal Problems of Codes of Conduct for Multinational Enterprises* (Deventer: Kluwer Law International, 1980).

H. Hosein, 'Unsettling: Bhopal and the Resolution of International Disputes Involving an Environmental Disaster' (1993) 16 *Boston College International and Comparative Law Review* 285.

A. I. Huff, 'Resource Development and Human Rights: A Look at the Case of the Lubicon Cree Indian Nation of Canada' (1999) 10 *Colorado Journal of International Environmental Law and Policy* 161.

The International Bureau of the Permanent Court of Arbitration, *International Investments and Protection of the Environment. The Role of Dispute Resolution Mechanisms* (The Hague: Kluwer Law International, 2001).

IFC, 'Response to the Compliance Advisor/Ombudsman Review on IFC Policy and Performance Standards on Social and Environmental Sustainability' (22 September 2005) <http://www.ifc.org/policyreview>.

IFC, 'Policy and Performance Standards on Social and Environmental Sustainability and Policy on Disclosure of Information: IFC Responses to Stakeholder Comments and Rationale for Key Policy Changes' (22 September 2006).

The International Council on Human Rights Policy, *Beyond Voluntarism: Human Rights and the Developing International Legal Obligations for Companies* (Versoix: International Council on Human Rights Policy, 2002).

The International Council on Minerals and Mining, *Position Statement on Mining and Protected Areas* (20 August 2003) <http://www.icmm.com/page/8602/21st-world-mining-congress >.

IUCN, *A Survey of Guidelines for Not-for-profit/Private Sector Interaction: Results and Recommendations for IUCN's Forthcoming Operational Guidelines for Private Sector Engagement* (Gland: IUCN, 2005).

N. Jägers, *Corporate Human Rights Obligations: In Search of Accountability* (Cambridge: Intersentia, 2002).

R. Jarashow, 'The Lessons for Multinationals of the Amoco Cadiz' (1986) *Energy Law* 789.

S. Jasanoff, 'The Bhopal Disaster and the Right to Know' (1988) 27 *Social Science and Medicine* 1113.

P. Jessup, *Transnational Law* (New Haven: Yale University Press, 1956).

S. Johnston, 'The Convention on Biological Diversity: The Next Phase' (1997) 6 *Review of European Community and International Environmental Law* 219.

P. Juillard, 'L'évolution des sources du droit des investissements' (1994) 250 *Recueils de Cours* 133.

S. Jungcurt and N. Schabus, 'Liability and Redress in the Context of the Cartagena Protocol on Biosafety' (2010) 19 *Review of European Community and International Environmental Law* 197.

C Kaeb and D Scheffer, 'The Paradox of *Kiobel* in Europe' (2013) 107 *American Journal of International Law* 852

M. T. Kamminga and S. Zia-Zarifi (eds), *Liability of Multinational Corporations under International Law*' (The Hague: Kluwer Law International, 2000).

C. Kamphuis, 'Contesting Indigenous-Industry Agreements in Latin America' in D. Newman and I. Odumosu-Ayanu (eds), *The Law and Politics of Indigenous-Industry Agreements* (London: Routledge, 2019).

N. Kanie and P. M. Haas (eds), *Emerging Forces in Environmental Governance* (Tokyo: United Nations University Press, 2004).

M. Karavias, *Corporate Obligations under International Law* (Oxford: Oxford University Press, 2013).

M. Karavias, 'Shared Responsibility and Multinational Enterprises' (2015) 62 *Netherlands International Law Review* 91.

P. Keenan, *Business, Human Rights, and Communities: The Problem of Community Contest in Development*, Illinois Public Law Research Paper No. 14–18 (2013) http://ssrn.com/abstract=2353493.

R. O. Keohane, 'The Concept of Accountability in World Politics and the Use of Force' (2003) 24 *Michigan Journal of International Law* 1121.

T. M. Kerr, 'What's Good for General Motors Is Not Always Good for Developing Nations: Standardizing Environmental Assessment of Foreign-Investment Projects in Developing Countries' (1995) 29 *The International Lawyer* 153.

A. Khokhryakova, 'Beanal v. Freeport-Mcmoran, Inc.: Liability of a Private Actor for an International Environmental Tort under the Alien Tort Claims Act' (1998) 9 *Colorado Journal of International Environmental Law* 463.

L. Kimball, 'Institutional Linkages between the Convention on Biological Diversity and Other International Conventions' (1997) 6 *Review of European Community and International Environmental Law* 239.

J. Kimerling, 'Disregarding Environmental Law: Petroleum Development in Protected Natural Areas and Indigenous Homelands in The Ecuadorian Amazon' (1991) 14 *Hastings International and Comparative Law Review*) 849.

A. King, 'The United Nations Human Rights Norms for Business and the UN Global Compact' (2004) <http://www.kingzollinger.ch/pdf/UN%20Norms.pdf>.

B. King, 'The UN Global Compact: Responsibility for Human Rights, Labour Relations, and the Environment in Developing Nations' (2001) 34 *Cornell International Law Journal* 481.

D. Kinley and R. Chambers, 'The UN Human Rights Norms for Corporations: The Private Implications of Public International Law' (2006) 6 *Human Rights Law Review* 447.

D. Kinley and J. Tadaki, 'From Talk to Walk: The Emergence of Human Rights Responsibilities for Corporations at International Law' (2003–04) 44 *Virginia Journal of International Law* 931.

A. Kiss, 'Un cas de pollution internationale: l'affaire des boues rouges' (1975) 102 *Journal du Droit International* 207.

A. Kiss, 'L'affaire de l'Amoco Cadiz: responsabilité pour une catastrophe écologique' (1985) *Journal du Droit International* 575.

A. Kiss, '"Tchernobale" ou la Pollution Accidentelle du Rhin par les Produits Chimiques' (1987) 33 *Annuaire Français de Droit International* 719.

A. Kiss and D. Shelton, *International Environmental Law*, 3rd edn (New York: Transnational Publishers, 2004).

A. Kiss, D. Shelton, and K. Ishibashi, *Economic Globalization and Compliance with International Environmental Agreements* (The Hague: Kluwer Law International, 2003).

P. Kohona, 'Implementing Global Environmental Standards: Is the Non-State Sector a Reluctant Convert or an Eager Devotee?' (2003–04) 11 *Asian Yearbook of International Law* 69.

P. Kohona, 'The Future We Wanted—The Future We Will Get' (2012) 42 *Environmental Policy and Law* 137.

K. Koufa, *Protection of the Environment for the New Millennium* (Athens: Sakkoulas Publications, 2002).

K. Koufa, *The New International Criminal Law* (Thessaloniki: Institute of International Public Law and International Relations of Thessaloniki, 2003).

L Krämer and E. Orlando (eds), *Principles of Environmental Law* (Cheltenham: Edward Elgar, 2018).

J. Ku, 'Kiobel and the Surprising Death of Universal Jurisdiction under the Alien Tort Statute' (2013) 107 *American Journal of International Law* 835.

K. Kulovesi, M. Mehling, and E. Morgera, 'Global Environmental Law: Context and Theory, Challenge and Promise' (2019) 8 *Transnsational Environmental Law* 405.

W. Lang (ed.), *Sustainable Development and International Law* (London: Graham & Trotman/Martinus Nijhoff, 1995).

L. Lambert, 'At the Crossroads of Environmental and Human Rights Standards: Aguinda v. Texaco Inc: Using the Alien Tort Claims Act to Hold Multinational Corporate Violators of International Laws Accountable in U.S. Courts' (2000) 10 *Journal of Transnational Law & Policy* 109.

M. Langton and J. Longbottom (eds), *Community Futures, Legal Architecture: Foundations for Indigenous Peoples in the Global Mining Boom* (Abingdon: Routledge, 2012).

M-L. Larsson, *The Law of Environmental Damage: Liability and Reparation* (The Hague: Kluwer Law International, 1999).

S. Leader, 'Human Rights, Risks and New Strategies for Global Investment' (2006) 9 *Journal of International Economic Law* 657.

R. Lefeber, 'The Legal Significance of the Nagoya–Kuala Lumpur Supplementary Protocol: The Result of a Paradigm Evolution' (Amsterdam Law School, 2012).
M. Leighton, *From Concept to Design: Creating an International Environmental Ombudsperson. Legal and Normative References: Environmental Human Rights* (Berkley: The Nautilus Institute for Security and Sustainable Development, 1998).
F. Lenzerini, 'Lo 'sfruttamento minerario sostenibile' come principio emergente nel dir-itto internazionale contemporaneo' (2004) 19 *Rivista Giuridica dell' Ambiente* 165.
F. Lenzerini, 'Sovereignty Revisited: International Law and Parallel Sovereignty of Indigenous Peoples', 42 *Texas International Law Journal* (2006) 155
F. Lenzerini (ed.), *Reparations for Indigenous Peoples: International and Comparative Perspectives* (Oxford: Oxford University Press, 2008).
A. Levi, 'Il Codice OCSE sulle Imprese Multinazionali' (1982) *Giurisprudenza Commerciale* 326.
L. Liberti, 'OECD 50th Anniversary: The Updated OECD Guidelines for Multinational Enterprises and the New OECD Recommendation on Due Diligence Guidance for Conflict-Free Mineral Supply Chains' (2012) 13 *Business Law International* 35.
J. Lin, 'Governing Biofuels: A Principal-Agent Analysis of the European Union Biofuels Certification Regime and the Clean Development Mechanism' (2012) 24 *Journal of Environmental Law* 43.
C. Lopez and B. Shea, 'Negotiating a Treaty on Business and Human Rights: A Review of the First Intergovernmental Session' (2015) 1 *Business and Human Rights Journal* 111.
V. Lowe, 'Corporations as International Actors and International Law Makers' (2004) 13 *Italian Yearbook of International Law* 23.
L. Lucchini, 'Le procès de l'Amoco Cadiz: présent et voies du future' (1985) *Annuaire Français de Droit International* 762.
B. Maheandiran, 'Calling for Clarity: How Uncertainty Undermines the Legitimacy of the Dispute Resolution System under the OECD Guidelines for Multinational Enterprises' (2015) 20 *Harvard Negotiation Law Review* 205.
S. Maljean-Dubois, 'Justice et société internationale: l'équité dans le droit international de l'environnement' in A. Michelot (ed.), *Equité et environnement* (Brussels: Lancier, 2012) 355.
P. Marchegiani, E. Morgera, and L. Parks, 'Indigenous Peoples' Rights to Natural Resources in Argentina: The Challenges of Impact Assessment, Consent and Fair and Equitable Benefit-sharing in Cases of Lithium Mining" (2020) 24 *International Journal of Human Rights* (224-240.)
M. Mason, *The New Accountability: Environmental Responsibility Across Borders* (London: Earthscan, 2005).
C. Mates, 'Project Finance in Emerging Markets: The Role of the International Finance Corporation' (2004) 18 *The Transnational Lawyer* 165.
D. McBarnet, Aurora Voiculescu, and Tom Campbell (eds), *The New Corporate Accountability: Corporate Social Responsibility and the Law* (Cambridge: Cambridge University Press, 2007).
A. McBeth, *International Economic Actors and Human Rights* (Abingdon: Routledge, 2010).
S. C. McCaffrey, 'The Work of the International Law Commission relating to Transfrontier Environmental Harm' (1987–88) 20 *New York University Journal of International Law and Policy* 715.
D. F. McClatchey, 'Chernobyl and Sandoz One Decade Later: The Evolution of State Responsibility for International Disasters' (1996) 251 *Georgia Journal of International and Comparative Law* 659.

R. McCorquodale, 'Waving Not Drowning: Kiobel Outside the United States' (2013) 107 *American Journal of International Law* 846.

J. McDonald, 'The Multilateral Agreement on Investment: Heyday or MAI-Day for Ecologically Sustainable Development?' (1998) 22 *Melbourne University Law Review* 617.

D. McGraw, 'The CBD: Key Characteristics and Implications for Development' (2002) 11 *Review of European Community and International Environmental Law* 17.

R. Meeran, 'Tort Litigation Against Multi-national Corporations for Violations of Human Rights: An Overview of the Position Outside the United States' (2011) 3 *City University of Hong Kong Law Review* 1.

M. Merle, 'Le pouvoir réglementaire des institutions internationales' (1958) 4 *Annuaire Français de Droit International* 341.

C. Metcalf, 'Corporate Social Responsibility as Global Public Law: Third Party Rankings as Regulation by Information' (2010–11) 28 *Pace Environmental Law Review* 145.

C. Methven O'Brien, A. Mehra, S. Blackwell, and C. Poulsen-Hansen, 'National Action Plans: Current Status and Future Prospects for a New Business and Human Rights Governance Tool' (2015) 1 *Business and Human Rights Journal* 117.

W. H. Meyer and S. Boyka, 'Human Rights, the UN Global Compact, and Global Governance' (2001) 34 *Cornell International Law Journal* 501.

A. Meyerstein, 'Global Adversarial Legalism: The Private Regulation of FDI as a Species of Global Administrative Law' in M. Audit and S. Schill (eds), *Transnational Law of Public Contracts* (Brussels: Bruylant, 2016) 799.

K. Miles, *The Origins of International Investment Law* (Cambridge: Cambridge University Press, 2013).

Millennium Ecosystem Assessment, *Ecosystems and Human Well-Being: Opportunities and Challenges for Business and Industry* (Washington DC: World Resources Institute, 2005).

J. K. Miller, 'Court of Appeals Ruling Re-Ignites Possibility that Texaco will answer for its Alleged Degradation of Ecuador's Rainforests in US Courts' (1999) *Colorado Journal of International Environmental Law and Policy Yearbook* 139.

A. Mistura, 'Is There Space for Environmental Crimes under International Criminal Law: The Impact of the Office of the Prosecutor Policy Paper on Case Selection and Prioritization on the Current Legal Framework' (2018) 43 *Columbia Journal of Environmental Law* 181.

E. Morgera, 'From Stockholm to Johannesburg: From Corporate Responsibility to Corporate Accountability for the Global Protection of the Environment?' (2004) 13 *Review of European Community and International Environmental Law* 214.

E. Morgera, 'An Update on the Aarhus Convention and its Continued Global Relevance', (2005) 14 *Review of European Community and International Environmental Law* 138.

E. Morgera, 'The UN and Corporate Environmental Responsibility: Between International Regulation and Partnerships' (2006) 15 *Review of European Community and International Environmental Law* 93.

E. Morgera, 'An Environmental Outlook on the OECD Guidelines for Multinational Enterprises: Comparative Advantages, Legitimacy and Outstanding Questions in the Lead-up to the 2006 Review' (2006) 18 *Georgetown International Environmental Law Review* 751.

E. Morgera, 'Significant Trends in Corporate Environmental Accountability: The New Performance Standards of the International Finance Corporate' (2006) 18 *Colorado Journal of International Environmental Law and Policy* 147.

E. Morgera, 'Human Rights Dimensions of Corporate Environmental Accountability' in P.-M. Dupuy, E.-U. Petersmann, and F. Francioni (eds), *Human Rights, Investment Law and Investor-State Arbitration* (Oxford: Oxford University Press, 2009) 511

E. Morgera, 'Bilateralism at the Service of Community Interests? Non-judicial Enforcement of Global Public Goods in the Context of Global Environmental Law' (2012) 23 *European Journal of International Law* 743.

E. Morgera, 'From Corporate Social Responsibility to Accountability Mechanisms' in P.-M. Dupuy and J. Viñuales (eds), *Harnessing Foreign Investment to Promote Environmental Protection: Incentives and Safeguards* (Cambridge: Cambridge University Press, 2013) 321.

E. Morgera, 'Against All Odds: The Contribution of the Convention on Biological Diversity to International Human Rights Law' in D. Alland et al. (eds), *Unity and Diversity of International Law. Essays in Honour of Professor Pierre-Marie Dupuy* (Leiden: Martinus Nijhoff Publishers, 2014) 983.

E. Morgera, 'Environmental Accountability of Multinational Corporations: Benefit-sharing as a Bridge between Human Rights and the Environment' in B. Boer (ed.), *Human Rights and the Environment* (Oxford: Oxford University Press, 2015) 37.

E. Morgera, 'Fair and Equitable Benefit-sharing at the Crossroads of the Human Right to Science and International Biodiversity Law' (2015) 4 *Laws* 803.

E. Morgera, 'Justice, Equity and Benefit-Sharing Under the Nagoya Protocol to the Convention on Biological Diversity' (2015) 25 *Italian Yearbook International Law* 113.

E. Morgera, 'Dawn of a New Day? The Evolving Relationship between the Convention on Biological Diversity and International Human Rights Law' (2018) 54 *Wake Forest Law Review* 101.

E. Morgera, 'Under the Radar: Fair and Equitable Benefit-sharing and the Human Rights of Indigenous Peoples and Local Communities connected to Natural Resources' (2019) 23 *International Journal of Human Rights* 1098.

E. Morgera and L. Gillies, 'Realizing the Objectives of Public International Environmental Law through Private Contracts: The Need for a Dialogue with Private International Law Scholars?' in D. French, V. Ruiz Abou-Nigm, and K. McCall Smith (eds), *Public and Private International Law: Strengthening Connections* (Oxford: Hart Publishing, 2018) 175.

E. Morgera and K. Kulovesi, 'Public-Private Partnerships for Wider and Equitable Access to Climate Technologies' in A. E. L. Brown (ed.), *Environmental Technologies, Intellectual Property and Climate Change: Accessing, Obtaining and Protecting* (Cheltenham: Edward Elgar, 2013) 128.

E. Morgera and K. Kulovesi (eds), *International Law and Natural Resources* (Cambridge: Cambridge University Press, 2016).

E. Morgera and J. Razzaque (eds), *Encyclopedia of Environmental Law: Biodiversity and Nature Protection Law* (Cheltenham: Edward Elgar, 2017).

E. Morgera and E. Tsioumani, 'The Evolution of Benefit-Sharing: Linking Biodiversity and Community Livelihoods' (2010) 15 *Review of European Community and International Environmental Law* 150.

E. Morgera and E. Tsioumani, 'Yesterday, Today and Tomorrow: Looking Afresh at the Convention on Biological Diversity', 21 *Yearbook of International Environmental Law* (2011) 3.

E. Morgera and A. Savaresi, 'A Conceptual and Legal Perspective on the Green Economy' (2012) 21 *Review of European Community and International Environmental Law* 14–28.

L. A. Mowery, 'Earth Rights, Human Rights: Can International Environmental Human Rights Affect Corporate Accountability?' (2002) 13 *Fordham Environmental Law Journal* 343.

P. Muchlinski, 'The Bhopal Case: Controlling Ultrahazardous Industrial Activities by Foreign Investors' (1987) 50 *Modern Law Review* 545.

P. Muchlinski, 'The Accountability of Multinational Enterprises and the Right to Development: The Compensation of Industrial Accident Victims from Developing Countries' (1993) *Third World Legal Studies* 189.

P. Muchlinski, *Multinational Enterprises and the Law* (Oxford: Blackwell, 1999).

P. Muchlinski, 'Human Rights, Social Responsibility and the Regulation of International Business: The Development of International Standards by Intergovernmental Organizations' (2003) 3 *Non-State Actors and International Law* 123.

P. Muchlinski, 'Caveat Investor? The Relevance of the Conduct of the Investor under the Fair and Equitable Treatment Standard' (2006) 55 *International and Comparative Law Quarterly* 527.

P. Muchlinski, 'Corporate Social Responsibility' in P. Muhclinski, F. Ortino, and C. Schreuer (eds), *The Oxford Handbook of International Investment Law* (Oxford: Oxford University Press, 2008) 637.

P. Muchlinski, 'Implementing the New UN Corporate Human Rights Framework: Implications for Corporate Law, Governance and Regulation' (2012) 22 *Business Ethics Quarterly* 145–77.

P. Muchlinski, F. Ortino, and C. Schreuer (eds), *The Oxford Handbook of International Environmental Law* (Oxford: Oxford University Press, 2008).

M. Mullen de Bolívar, 'A Comparison of Protecting the Environmental Interests of Latin-American Indigenous Communities from Transnational Corporations under International Human Rights and Environmental Law' (1998) 8 *Journal of Transnational Law and Policy* 105.

D. Murphy, 'The United Nations and Business: Global Partnership in Action' (2006) 4 *Partnership Matters* 19.

D. Murphy and J. Bendell, *Partners in Time? Business, NGOs and Sustainable Development* (Geneva: UNRISD, 1999).

J. Murray, 'A New Phase in the Regulation of Multinational Enterprises: The Role of the OECD' (2001) 30 *International Law Journal* 255.

V. Nanda and B. Bailey, 'Challenges for International Environmental Law—Seveso, Bhopal, Chernobyl, the Rhine and Beyond' (1988) 21 *Law and Technology* 1.

F. Nelli Feroci, 'Società multinazionali: verso un codice di condotta' (1978) 33 *La comunità internazionale* 325.

J. Nelson, *Building Partnerships. Co-operation between the United Nations System and the Private Sector* (New York: United Nations Global Compact Office, 2002).

V. Nilsson, 'The OECD Guidelines for Multinational Corporations in Practice' (Paper Presented at the OECD Global Forum on International Investment—Investment for Development: Forging New Partnerships, 19–21 October 2004) <http://www.oecd.org/dataoecd/6/61/33807212.pdf>.

A. Nollkaemper and I. Plakokefalos (eds), *The Practice of Shared Responsibility in International Law* (Cambridge: Cambridge University Press, 2017).

A. Nollkaemper and A. Reinisch (eds), *International Law in Domestic Courts: A Casebook* (Oxford: Oxford University Press, 2018).

K. Norwrot, 'The New Governance Structure of the Global Compact: Transforming a "Learning Network" into a Federalized and Parlamentarized Transnational Regulatory Regime' (2005) Essays in Transnational Economic Law No. 47.

J. C. Ochoa Sanchez, 'The Roles and Powers of the OECD National Contact Points Regarding Complaints on an Alleged Breach of the OECD Guidelines for Multinational Enterprises by a Transnational Corporation' (2015) 84 *Nordic Journal of International Law* 89.

OECD, *OECD and the Environment* (Paris: OECD, 1986).

OECD, *Codes of Corporate Conduct: Expanded Review of their Contents* (Paris: OECD, 2001).

OECD, *Global Instruments for Corporate Responsibility: OECD Guidelines for Multinational Enterprises Annual Report* (Paris: OECD, 2001).

OECD, *Relationships between International Investment Agreements* (Paris: OECD, 2004).

OECD, 'Roundtable on Corporate Responsibility: Encouraging the Positive Contribution of Business to Environment through the OECD Guidelines for Multinational Enterprises—Background Report' (2004) <http://www.oecd.org/document/1/0,2340,en_2649_34889_31711425_1_1_1_1,00.html>.

OECD, 'Roundtable on Corporate Responsibility: Encouraging the positive contribution of business to environment through the OECD Guidelines for Multinational Enterprises—Summary of the Roundtable Discussion' (2004) <http://www.oecd.org/document/1/0,2340,en_2649_34889_31711425_1_1_1_1,00.html>.

OECD, 'Key Messages' (OECD Workshop on Multilateral Environmental Agreements and the Private Sector, Helsinki, 16–17 June 2005).

Office of the High Commissioner for Human Rights and Global Compact Office, 'Consultation on Business and Human Rights—Summary of Discussions' (22 October 2004) <http://www.unglobalcompact.org/Issues/human_rights/business_human_rights_summary_report.pdf>.

D. Ong, 'International Legal Developments in Environmental Protection: Implications for the Oil Industry' (1997) 4 *The Australian Journal of Natural Resources Law and Policy* 55.

D. Ong, 'The Impact of Environmental Law on Corporate Governance: International and Comparative Perspectives' (2001) 12 *European Journal of International Law* 685.

D. Ong, 'From 'International' to 'Transnational' Environmental Law? A Legal Assessment of the Contribution of the 'Equator Principles' to International Environmental Law' (2010) 79 *Nordic Journal of International Law* 35.

D. Ong, 'Public Accountability for Private International Financing of Natural Resource Development Projects: The un Rule of Law Initiative and the Equator Principles' (2016) 85 *Nordic Journal of International Law* 201.

L. Oppenheim, *International Law—A Treatise*, 4th edn (London: Longmans, Green and Co Ltd, 1928).

E. Orlando, 'From Domestic to Global? Recent Trends in Environmental Liability from a Multi-level and Comparative Law Perspective' (2015) 24 *Review of European, Comparative and International Environmental Law* 289.

H. M. Osofsky, 'Environmental Human Rights under the Alien Tort Statute: Redress for Indigenous Victims of Multinational Corporations' (1997) 20 *Suffolk Transnational Law Review* 335.

A. Palmer, *Community Redress and Multinational Enterprises* (London: Foundation for International Environmental Law and Development, 2003).

L. Parks, 'Challenging Power from the Bottom Up? Community Protocols, Benefit-sharing and the Challenge of Dominant Discourses' (2018) 88 *Geoforum* 87.

L. Parks and E. Morgera, 'The Need for an Interdisciplinary Approach to Norm Diffusion: The Case of Fair and Equitable Benefit-sharing' (2015) 24 *Review of European, Comparative and International Environmental Law* 353.

D. Partan, 'The Duty to Inform in International Environmental Law' (1988) 6 *Boston University International Law Journal* 43.

U. Pascual, P. Balvanera, S. Díaz, G. Pataki, E. Roth, M. Stenseke, R. T. Watson, E. B. Dessane, M. Islar, E. Kelemen, and V. Maris, 'Valuing Nature's Contributions to People: The IPBES Approach' (2017) 26–27 *Current Opinion in Environmental Sustainability* 7.

J. Pauwelyn, R. Wessel, and J. Wouters (eds), *Informal International Lawmaking* (Oxford: Oxford University Press, 2012).

C. Pearson (ed.), *Multinational Corporations, Environment, and the Third World* (Durham: Duke University Press, 1987).

C. Pearson, 'An Environmental Code of Conduct for Multinational Companies?' in S. Rubin and T. Graham (eds), *Environment and Trade* (New Jersey: Allendheld Osman and Co, 1982) 154.

G. Pentassuglia, 'Indigenous Groups and the Developing Jurisprudence of the African Commission on Human and Peoples' Rights: Some Reflections' (2010) 3 *UCL Human Rights Review* 150.

J. L. Peters, 'Human Rights and the Environment: The Unocal Litigation' (1998) *Colorado Journal of International Environmental Law and Policy Yearbook* 199.

R. Pisillo Mazzeschi, 'Le Nazioni Unite e la codificazione della responsabilità per danno ambientale' (1996) *Rivista Giuridica Dell' Ambiente* 371.

A. Postiglione, 'Danno ambientale e Corte di Cassazione' (1989) *Rivista giuridica dell'Ambiente* 97.

R. Pound, *Social Control through Law* (New Haven: Yale University Press, 1942).

B. Pozzo, 'Il caso Seveso e la risarcibilità del danno morale' (2002) *Rivista Giuridica dell' Ambiente* 946.

R. Pritchard (ed.), *Economic Development, Foreign Investment, and the Law: Issues of Private Sector Involvement, Foreign Investment and the Rule of Law in New Era* (London: Kluwer Law International, 1996).

RAID, 'Unanswered Questions: Companies, Conflict and the Democratic Republic of Congo' (May 2004) <http://www.unites.uqam.ca/grama/pdf/RAID-DRC_Ex-Summary.pdf>.

RAID and SOMO, 'OECDWatch Review of National Contact Points for the OECD Guidelines for the period June 2003–June 2004 and Update of NCP cases filed by NGOs' (August 2004) <www.corporate-accountability.org/docs/OW_2004_Review.pdf>.

K. V. Raman, 'Corporate Responsibility to Protect the Global Environment: Emerging Issues of Law and Equity' (1998) C7 *Canadian Council on International Law, Proceedings of the Annual Conference* 93.

J. K. Rankin, 'US Laws in the Rainforest: Can a US Court Find Liability for Extraterritorial Pollution Caused by a US Corporation? An Analysis of Aguinda v Texaco, Inc.' (1995) 18 *Boston College International and Comparative Law Review* 221.

A. Rasche and G. Kell (eds), *The United Nations Global Compact: Achievements, Trends and Challenges* (Cambridge: Cambridge University Press, 2010).

T. Rathgeber, 'UN Norms on the Responsibilities of Transnational Corporations' (Friedrich-Ebert-Stiftung Occasional Geneva Papers no. 22, 2006).

S. Ratner, 'Corporations and Human Rights: A Theory of Legal Responsibility' (2001–02) 111 *Yale Law Journal* 488.

S. Ratner, 'Business' in D. Bodansky, J. Brunnee, and E. Hey (eds), *The Oxford Handbook of International Environmental Law* (Oxford: Oxford University Press, 2007) 807.

B. Richardson, 'Financing Sustainability: The New Transnational Governance of Socially Responsible Investment' (2008) 17 *Yearbook of International Environmental Law* 73.

B. Richardson, *Socially Responsible Investment Law: Regulating the Unseen Polluters* (Oxford: Oxford University Press, 2008).

F. Rivera, 'A Response to the Corporate Campaign against the Alien Tort Claims Act' (2003) 14 *Indiana International and Comparative Law Review* 251.

D. Robinson and J. Dunkley (eds), *Public Interest Perspectives in Environmental Law* (London: Wiley Chancery, 1995).

M. Robinson, 'Commentary on the Interim Report of the Special Representative on Business and Human Rights' (2006) <http://www.business-humanrights.org/Links/Repository/246742>.

P. Robinson, 'The Question of a Reference to International Obligations in the United Nations Code of Conduct on Transnational Corporations' (1986) UN Doc. ST/CTC/SER.A/1.

S. Robinson, 'International Obligations State Responsibility and Judicial Review under the OECD Guidelines for Multinational Enterprises Regime' (2014) 30 *Utrecht Journal of International and European Law* 68.

C Rodríguez-Garavito (ed.), *Business and Human Rights: Beyond the End of the Beginning* (Cambridge: Cambridge University Press, 2017).

M. J. Rogge, 'Towards Transnational Corporate Accountability in the Global Economy: Challenging the Doctrine of *Forum Non Conveniens* in In Re: Union Carbide, Alfaro, Sequihua, and Aguinda' (2001) 36 *Texas International Law Journal* 299.

M. Rolén, H. Sjöberg, and U. Svedin (eds), *International Governance on Environmental Issues* (Dordrecht: Kluwer Academic Publishers, 1997).

N. Rosemann, 'The UN Norms on Corporate Human Rights Responsibilities: An Innovating Instrument to Strengthen Business' Human Rights Performance' (Friedrich-Ebert-Stiftung Occasional Geneva Papers no. 20, 2005).

A. Rosencranz and R. Campbell, 'Foreign Environmental and Human Rights Suits against U.S. Corporations in U.S. Courts' (1999) 18 *Stanford Environmental Law Journal* 145.

C. Rossi, *Equity and International Law: A Legal Realist Approach to International Decision-Making* (The Hague: Martinus Nijhoff, 1993).

P. Roubier, *Théorie générale du droit: Histoire des doctrines juridiques et philosophie des valeurs sociales* (Paris: Dalloz, 1951).

J. Ruggie, 'Reflections concerning the United Nations Commission on Transnational Corporations' (1976) 70 *American Journal of International Law* 73.

J. Ruggie, 'Transnational Corporations and International Codes of Conduct: A Study of the Relationship between International Legal Cooperation and Economic Development' (1994–95) 10 *American University Journal of International Law and Policy* 1275.

J. Ruggie, 'Theory and Practice of Learning Networks: Corporate Social Responsibility and the Global Compact' (2002) 5 JCC 26.

J. Ruggie, 'Business and Human Rights: The Evolving International Agenda' (2007) 101 *American Journal of International Law* 819.

J. Ruggie, 'State Responsibilities to Regulate and Adjudicate Corporate Activities under the United Nations' core Human Rights Treaties' (May 2007) <http://www.humanrights.ch/home/upload/pdf/070410_ruggie_2.pdf>.

J. Ruggie, 'Presentation of the work of the Special Representative of the UN Secretary-General on Business and Human Rights to the 7th Inter-Committee meeting of the Human Rights Treaty Bodies' (Geneva, 24 June 2008) <http://www.business-human-rights.org/Documents/Presentation-Human-Rights-Treaty-Bodies-24-Jun-2008.pdf>.

J. Ruggie, 'Keynote Presentation by the Special Representative of the UN Secretary-General on Business and Human Rights to the Annual Meeting of National Contact Points of the Organization for Economic Cooperation and Development' (Paris, 24 June 2008) <http://www.reports-and-materials.org/Ruggie-presentation-OECD-Natl-Contact-Points-24-Jun-2008.doc>.

J. Ruggie, 'Global Governance and "New Governance Theory": Lessons from Business and Human Rights'(2014) 20 *Global Governance* 5.

J. Ruggie and T. Nelson, 'Human Rights and the OECD Guidelines for Multinational Enterprises: Normative Innovations and Implementation Challenges' (2015) 22 *Brown Journal of World Affairs* 99.

J. Ruggie and J. Sherman, 'Adding Human Rights Punch to the New *Lex Mercatoria*: The Impact of the UN Guiding Principles on Business and Human Rights on Commercial Legal Practice' (2015) 6 *Journal of International Dispute Settlement* 455.

L. Rutherford, 'Redressing U.S. Corporate Environmental Harms Abroad through Transnational Public Law Litigation: Generating a Global Discourse on the International Definition of Environmental Justice' (2002) 14 *Georgetown International Environmental Law Review* 807.

H. Saba, 'L'activité quasi-législative des institutions spécialisées des Nations Unies' (1964) 111 *Recueil des Cours* 607.

T. Sagafi-Nejad, 'Should Global Rules have Legal Teeth? Policing (WHO Framework Convention on Tobacco Control) vs. Good Citizenship (UN Global Compact)' (2005) 10 *International Journal of Business* 363.

J. Salmon, *Dictionnaire de Droit International Public* (Bruxelles: Bruylant/AUF, 2001).

M. Salmon, 'From NIEO to Now and the Unfinishable Story of Economic Justice' (2013) 62 *International and Comparative Law Quarterly* 31.

J. Salzman 'Decentralized Administrative Law in the Organization for Economic Cooperation and Development (2005) 68 *Law and Contemporary Problems* 189.

J. Salzman, 'The Organization for Economic Cooperation and Development's Role in International Law' (2011) 43 *The George Washington International Law Review* 255.

P. Sand, 'Environmental Summitry and International Law' (2003) 13 *Yearbook of International Environmental Law* 21.

P. Sands, 'The Environment, Community and International Law' (1989) 30 *Harvard International Law Journal* 393.

P. Sands, 'Present at the Creation: A New Development Bank for Europe in the Age of Environment Awareness' (1990) 84 *Proceedings of the American Society of International Law* 77.

P. Sands, *International Environmental Law. Emerging Trends and Implications for Transnational Corporations* (New York: United Nations, 1993).

P. Sands, *Principles of International Environmental Law*, 1st edn (Manchester: Manchester University Press, 1995).

P. Sands, *Principles of International Environmental Law*, 2nd edn (Cambridge: Cambridge University Press, 2003).

P. Sands and J. Peel, with A. Fabra and R. MacKenzie, *Principles of International Environmental Law*, 4th edn (Cambridge: Cambridge University Press, 2018).

A. Sanhoury, *Les restrictions contractuelles à la liberté individuelle de travail dans la jurisprudence anglaise. Contribution à l'étude comparative de la règle de droit et du standard juridique* (Paris: Marcel Giard, 1925).

A. Santner, 'A Soft Law Mechanism for Corporate Responsibility: How the Updated OECD Guidelines for Multinational Enterprises Promote Business for the Future' (2011) 43 *The George Washington International Law Review* 375.

B. Saper, 'The International Finance Corporation's Compliance Advisor/Ombudsman (CAO): An Examination of the Accountability and Effectiveness from a Global Administrative Law Perspective' (2011) 44 *NYU Journal of International Law and Policy* 1280.

S. Schlemmer-Schulte and K. Tung, *Liber Amicorum Ibrahim F.I. Shihata* (The Hague: Kluwer Law International, 2001).

G. Schuler, 'Effective Governance through Decentralized Soft Implementation: The OECD Guidelines for Multinational Enterprises' (2008) 9 *German Law Journal* 1753.

A. Schwabach, 'The Sandoz Spill: The Failure of International Law to Protect the Rhine from Pollution' (1989) 16 *Ecology Law Quarterly* 443.

T. Scovazzi, 'Immersione di sostanze inquinanti in mare e risarcimento del danno' (1986) *Rivista giuridica dell' ambiente* 105.

T. Scovazzi, 'State Responsibility for Environmental Harm' (2001) 12 *Yearbook of International Environmental Law* 43.

S. Seck, 'Environmental Harm in Developing Countries caused by Subsidiaries of Canadian Mining Corporations: The Interface of Public and Private International Law' (1999) 37 *The Canadian Yearbook of International Law* 139.

S. Seck, 'Transnational Corporations and Extractive Industries' in S. Alam, S. Atapattu, C. Gonzalez, and J. Razzaque (eds), *International Environmental Law and the Global South* (Cambridge: Cambridge University Press, 2015) 380.

S. Seck, 'Indigenous Rights, Environmental Rights, or Stakeholder Engagement? Comparing IFC and OECD Approaches to the Implementation of the Business Responsibility to Respect Human Rights' (2016) 12 *McGill Journal of International Sustainable Development Law and Practice*

A. Sen, 'Human Rights and the Limits of Law' (2005–06) 27 *Cardozo Law Review* 2913.

M. Shaughnessy, 'The United Nations Global Compact and the Continuing Debate about the Effectiveness of Corporate Voluntary Codes of Conduct' (2000) *Colorado Journal of International Environmental Law and Policy Yearbook* 156.

C. Shavin, 'Unlocking the Potential of the New OECD Due Diligence Guidance on Responsible Business Conduct' (2019) 4 *Business and Human Rights Journal* 139.

D. Shelton (ed.), *Commitment and Compliance: The Role of Non-binding Norms in the International Legal System* (Oxford: Oxford University Press, 2000).

I. Shihata, 'Implementation, Enforcement and Compliance with International Environmental Agreements—Practical Suggestions in Light of the World Bank's Experience' (1996–1997) 9 *Georgetown International Environmental Law Review* 37.

I. Shihata (edited by A. Parra, F. Tschofen, M. Stevens, and S. Schlemmer-Schulte), *The World Bank in a Changing World* (Boston: M. Nijhoff, 1995).

L. Siegele and H. Ward, 'Corporate Social Responsibility: A Step towards Stronger Involvement of Business in MEA Implementation?' (2007) 16 *Review of European Community and International Environmental Law* 135.

P. Simons, 'International Law's Invisible Hand and the Future of Corporate Accountability for Violations of Human Rights' (2012) 3 *Journal of Human Rights and the Environment* 5.

P. Simons and A. Macklin, *The Governance Gap: Extractive Industries, Human Rights and the Home State Advantage* (Abingdon: Routledge, 2014).

B. Sjåfjell and B. Richardson (eds), *Company Law and Sustainability: Legal Barriers and Opportunities* (Cambridge: Cambridge University Press, 2015).

G. Skinner, R. McCorquodale, and O. De Schutter, with A. Lambe, *The Third Pillar: Access to Judicial Remedies for Human Rights Violations by Transnational Business* (ICAR, CORE, and ECCJ, 2013).

M. Sornarajah, *The Settlement of Foreign Investment Disputes* (The Hague: Kluwer Law International, 2000).

M. Sornarajah, *The International Law on Foreign Investment* (Cambridge: Cambridge University Press, 2004).

M. Sornarajah, 'The Fair and Equitable Standard of Treatment: Whose Fairness? Whose Equity?' in F. Ortino, L. Liberti, A. Sheppard, and H. Warner (eds), *Investment Treaty Law, Current Issues II* (London: British Institute of International and Comparative Law, 2007).

J. Sorrentino, 'Flores v. Southern Peru Copper Corp' (2004) 17 *New York International Law Review* 133.

W. Sprote, 'Negotiations on a United Nations Code of Conduct on Transnational Corporations' (1990) 33 *German Yearbook of International Law* 331.

M. Stati, '*Le standard juridique*' (DPhil thesis, Paris, 1927).

R. Steinhardt, 'Kiobel and the Weakening of Precedent: A Long Walk for a Short Drink' (2013) 107 *American Journal of International Law* 841.

D. Stewart and I. Wuerth, 'Kiobel v. Royal Dutch Petroleum Co: The Supreme Court and the Alien Tort Statute' (2013) 107 *American Journal of International Law* 601.

C. Streck, 'The World Summit on Sustainable Development: Partnerships as New Tools in Environmental Governance' (2003) 13 *Yearbook of International Environmental Law* 63.

D. Strouss, 'Bringing Pesticide Injury Cases to US Courts: The Challenges of Transnational Litigation' (2019) 4 *Business and Human Rights Journal* 337.

TEEB, *The Economics of Ecosystems and Biodiversity in Business and Enterprise* (London: Earthscan, 2012)

W. L. Thomas, 'Wither from Here? American Enterprise and the Journey towards Environmentally Sustainable Globalization following WSSD' (2003) 12 *Review of European Community and International Environmental Law* 39.

P. Thornberry, *Indigenous Peoples and Human Rights* (Manchester: Manchester University Press, 2002).

C. Tomuschat, 'International Law: Ensuring the Survival of Mankind on the Eve of a New Century' (1999) 281 *Recueil des cours* 9.

E. Tourme-Jouannet, *What Is a Fair International Society? International Law between Development and Recognition* (Oxford: Hart Publishing, 2013).

T. Treves, 'Nazioni Unite e imprese multinazionali' (1978) 14 *Rivista di diritto internazionale privato e processuale* 900.

O. Triffterer (ed.), *Commentary on the Rome Statute of the International Criminal Court* (Baden-Baden: Nomos, 1999).

N. Tru, 'Les codes de conduite: un bilan' (1992) 96 *Revue Générale de Droit International Public* 45.

E. Tsioumani, 'Beyond Access and Benefit-sharing: Lessons from the Law and Governance of Agricultural Biodiversity' (2018) Journal *of World Intellectual Property* 1.

I. Tudor, *The Fair and Equitable Treatment Standard in the International Law of Foreign Investors* (Oxford: Oxford University Press, 2008).

S. Tully, 'The 2000 Review of the OECD Guidelines for Multinational Enterprises' (2001) 50 *International and Comparative Law Quarterly* 394.

S. Tully, 'Corporate-NGO Partnerships and the Regulatory Impact of the Energy and Biodiversity Initiative' (2004) 4 *Non-State Actors and International Law* 111.

UNCTAD, *Environmental Management in Transnational Corporations. Report on the Benchmark Corporate Environmental Survey* (New York: United Nations, 1993).

UNCTAD, *World Investment Report 1999: Foreign Direct Investment and the Challenge of Development* (Geneva: United Nations, 1999).

UNCTAD, *Social Responsibility* (Geneva: United Nations, 2001).

UNCTAD, *Environment* (Geneva: United Nations, 2001).

UNCTAD, *Voluntary Approaches to Corporate Responsibility: Readings and a Resource Guide* (Geneva: United Nations, 2002).

UNCTAD, *World Investment Report 2003: FDI Policies for Development: National and International Perspectives* (New York: United Nations, 2003).

UNCTAD, 'Disclosure of the Impact of Corporations on Society: Current Trends and Issues' (15 August 2003) UN Doc. TD/B/COM.2/ISAR/20.

UNCTAD, World Investment Report 2016—Investor Nationality: Policy Challenges (UNCTAD/WIR/2016).

R. Unger, 'Brandishing the Precautionary Principle through the Alien Tort Claims Act' (2001) 9 *New York University School of Law Environmental Law Journal* 638.

United Nations Development Programme (UNDP), Human Development Report 1999 (New York: Oxford University Press, 1999).

Union Académique Internationale, *Dictionnaire de la terminologie du droit international* (Paris: Librerie du Recueil Sirey, 1960).

United Nations Conference on Trade and Development (UNCTAD), *World Investment Report 2002* (New York: United Nations, 2002).

United Nations Environment Programme, *Assessing Environmental Impacts—A Global Review of Legislation* (UN, 2018).

UNRISD, 'Corporate Social Responsibility and Development: Towards a New Agenda?' (Report of the UNRISD Conference 17–18 November 2003, Geneva).

UNRISD, 'Corporate Social Responsibility and Development: Towards a New Agenda: Summaries of Presentations made at the UNRISD' (Geneva, 17–18 November 2003) <http://www.unrisd.org/80256B3C005BD6AB/httpNetITFrame?ReadForm&parentunid=3B9E23F717B84550C1256E23004DAB40&parentdoctype=eventauxiliarypage&netitpath=http://www.unrisd.org/unpublished_/tbs_/confsum/content.htm>.

E. J. Urbani and C. P. Rubin (eds), *Transnational Environmental Law and its Impacts on Corporate Behaviour* (Irvington on Hudson, NY: Transnational Juris Publications, 1994).

P. Utting, 'UN-Business Partnerships: Whose Agenda Counts?' (Paper presented at seminar on 'Partnerships for Development or Privatization of the Multilateral System', Oslo, Norway, 8 December 2000).

P. Utting, *Business Responsibility for Sustainable Development* (Occasional Paper n.2; Geneva: UNRISD, 2000).

P. Utting (ed.), *The Greening of Business in Developing Countries* (London: Zed Books in association with UNRISD, 2002).

P. Utting, 'The Global Compact: Why All the Fuss?' (2003) 40 *UN Chronicle* 1.

P. Utting, *Corporate Social Responsibility and Business Regulation* (Geneva: UNRISD, 2004).

D. Vagts, 'The Question of a Reference to International Obligations in the United Nations Code of Conduct on Transnational Corporations: A Different View' (1986) UN Doc. ST/CTC/SER.A/2.

D. Vagts, 'The UN Norms for Transnational Corporations' (2003) 16 *Leiden Journal of International Law* 795.

S. Vermeylen, 'The Nagoya Protocol and Customary Law: The Paradox of Narratives in the Law' (2013) 9 *Law Environment & Development Journal* 185.

S. Vermeylen, G. Martin, and R. Clift, 'Intellectual Property, Rights Systems and the Assemblage of Local Knowledge Systems' (2008) 15 *International Journal of. Cultural Property Rights* 201.

P. Vigni, 'A Liability Regime for Antarctica' (2005) 15 *Italian Yearbook of International Law* 217.

J. Viñuales, *Foreign Investment and the Environment in International Law* (Cambridge: Cambridge University Press, 2012).

J. Viñuales (ed.), *The Rio Declaration on Environment and Development: A Commentary* (Oxford: Oxford University Press, 2015).

L. Chand Vohrah (ed.), *Man's Inhumanity to Man: Essays on International Law in Honour of Antonio Cassese* (The Hague: Kluwer Law International, 2003).

K. Von Moltke, *A Model International Investment Agreement for the Promotion of Sustainable Development* (Winnipeg: International Institute for Sustainable Development, 2004).

M. Wagner, 'The International Legal Rights of Indigenous Peoples Affected by Natural Resource Exploitation: A Brief Case Study' (2001) 24 *Hastings International and Comparative Law Review* 491.

R. J. Waldmann, *Regulating International Business Through Codes of Conduct* (Washington DC: American Enterprise Institute for Public Policy Research, 1980).

C. D. Wallace, 'International Codes and Guidelines for Multinational Enterprises: Update and Selected Issues' (1983) 17 *The International Lawyer* 435.

C. D. Wallace, *The Multinational Enterprise and Legal Control* (The Hague: Martinus Nijhoff Publishers, 2002).

H. Ward, *Governing Multinationals: The Role of Foreign Direct Liability* (London: Royal Institute for International Affairs, 2001).

H. Ward, 'Securing Transnational Corporate Accountability through National Courts: Implications and Policy Options' (2001) 24 *Hastings International and Comparative Law Review* 451.

H. Ward, 'Towards a New Convention on Corporate Accountability? Some Lessons from the Thor Chemicals and Cape PLC Cases' (2002) 13 *Yearbook of International Environmental Law* 105.

H. Ward, The OECD Guidelines for Multinational Enterprises and Non-Adhering Countries: Opportunities and Challenges of Engagement' (Paper presented at the OECD Global Forum on International Investment: Investment for Development, New Delhi, 19–21 October 2004) <http://www.oecd.org/dataoecd/6/62/33807204.pdf>.

H. Ward, 'Corporate Social Responsibility—A Step Towards Stronger Involvement of Business in MEA Implementation?' (Paper presented at the OECD Workshop on Multilateral Environmental Agreements and the Private Sector, Helsinki, 16–17 June 2005).

H. Ward, 'Corporate Social Responsibility—A Step towards Stronger Involvement of Business in MEA Implementation?' (Paper presented at the OECD Workshop 'Multilateral Environmental Agreements and the Private Sector', 2005).

M. Warner, *The New International Benchmark Standards for Environmental and Social Performance of the Private Sector in Developing Countries: Will it Raise or Lower the Bar?* (London: Overseas Development Institute, 2006) <http://www.odi.org.uk/publications/opinions>.

C. Weeramantry, 'Human Rights and the Global Marketplace' (1999) 25 *Brooklyn Journal of International Law* 27.

P. Weil, 'Le droit international en quête de son identité. Cours général de droit international public' (1992) 237 *Recueil des Cours* 203.

T. Weiler, 'Balancing Human Rights and Investor Protection: A New Approach for a Different Legal Order' (2004) 27 *Boston College International and Comparative Law Review* 429.

F. Weiss, E. Denters, and P. de Waart (eds), *International Economic Law with a Human Face* (The Hague: Kluwer Law International, 1998).

D. Weissbrodt and M. Kruger, 'Norms on the Responsibilities of Transnational Corporations and Other Business Enterprises with regard to Human Rights' (2003) 97 *American Journal of International Law* 901.

R. Welford, *Environmental Strategy and Sustainable Development: The Corporate Challenge for the 21st Century* (London: Routledge, 1995).

A. Westing, *Global Resources and International Conflict: Environmental Factors in Strategic Policy and Action* (Oxford: Oxford University Press, 1986).
O. F. Williams (ed.), *Global Codes of Conduct: An Idea Whose Time Has Come* (Notre Dame, Ind: University of Notre Dame Press, 2000).
T. Williams and P. Hardison, 'Culture, Law, Risk and Governance: Contexts of Traditional Knowledge in Climate Change Adaptation' (2013) 120 *Climatic Change* 531.
M. Wilson, 'The New Frontier in Sustainable Development: World Summit on Sustainable Development Type II Partnerships' (2005) 36 *Victoria University of Wellington Law Review* 389.
G. Winter (ed.), *Multilevel Governance of Global Environmental Change: Perspectives from Science, Sociology and the Law* (Cambridge: Cambridge University Press, 2006).
J. Witte and C. Streck, *Progress or Peril? Partnerships and Networks in Global Environmental Governance* (Berlin: Global Public Policy Institute, 2003).
J. M. Witte and W. Reinicke, *Business UNusual* (New York: United Nations Global Compact Office, 2005).
R. Wolfrum (ed.), *Max Planck Encyclopedia of Public International Law* (Oxford University Press, online edition, 2010).
World Bank, *Greening Industry: New Roles for Communities, Markets and Governments* (Oxford: Oxford University Press, 2000).
World Bank, *The Final Report of the Extractive Industries Review* (Washington DC: World Bank, 2003).
World Resources Institute, *World Resources 2002-2004: Decisions for the Earth: Balance, Voice, and Power* (Washington DC: World Resources Institute, 2003).
World Resources Institute, *Mining and Critical Ecosystems: Mapping the Risks* (Washington DC: World Bank, 2003).
The World Wide Fund for Nature (WWF), *No Investment Agreement within the WTO: Re-Directing Investment to Promote Sustainable Development* (WWF Discussion Paper, October 2001).
The World Wide Fund for Nature (WWF), 'Guidelines for Investment in Operations that Impact Forests' (September 2003) <http://www.forestandtradeasia.org/files/WWF%20FOrest%20Investment%20Guideline.pdf>.
The World Wide Fund for Nature (WWF) (A. Durbin, S. Herz, D. Hunter, and J. Peck), 'Shaping the Future of Sustainable Finance: Moving from Paper Promises to Performance' (January 2006) <http://www.wwf.org.uk/researcher/issues/companiesandfinance/index.asp>.
WWF-US and International Institute for Sustainable Development, 'Private Rights, Public Problems: A Guide to NAFTA's Controversial Chapter on Investor Rights' (2001) <http;//www.iisd.org/pdf/trade_citizensguide.pdf>.
J. Wouters and C. Ryngaert, 'Litigation for Overseas Corporate Human Rights Abuses in the European Union: The Challenge of Jurisdiction' (2008-09) 40 *George Washington International Law Review* 939.
E. Yemin, *Legislative Powers in the United Nations and Specialized Agencies* (Leyden: Sijthoff, 1969).
A. Zammit, *Development at Risk. Rethinking UN-Business Partnerships* (Geneva: UNRISD, 2003).
J. Zerk, 'Corporate Liability for Gross Human Rights Abuses: Towards a Fairer and More Effective System of Domestic Law Remedies', report prepared for the Office of the High Commissioner for Human Rights (2012).

S. Zia-Zarifi, 'Suing Multinational Corporations in the US for Violating International Law' (1999) 4 *UCLA Journal of International Law and Foreign Affairs* 81.
C. Zilioli, 'Il caso Bhopal e il controllo sulle attività pericolose svolte da società multinazionali' (1987) *Rivista giuridica dell' ambiente* 199.
D. N. Zillman, A. R. Lucas, and G. Pring (eds), *Human Rights in Natural Resource Development* (Oxford: Oxford University Press, 2002).

Index

For the benefit of digital users, indexed terms that span two pages (e.g., 52–53) may, on occasion, appear on only one of those pages.

agri-business, 128, 162, 164–65, 170–71, 172, 175, 185–86, 191, 194, 198, 200, 202–3, 204–5, 207, 221, 223–24
Alien Tort Claim Act, 33–37

benefit-sharing, 146, 185–88, 189–90, 195, 202–10, 266, 267–71, 276, 281
bilateral investment treaties, 50, 59–60, 81–82, 91–92, 113–14
biodiversity, 3, 5–7, 105, 125–26, 132–34, 141–46, 149, 151–53, 154–55, 255–57

chemicals, 159, 163–64, 167–68, 173, 280–81, 287–88
climate change, 125–26, 132–34, 141–42, 149, 157, 164–65
compliance, 228–31
corporate accountability (definition) 12–13, 15–16, 18–22, 109–10
corporate governance, 21–22, 98, 128, 172, 288–89
corporate liability, 10–11, 13, 28–46, 53, 58, 67, 70–71, 125, 271–72
corporate responsibility (definition) 12–13, 15–18
corporate social responsibility (CSR), 15–16, 87–88
customary international law, 34–35

due diligence, 20, 22, 34, 40, 60, 81, 109–10, 111–12, 128, 144–46

ecosystem services, 5–6, 133–34, 151–53, 220, 257
environmental impact assessment, 25, 72–73, 118–19, 148–55, 235, 241, 251–52, 261–62, 263
environmental information, 72–73, 87, 125, 137, 153–57, 168–74, 199, 206–7, 253–55, 265–68, 279–84, 287
Equator Principles, 134–36

foreign direct investment, 10, 89–90, 91, 122–23

foreign direct liability, 30–33
freshwater, 156–57, 161–62, 265–66

gender, 133, 188–89
Global Compact, 14–15
green economy, 13–14

human right to water, 113–14, 143–44

indigenous peoples, 118–19, 133, 144–46, 151–54, 174, 175–76, 178, 181–210
integration, 70–71, 147–57
International Finance Corporation, 129–31
    Compliance Advisor/Ombudsman, 164–65, 222
international human rights law, 53–60, 71–72, 99–119, 126–27, 143–44, 148–49, 165, 173, 178, 181, 258
International Labour Organization, 105–6, 153
International Seabed Authority, 61–62, 82

local communities, 186–88

Millennium Development Goals, 94
Millennium Ecosystem Assessment, 5–7, 220
minerals, 128, 154–55, 191, 236–37, 240–41
multinational companies
    definition, 63–65
    status, 60–67

New International Economic Order, 89–91

Organization for Economic Cooperation and Development, 91, 106, 120–29, 135–36
    Committee on International Investment and Multilateral Enterprises, 231–32
    guidelines for multinational entreprises, 14–15
    National Contact Points, 124, 177–78, 231–47, 263–64, 278–79

polluter-pays, 35, 70–71, 96
precaution, 35, 70–71, 98, 105–6, 132, 137, 147, 149–50, 155–56, 165–68

318   INDEX

prevention, 70–71, 105–6, 111–12, 155–56, 158–65, 179–80, 216, 236, 287–89
principles of international environmental law, 35–36, 70–73, 96, 98
protected areas, 184, 211–16, 235–36, 256

remedies, 110–11
Rio Conference, 8–10, 87
Rio+20 Conference, 13–16

standards, 70–78, 86, 144–46
    operational, 76
    as soft-law, 78–80
    technical, 76
State liability, 40–42
State responsibility, 39–44
Stockholm Conference, 8
Supply chain, 126, 128
sustainable development, 8–9, 105, 124–25, 147
Sustainable Development Goals, 94
sustainable use, 72–73, 166, 216–24

tourism, 146, 153, 155, 162, 170–71, 173, 204–5, 221
transboundary environmental harm, 34, 40–43, 58–59, 158

United Nations
    Commission on Human Rights, 101–5, 108
    Commission on Transnational Corporations, 84–85, 87–88, 91
    Conference on Trade and Development, 87–88
    Economic and Social Council, 70–71, 84–85, 93
    Educational, Scientific and Cultural Organization, 235–36
    Environment Programme, 105–6, 153, 283
    Food and Agriculture Organization, 133, 162–63
    Framework on Business and Human Rights, 1, 17–18, 20, 22, 56, 60, 99–100, 108–19, 126, 129, 241, 248–49, 272–73, 275–76
    General Assembly, 5–6, 83–84, 96–97, 285
    Guiding Principles on Business and Human Rights, 14–15, 24, 53, 245–46, 281–82
    Human Rights Council, 195
    Secretary-General, 93, 96–97
    Security Council, 242–44
    Special Rapporteurs
        Human Rights and the Environment, 126, 143–44, 186–88, 222, 273–74
        Indigenous Peoples' Rights, 174, 184, 188, 195, 202, 203–4, 208, 275–79
        Toxics, 106, 119, 160, 163–64, 170–71, 173–74, 279–82
    Special Representative on Business and Human Rights, 76, 108–19, 233–34
        Working Group on Business and Human Rights, 114–17, 118–19, 185–86, 194–95, 199, 232, 272–73, 276

Waste, 162
World Bank, 82, 91–92, 129–35, 251–58
World Health Organization, 162–63
World Summit on Sustainable Development, 10–13, 94–95, 105, 125
World Trade Organization, 87–88, 90–92